Our Changing Coastlines

An International
Oceanographic Foundation
Selection

The International Oceanographic Foundation
10 Rickenbacker Causeway
Virginia Key
Miami, Florida 33149

McGraw-Hill Book Company

New York

San Francisco

St. Louis

Düsseldorf

London

Mexico

Panama

Sydney

Toronto

Our Changing Coastlines

Francis P. Shepard

Scripps Institution of Oceanography
University of California, San Diego

Harold R. Wanless

Department of Geology
University of Illinois

To Elizabeth and Grace

Our Changing Coastlines

This book was set in Linotype Fairfield by Holmes Typography, Inc., and printed on permanent paper by Halliday Lithograph Corporation and bound by The Book Press. The designer was Michael A. Rogondino. The illustrations were prepared for reproduction by Tom Tracy with the assistance of Doug Deluchi. The editors were Bradford Bayne and Ronald Q. Lewton. Charles A. Goehring supervised production.

Printed in the United States of America.

Library of Congress catalog card number: 72–139563

1234567890 HDBP 7987654321

07–056558–9

Foreword

In this exhaustive review of the coastlines of the United States, Francis P. Shepard and Harold R. Wanless provide a basic text suitable for both scholar and student. *Our Changing Coastlines* is a detailed yet readable description of the nation's coastal features. As such it will no doubt be required reading for those concerned with further scientific inquiry into the nature of our shorelines. Professors Shepard and Wanless are to be commended for the care and patience this book represents and congratulated upon the result. *Our Changing Coastlines* adds immeasurably to the knowledge about the physical characteristics of our nation.

These characteristics shape our society and help determine our public policies. The natural resources of a country—and a coastline is a natural resource of immense value—provide considerable insight into national capabilities and goals.

Life in the United States is greatly influenced by the coastal nature of the country's topography. Resource exploitation, trade and commerce, demographic patterns, military strength, and life styles all reflect the coastal nature of America.

Shepard and Wanless describe this nature and point up the constantly changing nature of our shorelines. This movement or evolution of the coast's physical characteristics is matched by the changing patterns of the population along the coast. Not surprisingly the population of the coastal areas is increasing rapidly. Already about 75 percent of the country's population live within the coastal zone, which accounts for but 5 percent of the nation's land area. The coastlines are becoming crowded. The demand for shoreline space is great. And sparsely populated coastal areas like Maryland's serene and lovely Eastern Shore will totally change in the next thirty years as America's population reaches 300 million people.

What the coastal areas of the United States, as described in this book, now require is a plan or management system. The system must prepare water and land use plans, decide upon competing demands within the coastal zone, allocate shoreline resources, and determine coastal benefits. Such planning is of course contrary to our tradition. But the coastal areas are finite, and the coastal "frontier" will shortly close. Planning thus becomes mandatory. A coastal management system is essential to assure continued public benefits of the coastal resources. Haphazard coastal policies no longer suffice.

A few states are already preparing coastal plans or systems. Others will do so when Congress enacts a coastal planning grant program in the 92nd Congress. Yet the complexities of management, paralleling the physical coastal complexities described in *Our Changing Coastlines*, cast considerable doubt on our ability to effect the necessary changes. What Professors Shepard and Wanless describe so well in this fine book may well prove to be a resource that we are unable to develop and use properly.

Joseph D. Tydings
United States Senator
October, 1970

Preface

In a few scattered localities along the coasts of the United States attempts have been made previously to show how the coastlines have changed during historical times. However, no one has provided information for our entire coast or has tried to coordinate this in such a way that general conclusions could be reached concerning what is likely to happen to coastal communities in the future. We realize that our information is limited for many areas, but hope that by offering what is available we may provide an incentive to other investigators to continue where we have left off.

With the rapidly increasing concern about environment and ecology, and with the realization that we will have to do something about them for future generations, it should be realized that it is not only pollution of streams, lakes, and the surrounding seas that is threatening our country but that large, important areas along the shoreline are in great danger of being ruined by erosion or even by deposition. We have to learn methods of stopping these destructive coastal changes. In order to do so, we need detailed information as to exactly what is happening. Why are some beaches rapidly disappearing and others growing too wide? Why are some coastal towns being undermined by the waves, and how serious is the future threat to others?

The U.S. Army Corps of Engineers, along with various academic engineers and geologists, have been investigating the effects of breakwaters, jetties, groins, and seawalls on coastal erosion. This book attempts to bring together much of this scattered information and coordinate it with the equally important changes produced by nature.

The effect of great inundations resulting from hurricanes and tsunamis (tidal waves) is treated in the book with emphasis on what has happened to our coasts when these catastrophes have occurred in recent years. It is our hope that these accounts will be of some help to city planners and engineers in minimizing the effects of future disasters of this sort.

In preparation for writing the book the authors made a field coverage of most of the coasts of the United States and Hawaii. This coverage was supplemented by the study of literature in geology and engineering of the coastal areas. We visited only a small part of the Alaska coast, so that in this area we had to rely heavily on the excellent coverage by the U.S. Geological Survey.

We have been somewhat amazed to find how distinctive in character the various coasts have proven to be as we made our tour clockwise around the conterminous United States, then around Alaska, and finally around the main islands of the State of Hawaii. Each area has its special problems and features. One could never say, "If you have seen one coast or beach, you have seen them all."

In compiling the information for the present book we have drawn heavily on the theses submitted at the University of Illinois that were directly related to studies of coastal changes. Wanless' students, Mohamed T. El-Ashry, Constance E. Gawne, and Paul L. Plusquellec, had particularly helpful material, and Wanless' son Harold Rogers Wanless provided us with a large fund of information. Many organizations have contributed directly or indirectly to the work. These include Scripps Institution of Oceanography, the Geology Department of the University of Illinois, the U.S. Coast and Geodetic Survey (ESSA), the Office of Naval Research (Grant 2216[23]), and the American Petroleum Institute (Project 51). The authors wish to acknowledge particularly the numerous suggestions of Margaret R. Miller relative to the style of the manuscript. We appreciate the comments and constructive criticism of Clifford A. Kaye, Turbid Slaughter, James P. Morgan, E. L. Winterer, J. S. Creager, D. S. McCulloch, D. C. Cox, and G. W. Moore, who read one or more chapters. James R. Moriarty made most of the line drawings and Neil F. Marshall was of help to us in many ways. Finally, we wish to express appreciation and sympathy to our wives for acting as critics during the reading and rereading of the manuscript.

Francis P. Shepard

Harold R. Wanless

My good friend and coauthor Harold R. Wanless passed away on June 3, 1970. It is especially unfortunate that after all the time and energy he put into the book he had no chance to see it in print. During his entire scientific career Wanless was a prodigious worker, and his was a very important role in unveiling the history of the Carboniferous period. Even in the field of marine erosion, which was rather far from his specialty, he made a fine contribution and I am most appreciative of the tremendous amount of work he did in helping to create this book.

Francis P. Shepard

Contents

Introduction

1   Ever since the earliest civilizations, the seacoast has held great appeal to man, and he has concentrated his habitations in that narrow belt, which lies directly landward from the edge of the ocean. The coast has attracted man—ancient and modern—because it has provided a source of food and of that vital mineral, salt. Climatically, the coasts of the world are preferable to the interior because of the amelioration of the climate that comes from the much less variable ocean temperatures. The slow cooling of the ocean in winter keeps the coast warmer and the slow heating in summer keeps it cooler. Most coastal belts have a higher rainfall, due to the nearby source of water and the onshore winds, caused by heating of the land and the resulting convection currents.

Presumably, early man was not particularly influenced by the esthetic beauty of the coasts; but, going back as far as the time of the early Greeks, man has given this factor great weight in choosing sites for his homes and temples. Finally, with the development of the automobile, there has been a tremendous growth of coastal highways. Because the public desires to look at beautiful scenery, our own western seaboard has an almost continuous highway extending along the coast from Mexico to the Strait of Juan de Fuca, which separates Washington and British Columbia. Coast routes along the East and Gulf Coasts are far less continuous, partly because of the intricate indentations that push the roads inland and partly because of the low swampy lands and shifting belts of sand dunes.

Advantages of coastal areas are somewhat offset by dangers. Now we are no longer harassed by pirates who made coastal habitation dangerous in ancient times, but coasts are definitely less stable than interior areas. Steep coasts are subject to landslides and soil creep and in many places are being undermined by wave erosion, causing homes and even sections of highways to fall into the attacking sea. Low sandy coasts are particularly unstable because sediments are shifted by the waves and currents. One of the effects of hurricanes is to raise the sea level, very much as do tsunamis (popularly called *tidal waves*) that result from sudden earth movements under the sea. The rising sea during hurricanes and tsunamis has destroyed property worth many millions of dollars in the United States. Although we have abundant evidence of hurricanes and tsunamis as far back as our records go, both may have become somewhat more prevalent during the past few decades.[1] During the early 1900s, residents of the northeastern coast of the United States were little concerned with the effects of hurricanes until September 21, 1938, when the first of a devastating series occurred.

In 1967, Sen. Joseph D. Tydings of Maryland reported that the annual damage to property along coasts between Maine and Texas caused by normal day-to-day processes is about $31 million, and an additional $83 million of annual damage is due to hurricanes and other major storms. Hurricane Hazel, in October 1954, the most destructive hurricane recorded in the United States, caused $1 billion worth of damage.[2] However, the hurricane that struck Galveston, Texas, in September 1900, caused the deaths of 6,000 people and almost destroyed the city.

For several generations, Hawaiians gave little thought to the great waves of tsunamis until 1946 when destructive seas rolled into all of the exposed north and east coasts of these islands. In Hawaii, these inundations have since been repeated three times.

The present writers' interest in a book on coasts and coastal changes resulted from several influences. Wanless had been working for many years with aerial photographs of the same areas taken at successive dates and had found that even during the short period since compilations of aerial photographs along the coast began (about 1930), significant changes are very easy to detect along the lowlands of the East and Gulf Coasts of the United States. Some of his stu-

dents at the University of Illinois became interested in his extensive collections of coastal photographs, and their interest resulted in several theses that documented the significance of these changes. Shepard has also been studying aerial photographs but has been particularly interested in collecting old photographs and periodically retaking pictures of the same sites, showing what has happened to the sea cliffs. Photos along the California coast dating back as far as the last century have been used. This study was first conducted with U. S. Grant IV, of the University of California, Los Angeles, about thirty years ago, and results were published at that time. Three decades have intervened, allowing further study with better controls and more points for comparison.

Another reason for the present book has been the frequent inquiries we have had about the safety of property built along the coast. However, predicting whether a house owner is likely to lose his property during his lifetime is a little like predicting when a war is going to end. About all we can do here is to give some evidence of what has happened during the past several decades and to make some attempt to show what factors have contributed either to stability or to rapid retreat of the coastal margin. Similarly, the changes in coastal lowlands are not easy to predict. The same sand point may alternately have been cut back and built forward. A cape, for example, may be cut away on the north side and prograded on the south; then, after a sudden shift of conditions, the process may be completely reversed. Much depends on wind direction and intensity of the storms that cause these changes, and those are hard to predict for the future. However, some areas appear to be less subject to the effects of storms than others, and we can attempt to point out some of the conditions underlying these differences. Actually, compiling the evidence from many areas along the extensive coasts of the United States has helped to clarify the picture for us. The effects of man's engineering projects are much easier to predict and are now well documented.

Because the changes which the various coasts are undergoing are greatly dependent on the character of the coasts, we will precede our descriptions by an attempt to classify the coasts of the United States. In fact, this classification could as well be considered a classification of the coasts of the world, because virtually every world type is represented. This would

[1] Because of the lack of or inadequacy of communications and areas being less populated, there was less general awareness of tsunamis and hurricanes, which may have occurred in the past with equal frequency; but now people are much more conscious of the effects of these catastrophes.

[2] Perhaps exceeded by Hurricane Camille in August 1969.

not have been true until 1959 and 1960 when statehood was granted to Alaska and Hawaii, with their glaciers, volcanoes, and sudden changes of level during earthquakes. These phenomena furnish three of the types. Some background in the nature of coastal processes is also necessary in order to understand the causes of the changes that take place.

A few coastal features will be referred to so much in the book that we should define them here. There is no unanimity among coastal investigators concerning these definitions, but to us they seem the most logical. First, the low ridges of sand that are separated from but parallel to many coasts we are calling *barriers*. They may be in the form of narrow beaches or of wide islands or spits of sand extending across or partly across embayments. Although these have been referred to as *offshore bars*, it seems far better to follow the example of mariners and confine the word *bar* to submerged sand ridges. The term *barriers* is now becoming standardized among most geologists. In relation to coastal embayments, two of the types are generally quite distinct, so to us it seems unwise to use the same name for both. These are shown in Figure 1.1. We are confining the word *estuary* to the type of bay that results from the drowning of a river valley.[3] These embayments, also called *rias*, usually extend into the land approximately at right angles to the coastal trends. The other common type of embayment lies roughly parallel to the coast and is protected by a sand barrier. This last type we are calling a *lagoon*. These and other terms that may cause confusion to some of the readers of this book are defined in the glossary at the end.

In the past, information regarding changes along the coasts of the United States has been derived principally from navigation charts of the U.S. Coast and Geodetic Survey and topographic maps of the U.S. Geological Survey. Since the early 1930s, however, several governmental agencies have systematically photographed the United States from the air at intervals, so that for some coastal areas, such as the North Carolina capes, as many as ten dates of photography are available for a 30-year period. The photographs show more detail than can be found on any map or chart and are thus excellent guides to changes that have taken place between dates of photography.

[3] Some other authors define *estuary* as any coastal embayment periodically affected by brackish oceanic waters.

1.1 Illustrating the difference between a lagoon and an estuary as the terms are used in this book.

Governmental photographs are commonly taken from a camera pointed vertically downward from the floor of a specially equipped photographic plane. These vertical aerial photographs show all features in their space relations near the center of the photograph and are excellent map substitutes. However, hills near the margin of a photograph are displaced away from the center beyond their true positions, while valleys are displaced toward the center. When the plane is caught in a wind eddy just as the photograph is taken, there may be an additional error due to tilt.

Most governmental map-making photographs are taken while flying north-south or east-west courses. During each flight, photographs are taken at regular intervals, so that each picture overlaps the preceding one by about 60 percent. By overlapping the two pictures in a pattern identical with that of the pattern of flight and with the use of a lens stereoscope, it is possible to view the overlapping portions in three dimensions, greatly increasing the ease of interpreting land forms. One stereo pair, illustrating Koko Head, Oahu Island, Hawaii, is included as Figure 15.42. For many illustrations of this book, two or more photographs have been combined to produce a composite picture of a large area. In some illustrations, small offsets at the junctions of the photographs are caused either by topographic relief of features shown or by slight tilt of the plane.

Aerial photographs are generally taken on panchromatic film, which permits the recognition of submerged shoals and sand ridges to depths of about 30 feet, as at Cape Lookout Shoals (Fig. 5.8). The infrared film used for some purposes causes the water surface to appear dark and reveals no detail of the shallow sea bottom. The photograph of old beach ridges on Chincoteague Island (Fig. 4.18) is illustrative of infrared photography.

Most aerial photography shows ground features with scales of 1:20,000 to 1:40,000, or from about 3 inches to 1.5 inches per mile. Many of the photographs in this book are reduced, so the scale is smaller than that of the original negative. Contact prints of high-altitude photography, which has been used increasingly in recent years, have a scale of about 1 inch per mile. Figure 6.23 of Florida Bay is illustrative of high-altitude photography. In sparsely settled areas, like parts of Alaska, many nine-lens photographs have been taken. One lens is pointed vertically toward the ground and the others are inclined at 45 degrees in eight directions. The inclined photographs are rectified in printing to show the ground without distortion. In Figure 13.49, the photo of Carlisle Volcano, and Figure 14.19 of Cape Krusenstern, are nine-lens photographs.

Many readers have probably taken photographs through airplane windows during commercial flights. These are oblique air photographs and are somewhat more easily interpreted by the uninitiated than are vertical photographs, although they are less useful in mapping. Many examples are included in this book.

The interpretation of features on black-and-white aerial photographs is dependent on the recognition of shapes and varying shades of gray. On a water surface one can distinguish the direction of wave advance toward shore, the spacing of wave crests, and interference patterns where two sets of waves meet at a point, as at Point Año Nuevo, California (Fig. 11.17). The line of breaking waves shows as a nearly white color. As most photographs are taken on bright days, one part of a photograph over water may appear light because of sun reflection from the water surface. Some governmental aerial photographs show clouds, which appear as light masses obscuring the ground features and produce shadows that darken ground areas.

Shades of gray on land are determined principally by vegetation and soil tones. Evergreen trees are generally darker colored than deciduous trees, and some dark soils or rocks are plainly distinguished from lighter soils or rocks. Sandy beaches are very light colored, and varying width of the beach can be measured easily, as at Cape May, New Jersey (Fig. 4.11).

This book treats the coasts of the Atlantic, Gulf of Mexico, and Pacific borders of the continental United States, Alaska, and Hawaii, giving descriptions and interpretations of selected areas with respect to their location, geological history, and circumstances favoring or opposing present-day coastal changes, with a few generalized predictions for the future changes of the areas described. With the use of charts (often of several dates going back a century or more), aerial photographs taken at various times within the past 40 years, and specialized reports on the geology, recent history, and intensity of present-day processes, we are able to say that certain changes have occurred and have left a record in the landforms, sediment distribution, or vegetation. In light of this history, it is then possible to conclude with some trepidation that similar processes will continue to operate and to evaluate the types of changes to be expected from them.

Major storms, often of hurricane intensity, have hit almost all parts of the Atlantic and Gulf Coasts many times within the past century, but it is impossible to predict just where the next storm will strike or the direction from which it will come. Somewhat less violent storms are experienced along our western coasts. Several writers have said that a single hurricane accomplishes as much coastal change as a century of the operation of normal processes.

Chapter 2 discusses the primary and secondary processes responsible for coastal evolution. For any particular coast, it may readily be said that it was or was not glaciated, elevated, faulted, composed of resistant rock or nonresistant sand or clay; that the rocks were or were not deformed or metamorphosed; that volcanic activity had or had not taken place; that the land behind the shore is flat, hilly, or mountainous; that tidal ranges are high or low; and that wave energy is strong or weak. The direction of prevailing longshore currents can be ascertained. The climate can be described as subtropical, temperate, frigid, or very humid or very arid. The effects of recent violent storms may or may not be evident, and it can be seen that human activities have or have not interfered with the normal course of coastal evolution. In addition, the recent geological history of an area is very significant in determining the origin of the present-day features, as well as the rates of change of a coastal area.

Because of the large number of variables mentioned in the preceding list, it is easy to understand why almost every 20- to 50-mile stretch of the United States coast is unique in certain respects and different from every other part. In choosing and illustrating the examples, the authors have attempted to cover as great a diversity of coasts, coastal features, and coastal histories as possible.

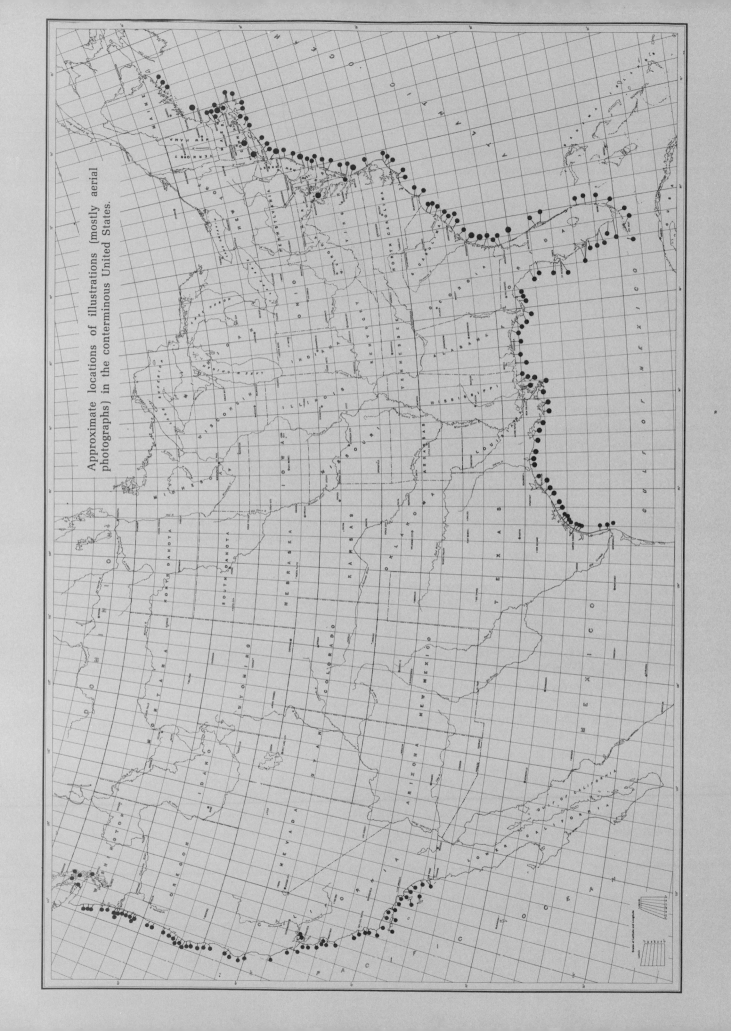

Approximate locations of illustrations (mostly aerial photographs) in the conterminous United States.

Types of Coasts

2 Marine forces are operating to varying degrees along all coasts. However, many land margins have scarcely been affected by the marine processes, so they are essentially in the same condition as they were when the sea came to rest against them. These virginal coasts we can refer to as *primary*. The form of these shorelines unmodified by the sea depends on what had happened to the area previously. Coasts that have been significantly modified by the waves and currents along the shore we shall call *secondary coasts*.

PRIMARY COASTS

DROWNED RIVER VALLEYS AND SEA-LEVEL CHANGES   Virtually all coasts of the world have been submerged, even since the time of the ancient civilizations. The reason for this is that prior to about 10,000 years ago, large parts of northern North America and northwestern Europe were covered by great ice sheets, similar to the Antarctic and Greenland ice caps. During those times of continental glaciation, even Antarctica had a thicker and more extensive glacial cover. The principal source for the ice was the ocean and, as a result, sea level went down. When the ice caps melted, the water returned and sea level rose. Several recent investigations along stable coasts have established that during the past 10,000 years the sea level rose approximately as indicated in Figure 2.1. Disagreement regarding this curve led Shepard and others to conduct an expedition to a group of islands in Micronesia to look for possible higher stands in the past few thousand years, a possibility that had been suggested by some well-known scientists. Thirty-three islands, all in a very stable area (free from earthquakes), failed to show

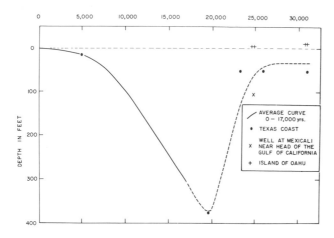

2.1 Approximate sea-level changes during the last 30,000 years due to fluctuations of continental glaciers.

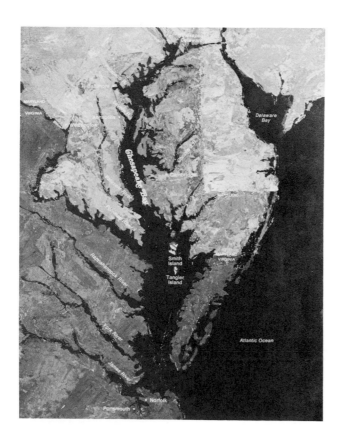

2.2 Outline map of Chesapeake Bay, a typical estuary formed by postglacial drowning of coastal plain rivers. Courtesy of *Oceans Magazine*.

any such evidence. All carbon-14 dated[1] material agreed well with the suggested curve. This and other evidence leads us to conclude that the sea has risen along all coasts except those where upward land movements have offset the effect. Unless crustal movements of the order of 100 feet in the past 10,000 years (Fig. 2.1) have occurred—and we know that most lands have not risen at any such rapid rate—most coasts can be considered as submergent.[2]

The ordinary result of submergence (whether it is due to rising sea level or sinking land) is that the river valleys become embayed. A classic example of the effect of drowning is Chesapeake Bay with its many arms, looking like a giant maple leaf (Fig. 2.2). Since the floors of river valleys slope outward and generally lack basins, the axes of the embayments due to drowning will also slope seaward unless later modified. If the river-eroded lands had hills and the submergence was sufficient to drown the margins of these hills, they would then appear as islands.

EFFECTS OF GLACIAL EROSION   In New England, northern Washington, and parts of Alaska, the hilly or mountainous coastal areas were covered by continental glaciers; and a different type of coast developed when the ice melted. The erosive effect of valley glaciers is to produce a straightening and steepening of the valley walls, along with the development of broad U-shaped cross sections and the excavation of deep basins. When the ice retreated, long straight arms of the sea extended for many miles into the excavated valleys. The water in these bays is much deeper than those of the drowned river valleys. Many of the deepest places are well inside the bay mouths, and these basin depressions are often a thousand or even several thousand feet deep. These drowned glacial valleys are called *fiords* (Fig. 2.3). For the most part, fiord coasts have not been subsequently modified because the waves are not very effective in the bays, and hard rock is prevalent on the marginal walls.

[1] Accurate measurement of the extent to which carbon-13 has changed to carbon-14 allows an estimate of the age of shells or wood fibers found in a deposit. This method is applicable if the object is not older than 30,000 years.

[2] One of the popular older classifications of coasts had submergence as a principal class, but obviously this type is far too widespread to justify any such classification.

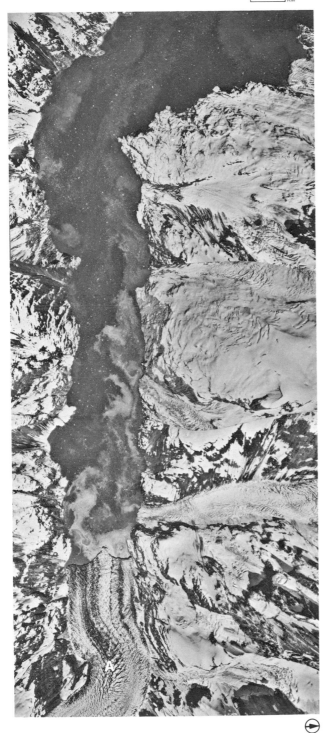

2.3 Johns Hopkins Fiord, Glacier Bay National Monument, Alaska. Johns Hopkins Glacier (A), at head of fiord, retreated 7 miles in 30 years. U.S. Coast and Geodetic Survey, June 1964. Letters refer to features mentioned in text or caption.

EFFECTS OF GLACIAL DEPOSITION AND DEPOSITION BY GLACIAL OUTWASH   At or near the outer margin of the continental glaciers, the melting of the ice caused extensive deposition of the debris transported along the bottom and in the interior of the ice. This deposition led to the development of *moraines* (irregular hilly ridges composed of glacial drift) and *drumlins* (elliptical hills steeper on the side from which the glacier was advancing). Some of the islands along the northeast coast of the United States, notably Long Island, are basically morainic in origin. The islands of Boston Harbor (Fig. 2.4) are slightly modified drumlins.

The quantities of debris carried out by braided streams from the margins of glaciers form fan deposits. Some of these accumulations occurred between lobes of ice. When the glaciers retreated, these glaciofluvial deposits were left behind, forming capes and islands along the newly established coast. Unlike the coasts left by glacial erosion, those resulting from glacial deposition and outwash were quickly modified, partly because the materials were unconsolidated sediments and partly because in most places there was nothing to protect them from the wave attack of the open sea.

DROWNED KARST TOPOGRAPHY   Where bedrock consists of limestone or gypsum, erosion by rain and running water produces a very special type of topography because of rapid solution of these types of rock. In such terrain, rivers flow for only short distances before running into caverns and disappearing. The roofs of the caves are unstable and often collapse, developing the circular pits or lakes called *sinkholes*. Because of the prevalence of this type of topography in the Karst area of Yugoslavia, along the east side of the Adriatic, the topography has been given this name. Where the limestone coasts have been submerged, karst features characterize the shoreline. Partly because of the general protection from wave action, the area along the limestone west coast of Florida, in the broad curve north of St. Petersburg, owes much of its form to drowning of such a limestone karst area.

COASTS FORMED BY RIVER DEPOSITION
Where rivers are introducing more sediment into the sea than can be carried away by the waves and cur-

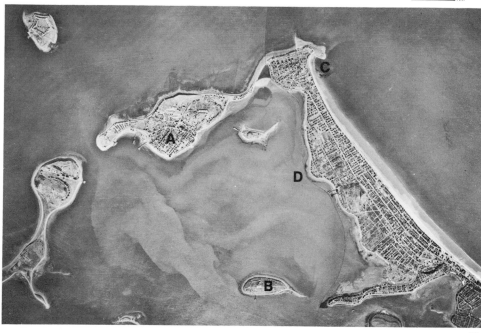

2.4 Nantasket Beach area of Boston Harbor, Massachusetts. A coast formed by barrier beaches tying together a series of drumlins. U.S. Geological Survey, 1938. Letters refer to features discussed in subsequent chapters.

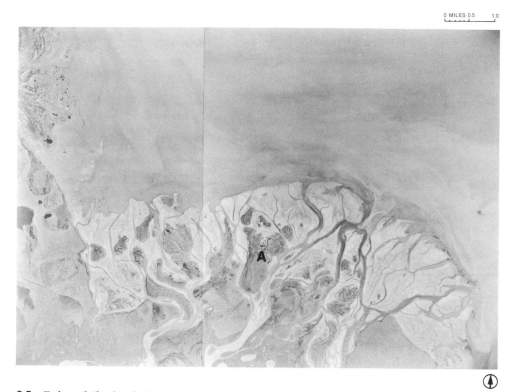

2.5 Delta of Ikpikpuk River, northern Alaska. U.S. Geological Survey, 1935.

0 MILES   .50   1.0

KM

2.6 Distributaries of Mississippi River forming small deltas in Garden Island Bay. All these deposits have formed during the past century. U.S. Coast and Geodetic Survey, 1956.

rents, the land progrades in the form of deltas (Fig. 2.5). Deltas are very common at the heads of bays where waves are of minimal effect; but deltas form also in the open ocean where enormous quantities of sediment are introduced, such as at the mouth of the Mississippi, and are even found on a small scale as tidal deltas at the mouths of some bays. Because the rivers develop distributaries at their mouths, the deltas are likely to have lobes separated by indentations, as in the Birdfoot Delta of the Mississippi (Fig. 2.6). However, in some places, delta deposition is so general that only one broad arc develops. The best

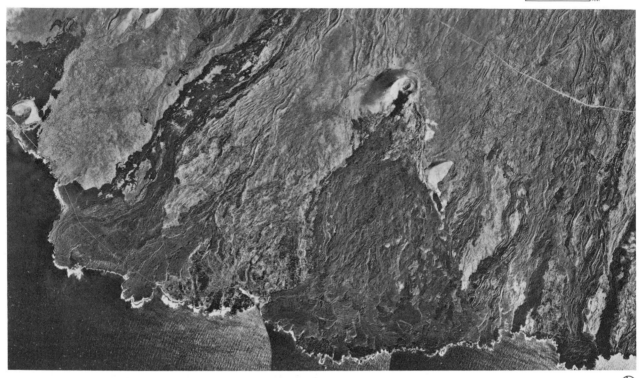

2.7 Volcanic coast of southwestern Maui, Hawaii. Lava flows on the southwest side of Haleakala Volcano, which occurred late in the eighteenth century. Paired lines are natural levees that confined flow. Four smaller cinder cones are partially buried by lava flows. U.S. Coast and Geodetic Survey, 1960.

examples of such arcs are in Africa at the mouths of the Nile and Niger, but the Yukon Delta also has an *arcuate* outline. A *cuspate* form develops if there is only one main channel, as at the mouth of the Brazos in Texas or the Tiber near Rome, Italy.

In an older classification of coasts that included submergence and emergence, deltas were considered as neutral. Actually, this was misleading because, as far as we know, all large deltas have been sinking at a faster rate than sea level has been rising in the past 6,000 years and are maintained above sea level only where rapid deposition is taking place. For example, some mouths of the Mississippi, abandoned in the past century, have sunk so deep that the area can now be traversed in boats. Elsewhere, the natural levee embankments of the old abandoned deltas are all that is left above sea level, forming discontinuous sand islands.

VOLCANIC COASTS   Where lava flows down the sides of volcanoes along the continental margin

or on oceanic islands, lava fans are built forward into the ocean with broad arcuate shapes (Fig. 2.7). Elsewhere, in volcanic areas, coastal indentations are formed where volcanoes either have been partly blown away or where one side has collapsed, allowing the sea to enter the breached crater. The resulting coast has broad, rounded embayments in contrast to the convexity of the lava fans.

FAULT COASTS   Where the earth's crust is unstable, as in most areas where large earthquakes occur, the initial form of the coast is likely to be closely related to faulting. The dropping of a broken block of land below sea level generally leaves a straight sea cliff (Fig. 2.8). Other cliffs may be the result of wave erosion, but there is one distinct difference. The sea floor along most fault scarps deepens rapidly —in fact, it may go down vertically—whereas along straight wave-cut cliffs there is a shelving bottom due to the effects of wave erosion.

2.8 Coast on northeast side of San Clemente Island, California, illustrating a fault coast. U.S. Navy photo.

2.9 The nature of water motion in various parts of a wave. Some of the common names applied to waves are included. Note that the water particle motion is much smaller at a depth equal to a quarter of a wave length.

SECONDARY COASTAL FORMS RESULTING FROM MARINE MODIFICATION

Actually, the term *primary coast* is somewhat deceptive since all coasts are secondary to some extent, because the sea begins to act on the primary coasts immediately after conditions stabilize. However, where the waves are small and where the rock is hard, the effects are slow to develop, so that the coast continues to be primary in such cases for a long time. Most coasts are a mixture of primary and secondary in varying degrees.

Although some coasts show little effect of marine processes since the sea approached its present level, most have extensive indications of changes produced by waves and currents, even during the few thousand years since the sea ended its rapid rise. During that time, most coasts have been worn back by wave erosion, especially exposed points of land; but some coasts have been prograded by marine processes, producing advances of the same order as the deposition of deltas at the mouths of rivers. Before discussing these types of marine-modified coasts, we shall present some of the background information relative to the nature of the waves and currents that produce these changes.

NATURE OF WAVES   A detailed discussion of wave mechanics is beyond the purpose of this book,[3] but some of the principles should prove helpful in demonstrating how the humping up and breaking of these waves along the shore cause many of the coastal changes with which we will be dealing. Most waves that roll into the shore are the product of wind blowing unevenly on the surface of the ocean, often at a great distance from the coast. A simplified type of wave is shown in Figure 2.9. The high points are the *crests* and the low, the *troughs*. Crest-to-crest distance is the *wave length*, and the vertical difference between crest and trough is the *wave height*. The time it takes for the passage of two crests by a fixed point, such as the end of a pier, is the *wave period*. As indicated in the diagram, the particles of water move in opposite directions at the crest and trough. Waves appear to be moving rapidly toward the shore, but actually the water particles progress shoreward only in the wave crest and away from the shore in the trough.

Waves change character while moving from deep into shallow water. Their crests become sharper,

[3] Books dealing with waves are listed in the References at the end of the chapter.

2.10

a　A plunging wave, north coast of Oahu, Hawaii. Photo by Ron Church.

higher, and closer together. Upon reaching depths slightly greater than the wave heights, the wave crests outrun the rest and therefore topple over or break. The water in the breaker rushes shoreward and surges up onto the beach, carrying sand or pebbles with it. This *uprush* is followed by *backwash*, which also produces a powerful flow and carries back some of the sediment, but not as much because of water sinking into the beach. The backwash tends to topple a bather and carry him seaward. The term *undertow* has been applied to the backwash, but actually it does not drag a person under the water surface. Ordinarily he can return with the next uprush.[4]

There are several types of breakers. If the waves along a shore are caused by a distant storm, they are likely to have long periods; and, in the open sea, as soon as these waves have moved out of the storm area, they become quite smooth in shape and are called *swells*. When these long-period waves come into the shore, they break in deeper water than short-period

[4] Exceptions are rip currents, described later.

b Spilling waves coming in along the Scripps Institution pier at La Jolla, California. Photo by Shepard, 1940.

waves of the same height, and their breakers have hollow fronts (Fig. 2.10*a*); but their crests pound down with great force, making them dangerous for swimmers if the waves are high. This force also enhances erosion. If the waves are the product of a local wind, they have shorter periods and are much more irregular. Outside the breakers, wind waves are more menacing to a small boat than are the smooth long-period waves. When short-period wind waves break (Fig. 2.10*b*), they usually have a steep front but lack the hollows and cascades of the long-period waves. The *spilling breakers* are less disastrous to a swimmer and have less effect on the beach or rocks beneath them. In general, long-period waves (10 to about 18 seconds) occur along the West Coast of the United States and short-period waves (commonly 6 to 8 seconds) along the East Coast.

The waves and breakers along the West Coast are usually higher than those of the East Coast. This is largely because, in addition to varying with the wind strength, the wave height is dependent on the *fetch* (the distance over which the wind has been blowing). There is rarely a great fetch on the East Coast because of the prevailing west winds, but the same winds have thousands of miles of fetch off the West Coast. Nevertheless, great storms occur along the East Coast, and the high onshore winds produce very high waves under exceptional conditions, especially in hurricanes.

CURRENTS INDUCED BY WAVES   Although the particles of water in a wave move back and forth, they usually have a net motion toward the shore in the same direction as the apparent motion of the

2.11 Atlantic City, New Jersey, illustrating oblique wave approach to coast, which causes a southward littoral current. U.S. Coast and Geodetic Survey, 1950.

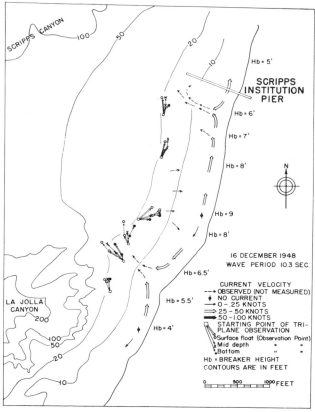

2.12 Circulation pattern associated with waves near Scripps Institution pier, La Jolla, California. Waves converging between La Jolla and Scripps Submarine Canyons. From Shepard and Inman (1950).

crests (Fig. 2.11). These diagonal approaches along with the net forward motion of the wave particles move the water along the beach in the same direction as the approach. Thus, in Figure 2-11, we can expect currents to be moving to the south along the shore. These are called *longshore currents*, and their effect is to move sediments in the same direction. For example, the prevailing northwest storm winds along most of the West Coast of the United States move sand to the south, whereas the prevalent northeast storm winds along the East Coast also move sand to the south. Some of the sand well south on the Florida East Coast, for instance, has come from the Carolinas, as can be determined by the comparison of the mineral content of the Florida beaches with that of the Carolina rivers.

Another type of current is developed as a result of deep submarine valleys that come in close to the West Coast, particularly in California. As shown in Figure

2.12, waves approaching the coast are largely dissipated at the head of a submarine valley, because they move faster in deep water than in shallow water. The energy is concentrated between the canyon heads by the same process. The effect is to pile up the water in the zones of convergence between canyons. This higher sea level develops a gradient, and the flow of water is away from the convergence in both directions, producing another type of longshore current.

Because waves have a tendency to carry water toward the shore, there must be return flow. In the case of the diagonally approaching waves, the return flow is likely to take place where there is a slight seaward bulge in the beach or where the flow encounters a projecting point. In the special condition produced by the submarine valley, the return flow is likely to be near or over the valley (Fig. 2.12). These return flows develop considerable velocity and can carry a swimmer seaward faster than he can swim. They are called *rip currents* (also *rip tides* and *sea pusses*). Along the West Coast, they are the most common cause of drowning. Most of these drownings can be avoided if a swimmer with any endurance will swim to one side of the rip where the current stops;[5] the danger lies in trying to swim against it.

CATASTROPHIC WAVES   Coastal changes are particularly great when unusual waves are produced by big storms, such as the East and Gulf Coast hurricanes. During these storms, in addition to the great heights of the pounding waves, the sea level is often raised as much as 10 feet, rarely 20 feet, above normal. When these *storm surges* come in at high tide, they often sweep over low sand islands and cause enormous destruction. Figure 2.13 shows a part of the Maryland coast one week before (*a*) and one year after (*b*) the 1962 Atlantic storm.

Another type of great wave is caused by sudden movements of the ocean bottom, such as accompany faulting of the sea floor and its attendant earthquakes. If the ocean floor drops, it carries water down to fill the void, thus initiating a series of waves of very long period, often 15 minutes or more. A sudden rise of the ocean floor causes a similar effect. These waves, called *tsunamis* or *tidal waves* (although they are not related to tides), are small in the open ocean but pile up along the shore, where they may surge up to heights of as much as 100 feet. The mainland of the United States has been quite free of disastrous tsunamis, but the Hawaiian Islands are right in the path of these waves caused by faulting in the deep trenches off Alaska, Japan, and the west coast of South America. Alaska has also been hit by tsunamis, but the generally embayed coasts of this northernmost state provide more protection than exists in Hawaii.

A third type of catastrophic wave comes from landslides. In Lituya Bay, Alaska, a large mass of rock broke off the steep wall of a fiord and, falling into the water, caused a surge on the opposite side that rose 1,700 feet. Waves of this sort are fortunately very rare and have caused little damage to man.

TIDAL CURRENTS   The effect of the moon and sun on the ocean is well known but is so complex that only a general description will be given here. The tide rises and falls twice a day—or actually during 24 hours and 52 minutes—because of the relative movement of the moon around the earth, total orbit being 28 days. The tides in the Bay of Fundy, Nova Scotia, have a range of as much as 60 feet; but along the coasts of the United States tides average only about 5 feet, and in the Gulf of Mexico and Arctic Alaska, they are mostly less than 2 feet.

One of the results of the rising and falling tides is the development of strong currents. These are especially powerful at narrow entrances of large bays. Tides flowing at a rate of several miles an hour cause a large amount of sand transport in and out of these bays. They are effective in keeping the entrance channels open and in many places have cut deep holes (more than 1,400 feet in the entrances to the Sea of Japan and 380 feet at the Golden Gate, San Francisco).

COASTAL EROSION   The pounding of the waves on the shore has produced large amounts of erosion in some places. The rate at which cliffs are worn back by wave attack depends on several factors. Soft rocks and sediments are particularly vulnerable to wave attack. So far as we know, in all places where cliffs are receding as much as several feet a year, the materials of the cliffs are unconsolidated sands, clays, and gravels, or a type of rock that can be cut by a shovel. The rate of recession is also dependent on the exposure of the cliffs to large waves. For that reason, the West Coast has more cliff erosion than the East Coast, due again to the prevailing west winds. If the coast is deeply embayed, wave erosion is important only at the headlands between bays where the waves converge.

Wave erosion produces two types of coasts. In general, if the sea cliffs are of uniform material, the waves are likely to straighten the sea cliffs (Fig. 2.14); whereas, if varying degrees of hardness exist in the coastal formations, the waves cut indentations into the softer material, leaving the hard rocks protruding as points. There is a marked contrast between an irregular wave-eroded coast and a drowned river-valley shoreline. The former lacks the extensive estuaries and is characterized by the type of cove

[5] Usually rip currents are narrow, rarely more than 100 feet in width.

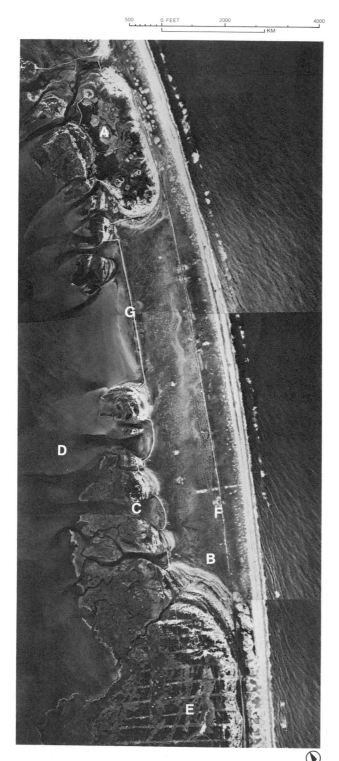

2.13

a A portion of the Maryland coastline on Assateague Island. This illustrates a broad sand plain formed at the site of a washover during an older hurricane. U.S. Coast and Geodetic Survey, April 1961.

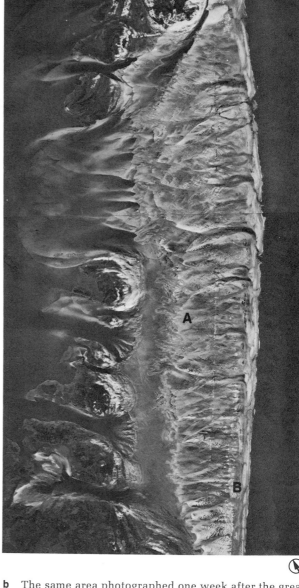

b The same area photographed one week after the great Atlantic storm of 1962. U.S. Coast and Geodetic Survey, March 15, 1962.

shown in Figure 2.15. If the prevailing trend of the rock structure is parallel to the coastal trend, wave erosion is likely to have a straightening effect; whereas, if the trend forms a large angle to the coast, erosion will ordinarily produce irregularities.

2.14 Wave-straightened coast at San Onofre, California. Shows also elevated marine terrace and eroded mountains in background. Photo by R. C. Frampton.

MARINE DEPOSITION COASTS   Along the Gulf Coast and the East Coast south of New York, the land has been extended seaward since sea level virtually stopped its rise. Unless offset by submergence, such extensions take place along those coasts bordered by shallow water where so much bottom sediment is stirred up by waves that longshore currents are incapable of transporting all of it along the shore, and a considerable amount is piled up onto the adjacent beach.

The seaward growth of a coast is the result of the processes of deposition. The waves may cause accretion to the beaches, building out sand plains, or, because of breaking well out from shore, the waves may build up sand bars. The latter may become emergent sand ridges that lie well out from the coast, enclosing lagoons on the inside. These barriers have been the typical development along the East and Gulf Coasts

2.15 Rocky headland and coves, the product of wave erosion near Pt. Sur, California. U.S. Department of Agriculture.

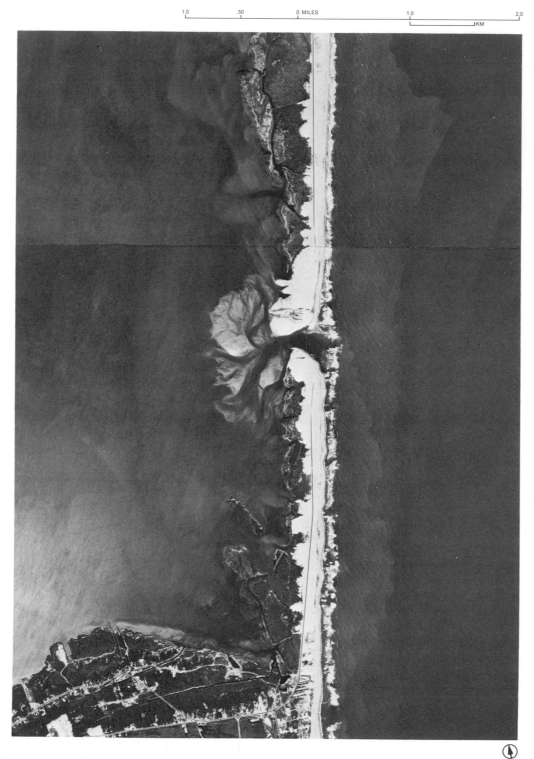

2.16 A barrier beach with tidal delta inside inlet about 6 miles north of Cape Hatteras, North Carolina. Inlet was opened by the March 1962 Atlantic storm. Tidal delta had formed in less than 2 months. About 10 months after being opened, the inlet was artificially closed by the U.S. Army Corps of Engineers. U.S. Coast and Geodetic Survey, May 3, 1962.

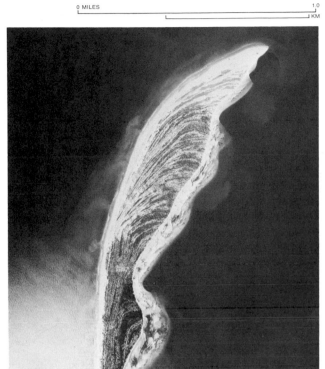

2.17 Tisbury Great Pond, Martha's Vineyard Island, Massachusetts. A glacial outwash plain was eroded by several small streams, which were drowned by post-glacial rise in sea level. The irregular shore has been straightened by building a barrier across the estuaries. U.S. Coast and Geodetic Survey, 1955.

2.18 St. Joseph Spit, western Florida Panhandle. Successive sand ridges with light tones alternating with swales reveal the growth history of this spit. U.S. Geological Survey, 1942.

of the United States where the bottom is much more gently sloping than off the West Coast. The sand barriers ordinarily flank the mainland. If they consist of only one low ridge, they are referred to as *barrier beaches* (Fig. 2.16). If they include more than one ridge with intervening marshy flats or if dunes are on the inside rising well above the beach, they are called *barrier islands*. A *bay barrier* is one that is built across the mouth of a bay (Fig. 2.17).

In the early stages of development, the barriers are commonly formed adjacent to points, and these are referred to as *spits* (Fig. 2.18). As the spits grow, they are apt to have their points turned by storm waves and develop hooks. Further extension of the spit may then proceed, and at the time of another storm a second hook may develop. Many spits have a succession of these hooks representing the effects of various storms during their growth (Fig. 2.18). Whether or not the spits will unite and close the bay depends largely on the strength of the tidal cur-

rents. This, in turn, is related to the tidal ranges in the area and to the size of the enclosed bay; large tides and large bays have the most powerful currents.

Barrier ridges may be continuous for a hundred or more miles along a coast, like Padre Island of southern Texas. The continuity of these ridges is very dependent on the frequency of great storms. Figures 2.13*a* and *b* show how a hurricane cut a series of channels across a barrier along the Maryland coast. These channels are likely to be of short duration, depending on storm frequency and on the tidal flows that tend to keep them open.

After the formation of barriers, the lagoons on the inside fill with sufficient rapidity that important changes may be seen in a few decades. Streams entering the lagoons deposit muddy sediment in these inland bodies of water, and tidal currents coming in through the passes from the outer ocean carry in large quantities of sand. As the lagoons become filled, they take on the character of marshes crossed by

TYPES OF COASTS

21

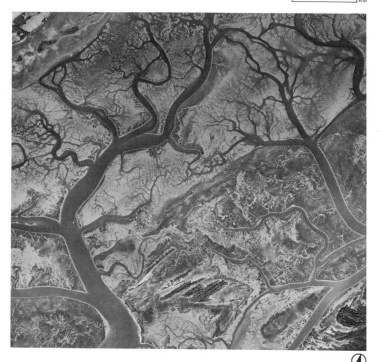

2.19 Tidal marshes and streams on St. Phillips Island, South Carolina. There are remnants of old beach ridges in the marsh, but most of the area was a tidal lagoon, now traversed by numerous small tidal channels. U.S. Department of Agriculture, 1955.

twisting channels, like those in Figure 2.19. Some of the marsh channels are the result of tidal currents and others of stream runoff from the land. At this stage, the area is virtually useless to man and very hard to traverse, either by boat or on foot. The sequence of lagoon filling is well illustrated by John Lucke's diagrams (Fig. 2.20).

Where large quantities of sediment are carried into a bay through a narrow inlet, either by tides or by a great storm, a tidal delta may form (Fig. 2.16). This is the opposite of a river delta and represents building toward the land rather than away from it. Another form develops, particularly during hurricanes when the water seeps over barriers, producing *wash-over fans* (Fig. 2.21). Sand spits often extend into lagoons, both from the inside of barrier islands and out from the mainland (Fig. 2.22). These *cuspate spits* may be partly the result of overwash but appear to be closely related to currents within the bays.

Another type of barrier represents the intersection of two arcuate beaches in a point protruding far into the ocean outside a low sand coast. This is called a *cuspate foreland* and is typified by Cape Hatteras (Fig. 2.23a). In some cases, forelands are connected with the mainland, as, for example, Cape Kennedy; but ordinarily they have wide lagoons on the inside and barrier island on their margins.

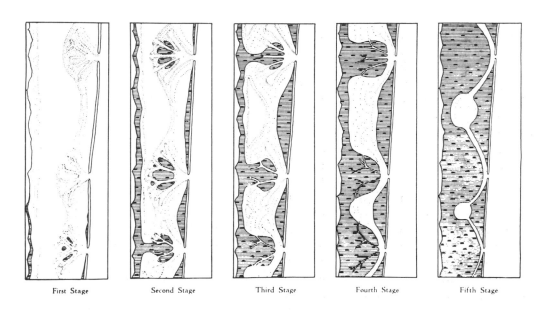

First Stage   Second Stage   Third Stage   Fourth Stage   Fifth Stage

2.20 Idealized stages in the filling of a tidal lagoon. From Lucke (1934).

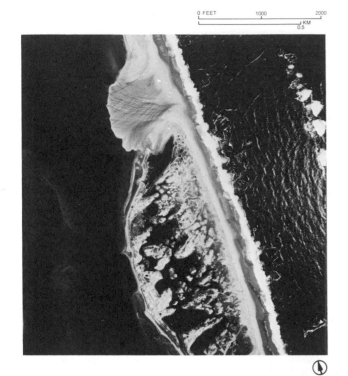

Deposition also takes place on the upcurrent side of projecting capes or rocky islands. These islands become connected with the land, and they are then termed *tombolos*. Spits may develop on both sides, forming a double tombolo with a completely enclosed lagoon. Where man has built jetties out into the sea, deposition takes place on the side toward which the dominant current is running (Fig. 2.24). Smaller walls, called *groins*, produce the same effect. On the downcurrent side of these projecting walls, erosion may have serious effects on beach and shore property.

2.21 Nauset Beach barrier near Chatham, Cape Cod, Massachusetts, illustrating two generations of washover fans. A new barrier was built on seaward side of the washover, and a very narrow barrier seals lagoon side. A major storm in 1961 formed a new beach to the north, and a new washover fan formed. The March 1962 Atlantic storm formed a breach through the 1961 washover fan. U.S. Coast and Geodetic Survey, April 1961.

2.22 Cuspate spits in the lagoon inside Santa Rosa Island, western Florida Peninsula. Photo by D. L. Inman, 1951.

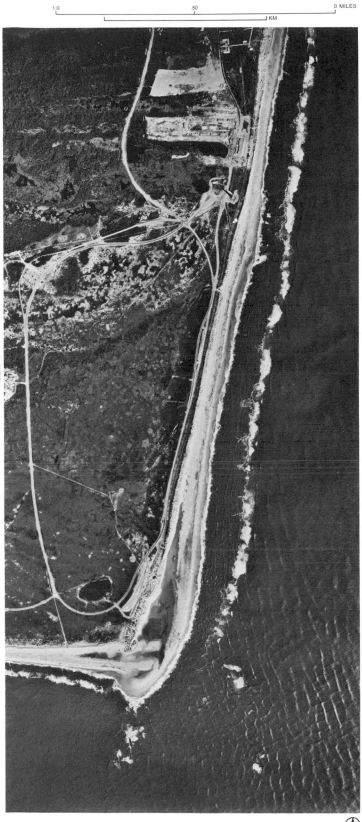

2.23

a Cape Hatteras, North Carolina. This well-known cuspate foreland forms nearly a right-angle bend in shoreline. Littoral currents from the north extend the cape southward, while currents from the west extend it eastward. The latest littoral current was from the north. U.S. Coast and Geodetic Survey, 1958.

b Small cuspate foreland on Lacosta Island, southwest Florida. This was formed in an area protected by an offshore cuspate sandkey. Photo by D. L. Inman, 1951.

2.24 Lake Worth Inlet, Palm Beach, Florida. Jetties were built to protect the harbor entrance. The predominant littoral current is southward, indicated by growth against north jetty. There has been some erosion next to south jetty. U.S. Coast and Geodetic Survey, 1945.

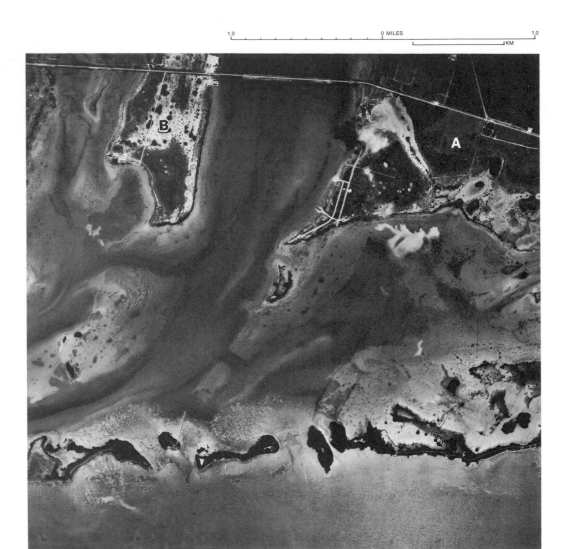

2.25 Coral reef coast, Florida Keys. Overseas highway (U.S. Route 1) crosses Big Pine (A) and Little Torch (B) Keys, islands composed of Miami oölite. The narrow chain of islands to the south is an old coral reef. U.S. Coast and Geodetic Survey, 1955.

COASTS BUILT OUT BY ANIMALS AND PLANTS   Certain lime-secreting animals are capable of building out coasts, although they normally do not build above sea level. Of these, corals are the most important. Coral reefs are found exclusively in warm seas and in localities where the water is relatively clear, that is, away from the mouths of muddy streams. The corals grow up to low-tide level; but the reefs often are built higher by large waves that break off portions of the growing or dead coral and throw it onto the growing reef so that it may build above sea level, even sufficiently for habitation of

man (Fig. 2.25). Most of the coral islands of the Pacific and many of the Atlantic are the result of this combined activity. Associated with the corals are other abundant organisms, notably the algal plants. Some of these plants can grow slightly above low tide because they can be kept alive by ocean spray. This causes the raised margins, called *lithothamnion ridges*, which are exposed at low tide along the outer edge of many growing reefs.

Small additions to the coast can be formed by serpulid worms that develop solid lime tubes that become cemented onto the outer beach. These worm reefs also are virtually confined to the tropics and subtropics. Oyster reefs develop mostly in bays. Masses of dead shells are brought up by waves and form islands but occur mostly as submerged bars.

Some trees, notably mangroves, are able to grow in salt water. These are capable of prograding coasts and are particularly common in tropical embayments (Fig. 2.26). Extensive coasts with mangrove projections are found in southwest Florida. Generally, these develop inside sand islands, but in some places wave action is small and mangroves grow out into the open sea. Vegetation also forms coastal protrusions in many partially filled bays, due to the growth of marsh grass and various types of sedges in the shallow waters. Sediment is entrapped around these grasses until they become islands or even a part of the mainland.

2.26 Mangroves bordering limestone islands at Big Pine Key, Florida. Photo by D. L. Inman.

REFERENCES

Johnson, D. W., 1919. *Shore Processes and Shoreline Development.* John Wiley & Sons, New York, pp. 159–403.

Lucke, J. B., 1934. A study of Barnegat Inlet, New Jersey, and related shoreline phenomena. *Shore and Beach,* Jour. Amer. Shore and Beach Preservation Assn., vol. 2, no. 2, pp. 5–54.

Shepard, F. P., 1963. *Submarine Geology,* 2d ed. Harper & Row, New York, pp. 152–166.

————, and D. L. Inman, 1950. Nearshore water circulation related to bottom topography and wave refraction. *Trans. Amer. Geophysical Union,* vol. 31, no. 2, pp. 196–212.

For additional discussion on wave mechanics, see:

Bascom, Willard, 1964. *Waves and Beaches.* Doubleday & Company, Garden City, N.Y., chaps. 2–4.

Inman, D. L., 1963. In F. P. Shepard, *Submarine Geology,* Harper & Row, New York, chap. 3.

Kinsman, Blair, 1965. *Wind Waves, Their Generation and Propagation on the Ocean Surface.* Prentice-Hall, Englewood Cliffs, N.J.

Wiegel, R. L., 1964. *Oceanographic Engineering.* Prentice-Hall, Englewood Cliffs, N.J., chaps. 2–5.

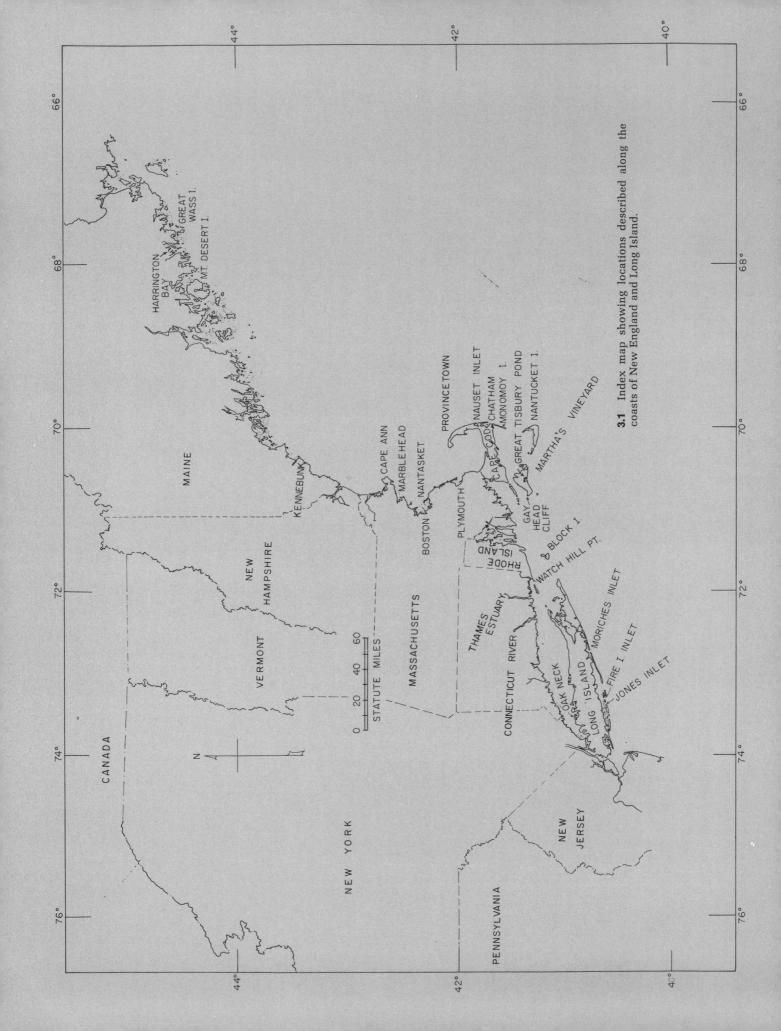

3.1 Index map showing locations described along the coasts of New England and Long Island.

Glaciated Coasts

New England and Long Island

3 The only East Coast areas with rocky bluffs and shores are found between northeastern Maine and Staten Island, New York (Fig. 3.1). All this region was glaciated during the Pleistocene ice age, and the continental glaciers extended beyond the present shoreline as far south as Nantucket Island, Massachusetts. The outermost margin of the ice traversed Nantucket, Martha's Vineyard, Block Island, and Long Island, but west of New York Harbor it curved inland away from the coast. The glacier was a powerful erosive agent and removed much of the surface soil and weathered rock. As it moved slowly over the New England terrain, rock fragments embedded in its base scratched and polished the solid rock beneath. These scratches, called *striations,* and the polished rock surfaces are still to be seen at many places, even a few feet from the present seashore. At such places, virtually no erosion has occurred since the disappearance of the latest glacier some 12,000 years ago. The study and mapping of the directions of these striations permits the reconstruction of the flow pattern of the vanished glaciers. In favorable locations, the glaciers were able to erode the sea floor far below the contemporary sea level.

The substratum in New England varies in its resistance to erosion from weak clays and sands, such as those exposed in western Martha's Vineyard and outer Cape Cod, to the granites and other equally hard rocks that characterize the Maine coast. Before the glacial period, areas of weaker rock had been worn down to lower relief than those with the more resistant rocks. In general, where exposed along the coasts, the weak rocks have undergone more glacial excavation as well as more postglacial wave erosion than areas with granitic bedrock. However, there are spectacular wave-steepened cliffs along the northern Maine coast where soft rocks were left in juxtaposition with the rugged granite hills, and the waves have accentuated the relief after the glaciers retreated. Before glaciation, areas such as Passamaquoddy Bay, at the Canadian border, and the Boston and Narragansett Bay areas were lowlands and now form major indentations of the coast.

The advance of the continental glacier over New England created a great additional load, under the weight of which the land was depressed to degrees dependent on the weight of the glacial ice at any particular place. Near the Maine–New Brunswick border, the bedrock is found as deep as 400 feet below the present sea level. This is partially due to the glacial scour. Subsidence under the load of the glacier made this even deeper; but, as the glacial ice melted, the load diminished, permitting a rebound. However, the glacier melted more quickly than the rate of uplift of the land. As far as is known, when the ice had disappeared from the coast, the margin of the sea advanced, keeping contact with the retreating glacier until the ice margin was higher than the contemporary sea level. Prior to that time, the melting ice discharged its load of debris directly into the sea. Much of this load was finely pulverized "rock flour," which was distributed by waves and currents to form an extensive deposit of marine clay, with a base locally as deep as 300 feet below the sea floor. Gravels and sands accumulated close to the margin of the glacier but were not extensively reworked in the sea. Icebergs dropped rocks as they drifted, and these are now found surrounded by fine marine clays.

Soon after the glacier had disappeared, the land, freed from the load of glacial ice, began to rise. The amount of rebound can be measured by the heights above present sea level where clays containing sea shells are found overlying glacial deposits or glacially eroded rock. The rebound was not uniform, but ranged from about 350 to 400 feet above present sea level at the Maine–New Brunswick border to zero (sea level) about 100 miles south of Boston. This means that near the Canadian border the land subsided more than 400 feet under the load, while the subsidence was negligible south of Cape Cod.

Although the crust of the earth is more rigid than wet clay and reacts much more slowly to loading and subsequent unloading, the following example will illustrate the causes behind the elevation and depression of parts of New England and other glaciated areas during and after the ice age. If a heavy load, such as a pile of iron ore, is placed on wet clay, the load will settle into the ground and a bulge will form around it as the clay is squeezed toward the side of the loaded area. If the load is later removed, the ground under it will rise gradually and the bulge will eventually disappear. The southernmost New England coast was covered by much thinner glacial ice than the northern area, and therefore may have bulged slightly, while the northern area was depressed.

As explained in Chapter 2, another factor enters the complicated story of sea-level change on the New England coast. The water to form the Pleistocene[1] glaciers came from the oceans of the world; and, at the climax of late glaciation, the world sea level was at least 300 feet lower than at present. With the melting of the glaciers, the meltwater largely returned to the sea, virtually restoring its preglacial level. Such worldwide changes in sea level are called *eustatic,* while the depression of the land under the weight of an ice sheet and its subsequent rebound is called *isostatic adjustment.*

Thus, on the coast of northern New England, after deglaciation, the land was rising following the removal of the glacial ice, while at the same time the sea level was also rising because of the return of meltwater to the ocean. Some areas probably maintained a stable sea level for some time, because the rebound on the land nearly matched the rate of sea-level rise. Different parts of the coast might have been emerging or submerging simultaneously, depending on which process was dominant at each place.

Tide gauge records show that parts of the land depressed by glacial ice have not entirely rebounded as yet. The amount of settling under glacial load is difficult to determine, because the glaciers eroded extensively below sea level. Since huge glaciers still exist in Antarctica, Greenland, and smaller ice-covered areas, sea level is still about 100 to 200 feet below that of an ice-free world; therefore, future drowning may be expected.

The discovery that rather accurate dates, within the past 30,000 years, can be determined from the proportions of carbon-14 in long-buried plant detritus and in marine or freshwater shells, has permitted the postglacial dating of sea-level changes at many places along the New England coast.

---

[1] A time scale of geological periods may be found at the end of the book.

According to the investigations of A. L. Bloom, C. A. Kaye, and E. S. Barghoorn, a general sequence of events has been approximately as follows:

12,000 to 13,000 years before the present (B.P.) —Melting glaciers exposed most of the New England coast. World sea levels were still about 150 feet below the present level. However, because all of northern New England had been pushed down by the great weight of the ice to a level lower than the 150 feet, the sea encroached beyond the present coast in these northern areas; and marine clays were deposited landward of the present coast. In southern New England, where the thin ice had had little weighting effect, the shoreline was many miles seaward of its present location.

12,000 to 10,000 years B.P.—Sea level rise and land rebound approximately offset each other in northern New England, so that the submerged condition of the coast was maintained with little change.

12,000 to 300 years B.P.—Southern New England became submerged more or less continuously at rates that decreased markedly about 6,000 years B.P.

10,000 to 3,000 years B.P.—Rebound in northern New England greater than sea-level rise, resulting in gradual emergence of the coast.

7,000 to 3,000 years B.P.—General stability in Boston area due to balance of rebound and sea-level rise.

3,000 to 300 years B.P.—General submergence of all New England by a few feet.

300 years B.P. to present—Virtual stability of sea level along most of the coast.

The lack of recent change in sea level is substantiated by soundings and by barnacle accumulations on rocks and pier pilings during the past 100 years and by the position of kitchen-midden heaps of discarded oyster shells (prehistoric).

Thus, the New England coastline, which has somewhat the aspect of a recently drowned coast, has had a complex history of glacial scour below sea level, subsidence under load, rebound, and sea-level rise following deglaciation. The uplift did not exceed the downwarping; therefore, the coast today retains many characteristics of drowning. Since only slight changes in sea level have occurred during the past 3,000 years, the waves, littoral currents, and tidal currents (where conditions were favorable) have had time to erode, transport, and deposit detritus in adjusting the shoreline to present sea level.

Factors generally unfavorable to present-day wave erosion in New England are

1. The earlier removal of soil and weathered rock by glacial erosion left hard rock at the coast.

2. The intricacy of the coastal outline, with many islands, especially in Maine, and headlands elsewhere, protected localities from direct wave attack.

3. Vegetative cover is extensive, due to cool climate and adequate rainfall.

Factors locally favorable to marine erosion include

1. Glacial till, outwash sands and gravels, and marine clays, where found along the coast, are relatively easy to erode.

2. Many of the rock cliffs are extensively jointed or have been disrupted by faulting, so that they may be undermined and fall to the shore in large blocks.

Sand is not so plentiful on most parts of the New England coast as elsewhere, because the hard rocks of the area do not produce much sand upon weathering, and the rivers generally discharge into drowned valleys, so do not introduce sand to the open coast. Such sand as there is comes mainly from erosion of cliffs of glacial drift and outwash.

Rock fragments in the form of large and small boulders, picked up by glaciers, may have been moved hundreds of miles from their parent ledges. At the margin of the great ice sheet, the warmer climate caused melting to keep pace with glacial advance; and the load brought to the perimeter was deposited. When the ice front remained in nearly the same position for some time, rock debris continued to be brought to this terminus and dropped where melting at the front balanced the forward movement. Thus, after the glacier had disappeared, the deposit along this line was thicker than in other parts of the glaciated area and formed what is called an *end moraine*. There may be more than one end moraine of a particular glacial stage, because while the glacier is wasting away, its front may again become nearly stationary behind the outermost position reached by the glacier during this stage. Long Island, New York, has two such end moraines, one at or near the north shore and the other at the west end near the middle of the island but approaching the south shore at the eastern end.

At times, glaciers retreat rather slowly, and all of the load from the largest boulders to the finest clay is deposited together. This forms what is called *glacial till*. A layer of such material, ranging from a few feet to several hundred feet in thickness, is distributed over most of the region once covered by the New England glaciers.

Where glaciers covered extensive areas in which the topography is hilly, the glacial ice was much thicker over the lowlands than over the hills. During glacial wastage in New England, ice masses in the valleys were cut off from other parts of the glacier and became stagnant. In such regions, there is no position that can be mapped as an end moraine of a certain stage in glacial wastage. In New England, the ice disappeared first from hilltops where it was thin and remained longest in lowlands, such as the present Long Island Sound. Therefore, no substantial end moraines are found north of those on Long Island, except those on Block Island, Elizabeth Islands, Martha's Vineyard, Nantucket, and southern Cape Cod.

When a glacier is overloaded with debris, generally close to its outer margin, this debris accumulates at the base of the glacier, and the moving ice shapes it into oval masses, called *drumlins*. These may be half a mile or more in length, and sometimes as high as 200 feet. The glacial till in them is very compact, because it was deposited under a considerable weight of ice. Drumlins generally occur in large groups, all with their long dimensions pointing in the direction of movement of the now-vanished glaciers. Because the drumlins are compact, they erode less easily than the till formed higher in the glacier. A large group of drumlins is located in and near Boston, some forming the islands of Boston Harbor.

When a glacier stagnates, most of its load is deposited where the ice melts. When a glacier is still moving but the melting at the front balances its rate of advance, the meltwaters flowing from the ice margin toward the sea carry away much of the debris. The streams redistribute the material as outwash, with the boulders and cobbles dropped close to the ice front and the lighter sand and pebbles washed away from it, forming either a sloping plain against the end moraine, known as an *outwash plain*, or extending for miles away from the ice front along rivers that carry the meltwater toward the sea, the latter called *valley trains*. The average size of fragments transported down river valleys decreases with distance from the end moraine. Outwash material is eroded more readily than glacial till, because the clay in till tends to make it more compact.

Outwash sands and gravels are extensively distributed in front of end moraines on Cape Cod and the islands to the south. Along eastern Cape Cod, the ease of erosion of these deposits has caused rapid retreat of the sea cliffs, in contrast to the jagged rocky coasts of northern New England. Similarly, along the northern shore of Long Island, bluffs with outcrops of glacial deposits associated with one of the end moraines have receded extensively during the past century.

GREAT WASS ISLAND, MAINE (Fig. 3.2)
Great Wass (A)[2] is typical of the complex coast of Maine, with many islands, some of which are separated from the mainland by as much as 30 miles. The area was intensively glaciated, and bedrock[3] is exposed along all the coasts as well as on the island hills. The bedrock is principally granite, although the darker shades as at B indicate volcanic rocks. In the embayments, water depths are generally 20 to 40 feet, except at the lower right where a small area near the center of the photo has water depths of 80 feet. The tidal range is 11 to 13 feet, and many of the lighter areas in the upper part of the photo are mud flats exposed at low tide. None of the islands have sand beaches. The sharp truncation of Great Wass Island (with a tone change in the adjacent water) (C) represents a submerged escarpment, where water depth increases from about 40 to 220 feet in a short distance. Douglas Johnson called this the Fundian Fault, named for the Bay of Fundy; but it was interpreted by Shepard as the rim of a broad glacially gouged fiord, an interpretation that has now

[2] Letters refer to marked points in aerial photographs.

[3] Rock exposures generally have a lighter tone in aerial photographs.

3.2 Great Wass Island, Maine. A glacially eroded area of granite, which was drowned by postglacial rise in sea level. Letters refer to features described in text. U.S. Coast and Geodetic Survey, 1959.

been confirmed by reflection profiling. It is believed that the glacier advanced southwest, down the Bay of Fundy, and sent arms up smaller tributary valleys between the islands. The incoming tides have stronger flow than the ebb tides and probably carry mud in suspension to be deposited in sheltered places between islands (D). The sediment is largely reworked marine clay. Glacial striae are found within a few feet of sea level at various places, showing negli-

gible erosion in recent times. Tree stumps are visible offshore, indicating slight subsidence of relatively recent date.

The principal change to be expected here is continued silting of bays, so that some small boat channels may require dredging. The rock shores will remain virtually unchanged for a long time. The irregular coast and varied water depths are typical of topography affected by extensive glacial erosion.

3.3 Harrington Bay area, Maine, showing the heads of stream valleys converted into tidal flats by deposition from strong inflowing tidal currents. U.S. Coast and Geodetic Survey, 1959.

HARRINGTON BAY AREA, MAINE (Fig. 3.3)
The coast of Maine is deeply embayed. These bays were partially filled with glaciomarine clays formed just after the glaciers had melted. Subsequent rebound of the lands following glacial unloading has exposed the clays above sea level. Much clay has since been washed down to form new deposits at lower elevations. Fine clays and silts eroded from the margins of the Bay of Fundy are carried by incoming tides up into the heads of small estuaries and creeks, where they accumulate as tidal mud flats. Such mud

flats are even commoner in New Brunswick and Nova Scotia, where the tidal range is as much as 60 feet compared with 11 feet at Harrington Bay.

The Harrington Bay area (Fig. 3.3) is about 15 miles northwest of Great Wass Island. Bedrock hills form islands in the lower part of the bay, but tidal flats are very conspicuous in the heads of the three bays: (from left to right) Black Bay, Flat Bay, and Harrington "River." Tidal currents scour mud from the channels through which they flow but drop the sediment on the flanking mud flats. Water depth at the junction of the Harrington "River" and Flat Bay tidal channels is 35 feet, and very narrow central channels are visible up to the tidal limit in several creeks. Here, the principal effect of coastal change is the filling of harbors with clay and silt.

MT. DESERT ISLAND, MAINE   Although the rocky coast of Maine is predominantly low, an east-west ridge of granite forms the highest elevation on the entire Atlantic coast of the United States. This centers in the 1,532-foot Cadillac Mountain of Acadia National Park. The granite ridge is cut by a series of deep notches, extending generally north-south. Many of these form elongated ponds, but Somes Sound (A in Fig. 3.4) is an embayment of the seacoast with water depths as great as 150 feet and marginal cliffs that rise to more than 800 feet above sea level. This is the best example of a fiord on our Atlantic coast. The broad bay south of Mt. Desert Island is about 50 feet deep. The features of this area were produced by a continental glacier advancing from the north, which met an obstruction in the east-west granite ridge. Following a series of notches formed by faults or dikes of basaltic rock, the glacier scoured U-shaped valleys across the granite ridge and, in the case of Somes Sound, cut a particularly deep valley. When sea level rose, following the melting of the glaciers, the margin of the sea terminated against steep walls of granite cut by the glacier. These walls might give the impression of being great wave-cut cliffs, but actually they have been very little modified by wave erosion.

In this area, a very few narrow glacial valleys have been closed by small gravel bars. Otherwise, during the past 3,000 years, while the sea has been near its present position, almost no changes have been made by waves, and very little change is to be expected in the near future.

KENNEBUNK–CAPE PORPOISE AREA, MAINE

[Fig. 3.5]   In southern Maine, New Hampshire, and northern Massachusetts, offshore rocky islands are smaller and less numerous. Here, the shoreline has frequent alternations between rocky headlands and sandy or gravelly beaches. Much of the sand and gravel is derived from outwash deposits formed by streams that transported glacial meltwater to the sea. Most of the outwash was not deposited in the sea. The sand and gravel of beaches was largely derived from nonmarine sediments along the shore. Other sources of sand and gravel are wave erosion, sorting of glacial deposits, and sediments carried to the seashore by rivers, such as the Merrimac in northern coastal Massachusetts.

The well-known summer resort coast at Kennebunk (A) and Cape Porpoise (B), located 20 miles south of Portland, represent a considerable change from the deeply embayed areas north of Portland, where myriads of islands are separated by deep passages. In this more southerly Maine region, there are only minor embayments and a few protecting islands, so that boats are more exposed to storm waves and yachting is less popular.

The effect of glaciation is much less pronounced along this part of the coast. The embayments are more typical of drowned river valleys. A few relatively long estuaries extend into the land, as at the mouth of the Kennebunk River and at Cape Porpoise. These estuaries are being filled at their heads by silt and clay deposits introduced by small streams and by sand carried in from the coast by strong tides. Because of the tides, these estuaries are deep enough to be used as harbors for small boats.

Pocket beaches can be seen on both sides of the Kennebunk–Cape Porpoise area. These narrow beaches are cut away by winter storms and are built up each summer. On the east end of Kennebunk Beach, the west jetty of the Kennebunk estuary shows some buildup of sand, indicating the effect of the southwesterly approach of the waves during summers. A sand tidal flat (C) is exposed at low tide on the west side of the Goosefair Beach at the mouth of the small estuary. Farther east, the sand is developing a spit (D) outside the small point. This may become connected to the rocks, developing a tombolo.

CAPE ANN, MASSACHUSETTS   Cape Ann, a rocky peninsula about 25 miles northeast of Boston,

3.4 Somes Sound, Mt. Desert Island, Maine, the best example of a fiord along the Atlantic coast of the United States. U.S. Department of Agriculture, 1966.

3.5 The Kennebunk–Cape Porpoise area in southwestern Maine. Glacial scour was less intense than in northeastern Maine, shows bedrock in promontories and offshore islands. Coasts with glacial till or sand and gravel have been cut back, leaving small coves with sand or gravel beaches. Drowned river valleys form boat harbors. U.S. Department of Agriculture, 1962.

is composed largely of granite bedrock. The average elevation of uplands on Cape Ann is 100 to 150 feet, so the peninsula is much less rugged than Mt. Desert Island. Cape Ann was glaciated, and coastal lowlands and inland areas are thinly covered with glacial drift. The area illustrated (Fig. 3.6) shows Gloucester Harbor and Eastern Point, a promontory at the southeastern border of the cape. Eastern Point is

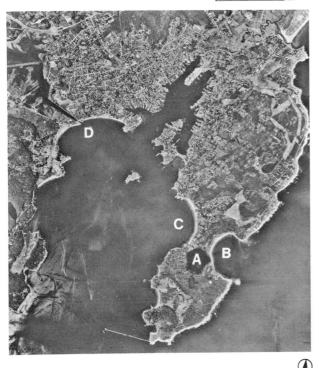

3.6 The southern part of Cape Ann, Massachusetts, including Gloucester Harbor and Eastern Point. Rocky coast with rounded coves and narrow beaches. U.S. Department of Agriculture, 1952.

3.7 Marblehead and Marblehead Neck, Massachusetts. The Neck is a tombolo tied to the mainland by a sand barrier. U.S. Army Map Service, 1945.

nearly separated from areas to the north by a narrow neck of land, with Niles Pond (A) in the center. The coast is low and rocky except for two sandy bays, Brace Cove (B) and Southeast Harbor (C), on each side of the neck and a small cove with a sandy beach (D). Waves striking this indented coast have drifted sand and gravel from both ends toward the center of the cove. This is probably a place where glacial drift extended to or below sea level.

Evidently this area was partially drowned by postglacial rise of sea level, and the site of the neck was formerly a lowland. After partial drowning, Eastern Point became an island about half a mile offshore. Then sand and gravel, washed from the headlands on each margin of the mainland and the island, accumulated in the passageway and formed a land-tied island. The Eastern Point tombolo was broadened and built up until part of it is now 20 feet above sea level. Sand drifting into the embayed area from each side has widened the "neck." A few offshore rock

stacks are outlined by the white foam of breaking waves.

Granite along this coast will erode very slowly, but a major storm may remove much of the sand from the pocket beaches, leaving a residue of cobbles and gravel, as found on many New England beaches.

MARBLEHEAD AND MARBLEHEAD NECK [Figs. 3.7, 3.8 and 3.9]   Few localities have been so badly named as the historical town of Marblehead and the neighboring Marblehead Neck. There is no marble within scores of miles. Our forefathers, evidently weak in geology, must have been fooled by the intrusions of Quincy granite or the relatively white Dedham granodiorite. The Neck, connected by a tombolo, might be more properly called the Head.

Marblehead (Fig. 3.7) is known as the birthplace of the United States Navy. It was formerly an important fishing port and now in summer the harbor shelters one of the largest fleets of sailing yachts in

3.8 A small area on the rocky Marblehead coast, showing very little change in coastal features in 58 years.

a June 17, 1892, photo. The costumes and the rigging of sailboats look out of place today. Photographer unknown.

b Summer 1950. The tide is similar to that of the 1892 photo, but many details of the rocky shore show no change. Photo by Shepard.

the country. It is well protected except for occasional northeast storms during which the wind blows directly into the harbor. The fetch is only 4 miles, so the waves do not build up to great heights; but these storms often cause anchors to drag and yachts to pile up on the harbor side of the causeway. The rock is sufficiently indurated so that even at the entrance to the harbor, erosion from these easterly storms is so slow that no appreciable changes have occurred since 1890 (Figs. 3.8a and b). Much larger waves develop on the outside of the Neck during easterly storms. As a result, the indentations have little sand, and storm beaches are built up between the headlands (Fig. 3.9).

The tombolo that connects Marblehead Neck to the mainland was entirely due to natural causes in prehistoric times. The prevalent southwest winds, which still carry sand along this northeasterly trending coast, deposited sand where a former crystalline rock island, now the Neck, provided some protection from northeast storms. There is no evidence that the situation has changed appreciably in historical times. A similar tombolo connects nearby Lynn with the two crystalline rock islands of Nahant.

In 1894, an attempt was made by Bostonian John H. Sears to show that the ledges around Marblehead and Salem had sunk about 2 feet since the Nathaniel Bowditch[4] surveys of 1804. In 1935, this evidence was critically reexamined by J. W. Goldthwait, who concluded that Sears had based his conclusions on comparisons of rather remote ledges where the old surveys had failed to define clearly the relation of depths to the extreme low tides. Other descriptions from the Bowditch survey showed that in 1804 some ledges near Peach's Point, Marblehead, were laid bare only during low spring tides, and exactly the same phenomenon was observed by Goldthwait in 1935. Shepard, coming from a yachting family who had a summer home on Peach's Point, can verify this observation. In fact, he is most familiar with the rocks in the area, because his father used to hit them with his yacht whenever he miscalculated the height of the tide in approaching his mooring.

BOSTON HARBOR, MASSACHUSETTS [Figs. 3.10 and 2.4]   According to Kaye and Barghoorn,

[4] Bowditch wrote the first edition of the still available *The American Practical Navigator.*

3.9 A storm beach composed of gravel west of Marblehead, 1950. Note that the seaward slope is steeper than that on the sandy beaches. Photo by Shepard.

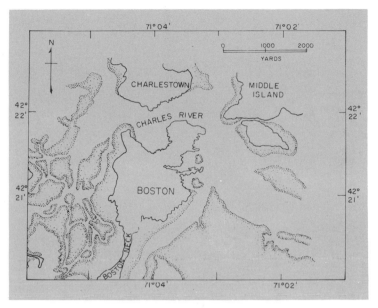

3.10

a Boston Harbor area mapped in 1765 by the British Admiralty. Note that Boston was connected with surrounding areas only by the narrow Boston Neck. Marshes just west of Boston later became the Back Bay district. From *The Atlantic Neptune*, reprinted in 1966.

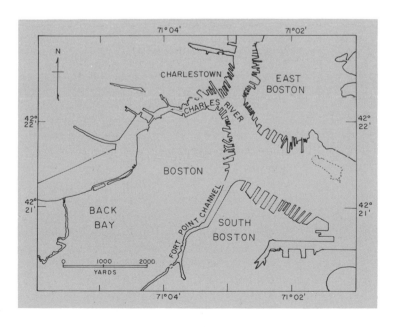

b Boston Harbor area as shown on the 1966 navigation chart of the U.S. Coast and Geodetic Survey. Much of the new land is the result of artificial fill.

when the glaciers retreated from the present site of Boston, the area was more submerged than at present; but, as a result of crustal rise due to rebound, the sea soon withdrew well beyond the present coast and left a relatively flat plain of glacial deposition with drumlins rising above it. Valleys were cut into this plain by streams. Later, with a reduction of rebound, the effect of sea-level rise caused a drowning of these valleys, leaving wide-mouthed estuaries and many of the drumlins as islands in the present harbor (Fig. 2.4).

When Boston was first settled in 1630, the harbor was very different from what it is now. The 1765 edition of the British Admiralty chart (Fig. 3.10*a*), published in *The Atlantic Neptune*, shows Boston as a tombolo connected to Roxbury by a narrow neck of land. The present Back Bay was literally a bay consisting of a network of channels separating extensive shoals. Many of the shoals became land due to river and tidal marine deposition, but most of the present land has been filled in artificially (Fig. 3.10*b*). The estuaries of Fort Port Channel, Charles River, and Mystic River have been considerably narrowed in the past two centuries.

Since the sea reached its present level, there have been many changes in the outer harbor. These were described by Douglas Johnson with particular refer-

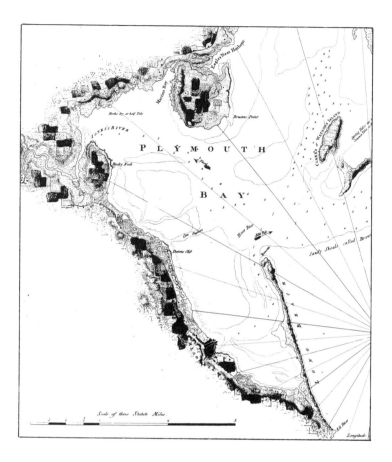

3.11 Changes in Plymouth Bay and Harbor between 1765 and 1960.

a 1765 chart of the British Admiralty. The rectangular patches are land holdings of rural residents. Depths in Plymouth Bay are in fathoms. From *The Atlantic Neptune*, reprinted in 1966.

thus forming a complex peninsula with the sharp change of direction (C). Where the drumlins continued to be exposed to wave attack, they were gradually eroded, leaving a bulge in the shoreline or a concentration of cobbles on a shoal outside the coast. Such a bulge is seen on the west side of the Nantasket Beach tombolo (D). The last remnants of a drumlin, called Skull Head, at this location were removed for road material early in the present century.

A small remnant of a drumlin, Little Hill (C), is found at a point of land forming the sharp angle in the tombolo. This remnant would have been destroyed by now if it had not been protected by a stone seawall built at its base. The drumlins may be considered as anchor points in maintaining the complex shoreline of Nantasket Beach. As soon as one of these points has been eroded, the coast may be expected to suffer rapid retreat unless artificially protected. Thus the small remnant of Little Hill with its seawall protects the large drumlin, Great Hill, at a sharp angle in the coast, preventing erosion of a densely populated coastal area.

Clifford Kaye, of the U.S. Geological Survey, has studied the erosion of a sea cliff at the west end of Long Island, well within the protected waters of Boston Harbor. He found that over a period of four years the cliff had retreated from a quarter to half a foot each year. The year with the greatest erosion was the one with the highest rainfall, suggesting that rain is more important than wave attack. During most of the time, the cliff was protected from wave erosion by talus, so that the surf was able to attack the cliff only for short periods. Mass movements on the face of the cliff were observed after the spring thaw had melted the ice in the soil interstices.

Boston Harbor is the only ocean coast in a drumlin belt in the United States, but other examples are found along the coasts of Nova Scotia and western Ireland. Drumlins are also along the south shore of Lake Ontario in western New York, where the waves of the lake are eroding and straightening the coast.

PLYMOUTH HARBOR, MASSACHUSETTS
[Fig. 3.11]   The harbor of Plymouth, the site of the second permanent British settlement in what is now the United States, offers the possibility of studying coastal changes for a longer span of years than in most other places on the northeast coast. After a short anchorage at Provincetown on outer Cape Cod,

ence to the drumlins in the Nantasket area (Fig. 2.4). Many of the drumlins were destroyed or partly destroyed by wave erosion. Others were cliffed on their exposed sides. The sediment derived from this erosion was redistributed by currents; and a barrier, now called Nantasket Beach, was built between some of the outer drumlins. The beach then protected the inner drumlins. The 1765 chart indicated that this barrier was narrower and less extensive in early colonial times and has now been lengthened to include Hull (A) and the mainland to the south. An illustration (Fig. 2.4) of the beginning of such a deposit is the narrow light band extending southeastward from Bumkin Island (B). Eventually these drumlins were tied together by sand and gravel bars (tombolos), the *Mayflower* crossed Massachusetts Bay to the mainland where the Pilgrims landed in 1620 and built a settlement, which they named Plymouth (A in Fig. 3.11b) after the English seaport from which they had sailed. According to tradition, they stepped out on a rock that has since become celebrated as Plymouth Rock. The original landing was about 3 miles north of the present town of Plymouth.

The oldest map of Plymouth that the present authors were able to locate was made in the 1760s by the British Admiralty (Fig. 3.11a) and was published in *The Atlantic Neptune* in 1776, along with numerous other New England coastal maps.

Plymouth Harbor is separated from Massachusetts Bay by Duxbury and Squamish Beaches, a long spit extending from the north and northeast, and by Long Beach (B in Fig. 3.11b). The bay inside these spits is mostly less than 6 feet deep except in a few tidal channels, the deepest of which is about 40 feet.

A comparison of *The Atlantic Neptune* map with aerial photos taken in 1943 (Fig. 3.11b) and in 1960 (not illustrated), shows very little change in this 170- to 190-year period. Long Beach had approximately the same length, location, and configuration and about the same tidal channels as on the old map. One may wonder how the *Mayflower* could have been piloted to a nearshore anchorage through a shallow mud flat without navigation charts showing locations of the tidal channels. The flats between the channels were less than 1 fathom (6 feet) deep at low tide, and photographs show that they must still be very shallow today.

It is probable that Plymouth Bay, protected by spits from the more turbulent water of Massachusetts Bay, has shoaled somewhat and that in the near future tidal mud flats will occupy more of it. The channel leading to Plymouth has been dredged to give a uniform depth of 15 feet to the docking area near Plymouth Rock.

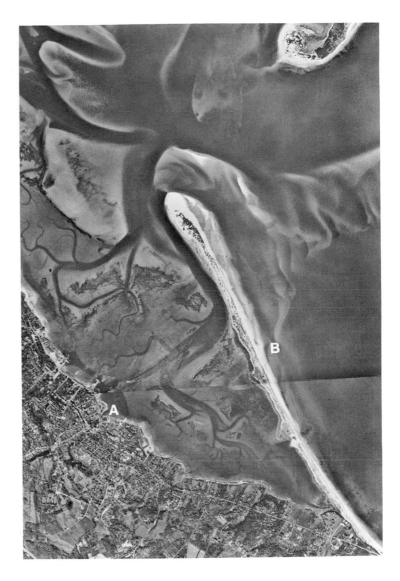

b Aerial photograph of southern part of Plymouth Bay and Long Beach, showing Plymouth Rock (A). The bay behind Long Beach appears shallower than in 1765, but otherwise there is little change. U.S. Department of Agriculture.

PROVINCETOWN AND EASTERN SHORE OF OUTER CAPE COD [Fig. 3.12]   The outer 20 miles of Cape Cod form a curving coast from Nauset Coast Guard Station, where the shore trends nearly north-south, to Race Point, where it trends nearly east-west. The peninsula in this area is largely composed of outwash sand and gravel, but the Sandwich moraine of southwestern Cape Cod may reach the eastern coast a little south of Nauset Coast Guard Station. The central and southern parts of this coast include uplands behind the beach, which rise abruptly 120 to 180 feet above sea level. At one point, the cliffs are surmounted by Cape Cod Light (formerly called Highland Light). Historical records show that because of the rapid cliff recession, the lighthouse had to be relocated at last three times dur-

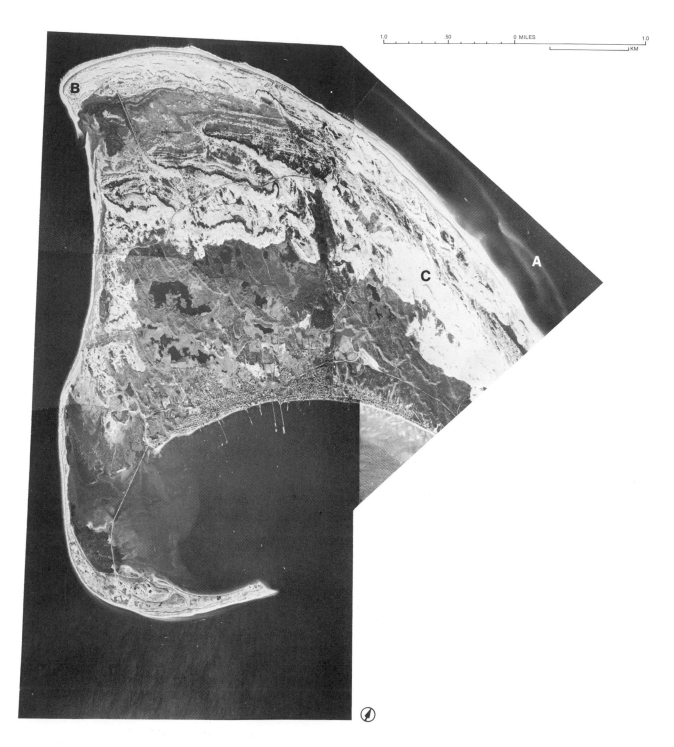

3.12 The Provincetown area, northern Cape Cod, Massachusetts. Sand has drifted from eroded bluffs of glacial outwash westward to Race Point (B). Behind the beach are large active sand dunes (C). Shore currents have shifted sand southward and eastward in a spit protecting Provincetown Harbor. U.S. Geological Survey, 1938.

ing the nineteenth century. Storms strike outer Cape Cod from all directions; but the most violent are those induced by strong northeast winds, the famous "nor'easters" of coastal New England. Such storms cut back the beach significantly; and, when waves are sufficiently high, the lower 10 to 30 feet of the cliffs is attacked. Because the cliffs are largely composed of unconsolidated sand and gravel of the glacial outwash plain, extensive slumping often follows. The slumped material accumulates near the base of the cliffs, which then remains comparatively stable until the next destructive nor'easter, perhaps several years later.

Attempts have been made to calculate the amount of cliff recession at Cape Cod since the waves first began to break against the shore at or near the present sea level. Johnson proposed that 3 miles of total recession had occurred in the narrow neck of the cape near Cape Cod Light. In 1957, John Zeigler and his associates studied rates of cliff retreat in outer Cape Cod. Compared with recent shorelines and careful surveys of the same coast made in 1887 by H. L. Marindin, Zeigler found that the cliffed part of the coast had retreated an average distance of 2.5 feet per year during a 70-year period, or a total of 175 feet. Erosion rates at different points along this stretch of coast vary from a minimum of 1 foot to a maximum of 4 feet per year. If this rate of recession is projected 3,000 years into the past (when sea level was close to its present stand), a total recession of 7,500 feet is indicated. This should probably be considered a minimum, since at the end of the rapid rise of sea level, waves lost less of their energy before reaching the coast because relative stability was necessary before a longshore bar could develop. These rapid rates of erosion contrast markedly with those on the granite coast of Maine.

Usually, when a rocky coast has been eroded, a rock bench a few feet below mean sea level extends seaward from the shore (Fig. 10.12). Storm waves break at the edge of this wave-cut platform and then lose much of their force before reaching the beach or coastal cliff. As a result, erosion decreases with the widening of the bench. However, there is no bench off the cliffs of Cape Cod. Aside from a narrow coastal bar (A in Fig. 3.12), the slope descends quite uniformly to depths of 500 feet or more outside the coast where all the erosion has taken place. Probably the strong tidal currents that flow along the coast are

capable of eroding the slope at a rate comparable to the retreat of the coast from wave attack. This is presumably possible because of the unconsolidated material in the slope.

Off outer Cape Cod, a nearshore bar is exposed at low tide 600 feet out from the beach; and along much of the coast a longshore bar, 20 to 30 feet below mean low tide, lies about 2,000 feet offshore. North of Provincetown, the longshore bar is plainly visible from the air (A). Zeigler and his associates have shown that if there is a breach in the longshore bar, the adjacent beach is eroded much more rapidly during storms than are beach areas protected by the bar. They also found that 44 percent of material eroded from the cliffs, beach, or shallow sea bottom, drifts along the shore, replacing sand lost from eroded beaches; 36 percent replaces sand eroded from the offshore bar; and only 20 percent is lost. Much of the latter is carried into deep water; but some is blown inland by the wind, forming dunes (C).

Under some conditions, the sand eroded from the beach or cliffs drifts westward toward Race Point, the northwestern tip of Cape Cod (B). Much sand that had accumulated on this east-west part of the cape has been blown inland to form the prominent belt of sand dunes north and northwest of Provincetown. During rising tides at Race Point, currents of considerable strength flow southeastward to fill Cape Cod Bay. Some of the sand drifts southward from Race Point and then to the east and finally northeast to Long Point, extending the spit that partially encloses Provincetown Harbor. West of Race Point, water is 100 feet deep 0.3 mile offshore and nearly 200 feet deep 0.6 mile offshore, illustrating the rapid advance of the cape end into Massachusetts Bay.

The whole complex hooked spit of the Provincetown area has been built of debris eroded from the 16 miles of cliffs of outer Cape Cod. Studies of the Provincetown–Cape Race area during the 70-year period from 1887 to 1957 show that beaches have prograded along the north coast of Cape Cod at rates varying from 0.5 foot to 5 feet per year. From time to time, these newer beaches are temporarily cut back by storms striking the coast from the north or northeast, but the beaches redevelop rapidly.

Along the southern part of the cliffed coast of outer Cape Cod, storm winds from the north to northeast generate shore currents that cause southward drifting. This drift formed Nauset Beach, a

1.0   0 MILES   1.0   2.0   3.0   4.0   5.0

KM

3.13 Straightening of the western shore of Cape Cod at Wellfleet Harbor by littoral currents, which have formed a barrier spit. Gyrol flow has carried much sediment southwest from the spit, forming Billingsgate Shoal (B). U.S. Army Map Service, 1960.

spit that has been built a total of 11 miles southward from the end of the cliffed coast and is still rapidly growing. Present-day changes in Nauset Beach are described later in this chapter.

WESTERN SHORE OF OUTER CAPE COD

The outwash plain responsible for the cliffs near Cape Cod Light slopes southwestward, and the plain eventually dips below present level of Cape Cod near Wellfleet Harbor (Fig. 3.13). The coast is quite uneven because of irregularities in the topography of the outwash plain where it passes below sea level. Cape Cod Bay has smaller waves than those of the open Atlantic; but north winds cause some southward beach drifting, and a spit partially protects the western entrance to Wellfleet Harbor. This spit has grown southward a total of about 3 miles. Photos of Wellfleet Harbor taken in 1938 and 1960 reveal that the spit has lengthened about 0.5 mile in 22 years, an

average rate of 120 feet per year (Fig. 3.13). Great Island (A), in line with the spit, has been tied to the mainland. For a mile south of the spit, water depths are less than 2 feet, and a part of this shoal is exposed at low tide.

Billingsgate Shoal extends 6 miles southwest from the tip of the sand spit. The photo shows the general bottom configuration to depths of about 18 feet. Although the entire shoal is V-shaped in ground plan, with the apex of the V to the southeast, it consists largely of a succession of sand waves and troughs that trend nearly north-south along the shore of the spit. The southwestward trend of this shoal probably results from eddying of the tidal currents that enter Cape Cod Bay around Race Point.

SOUTHEAST COAST OF CAPE COD, MASSA-CHUSETTS[5]   Just south of Nauset Coast Guard Station, the coastal cliffs end. From here to the tip of Monomoy Island, a distance of 20 miles, the coast consists of a series of barriers except for a mile at Nauset Highlands, where the terrace of the outwash plain terminates in a low cliff. All parts of this barrier coast have been subject to striking changes during historic time. Sources of information include (1) sketches or maps of parts of the coast back to 1606 compiled by Douglas Johnson, (2) charts of the Coast and Geodetic Survey back to about 1840, and (3) aerial photographs taken in 1938, 1951, 1953, 1955, and annually from 1958 to 1962. The changes will be described in three parts: (1) history of Nauset Inlet; (2) history of the Chatham area; and (3) history of Monomoy Island. The illustrations provide a span of 356 years of shoreline evolution in the Chatham area, probably as long as any records in the United States.

Nauset Inlet (Fig. 3.14) is now located at the southern end of a spit about 2 miles long, the northern end of which adjoins the Cape Cod cliffs. Photos show that during the century before 1956 this inlet had migrated from directly north of Nauset Highlands (A in Fig. 3.14)[6] to more than a mile farther north, an average rate of 53 feet per year.

In 1938 (Fig. 3.14a), when the inlet was immediately north of Nauset Highlands, the spit on the

[5] Largely based on a report by Harold Rogers Wanless.

[6] A and B in common for Figures 3.14a, b, c, and d.

3.14 Coastal changes at and near Nauset Inlet, Massachusetts, eastern Cape Cod, from 1938 to 1962.

a 1938. The inlet is directly north of the village of Nauset Highlands (A). A narrow channel separates the barrier spit north of the inlet from a marshy island (B) behind it. U.S. Geological Survey.

north side was almost directly in line with the beach to the south. Behind the hook at the southern end of the spit was a narrow channel adjoining a marshy island (B) about 0.7 mile long.

In 1951 (Fig. 3.14b), a spit from the south (C), missing in 1938, had grown to a length of 0.6 mile, and the north spit had receded about 0.2 mile, so that the inlet was opposite the southeast tip of the marshy island (B). Some sand had been deposited over the marsh nearest the inlet, and the island may have suffered slightly from wave erosion.

In 1953 (Fig. 3.14c), the new south spit had developed a hook 0.2 mile long; and the remnant of the end of the north spit had merged with the east side of the marshy island, destroying the narrow channel behind the spit. The remnants of the 1938 spit, which formed the northern margin of Nauset Inlet, had retreated landward about 0.15 mile. A major storm evidently occurred shortly before the 1953 photography, for a channel had been cut across the spit at the north end of the marshy island (D).

A new shoal, partially exposed at low tide, had developed near the southern end of the spit (C). Seaward from the spit, a series of diagonal shoals trending northwest to southeast suggests that sand had been swept out through the inlet during a recent flood. A series of arcuate and S-shaped longshore bars (E) are seen just north of Nauset Inlet.

John Zeigler and others have shown that the beach area just north of Nauset Inlet has been receding at the rate of 3 to 5.5 feet per year, the most rapid erosion occurring just north of the inlet. They suggest that because the coast south of the inlet is more

b 1951. A spit has grown 0.6 mile north from the village, shifting the inlet location. U.S. Coast and Geodetic Survey.

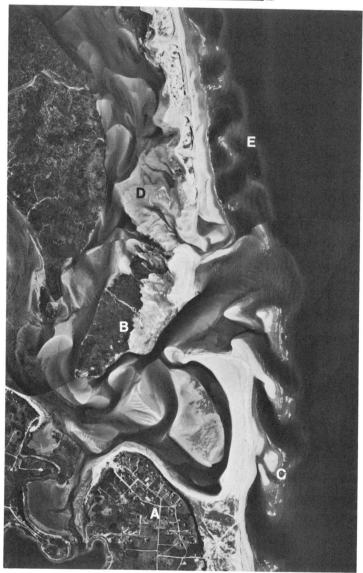

d 1962. The spit north of the inlet has shifted 0.3 mile shoreward, and most of the marshy island (B) has been buried with sand. U.S. Coast and Geodetic Survey.

3.14

c 1953. A hook has developed at the end of the new spit. The spit north of the inlet has shifted shoreward and is in contact with the marshy island (B). A breach in the northern spit (D) has opened. Underwater bars north of the inlet display a series of loops, like those on Horn Island, Mississippi (Fig. 7.35). U.S. Coast and Geodetic Survey.

nearly parallel to the direction of storm approach, the beach to the north erodes more rapidly than the beach to the south.

By 1962 (Fig. 3.14*d*), the barrier north of Nauset Inlet had shifted 0.3 mile landward of the

spit south of the inlet (C). This landward move had buried with sand all but a small area at the southwest tip of the bordering marshy island (B). This photo was taken about two weeks after the great Atlantic storm of 1962, and much of the beach erosion probably had occurred at that time.

Nauset Beach, (Fig. 3.15), a barrier spit, extends 8.5 miles from Nauset Highlands to the vicinity of Chatham. Three miles north of its southern tip, Nauset Beach has twice been breached by major storms (Fig. 2.21). At the left of the aerial photograph one can see where earlier storm waves had broken across the beach, forming a washover fan or delta 1.5 miles wide and extending about 0.5 mile into the bay. Subsequently, an arcuate bar enclosed this washover deposit on the lagoonal side. The 1961 photograph (Fig. 2.21) shows that a new breach 0.1 to 0.2 mile wide had developed just north of the older washover. The photograph also shows the flow patterns of the sand, which had formed a fan in the quiet waters of the bay. A year later, during the Atlantic storm of 1962, storm waves and tides broke through the center of the 1961 fan, building a new deposit farther into the bay.

The southern end of Nauset Beach, opposite Chatham, has had exceptionally rapid changes. Douglas Johnson, using old charts, illustrated outlines of this coast at several dates between 1606 and 1902. Later changes were determined from aerial photographs from 1938 to 1962. The oldest of Johnson's sketches is from the French explorer Samuel de Champlain and is more generalized than later sketches. This 1606 sketch shows a barrier reaching southward as far as the present tip of Nauset Beach. A gap of more than 200 years follows. Later sketches suggest that the barrier of 1606, or perhaps a later one, was shifted shoreward and was broken up by new inlets during major storms.

By October 1951 (Fig. 3.15a), Nauset Spit had grown a little south of Chatham. A prominent longshore bar is shown by a line of breakers 0.4 mile from the beach. About 1.3 miles northeast of the end of the spit, the bar extended south for 2 miles (A), while the beach gradually curved toward the mainland shore. Near the tip of the beach, three successive hooks were formed as sand was swept around the end of the spit by incoming tides entering the lagoon behind the barrier. The lagoonal side, however, had been straightened by the building of narrow bars connecting the tips of earlier hooks to the mainland. Seven such bars are visible (B). By May 1951, a short southward addition had begun to form at the end of the spit.

By 1953 (Fig. 3.15b), this new spit had been lengthened and curved sharply shoreward, developing an additional hook (C). At this time, the longshore bar showed more plainly than in 1951, probably because the ocean was less agitated by waves at the time the 1953 photo was taken. The northern end of the bar was connected with the beach by a number of shoals extending diagonally (southeastward) from the beach to the bar (B). The gaps between the shoals are probably rip current paths, which generally occur more at right angles to the shore. These same features also appear in the photograph of August 1958 (Fig. 3.15c). By 1953, the longshore bar of the 1951 photograph had been driven landward to join the center beach, while the 1953 bar was a new feature (C). From observations of this coast between 1958 and 1960, John Shelton suggested that littoral currents had frequently driven a longshore bar landward, but each time a new one developed it diverged from the beach farther along the lengthened spit. Our available photographs and those used by Shelton indicate that each new longshore bar that shifted landward was the beginning of a new hook at the end of the spit. Shelton estimated that since 1940 an average of a quarter of a million cubic yards of sand have been added annually to the tip of Nauset Beach.

The 1953 and 1958 photographs (Figs. 3.15b and c) show complicated bends in the longshore bar beyond the tip of the spit (C). Seaward trends are due to ebb tidal currents emerging from the lagoon. Two very shallow bars at right angles to the coastline, more than a mile south of the tip of Nauset Beach, may be remnants of an older spit or may represent new hooks developing offshore.

Monomoy Island (Figs. 3.16 and 3.17) extends 7 miles south from the southeast corner of the Cape Cod mainland. As far as is known, until about 1960, Monomoy was a spit connected to the coast. Then, after its separation, beach drifting began to close the breach until the great Atlantic storm of March 1962 cut a new gap nearly a mile wide between the mainland and Monomoy (A in Fig. 3.16). At the same time, several other sluiceways were cut through narrow parts of the island; and great quantities of beach sand were washed through the narrow breaks, burying soil and vegetation. According to Henry Mitchell, Monomoy Point grew southward 2 miles in the century between 1772 and 1872. A chart dated 1919 shows a northward continuation of Monomoy Point past Chatham, where it occupied the present site of the southern end of Nauset Beach. This northern extension probably migrated landward and joined the mainland at Chatham.

The southern part of Monomoy Island illustrates very well the part played by hooks in the development of a projecting point or cape. A series of hooks, each curving southwestward toward the quieter waters of Nantucket Sound, record outlines of the

3.15 Changes in the spit at southern end of Nauset Beach, near Chatham, Massachusetts, between 1951 and 1958.

a 1951. During the rapid southern extension of the barrier spit several hooks had formed, but part of them had been tied together on the lagoon side by narrow barriers. A shoal (A) extends south from the end of the spit. U.S. Coast and Geodetic Survey.

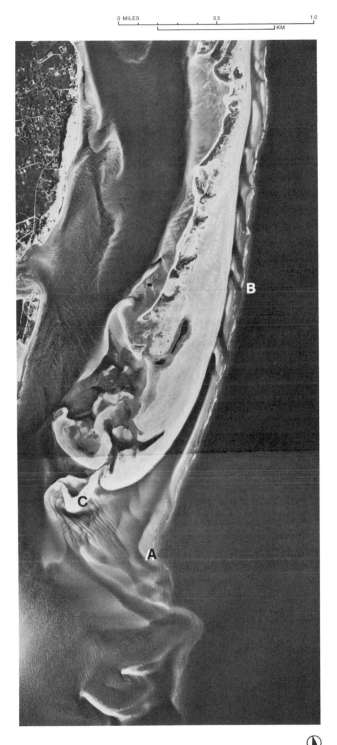

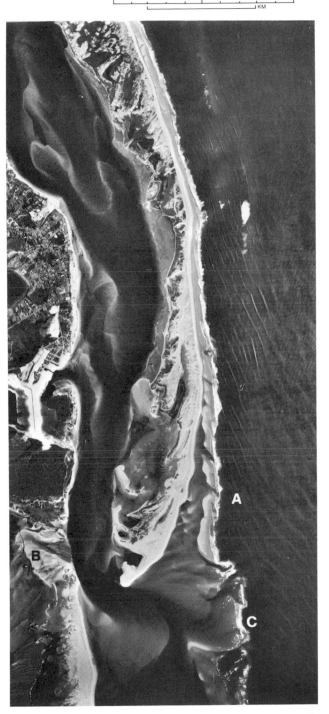

b 1953. An additional hook has formed, and the offshore shoal (A) has lengthened with curving trends. The barrier has lengthened slightly, so as to be opposite the northern end of Monomoy Island. U.S. Coast and Geodetic Survey.

c 1958. The shoal (A) is nearer surface. Note that Monomoy Point (B) is still connected to mainland. U.S. Coast and Geodetic Survey.

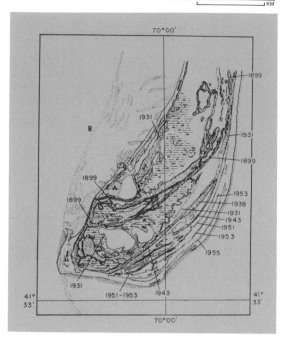

3.16 Monomoy Point (Fig. 3.15c) has now become Monomoy Island because of a breach opened March 5, 1962, by the great Atlantic storm. U.S. Coast and Geodetic Survey.

3.17 The southern part of Monomoy Island, Massachusetts, showing its pattern of growth between 1899 and 1955, as illustrated by a series of dated beach ridges. The straight southern end of the island was developed by erosion during the 1962 Atlantic storm. Prepared by Harold Rogers Wanless.

"Point" at various earlier dates. Figure 3.17 gives the ages of the successive dune ridges formed directly behind shorelines dating as far back as 1899. A dune ridge built along the shore in 1943 truncates the northern ends of a series of the older ridges. Successively younger ridges, however, are nearly parallel to the present shoreline. At the southern end, a formerly rounded shoreline was cut back between 1960 and 1961, truncating former dune ridges as old as 1938. However, within a few months a new dune ridge had formed parallel to the new shoreline.

On the western coast of Monomoy, a substantial reentrant bay (A), a mile from the end, was probably formed before 1899. This is partially occupied by a small lake or lagoon, largely cut off from Nantucket Sound by a narrow baymouth bar with a small tidal inlet. Evidently this bar was formed partly by

beach sand swept around the point by tidal currents and partly by a southward longshore drift of sand along the western side of the island. A prominent longshore bar (B) can be traced for 5 miles, meeting the coast just north of the southwest corner of the peninsula. Shoreward from the bar, water depths vary from 3 to 8 feet and outside the bar, from 15 to 20 feet.

The narrower parts of Monomoy Island are subject to active erosion at times of great storms from the east or northeast. However, the eastern shore has prograded between storms whenever there was a plentiful supply of sand for beach drifting. At such times, the island has lengthened by accretion at its southern tip. If a hurricane should strike this coast from the west, the very narrow beach, lacking protecting dune ridges, would probably undergo extensive erosion on that side.

SOUTH SIDE OF CAPE COD [Figs. 3.18 and 3.19]
The southern coast of Cape Cod is formed along an

outwash plain and the end moraine of a late Pleistocene glacier. Wave erosion on this coast is less active than on the east side of the cape, because Nantucket Sound is partly shielded from Atlantic waves by Monomoy Island and the most destructive storms generally come from the northeast, not the south.

The outwash plain is drained southward by small streams, which head in or pass through freshwater ponds. These ponds are *kettle holes* and mark large masses of glacial ice that were buried by outwash sand and gravel. Later, these buried glacial remnants melted away and left depressions, or ponds. Figure 3.18, near West Dennis, shows the small deltas built into Nantucket Sound by Parkers River (A) and Bass River (B). Parkers River heads in a pond of the type just described. The delta of Parkers River is deflected to the right, because of beach drifting in that direction; and the delta of Bass River was similarly

3.18 Small deltas built by Parkers River (A) and Bass River (B) on the southern shore of Cape Cod. U.S. Geological Survey, 1938.

3.19 The straight southern coast of Cape Cod near Harwichport modified by the construction of short jetties to protect boat harbor entrances and numerous groins which impede the littoral current drifting sand. U.S. Coast and Geodetic Survey.

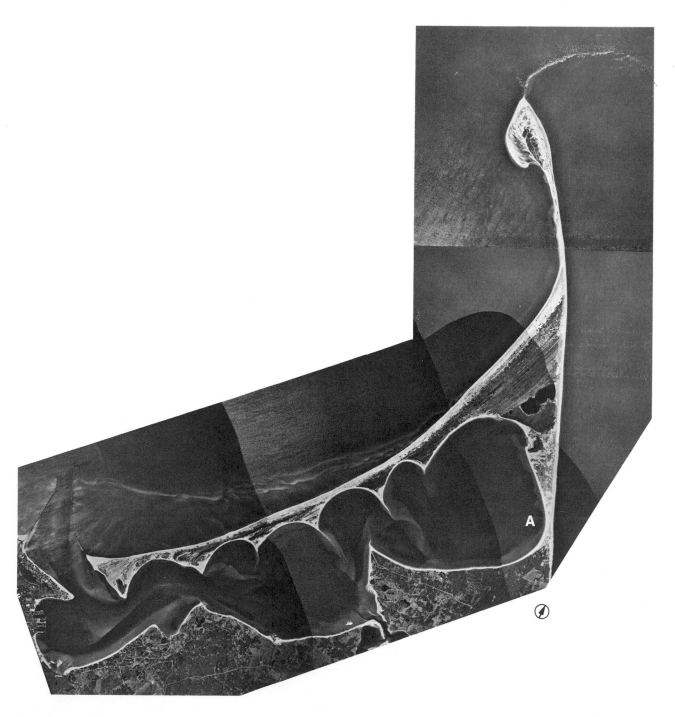

3.20 Great Point, the northern tip of Nantucket Island and Nantucket Harbor. A series of six large cusps have formed on the inside of the barrier spit enclosing Nantucket Harbor and three on the southeast side of harbor. U.S. Geological Survey, November 1938.

deflected until a jetty was built along its right bank, so that a channel could be maintained with adequate draft for small boats. Underwater sand ridges resulting from redistribution of delta sands by waves and by shore currents are visible to depths of 18 to 20 feet. Tidal currents move up a left fork of Parkers River, forming the small tidal delta of Lewis Pond (C).

To check beach erosion, a portion of the southern coast near Dennisport has been protected by building a series of thirty-two groins in the 2 miles between Swan Pond (A in Fig. 3.19) and Herring River (B). The shore has a sawtooth pattern, due to the deposition on the upcurrent (west) side of each groin and erosion on the downcurrent side.

At Herring River, a jetty about 500 feet long was built on the west side of the river mouth and a much shorter jetty on the east. A sandy beach, about 250 feet wide, has accumulated against the west jetty, but the beach is only about 50 feet wide beside the east jetty. Most of the sand is kept between successive groins and jetties, rather than being shifted farther along the shore.

NANTUCKET ISLAND   [Figs. 3.20 and 3.21] South of the elbow of Cape Cod, the island of Nantucket also has a core of glacial deposition, including a moraine to the north and an outwash fan to the south. Along the northeast coast, the rather shallow harbor, which includes a 5-mile lagoon, is protected from the open sea by a barrier consisting of one arm of a cuspate foreland (Fig. 3.20). The glacial deposits at the outer end of the foreland, reported by F. P. Gulliver, indicate that the point is a land-tied island. This tombolo was cut back about 1,400 feet between 1784 and 1874 but has been relatively stable since then. In 1896, according to Gulliver, a storm broke through the narrow barrier on the northeast side of the bay (A), and a new entrance was developed that was maintained for about ten years.

The series of six cuspate spits that have grown into the harbor from the protecting barrier have been in existence for at least 200 years. They have been interpreted in several ways. In 1889, N. S. Shaler suggested that eddies related to the tide running along the length of the bay were the cause. Thirty-five years later, Douglas Johnson decided that the points represented modified hooked spits (see Fig.

2.18), which formed in succession as the spit was gradually built to the southwest. They also might be overwash fans (Fig. 2.21) that have since been given the cuspate form. Thanks to the aerial photographs, it is possible to see which of these ideas is favored by the growth lines along the spit (Fig. 3.20). The two eastern spits near the present inlet show a slight indication of being recurved spits, although they differ markedly from other good examples of overlapping hooks (Fig. 2.18). The beach-ridge structure of the other cuspate spits is clearly truncated, showing that currents of the type described by Shaler are important. If overwashes have contributed to the spits, the aerial photos provide no evidence. Therefore, we conclude that at least these cuspate spits are largely the result of current eddies operating in the lagoon. Photographs and charts dating back to 1776 show little indication of a change in the location of the spits, but the underwater bars that continue into the bay beyond them have been shifted back and forth to a moderate degree.

The spit west of the western end of Nantucket is much less stable than the one that protects the harbor (Fig. 3.21). In 1776 (Fig. 3.21a), the spit's total length was 2.5 miles and was shown as extending past Tuckernuck Island (A). Shaler's 1889 map shows about the same extent. However, a 1919 chart reveals a break in this spit southeast of Tuckernuck, and the end had grown west for 1.5 miles past Muskeget Island to point B in Figure 3.21b. The 1960 aerial photo (Fig. 3.21b) indicates that all the western portion of the spit had disappeared, leaving only the part between Tuckernuck and Nantucket. A channel can be seen along the south end of Tuckernuck. The 1966 chart shows still further attrition, and the remnant of the spit is left as a barrier island separated from Nantucket by a shallow channel. Because of this reversal between growth and attrition since 1889, it would seem unwise to predict the future.

Tuckernuck and Muskeget Islands are the western continuation of Nantucket and represent a portion of an end moraine. The 1776 chart shows both these islands, but both have been considerably decreased in size (compare Figs. 3.21a and b). The islands have an uneven topography, both above sea level and in the submerged areas that surround them. Deposition of sand has somewhat smoothed the bottom, so

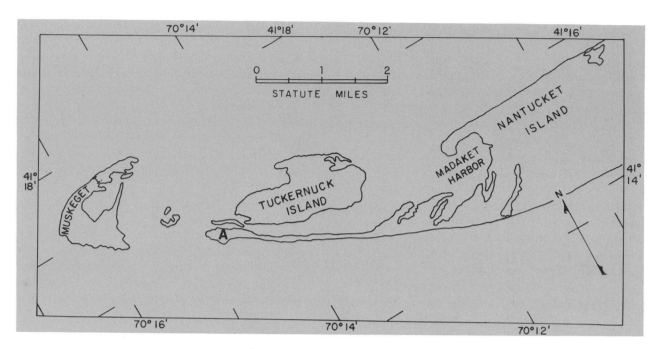

3.21 Changes in the configuration of western Nantucket Island and Tuckernuck and Muskeget Islands between 1765 and 1960.

a 1765. A barrier spit of southern shore of Nantucket Island extended beyond the western end of Tuckernuck Island. Tuckernuck and Muskeget Islands were larger and more irregularly shaped than at present. From British Admiralty chart in *The Atlantic Neptune.*

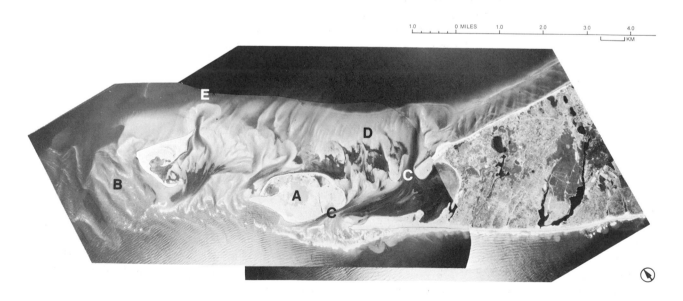

b 1960. The barrier spit extends to east of Tuckernuck Island, which is more rounded. Muskeget Island is much smaller. Water depths and sediment distribution patterns are clearly shown to depths of about 25 feet. Black areas (D) are kelp beds. U.S. Army Map Service high-altitude aerial photography.

that water depths on the Tuckernuck Bank are shown on recent charts as 1 to 10 feet. The shoal bank extends about 9 miles west of Nantucket Island and constitutes a barrier, not only to navigation but also to tidal inflow and outflow between the ocean and Nantucket Sound. Tidal currents scour channels across this shoal through which the strongest flow takes place. The principal channel (C) lies eastward along the southern shore of Tuckernuck Island, thence northeastward across the bay separating the two prongs of Nantucket Island, and then north to the margin of the bank. According to the Coast and Geodetic Survey charts of 1959, the channel ranges in depth from 8 to 21 feet.

Sand drifting to the side makes a series of arcuate fronts at the ends of minor channels (northeast of the northern tip of Muskeget Island, E). Great kelp beds (which appear black in Fig. 3.21b) are growing in areas sheltered from tidal currents, as north of Tuckernuck Island and in the bay between the two western points of Nantucket Island. At times of major storms, currents carrying sand invade these areas, partially burying the kelp beds. Photographs from 1955, 1960, 1961, and 1962 have been compared and show the direction and amount of shift in position of these shoals and channels. Photographs of the last three dates (not shown) are in color, permitting better differentiation of bottom materials. For example, the deeper channel south of Tuckernuck Island appears quite different from the kelp beds north of the islands. The October 1960 photographs also show that the tidal channel east of Tuckernuck Island is distinctly shoaler than the depths shown on the Coast and Geodetic Survey charts published at about the same date.[7]

Unless soundings have been taken very recently in an area of shoals, they are subject to considerable uncertainty. Large storms produce major shifts. After a 70-mile-per-hour blow in June 1945, Shepard was sailing across one of the shoals near Tuckernuck and struck bottom in a position where the chart of recent date showed ample water. Grounding on such a shoal is not generally serious provided the seas are calm, as was the case in this instance.

Aerial photographs identify shoals that are navigation hazards and aid in understanding present-day patterns of sediment shift in shallow water.

TISBURY GREAT POND AREA, MARTHA'S VINEYARD [Fig. 2.17]

Glacial deposits of the last two glacial epochs, the Illinoian and Wisconsin, are found on Martha's Vineyard. The end moraine of the older (Illinoian) glacier is located in the northwest part of the island, and the outermost (although not the youngest) end moraine of the Wisconsin glaciation is on the northeast. Figure 2.17 represents an area in the center of the south coast that is almost entirely a part of the Wisconsin outwash plain. This sand and gravel plain was drained largely by southwestward flowing streams. After the glaciers disappeared, sea level rose about 300 feet, because of the return of glacial meltwater to the ocean. These small streams were drowned in their lower courses, leaving an extremely irregular coast, about 3,000 years ago when sea level attained approximately its present position. Subsequently, wave erosion cut off projecting headlands of sand and gravel; and the eroded debris was shifted along the shore, accumulating as a series of baymouth barriers. The drowning of the junction of several streams (A in Fig. 2.17) formed what is now Tisbury Great Pond. At first, bars were built across the mouths of several small tributary estuaries (B) in this area. Three such baymouth barriers are seen on the right side of the "pond" and two on the left. Later, erosion had cut away the headlands that projected farthest south, and in a new episode of coastal straightening the whole broad bay was enclosed by a straight east-west shoreline.

Aerial photographs for 1938, 1955, and 1962 show very little change except that the sand has been washed or blown inland a short distance, varying from 100 to 200 feet. In both 1938 and 1962, there was a small inlet through the baymouth bar across Tisbury Great Pond, whereas none was visible in 1955 (Fig. 2.17). The 1962 photograph, taken about two weeks after the great Atlantic storm, shows a series of small washover fans all along the coast, ex-

---

[7] Indicating that the survey had been made somewhat previously.

tending 100 to 200 feet inland from the landward margins of the barrier as it was in 1938 and 1955.

The shoreline on the south side of Martha's Vineyard is evidently quite stable, but the baymouth sand bars and dune ridges are subject to breaching at times of great southerly storms.

GAY HEAD CLIFFS AND VICINITY, MARTHA'S VINEYARD[8] [Fig. 3.22]

At the west end of Martha's Vineyard, several cliffs consisting of soft formations are exposed to erosion. The most interesting are the colorful cliffs at Gay Head. The nature of these cliffs and their origin was first determined by J. B. Woodworth and Edward Wigglesworth. The cliffs include Upper Cretaceous and Miocene sands, clays, gravels, lignites, and greensand. Because of the effect of the Illinoian glaciers, these older formations have been ploughed up and piled into hummocks, being greatly contorted in the process. In places, glacial till covers this disturbed mass of sediment. Large boulders are found in the cliffs and along the beach, as well as some distance out from shore.

The retreat of the cliffs at Gay Head has been irregular because of the extensive creeping slides that are still occurring. Masses from the upper cliffs fall to or beyond the shore, where they can be seen in the 1917 photo (Fig. 3.22a) and also in that of 1968 (Fig. 3.22b). These boulders appear to have stayed for the most part in the same locations, so they were useful in finding the site of the 1917 photo. It was impossible to get to the exact place because the terrace edge, from which the picture was taken, had been eroded; but a point was chosen that appeared to be a few feet directly below the old site. Erosion is evident on the various ridges and the small plateau where the old Coast Guard Station was located until 1960. By that time, the plateau had retreated so much that the buildings had been dismantled and moved to the east. Because of landslides, the foot of the cliffs had not receded, and, in some

[8] Helpful information was provided to us by Clifford A. Kaye, of the U.S. Geological Survey.

3.22 Changes in Gay Head cliffs, western Martha's Vineyard, Massachusetts, between 1917 and 1968. Photos by Shepard.
a 1917. Gully erosion, with vegetation covering landslide behind foreground ridge.
b 1968. Building on distant promontory is gone, landslides seem more widespread, having blocked some of the gullies of 1917.

places outside the shore, the bottom has been pushed up due to the plastic movements of the clays.

Nashaquitas Cliffs, 5 miles east of the Gay Head Cliffs on the south shore of Martha's Vineyard, are much straighter in outline. According to Clifford Kaye, the average recession of the cliff tops has been 5 feet a year. The formations here are also unconsolidated and are extremely variable in composition. Landsliding is also important in the retreat of these cliffs.

The future development of the cliffed sections of Martha's Vineyard is fairly clear. The cliffs will retreat in an irregular fashion; and, no doubt, as time goes on, houses located close to the cliff edge will either fall over or have to be moved. It would appear that the retreat will generally be so slow as to cause no great damage.

COAST OF SOUTHEASTERN RHODE ISLAND

Eastward from the mouth of Narragansett Bay, the bedrock throughout is the hard crystalline Dedham granodiorite, a massive granitic rock. After preglacial river erosion, the glacier moved southward across the area toward its terminal position, now submerged beneath the water of Rhode Island Bay. The subsequent sea-level rise, due to deglaciation, left an extremely irregular coast with estuaries at intervals of about a mile. Because this low coast is not protected by offshore islands, some erosion of the bedrock and of glacial till has taken place at Sakonnet Point (A in Fig. 3.23) at the outlet of Narragansett Bay. Several rock stacks, remnants of erosion, are visible offshore. These appear white in the photo because of waves breaking against them.

The erosion of glacial till and the underlying bedrock has provided sediment that has formed a series of eleven baymouth bars across the estuaries. One of these appears to be compound (B). Probably it originated as a double tombolo. The seaward point in the middle of the loop was evidently a remnant of a bedrock divide between two small valleys.

The sediment to build the baymouth barriers was largely derived from the headlands at each end. By the building of the barriers, the coastline has been greatly straightened, leaving gently curved barrier loops between headlands.

Some seawater seeps through the sand and gravel, but surface drainage from rainfall tends to freshen the water in the bays. At times of major storms or

3.23 Southeastern Rhode Island coast east of Narragansett Bay. Several small stream valleys were drowned, producing an uneven coast. These have been closed by barrier bars, some of which are breached by small inlets with tidal deltas inside. U.S. Coast and Geodetic Survey, 1961.

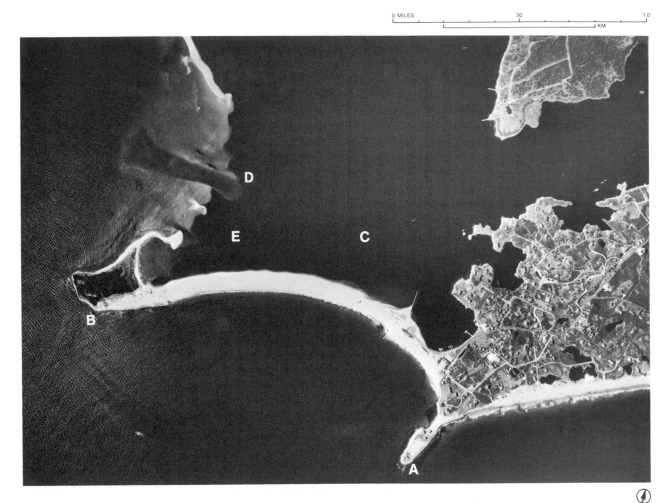

3.24 Watch Hill Point (A), Rhode Island. This coastal resort was severely damaged by the 1938 New England hurricane, resulting in the breaching of the spit extending toward Sandy Point at D, and the rotation of the spit remnant about 30 degrees. U.S. Coast and Geodetic Survey, 1954.

unusually high tides, waves break through the narrow barriers, opening new inlets (C). In April 1961, when the photograph was taken (Fig. 3.23), six of the bays were connected with the sea by very narrow inlets. Although they were then newly opened, sand or fine gravel had been washed through these inlets, forming small tidal deltas (D) on the inside. Such deposits can be seen adjacent to four of the six inlets, but they are missing in the two smallest bays. The growth of such tidal deltas tends to decrease the flow of tidal currents through the small inlets; eventually they may close. In two of the bays, there is evidence of former inlets that have been closed, but new inlets were opened at other places along the barriers.

The continual transfer of sediment from the ocean side to the bay side of the beach will gradually shift the barriers landward. Photos taken in 1951, 1961, (Fig. 3.23), and 1962 show very little change. The 1962 photos were taken about a month after the great Atlantic storm (see later chapters). If the bars include large proportions of gravel, they are less easily shifted than similar bars composed entirely of sand. The New England hurricane of September 21, 1938, greatly damaged buildings and other man-made structures along this coast.

In the future, the rate of change should be moderate, with the likelihood that from time to time new inlets will be opened in the baymouth barriers.

WATCH HILL POINT, RHODE ISLAND [Fig. 3.24]   Watch Hill Point (A) is a seaside resort at the end of the barrier coast of Rhode Island, west of Narragansett Bay. The point has an oceanside cliff exposing glacial till and outwash, and rises 50 feet above sea level. The point is protected by a seawall. The hill is a tombolo and prior to the 1938 hurricane was connected to Napatree Point (B) to the west, as it is at present. Napatree Point joins a spit extending north to Sandy Point (not shown). Napatree Point contains glacial till partially protected from erosion by a veneer of gravel. Together, the tombolo and spit form adequate protection for Little Narragansett Bay (C).

This portion of the Rhode Island coast was struck by the full force of the 1938 New England hurricane (described by R. L. Nichols and A. F. Marston). Storm tides rose 15 feet above normal high tide, and wind velocities were more than 100 miles per hour. At Watch Hill Point, many buildings were reduced to piles of rubble or were moved from their foundations. The 50-foot sand cliff was cut back 30 feet in spite of the seawall protection. Much sand was washed over Napatree Beach from the ocean to the bay side, and an inlet was temporarily opened. The dune ridges were extensively eroded. Some houses were left balanced on remnant pillars of sand; some collapsed later as the sand was removed from beneath them. Damage of more than $1 million resulted.

Sandy Point (not illustrated) was cut by three inlets during the hurricane, but only the one closest to Napatree Point survived in 1960 (D). Tidal currents now enter and leave Little Narragansett Bay (E) through this inlet. The trend of the spit that connects Sandy Point with Napatree Point has been rotated counterclockwise about 30 degrees. Although a tidal channel is still evident near the center of the inlet, lunate bars of sediment have formed at each end of the channel, and shoals have developed between the channels and the bordering sand spits. Exposed sand barriers such as these are subject to great damage by storms of hurricane strength, even when protected by seawalls. The Sand Point area was inadequately prepared for such a storm, partly because nothing approaching this wind velocity had occurred since 1815.

EASTERN CONNECTICUT SHORELINE   The inner of two end moraines of Pleistocene continental glaciation passes through Fishers Island, southeast of the eastern Connecticut shore, and reaches the New England mainland shore at Watch Hill Point. Thus the entire coast of Connecticut lies inside the end moraines and was subject to glacial erosion and deposition. Glacial deposits are generally 40 feet or less in thickness, so that at many places Holocene coastal erosion has removed all glacial deposits from the headlands, leaving exposed crystalline rock (in Connecticut, principally gneiss), which is much more resistant to wave erosion.

Eustatic rise of sea level has drowned much of the topography, leaving a very irregular coast embayed by many estuaries, including those of the Connecticut River (Fig. 3.25) and the nearby Thames. The Connecticut River, heading in the province of Quebec, is the largest in New England, with a length of 280 miles and a drainage area of 11,320 square miles; whereas the 65-mile-long Thames heads in Massachusetts. Along this part of the coast, many smaller streams enter estuaries, some of which have been filled with marsh deposits.

The Connecticut shore is partially protected from major storm erosion by Long Island and locally by Fishers Island. The major storm winds producing erosion generally come from directions ranging from northeast to southeast. There is no consistent direction of beach drifting along this coast, but the shift of sediment within an embayment or cove between two headlands depends on the storm direction and the degree of protection from such storms. In 1929, Henry Sharp illustrated these points by showing that beach drifting on three adjacent beaches near the New York–Connecticut line was in different directions on each beach.

Exposures of glacial drift consist of glacial till, which usually contains many large or medium-sized boulders in a matrix of finer sediments, and waterlaid deposits of sand and gravel, in which boulders are generally absent. The larger fragments removed by waves tend to remain near their source, while progressively smaller particles are sorted and transported farther away. Thus a beach near a deposit of till or bedrock outcrop is likely to be cobbly or even have boulders. Beach drifting in favorable areas may produce sand beaches suitable for recreation. Griswold Point, the sand spit just east of the Connecticut River estuary (A) is one of the longest beaches in the state. Henry Sharp presented evidence that this

0 MILES   .50   1.0

KM

3.25 The mouth of the Connecticut River into Long Island Sound. Although the Connecticut is the largest New England river and has been subject to disastrous flooding, it has built no delta into the sound. The river does not seem to contribute sand for beach development. U.S. Department of Agriculture, 1963.

beach had retreated shoreward about 0.25 mile since its formation, indicating that beach cottages along such a sand spit were especially subject to destruction. The U.S. Army Corps of Engineers has been called upon at several Connecticut beaches to check beach erosion where it was becoming harmful to the beach-resort character of the community. In several places, groins have been erected along the shore to trap sand. To replace it on the beaches where erosion had occurred, sand has been dredged from offshore deposits. This sand transfer has oversteepened the subaqueous profile, causing accelerated beach erosion, and a few years later the dredging process has had to be repeated. This type of costly maintenance of sand beaches has been attempted at several places along the Connecticut shore.

The Connecticut River has been subject to catastrophic floods, especially in March 1936 and September 1938, the latter at the time of the New England hurricane. The effects of these floods on the Massachusetts part of the valley were fully documented by Richard Jahns in 1947. The 1936 flood followed a rapid thaw of snow and frozen ground. Discharge at Hartford, Connecticut, increased from 15,000 cubic feet per second on March 12 to 310,000 cubic feet per second on March 20. The river stage was 20 feet above normal, and it inundated about 10 percent of the bottomland. Additions to floodplain deposits of about 8 inches occurred during the 1936 storm and 6 inches during the 1938 storm. Although much sediment must have been carried to Long Island Sound, there appears to be no report of the effects of these floods on the Connecticut coast. A few large sand-bar islands are seen in the river in the upper part of Figure 3.25, but much of the permanent deposit was probably dropped above the head of the estuary at Middletown, 25 miles from the coast. No delta is evident at the present time. The extension of the Griswold Point spit (A in Fig. 3.25) westward toward the Connecticut River indicates that the river must be a very minor source of coastal sand.

Here, also, the New England hurricane of September 1938 left much destruction of human property. At Ocean Beach, just south of the New London area on the west side of the Thames estuary, the high storm tides lifted fifty or more beach cottages from their foundations, tumbled them end over end, and piled them in heaps across the main thoroughfare.

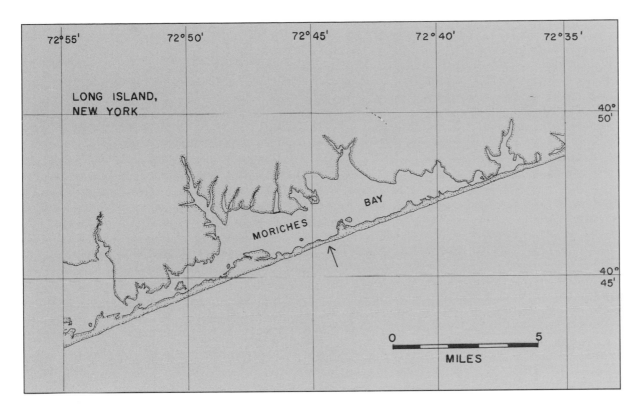

3.26 Outline of Moriches Bay on the south coast of Long Island, prior to the opening of Moriches Inlet in 1931. Arrow marks location of the inlet. U.S. Geological Survey, Geological Map of Long Island, 1913.

The shore road that passes the New London lighthouse was completely destroyed. River floods associated with the hurricane were slightly lower than those of the 1936 flood.

Most of the coastal areas adjacent to the mouths of the Connecticut (Fig. 3.25) and Thames estuaries have low cliffs of glacial deposits, although bedrock forms the cores of the two small islands just east of the Thames estuary. As the erosion progresses in the future, the thin mantle of glacial till will be removed from bedrock hills, and rocky headlands will gradually replace the headlands of glacial deposits that now predominate. The shore will then become more irregular, and there will be less sand on beaches than at present. On the other hand, in the far future, the Connecticut and Thames estuaries probably will fill with sediment, and sand transported to Long Island Sound by the rivers will become a major additional source of sand for replenishment of eroding beaches.

MORICHES INLET, LONG ISLAND, NEW YORK [Figs. 3.26 and 3.27]   South central Long Island is formed by an outwash plain that dips below sea level to the south. During the low stages of sea level, small stream valleys had been cut into this plain, and these were drowned by the rise that virtually terminated a few thousand years ago. Later, a barrier island developed outside the seaward limit of the drowned plain and extended along most of Long Island. Locally, the barrier touches the plain, but elsewhere it is separated by as much as 8 miles. Prior to 1931, the barrier was without a break for 50 miles from Southampton to Fire Island Inlet. At that time, the present Moriches Inlet had no connection with the sea (Fig. 3.26), but an inlet was opened in 1931 and has been maintained subsequently.

In June 1938, the inlet (Fig. 3.27a) was about 1,000 feet wide, and portions of the old barrier on each side had been rotated about 20 degrees toward

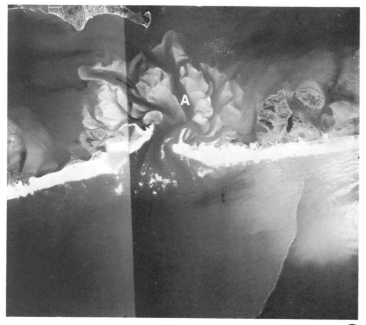

3.27 Changes in Moriches Inlet, Long Island, New York, 1938 to 1947.

a 1938. The inlet, opened in 1931, was 1,000 feet wide in 1938, and a tidal delta had formed in the lagoon. Photo was taken in June, three months before the New England hurricane. U.S. Department of Agriculture.

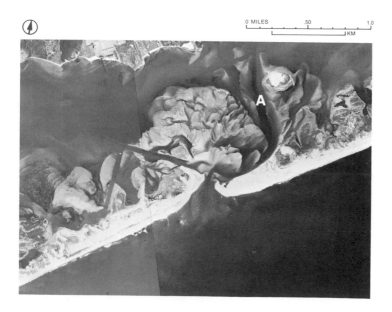

the inlet. Small hooks had formed at the ends of the new spits. A tidal delta, about 2 miles wide and projecting more than a mile into the bay, had formed in the 7 years since the opening of the inlet. Tidal currents at various times have entered Moriches Bay through five channels, the middle one (A) being least obstructed by sand. Most of the sand accumulated in shoals between the channels.

The hurricane of September 1938 raised the water level at Moriches Bay to a maximum of 15 feet above normal high water. Waves swept across the low sandy island, opening two new inlets, and moving large quantities of sand over the barrier into Moriches Bay. Several marshes on the bay side of the barrier do not correspond with those of June 1938. They are probably the results of washovers that occurred during the September storm.

By 1947 (Fig. 3.27*b*), the delta had been rebuilt to about its prehurricane dimensions, but its central part was more completely filled with sand than in 1938. The principal central channel of 1938 was on the east side and had been dredged for small boats. Another channel had also been dredged at the extreme left margin of the tidal delta; but its lower end, just inside the inlet, already had been largely blocked by sand. The boat channel to the east will require frequent dredgings, especially just inside the inlet.

In spite of the transfer of large quantities of sand through the inlet by the 1938 hurricane, the offshore barrier did not shift landward in the 9-year period from 1938 to 1947 and still occupied virtually the same position as on the geologic map made in 1913 (Fig. 3.26). This indicates that additional supplies of sand had restored the beach to its earlier dimensions after it had been greatly eroded during the major 1938 storm.

FIRE ISLAND INLET, LONG ISLAND [Figs. 3.28 and 3.29]   To the west of Moriches Inlet, the next opening through the barrier is at Fire Island (Fig. 3.28). This inlet is unusual in that the eastern bar-

b 1947. The coast near Moriches Inlet was greatly disrupted by the New England hurricane, with the opening of temporary inlets and widening of the present one. By 1947, the temporary inlets were closed, and a new tidal delta had developed. Two channels, dredged for small boat use, have become partly blocked by sand. U.S. Department of Agriculture.

rier (Fire Island) overlaps the western barrier (Oak Beach) by a distance of 3 miles. The history of Fire Island Inlet has been traced back to 1825 by S. Gofseyeff, of the U.S. Army Corps of Engineers. Some of his maps are reproduced in Figure 3.29. In 1825, the tip of Fire Island, Democrat Point, lay 4.6 miles to the east of its position in 1941 when the jetty was completed at the end of the point. The old Fire Island Light was at the end of the point in 1825 and is still maintained at the same location. The growth of the island took place at a highly irregular rate. Over one 6-year period, for example, it advanced at an average rate of 838 feet a year, but in one unusual year it was actually cut back 600 feet. While the island was growing spasmodically toward the west, its ocean shoreline was retreating but only at an average of 2.1 feet per year during the 120 years of observations.

During the same historical period, Oak Beach was being cut back at an average rate of 19 feet per year. In 1834, Oak Beach was in two parts, separated by Oak Island Inlet, but this inlet had been filled by 1887 and essentially the present outline of the western spit had been developed.

A strong tidal current maintains an irregular channel in the inlet. During the 120 years of surveys, the natural channel (Fig. 3.29, dashed lines) migrated to the west, keeping a rough S-shape. The deepest water has been generally close to Democrat Point, then bending northward until it approached Oak Beach, and then up the inlet switching to the Fire Island side, with still another bend carrying it close to the east end of Oak Beach.

When army engineers built the Democrat Point jetty (1939 to 1941), several changes resulted. The westward growth of the point was temporarily stopped. Sand built the outer beach of Fire Island out to the end of the jetty in a few years; a new projection grew northward from the point across half of the inlet (B in Fig. 3.28a); and, by 1946, a bar had built most of the way across to Oak Beach. The strong current in the channel increased as a result of the growth of this bar and attacked the western portion of Oak Beach, cutting it back variously from 150 to 200 feet, and threatening many homes. Consequently, the beach was built out artificially and a new channel was cut by the state of New York at about the middle of the inlet. This channel soon filled, necessitating more drastic action, so a jetty

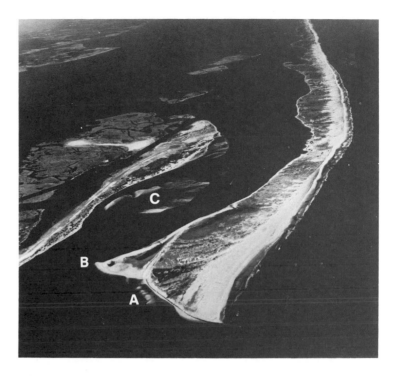

3.28 Changes at Fire Island, Long Island, New York. This inlet, an important entrance, is located where Fire Island, lengthening from the east, overlaps Oak Beach, lengthened from the west. Changes between 1946 and 1962 are shown.

a 1946. About five years after the construction of a jetty to protect the inlet from silting, a spit (B) had extended nearly halfway across the channel. U.S. Army Corps of Engineers.

was built across the north channel. The erosion has stopped; but, according to the 1960 chart, no adequate channel now enters the bay. In recent years, the point has grown 0.5 mile west of the jetty (Fig. 3.28b).

An interesting U-shaped bar a mile inside the inlet has apparently resulted from the building of the jetty (C in Fig. 3.28a). This bar, which forms an arc with points projecting toward the inlet, may be partly the result of blocking of an old channel.

The future of Fire Island Inlet will depend considerably on how much the shore is controlled by man. Probably, if left alone, the large overlap of Fire Island will not persist. The erosion of Oak Beach should continue until storm waves cut through it; and, having developed a closer connection with Great South Bay, the new inlet should remain open and the

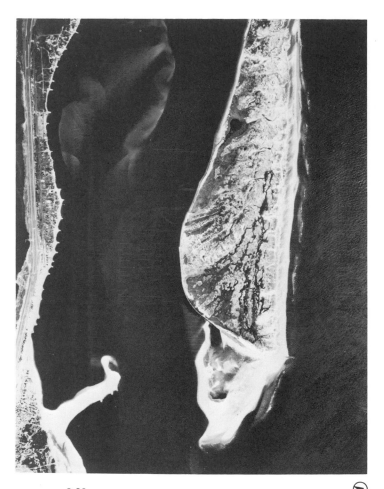

3.28

b 1962. The spit (B) of Figure 3.28*a* has been removed or eroded, and a new very similar point has grown to the west. Note also the new sand spit across the channel. U.S. Coast and Geodetic Survey.

old one become filled. It is surprising that this had not happened before human activities interfered.

JONES INLET, LONG ISLAND, NEW YORK [Fig 3.30]   The southwestern end of the series of offshore barriers south of Long Island provides large recreational beaches for metropolitan New York and has become densely populated. A single barrier island extends from Fire Island Inlet to Jones Inlet, a distance of about 15 miles. In 1913, the inlet was mapped as 1.5 miles wide, but had narrowed to about 0.5 mile by 1936.

Prior to 1913, in the bay behind the inlet a complex of marshy islands formed a tidal delta at the

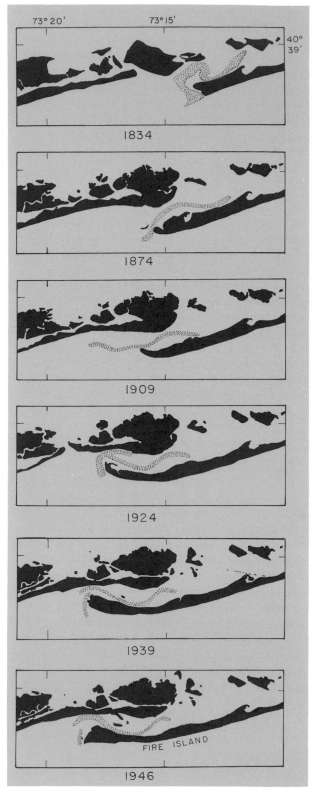

entrance to Jones Inlet. Today, these marshes are being drained by closely spaced ditches, which are evident on the aerial photos (A in Fig. 3.30b). Residential areas and major highways are being built on these reclaimed marshes.

Like Fire Island, Jones Beach has been building westward. It was extended 1.5 miles between 1913 and 1942. In 1942, after the beach had lengthened southwestward, considerable sand was swept through the narrowing inlet where the sand had been accumulating between the marshy islands (Fig. 3.30a). The beach lengthened 0.5 mile between 1942 and 1953 (Fig. 3.30b) and developed a hook projecting into the bay (B), which threatened to block the inlet for small boats.

On the east side of the inlet, between 1953 and 1960, a jetty (B in Fig. 3.30c) was built nearly a mile seaward from the point. By 1960, sand had accumulated against almost half the length of the jetty in less than 7 years. The effect of this deposition on the upcurrent side of the jetty has been to subject the western beach to serious erosion (C in Fig. 3.30c). A comparison of charts of the Coast and Geodetic Survey for 1934 and 1965 shows that this beach has already been narrowed 0.25 mile. A shoal outlined by a line of breakers remains where the beach was formerly located (D in Fig. 3.30c).

In a comparable situation at Santa Barbara, California, sand is being pumped from the area of accumulation on the upcurrent side of the harbor jetty and placed on the beach on the downcurrent side where erosion had taken place.

OAK NECK AREA, NORTH COAST OF LONG ISLAND, NEW YORK [Fig. 3.31]   The northern shore of Long Island is largely an end moraine composed of sand and gravel with some till deposits. To the north, the moraine rises 50 to 100 feet above Long Island Sound. Although this Long Island shore is protected from major northeast storms, erosion has been rapid. High points on the moraine form headlands, because the shore has been cut back more rapidly where cliffs are low. Many bays along the shore were formed by the drowning of lows in the morainic topography, as for example, Oyster Bay, on

3.29   Sketch maps showing changes at Fire Island Inlet between 1834 and 1946. After S. Gofseyeff, U.S. Army Corps of Engineers.

3.30   Changes at Jones Inlet, Long Island, New York, between 1942 and 1960. A is same in a, b, and c.
a   1942. Prior to construction of the jetty. Note rounded edge of point.

the eastern side of the aerial photograph (A) where Theodore Roosevelt had his estate. Sediments drifting alongshore, largely from the east, have produced spits or baymouth bars across small inlets; and some such lagoons have filled with tidal delta deposits and marsh vegetation. Broader sandy beaches along these shallow coastal bays protect the marshes from erosion, while the intervening headlands are open to attack.

The portion of the coast illustrated in Figure 3.31 includes, from west to east: Matinicock Point (B), Peacock Point (C), Fox Point (D), Oak Neck (E), and Rocky Point (F). In 1833, according to Douglas Johnson, a series of triangulation monuments were

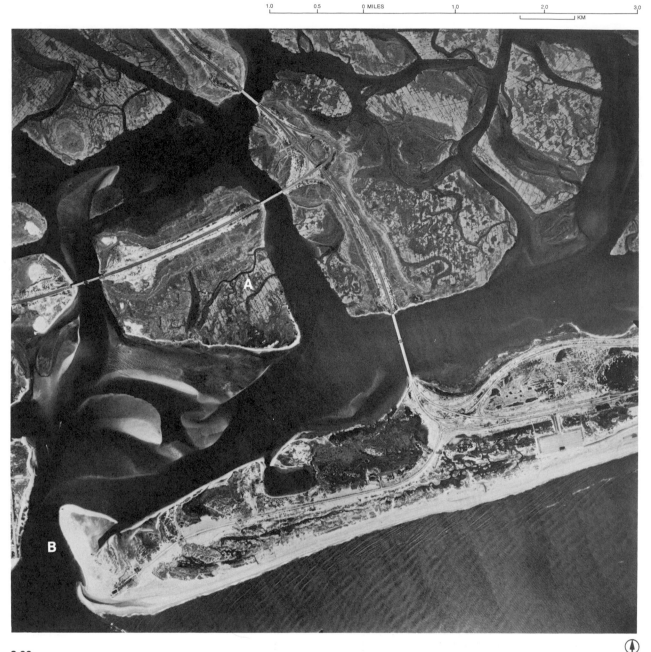

1.0   0.5   0 MILES   1.0   2.0   3.0
                                    KM

3.30
b 1953. During construction of jetty, a V-shaped spit (B) has built halfway across
the inlet. Note also change in shape of shoals inside the inlet.

placed by the Coast and Geodetic Survey on hilltops at four of these headlands. Fifty years later, the Survey attempted to relocate the monuments but found only one of the original four remaining. The site of the Matinicock Point monument was found to be 50 feet offshore in 6 feet of water, suggesting an amount of cliff erosion of about 3 feet per year. At Peacock Point, the monument, the promontory on which it had been located, and the homes of fishermen had all been destroyed. A new triangulation station was

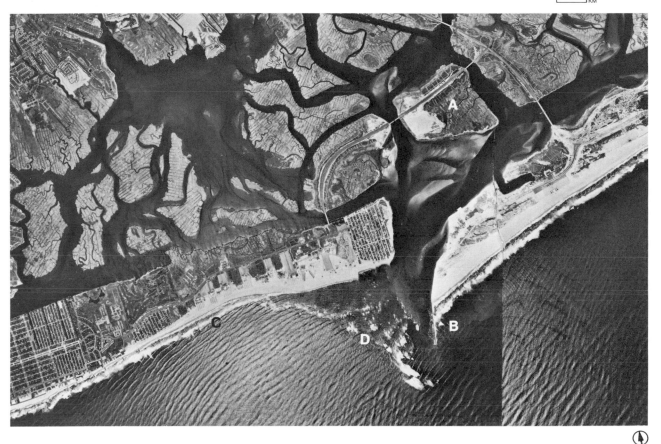

c 1960. After completion of jetty, east side shows progradation. The spit in 1953 photo has disappeared. Serious erosion has occurred on the west side of the inlet (C). Note urbanization of marsh area.

established at Oak Neck Point in 1883, but it had been eroded by 1915, and a third monument was erected 20 feet back from the edge of the cliff. By 1922, the cliff here had already receded 7 feet toward the third monument. Johnson published a series of accurate descriptions of the margins of the cliffs at Oak Neck and Fox Points, as to direction and distance from local landmarks, so that the amounts of change after 1922 could be accurately determined. He estimated that the cliffs have retreated a minimum distance of 500 feet in 250 years and that cutting was more rapid prior to the erection of strong seawalls in the 1880s. However, even the concrete seawalls have been pounded to pieces and erosion continues. Much of the erosion has been associated with oversteepening of the shore cliffs by waves, after which slumping of upper parts of the cliffs has provided more loose material for the waves to attack.

Johnson described a legal complication resulting from the movement of a barrier spit connecting Oak Neck with Fox Point. The waves removed the spit from land belonging to one owner and deposited it on that of another. A part of the litigation concerned the date when the barrier had moved. Because sufficiently accurate surveys were not at hand, this point could not be resolved satisfactorily.

The aerial photographs in Figure 3.31 were taken in 1947, 25 years after the last studies by Johnson; and the cliffed shorelines should have receded 50 to 75 feet or more, especially because this area was in the path of the 1938 New England hurricane. Changes noted on the photographs subsequent to the time of Johnson's map include the construction of a series of groins at several of the points to trap sediment and widen the beaches, thus retarding wave undercutting of the cliffs. Because Johnson's map

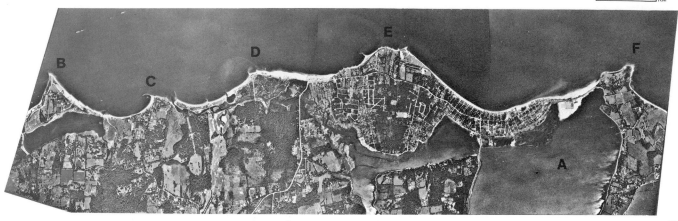

3.31 North shore of Long Island, New York, near Oyster Bay, showing straightening by barrier building and cuspate spits. Erosional history of this area has been traced back for a century. See text. U.S. Coast and Geodetic Survey, 1947.

does not show roads or buildings, it is difficult to locate changes. Most of the sand trapped by the groins is on the eastern sides, indicating littoral current drift is to the west. The latest chart indicates cobble beaches near Matinicock, Oak Neck, and Rocky Points. The village of Bayville at and near Oak Neck Point will probably suffer continued erosion of the bluff, and some homes near the crest of the point may be destroyed. However, all such predictions are dependent on the measures taken by man.

REFERENCES

Bloom, A. L., 1963. Late-Pleistocene fluctuations of sea level and postglacial crustal rebound in coastal Maine. *Amer. Jour. Sci.*, vol. 261, pp. 862–879.

Fuller, M. L., 1914. Geology of Long Island. *U.S. Geol. Survey Prof. Paper* 82.

Gofseyeff, S., 1953. Case history of Fire Island Inlet, New York. *Council on Wave Res., Engr. Found., Proc. 3rd Conf. Coastal Engineering*, pp. 272–305.

Goldthwait, J. W., 1938. Vertical stability of the coast at Marblehead, Massachusetts. *Amer. Jour. Sci.*, vol. 35, no. 206, pp. 81–93.

Gulliver, F. P., 1904. Nantucket shorelines, I. *Geol. Soc. Amer. Bull.*, vol. 14, pp. 555–556.

———, 1904. Nantucket shorelines, II. *Geol. Soc. Amer. Bull.*, vol. 15, pp. 507–522.

Howard, A. D., 1939. Hurricane modification of the offshore bar of Long Island, New York. *Geog. Rev.*, vol. 29, no. 3, pp. 400–415.

Jahns, Richard Henry, 1947. Geologic features of the Connecticut Valley, Massachusetts, as related to recent floods. *U.S. Geol. Survey Water-Supply Paper* 996.

Johnson, D. W., 1925. *The New England–Acadian Shoreline.* John Wiley & Sons, New York.

Kaye, C. A., 1964. Outline of the Pleistocene geology of Martha's Vineyard, Massachusetts. *U.S. Geol. Survey Prof. Paper* 501-C, pp. C134–149.

————, 1967. Erosion of a sea cliff, Boston Harbor, Massachusetts. In O. C. Farquhar (ed.), *Economic Geology in Massachusetts*, Univ. Mass. Grad. School, Amherst, pp. 521–528.

————, and E. S. Barghoorn, 1964. Late Quarternary sea-level change and crustal rise at Boston, Massachusetts, with notes on the autocompaction of peat. *Geol. Soc. Amer. Bull.*, vol. 75, pp. 63–80.

Mitchell, Henry, 1873. Report concerning Nauset Beach and the peninsula of Monomoy. *Mass. Board of Harbor Comm.*, 7th Ann. Rept.

Nichols, R. L., and A. F. Marston, 1939. Shoreline changes in Rhode Island produced by hurricane of September 21, 1938. *Geol. Soc. Amer. Bull.*, vol. 50, pp. 1357–1370.

Shaler, N. S., 1889. Geology of the island of Nantucket. *U.S. Geol. Survey Bull.* 53.

Sharp, Henry S., 1929. The physical history of the Connecticut shore line. *Connecticut Geol. and Nat. History Survey Bull.* 46.

Shelton, J. S., 1966. *Geology Illustrated.* W. H. Freeman and Company, San Francisco, pp. 190–191.

Woodworth, J. B., Edward Wigglesworth, and others, 1934. *Geography and Geology of the Region Including Cape Cod, the Elizabeth Islands, Nantucket, Martha's Vineyard, No Mans Land, and Block Island.* Harvard Coll. Mus. Comp. Zool. Mem. vol. 52.

Zeigler, J. M., S. D. Tuttle, G. S. Giese, and H. J. Tasha, 1964. Residence time of sand composing the beaches and bars of outer Cape Cod. *Amer. Soc. Civil Engineers, Proc. 9th Conf. on Coastal Engineering*, pp. 403–416.

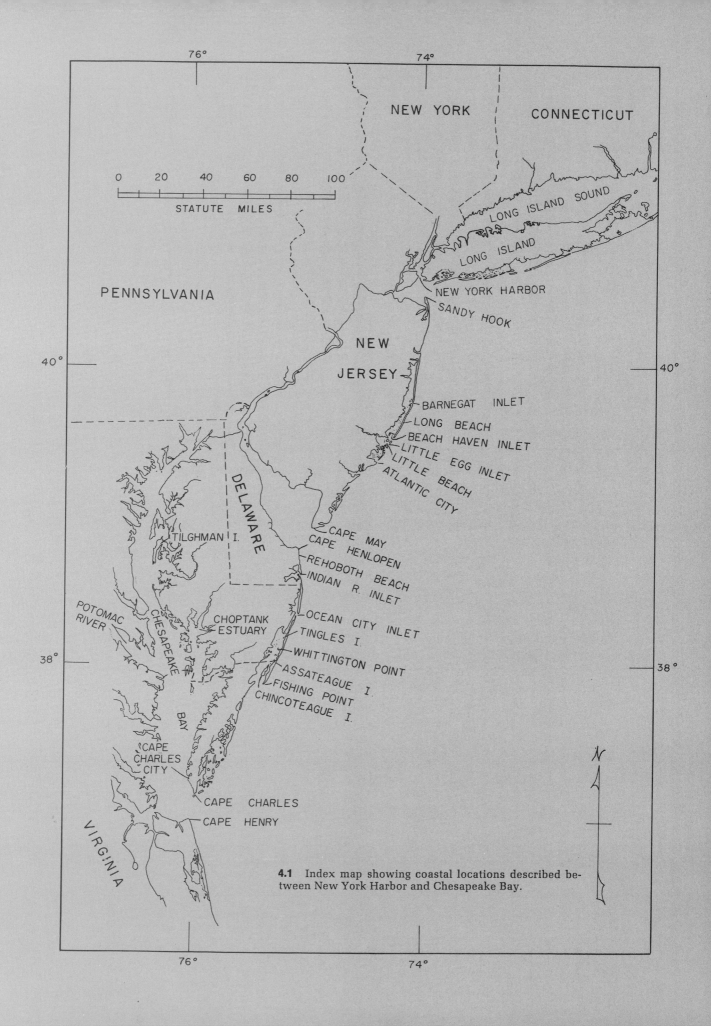

NEW YORK   CONNECTICUT

0   20   40   60   80   100

STATUTE MILES

PENNSYLVANIA

LONG ISLAND SOUND

LONG ISLAND

NEW YORK HARBOR

SANDY HOOK

NEW

JERSEY

40°

BARNEGAT   INLET

LONG BEACH

BEACH HAVEN INLET

LITTLE EGG INLET

LITTLE BEACH

ATLANTIC CITY

DELAWARE

TILGHMAN I.

CAPE MAY

CAPE HENLOPEN

REHOBOTH BEACH

INDIAN R. INLET

POTOMAC
RIVER

CHESAPEAKE

CHOPTANK
ESTUARY

OCEAN CITY INLET

TINGLES I.

WHITTINGTON POINT

ASSATEAGUE I.

FISHING POINT

CHINCOTEAGUE I.

38°

BAY

CAPE
CHARLES
CITY

CAPE CHARLES

CAPE HENRY

VIRGINIA

N

4.1 Index map showing coastal locations described between New York Harbor and Chesapeake Bay.

Straight Barriers and Long Estuaries

New York City to Chesapeake Bay

4 South of Long Island, we leave the glaciated coasts and encounter a type that characterizes most of the land margins of the remainder of the East Coast and the Gulf Coast down to and beyond the Mexican border. This type is deeply embayed, with the mainland coastal plain fringed by long sand barriers. Locally, the sand barriers lie in contact with the mainland, but mostly they are separated by lagoons. The latter are partly filled, and large tracts of marsh exist where the fill has been almost complete. Well-known seaside resorts, such as Atlantic City, Ocean City, and Virginia Beach, were built on the barriers which are cut by many inlets.

In this part of the coast (Fig. 4.1) there are three long estuaries. At the north end, New York Harbor, with its branching bays, is a combination of a partially filled fiord cut by the glaciers and drowned river valleys that were somewhat modified at the outer margin of the ice sheets. Delaware Bay and Chesapeake Bay to the south are drowned river valleys, and the latter has the longest arms of any in the United States, extending inland for as much as 180 miles.

The area south of New York Harbor was not glaciated, although some of the glacial outwash extends into northern New Jersey, accounting for the numerous gravel deposits. The effects of sea-level changes on this coast are somewhat complicated because, in addition to the drowning due to melting glaciers at the end of the last glacial stage, the earth's crust has undergone independent warping, particularly near the mouth of Chesapeake Bay. Wyman Harrison and others have found that the crust was being uplifted between 13,000 and 4000 B.C. at about the same rate that the sea was rising. After 4000 B.C., the land subsided for about 4,000 years and then has been slowly rising during the past 2,000 years. In New England, glaciation destroyed the

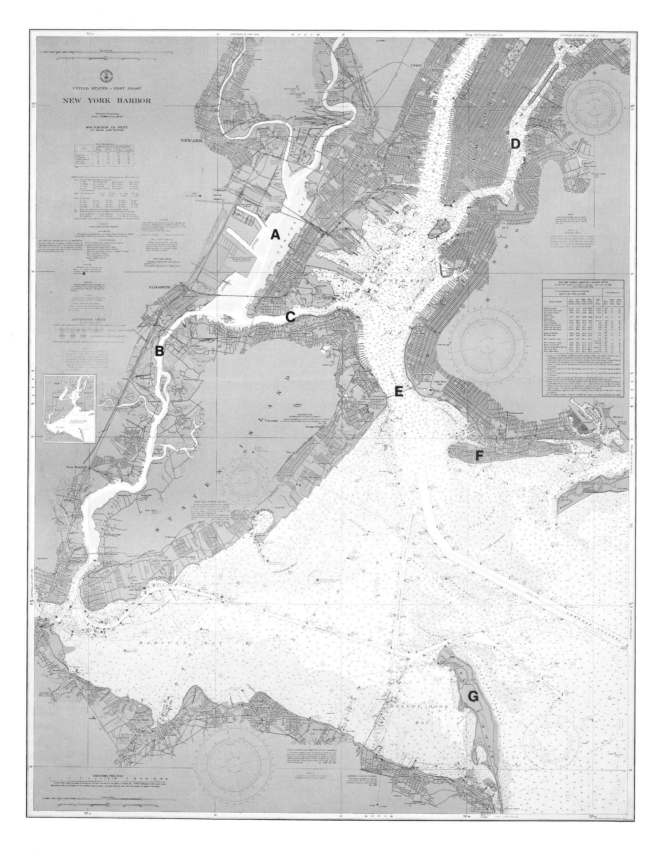

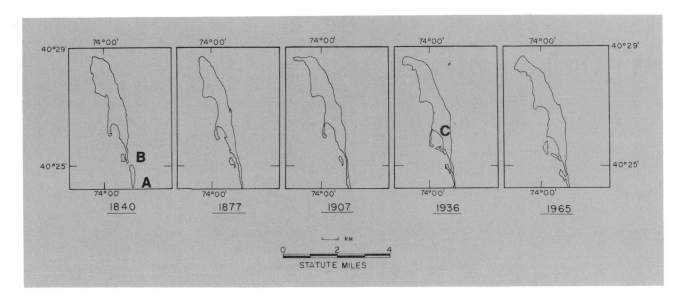

4.3 Sketches showing evolution of the Sandy Hook spit, 1840 to 1965. From U.S. Army Corps of Engineers.

effects of high stands of sea level during interglacial stages; but along the coast of New Jersey, beyond the edge of the former ice sheets, it is possible to recognize the high stand of about 100,000 years ago by the 25-foot terrace.

The barrier coasts south of New York are all exposed to the full force of East Coast hurricanes and severe northeasters. The storm of March 6 to 8, 1962, has had the greatest effect of any in recent years and caused extensive erosion of the barriers and sand islands all along the open coast of New Jersey, Delaware, and Maryland. Unlike most East Coast storms that produce only one episode where high tides are combined with destructive waves, the long-lasting 1962 storm continued through five successive high spring tides. During each of these, the waves cut away more and more of the barriers, and there was no time to repair the damage between the high tides. As a result, many man-made structures along the coast were destroyed.

NEW YORK HARBOR ENTRANCE AND SANDY HOOK, NEW JERSEY [Figs. 4.2, 4.3 and 4.4] New York City has the most important har-

4.2 Navigation chart of New York Harbor. U.S. Coast and Geodetic Survey Chart 369, 1966 edition.

bor on the North American continent (Fig. 4.2). It lies at the lower end of the Hudson River estuary where the river is essentially at sea level as far up as Albany, 150 miles north of its mouth. The preglacial Hudson Valley was later occupied by a lobe of continental glacier that deepened it as a fiord. Bedrock is more than 800 feet below sea level at Storm King Mountain, 50 miles north of New York City where the city's aqueduct crosses the river through a rock tunnel in granite 1,100 feet below sea level.

The west bank of the Hudson includes the Palisade sill, an intrusion of *diabase* (dark colored igneous rock). Farther west, Newark Bay (A in Fig. 4.2) is formed from the confluent estuaries of Passaic and Hackensack Rivers. Formerly, the valley occupied by Newark Bay drained southward through what is now Arthur Kill (B), along the west side of Staten Island; but later it was captured by a western tributary of the Hudson and deflected through Kill van Kull (C), north of Staten Island. Thus Staten Island is bounded on the north and west by drowned valleys of the Passaic and Hackensack Rivers. East River (D), which divides Manhattan Island from Long Island, is the drowned valley of a river that carried drainage southwestward into the Hudson from what is now Long Island Sound.

4.4 Aerial photo of Sandy Hook spit, New Jersey. U.S. Coast and Geodetic Survey, 1952.

Most of the shoreline features of New York Harbor are man-made, with multitudes of piers, docks, jetties, and dredged channels. The harbor has an Upper and Lower Bay, separated by the mile-wide Narrows (E) between Long Island and Staten Island, where the Narrows-Verrazano bridge was constructed in 1964. The Narrows are located at the crossing of the outermost end moraine at the margin of the continental glaciation. This is the point where the moraine curves inland to the west of Staten Island. Seaward of the Hudson River mouth, the Hudson Sea Valley is virtually a continuation of the estuary, extending out for 90 miles across most of the continental shelf.

Spits have been built into the Lower Bay from the east and south. Coney Island (F) is located at the western end of the chain of barriers along the south coast of Long Island, in which Moriches, Fire Island, and Jones Inlets (Chap. 3) are situated. Sandy Hook (G) has grown north for more than 5 miles from the Atlantic coast of New Jersey into the Lower Bay.

Outlines of Sandy Hook for 1840, 1877, 1907, 1936, and 1965 are shown in Figure 4.3. Earlier records are not at hand, but some of the events prior to 1840 are known. First, at some undetermined time, a spit grew northward from a barrier that had formed seaward from the estuaries of the Navesink and Shrewsbury Rivers (south of present Sandy Hook). After the spit had extended about 2 miles into New York Bay, it curved westward and southwestward, developing a hook. Then northward growth was resumed until the spit projected about 3.5 miles into the bay, and again a hook developed. Later growth continued until the present length of 5.3 miles was attained by 1840.

In 1840, the slender base of Sandy Hook had been breached in two places; one at Shrewsbury Inlet (A in Fig. 4.3), near the estuary of Navesink River, and the other 1.1 miles farther north, opposite the southeastern tip of Sandy Hook Bay (B). These inlets were probably opened at times of major storms. They were both closed in 1877 and, according to charts and available aerial photos, have remained closed since then. In 1840, a main ship channel passed westward just north of the tip of Sandy Hook, and there has been a channel in approximately the same location ever since. Dredging operations for this channel have probably prevented further lengthening of the spit or an increase in development of a recurved hook.

Between 1907 and 1936, spits were lengthened from the north and southeast to partially enclose a lagoon, Spermaceti Cove (C), near the oldest of the three hooks. The spit from the north was present in 1840, and the southeastern one formed between 1877 and 1907. By 1907, a hook had developed westward from the northern end of the spit. Between 1952 and 1955, the southeastern spit (A in Fig. 4.4) was separated from the main Sandy Hook spit; and between 1955 and 1962, the northern one was breached at B in Figure 4.4. In photographs for 1962 and 1963, both of the spits enclosing Spermaceti Cove had become islands.

The U.S. Army Corps of Engineers surveyed portions of the eastern exposed shore of Sandy Hook on seven dates between 1836 and 1953. The comparison of their lines shows that the coast has fluctuated back and forth with maximum changes of 900 feet. Arthur N. Strahler made a three-year study of changes at two of the old army stations. Many of his marker stations were destroyed when Hurricane Donna struck the area in late August 1960. Strahler states that here beach profiles are restored within a few days after major tropical storms. The beach includes both sand and medium gravel, the latter probably derived from glacial outwash. Just below low tide, a gravel step about 0.5 foot high is a characteristic feature of the Sandy Hook profile.

A small amount of change in outline displayed in the Sandy Hook spit between 1840 and 1936 suggests that it is essentially in equilibrium.

BARNEGAT INLET, NEW JERSEY [Fig. 4.5]
Barnegat Inlet, about 55 miles south of Sandy Hook, has been open for at least 300 years since the earliest surveys. It is now the northernmost of the natural New Jersey inlets, although inlets have opened and closed during the past three centuries; and Manasquan Inlet, 20 miles south of Sandy Hook, was opened and maintained artificially. A natural inlet, about 10 miles north of Barnegat, was formerly used by small boats but was closed by deposition in 1812. Before that time, Barnegat Inlet seems to have remained approximately in one location; but since 1812 it has shifted southward about a mile. The direction of beach drifting along this area is southward; sand and gravel are supplied to the beaches from erosion of Atlantic Highlands, about 50 miles to the north.

Incoming tides sweep sand through Barnegat Inlet, so that much of the southerly transported sand never reaches the next inlet down the coast. When an inlet is closed, the amount of sand arriving at the next downcurrent opening increases, and the inlet begins to shift location in the direction of beach drifting. Thus the closing of Cranberry Inlet started the southward shift in location of Barnegat Inlet.

The history of Barnegat Inlet and the growth of the tidal delta inside it were described and illustrated in 1934 by John Lucke. Between 1934 and 1940, jetties (A and B in Fig. 4.5b) 0.6 and 0.4 mile in length were constructed at the entrance to the inlet, and a boat channel was cut across the southward loop of the tidal channel inside the inlet (C). As the jetties trapped much of the sand reaching Barnegat Inlet, the tidal delta has grown very little since 1940 (shown by aerial photographs in 1950, 1956, and 1963). The 1963 photograph shows that a residential subdivision was being laid out on the southern part of the tidal delta (D) where the land had been filled artificially.

LITTLE EGG AND BEACH HAVEN INLETS, NEW JERSEY[1] [Figs. 4.6 through 4.10]   The largest gap in the series of barriers along the New Jersey coast is located 10 miles north of Atlantic City. Here, Little Egg Inlet and Beach Haven Inlet, on the north, form a combined breach in the barrier system 3 miles across (Fig. 4.6). On the north side of the combined inlet, Long Beach extends without a break for 20 miles to Barnegat Inlet. On the south, the situation is very changeable; and the irregular-shaped sand island, generally referred to as Little Beach, was in 1964 only about 2 miles long. Directly inside the main inlet is the voluminous Great Bay, which is separated from Little Egg Harbor by a large abandoned tidal delta. The barriers here are separated from the mainland shore by 4 to 8 miles; but the lagoon inside has been considerably modified by tidal deltas and marsh growth, so that it has reached what appears to be stage three of the Lucke classification (Fig. 2.20).

The history of the inlet has been traced back to 1769; a crude map of that date shows a single opening in the barrier at about this location, labeled "Little

---

[1] Largely based on an unpublished report by Paul Plusquellec, illustrated by Judith Greer and Janet Garrell.

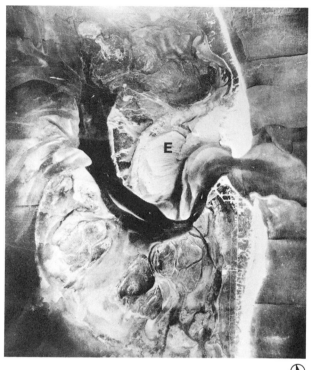

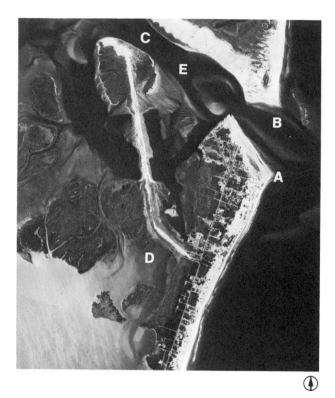

4.5

a Barnegat Inlet, New Jersey, showing tidal delta as photographed in early 1930s. Airview Inc., Long Branch, New Jersey; an aerial mosaic.

b Same locality 1950, showing navigation channel cut through tidal delta. Point E is in common to both photos. U.S. Coast and Geodetic Survey.

Egg Harbour." The first chart to give details of the barrier system was published in 1840 (Fig. 4.7*a*). It shows two inlets; the one to the north, called "Old Inlet" (A in Fig. 4.7), is apparently the same as shown in the 1769 map; but the one to the south, "New Inlet" (B), was opened about 1800. Each was about a mile wide; and Tucker Island, with a length of 2 miles, lay between them. The subsequent history is best described by first considering the development of the south end of Long Beach and then the evolution of Little Beach, although the series of maps (Fig. 4.7) so far as possible combines both developments. Charts used to show the history of the two areas are dated 1840, 1870, 1885, and 1904. Aerial photos continue the history with dates of 1932, 1940, 1944, 1950, 1955, 1963, and 1964.

Long Beach grew 3 miles to the south between 1840 and 1870, having built across Old Inlet and around the south end of Tucker Island. A further

extension of Long Beach in 1885 connected it with Tucker Island and left only a mile-wide inlet into Great Bay. Just inside the inlet, a north branch developed west of Tucker Island and led to Little Egg Harbor. Between 1904 and 1932, Long Beach was severed by another wide opening, called Beach Haven Inlet (C), which was formed at about the same place as Old Inlet. This reestablished Tucker Island with a new length of more than 2 miles. The island was now deprived of its source of sediment by the new inlet, and the 1940 aerial photographs show a remarkable change (Fig. 4.10*a*). These photos cover only 0.75 mile of the area where the southern end of the island had been, but in this area not even a shoal is indicated. The 1944 photographs (not shown) cover the entire site of the 1932 island, and

4.6 Long Beach–Little Egg Inlet area, New Jersey, showing general geography. U.S. Coast and Geodetic Survey Navigation Chart 826, 1964.

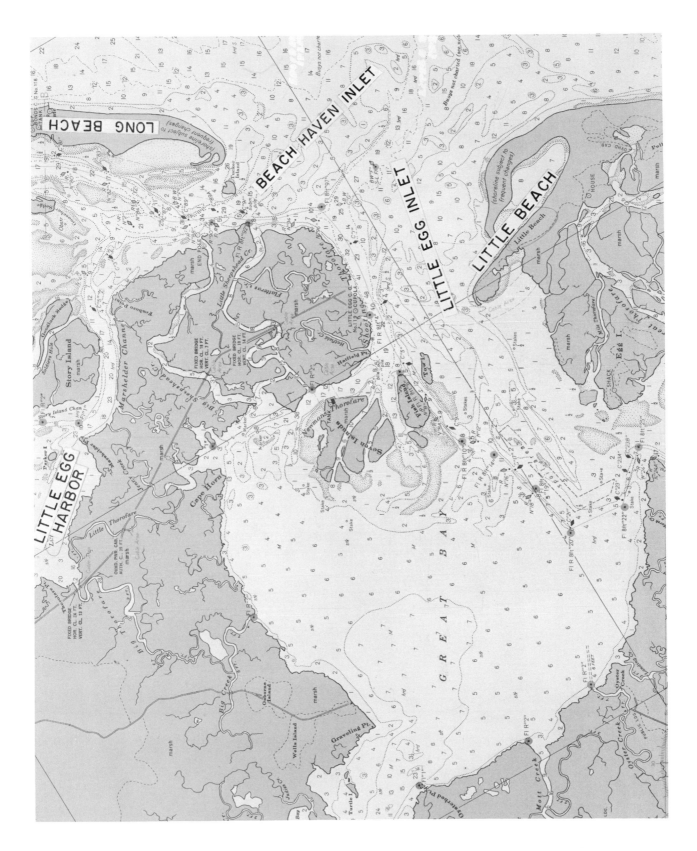

indicate that the south end had been cut back about a mile and separated into two small remnants. At the same time, Beach Haven Inlet was largely filled with longitudinal sand bars.

Apparently, after the 1769 map, a large tidal delta was built into what had been called Flat Bay, virtually cutting the bay in two, leaving Great Bay on the south and Little Egg Harbor on the north. This tidal delta has had a much more recent enlargement. Slightly before 1950, while Tucker Island was still of significant size, a storm tide appears to have developed a north flow on the west side of the island and built a new tidal delta into the southern end of Little Egg Harbor (A in Fig. 4.8). This left only a narrow eastern channel into the harbor.

By 1950, Tucker Island (B in Fig. 4.8) had virtually disappeared and was represented only by a shoal in the May 1962 photographs (A in Fig. 4.9). Long Beach continued to grow southward and by early March 1962 had reached the position of the remnant of Tucker Island, developing a hook that considerably restricted the entrance to Little Egg

Harbor. However, on March 6, 1962, the great storm that affected so much of the East Coast was devastating in its attack on Long Beach. This was described in the *National Geographic Magazine* (Dec. 1962), and their fold-in illustration shows the numerous sluiceways cut across the island and the many blocks of property destroyed in Beach Haven. Ten miles farther north, the storm obliterated the small town of Harvey Cedars. However, the waves did not permanently change the beach outline. Two months later, a new outer beach had redeveloped, bringing back the old shoreline, although sluiceways from the storm (B in Fig. 4.9) were still conspicuous (compare Figs. 4.8 and 4.9). The new beach connects with the wide belt of sand built westward by the overwashes (B in Fig. 4.9). By 1964, the outer beach of the island showed some southward growth but no other major change.

Little Beach, to the south of the inlets, has had quite a different history from that of Long Beach. After the development of New Inlet about 1800, when there was a considerable growth to the north,

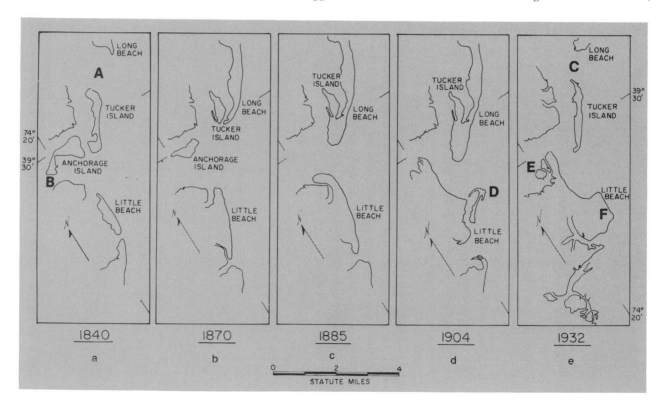

4.7 Sketch maps showing coastal changes in Long Beach–Little Beach area, New Jersey, between 1840 and 1932. Prepared by Paul Plusquellec.

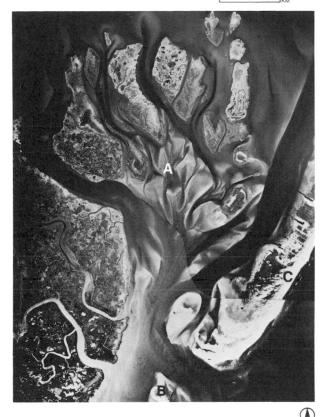

4.8 Tidal delta formed in Beach Haven Inlet, near Long Beach (C), New Jersey. U.S. Coast and Geodetic Survey, 1950.

the north end of Little Beach appears to have maintained approximately the same position (Fig. 4.7). However, Little Beach has changed extensively in shape. In 1840 (Fig. 4.7*a*), there were two islands; but, by 1870 (Fig. 4.7*b*), these had merged and the spit had grown somewhat to the east. By 1885 (Fig. 4.7*c*), the eastern arm of the beach had grown to the north and then curved to the west with a total lengthening of 0.7 mile. By 1904 (Fig. 4.7*d*), the island had had its greatest growth, having advanced 0.75 mile to the north. During this interval, a cuspate point had developed along the southeast coast of the island; and, directly outside it, a new island (D in Fig. 4.7*d*) 1.5 miles long had been formed, with two curved spits at its northeastern end. By 1932, the northern end of the island was partly submerged, leaving two marshy islands (E in Fig. 4.7*e*) on the west side and a spit to the east. The island off the southeast coast had been incorporated into the main island (F in Fig. 4.7*e*).

4.9 Southern end of Long Beach and northern end of Little Beach, New Jersey, two months after Atlantic storm of 1962, showing numerous washovers. U.S. Coast and Geodetic Survey, May 4, 1962.

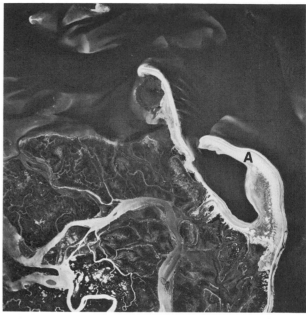

b 1950. Showing rotation of older spit and lengthening of new spit. U.S. Coast and Geodetic Survey.

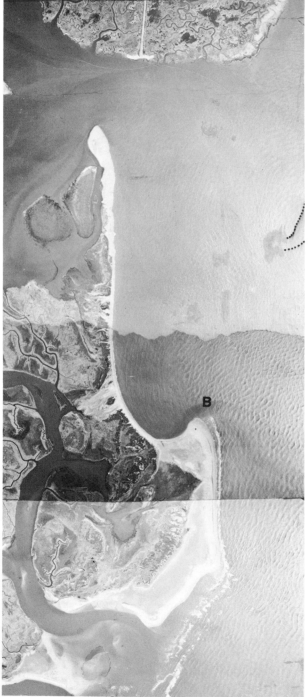

4.10 Coastal changes at Little Beach, New Jersey, 1940 to 1964.

a 1940. Before growth of new eastern spit. Dotted line shows part of Tucker Island in 1932. Not even a shoal is indicated in 1940. U.S. Department of Agriculture.

The 1940 aerial photographs (Fig. 4.10a) show little change in the spit and the marsh islands, and the point to the south (B) had only grown slightly beyond its condition in 1932. By 1944, the narrow spit (A) had started to grow northward from the one of the marshy islands. At the same time, a new spit (B) had started to grow northward from the easterly bulge farther down the island. By 1950 (Fig. 4.10b), the northern point had moved still farther to the west until it covered most of the western portion of the marshy islands. The new spit had grown about a mile to the north and was also hooking to the west. From 1950 to 1964, the eastern spit continued to grow to the north until it reached the same latitude as the inner spit (Fig. 4.10c). The 1962 storm had cut sluiceways across this outer spit but did not change its outline. In the new bay between the spits, a tidal delta (A in Fig. 4.10c) formed and had become well developed by 1964, nearly closing the bay entrance. Probably the 1962 storm introduced much of the sand, which was later reworked into this delta. The western spit (B) had meantime been shrinking, due to either subsidence or erosion. The north-growing easterly spit gradually moved westward, en-

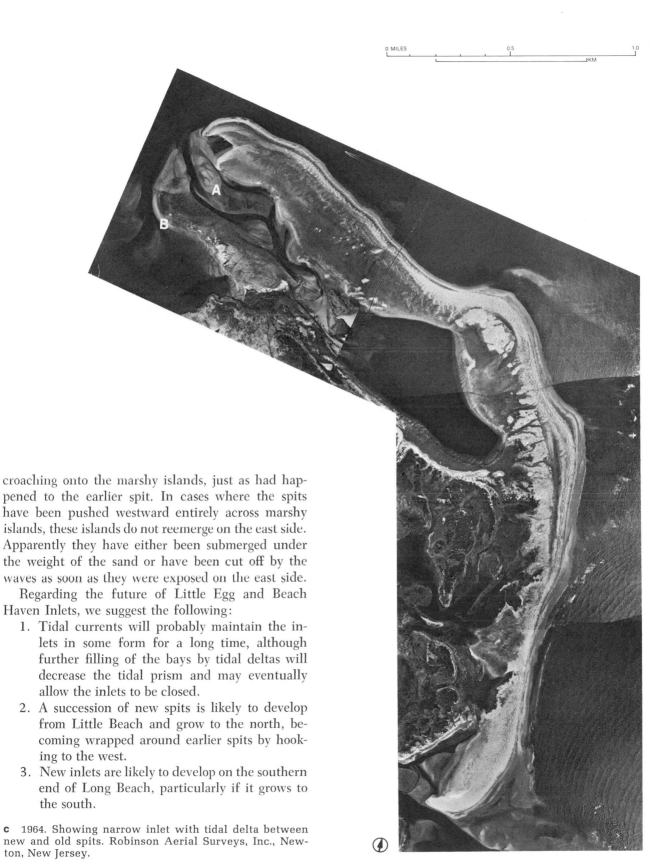

croaching onto the marshy islands, just as had happened to the earlier spit. In cases where the spits have been pushed westward entirely across marshy islands, these islands do not reemerge on the east side. Apparently they have either been submerged under the weight of the sand or have been cut off by the waves as soon as they were exposed on the east side.

Regarding the future of Little Egg and Beach Haven Inlets, we suggest the following:

1. Tidal currents will probably maintain the inlets in some form for a long time, although further filling of the bays by tidal deltas will decrease the tidal prism and may eventually allow the inlets to be closed.

2. A succession of new spits is likely to develop from Little Beach and grow to the north, becoming wrapped around earlier spits by hooking to the west.

3. New inlets are likely to develop on the southern end of Long Beach, particularly if it grows to the south.

c 1964. Showing narrow inlet with tidal delta between new and old spits. Robinson Aerial Surveys, Inc., Newton, New Jersey.

4.11 Changes in coastline at Cape May, New Jersey, 1944 to 1963.
a 1944. Shortly after the jetty was built. Airport partly eroded and beach at Cape May largely destroyed. U.S. Department of Agriculture.

ATLANTIC CITY, NEW JERSEY [Fig. 2.11] South of Little Egg Inlet, there are two long straight beaches. The southern of these includes Atlantic City with its famous Boardwalk. The Atlantic side of the island extends for 8 miles without any appreciable change of direction. The valuable sea front with its resort hotels is sufficiently protected artificially so that little damage has resulted from the East Coast storms. However, the steel pier (A in Fig. 2.11) was snapped in two during the great storm of 1962.

The jettied north end of the island (not shown) projects seaward 0.5 mile beyond the south end of Brigantine Island, suggesting that the current here is dominantly north. This is not supported by any appreciable sand buildup on the north side of the piers and groins. At the time of the aerial photograph (Fig. 2.11), the current was definitely moving to the south, and such a direction should be favored by the predominant northeast storms.

CAPE MAY, NEW JERSEY [Figs. 4.11a and b] Cape May forms the southern tip of the New Jersey coast adjoining Delaware Bay and is about 11 miles northeast of Cape Henlopen, on the other side of the estuary. At present, the gently curving southern end of New Jersey is about 6 miles broad, in contrast to

the narrow sharp point at Cape Henlopen. The city of Cape May (A) is located along the straight outer coast, 2 miles east of the Cape (B). A canal (C) crosses the Cape May Peninsula 2 miles north of the point. A pair of jetties (D) maintain the entrance to Cape May Harbor by concentrating the tidal flow. The eastern jetty, 0.4 mile long, has trapped much sand against its eastern side, showing a predominant westward beach drifting at this locality. The city of Cape May is protected by a seawall nearly 3 miles long. Five groins project from the western part of this wall and, by 1963 (Fig. 4.11b), all had trapped sand on their east sides. There is no seawall at Wildwood (E) or at Cape May Point, but five groins at the point have trapped sand on their eastern and southeastern sides.

Although all groins and jetties along the Atlantic shore of Cape May show sand trapped on their eastern sides, inside Delaware Bay the jetties at the western entrance to the Cape May canal (not illustrated) have trapped sand about equally on the north and south, indicating that some sand has been swept into the lower bay from beaches on the open coast, and some has been brought down the bay perhaps at times of Delaware River floods.

A town called South Cape May (F in Figs. 4.11a and b) formerly existed in the coastal stretch between

b 1963. Beach at Wildwood northeast of jetty has broadened. More destruction at airport. South Cape May (F) has been entirely eroded. U.S. Department of Agriculture.

Cape May Point and the western end of the seawall of the city of Cape May, but South Cape May has been destroyed by beach erosion during the past 50 years. Portions of two coastal roads, which formerly extended to South Cape May, are visible on the 1944 aerial photograph (Fig. 4.11a) but were missing in 1963 (Fig. 4.11b). Senator Joseph D. Tydings of Maryland reported in 1967 that two Roman Catholic convents, two lighthouses, a Coast Guard radar station, and nearly a fourth of the land area of the old town had been lost.

A comparison of photographs of the Cape May area in 1944 (Fig. 4.11a) and 1963 (Fig. 4.11b) shows other changes during that 19-year period. In 1944, the beach at southwestern Wildwood (G in Fig. 4.11a) was suffering erosion, because there is no seawall there; but, by 1963, the trapping of sand behind the Cape May Harbor jetty had resulted in a straight beach at Wildwood, broader than in 1944 (G in Fig. 4.11b). Southwest of the harbor entrance, the coast at the Cape May airfield had been cut back about 0.3 mile (H in Fig. 4.11b), because of the lack of sufficient sand to replenish that eroded during storms.

The city of Cape May is now largely protected by a seawall, so it has not suffered much recession; but Figure 4.11b shows that all of the beach sand has

been eroded from the eastern half of the city waterfront, a serious loss as Cape May is predominantly a beach resort town. The protection of the town by the seawall and groins is shown by the 400-foot setback of the shoreline just west of the end of the seawall and the westernmost groin. Cape May Point is supplied with sand eroded from the site of the former town of South Cape May. Because of the groins, the cape will probably continue its present form as the unprotected shore between it and the city of Cape May continues to erode and supply replacement of sand for Cape May Point.

South and southwest of the Cape May shore (not illustrated), coastal charts show a series of shoals with water depths of 20 feet or less, extending about 7 miles into the ocean at the mouth of the estuary. Their form suggests the former existence of at least seven successive arcuate barriers separated by slightly deeper water. The outer barriers may be remnants of Pleistocene shorelines formed when world sea level had not yet reached its present position following the last ice age. Alternatively, the barriers may be in part subaqueous sand bars due to the reworking of sand introduced into the sea from the Delaware estuary, and the inner shoals may be benches marking the positions of recent shorelines abandoned during modern shore recession.

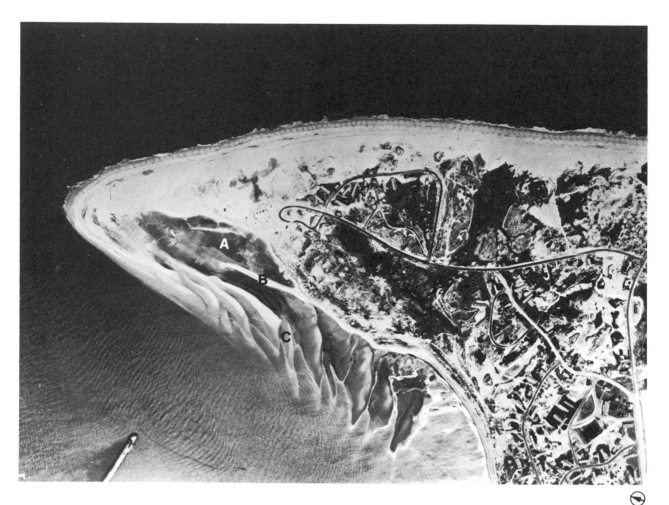

4.12 Changes at Cape Henlopen, Delaware, south side of Delaware River estuary.
a 1948. U.S. Army Map Service.

CAPE HENLOPEN, DELAWARE [Fig. 4.12] Cape Henlopen, on the southwest side of the entrance to Delaware Bay, is a cuspate foreland with a spit built onto the end that bends into the bay. The spit, unlike Cape Charles, has been built up across the shoals along this side of the entrance and is bordered by water 60 feet deep. The aerial photographs of 1948, 1953, 1955, and 1962 (Fig. 4.12) show a progressive advance of the cape with a total growth of 800 feet. Thus this cape is bordered by relatively deep water and is being built forward; whereas on the other side of the entrance, Cape May, bordered by shallow water, has undergone recent erosion and needs to be protected by artificial struc-

tures. This is particularly surprising because in rivers in which the channel approaches the bank, as on the outside of bends, erosion is taking place and deposition is occurring on the other side where the water is shoal.

The aerial photographs all show a relatively straight east side of the spit; but the west side is made irregular by bars and spits, which extend out from the land to the southwest and west and are extremely variable in location. Examination of the 1948 photo (Fig. 4.12a) shows that the west side of the spit had a considerable embayment (A) near the end of the point. A spit (B) had been built from the south halfway across this bay. Subsequently, sedi-

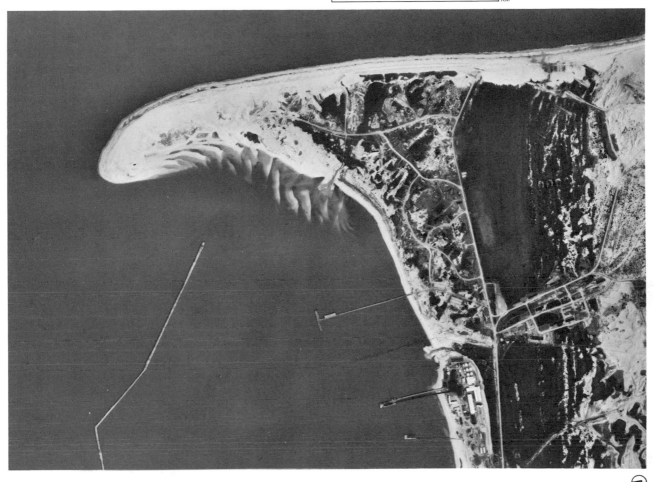

b March 15, 1962. One week after great Atlantic storm. Note deflection of tip of peninsula to west. U.S. Coast and Geodetic Survey.

ment had been carried around the end of the spit; and a series of diagonal bars had been built toward the southwest, each bar overlapping the one to the south (C), like shingles on a roof. By 1953 (not shown), the end of the point had grown 0.25 mile and had turned to the west. The spit that crossed the embayment was largely covered by a new spit, which extended from near the end of the point down across the entire bay. Also, part of the bay had been filled by deposition. The diagonal bars were not so prominent as in the 1948 photo, perhaps due to the water not being as clear or because the photo was taken at high tide. In 1962 (Fig. 4.12b), a week after the March storm, the point had grown another 0.15 mile

and had been turned still farther to the west. The bay had been almost entirely filled, apparently as a result of the general migration of the point to the west. The bars show prominently in the 1962 photo but appear a little shorter, probably also due to the migration of the point to the west.

The effects of the great 1962 storm are far less visible in the photo of Cape Henlopen (Fig. 4.12b) than at most other places along this part of the coast. However, the northern end of the road appears to have been largely covered with sand, and the loop of the road near the coast has also been buried. The storm may have caused the filling of the old bay and also the bending of the point to the west.

4.13 Indian River (D) and Rehoboth (E) Bays, Delaware, showing inlet and three tidal deltas of different ages. High-altitude photography by U.S. Army Map Service, 1960.

REHOBOTH BAY AND INDIAN RIVER INLET, DELAWARE [Figs 4.13 and 4.14]   The coast is very straight for 25 miles south of the entrance of Delaware Bay, then curves more to the west, but continues all the way to Cape Charles as a barrier island. In some places, the lagoons inside have been filled. The first unfilled embayments are Rehoboth and Indian River Bays (Fig. 4.13), both drowned river valleys. This is an example of an uneven coast resulting from postglacial rise in sea level that has been entirely straightened by erosion of projecting points and construction of barriers across the mouths of the estuaries.

The bays connect with the sea through Indian River Inlet (A in Fig. 4.13), which was artificially constructed in the twentieth century. The inlet is protected by small jetties, and a tidal delta has formed in the bay inside the entrance. The earliest topographic map available, made in 1918, shows a natural inlet just north of the present entrance (B).

4.14 Dewey Beach (A) and Rehoboth Bay, Delaware, showing many sluiceways formed by 1962 Atlantic storm. U.S. Coast and Geodetic Survey, March 15, 1962, one week after storm.

Although this old inlet closed in 1920, its former position is marked by a small tidal delta inside the beach. A little farther north, there are remains of a still older tidal delta (C), called Rehoboth Marsh. The beach was evidently farther seaward when this older tidal delta formed, because now only the landward portions of the distributary channels survive. However, there has been little if any change between 1938 and 1960, according to the aerial photos of these two dates.

The positions and relative ages of the two closed tidal inlets suggest that the predominant littoral current has been southward, although at Indian River Inlet the beach has built out a little farther on the south than on the north side of the jetty.

This low barrier coast was struck with the full fury of the great Atlantic storm of March 1962. Many washovers of sand from the beach occurred, averaging one or two in the length of a city block at Dewey Beach (A in Fig. 4.14). Many reached the coastal road, and beach sand swept clear across the barrier to Rehoboth Bay in a belt about 0.5 mile wide (B). At Dewey Beach, a seaside resort, many homes were destroyed. Washovers swept down each street in the town. The photograph, made about a week after the beginning of the storm, shows that a narrow and interrupted longshore bar had already formed seaward from the beach.

OCEAN CITY INLET AND BARRIER, MARYLAND[2] [Fig. 4.15]   Ocean City, the principal seaside resort on the Atlantic coast of Maryland, is situated at the southern end of the Fenwick Island barrier and about 21 miles south of the beach at Indian River Inlet. The barrier is separated from the irregular mainland coast by a lagoon of variable width, 0.5 mile at its narrowest at Ocean City, where the bridge connects Fenwick Island with the mainland.

Inlets have opened and closed several times along this barrier island; but in early 1933 it was unbroken for 40 miles, from the Delaware line across Maryland to Chincoteague Inlet in coastal Virginia. However, in August 1933, a hurricane opened an inlet immediately south of Ocean City, and this inlet has persisted until the present. The part of the barrier south of the inlet to Fishing Point, Virginia, is called Assateague Island. The inlet was stabilized in 1935 when the U.S. Army Corps of Engineers built jetties

[2] Largely based on a report by Constance Gawne, 1966.

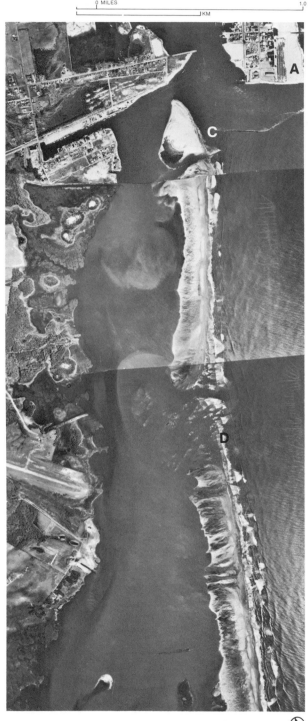

4.15 Ocean City, Maryland, showing offset in shoreline due to building of jetty on northern side of Ocean City Inlet. A is same in *a* and *b*.

a 1955. Beach extended north of jetty. U.S. Coast and Geodetic Survey.

b March 24, 1962. Showing that the northern end of Assateague Island had been cut back beyond landward end of the southern Ocean City jetty, and deeply eroded by the 1962 Atlantic storm of March 5. U.S. Coast and Geodetic Survey.

on each side of the inlet. The north jetty borders the south end of Ocean City and extends 1,100 feet east of the Boardwalk. The south jetty is 1,850 feet in length out from the north end of Assateague Island.

A strong littoral current flows southward. In order to check erosion of the Fenwick Island beaches, a series of groins were placed at 450-foot intervals outside Ocean City and at 900-foot intervals north to the Delaware line during 1954 and 1955. So much sand was trapped that many groins were covered within a week of their construction. Since 1935, the north jetty at the Ocean City Inlet has trapped sand, forming a triangular beach nearly a mile long. However, because of the jetties, an inadequate supply of sand on the south side of the inlet has caused the beach to recede rapidly. Figure 4.15a shows the area in 1955 when the jetties were 20 years old. The north beach has extended seaward nearly to the end of the Ocean City pier. Assateague Island beach, south of the south jetty, had receded about 1,500 feet. By April 1961, this beach was no longer connected with the inner end of the south jetty, and the hooked spit in the inlet began to erode. A major storm occurred between April and November 1961, and the photographs of the latter date (not illustrated) show the beach separated from the inner end of the south jetty by almost 800 feet of open water (as shown in March 1962, C in Fig. 4.15b).

At the time of the 1961 storm, the Assateague Island barrier was cut by four new breaches in the 2 miles directly south of the inlet. This area became seriously impoverished for sand during the 26 years since the jetties had been built and resulted in an offset of about a mile between the beach at Ocean City and that to the south.

In March 1962, this coast felt the full intensity of the Atlantic storm, and the northern Assateague Island coast was further eroded, leaving much of it a shoal barely exposed at high tide (D in Fig. 4.15b). A breach nearly a mile wide opened about 2 miles south of the Ocean City inlet. Following the storm, dredging operations reconnected the south jetty to the mainland. The April 28 aerial photograph shows that the gap had been largely filled, and a photograph taken in March 1963 indicates that the north end of the island had been restored completely. The next major storm could easily cause a new separation of the barrier from the landward end of the jetty.

TINGLES ISLAND AND WHITTINGTON POINT AREAS, ASSATEAGUE ISLAND, MARYLAND[3] [Figs. 4.16 and 2.13]

Assateague Island, near the Maryland-Virginia line, is broader than at its northern end near the Ocean City inlet, averaging 0.75 to 1 mile in width. The Atlantic shoreline extends south-southwestward to Green Run Bay, the site of an inlet abandoned between 1850 and 1900. Here, it curves more toward the southwest.

The inner shoreline adjoining Chincoteague Bay is very irregular as a result of old tidal deltas and washovers formed during major storms and hurricanes. Aerial photographs of the island show dunes, sluiceways, washover deltas, reticulate bars, sand plains, and washarounds, making this one of the most spectacular areas along the Atlantic coast.

The oldest aerial photography available to us is from 1955, but high-altitude photography in 1959 and lower altitude for April (Fig. 4.16a) and November 1961, and for March 15 (Fig. 4.16b) and March 24 and April 28 (Fig. 4.16c), 1962, provide seven photographic records within as many years.

Prior to this photography of the area, sand dunes had formed between 0.25 and 1 mile behind the beach (A in Fig. 2.13a), and many were stabilized by vegetation. At an undetermined date before 1955, a major storm or hurricane produced three wide washover fans at Sugar Point (Figs. 2.13a and b), about 3 miles wide; Tingles Island (Fig. 4.16), about 0.75 mile wide; and Smith Hammocks, farther south, about 3 miles wide. There were also many narrower washovers and many sluiceways. Where these flows broke through dunes near the coast, the sand was washed along the sides of the eroded dunes; and some sand was banked against their margins (B in Fig. 2.13a). Narrower breaches were made in a second belt of dunes about 0.5 mile behind the beach (Fig. 4.16; C in Fig. 2.13a). The storm waters cut a series of sluiceways through lower marsh deposits and into Chincoteague Bay (D in Fig. 2.13a), where some of the eroded sand accumulated in washover deltas and reticulate bars.

Tingles Island has good examples of what W. Armstrong Price has named *washarounds*. These are still poorly understood by geologists. The best ex-

[3] Largely based on an unpublished report by Constance Gawne, 1966.

4.16

a April 21, 1961. Hurricane effects on part of Assateague Island just south of Tingles Island, Maryland, showing large washover formed by an older hurricane, and several washarounds (A and B). U.S. Coast and Geodetic Survey.

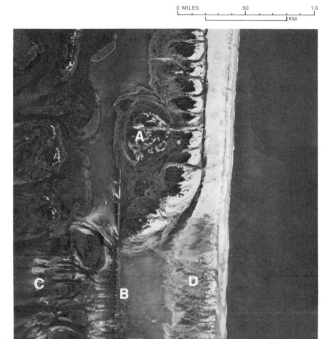

b March 15, 1962, one week after Atlantic storm, showing reticulate bars (D) and small sand dunes (E) formed during first week after storm. B is same in *b* and *c*. U.S. Coast and Geodetic Survey.

c April 28, 1962, seven weeks after Atlantic storm, showing reworking and smoothing of reticulate bars. U.S. Coast and Geodetic Survey.

ample (A in Fig. 4.16*a*) will illustrate their character. During a great storm, a vegetated portion of a dune ridge is apparently isolated as an island, and the currents of water flowing past on either side evidently develop its rounded shape. Deposition from the sand-laden currents against the sides of the hill may account for the rings that surround these temporary islands; and, after the water has gone down, wind drift may add further to these terraces around the hills. Additional concentric layers (A) may be added during later storms. Several smaller examples (B) are seen farther south in the same photograph. These washarounds occur also along the south Texas coast (Fig. 9.24), where they were first described by Price.

Southern Assateague Island was planned for development as a beach resort before 1962, and streets had been laid out (E in Fig. 2.13*a*) and a few houses built. To protect this low island from destructive beach erosion by future storms, a series of low walls were built across the sluiceways (C in Fig. 4.16; F in Fig. 2.13*a*), cutting the dune belt adjoin-

ing Chincoteague Bay; and another line was built across the sand plain behind the beach (C in Fig. 4.16*b*; G in Fig. 2.13*a*).

During the March 1962 storm, the beach was extensively eroded, and large volumes of sand were washed in across the sand plain, eroding or burying most of the protective barriers (Figs. 4.16*b* and 2.13*b*). The bulk of the eroded beach sand accumulated on the broad sand plains as a series of narrow washover fans, each with a pointed end (A in Fig. 2.13*b*). Where the sand was carried through an older sluiceway into the bay, it formed new reticulate bars (C in Fig. 4.16*b*). Small sand dunes (B in Fig. 2.13*b*) had already formed within a week after the storm.

In the narrower washover near Tingles Island (Fig. 4.16*c*), most of the washover fan had accumulated seaward from the sand dike that had been built across the head of the sluiceway. However, the dike was obliterated at many places (compare Figs. 4.16*b* and *c*). The Tingles Island area was rephotographed on April 28, seven weeks after the storm (Fig.

4.17 Chincoteague Island (B) and Bay, the southern end of Assateague Island (F), including Fishing Point (G) and the northeastern end of Wallops Island (H), all Virginia. High-altitude photography by U.S. Army Map Service, 1959.

4.16c). This provides an illustration of what changes may be expected in a sandy coastal area in a short time after it has been devastated by a major storm. The wind had redistributed the sand so that the washover features, so prominent in Figure 4.16b, had been smoothed. Some of the sand had been blown against dunes covered with vegetation, forming new sand ridges. A part of the sand remained in the flats, building the sand plain a little higher. Later, it was somewhat drifted by wind until the flat was stabilized by vegetation.

After the 1962 storm, private plans to develop a beach resort on Assateague Island were abandoned; and the island was made a part of the National Sea-

shore Reserve, administered by the National Park Service.

CHINCOTEAGUE ISLAND–FISHING POINT AREA, VIRGINIA[4] [Figs. 4.17, 4.18 and 4.19] The southern end of Assateague Island, Virginia, shows evidence of a complicated history. The principal features, given by letters in Figure 4.17, are Chincoteague Bay (A); Chincoteague Island, marked by very irregularly spaced dune (or beach) ridges (B); Chincoteague Inlet southwest of Chincoteague Island (C), connecting Chincoteague Bay with the

[4] Partly based on a report by Constance Gawne, 1966.

ocean; Assateague Channel, southeast of Chincoteague Island (D); Assateague Point 1 (E), a series of low beach or dune ridges southeast of Assateague Channel; Assateague Point 2 (F), a hooked spit south of point 1, interrupted by a tidal stream; Fishing Point, the prominent hooked spit (G); and Wallops Island (H), the barrier extending southwest from Chincoteague Inlet. E, F, and G indicate a succession of three hooked spits at the south end of Assateague Island.

Chincoteague Island (B) is probably the oldest feature in this area. During its growth, at least fifty dune or beach ridges (Fig. 4.18) were formed by littoral currents coming from the southwest. At their northeastern ends, these ridges diverge and curve eastward, as though they were growing toward a cape no longer existent. Cape Kennedy, Florida, has a similar growth pattern (see p. 148). The chart of the Maryland-Virginia coast (Coast and Geodetic Survey Chart 1220) shows a series of offshore shoals seaward from Assateague Island with trends similar to those of the ridges on Chincoteague Island. These may be remnants of a cuspate cape between Delaware and Chesapeake Bays, which has been largely destroyed. No similar structures are seen on Wallops Island (H) or on Assateague Island. The northeastern end of the Chincoteague Island ridges is abruptly cut off along the north-south trending shore (A in Fig. 4.18), and the southwestern end is also cut near Chincoteague Inlet (I in Fig. 4.17).

Some time after the extensions of Chincoteague Island and the cape were destroyed, Assateague Island began to grow southwestward. Its growth was favored by the strong littoral current, of which present-day effects are also evident at Ocean City, Maryland (p. 89). Because Assateague Island was growing southwestward more actively than the northeastward growth of Wallops Island (H), there was, and continues to be, an offset between these barriers. As Assateague Island approached junction with Wallops Island, it formed a succession of hooked spits (Fig. 4.19). Assateague Point 1 was the oldest. Later, Assateague Island continued its southwestward growth, abandoning point 1 and forming point 2 (F), shown on the 1849 chart as the end of the island.

Some time between 1859 and 1887, addition to Assateague Point 2 spit ceased, and the island was extended southwestward for 3 miles until in 1904

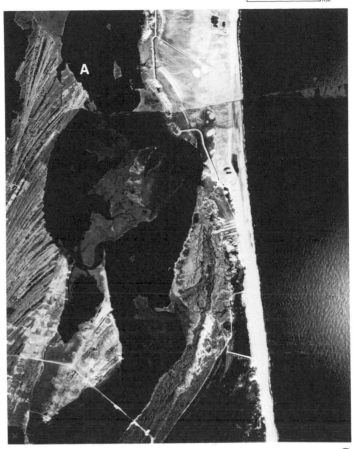

4.18 Chincoteague Island and southern Assateague Island, showing remarkably regular beach ridges on Chincoteague Island. Infrared photography. U.S. Geological Survey, 1963.

Fishing Point hook began growing northwestward toward Chincoteague Inlet. Between 1904 and 1963, Fishing Point (G) had grown more than 2 miles in that direction.

Constance Gawne was able to identify on Fishing Point thirty-nine successive dune ridges, which developed between 1908 and 1963. Six growth stages are illustrated in Figure 4.19. The ridges are not traceable as continuously as those on Chincoteague Island; but groups of ridges were truncated in 1940, 1949, and 1962, probably because of rapid erosion at times of hurricanes and other major storms.

In the future, Chincoteague Inlet should remain open unless a new inlet is cut, allowing tidal flow to

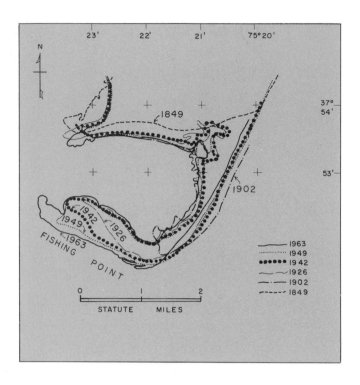

4.19 Sketches showing growth of Fishing Point, Assateague Island, Virginia, between 1849 and 1962. Prepared by Constance Gawne.

enter and leave Chincoteague Bay by a shorter route. If Assateague Island extends southwestward, it may overlap Wallops Island, as at Fire Island Inlet (p. 62). Alternatively, the northeast end of Wallops Island may be eroded.

CAPE CHARLES AND DELMARVA PENINSULA [Figs. 4.20 through 4.23]   The long narrow peninsula that forms the east flank of Chesapeake Bay and terminates in Cape Charles, we are designating as *Delmarva Peninsula* (Fig. 4.20), a name used by the *National Geographic Magazine* because of the three states involved. The lower end of this peninsula is divided in two along a north-south line. To the east, the area is largely marsh and lagoons with a barrier island along the seaward margin, while on the west side, the land is higher and mostly well drained. The marsh and lagoon on the eastern side

is perhaps the wettest coastal region in the forty-eight contiguous states. Maps published up to 1912 show continuous lagoons without marshes covering nearly all of the area, but more modern charts show a preponderance of marsh that is exposed at low tide. Both interpretations are probably generalized, but it is possible that the coast has become more emergent in recent years. The aerial photographs, of which we include two (Figs. 4.21, 4.22), indicate a mixture of marsh and shallow-water area along with marginal sand barriers. A network of channels maintained by tidal scour traverse this region and locally there are depths as great as 70 feet.

Hog Island, about 25 miles north-northeast of Cape Charles, is part of the barrier chain that forms a rim along most of the swampy coast. Wyman Harrison and others reported finding peat 5 feet above sea level overlying a shell bed in the seaward face of the beach of Hog Island. A sample of peat was dated as A.D. 800, and oyster shells from the shell bed were dated as A.D. 50. Because this shell assemblage indicated that the depth of water at the time of deposition was about 20 feet, whereas the peat grew at or a little below sea level, the area appears to have been elevated about 25 feet in the past 1,900 years, and 10 feet in the latest 1,100 years.

Cobb Island, south of Hog Island, is another in the chain of barriers. Behind this island there is a very shallow bay, probably drained at very low tide, which includes a linear chain of narrow marshy islands known as Gull Marsh (Fig. 4.21). This marsh probably formed on top of a beach ridge, which was later drowned by rise in sea level. Following that period, the rise of land in the past 2,000 years has again exposed the old beach ridge, but it is still covered with peat. Gull Marsh is crossed by eleven tidal stream channels, which may have originated during the recent reemergence. If the land should continue to rise, the marsh deposits will be eroded and the beach will be exhumed.

Figure 4.22, a high-altitude aerial photo, shows a section near the southern end of this coast from Ship Shoal Island (A) at the north to Smith Island (B) at the south. Depths in Ship Shoal Channel (C) generally range between 20 and 40 feet. Its southern distributary has built a large tidal delta (D). Mockhorn Island (E), an old beach ridge, trends nearly north-south and rises slightly above sea level between the tidal delta and a shallow bay to the west. Other

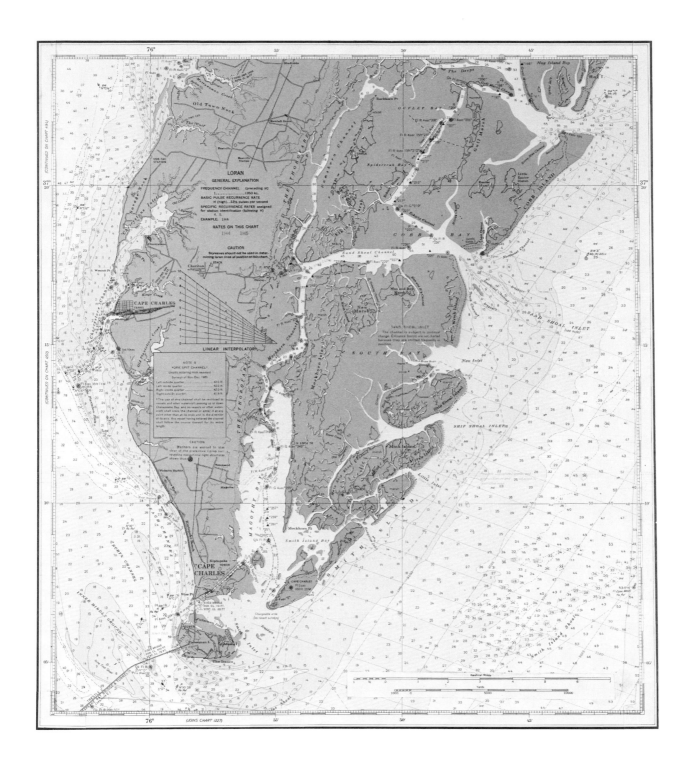

4.20 Chart showing southern end of Delmarva Peninsula and the entrance to Chesapeake Bay, with marshy area on east and dry land on west. Unusual depths in channel are due to tidal scour. U.S. Coast and Geodetic Survey Chart 1222, 1966 edition.

4.21 Gull Marsh (A), a partially exhumed beach ridge in Outlet Bay, Virginia. U.S. Department of Agriculture, 1949.

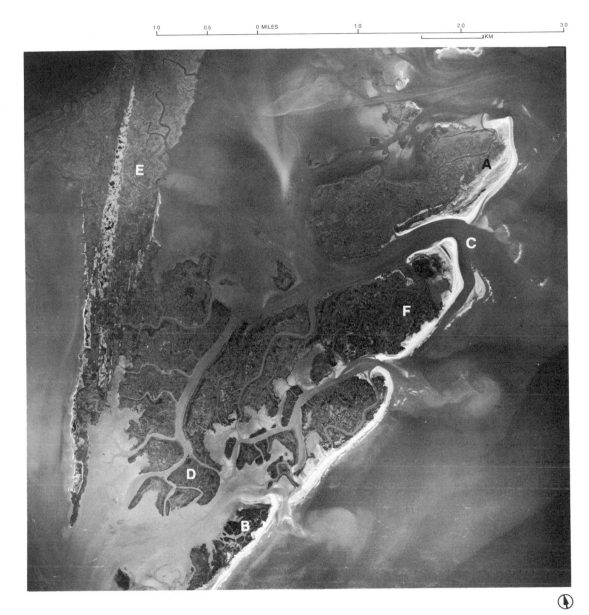

4.22 Coastal barriers including Ship Shoal Island (A), Myrtle Island (F), Smith Island (B), and Mockhorn Island (E), an exhumed barrier island. High-altitude photography by U.S. Army Map Service, 1959.

indistinct traces of parallel beach (or dune) ridges are indicated to the east and west of the more prominent beach. Mockhorn Island is probably older than Hog Island, which is about 2,000 years old; and Mockhorn Island was first drowned by a rise in sea level more than 2,000 years ago. Later, because of the recent upwarping of the land (see p. 94), the beach was uncovered and marsh vegetation grew upon it. With a continued rise of the land, the marsh

peat has been oxidized or eroded, reexposing the beach.

The modern barrier islands between the inlets are narrow, and the narrow hooks built into each inlet suggest that the predominant littoral current is to the northeast. Evidently the supply of sand is inadequate to replace that washed into the four inlets (Fig. 4.22).

Cape Charles and Fishermans Island (Fig. 4.23),

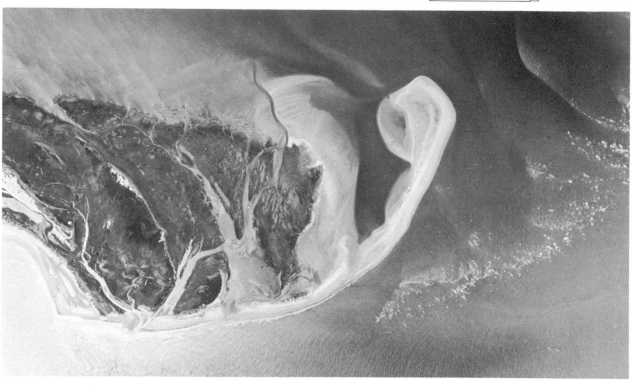

4.23 Fisherman Island and Cape Charles at the northern entrance to Chesapeake Bay. U.S. Department of Agriculture, 1949.

a mile south of the tip of the mainland, directly adjoin Chesapeake Bay. Most of the island and cape are marshy; but the southern side of the island is a narrow sand barrier, extending northeastward as a spit. This configuration indicates that flow at ebb tide is stronger than that at flood tide, due to the many large rivers that drain into Chesapeake Bay.

If very slow emergence continues, as during the past 2,000 years, many parts of the bays will become shallow enough to support plant growth and will change into a complex of marshes and tidal streams, such as are common elsewhere along the Atlantic coast. The Atlantic beaches should be shifted eastward; and, with partial drainage of the shallow bays, some of the fifteen inlets between Chincoteague Island and Cape Charles will probably close.

EASTERN SIDE OF CHESAPEAKE BAY, VIRGINIA   Chesapeake Bay, the longest drowned river valley in the United States, is almost wholly cut

into the coastal plain province. It is 180 miles long from the mouth of the Susquehanna River to Cape Charles. The drowned valleys of the Susquehanna, Potomac, and other major rivers have water depths ranging to about 70 feet. The widespread flat floors of the bay commonly have depths of 15 to 30 feet. All coastal plain rocks exposed in Chesapeake Bay and its tributary estuaries are relatively unconsolidated sands, muds, and marls. The fetch of the prevailing winds is small, but somewhat larger with north or south winds. In spite of greater protection than exists on the open Atlantic, the east shores of Chesapeake Bay have been seriously eroded during the past century. Littoral currents drift sand along the shore; but in many places sediment has accumulated in the deeper areas, notably in the drowned valleys of major rivers.

Along the eastern shore north of the city of Cape Charles (Fig. 4.24), about 12 miles north of Fishermans Island, a drowned valley, Cherrystone Inlet

(A), enters the bay from the northeast. The depth of this channel increases irregularly to the south, reaching about 10 feet at the city of Cape Charles, where a 15-foot channel (B) was dredged for the automobile and rail ferries that cross Chesapeake Bay.

A south-flowing littoral current has formed a spit across part of Cherrystone Inlet (C), which continues southward as a shoal beyond the end of the spit. Nearly all coasts in this area have additional protection from wave attack by these longshore shoals. In 1949 (Fig. 4.24), a broad longshore bar entered from the north (D), 0.5 mile from the Cherrystone spit. Farther south, this bar disappears and is replaced by six or more north-south parallel bars; and near the shore irregular sand bars are seen extending mostly northeast-southwest but crossed locally by northwest-southeast bars. South of the city of Cape Charles, the bars become more regular inside the channel and converge onto the shore.

Because of the very acute angle between the spits and the drowned valley of Cherrystone River, no tidal delta has formed; but where angles between littoral currents and estuary mouths of smaller creeks are more favorable, there are tidal deltas in the drowned creek valleys. About 18 miles north of the city of Cape Charles, a large tidal delta (not illustrated) partially blocks the lower end of Nassawadox Creek estuary; and a smaller one enters the adjacent Waterhouse Creek.

CHESAPEAKE BAY, INCLUDING ISLANDS
[Figs. 4.25 and 4.26]   The western shore of Chesapeake Bay adjoins a part of the coastal plain that lies 100 feet or more above sea level, and cliffs of soft Miocene rocks 80 to 100 feet high are common. The eastern shore of the bay and the islands are much lower, generally 10 to 20 feet above sea level. The central portion of Chesapeake Bay has a mean tidal range of only 1.3 feet, but extreme tides during a 50-year period at Baltimore had a total range of 12.8 feet. The highest tides commonly occur at times of high winds and waves, which increase the capacity of the waves to erode the relatively unconsolidated sands and clays that form the shores of the bay and its islands. Chesapeake Bay generally has westerly or northwesterly winds, so the fetch and wave heights are usually larger on the low eastern shores of the mainland and on the northern and western shores of

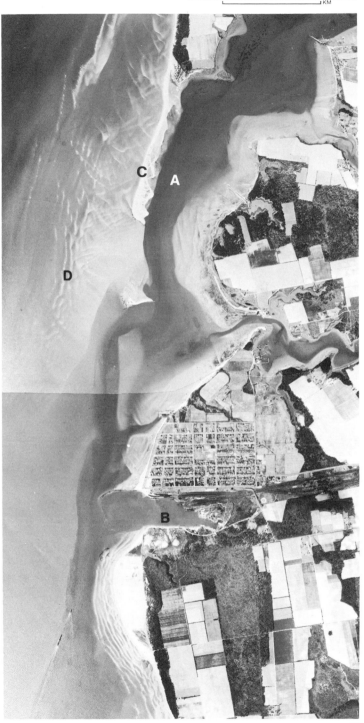

4.24 Cape Charles City and Cherrystone Inlet, eastern shore of lower Chesapeake Bay, showing spits and underwater sand ridges formed by southward-flowing littoral currents. U.S. Department of Agriculture, 1949.

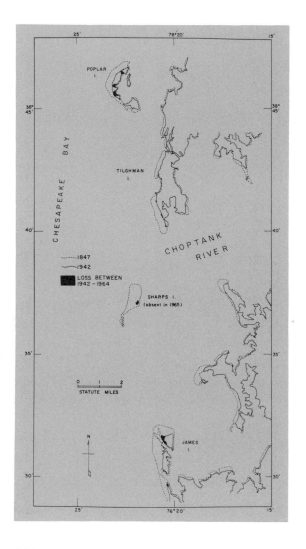

4.25 Map of Chesapeake Bay islands, showing erosion between 1847 and 1964. Compiled from maps by J. Fred Hunter and G. F. Jordan.

the islands in the bay. On the western shore of the bay, however, slumping and landslides have contributed substantially to shore erosion.

Erosion of the shores of Chesapeake Bay was studied by J. Fred Hunter in 1914, Joseph T. Singewald, Jr., and Turbit Slaughter in 1949, and G. F. Jordan in 1961. Singewald and Slaughter reported that the mainland shores had suffered a net loss of 17,000 acres in an 89-year period. About two-thirds of this loss was on the low eastern shore. Islands in the bay lost a net amount of 7,600 acres in the same period.

Studies of erosion by Hunter and Jordan were

concentrated on the islands and eastern mainland near the mouth of the Choptank River estuary, about midway along the north-south axis of the bay. Here, the bay west of the island fringe is 10 to 12 miles wide, giving sufficient fetch to the winds so that the western faces of the islands and the mainland of the eastern shore have experienced substantial erosion. Where the eastern shore lies in the lee of these islands, it has suffered much less erosion. A map (Fig. 4.25) derived from the studies of Hunter and Jordan indicates the amount of loss in area between 1847 and 1942, and also shows further losses up to 1964 (Fig. 4.25). The four islands investigated include, from north southward, Poplar Island, Tilghman Island, Sharps Island, and James Island. These are composed of Pleistocene sandy clay loam, occupying the upper portion of the formation with layers of gravel and scattered boulders. The lower half is clay, sand, gravel, boulders, and peat.

Poplar Island, as photographed in 1964 (A in Fig. 4.26), was a string of four islands forming an arc curved to the west and a straight north-south island east of the arc. In 1847 (Fig. 4.25), these four islands were joined, and the island was much broader than in 1964. In 1942, the three northern islands were connected, but by 1964, the northern and southern had been separated by narrow necks of land, and the middle of the three northern islands had been almost divided into two islands. The map comparing shorelines in 1847, 1942, and 1964 (Fig. 4.25) shows that virtually all the erosion had taken place on the western and northwestern sides. Rates of erosion have amounted to about 9 feet per year during the past 116 years. According to aerial photographs of Poplar Island (Fig. 4.26), sediment has been drifted southwestward from the exposed western shore of the island chain.

Tilghman Island, about 3.5 miles long and separated from the mainland by a narrow strait, is the site of two towns, both at the north end. The island area decreased from 2,015 acres in 1848 to 1,686 acres by 1901. Nearly all the erosion had occurred on the west side. By 1964, the southern tip of the island had been nearly separated by a new strait, otherwise little change had occurred since the 1901 chart. Hunter estimated in 1914 that Tilghman Island would disappear in about 570 years, but the recent chart suggests that the island may last longer. Except for a few houses, the settlements are on the

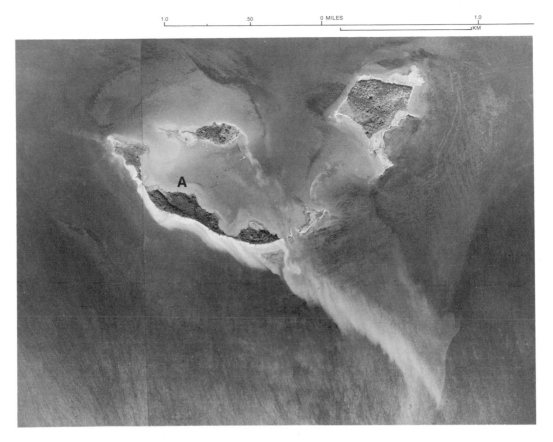

1.0   .50   0 MILES   1.0
                     KM

4.26 The small remnants of Poplar Island, Chesapeake Bay, Maryland, showing erosion of western shores and southwestward drift of eroded material. U.S. Department of Agriculture, 1964.

east side, so they are in no immediate danger.

Sharps Island had an area of 438 acres in 1848, 91 acres in 1900, 53 in 1910, and only 6 acres in 1946. Erosion was most rapid at the north where clay and sand predominate, and slowest in the marshland at the south end of the island. In 1914, Hunter predicted that Sharps Island would be gone by 1951. This was about correct. The 1965 charts show no remnants of the island. At one time, it was a well-wooded island supporting a summer resort and was a favorite spot for hunting. By 1910, an abandoned hotel in the center of the island was the only surviving building, and an old artesian well stood out in the waters of Chesapeake Bay.

James Island had an area of 976 acres in 1848, was reduced to 555 acres by 1901, and to 490 acres by 1910. Where the land is high, consisting of a silty clay, erosion rate is greater than in the low-lying marshes. Hunter's 1914 prediction was that James

Island would survive for about 150 years.

Chesapeake Bay has varied underwater topography, the greatest depths near the bay islands being 117 and 130 feet west of Sharps and Tilghman Islands respectively. The major currents through the bay follow the linear depressions of drowned river channels. Sediment eroded from the islands or mainland coastal cliffs has partly filled topographic depressions in the bay and has also accumulated in shoals in the lee of protecting islands. Studies reported by Jordan indicate that after erosion of island areas, benches about 3 feet below low tide develop briefly, but within a few years 6-foot depths are commonly attained. Maximum depths of 14 or 15 feet occur where there was actually land within the past century. This present-day erosion below sea level makes it nearly impossible to identify the time of subaqueous benches formed before sea level had risen to its present position.

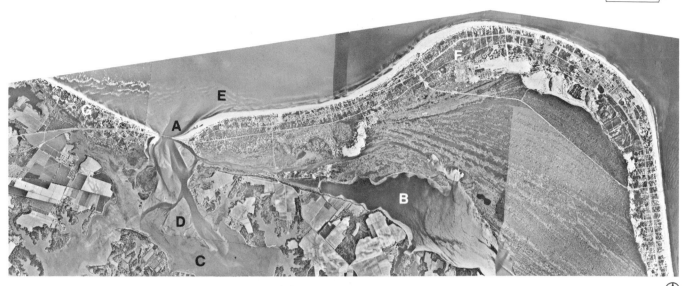

4.27 The southern entrance to Chesapeake Bay with Cape Henry (F), Lynnhaven Inlet (A), and Broad Bay (B). Cape Henry shows a long series of dune ridges, illustrative of the growth history of the cape. U.S. Department of Agriculture, 1949.

CAPE HENRY, VIRGINIA [Fig. 4.27]   Cape Henry, at the south side of the entrance to Chesapeake Bay, is about 13 miles east of Norfolk. Unlike the low marshy Fishermans Island, on the north side of the strait, Cape Henry has a series of dune ridges, some about 50 feet high. The land to the south of the dune ridges is low with extensively embayed small streams. An old abandoned shoreline extends from the west side of Lynnhaven Inlet (A) east-southeast along the southern side of Broad Bay (B) toward the ocean. Lynnhaven Inlet drains most of the lowland through Lynnhaven Bay and Broad Bay. Lynnhaven Bay (C) is a typical drowned stream valley or estuary, while Broad Bay is a coastal lagoon that formed after the original barrier had separated it from the ocean. A tidal delta (D) has formed in Lynnhaven Bay.

As the barrier grew, a northward projection developed; and the cape has been shifted about 3 miles north and 2 miles east of the old shoreline (Fig. 4.27). This migration resembles that of Cape Kennedy (p. 148). More than forty subparallel dune or beach ridges may be traced around the cape. At several places, one ridge may be observed to truncate a series of older ones. Nearly all ridges appear to be cut off to the north and east by the present ocean

shore. The highest dunes, probably representing the longest period of static shore position, are about 0.5 mile inland from the present shore.

The coastal change, as interpreted from a study of the dune ridges, starts with an Atlantic shore which had a cape to the west of the present very straight shore. Sand swept into the bay by incoming tides and by storms from the east and southeast built up a succession of ridges over a period probably several centuries in length, extending the shore farther east than it is at present. The strong winter northeast winds piled up sand, forming low dune ridges back of the beach, generally to heights of less than 5 feet. Beach drifting carried the sand around the point and along the shore beyond Lynnhaven Inlet (G). Part of the sand built longshore bars (E). At times of major storms, these may have been driven inshore to initiate new beaches which later developed adjacent dune ridges.

The longshore bars, shown in the photograph, bend out around a small shoal due to a tidal delta outside Lynnhaven Inlet. Westward, they continue along the south side of Chesapeake Bay; and beyond the inlet, a series of short bars reach out obliquely northwest from the shore.

Photographs of Cape Henry in 1949 (Fig. 4.27)

and 1964 (not illustrated) show very slight changes in this 15-year period. A pier or jetty about a mile northeast of Lynnhaven Inlet was constructed between the two dates of photography; but there was no sign that sand had accumulated on its upcurrent (east) side. The apparent lack of further accretion of new dune ridges during that period suggests that the beach may have nearly attained equilibrium. By 1964, the area just north of Broad Bay, including the oldest dune ridges, had been cleared of forest and laid out as a residential subdivision; and another had been developed for a mile east of Lynnhaven Inlet.

REFERENCES

Gawne, Constance E., 1966. Shore changes on Fenwick and Assateague Islands, Maryland and Virginia. Univ. Illinois, honors bachelor's thesis in geology.

Harrison, W., R. J. Malloy, G. A. Rusnak, and J. Terasmae, 1965. Possible Late Pleistocene uplift, Chesapeake Bay entrance. *Jour. Geol.*, vol. 73, pp. 201–229.

Hunter, J. Fred, 1914. Erosion and sedimentation in Chesapeake Bay around the mouth of Choptank River. *U.S. Geol. Surv. Prof. Paper 90*, pp. 7–15.

Jordan, G. F., 1961. Erosion and sedimentation, eastern Chesapeake Bay at the Choptank River. *U.S. Coast & Geodetic Survey, Tech. Bull. 16.*

Kenny, N. T., and B. A. Stewart, 1962. Our changing Atlantic coastline. *Nat. Geographic Magazine,* vol. 122, no. 6, 860–887.

Lucke, J. B., 1934. A study of Barnegat Inlet, New Jersey, and related shoreline phenomena. *Shore and Beach*, vol. 2, no. 2.

———, 1934. A theory of evolution of lagoon deposits on shorelines of emergence. *Jour. Geol.*, vol. 42, no. 6, pp. 561–584.

MacClintock, P., and H. G. Richards, 1936. Correlation of Late Pleistocene marine and glacial deposits of New Jersey and New York. *Geol. Soc. Amer. Bull.*, vol. 47, pp. 289–328.

Plusquellec, P. L., 1966. Coastal morphology and changes of an area between Brigantine and Beach Haven Heights, New Jersey. Univ. Illinois, unpublished M.S. thesis, ill. by Judith Greer and Janet Garrell.

Price, W. Armstrong, 1958. Sedimentology and Quaternary geomorphology of South Texas. *Gulf Coast Assoc. of Geol. Soc., Trans.*, vol. 8, pp. 41–75.

Singewald, J. T., Jr., and Turbit Slaughter, 1949. Shore erosion in tidewater Maryland. *Maryland Dept. Geol., Mines, and Natural Resources Bull. 6.*

Strahler, Arthur N., 1966. Tidal cycle of changes in an equilibrium beach, Sandy Hook, New Jersey. *Jour. Geol.*, vol. 74, no. 3, pp. 247–268.

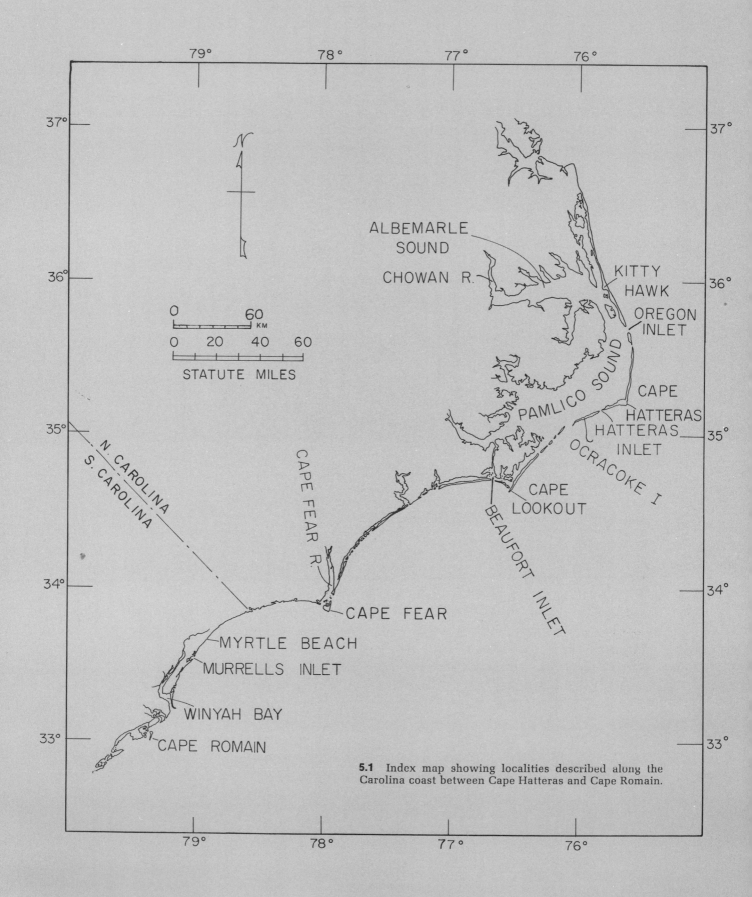

5.1 Index map showing localities described along the Carolina coast between Cape Hatteras and Cape Romain.

Cuspate Foreland Coasts

Cape Hatteras to Cape Romain

5 The Atlantic coasts of the Carolinas are characterized by a series of seaward projecting barriers called *cuspate forelands*. These include Capes Hatteras, Lookout, and Fear, in North Carolina, and Romain, in South Carolina (Fig. 5.1). Distances between these capes are, respectively, 72, 101, and 98 miles. The arcs between the capes are smoothly curved with midpoints 15 to 25 miles landward of straight lines connecting the successive points.

South of Chesapeake Bay, the estuaries are of smaller size, but the lagoons are larger. Pamlico Sound, in the vicinity of Cape Hatteras, is the largest body of water inside a barrier along the entire coast of the United States. The longest estuary in the area, Albemarle Sound, and the drowned entrance to Chowan River extend inland for 70 miles; and Pamlico Sound, a 30-mile-wide lagoon combined with estuaries, follows the inside of the cuspate foreland for 80 miles.

In this coastal stretch, the inner margin of the Gulf Stream, with a current velocity of about 1 to 4 knots, ranges from 15 to 60 miles offshore and is particularly close to Cape Hatteras and Cape Lookout. Although the Gulf Stream flows northeastward, the predominant direction of longshore sediment drift is in the opposite direction due to countercurrents.

According to the U.S. Army Corps of Engineers, net erosion of the total North Carolina coast averages 0.9 foot per year. Erosion rates vary from 0 to 21 feet per year, the highest at Cape Hatteras. Accretion of as much as 2.2 feet per year occurs midway between Cape Lookout and Cape Fear. The sediment accretion has a source predominantly from the northeast, but contributions also come from the cape points to the southwest.

Barrier islands fringe the coast throughout all this area except northeastern South Carolina, in the vicinity of Myrtle Beach. Coastal lagoons are connected

Much material on the North and South Carolina coasts in this chapter was derived from reports by Mohamed T. El-Ashry.

with the ocean by about fifty relatively permanent tidal inlets, and many others are opened temporarily during major storms. Because of the predominant southwestward beach drifting, many of the inlets have migrated southwestward during historic time.

This area has the best examples in the world of cuspate forelands. Explanations of this series of capes with reentrant arcs between have included (1) a series of gyrols developed between the northeastward-flowing Gulf Stream and the southwestward littoral current, (2) deposition inside a framework constructed by organic reefs or coquina limestones, and (3) capes formed at divides between streams draining southeastward across the coastal plain.

An earlier idea, now abandoned, was that they developed over buried mountain systems, such as the Appalachians. Deep drilling, as at Cape Hatteras, gives no support to this old explanation.

William A. White studied the evolution of cuspate forelands and developed a comprehensive explanation, which includes the following points: (1) The capes tend to lie a little west of the outlets of important coastal plain rivers, marking positions of Pleistocene drainage divides. (2) A study of the exposed Pleistocene shorelines, recording high-level stages during interglacial times, suggests that capes then existed at comparable locations. (3) The lack of detailed study of low sea-level (glacial-age) shorelines prevents us from substantiating the existence of capes at such times. (4) Where beach drifting continually brings sediments southwestward to a sharp point in the coast, much of the sediment continues such drifting offshore from the cape, building up shoals in the direction of drift. Such shoals are found today and probably were developed at all Pleistocene sea levels. Once formed, they would tend to perpetuate the cuspate outlines of the coast, both during submergence and emergence. (5) Early cementation of shell beds has produced coquina limestone on the beaches near Cape Fear and a short distance offshore near Capes Lookout and Hatteras. This limestone is more resistant to erosion than loose sand or shell beds, with a stabilizing result. (6) A major geomorphic boundary seems to occur near the Virginia–North Carolina line. North of this line, major drainage of the Susquehanna and Delaware Rivers is deflected

5.2 Coastal barrier with sand dunes near Kitty Hawk, North Carolina. U.S. Coast and Geodetic Survey, 1962.

southward of the more direct southeastward trends across the coastal plain. The rivers of North and South Carolina do not show such southward drift.

White proposes that during times of Pleistocene lower sea level, the Chesapeake drainage may have continued southward off modern North Carolina, so that the now-drowned streams of Albemarle and Pamlico Sounds flowed eastward into "lower Chesapeake Bay," the system ending a little north of Cape Hatteras.

Despite the significance of these suggestions by White, there can be little doubt that the effect of countercurrents of the Gulf Stream has been of vital importance in developing the cuspate forelands.

KITTY HAWK AREA, NORTH CAROLINA [Fig. 5.2]   From near Cape Henry, Virginia, southward to Cape Hatteras, the coast is a continuous barrier island about 100 miles long with only one major break, Oregon Inlet, 40 miles north of Cape Hatteras. Parts of the long barrier island include sand dunes 30 to 50 feet high. At Kitty Hawk, on one of these dunes, Killdevil Hill (A), the Wright brothers initiated the age of aviation. Such sand dunes occur back of the beach at many places along the Atlantic Coast. Where they form continuous ridges, as near Kitty Hawk, they constitute an effective barrier during major storms to prevent beach sand from being swept across the islands into the lagoons behind them.

CAPE HATTERAS AREA, NORTH CAROLINA [Figs. 5.3, 2.16, and 2.23a]   Cape Hatteras, the northernmost of the series of cuspate forelands, projects more than 30 miles out from the mainland (Fig. 5.1). Almost continuous barrier islands on either side of the cape protect the waters of Pamlico Sound. North from the cape, Hatteras Island now extends continuously for 30 miles; and, to the west, another arm of the island has a length of 12 miles. By bridging the narrow northern inlet, it has been possible to build a road for about 53 miles between Oregon Inlet on the north and Hatteras Inlet on the southwest. Therefore, tourists are now able to visit this interesting graveyard of the Atlantic, with its many old wrecks still visible along the outer shore and its historic lighthouse.

We have a record of the changes that Cape Hatteras has undergone since 1852. The most significant modification of the outline has been from a V-shape

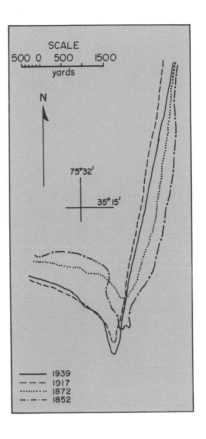

5.3 Diagram showing changes in Cape Hatteras between 1852 and 1962. Compiled by Mohamed T. El-Ashry. **a** 1852 to 1939. From U.S. Coast and Geodetic Survey maps.

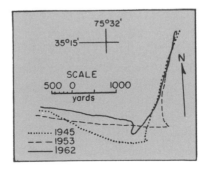

b 1945 to 1962 from aerial photographs of various agencies.

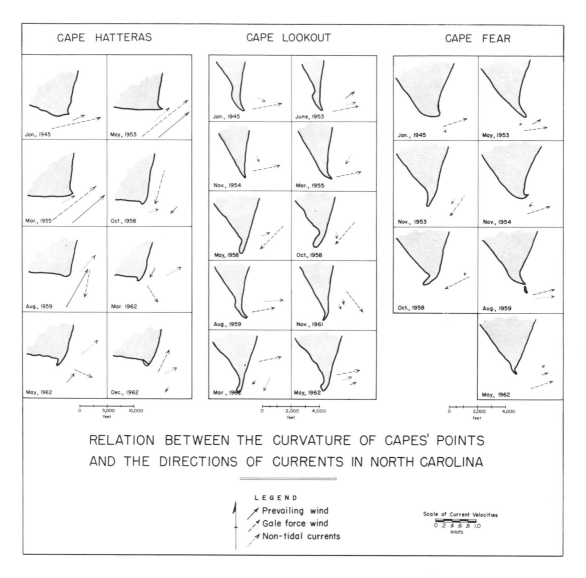

5.4 Relation between the curvature of the points of Capes Hatteras, Lookout, and Fear, and the directions of currents and winds during the month preceding photography, North Carolina. Compiled by Mohamed T. El-Ashry from aerial photographs and U.S. Weather Bureau records.

pointing to the south, which persisted from 1852 until about 1940, to a right-angle bend (Fig. 5.3*a*). The change in shape took place largely by the projecting point being cut off and also by a wearing back of the north-south coast. Between 1852 and 1917, this erosion had amounted to 2,500 feet, but since then it has built back 750 feet, leaving a net loss of 1,750 feet. However, according to a 1947 report by the U.S. Army Corps of Engineers, a few miles to the north of the cape there has been a net accretion dur-

ing the past 86 years. The general thinness of the barrier to the north seems to indicate that any such accretion was of short duration. North of the cape, the average width of the barrier is 0.5 mile; but, to the west, it is 2 miles wide. This change suggests that accretion has been dominant on the southwest side of the cape in contrast to the erosion to the north. Although the beach ridges, such as are shown in Figure 2.23*a*, are convincing evidence of this accretion, the cutting off of the south projecting point (Fig.

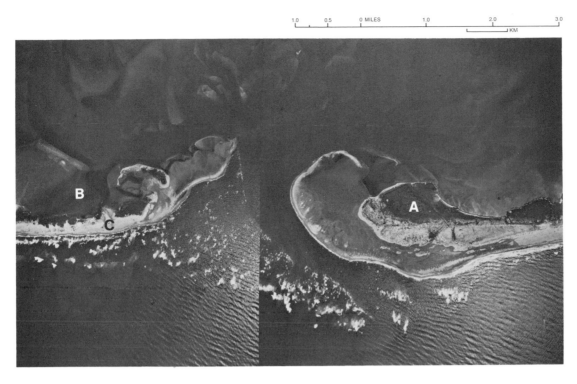

5.5 Changes in the configuration of Hatteras Inlet, North Carolina, between 1953 and 1962.

a 1953. A small washover (C), formed during a storm, later became the site of a new inlet. U.S. Coast and Geodetic Survey.

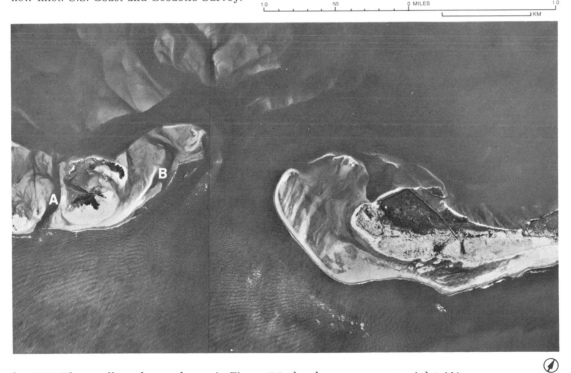

b 1955. The small washover shown in Figure 5.5a has become a narrow inlet (A). U.S. Coast and Geodetic Survey.

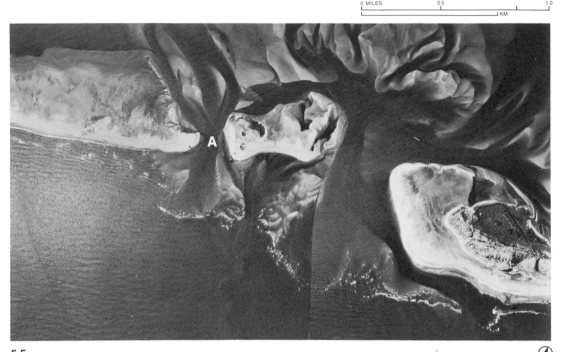

5.5

c   May 4, 1958. Before Hurricane Helene of September 30, 1958. The new inlet has widened and a tidal delta has developed on the Pamlico Sound side. U.S. Coast and Geodetic Survey.

1.0   .50   0 MILES   1.0

KM

d   March 13, 1962. Resulting from two severe storms, the new inlet has become as wide as the old one, and most of the land between them has been eroded. Photographed one week after the great 1962 Atlantic storm. U.S. Coast and Geodetic Survey.

5.3) shows that the latest effects have been erosion. Examination of the truncated beach ridges along the south-facing coast (Fig. 2.23a) confirms this reversal of trend.

The nature and cause of recent changes can be shown by comparing the shape of the point with the direction of the prevailing wind and of the gale-force winds during the month preceding the photography and with the general direction of the nontidal currents during the same period (Fig. 5.4). This comparison is indicated in Figure 5.4; and a very distinct relation is shown, especially between the direction of the gale-force winds and the development of small protruding points. Thus, the easterly pointing spits in 1945, 1953, and 1955 (Fig. 5.4a) were preceded by westerly or southwesterly winds and currents in the same direction, and the southward-extending tips in October 1958 and again in 1962 were caused by southward-trending winds and currents. Similar influences were involved in changes shown at Cape Lookout and Cape Fear (Figs. 5.4b and c).

The inlets in the vicinity of Cape Hatteras have undergone notable changes. During the Atlantic storm of March 1962, a new inlet was opened 5 miles north of the cape, and it widened rapidly to about 500 feet. The widening cut away parts of the new road. Sand swept through this new inlet and after 5 days had formed a tidal delta with an area of 60 acres. This had increased to about 150 acres 2 months later (Fig. 2.16). After a period of 10 months, army engineers dredged away part of the tidal delta and piled sand back into the inlet, closing it, and then constructed artificial dunes behind the beach to prevent later reopening.

Hatteras Inlet, 12 miles west of the cape, separates Hatteras Island (A in Fig. 5.5a) from Ocracoke Island (B). The inlet was open, so far as known, from 1585 to about 1800. Then, after being closed for a few years, it reopened during a hurricane in 1846. The aerial photos show its changes between 1953 and 1962 (Figs. 5.5a to d). The 1953 photo (Fig. 5.5a) shows a single inlet with a channel hugging close to Hatteras Island. Both islands reveal evidence of prograding toward the inlet, with narrow, partly submerged hooked spits that curve toward Pamlico Sound. Inside the hooked spit of Ocracoke Island, a small washover was the result of a storm that carried sand across the narrow barrier (C). By 1955, a breach (A in Fig. 5.5b) had developed across the

eastern hook of Ocracoke Island at the same place as the earlier washover. Farther east, another small inlet is also shown (B). By 1958, the western of these two breaches had been widened to about 500 feet (A in Fig. 5.5c). The photo of this date also provides a clear outline of the tidal deltas inside both inlets. By 1962, the new western inlet (A in Fig. 5.5d) is shown to be as wide as the original Hatteras Inlet (B), with only a small remnant island separating the two. The eastern end of Ocracoke Island may be subject in the future to still further loss. The small washover (C) shown in the 1962 photo may be advance warning of a further change of this nature.

This evolution of Hatteras Inlet between 1953 and 1962 appears to be a common event when the sediment for barrier islands is derived principally from one side (the east, in this case). Most of this sediment is washed into the inlet and starves the downcurrent island. Preservation of the latter can be helped by closing such inlets.

Examination of the charts for the vicinity of Cape Hatteras shows that seaward from this point, Diamond Shoals extend directly across the continental shelf, terminating just inside the break in slope. This irregular series of submerged sand bars has an average width of about 2 miles, subject to frequent depth changes that make navigation across it extremely hazardous. These shoals are evidence of the seaward bending of currents that takes place off most of these cuspate capes. Inside Cape Hatteras, Long Shoal constitutes another example of a transverse sand bar, but this is located to the northeast, rather than being a landward continuation of Diamond Shoals. Long Shoal may have formed off an old cuspate foreland before Pamlico Sound was enclosed by the Cape Hatteras barriers.

OCRACOKE TOWN AND VICINITY, NORTH CAROLINA [Fig. 5.6]   Ocracoke, a town settled in Colonial times on the southwestern end of Ocracoke Island, was built on a shield-shaped dune. Much of the dune area is about 15 feet above sea level, but most of the surroundings have an elevation of only 5 feet.

In late September 1944, a destructive hurricane hit the area. The winds at the town of Hatteras, 19 miles to the northeast, were clocked at 90 to 100 miles an hour, and the water rose 7 feet above normal

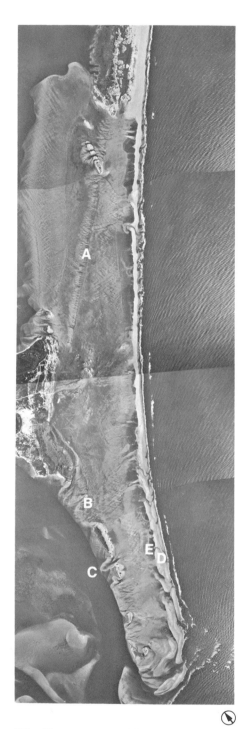

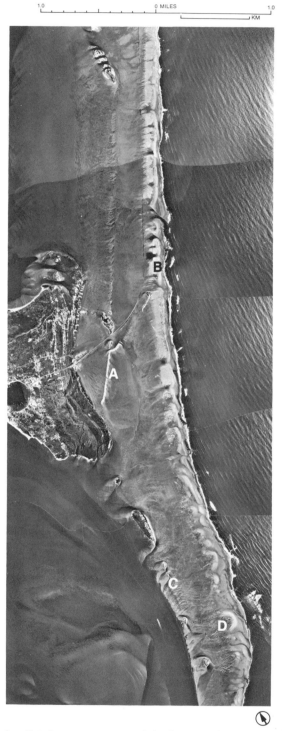

5.6 Changes caused by great storms on the straight sandy coast at Ocracoke, North Carolina.

a January 24, 1945. Aerial photo four months after a hurricane, showing a scarp cut behind beach (A) and numerous washovers (B). U.S. Coast and Geodetic Survey.

b October 10, 1958. Aerial photography 12 days after Hurricane Helene. A new scarp (A) was cut, although remnants of the 1945 scarp can be seen. Many small washovers along the beach failed to cross the island, while a few (C) reached Pamlico Sound. The coastal road was buried by sand in many places. U.S. Coast and Geodetic Survey.

high tide. The effects of the hurricane at Ocracoke are indicated in photos of January 1945 (Fig. 5.6a). During this storm, a scarp was cut in the interior of the present island (A), extending slightly diagonal to the island trend from the southeast corner of Ocracoke for 2 miles east to an interrupted line of low dunes. After the hurricane, the scarp had been deeply gullied by rain wash, before the 1945 photos. Another effect of the storm was the cutting of a series of washover channels across the narrow dune ridge (B) southwest of the town. Lagoonward from these cuts are U-shaped tidal deltas (C) extending into the edge of Pamlico Sound. The storm had apparently cut some small breaches into the low Atlantic shoreline south of the scarp; but, before the 1945 photos, beaches had built across the gaps (D), straightening the shoreline and leaving a lagoon (E) on the inside.

The next great storm to hit the area was Hurricane Helene, September 28 and 29, 1958. As shown on the October 10 photos (Fig. 5.6b), this storm cut a new scarp (A) seaward of that of 1944. Despite the series of sand fences, Helene caused the burial of much of the coastal road that had been built after the 1945 photo. A series of new washovers produced breaks in the Atlantic beach; but, by October 10, they were partly closed by beach drifting (B). Several remnants behind the beach formed small ponds.

West of the town, the water swept completely across the island, forming new washover deltas (C) in Pamlico Sound. Near the Atlantic shore southwest of the town, there are several very low U-shaped sand ridges (D), which are convex toward the sea. These may represent the frontal margins of washovers coming from Pamlico Sound. This reverse of the usual direction of overwash could be caused by water piling up at the southwest end of the sound until not all of it could escape through Ocracoke Inlet (to the southwest) but had to pour over the island. The U.S. Army Corps of Engineers report that many new inlets are opened across barrier islands in this way. An alternative origin for the curved edges is that they may have resulted from washovers from the west that cut narrow gaps in a low dune ridge, turning the ridge landward on either side of the gaps.

In viewing photographs, such as those of Figures 5.6a and b, it should be realized that many of the features have resulted from storms over a long period before the photos were taken. The patterns may differ from those features produced by the latest storms,

depending on the directions of strong winds during the storms and the heights of the storm tides. In considering the possibility of protecting an open sand coast, like Ocracoke, it may be helpful to study features formed by ancient storms. The history of the two hurricanes at Ocracoke indicate how difficult it is to protect such an area, and how ineffective sand fences are in reducing damage to roads and buildings.

CAPE LOOKOUT AREA, NORTH CAROLINA [Figs. 5.4b, 5.7 through 5.10]   Cape Lookout, 72 miles southwest of Cape Hatteras, is at the southwestern tip of the 24-mile barrier island called Core Banks[1] (Fig. 5.7). The cape is V-shaped, with a point that varies in length and in orientation (Fig. 5.4b). The island called Shackleford Banks (A in 5.7) extends northwestward from Cape Lookout to Beaufort Inlet, terminating 3 miles north of the cape. Core Sound, behind Core Banks Island, connects with the ocean through Barden Inlet (B) at the east end of the Shackleford Banks Island. Evidently Cape Lookout was formerly 3 miles north of its present location at the point where Core and Shackleford Banks were formerly joined; but, because of southwestward beach drifting, the cape has been shifted 3 miles to the south. A spit (D) has now been formed from Cape Lookout northwest in the direction of Shackleford Banks.

The tip of Cape Lookout was lengthened 1,300 feet between 1945 and 1953, but was cut back 3,300 feet between 1953 and 1962. Barden Inlet (B) was opened by a storm in 1933 and supplied some of the sand responsible for lengthening the cape point. However, in 1945, a water-level jetty (E) at the northwest end of the cape peninsula was constructed; it trapped much sand and was largely the cause of the subsequent erosion of the cape.

When the 1958 Hurricane Helene struck the shore of Core Banks, two washovers (F and G in Fig. 5.7) occurred just northeast of the Cape Lookout Peninsula. Some of the sand eroded from the beach was drifted to the cape point, lengthening it several hundred feet between the time of the aerial photos of May and October 1958. The slender cape

[1] The local custom of referring to barrier islands as *banks* is confusing because the term ordinarily refers to broad offshore shoals, like Georges Bank.

5.7 Cape Lookout at the south end of Core Banks Island (C). Barden Inlet (B) separates Core and Shackleford Banks (A). Sand trapped by water-level jetty (E) has resulted in erosion of the cape points. These photos, 12 days after Hurricane Helene, show washovers (G) north of Cape Lookout. U.S. Coast and Geodetic Survey, October 10, 1958.

point was slightly eroded after the storm, as illustrated in the 1959 photos (Fig. 5.8).

Cape Lookout Shoals extend for 17 miles south-southeast of the cape. Their depths of 2 to 20 feet rise from marginal depth of 60 to 90 feet. Aerial photography of August 1959 (Fig. 5.8) shows the underwater patterns of the inner 6 miles of these shoals. Beyond the cape, the first 3 miles have a trend suggesting seaward migration of longitudinal ridges forming a cover over a relatively smooth sand plain, which extends for another 1.5 miles seaward. Beyond that, more longitudinal ridges continue nearly to the margin of the photo. These longitudinal ridges also give the impression of an encroachment onto the deeper sea floor. The remaining 4-mile shoal area is partly depicted by a large-scale chart (Coast and Geodetic Survey Chart 1110). Here, somewhat deeper shoals (F in Fig. 5.8) trend east-northeast across the longitudinal shoals. This change in direction is similar to that on Georges Bank (east of Cape Cod), where northwest-trending shoals are seen overlapping onto northeast-trending sand ridges. Apparently, in each case an older pattern, possibly related to a slightly lower stand of sea level, is being overlapped by sand being carried to the southeast (A to E in Fig. 5.8). The successive overlaps off Cape Lookout may be related to different storms that intensified the circulation. Photos of these and other shoals taken at consecutive dates should provide evidence of pattern changes and of the nature of depth modifications over the shoals. Unfortunately, there appear to be no available sequential photographs of any of these shallow banks.

Beaufort Inlet (Fig. 5.9), 10 miles northwest of Cape Lookout, separates the two barriers, Shackleford Banks (A) and Bogue Banks (B). This inlet leads to several estuaries and lagoons. A relatively deep channel (C) provides a shipping lane to Morehead City (D) and has a northerly branch that passes Beaufort. Farther up the south branch, beyond the large tidal delta, is the shallow Newport River estuary (E). Inside Beaufort Inlet, the right-hand arm breaks into two branches, passing on either side of Middle Marshes (F); the right-hand channel extends into Back Sound (G), and the left leads into the estuary of North River (H). Here, another large tidal delta is seen partly blocking the entrance (I). Currents with velocities of 2 to 3 knots are found in the entrances to both of these large estuaries.

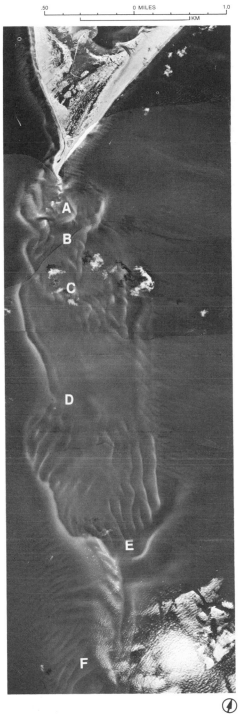

5.8 Cape Lookout Shoals, North Carolina. Littoral currents transport sand several miles seaward from the points of most cuspate forelands. Cape Lookout Shoals extend 17 miles beyond the cape point. Aerial photographs show the inner 8 miles of underwater sand bars to depths of about 20 feet. Shoals beyond other Carolina capes have not been photographed. U.S. Coast and Geodetic Survey, 1959.

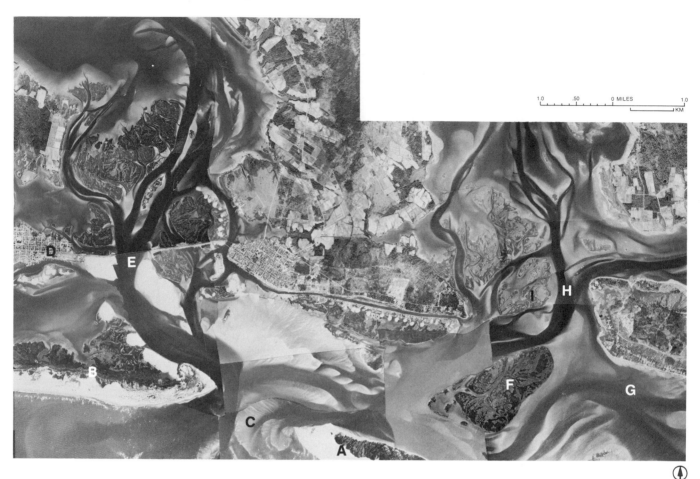

5.9 Beaufort Inlet, North Carolina, 1939, is kept open largely by tidal currents. The inlet connects with Newport River estuary (E) and North River estuary (H) and coastal lagoons east and west of the inlet. Tidal deltas have been formed into Newport and North Rivers estuaries. A 20-foot channel is maintained to the port of Morehead City (D). Fort Macon, a Civil War fort (J), is just west of the inlet. U.S. Department of Agriculture.

Beaufort Inlet was reported open as long ago as 1708 and has remained open, as far as we know, since that time. Our available aerial photographs cover the period of time from 1939 to 1962. In 1939 (Fig. 5.9), the left branch of the inlet, which joins the Newport River, appears to have had a deeper channel than the right branch heading toward the North River and Back Sound. As a result, curlicue-patterned bars (C) developed on both sides of Beaufort Inlet. By 1959 (Fig. 5.10), the bars west of Shackleford Banks had been built partly to sea level, adding a mile to the island (A). On the other side of the right branch, deposition had built a bow-shaped

sand bar that was also partly above water (B).

The growth of the Shackleford barrier has been somewhat matched by a retreat of the east end of Bogue barrier. The Civil War's Fort Macon (J in Fig. 5.9; C in Fig. 5.10), now a state park, was in 1939 a safe distance from the edge of Bogue Banks; but in 1958 Hurricane Helene eroded the island, bringing the inlet to the edge of the fort. This erosion exposed six short groins that had been constructed around the inlet side of the fort when Robert E. Lee was its commandant.

Despite the evidence indicating a westerly migration of Beaufort Inlet, the Army Corps of Engineers

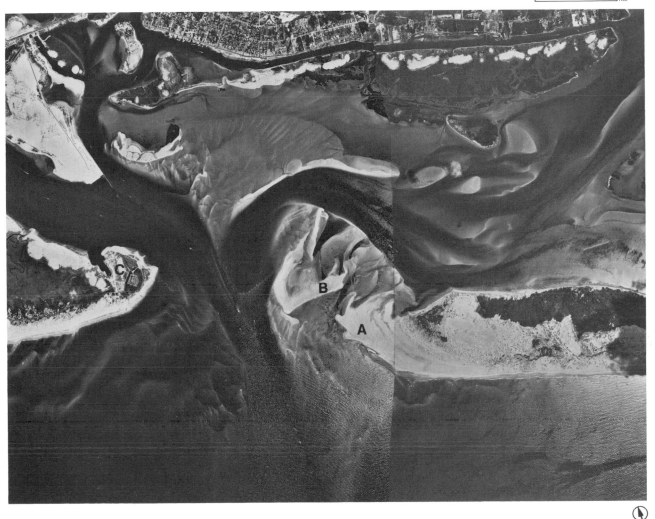

5.10 Beaufort Inlet, North Carolina, 1959, showing shore erosion at Fort Macon, and an addition to the sandy barrier east of the inlet (compare Fig. 5.9). U.S. Coast and Geodetic Survey.

report that 29,500 cubic yards of sediment per year are carried eastward past Fort Macon. We are not able to explain this apparent inconsistency. It would seem more reasonable to expect that the drift along the coast would be westward, due to a back eddy from the Gulf Stream outside. Apparently, frequent dredging will be necessary to maintain the channel for ocean-going ships.

CAPE FEAR AREA, NORTH CAROLINA [Figs. 5.11, 5.12, and 5.13]   Cape Fear, the next large cuspate cape, unlike Hatteras and Lookout, lies close

to the mainland and is separated from it by the north-south estuary of the Cape Fear River. The cape is V-shaped like Cape Lookout. At the tip, a narrow point projects seaward, either to the south or to the west, depending on preexisting storm conditions (Fig. 5.4c). A long barrier exists only on the north side of this cape. The south flank of the cape itself has a thickened barrier, as at Cape Hatteras. Aerial photographs (Fig. 5.11) show beach ridges parallel to the southwest-facing coast, indicating that the thickness is due to accretion on this protected side. West of the estuary mouth there is now only a short barrier, al-

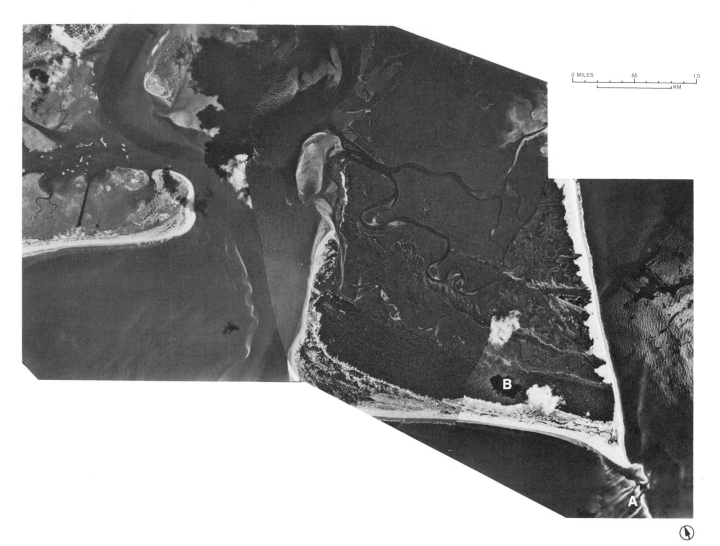

5.11 Cape Fear and the mouth of Cape Fear River, entrance to the port of Wilmington, North Carolina. The coastal offset of about 1.5 miles on the two sides of Cape Fear is due to the predominant northeastern source of sediment. The innermost part of Frying Pan Shoals (A) south of Cape Fear is illustrated. Dark patches (B) are due to cloud shadows. U.S. Coast and Geodetic Survey, 1959.

though the filled marsh indicates that it was formerly much larger. The U.S. Army Corps of Engineers report that the east-facing barrier lost about 1,600 feet by erosion between 1849 and 1929, while the south face added 640 feet. The loss of the east face continued at least until 1962, amounting to an additional 200 feet, and there was a gain of about the same amount on the south face.

Frying Pan Shoals extend about 18 miles south-southeast of the cape, with an eastward curve at their outer end. As off Cape Lookout, the shoals have longitudinal ridges in their inner portion where heavy breakers are quite continuous, and transverse ridges in the outer portion where the water depths at low tide exceed 14 feet. Drillings show that these shoals are underlain by Miocene deposits.

In many respects, the most interesting history of Cape Fear relates to the changes of the east-facing barrier (Fig. 5.12*a*), where army engineers built a 3-mile jetty from 1883 to 1889. The purpose of the jetty was to prevent a major breakthrough of the barrier that would allow the Cape Fear Estuary, with its strong tides and river flow, to take a short cut to the sea and hence bypass Southport, which is important to shipping of the Wilmington area. Repeated breaks in the barrier occurred prior to the building of the jetty. It is said that during the Civil War the North tried to blockade the Wilmington port by lying in wait off the estuary; but the Confederate ships escaped through a break in the north-south barrier, formed in 1862 as a product of a hurricane. The history of the barrier and its inlets from 1926 to 1950 is interpreted from charts and topographic maps (Figs. 5.12*b* to *d*), which cover the portion of the area of Figure 5.12*a* in the vicinity of Corncake and New Inlets. Before 1926, a sand spit had extended north from Cape Fear for 7 miles. The northern 2 miles of the spit was cut off by 1926 by the formation of Corncake Inlet (Fig. 5.12*b*). In 1926, New Inlet separated the northern remnant from a narrow spit that had grown southward. After 1926, New Inlet was closed; and, by 1935 (Fig. 5.12*c*), the narrow spit had grown southward outside of the disrupted spit as far as Corncake Inlet. The latter had been partially closed by 1935 by a new spit from the south. In 1946 (not shown), the northward-growing spit had doubled in width. By 1950 (Fig. 5.12*d*), Corncake Inlet had migrated southward 400 feet and was largely closed by the growth of the north spit. At the same time, New Inlet had reopened. The history is continued in aerial photographs between 1950 and 1962. Figure 5.13*a* shows more graphically the conditions in 1953, which were not greatly different from those in 1950. Corncake Inlet was partly reopened by a hurricane in 1954 but was subsequently entirely closed by 1958. This closed condition shows also in 1959 (Fig. 5.13*b*). It will be observed that by 1959 New Inlet had migrated north 0.5 mile as compared with 1953. A large tidal delta had formed inside New Inlet by 1959. Further breakthroughs and other changes in the spits can be anticipated for the future.

This complicated history of the Cape Fear north-south barrier and its inlets illustrates the conflict between northward growth exemplified by the oldest spit and the southward growth by the younger spit. Evidently the currents change from time to time, first favoring one direction and then the other. This history is greatly complicated by the occasional hurricanes. On October 15, 1954, Hurricane Hazel opened three new inlets, disrupted the southward-building spits, and developed many temporary washovers.

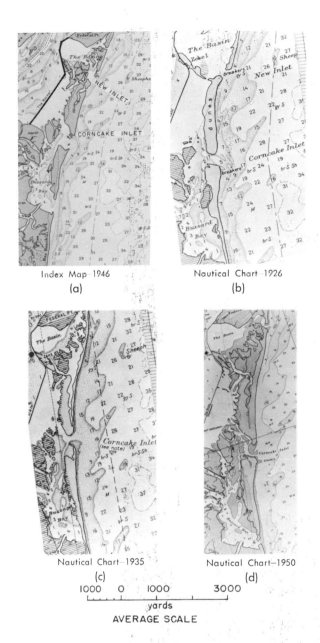

Index Map 1946
(a)

Nautical Chart 1926
(b)

Nautical Chart—1935
(c)

Nautical Chart—1950
(d)

1000   0   1000   3000
yards
AVERAGE SCALE

5.12 Index map of the barrier on the north side of Cape Fear (*a*) and changes in Corncake Inlet between 1926 and 1950 (*b* to *d*). From charts of the U.S. Coast and Geodetic Survey compiled by Mohamed T. El-Ashry.

The south-facing stub end of the Cape Fear Peninsula (Fig. 5.11) is terminated by the entrance to Cape Fear Estuary. The entrance is a mile across, and the westward continuation of the coast is offset northward for a mile. This offset indicates that accretion of the south-facing side of Cape Fear Peninsula is

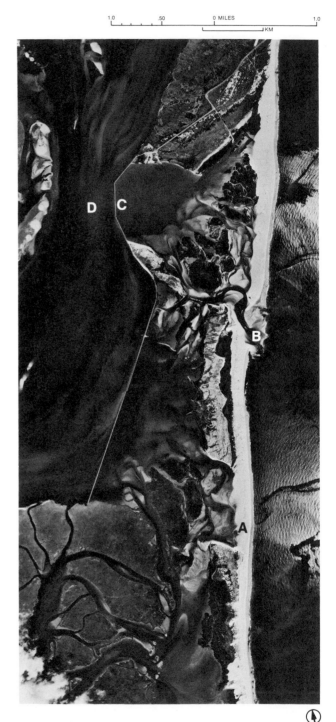

5.13 History of opening and closing inlets in barrier north of Cape Fear, North Carolina, from aerial photos.

a November 24, 1953. Corncake Inlet (A) has been partially closed by spit lengthening. New Inlet (B) had been recently opened. The older spit (C, D) farther west was formed by a littoral current from the south, while the newest spit (E) was formed by a current from the north. U.S. Coast and Geodetic Survey.

b August 16, 1959. A long jetty (C) was constructed by the U.S. Army Corps of Engineers to prevent floodwaters of Cape Fear River (D) from escaping into the Atlantic Ocean and bypassing the port of Wilmington. Between 1953 and 1959, New Inlet (B) had shifted southward and Corncake Inlet (A) had been closed. U.S. Coast and Geodetic Survey.

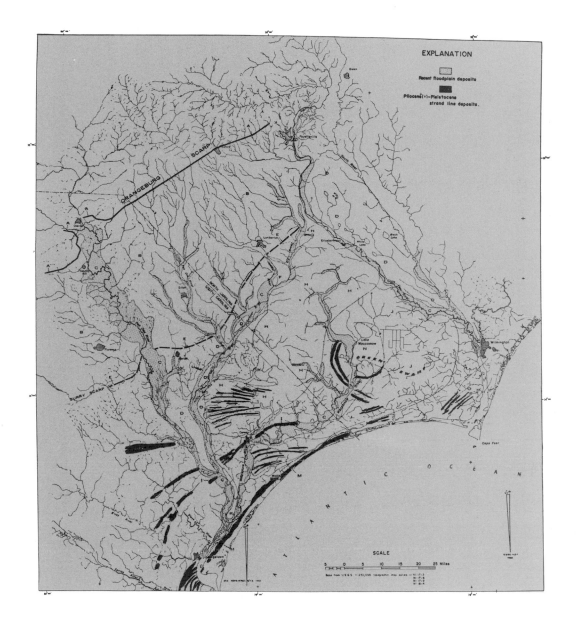

5.14 Sketch map of area between Cape Fear, North Carolina, and Georgetown, South Carolina, showing Pleistocene strand line deposits and bars. Adapted from a map by Henry Johnson and Jules Du Bar.

from the east, the sediment perhaps coming in part from Frying Pan Shoals. The accretion stops at the estuary where sediment is building a tidal delta on the inside.

MYRTLE BEACH AREA AND THE "CAROLINA BAYS," SOUTH CAROLINA [Figs. 5.14 and 5.15] West from the mouth of Cape Fear (Fig. 5.14), a

narrow barrier and lagoon extend to Cherry Grove Beach, South Carolina (6 miles southwest of the North Carolina line). From there southward for 25 miles past Myrtle Beach, there are neither barriers nor lagoons nor even coastal marshes, an unusual condition along the East Coast of the United States. The history of development of this coastal area was described by Henry Johnson and Jules Du Bar in

5.15 Pleistocene beach and dune ridges north of Myrtle Beach, South Carolina, interrupted by oval depressions known as "Carolina bays." Note that several of the bays have slightly elevated rims on their southeast ends (A). U.S. Department of Agriculture, 1939.

1964, and by Bruce Thom in 1967. Thom reported that the recent beach and coastal dunes average less than 0.25 mile in width. At Myrtle Beach, 3,000-year-old freshwater peat deposits are exposed beneath beach sand. Behind this narrow beach is the scarp of an older beach-dune complex, called Myrtle Barrier. This is too old to be dated by carbon-14, and probably formed during high sea level of the last interglacial stage, about 100,000 years ago. The Myrtle Beach dune complex is about 1.5 miles wide and is backed by remnants of a marshy lowland, the Myrtle backbarrier flat.

Behind the Myrtle barriers lies a still older barrier complex, the Jaluco, locally 8 miles wide, formed during the Yarmouth (second interglacial) stage, about 450,000 years ago. Northwest of Myrtle Beach, Thom reported seventy-one curved dune-beach ridges, each 3 to 10 feet high (Fig. 5.15). A map of northeastern South Carolina prepared by Thom and by Johnson and Du Bar (Fig. 5.14) suggests that the beach ridges of the Jaluco stage formed at a time when the seacoast in the Myrtle Beach area was much more cuspate than at present and that during a stage of the middle Pleistocene there were two capes between Cape Fear and Cape Romain: one about 20 miles south-southwest of Myrtle Beach and the other offshore not far from the North Carolina–South Carolina line. Myrtle Beach would have been near the center of the arc between these now vanished capes.

Today in North Carolina, maximum erosion is taking place at the capes, and there is slight accretion in the centers of the arcs between. The Myrtle Beach area, however, is near the center of the arc between Capes Fear and Romain; yet this coast has been eroded back so far that it is within 3 miles of where the coastline was in mid-Pleistocene time, a distance far less than along the rest of the coastal plain. The reshaping of the coastline is probably a product of differential erosion by waves after the lowered sea level of the last glacial stage. Erosion is still occurring, as shown by the exposure of peat deposits on the modern strand at the town of Myrtle Beach.

Also present in the belt are numerous oval marshy lowlands with long axes from northwest to southeast, ranging in length from about 0.25 mile to more than a mile. These have been called the "Carolina bays." It is estimated that there are more than half a million of them on the Atlantic coastal plain, mostly in the Carolinas and Georgia. These were described and interpreted in reports by Frank Melton and William Schriever in 1933, Douglas Johnson in 1942, and William Prouty in 1952, as well as in papers by many other scientists.

Among the theories proposed to explain the oriented elliptical marshes are the following: (1) the impact of a vast shower of meteorites striking the area from the northwest and raising low sand rims toward the southeast (A in Fig. 5.15); (2) lagoons segmented by elliptical currents controlled by a prevailing northwest wind during earlier periods, forming a chain of oval "bays"; (3) a combination of solution, artesian springs in lakes, and a prevailing northwest wind; and (4) development of thaw lakes on permafrost at the time of one of the glacial maxima but outside the glaciated area. Oriented lakes of northern Alaska (p. 485) are explained by this last hypothesis.

Little attempt is made here to interpret the origin of the Carolina bays, but note is made of the following facts: (1) they are reported in formations of various ages, at elevations up to more than 500 feet above sea level, and at distances of as far as 150 miles inland from the coast; (2) all but a few of the bays are on sandy-surface soils and on the coastal plain; (3) where beach or dune ridges are also present, as in Figure 5.15, the bays truncate the ridges, showing that they were formed later; (4) some bays occur on upland flats, some on gentle slopes, and others on flat-bottom lands; (5) the innermost Carolina bays are so much higher than the highest interglacial sea levels that not all of them appear to be related to coastal lagoons; and (6) according to the latest reports, there are no magnetic highs near the bays, as there should be if iron meteorites were buried nearby.

MURRELLS INLET, SOUTH CAROLINA [Fig. 5.16]   At Murrells Inlet, 14 miles southwest of Myrtle Beach, the coast again has barrier islands, lagoons, and marshes. The lagoon at Murrells Inlet is about a mile wide, and its tidal streams from the northeast and southwest join at the inlet. Most of the lagoon behind the barrier is filled with marshes, through which a network of small tidal streams alternately flood and then drain the surface. No significant drainage from the land enters this lagoon. Directly outside the inlet, the aerial photograph (Fig. 5.16)

0 MILES   .50   1.0

KM

5.16 Murrells Inlet, South Carolina, showing a large tidal delta built into the ocean. No major river reaches the coast at this inlet. U.S. Department of Agriculture, 1950.

shows a slightly submerged delta extending seaward for a mile. A channel cuts through this delta, suggesting powerful outward flow through the inlet with deposition on the sides. Submarine deltas usually build in the other direction because erosion inside bays is slight. If a large river entered the lagoon causing a powerful flow out through the inlet, one might expect a submerged delta of this type. Since this is not the condition, the explanation is not apparent.

WINYAH AND SANTEE BAYS, SOUTH CAROLINA [Figs. 5.17 and 5.18]   South of Myrtle

Beach, the coast bows outward as if approaching the next cuspate cape. A north-trending estuary, Winyah Bay, comes into the coast looking like Cape Fear River, but actually the cuspate cape does not appear for another 18 miles beyond Winyah Bay where the cuspate Cape Romain looks as though it had been displaced from its natural position (see Fig. 5.1). Winyah Bay is the estuary and lagoon at the mouths of the Peedee and Waccamaw Rivers. The entrance (Fig. 5.17) is bounded on the north by an arcuate spit called North Island and on the south by what was formerly a cuspate key and is now a barrier island connected to the mainland by a long east-west jetty (Fig. 5.18). Landward of the barrier, a narrow spit reaches into South Island. Farther down the coast, North and South Santee Rivers empty into a long estuary. In both cases, a long spit has grown from the north and displaced the estuary mouth southward. Southwest from the south barriers of Winyah Bay, shoals extend directly seaward for 12 miles. These shoals provide another indication that a cuspate cape did exist here, and that Cape Romain represents a shift of the cape to the south.

The history of the entrances to Winyah and Santee Bays is shown from the tracings of numerous charts and aerial photographs covering the period from 1890 to 1962 (Figs. 5.17 and 5.18). The names North Island and South Island are technically correct because they are severed from the mainland by the Intracoastal Canal, although in 1890 they were definitely connected, and the shore of South Island was smoothly curved with a south trend at Winyah Bay, bending to southwest where it approached the mouth of North Santee Bay. Between 1890 and 1896, a jetty 1.5 miles long was built southeast and east from the tip of North Island; and, between 1896 and 1908, a jetty 4 miles long was constructed due east from the South Island shore, 1 mile south of the position of the north jetty.

Between 1890 and 1949, the North Island spit grew southward 4,200 feet, and the island width increased 900 feet. Shortly after the jetties were constructed, the South Island beach just north of the south jetty suffered erosion, probably because the north jetty had cut off the sand supply for beach maintenance.

By 1929, a new and very narrow arcuate sand spit 3 miles long (Fig. 5.17) had formed from a point 2 miles out on the south jetty southwestward toward

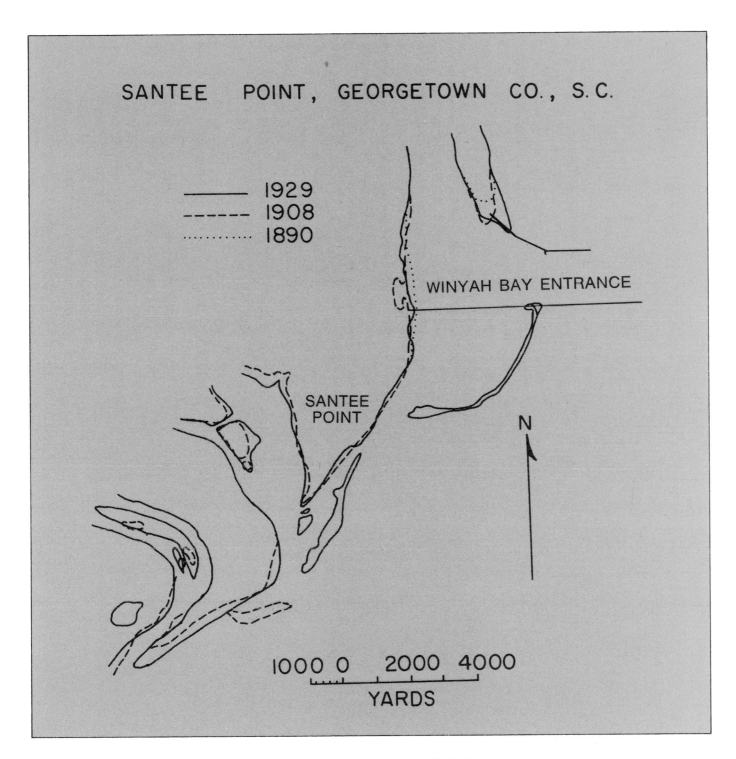

SANTEE POINT, GEORGETOWN CO., S.C.

———— 1929
– – – – 1908
.... 1890

WINYAH BAY ENTRANCE

SANTEE POINT

N

1000 0 2000 4000
YARDS

5.17 Shoreline changes near Winyah Bay, South Carolina. Jetties were built between 1890 and 1896 to protect the entrance to the harbor at Georgetown. This resulted in extensive change south of the south jetty, shown by sketches for 1890, 1908, and 1929. Compiled by Mohamed T. El-Ashry from charts of the U.S. Coast and Geodetic Survey.

5.18 Shoreline and jetties near entrance to Winyah Bay in 1949, showing triangle of new land barriers and marsh south of south jetty. U.S. Department of Agriculture.

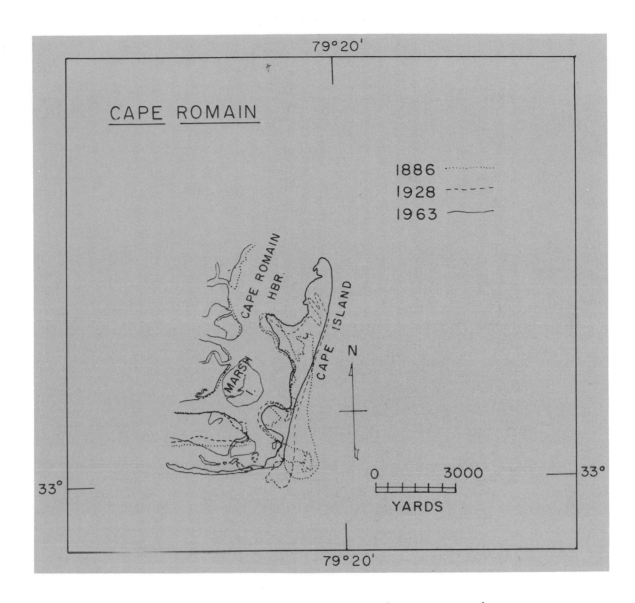

5.19 Changes in configuration of Cape Romain, South Carolina, between 1886 and 1963, sketched from charts of the U.S. Coast and Geodetic Survey.

South Island. By 1943, the point of junction of this spit with South Jetty had moved landward 3,000 feet, the spit had shortened to about a mile, and a new spit with the same orientation had grown more than 2 miles northeastward from South Island, partially enclosing a new bay 3.5 square miles in area bounded by South Jetty, South Island, and the two spits. By 1949 (Fig. 5.18), tidal currents had built a double tidal delta. Marsh vegetation, established at the shallow margins of the inner bay, had filled half of this lagoon by 1962 (not shown). Future filling with

sediment should add this area to South Island.

On the other side of South Jetty, a hooked spit had begun to develop by 1949 and was building northwestward toward the shipping channel. By 1962, it had lengthened to 0.75 mile. Further extension of this spit may require dredging to maintain the 25-foot channel for ocean-going vessels.

Beach drifting in this area must be from north to south. The building of the two jetties disturbed the balance and trapped sediment on North Island, allowing river sediment to be carried out into deeper

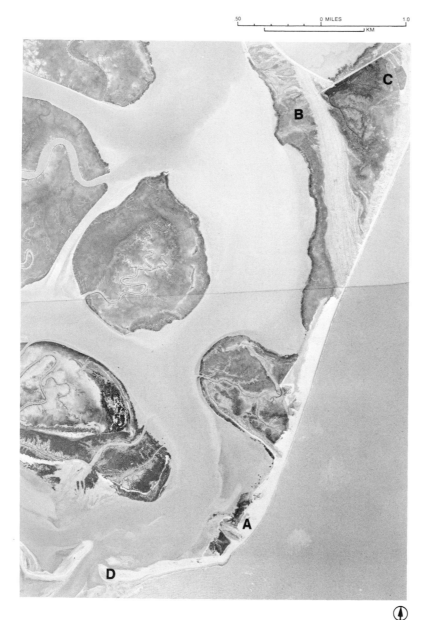

5.20 Changes at Cape Romain, South Carolina from 1941 to 1963. U.S. Department of Agriculture.

a November 2, 1941. North of Cape Romain (A) the nineteenth-century north-south spit (B) had been destroyed, while a new spit (C) extended to the northeast. A narrow barrier had built west from Cape Romain (D), but was cut by an inlet. (See Fig. 5.19.)

water. The south currents constructed a spit, and another spit developed due to overflow of South Jetty.

CAPE ROMAIN AREA, SOUTH CAROLINA [Figs. 5.19 and 5.20]   Cape Romain, 17 miles miles southwest of the mouth of Winyah Bay, has its apex on Cape Island, 5 miles off the mainland shore.

Although the outer 0.5 mile of this belt is mostly an open lagoon, the remaining 4.5 miles consist largely of tidal marshes and channels. Information about the history of Cape Romain is derived from charts dating back to 1886 and aerial photos taken in 1941, 1949, 1957, and 1963.

In 1886, Cape Island was about 3.5 miles long

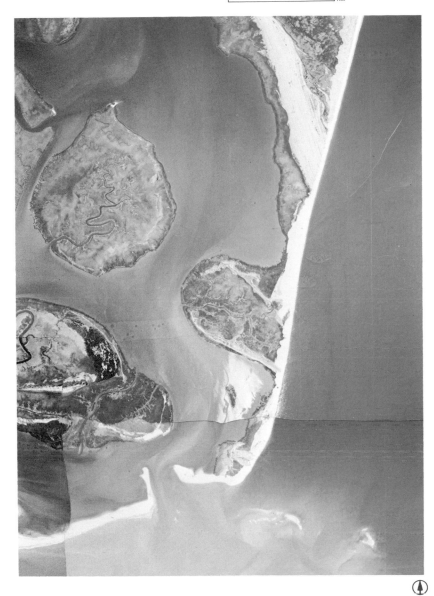

b March 4, 1949. The barrier west of Cape Romain has lengthened, and the inlet has been displaced eastward.

and had a north-south orientation (Fig. 5.19). By 1928, this orientation had changed 30 degrees in a counterclockwise direction, and the island length had increased to 4 miles. The new shape was the result of the north-northeastward growth of a small point of the 1886 shoreline, developing two shoreward-facing hooks. At the same time, the south end of the island was shifted westward. By 1938 (not shown), the southern end of the island had been reduced in width; and the chart shows a small hook to the west, the first indication of the development of the cuspate foreland at Cape Romain. By 1941 (Fig. 5.20a), new barriers extended westward for 1.4 miles, but with an inlet separating them, while Cape Island had

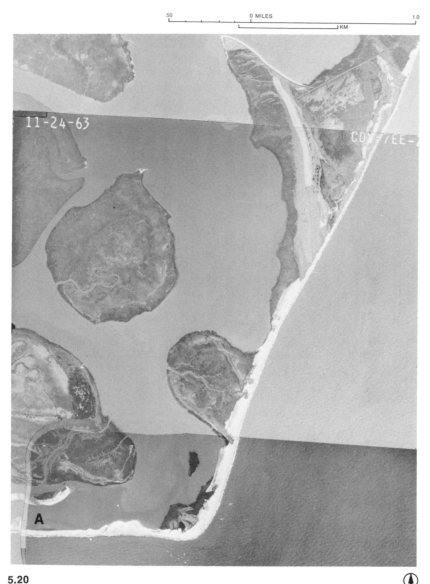

5.20

c November 24, 1963. The spit west of Cape Romain has lengthened farther and the inlet closed. A small barrier (A) inside the bay is of uncertain origin. The 1949 barrier may have migrated shoreward, while a new barrier formed outside, or it may have formed in the bay behind the present barrier.

grown slightly farther north. By 1949 (Fig. 5.20*b*), the west-trending barriers had reached a total length of 2 miles, and the inlet between the barriers had shifted closer to Cape Romain. By 1963 (Figs. 5.19 and 5.20*c*), a full-fledged cuspate foreland had developed with the westward barriers having a length of 2.3 miles without any break. Inside this arm, a new sand key had developed. Also, the north-trending barrier had lengthened to 4.6 miles.

The preceding history of the development of a new cuspate foreland at Cape Romain appears to be further confirmation of the southward shift of an older cape, thus increasing what had been remarkably even intervals between all four of these prominent points. However, the extensive southeastward-trending shoals off the present Cape Romain make one inclined to believe that this promontory has had a rather lengthy existence, even if the cuspate barriers are rather recent. Still further shift southward of Cape Romain may occur. Alternatively, the west arm of the cape may grow so as to enclose most of the marsh coast, which is an eastern flank of Bull Bay.

REFERENCES

Athearn, W. D., and F. C. Ronne, 1963. Shoreline changes at Cape Hatteras: an aerial photographic study of a 17-year period. *Office Naval Res., Res. Reviews*, vol. 16, no. 6, pp. 17–24.

Black, D. M., and W. L. Barksdale, 1949. Oriented lakes of northern Alaska. *Jour. Geol.*, vol. 57, no. 2, pp. 105–118.

Cooke, C. Wythe, 1934. Discussion of the origin of the supposed meteorite scars of South Carolina. *Jour. Geol.*, vol. 42, no. 1, pp. 88–104.

Corps of Engineers, U.S. Army, 1947. *North Carolina Shoreline, Beach Erosion Study*. House of Representatives, 80th Congr., 2d Sess., Document 763.

El-Ashry, M. T., 1966. Photointerpretation of shoreline changes in selected areas along the Atlantic and Gulf coasts of the United States. Univ. Illinois Ph.D. thesis in geology.

————, and H. R. Wanless, 1965. The birth and early growth of a tidal delta. *Jour. Geol.*, vol. 73, no. 2, pp. 404–406.

————, and H. R. Wanless, 1968. Photo interpretation of shoreline changes between Capes Hatteras and Fear (North Carolina). *Marine Geol.*, vol. 6, no. 5, pp. 347–379.

Johnson, D. W., 1942. *Origin of the Carolina Bays*. Columbia University Press, New York.

Johnson, H. S., Jr., and J. R. Du Bar, 1964. Geomorphic elements of the area between the Cape Fear and Peedee Rivers, North and South Carolina. *Southeastern Geol.*, vol. 6, no. 1, pp. 37–48.

Melton, F. A., and William Schriever, 1933. The Carolina "bays"—are they meteorite scars? *Jour. Geol.*, vol. 41, no. 1, pp. 52–66.

Newman, Walter S., and Gene A. Rusnak, 1965. Holocene submergence of the eastern shore of Virginia. *Science*, vol. 148, no. 3676, pp. 1464–1466.

Prouty, W. F., 1962. Carolina bays and their origin. *Geol. Soc. Amer. Bull.*, vol. 63, no. 2, pp. 167–224.

Thom, B. G., 1967. Coastal and fluvial landforms: Horry and Marion counties, South Carolina. *Louisiana State Univ. Coastal Studies Inst., Tech. Rept.* 44.

White, W. A., 1966. Drainage asymmetry and the Carolina capes. *Geol. Soc. Amer. Bull.*, vol. 77, no. 3, pp. 223–240.

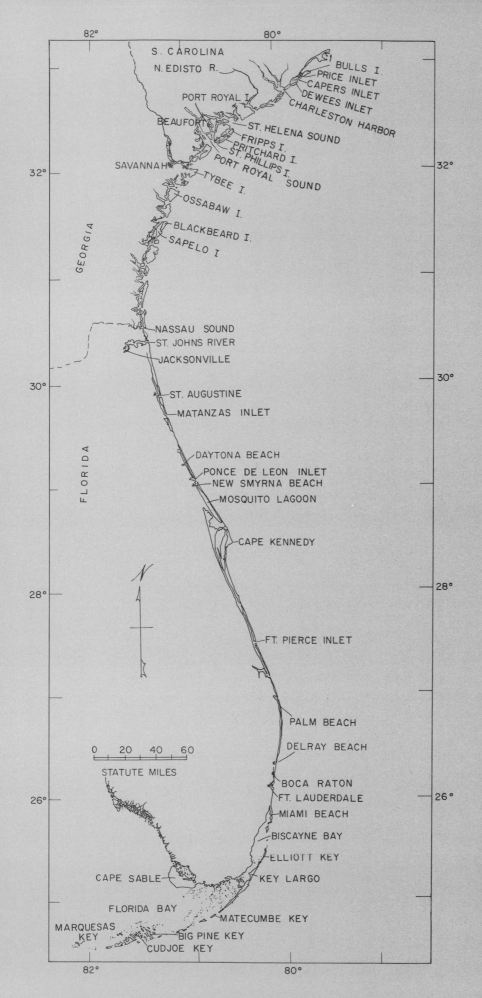

6.1 Index map of the Atlantic Coast from Cape Romain, South Carolina, to Florida Keys, showing locations described.

Straight Barrier Coasts

Cape Romain to Florida Keys

6 South of Cape Romain, the coast becomes much straighter (Fig. 6.1); and only at Cape Kennedy is there a cuspate foreland comparable with those to the north. The barriers along the South Carolina and Georgia coast are short, thick, stubby islands, separated from each other by rather deep penetrating estuaries. Near the Georgia-Florida line, the barrier islands become relatively thin and extend for as much as 100 miles without a break. The lagoons on the inside are mostly narrow and in some places would be entirely filled marshes if they had not been reopened by the Intracoastal Canal. At Cape Kennedy, the lagoons widen; but to the south they continue to be very narrow or completely filled as far as Biscayne Bay at Miami.

In the Miami area, the supply of quartz sand from the north has become scarce, due to the great distance from the source and to the proximity of the powerful north-flowing Gulf Stream, which counteracts the south-moving coastal currents. Also the narrowness of the continental shelf allows beach sand to disappear down the outer slope. As a result of the small supply and despite the building of many groins and jetties, the Miami area is faced with serious beach erosion; and the hotels are having great difficulty in keeping enough sand for their beaches.

South of Miami, the wide lagoons are protected by slightly elevated coral reefs that appear to be a continuation of the sand barriers to the north. These islands, called *keys* (the equivalent of the British *cays*), extend around the southern end of the Florida mainland but die out west of the peninsula. Inside the keys, the shallow Florida Bay widens to the west until the width is 30 miles at Cape Sable, the southwest promontory of the mainland. The outermost keys lose the barrier shape of the northern keys and instead become elongated in a northwest-southeast direction. Beyond Key West, only small isolated islands are found, and the Marquesas and Dry Tortugas are oval-shaped rings resembling atolls.

PRICE, CAPERS, AND DEWEES INLETS, SOUTH CAROLINA[1] [Figs. 6.2 and 6.3]

Along the South Carolina coast 12 to 30 miles north of Charleston, we have an example of these blocklike islands (Fig. 6.2a) that characterize this part of the coast. The islands are 0.5 to 0.75 mile wide and include outer beaches, beach or dune ridges, and inner flats and marshes. The lagoons on the inside have intricate channels with intervening marsh areas. No major streams drain into these lagoons, but the tidal currents are strong enough to keep the inlets between the islands open for small boat navigation. Also the outgoing tides, probably accentuated by run-off into the bays, have carried sand seaward at the mouths of the estuaries and have formed bars and cuspate islands that are constantly changing shape. There is, however, a conspicuous absence of tidal deltas inside. The 1954 aerial photographs (Fig. 6.2a) show that the island on the southeast side of each inlet is built farther seaward than the island on the northeast side. This suggests a northeast current, but comparison of Figure 6.2a with Figure 6.2b and Figure 6.3 shows that this relationship is variable and that the currents change direction from time to time.

Price Inlet (A in Fig. 6.2a) has had a history that is well documented in charts as far back as 1896 (Fig. 6.3). The changes at the mouth of this inlet are illustrative of these variable current conditions. In 1895, the southwest side was 3,000 feet seaward of the northeast, but this situation had reversed by 1929. By 1938, it had reversed again and the southwest side was 2,400 feet farther seaward; and this protrusion had increased to 4,500 feet by 1941. In 1963 (not shown), this extension had been entirely cut away, and again the northeast side was farther seaward. Another change at Price Inlet is shown on

[1] Contains information from a thesis by Mohamed T. El-Ashry.

6.2 Features of a portion of the South Carolina coast from Bulls Island to Isle of Palms.

a November 30, 1954, one month after Hurricane Hazel. Note lunate key at Price Inlet, also changes in Capers Inlet and Dewees Island from conditions shown in Figure 6.2b. U.S. Coast and Geodetic Survey.

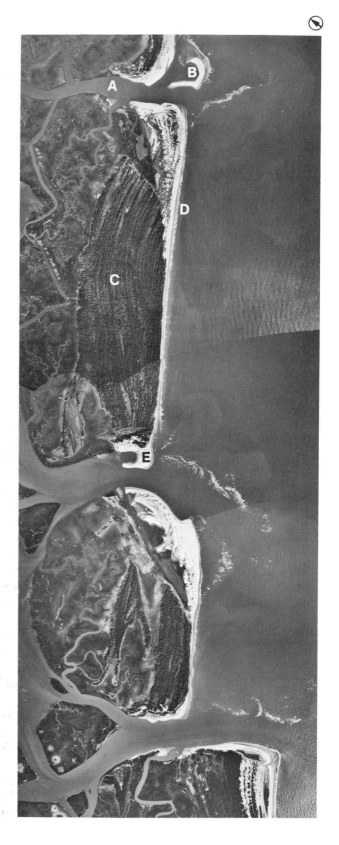

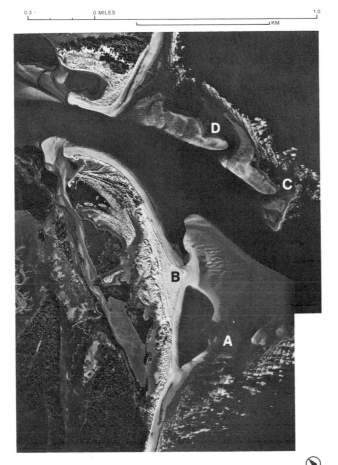

b November 23, 1953. Dewees and Capers Islands and Capers Inlet, showing two lunate bars and a small cuspate foreland on Dewees Island. These features were largely destroyed by Hurricane Hazel. U.S. Coast and Geodetic Survey.

6.3 Map sketches of Price Inlet, South Carolina, showing shorelines in 1896, 1929, 1941, and 1957. The northeastern and southwestern barriers adjoining the inlet have alternately projected farther seaward. Compiled by Mohamed T. El-Ashry.

the 1954 aerial photo (Fig. 6.2a), where a cuspate key (B) developed apparently as a result of Hurricane Hazel that hit the coast with winds from the south of 100 miles an hour. This key had disappeared by the time of the 1957 aerial photos (not shown), but a spit still existed (Fig. 6.3).

The entrance to Capers Inlet has also been the site of changes. One of these is illustrated by comparison of Figures 6.2a and 6.2b. In 1953 (Fig. 6.2b), the smaller Dewees Island to the south had a more rounded outline than Capers Island on the other side of the pass. Sediment drifting from both north and south had formed a cuspate bar (A) with a small gap in the middle. On the north end of this obstruction, sand had accumulated, temporarily form-

ing a spit (B). Shoals indicated by breaking waves suggest a large lunate bar (C) outside these features. At the same time, hooks had been formed by sand drifting toward Capers Inlet from both sides. Also in 1953, shoals extended straight seaward for 0.75 mile on the northeast side of the inlet (D). These may be interpreted as the result of sand carried out of the inlet by the outgoing tide and deposited at the edge of the tidal channel. A month before the 1954 photos (Fig. 6.2a), Hurricane Hazel cut away the cuspate and lunate sand bars that had been present off Dewees Island in 1953.

Beach ridges are very prominent in the central part of Capers Island (C in Fig. 6.2a). These ridges, older than 1896 as shown by the chart of that date,

6.4 Entrance to harbor of Charleston, South Carolina, showing Fort Sumter, at which the first shots of the Civil War were fired. U.S. Coast and Geodetic Survey, 1959.

are truncated on their seaward face as well as by the inlets where younger beach ridges and hooks have formed (D and E). Similar remnants of older ridges also occur on the other islands.

CHARLESTON HARBOR AND FORT SUMTER, SOUTH CAROLINA [Fig. 6.4]   Historic Fort Sumter (A), where the first shots of the Civil War were fired, was built in the middle 1800s on a rather muddy island at the south entrance to Charleston Harbor. The fort had gun emplacements to protect both sides of the harbor entrance. In 1860, the island was only a short distance offshore and was nearly connected with the adjacent marshy land. The island fort, held by Union troops, was besieged by the Confederates using guns located near the ends of the two spits that flanked the harbor entrance.

At the time of the Civil War, land approaches to the fort were poorer than when it was constructed,

and it was necessary to cross mud flats to reach the fort. Now, most of these flats are covered by 1 to 3 feet of water. When photographed in 1959 (Fig. 6.4), the hexagonal fort was entirely surrounded by water except for a narrow mud flat (B) at the south, covered at high tide. The photograph shows a shoal (C) about 0.2 mile southwest of the fort, but a nautical chart dated 1936 shows an island 1,500 feet long at the site of this present shoal. Evidently, erosion in the years from 1850 to 1959 almost entirely removed the mud-flat island on which Fort Sumter was constructed. The harbor channel, 28 to 34 feet deep, immediately adjoins Fort Sumter on the north; and the fort, a national monument, is now reached only by boat.

On each side of the harbor entrance, hooked spits are now seen curving toward the west. Because a map of the harbor at the time of the Civil War is not at hand, the amount of growth of these spits in the past century is not known to the authors.

NORTH EDISTO RIVER ESTUARY, SOUTH CAROLINA [Fig. 6.5]   North Edisto River is a drowned coastal-plain estuary about 25 miles southwest of the entrance to Charleston Harbor. It enters the ocean between Seabrook (A) and Edisto (B) Islands. The channel is 50 to 75 feet deep at the inlet. In 1954, Seabrook Island projected seaward about 4,500 feet beyond the shore of Edisto Island (Fig. 6.5). Although this is contrary to the island relationships in Figure 6.2a, it might be expected since the predominant littoral current along the coast is southwestward. The Seabrook Island barrier is 1.5 miles wide just northeast of the river mouth. The channel at the inlet is flanked by shoals on each side and these extend about 3 miles seaward. In 1954, just southwest of the channel and 1.5 miles offshore from Edisto Island, there was a horseshoe-shaped lunate sandkey nearly a mile long, open toward the inlet (C in Fig. 6.5a). This sandkey appears to have been the product of reworking of a sand shoal representing sediment brought into the sea during ebb tides. It is more restricted in size but otherwise resembles lunate bars formed at the seaward margins of many channels along the West Coast. The same lunate sandkey and adjoining shoals are shown probably at a lower tidal stage in 1953 (Fig. 6.5b). At this earlier date, a small tidal delta can be seen on the inside of the lunate bar. The 1957 and 1963 aerial

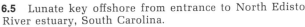

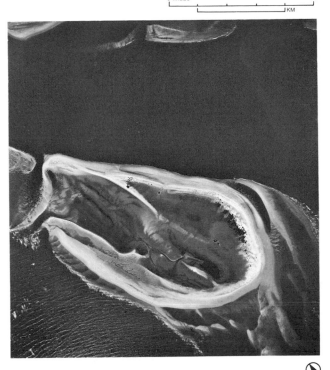

6.5 Lunate key offshore from entrance to North Edisto River estuary, South Carolina.

a April 7, 1954. U.S. Coast and Geodetic Survey.

b December 23, 1953. This photo, taken at a lower tidal stage than Figure 6.5a, shows a small tidal delta inside the key. U.S. Coast and Geodetic Survey.

photographs (not included) show that the lunate sandkey had narrowed, had become more rectangular, and had been shifted toward Seabrook Island about 0.3 mile.

A remarkable feature of the South Carolina coast is the large number of cuspate spits, lunate bars, and tidal deltas built into the ocean outside inlets of tidal streams or small coastal plain estuaries. On the other hand, the building of tidal deltas into lagoons, so common from southern New England to North Carolina, is relatively rare in South Carolina. The tidal inlets migrate less than most of those of North Carolina. Perhaps the location and stability of inlets and the accumulations of sediment offshore may be related to a system of gyrols between the Gulf Stream and the predominant southwestward littoral current. Also, the cuspate capes to the north may provide some protection from the full force of northeast storms.

FRIPPS ISLAND TO ST. PHILLIPS ISLAND AREA, SOUTH CAROLINA [Figs. 6.6 and 6.7]

The southwestern portion of the South Carolina coast represents a return to the deeply embayed coastal

plains found farther north (see Fig. 6.1). St. Helena Sound and its tributaries extend 25 miles inland, and Port Royal Sound, to the southwest, 30 miles. The coast consists of a series of "sea islands" separated from each other by tidal channels and by marshy bays from islands nearer the mainland. This belt continues southwestward into Georgia. The old mid-Pleistocene shorelines, about 3 miles from the present coast in northeastern South Carolina, are here as far as 40 miles inland. All the area seaward from the emerged Pleistocene coastal terraces is a maze of old beach ridges, modern marshes, and shallow lagoons nearly filled with marsh and crossed by many tidal channels. The area selected to illustrate the southern part of the South Carolina coast is between St. Helena and Port Royal Sounds, about 10 miles southeast of Beaufort and 40 miles northeast of Savannah, Georgia.

Fripps Island (A in Fig. 6.6) is separated from Prichard Island (B) to the southwest by the meandering channel of Skull Inlet (C). Harbor "River" (D) is a very shallow lagoon about 1.5 feet deep, but with mud flats exposed at low tide. The area is drained southward and eastward by an intricate series

6.6 Fripps Island, South Carolina. This coastal area consists largely of low marsh traversed by many tidal stream channels. There are a series of prograding beach ridges near the present coast and remnants of older beach ridges rising out of the marsh 2 miles inland. The marshes represent filled coastal lagoons of two stages. U.S. Department of Agriculture, 1951.

of tidal streams into Story River (E), which is 15 to 25 feet deep. Harbor and Story Rivers are parts of a lagoon largely filled with silt and sand, and supporting grassy marshes. Small remnants (F) of old beach ridges in these marshes are shown. South of Story River is a well-displayed series of beach ridges (G) with hooks sharply recurved toward the river. Oldhouse Creek (H) and Skull Creek (I), two tidal streams, drain a marshy area just south of the abandoned beach with hooked ridges. The old beach has been partly cut away, evidently by a former tidal inlet, now drained by tributaries of Oldhouse Creek (J). The old beach line is about 2 miles inland from the present coast. Former inlets are now filled with grassy marshes, which extend south to the younger ridges.

After the disruption of several older sets of beach ridges, a new barrier began to form about 2 miles offshore (K); and, as shown by a series of beach ridges, it prograded southward about a mile to or beyond the present shoreline. Some of these beach ridges can be observed to truncate other ridges, suggesting that the seaward growth of the new beach was frequently interrupted by erosion. Fripps Inlet (L), at the east end of Fripps Island, has evidently existed for a long time, because the beach ridges are somewhat hooked in the direction of this inlet. However, Skull Inlet (C) appears to have been opened later because beach ridges are not recurved toward it.

Near Fripps Inlet, Fripps Island was still prograding in 1951, as shown by the new unvegetated ridges (M), which curve slightly seaward at the northeast end of the island. Southwest toward Skull Inlet, the beach ridges are being cut away by erosion; and, a little farther in this direction, in 1951, the main barrier ridge (B) of Pritchard Island had been cut away. Hooked spits at this time show that sand was being washed into Skull Inlet, but photos taken 2 years later (not illustrated) show a tidal delta fronted by a lunate bar built out into the ocean.

No carbon-14 dates are available to provide information as to the age of the beach ridges of these islands, either along the present shore or along the somewhat older shore 3 miles inland. Evidently the seaward slope here is very gradual since both older and newer beaches are near modern sea level. The abandonment of the older beaches and the building of a new beach may have resulted from a slight lowering of sea level or, more likely, from shoaling of the

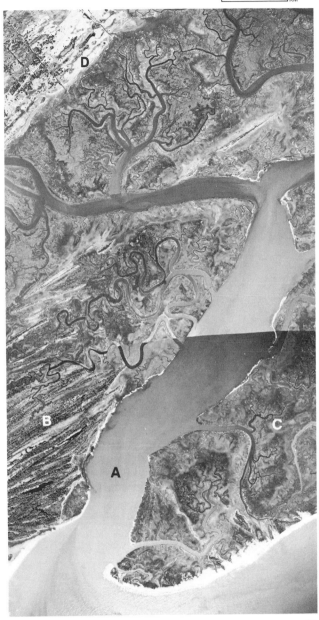

6.7 Trenchard Inlet (A) separates Pritchard and St. Phillips Islands, South Carolina. The modern beach ridges of Fripps Island (Fig. 6.6) northeast of this area, have been largely cut away, and the coast of Pritchard Island (C) is marsh fringed with a beach. A somewhat older series of beach ridges occurs near the coast on St. Phillips Island (B). A Pleistocene shoreline (D) is shown inland from a belt of tidal marshes. U.S. Department of Agriculture, 1951.

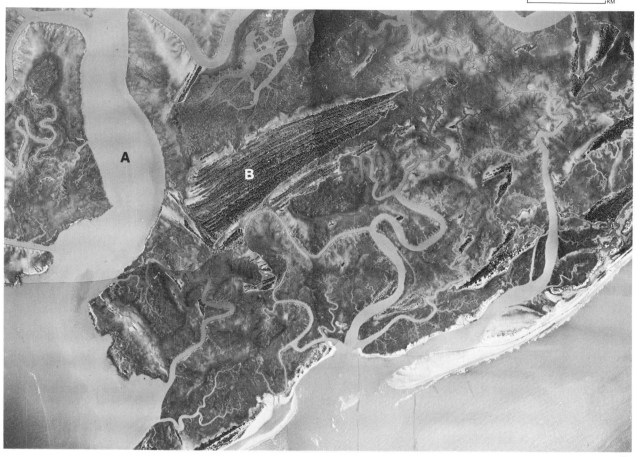

6.8 Tybee Island, northern coastal Georgia. This area, southwest of the mouth of the Savannah River, is a low marshy coast, with narrow barrier spits formed by littoral currents flowing southwestward. One large remnant of an old series of beach ridges (B) and several small patches rise from the marshes. U.S. Department of Agriculture, 1952.

offshore flat by sediment accumulation. However, dismembered remnants of an old beach rising out of modern coastal marshes suggest subsidence of the land or rise of sea level. Probably both rise and fall in sea level may be recorded in this area, especially if some of the beach ridges are as old as the last interglacial.

In 1965, Wanless visited Hunting Island State Park, about 2 miles northeast of Fripps Inlet, and found that recent storm erosion had destroyed pavement in a parking lot, toppled large trees, and cut back a coastal sand dune to form a cliff 15 to 20 feet high.

Figure 6.7 shows the 1951 configuration of Trenchard Inlet, which separates Pritchard Island from St. Phillips Island. The inlet, according to the most recent chart, is 20 to 68 feet deep but is subject to rapid variations, depending on the strength of the tidal currents at different times. The remnants of a beach with many subparallel ridges to the southwest (B) correspond with the ridges 2 miles inland, shown in Figure 6.6. The younger beaches of Fripps and Pritchard Islands (Fig. 6.6) have been entirely cut away here, and there is only a very narrow sand beach adjoining marshes northeast of Trenchard Inlet.

On St. Phillips Island, about 3 miles inland from the modern shore, a still older barrier (D) is now permanently above high tide and is cultivated by farmers. Its composition of sandy beach ridges and intervening swales is indicated by soil shade patterns. This beach is almost certainly of Pleistocene age, formed at a time of higher sea level, perhaps during the Sangamon interglacial stage, about 100,000 years ago. Even this older shoreline approaches present sea level, indicated by the tidal channels and marshes adjoining it.

TYBEE ISLAND, GEORGIA [Fig. 6.8] The nine major Georgia "sea islands" are segments of a series of barriers separated by estuaries that extend inland 10 miles or more. As a rule, the landward portions of the sea islands include one or more barriers dating to times of higher sea level during the Pleistocene interglacial stages. In northeastern coastal Georgia, the Silver Bluff shore, the latest Pleistocene barrier, is about 5 miles inland from the present coast.

Tybee Island, about 17 miles east of Savannah, is the northeasternmost of the Georgia sea islands. The area illustrated in Figure 6.8 is in the southwestern part of this island. Here, all the features are postglacial. Tybee River, a tidal stream (A), is 15 to 40 feet deep; and some of the smaller tidal streams are locally more than 20 feet deep. The depth evidently results from tidal scour. To the northeast (beyond the aerial photo), the barrier forms Savannah Beach, but the barrier does not continue as far south as the photo, where the coast is largely marshy with only a thin beach at the shoreline.

A strong southwestward littoral current has resulted in two separate spits fronting the sea (Fig. 6.8). These spits were apparently missing when the surveys were made for the 1928 chart.

In the marshes behind the modern shore, a wedge-shaped segment of an older beach (B), as reported by J. H. Hoyt and V. J. Henry, is about 2 miles long and 0.5 mile wide at the widest. It displays a series of fifteen or more beach ridges nearly parallel to the present shoreline. Other small segments of single ridges or small groups appear randomly above the surrounding marshes. These probably represent shorelines of short duration, along with narrow beaches or spits that had developed. While still exposed to wave attack, parts of these older beaches were cut away. The prograding of a modern lagoon-barrier complex in this area, which is broader than elsewhere along the Georgia coast, many have re-

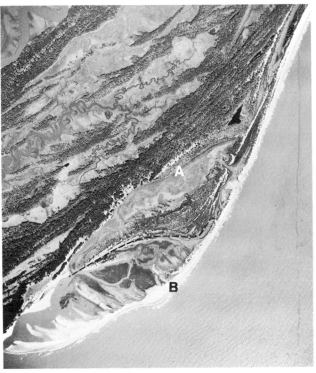

6.9 Ossabaw Island, Georgia. A series of somewhat older beach ridges are beveled by erosion just inside the modern beach. Three successive beaches, all near the coast, have prograded and developed a succession of hooks curving southwestward. These hooks must have formed recently, as they are not shown on a 1939 chart. The 1939 shore is marked by a dashed line. U.S. Department of Agriculture, 1952.

sulted from the supply of sediment introduced into the sea by the Savannah River a few miles to the northeast.

OSSABAW ISLAND, GEORGIA Ossabaw Island, the third from the northeast of the Georgia sea islands, is located between Ossabaw Sound (Ogeechee River) to the northeast and St. Catherines Sound (Medway River). In the northern part of Ossabaw Island, the broad lagoon-marsh complex of the Tybee Island area has been reduced to about 2 miles. In the southern part, this belt is entirely truncated, and the postglacial barrier immediately adjoins the Silver Bluff barrier of late Pleistocene date.

In Figure 6.9, half-way along the island, the old ridges are bordered by several narrow somewhat in-

6.10 Blackbeard (B) and Sapelo (A) Islands, Georgia. There are no visible beach ridges on Sapelo Island, which consists of marine sand formed during higher sea level of the later Pleistocene. Blackbeard Island consists largely of a succession of beach ridges. A marsh with tidal streams between the islands is a filled coastal lagoon. U.S. Department of Agriculture, 1953.

terrupted beach and dune ridges separated by tracts of coastal marshes. These features have all been added since the 1939 edition of the Coast and Geodetic Survey chart, which showed the coast where the dashed line has been placed on Figure 6.9. The shoreline at this time formed a cuspate point and a broad marshy area exists on the inside. A still older shoreline (A) is indicated at the border of the old vegetated ridges. Here, also, there was a cuspate cape with a small pond on the inside. Apparently the coast is growing southward with the addition of these points; and a new one may be in the process of development, as seen in the aerial photo (B).

SAPELO AND BLACKBEARD ISLANDS, GEORGIA [Fig. 6.10]

The conjoined Sapelo and Blackbeard Islands form the fifth in the series of Georgia sea islands. Sapelo Island (A) is about 10 miles long from northeast to southwest and is separated from Blackbeard (B) to the east by a marshy belt averaging about 1 mile in width and drained by Blackbeard Creek (C). Blackbeard Island is 6 miles long and lies seaward from Blackbeard Creek marsh along the northern 60 percent of Sapelo Island. Blackbeard Island varies in width from 2 miles at its northern end to a narrow spit about 600 feet wide at its southern tip.

This area has had substantial study by John H. Hoyt, John M. Zeigler, and Clifford A. Kaye. Zeigler classifies Sapelo Island as an erosional island of Pleistocene age. He reported that it is composed of horizontally bedded sand layers with marine fossils. The margin of this marine sand is tentatively referred to by Hoyt as the late Pleistocene Silver Bluff shoreline, formed when sea level was a few feet higher than at present. The old Sapelo Island barrier does not display any parallel beach ridges; and, because the sand yields marine fossils, it may have formed at or slightly below sea level. Blackbeard Island was formed after the postglacial sea level had stopped rising. Unlike Sapelo Island, Blackbeard displays a long succession of beach ridges.

Kaye suggested the increasing width of Blackbeard Island at its northern end is a result of active present-day accretion except at the northeastern face (D), where present-day erosion has yielded some of the sand contributing to a modern spit to the south. This spit, about a mile long in 1953, had developed largely between 1927 and 1953. However, the slender spit

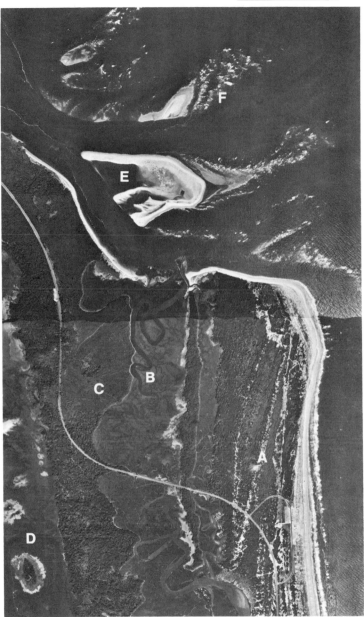

6.11 Nassau River estuary and Talbot (C) and Little Talbot (A) Islands, Florida. Little Talbot Island is a modern beach, while Talbot Island consists of marine sand formed during a higher sea-level stage in the Pleistocene. A lunate sandkey is near the entrance to the estuary. U.S. Coast and Geodetic Survey, 1962.

6.12 St. Johns River estuary and entrance to Jacksonville Harbor, Florida. Sand has accumulated against both jetties. Just north of St. Johns River, Fort George Inlet connects with a tidal lagoon, and a hook on the southern side of this inlet has been growing rapidly. U.S. Department of Agriculture, 1960.

just south of the outlet of Blackbeard Creek shows evidence of northward beach drifting. The south spit is overlapped by the wider spit on the north. Kaye recognized nine cycles of erosion and construction in the northern part of Blackbeard Island during the past several thousand years, the net effects of which resulted in advancing the island seaward 2.3 miles.

Thus, Figure 6.10 offers an illustration of the difference in structure and aspects between a late Pleistocene sand island (Sapelo) deposited under marine conditions and a recent barrier with beach ridges (Blackbeard).

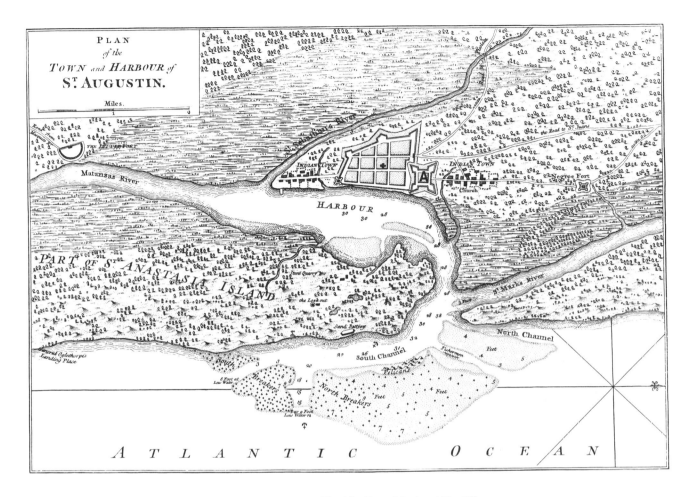

6.13 Map of the town and harbor of St. Augustine, Florida. Fort Marion (A) still exists. T. Jefferys, 1762.

NASSAU SOUND, FLORIDA [Fig. 6.11]   Nassau Sound, at the mouth of Nassau River, is located about 8 miles north of the entrance to the port of Jacksonville. On the south side of the entrance to the sound, a series of parallel barriers are indicated in Figure 6.11. The youngest, Little Talbot Island Beach (A), follows the present coast. A tightly meandering tidal stream, Simpson Creek (B), occupies most of the filled lagoon behind the modern barrier. The next older barrier, Talbot Island (C), can be seen to the left of the meandering creek. There is another filled lagoon behind Talbot Island, marked by piles of debris dredged in constructing the Intracoastal Waterway (D), and a third barrier, Black Hammock Island (not shown), lies west of the second filled lagoon.

In 1950 (not shown), a distorted lunate sandkey was found near the center of the sound entrance. Between 1950 and 1962, a second lunate sandkey had formed around the first one (E). In 1962, another shoal, nearly exposed at low tide (F), lay just north of the lunate sandkey, across the Nassau River tidal channel.

ST. JOHNS RIVER OUTLET, FLORIDA [Fig. 6.12]   The St. Johns River estuary winds in for 23 miles to the busy port of Jacksonville (Fig. 6.1). The entrance has a shipping channel maintained at 34 feet and is protected by jetties more than a mile long. Sand has accumulated against the south jetty and built out about 1,200 feet beyond the general beach line, possibly indicating a northward drift, al-

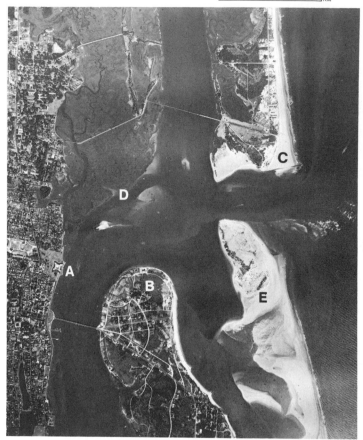

6.14 Aerial photograph of St. Augustine taken in the 1930s. For comparison with Figure 6.13, note Fort Marion and Anastasia Island (B). A new barrier island has been formed seaward from Anastasia. An artificial inlet was opened east of the city and is protected by jetties. U.S. Coast and Geodetic Survey.

ST. AUGUSTINE, FLORIDA [Figs. 6.13 and 6.14]
St. Augustine, 40 miles south of Jacksonville, has the reputation of being the oldest town in the United States. Juan Ponce de Leon landed here in 1513 in search of a magic fountain that was reputed to restore youth. He stayed in the area only five days, leaving no permanent settlement. Don Pedro Menéndez de Avilés, a Spanish admiral, took possession of the site of St. Augustine for the king of Spain in September 1565, and the town dates from that landing. At that time, the French fleet under Jean Ribault was preparing to attack the Spanish at St. Augustine, but the fleet was blown to sea by a hurricane. The town was fortified and was the Spanish military headquarters for North America for 40 years. In 1586, the town was sacked and burned by the British freebooter Sir Francis Drake but was rebuilt by the Spanish shortly afterward. After the English established Charleston, South Carolina, the Spanish constructed a stone fort, San Marcos (A in Figs. 6.13 and 6.14), later renamed Fort Marion; it is still standing. In 1740, James Oglethorpe, governor of Georgia, attacked St. Augustine and temporarily ended Spanish rule in Florida. The Spaniards fled to Cuba, and the British took over the town. During the Revolutionary War, St. Augustine became a headquarters for Tories and was never taken by American forces. At the end of the war, Spain again took over Florida, but in 1820 it was sold to the United States with St. Augustine as its first capital. The city was involved in warfare with the Seminole Indians between 1835 and 1842. Throughout the Civil War, it was controlled by Union troops.

St. Augustine was built on the mainland inside an inlet, where the land is protected by Anastasia Island (B in Fig. 6.14) on the south and by a long sand spit on the north (C). The harbor is connected with the ocean by an inlet almost directly east of the town. Although surrounded by water, it has not become an important port because shifting sand bars (D) at the mouth of Matanzas River have constituted a hazard to all but shallow-draft vessels. The barrier, Anastasia Island, is unlike most other Florida barriers, having a series of Pleistocene coquina limestone outcrops along the beaches that diminish the destructive effects of wave erosion. This limestone has been quarried extensively and used to build many of the oldest structures in St. Augustine, including Fort Marion, the old city gate, and many old houses.

though a south drift may carry sediment into Fort George Inlet (A), just north of the jetty, which leads into a largely filled lagoon behind the modern beach.

St. Johns River and Fort George Inlet are separated by a hooked spit (B) that curves westward toward Fort George Inlet. Comparison of the aerial photographs of 1947 (not included) and 1960 (Fig. 6.12) shows that the hooked spit had nearly doubled in size and a second hook had been initiated. The second hook showed still further growth in the 1962 photos (not shown). During this same period, the hook had retreated 0.3 mile but had become broadened. The same interval showed no appreciable growth adjacent to the south jetty.

A map published by T. Jefferys, an Englishman, in 1762, modified from an Italian map of similar date, is the oldest map of the St. Augustine coast located by the present authors (Fig. 6.13). When this map is contrasted with modern navigation charts and aerial photographs (Fig. 6.14), many changes are observed. Fort Marion (A) provides a good landmark for comparing the features in 1762 with those in the middle twentieth century. The small eighteenth-century town was built around the fort, but the present site of most of St. Augustine lies farther south and extends across St. Sebastian River into what was still uninhabited marsh land in 1762. Marshes are still present on both banks of the Matanzas River south of town. Anastasia Island is now connected with the town by a bridge, and the island's northern end is entirely urbanized.

In 1762, the barrier north of the inlet was narrow and separated from the marshy mainland by St. Mark's River (now Tolomato River), and the main South Channel, with depths of 15 to 20 feet, curved southward from this inlet for about 2 miles. Outside the channel lay shoal banks, called North and South Breakers, with water 4 to 7 feet deep. Today the channel has been artificially dredged across the barrier directly east of the inlet. A portion of the shallow banks of North and South Breakers has now become land, Conch Island (E in Fig. 6.14), and this is separated from Anastasia Island by a shallow lagoon in the position of the old South Channel.

At the dredged entrance, a jetty was built first on the north side (Fig. 6.14); and, as shown in the photograph, this led to a growth of the outer barrier on that side. Subsequently a south jetty (not shown) was constructed, and Conch Island has now grown out farther than the north barrier. Conch Island is at the site of the North Breakers in the old map.

Many hurricanes have struck the St. Augustine coast, some coming from the west after crossing the Florida Peninsula. The coquina limestone will probably prevent serious erosion on the St. Augustine coast.

MOSQUITO LAGOON AREA, FLORIDA

Between St. Augustine and Cape Kennedy (Fig. 6.1), a distance of 110 miles, the Florida coast is almost straight, broken only by Matanzas and Ponce de Leon Inlets, 12 and 60 miles south of St. Augustine. This straight east Florida coast includes the famous resorts Daytona Beach and New Smyrna. South of Ponce de Leon Inlet, the lagoon behind the coastal barrier widens from less than 1 mile to more than 6 miles, the wider part being called Mosquito Lagoon, which ends southward against the northern flank of Cape Kennedy.

The low areas inland from these east Florida beaches are principally underlain by limestones or marls, which yield little quartz sand. Therefore, the quartz in the beaches has been derived almost wholly from sand carried to the sea by Carolina and Georgia rivers and drifted southward by littoral currents. As at St. Augustine, there are various outcrops of coquina, a cemented shell rock of Pleistocene age. Detached blocks of this are found on the beaches near outcrops, and loose shells derived from the disintegration of the coquina are abundant in the sand for several miles south of each coquina outcrop. According to James Martens, the beach at the Mosquito Lagoon Coast Guard Station contains 48 percent of shell debris, suggesting a nearby outcrop of coquina, either on the beach or in the shallow water offshore.

The modern beaches in this area average about 300 feet in width and lie in front of a belt of low vegetated dune ridges ranging in width from 600 feet to 0.5 mile. Landward from this modern beach-dune belt is Mosquito Lagoon, 2 to 2.5 miles wide. Although Mosquito Lagoon farther south is an open body of water 6 miles wide and 1 to 7 feet deep, the northern part is filled with abundant small marshy islands, evidently parts of a tidal delta formed through Ponce de Leon Inlet. The Intracoastal Canal has been constructed along the western margin of the partly filled lagoon.

West of Mosquito Lagoon is an old beach and dune ridge and swale complex 1.25 miles wide, on which about fifteen nearly parallel dune ridges can be observed. This beach complex evidently was formed when sea level was relatively static and slightly above present sea level during a late Pleistocene interglacial. West of this belt is a wooded sandy ridge representing a still older beach, formed when sea level stood even higher. Although these beaches are close together at Mosquito Lagoon, farther south they diverge about 3 miles and are separated by Indian River, a coastal lagoon 130 miles long.

Significant erosion of the present coast is possible, although because it is flanked with dunes, it is more

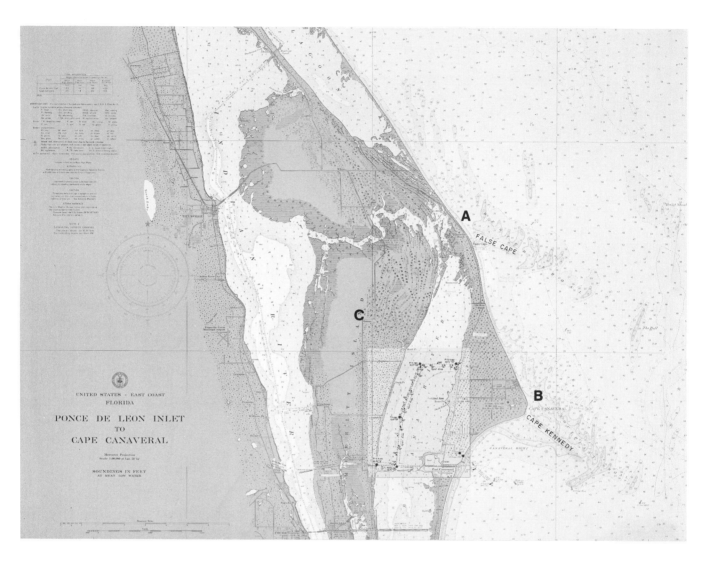

6.15 Chart showing Cape Kennedy and False Cape, an older cuspate foreland. U.S. Coast and Geodetic Survey, 1931.

resistant to erosion than many other parts of the sandy Atlantic shoreline.

CAPE KENNEDY (CANAVERAL), FLORIDA [Figs. 6.15 to 6.18]

As our chief rocket launching site, Cape Kennedy has received international recognition; but, of course, because of security, we are not in a position to obtain evidence of changes that this cuspate foreland has undergone since the base was built. Douglas Johnson referred to Cape Kennedy (then Canaveral) as an example of a cuspate foreland that had developed by aggradation of symmetrical ridges on both sides, developing False Cape (A in Fig. 6.15), and then had prograded to the south, building the present cape (B). Just prior to the construction of the missile site, Maurice Rosalsky, of the College of the City of New York, studied the cape. With the help of excellent U.S. Geological Survey topographic maps (5-foot contours), he was able to determine the nature of the ridges. In some respects, these are shown still better in aerial photos (Fig. 6.17). Studying the pattern of the ridges, Rosalsky found, as did Johnson, that the cape had migrated southward and eastward (Fig. 6.16). Mer-

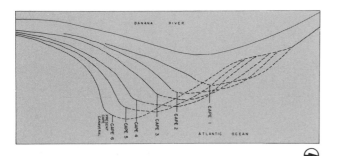

6.16 Stages in the evolution of Cape Kennedy (formerly Cape Canaveral). From Rosalsky (1960).

6.18 Truncation of old beach ridges by modern beach just north of False Cape, Florida. U.S. Coast and Geodetic Survey, 1948.

6.17 Aerial photo of Cape Kennedy showing successive beach ridges, which permit reconstruction of history of growth. U.S. Department of Agriculture, 1943.

ritt Island (C in Fig. 6.15) appears to represent a still earlier stage of the cape. The new cape is about 9 miles south of the point shown by the remnants of barriers at the end of Merritt Island. As in the cuspate forelands to the north, there is evidence of deposition on the southeast face of Cape Kennedy, and the old beach and dune ridges on the northeast face are clearly truncated (Fig. 6.18). The curve, representing an earlier point (A in Fig. 6.17), is obviously to the northwest of its present position.

Shoals extend seaward 8 miles to the east-southeast of Cape Kennedy. Here again, as off the

northern cuspate forelands, we can see longitudinal ridges in the shoals near the coast and transverse ridges on the outside. Another shoal, parallel to that of Cape Kennedy, was built out from near the end of the old cape at the outer point of Merritt Island. Here, the ridges are all transverse to the general direction of the shoal.

Cape Kennedy differs from the other cuspate forelands to the north in showing more symmetry on the two sides (Fig. 6.15). This was also true of the old cape represented by Merritt Island. In both cases, a thick land mass developed with an alternation of beach or dune ridges and intervening marshes. Cape Kennedy is also distinct from the Hatteras group of forelands in the great extent of thin barriers on both sides. The nearest natural inlets are 50 miles north and 40 miles south, although an artificial inlet was dug 5 miles south of the cape.

6.19 Lake Worth, Florida, a narrow coastal lagoon and a town of the same name on an old beach ridge inland from the lagoon. In the western part of the illustration is a limestone plain pitted by small sinkholes with tree islands, which constitute the eastern edge of the Everglades. U.S. Department of Agriculture, 1940.

The explanation of this cuspate foreland, which represents the only protrusion beyond an otherwise straight Florida coast, is not immediately apparent. The mapping of ancient shorelines by F. S. MacNeil indicates that the coast may have been straight in Pamlico time, during the last interglacial stage some 100,000 years ago. The cape probably developed when the sea rose to nearly its present level in a relatively warm period, about 25,000 to 40,000 years ago. The Gulf Stream, flowing north from the Florida Straits, first diverges significantly at Cape Kennedy. This divergence produces countercurrents that eddy in such a way as to allow deposition outside the shore, thus producing the two sets of beach ridges that grew together to develop a cuspate foreland.

PALM BEACH–DELRAY BEACH AREA, FLOR-IDA [Figs. 6.19 and 2.24]   Palm Beach (A in Fig. 2.24), 120 miles south of Cape Kennedy, is located on the barrier on the ocean side of Lake Worth, a narrow coastal lagoon inland from a 0.5-mile-wide barrier. Jetties at the inlet, built between 1918 and 1925, resulted in the accumulation of 1,500 feet of sand on the north side. The beach front is now offset at the inlet by that amount. A trace of the prejetty beach can be observed by a line of vegetation (B in Fig. 2.24). A 1959 coastal chart shows that this new land has now been subdivided into homesites. Peanut Island, just inside the inlet, is a tidal delta formed before the jetties were constructed.

North of Palm Beach, the continental shelf has narrowed gradually in approaching the northern entrance to the Straits of Florida. At Lake Worth Inlet, a 2-mile-wide shelf terminates at 90 feet, and the water 5 miles offshore is 600 feet deep.

The general width of the sand beach at Palm Beach is only 50 to 100 feet. This sand contains about 40 percent shell detritus coming mostly from offshore. Outcrops of coquina limestone occur also on the shore 7 miles south of Palm Beach and at Boca Raton, 14 miles farther south.

Behind the modern beach and coastal lagoon, there is an older Holocene beach (A in Fig. 6.19) at the town of Lake Worth, 6 miles south of Palm Beach. Most of the East Coast cities of southern Florida are located on a continuation of this older beach landward from the coastal lagoon. A marshy belt with two lakes just west of the town is largely a filled lagoon (B) behind the older beach. These blocked lakes at the town of Lake Worth seem to indicate two former inlets into this lagoon. The photograph also shows the eastern portion of the great swamp area known as the Everglades (C). It extends west from Palm Beach and Lake Worth about 80 miles to Lake Okeechobee. Soil in the Everglades is very thin and is derived largely from peat and muck formed by marsh vegetation. This thin soil rests on limestone bedrock throughout the area. The numerous small ponds are water-filled sinkholes in the limestone. When the Florida Peninsula was emerged by the lowered sea level of glacial stages, the limestone, which makes up the bedrock of most of the Florida Peninsula, was extensively dissolved because of increased circulation of ground water. Many caves were formed and connected with the surface by a multitude of sinkholes. When sea level rose after the latest glacial stage, the caves filled with water; and, in southern Florida, which is very flat and near sea level, the sinkholes were also filled. Shrub and tree islands often start in partly filled sinkholes where peaty soil is a little thicker. Many of the lighter patches in the central parts of small ponds (D) are the early stages of such "tree islands."

The Lake Worth lagoon ends about 12 miles south of Palm Beach; and, from there for 35 miles to Hollywood (just north of Miami), the old narrow coastal lagoon is mostly filled with sediment, but the Intracoastal Waterway has been dredged or cut through between Lake Worth and Biscayne Bay near Miami. Between Delray Beach and Boca Raton, the Intracoastal Waterway lies behind the narrow beach. Although sand has been trapped on the north side of the jetty at Boca Raton Inlet, the accumulation is only about 100 feet wide compared with the 1,500 feet at Palm Beach. The narrower beaches and smaller amount of beach drifting in southern Florida are related to the increasing distance from the northern source of quartz sand and to man's interference with littoral current movement of sand by jetty and groin construction. Southern Florida has been struck by many hurricanes which erode its beaches; and, unless they are replenished artificially, recovery is problematic.

MIAMI BEACH–NORTHERN BISCAYNE BAY AREA, FLORIDA[2] [Figs. 6.20 and 6.21]   Miami Beach lies near the very southern end of the long belt of sandy barriers (described in Chapters 3 to 6) that extend north to Long Island. The beach (Fig. 6.20) is about 9 miles long from Bakers Haulover Inlet (A) on the north to Government Cut (B), the entrance to Miami Harbor. The former was opened artificially in 1924 and the latter in 1905. To the south (Fig. 6.21) are three islands with small intervening channels; the small Fisher Island, the 2-mile Virginia Key, and the 4-mile Key Biscayne. The last two are now connected to the mainland by bridges (built after the date of the aerial photo).

Two separate bedrock ridges diverge at the northern end of the Miami area and control its configuration. The more inland of these is the Miami oölite ridge, which includes the eastern part of the city of Miami (C in Fig. 6.20). This was a shallow-water marine limestone bank formed during the higher sea level of the last interglacial stage about 100,000 years ago. Beginning at the northern end of the bay near North Miami, this bank forms the western shore of Biscayne Bay. Farther north on the Florida East Coast, the Miami oölite interfingers with a coquina limestone of similar age. To the southwest, the ridge curves inland for 30 miles as far as Homestead and then continues westward under the Everglades toward Cape Sable, the southwest point of the Florida mainland.

The other bedrock feature, formed by the Key Largo limestone, is an ancient coral reef of about the same age as the Miami oölite but formed farther seaward in slightly deeper water. Its upper surface lies about 10 feet below sea level in the Miami Beach area but nearly merges with the Miami oölite ridge at North Miami. It extends for 15 miles southward from Miami as a shoal (A in Fig. 6.21) separating Biscayne Bay from the ocean and from Soldier Key,

[2] Much information has been derived from a 1968 report by Harold Rogers Wanless.

15 miles south of Miami Beach, and is exposed in the Florida Keys for 125 miles to Big Pine Key.

Between the Miami oölite ridge and the Key Largo limestone, the shallow depression forming Biscayne Bay (D in Fig. 6.20) broadens southward to a width of about 10 miles near Soldier Key, at the southern end of the Miami area (Fig. 6.1). Farther south, this passes through a succession of narrower bays and broadens to about 35 miles in Florida Bay, separating mainland Florida from the Florida Keys. It was in Manatee Bay of this area, in 1893, that an attempt was made to rid the water of hyacinths, which were clogging the bay, by breeding manatees (sea cows) because they feed extensively on vegetation. Unfortunately, the attempt was not successful.

The Miami oölite ridge, which rises to nearly 25 feet above sea level in Miami, slopes gently westward under the swamp deposits of the Everglades just west of Miami. Sinkholes are found throughout this region.

A little quartz sand and some worn shell material on the outer beaches of Miami are derived from local limestone or coquina outcrops to the north. The proportion of shell in the sand increases as quartz diminishes. James Martens has reported 40 percent shell detritus 5 miles north of the entrance to Miami Harbor and 70 percent 5 miles farther north. Because of the shell, the beach sand is much coarser than in most beaches farther north, such as the very fine sand of Daytona Beach, which is all quartz.

The continental shelf off Miami Beach is 2 miles wide, a continuation of the narrow, shallow shelf that extends as far north as Palm Beach. To the south off Key Biscayne, the shelf widens to 4 miles and then to more than 10 miles where Biscayne Bay has only shoals on its eastern margin separating it from the Straits of Florida. East of the 40-foot-deep shelf margin, the slope descends to 1,000 feet in 3 miles. Partly because of the proximity to the margin of the continental shelf, there are relatively steep slopes near shore. Profiles made by the Army Corps of Engineers all along Miami Beach in 1937 generally showed depths of 10 feet about 600 feet offshore and 20 feet between 2,000 and 4,000 feet

6.20 Miami and Miami Beach, Florida. Miami Beach extends from Bakers Haulover Inlet (A) to Government Cut (B), both artificial inlets. In Biscayne Bay, there are numerous man-made islands. U.S. Department of Agriculture, 1940.

farther out. More recent profiles show still steeper slopes, including bedrock in 25 feet of water 500 feet offshore. This steepening of slopes should result in disastrous loss of sand.

Some 3,000 years ago, much of the Key Largo limestone ridge was at or near sea level, and a little inland from the present beach. Behind it was a shallow lagoon in which marine mollusks lived, perhaps with mangroves growing on bedrock in slightly shoaler places. This is recorded by lagoonal clays that were deposited behind the protection of the bedrock ridge, and which are preserved beneath the sands of the present barrier islands. Mangrove peat near the present surface of Virginia Key and Key Biscayne (B in Fig. 6.21) accumulated on sands on the bay sides of the barrier islands. About 2,000 years ago, barrier spits began extending southward, bringing in quartz sand and shells from coquina limestone to the north. This was the beginning of the barrier sand beaches in the Miami area.

Successive beach ridges formed as the spits were lengthened southward, and each one hooked westward at its southern terminus. Although the evidence of these beach ridges has been virtually destroyed from Miami Beach by urban development, they are still readily discernible on the aerial photographs of Virginia Key and Key Biscayne taken in 1940 (C). Probably the beach lay seaward about 0.5 mile from the present shore, as suggested by the light-colored shoal (D), and formed a continuous sand spit until erosion cut back the beach and new inlets opened. The inlets separating Virginia Key from Miami Beach to the north and Key Biscayne to the south may have opened either at times of hurricanes or perhaps because of a change in direction of offshore tidal currents before the arrival of the white men. On the present beaches of both keys, fossil mangrove roots are found at beach level. These had grown in a lagoon that lay behind the now-eroded beach. Erosion of these keys has been accelerated because the source of sand from the north was cut off by construction of the Miami Harbor jetties. Three months after destructive Hurricane Betsy of September 1965, abundant evidence of beach erosion was seen on these keys.

Cape Florida (E), at the southern tip of Key Biscayne, is the end of the chain of Atlantic barrier islands. Immediately south of this, shoals over the submarine Key Largo ridge form a continuous wave baffle between the ocean and Biscayne Bay. Storms

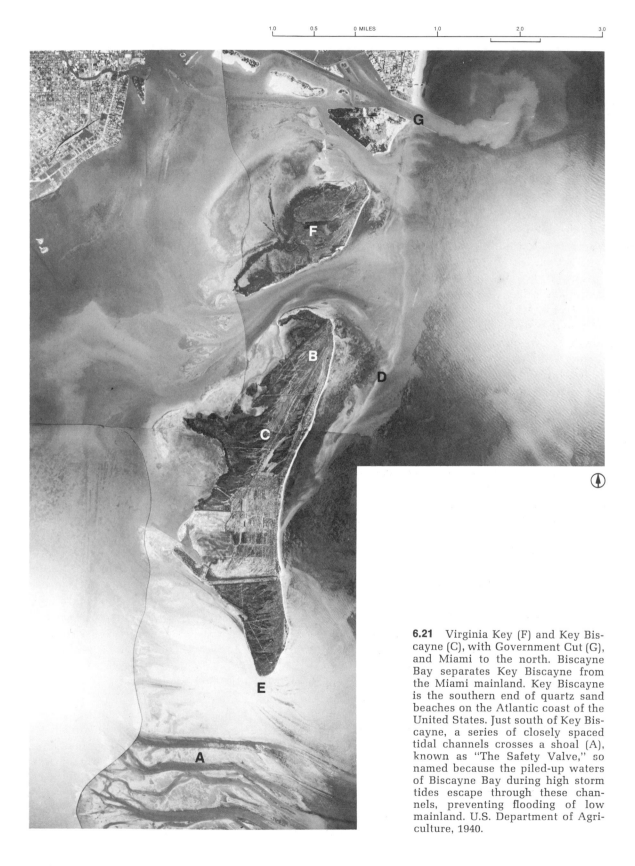

6.21 Virginia Key (F) and Key Biscayne (C), with Government Cut (G), and Miami to the north. Biscayne Bay separates Key Biscayne from the Miami mainland. Key Biscayne is the southern end of quartz sand beaches on the Atlantic coast of the United States. Just south of Key Biscayne, a series of closely spaced tidal channels crosses a shoal (A), known as "The Safety Valve," so named because the piled-up waters of Biscayne Bay during high storm tides escape through these channels, preventing flooding of low mainland. U.S. Department of Agriculture, 1940.

have cut a series of closely spaced sluiceways across these shoals, perhaps when sea level was a little lower than at present. They are called the "Safety Valve" (A) because this shoal area, with its tidal channels, controls much of the water entering and leaving the bay during hurricanes. A total of twenty-six hurricanes were recorded in the 70-year period from 1874 to 1944.

Two years after the Bakers Haulover Inlet (A in Fig. 6.20) had been opened in Miami Beach, the jetties and other shore structures were wholly destroyed in the severe hurricane of September 19, 1926, leaving the concrete highway bridge standing alone in the ocean waves. Some of the great loss of life in this hurricane in the Miami area occurred because people on the mainland drove across the causeway over Biscayne Bay to Miami Beach to see the damage. The temporarily quiet weather in which they ventured out was during the passage of the huge eye of the hurricane. Many were caught on the causeways after the eye had passed. Then the waters rose and the gales were renewed. The Bakers Haulover Inlet was reconstructed by 1928. Here, the jetties are 150 feet long. At the entrance to Miami Harbor (B), the north jetty is 4,000 feet long and the south jetty 3,000 feet. Contrary to the name, not all of the island of Miami Beach has sand in front of the seawalls, and most of the beaches are private, being maintained by hotels and motels. To protect these beaches from excessive erosion, a series of groins 170 to 200 feet long and 250 feet apart have been constructed for several miles. According to a report by the U.S. Army Corps of Engineers, erosion between 1884 and 1944 had caused about 500 feet of beach recession. This erosion took place principally at times of major storms, nearly half during the 1926 hurricane. Another hurricane as violent as the 1926 storm might destroy most of the rest of the sand beaches on the island.

Littoral currents are predominantly to the south, although north currents induced by southeast and south winds are also important. The shore jetties at Bakers Haulover Inlet have trapped little sand, but the beach is wider than average for a distance of about a mile north of the long jetty at the Miami Harbor entrance, whereas Virginia Key and Key Biscayne, south of the harbor entrance, have suffered increased beach erosion since the jetty was constructed.

KEY LARGO–ELLIOTT KEY AREA, FLORIDA[3] [Fig. 6.22]   The northeastern tip of Key Largo (A in Fig. 6.22) is 30 miles southwest of Miami and near the northern end of the coral reef chain constituting the Florida Keys. The narrow shoals and low islands formed by the Key Largo Pleistocene reef limestone separate the Atlantic Ocean (B) from the southwestern end of Biscayne Bay (C). A modern coral reef is growing in a belt 1 to 3 miles offshore in water a few feet deep. The beaches are entirely calcareous sand because this area is beyond the southern margin of quartz sand. Limestone, lime mud, and mangrove peat are the only sedimentary types present.

Key Largo limestone, although only about 90,000 years old, is completely lithified; and quarries are operated in it for building stone. In the intertidal zone, the limestone has been extensively weathered by a combination of boring organisms and solution, giving it a rough honeycombed surface. The old coral reef can be observed in the cut where the Key Largo Canal is crossed by U.S. Route 1. Broad Creek (D) and Caesars Creek (E) have channels about 10 to 22 feet deep cut through the reef rock by the combined effects of tidal currents and accelerated erosion during hurricanes. Because flow in these "creeks" is reversed between times of flood and ebb tide, they have formed double tidal deltas, the larger deltas being on the ocean or modern reef side. The reason for the larger seaward deltas appears to be that water from prevailing easterly winds tends to pile up in Biscayne Bay coming in through the "Safety Valve." This water then moves south in Biscayne Bay behind the protection of Elliott Key (F) and exits through the first available channel, which is Caesars Creek. This southward drift of water in the area produces a lop-sided delta (G) at Caesars Creek.

Another type of change in this vicinity is indicated from comparison between the 1940 aerial photos (not shown) and those of 1964. Several of the small islands have become connected during this interval. Apparently this is the result of sediment fill nearly to sea level and then growth of mangrove peat filling the shallow passages between the islands. Thus the land area is increased, although marshy conditions will exist in the new land until the marshes are drained or filled artificially.

[3] Much information has been derived from a 1968 report by Harold Rogers Wanless.

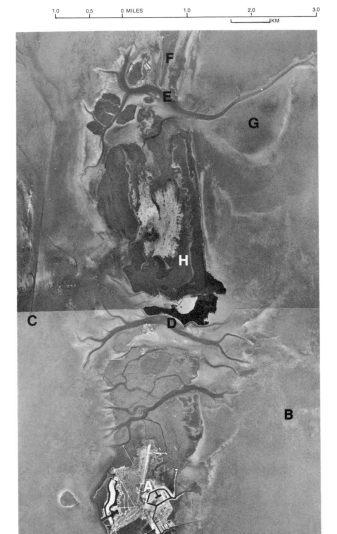

Scale: 1.0 — 0.5 — 0 MILES — 1.0 — 2.0 — 3.0 / KM

6.22 The northeast end of the Florida Keys, showing Key Largo (A), a series of tidal channels, called Broad Creek (D), Old Rhodes Key (H), Caesars Creek (E), and Elliott Key (F). The channels, cut in old reef rock, are double tidal deltas on the ocean and bay sides. From color photographs by U.S. Coast and Geodetic Survey, 1964.

FLORIDA BAY–MATECUMBE AREA, FLORIDA [Fig. 6.23]   Florida Bay, illustrated here by high-altitude photography, is about 40 miles southwest of the Key Largo–Elliott Key area. The aerial photo shows from the north (top) down the southern margin of the Florida mainland (H), called the Everglades; Florida Bay, here about 18 miles wide (I); a portion of the Key Largo limestone ridge, including Upper Matecumbe Key and other keys along U.S. Route 1 (D); the modern reef tract south of the keys (A), shown by lighter gray tones, 1 or 2 miles offshore; and the western margin of the Straits of Florida (B), where the water deepens within less than a mile from shore 20 to 250 feet. Light bands elongate parallel to the shore show some of the outer luxuriant reefs.

The water between the growing reef and the exposed reef rock of the keys (shown by a darker tone at D) is mostly 10 to 15 feet deep, but some of the lighter-toned outer zones are even deeper, and some are gray colored due to clear water.

This portion of the Florida Keys is about 0.5 mile wide, and is interrupted by five bedrock channels 15 to 20 feet deep, each with a tidal delta at each end. The bridge on the overseas highway between Upper and Lower Matecumbe Keys (E) crosses three of these channels (called "creeks" farther north) and is about 2 miles long.

In 1935, the Florida East Coast Railroad was in the process of constructing a line from Miami to Key West, and many of the bridges were completed so that some local trains were running. On September 2 of that year, one of the most intense hurricanes ever recorded in the Western Hemisphere struck this area. A barometer on Lower Matecumbe Key registered 26.35 inches, said to be next to the lowest barometric reading ever recorded on earth.[4] Winds in the Florida Keys exceeded 200 miles per hour, and virtually no structure on these low keys was able to withstand the combined forces of the wind, hurricane tides, and waves. The loss of life was about 400 persons, many of them railroad construction workers. Plans to complete the overseas railroad were given up, and the keys were left as a belt of tremendous

---

[4] The lowest was 26.18 inches in the Pacific east of the Philippines in 1927. The 1969 Hurricane Camille may have had a slightly lower barometer.

desolation. A few years later, the route intended as a railroad was reconstructed as the overseas highway.

M. M. Ball, E. A. Shinn, and K. W. Stockman studied in detail the effects of Hurricane Donna, September 9–10, 1960, on a portion of the Florida Keys about 10 miles east of Upper Matecumbe Key. Wind velocities in the study area were 140 to 180 miles per hour. A careful survey of the area before the storm was available. They found that the amount of boulder-sized rubble accumulated during the hurricane far exceeded that produced under normal conditions and concluded that most rubble in reef tracts is formed during hurricanes. At the same time, much sand-sized skeletal debris was moved and redeposited in flats behind the reef. Much life was destroyed by the storm. Supratidal flats acquired additional layers of stranded lime mud. In Biscayne Bay, after each of three hurricanes, a layer of coarse sand was found to be present at the surface in areas of normal lime mud accumulation. However, within ten months, burrowing mollusks had already destroyed this layer each time.

In this region, Florida Bay is largely 2 to 9 feet deep. Much of it has a bedrock floor away from the conspicuous mud banks floored with fine lime mud which, upon lithification, would form a fine-textured limestone, a very common type in the geological record. In the bay, a series of mounds and shoals (F in Fig. 6.23) form an interlacing network. Some of these have been built so nearly to sea level that mangrove trees have begun growth on the higher parts of the shoals. The mound type of accumulations in Florida Bay were largely unaffected by the 1960 storm.

The southern border of the Everglades is a narrow band of mangrove trees (G), behind which there is an immense saw-grass flat (H); and, in the deeper part, open ponds are still unfilled. Because of seasonal rainfall, standing water is deeper in the Everglades during the summer than during the winter.

6.23 High-altitude photography showing the overseas highway and the Florida Keys interrupted by several tidal channels with double tidal deltas; Florida Bay, with a branching series of lime mud islands; and the Everglades, at the southern end of mainland Florida. U.S. Army Map Service, 1951.

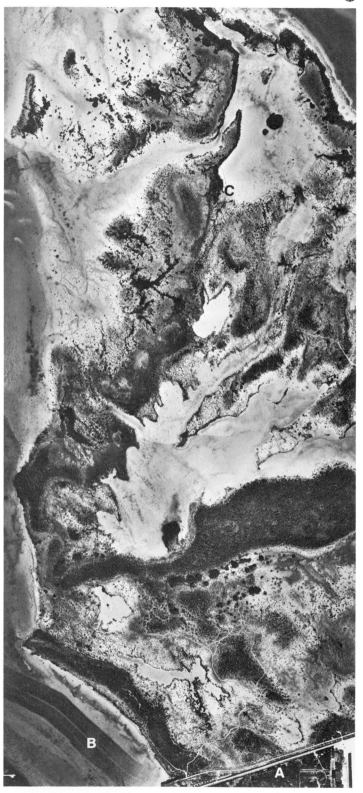

BIG PINE TO CUDJOE KEY, FLORIDA [Figs. 6.24 and 6.25] For 35 miles southwest of Lower Matecumbe Key, the islands continue to conform in their long dimensions to the general curve of the great arc made by the Florida Keys. However, beyond that point, a striking change takes place and the predominant elongation is at right angles to the arc (Fig. 6.25). Big Pine Key is the easternmost and largest of these northwesterly trending islands. After an almost straight course for 75 miles, the overseas highway makes its first large bend when it reaches Big Pine Key and for a few miles follows the northwesterly trend of the key. In this area, the islands are larger, with axes as long as 6 or 7 miles. Unlike the islands to the east, they are composed not of the coralliferous Key Largo limestone but of the Miami oölite, a rock of oval pellets of limestone, which directly overlie the reef rock. As at Matecumbe, the modern reef belt lies to the southeast of this group of keys.

J. E. Hoffmeister, K. W. Stockman, and H. G. Multer have proposed that during the last interglacial stage of high sea level the Miami oölite accumulated in banks piled up by currents on the back reef area, while reefs were forming in slightly deeper water. Tidal currents cut channels across the oölite banks at intervals, explaining their present separation into a string of keys. Then the oölites were lithified, forming a hard limestone; and the forms of the banks were preserved. When sea level lowered at the time of the last glaciation, solution weathering destroyed parts of the oölitic limestone. In postglacial time, with rise in sea level, the banks were again nearly submerged; but on the flats at the very irregular margins of the sea, mangrove trees have grown.

Cudjoe Key (Fig. 6.24), about 20 miles northeast of Key West, extends principally north of the overseas highway (A). The waters bordering the key are less than 6 feet deep, with a channel dredged to 10 feet just west of the island (B). The island rises only a few feet above sea level, and most of its lighter portion seen in the photo consists of somewhat disaggregated Miami oölite. Along the borders of the key and fringing a brackish-water lagoon in the north-

6.24 Cudjoe Key, one of the Miami oölite islands, showing many mangrove shorelines (dark tone). The channels separating these limestone islands were largely cut by hurricanes before lithification of the oölite deposits. U.S. Coast and Geodetic Survey, 1957.

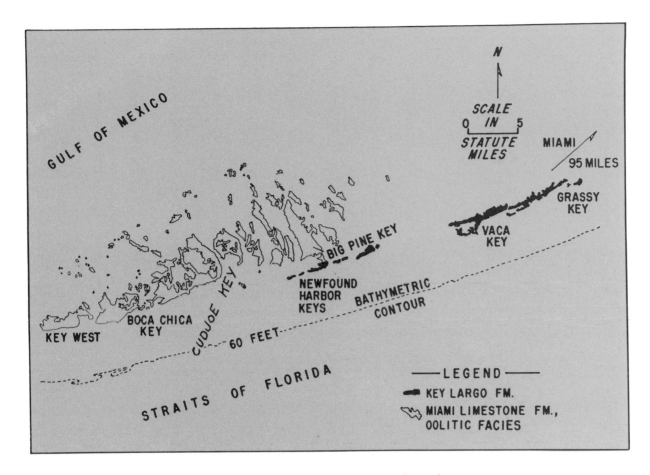

6.25 Geologic map of the Lower Keys of Florida, showing narrow keys elongate from northeast to southwest composed of Pleistocene reef limestones of the Key Largo Formation and wider keys elongate from the northwest to southeast composed of the Miami oölite (not a reef rock). From Hoffmeister, Stockman, and Multer (1967).

ern part (C) are mangrove trees rooted in the shallow water. Lime mud deposits are forming in the shallow lagoons and passages between the islands.

Although the area has had a long history of destructive hurricanes, the stiffness of the lime mud and induration of the Miami oölite have permitted little coastal change during the major storms; but vegetation that was inundated by hurricane tides has been killed and man-made structures have been destroyed.

MARQUESAS KEYS, FLORIDA [Fig. 6.26]
Marquesas Keys, 30 miles west of Key West, are in appearance about the closest approach we have to the atolls of the South Seas. The keys form a subcircular chain enclosing a lagoon 2 to 3 miles in diameter.

The largest island lies along the northern half of the lagoon, and a string of eight islets partly enclose the remainder. The lagoon has depths ranging to 10 feet. It is connected with the sea by six tidal channels.

In spite of the atoll-like form of these keys, they are reported to be composed of Miami oölite and are not actively growing coral reefs. Lime mud or sand forms very narrow beaches on the outside of the keys, and lime floors the lagoon. The Marquesas Keys are a part of the chain extending from Key West to the Dry Tortugas Islands, 50 miles farther west. The belt of modern reefs lies about 5 miles south of Marquesas Keys and is separated from them by water locally 50 feet deep. The southwest end of the Atlantic coast of the United States may be considered to be at the Dry Tortugas Islands.

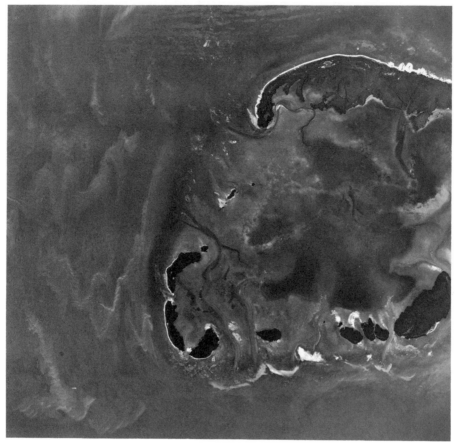

6.26 Marquesas Keys, west of Key West, Florida. A circular group of islands resembling an atoll, composed of Miami oölite. From color photo by U.S. Coast and Geodetic Survey, 1960.

REFERENCES

Ball, M. M., E. A. Shinn, and K. W. Stockman, 1967. The geologic effects of Hurricane Donna in South Florida. *Jour. Geol.*, vol. 75, pp. 583–597.

Corps of Engineers. U.S. Army, 1935. *Beach Erosion at Folly Beach, South Carolina.* House of Representatives, 74th Congr., 1st Sess., Document 156, pp. 1–17.

————, 1936. *Beach Erosion Study of Bakers Haulover Inlet, Florida.* House of Representatives, 79th Congr., 2d Sess., Document 527.

————, 1937. *Current and Sand Movement Study at Miami Beach, Florida.* House of Representatives, 75th Congr., 1st Sess., Document 169.

————, 1948. *Palm Beach, Florida, Beach Erosion Study.* House of Representatives, 80th Congr., 2d Sess., Document 772.

————, 1948. *Jupiter Island, Florida, Beach Erosion Study.* House of Representatives, 80th Congr., 2d Sess., Document 9.

El-Ashry, M. T., 1966. Photointerpretation of shoreline changes in selected areas along the Atlantic and Gulf coasts of the United States. Univ. Illinois, Ph.D. thesis in geology.

Ginsburg, R. N., 1953. Intertidal erosion on the Florida keys. *Bull. Marine Sci. of Gulf and Caribbean*, vol. 3, no. 1, pp. 55–69.

Hoffmeister, J. E., K. W. Stockman, and H. G. Multer, 1967. Miami limestone of Florida and its recent Bahamian counterpart. *Geol. Soc. Amer. Bull.*, vol. 78, pp. 175–190.

Hoyt, J. H., 1967. Barrier island formation. *Geol. Soc. Amer. Bull.*, vol. 78, pp. 1125–1136.

————, and J. R. Hails, 1967. Pleistocene shoreline sediments in coastal Georgia: deposition and modification. *Science*, vol. 155, no. 3769, pp. 1541–1543.

————, and V. J. Henry, 1964. Late Pleistocene and Recent sedimentation, central Georgia coast. In *Developments in Sedimentology*, vol. 1, *Deltaic and Shallow Marine Deposits*, Elsevier Publishing Company, Amsterdam, pp. 170–176.

Johnson, D. W., 1938. *Shore Processes and Shoreline Development.* John Wiley & Sons, New York.

Kaye, Clifford A., 1961. Shore-erosion study of the coasts of Georgia and northwest Florida. *U.S. Geol. Survey Rept. for U.S. Study Comm., Southwest River Basins.*

MacNeil, F. S., 1949. Pleistocene shorelines in Florida and Georgia. *U.S. Geol. Survey Prof. Paper 221-F*, pp. 95–107.

Martens, J. H. C., 1931. Beaches of Florida. *Florida State Geol. Survey, 21st-22nd Ann. Rept.*, pp. 69–119.

Richards, H. G., 1938. Marine Pleistocene of Florida. *Geol. Soc. Amer. Bull.*, vol. 49, pp. 1267–1296.

Rosalsky, Maurice B., 1960. The physiography of Cape Canaveral, Florida. *Rocks and Minerals*, Mar.–Apr., pp. 99–102.

Shinn, Eugene, 1963. Spur and groove formation on the Florida reef tract. *Sedimentary Petrology*, vol. 33, pp. 297–302.

Wanless, Harold Rogers, 1968. Recent depositional history, Biscayne Bay area, Florida. Univ. Miami, M.S. thesis in marine science.

Zeigler, J. M., 1959. Origin of the Sea Islands of the southeastern United States. *Geographical Rev.*, vol. 49, no. 2, pp. 222–237.

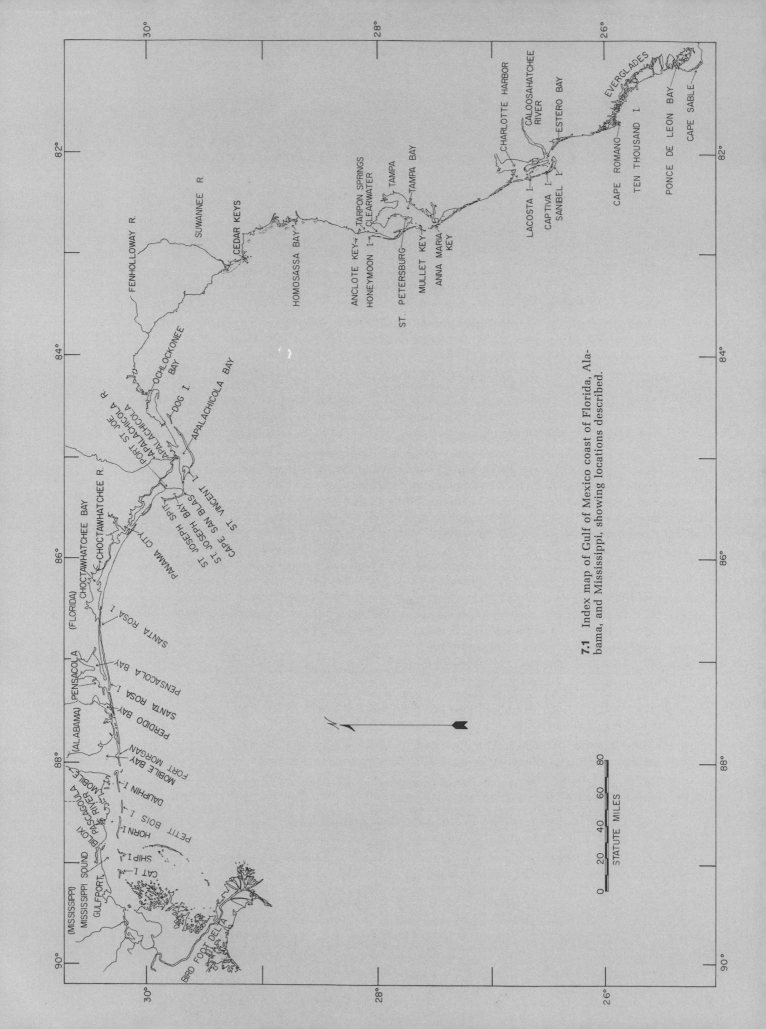

7.1 Index map of Gulf of Mexico coast of Florida, Alabama, and Mississippi, showing locations described.

90°   88°   86°   84°   82°

(MISSISSIPPI)
MISSISSIPPI SOUND
BILOXI
GULFPORT
PASCAGOULA RIVER
MOBILE RIVER
CAT I.
SHIP I.
HORN I.
PETIT BOIS I.
DAUPHIN I.
MT.
BIRD FOOT DELTA

(ALABAMA) PENSACOLA
(FLORIDA)
FORT MORGAN
MOBILE BAY
PERDIDO BAY
SANTA ROSA I.
PENSACOLA BAY
SANTA ROSA I.
CHOCTAWHATCHEE BAY
CHOCTAWHATCHEE R.

PANAMA CITY
ST JOSEPH SPIT
ST JOSEPH BAY
CAPE SAN BLAS
PORT ST JOE
APALACHICOLA R.
APALACHICOLA
APALACHICOLA BAY
ST VINCENT I.
DOG I.
OCHLOCKONEE BAY

FENHOLLOWAY R.
SUWANNEE R.
CEDAR KEYS
HOMOSASSA BAY

ANCLOTE KEY
TARPON SPRINGS
HONEYMOON I.
CLEARWATER
TAMPA
ST. PETERSBURG
TAMPA BAY
MULLET KEY
ANNA MARIA KEY

CHARLOTTE HARBOR
CALOOSAHATCHEE RIVER
ESTERO BAY
LACOSTA I.
CAPTIVA I.
SANIBEL I.
EVERGLADES
CAPE ROMANO
TEN THOUSAND I.
PONCE DE LEON BAY
CAPE SABLE

30°   28°   26°

N

0   20   40   60   80
STATUTE MILES

Alternating White Beaches and Swamps

West Florida to Mississippi Sound

7   The 700-mile coast from Cape Sable of southern Florida to the Mississippi Delta includes, besides the long west coast of Florida, an island-fringed south shore of Alabama and Mississippi (Fig. 7.1). The Florida portion, constituting 80 percent, has an alternation between raggedly indented swamps and long sand beaches with many barrier islands. The swampy coast reaches from Cape Sable to Cape Romano, where the sand barriers take over as far north as Tarpon Springs; then there is a long stretch of swamp around the coastal bend to the Ochlockonee River, near Tallahassee, where more sand barriers exist. The latter extend all the way to the Mississippi Delta.

All this coast is low and flat, and the average wave energy is decidedly less than along the Atlantic coast because of being in the lee of predominant east winds and because of the short fetch of the occasional westerlies. Nevertheless, hurricanes have frequently struck nearly all parts of this coast, including the 1969 Hurricane Camille, one of the worst in history.

As along the East Coast, all parts of the Gulf Coast were drowned by postglacial rise in sea level. The largest estuaries are Charlotte Harbor and Tampa Bay, Florida, and Mobile Bay, Alabama. There is one prominent cuspate foreland, Cape San Blas, in peninsular western Florida; and there are some other smaller ones.

CAPE SABLE AREA, FLORIDA [Fig. 7.2]   The Cape Sable area, at the southwest tip of the Florida mainland, is a coastal belt about 20 miles long with three slightly projecting capes. Bedrock is the Miami oölite, which lies about 5 feet below sea level along much of the coast and is covered with peat, marl, and shell sand.

Extensive studies in this area by David Scholl, William Spackman, and

7.2 Cape Sable consists of three small cuspate fore-lands at the southwestern tip of the Florida mainland. There are beaches at the cape points, but the rest is largely a red mangrove coast. Positions of five shorelines are indicated by lines. Photo mosaic of old shoreline demarcation from Spackman, Scholl, and Taft (1964).

others, have shown that sea level has risen about 12 feet in the past 4,400 years; amounting to 1 foot per century from 2400 to 1500 B.C. and 0.15 foot per century between 1500 B.C. and the present. This rise in sea level is considered the result of glacial melting in a region that has been tectonically stable during the entire postglacial period.

About 4,400 years ago, the Miami oölite rock ridge stood 7 feet above sea level and formed a southern rim for the Everglades. At the same time, a lower area to the north was swampy with freshwater lakes. Some 3,000 years ago, the rising sea level had buried the rock ridge; but red mangroves, encroaching from the Gulf border of the Everglades, began to grow in the shallow marine water and contributed layers of

peat, while seaward from the peat-forming area, marine marls composed of shells and shell detritus were accumulating. As the rate of subsidence had slowed greatly, the shore was able to prograde seaward because the mangroves growing out into the shallow water trapped longshore drifting marl sediment. However, during major storms, the trees were toppled and the peat near the sea border was eroded; but, between storms, the mangroves renewed a progradation of the shore. Thus in the 5-foot interval above bedrock there is an interfingering of peat and marine marl.

Today, at the northern cape, black mangrove stumps stick up through the marine shell layer that forms the beach. Since the black mangrove generally develops a swamp a little inland behind the red mangrove, this buried forest shows that formerly the mangrove swamp extended farther seaward than at present. No sand or clay is available here, so pure shell deposits overlie pure peat. This association, upon lithification, would form a coal bed overlain by a marine limestone. Many commercial coals of the Midwest have immediate roofs of limestone, evidently indicating that coastal swamps were inundated as the ancient seas transgressed, just as has occurred recently in the Cape Sable area. The extensive marshes of southwest Florida today probably resemble the landscapes in which ancient widespread coals of the world formed.

In the Cape Sable area, Spackman has recognized four shorelines older than the present, all shown on the aerial photo mosaic (Fig. 7.2). The earliest three shorelines lie inland from a narrow coastal lagoon behind the Middle Cape. The fourth shoreline evidently developed as a barrier built up by the storm waves of a hurricane, and the beach in 1964 shows that erosion of arcs has produced a group of cuspate forelands extending seaward of the coast during the fourth stage. A photograph of the Middle Cape made in 1951 (not illustrated) shows a seaward projecting hooked spit pointing northward, which had been cut away by 1964 when the photographs for Figure 7.2 were taken.

This shore is the first area we have described in which beaches are composed wholly of shells piled up by storms from offshore marl deposits. Here we have also an illustration of how mangroves can prograde a shoreline seaward while slow subsidence is in progress.

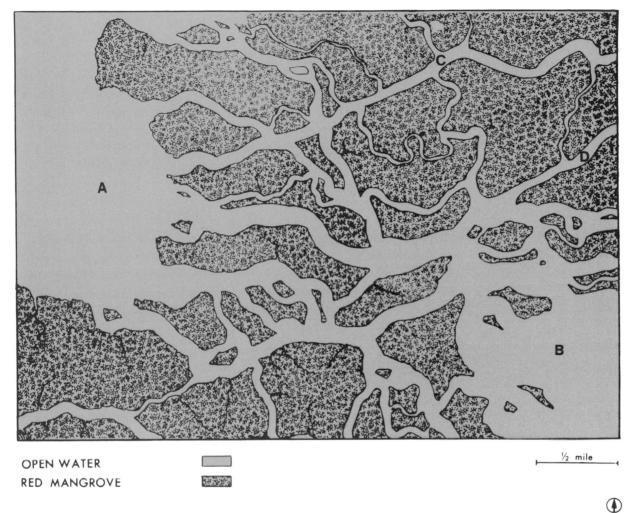

OPEN WATER

RED MANGROVE

½ mile

7.3 Ponce de Leon Bay (A), at the mouth of Shark River (C), is the entrance to Oyster Bay (B) and Whitewater Bay. The coast is entirely mangrove. Channels about 10 feet deep have been cut through mangrove peat to limestone bedrock. From Spackman, Scholl, and Taft (1964).

PONCE DE LEON BAY AND THE EVER-GLADES, FLORIDA [Figs. 7.3, 7.4, and 7.5] North of the Miami oölite ridge, the bedrock contains the Miocene Tamiami Formation, which is less resistant to erosion, and now lies 10 to 14 feet below sea level along the Gulf Coast. Ponce de Leon Bay (A in Fig. 7.3) connects inland with Oyster Bay (B) and Whitewater Bay, forming a series of open-water lagoons in the mangrove swamps, which extend southeastward about 15 miles. Shark River (C), an Everglades stream, also enters the sea at Ponce de

Leon Bay. Here, there is no beach, and red mangroves grow in seawater 2 to 4 feet deep. Coastal channels of Shark River and Little Shark River (D) are locally as deep as 10 feet below sea level. Whitewater Bay, behind the marshy islands fronting Ponce de Leon Bay, is brackish to normal marine in salinity, varying with the season. During the rainy summers, drainage from the Everglades is strong enough to fill the bays with fresh water; but, during the dry winters, sea water flows in through the channels, and marine shells are found on the bay floors several miles

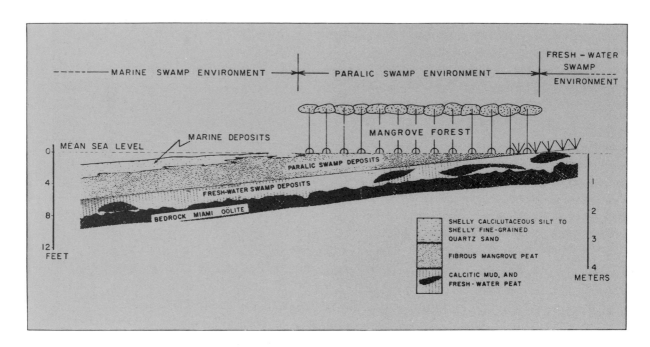

7.4 Cross section of the southwestern Florida coastal swamps, showing successive stages in a marine transgression, which has resulted in rise in sea level of about 12 feet in the past 4,000 years. From Scholl and Stuiver (1967).

inland from the open Ponce de Leon Bay.

Although drainage slopes in the marshes are gentle, river currents are strong. The river water is commonly dark colored to nearly black, because of the abundance of organic material transported from the marshes and accumulated in fine-grained marine sediments. Erosion of the channels, as in the Ponce de Leon Bay area, has often produced vertical sides down to or nearly to bedrock. In one place, a mangrove tree was found growing on top of a pillar of peat 7 feet high and only 1 foot wide.

The history of Everglades sedimentation during the past 4,400 years of gradual sea level rise has been developed by Scholl from his studies of drill cores throughout the area. He has dated events by carbon-14 measurements. Figure 7.4 is a cross section prepared by Scholl through the sediments resting on the Miami oölite in the Everglades. The initial sediment in many places is a freshwater marl such as would form in lakes, like Lake Okeechobee of central Florida. This is overlain by freshwater peat largely composed of the saw grass that fills most of the vast swamps of the Everglades (A in Fig. 7.5). Overlying this peat is the mangrove peat, generally black man-

grove underlying red mangrove. The black mangrove has a lower tolerance to salt water and could not stand the later full invasion of the sea so the red mangrove flourished when normal shallow marine water covered the area. The saltwater peat is usually overlain by marine marl. Indicative of a former low sea level, peat has been cored 2 miles offshore in the Gulf of Mexico in more than 10 feet of water. Since the sea level has gradually risen about 12 feet during the past 4,400 years, as described in connection with Cape Sable, each environmental border has shifted landward so that the sequence of sediments overlying the bedrock of southwest Florida presents a clear history of this transgression.

Broad River, a few miles north of Ponce de Leon Bay (Fig. 7.5), shows the saw-grass prairie marsh in interstream divides (A), margined by black mangrove (B), with a coastal fringe of red mangrove (C). Marine marl, not visible, is now forming offshore (D).

TEN THOUSAND ISLANDS AREA, FLORIDA [Fig. 7.6] East of Cape Romano (A) and 40 miles northwest of Ponce de Leon Bay, is a 20-mile

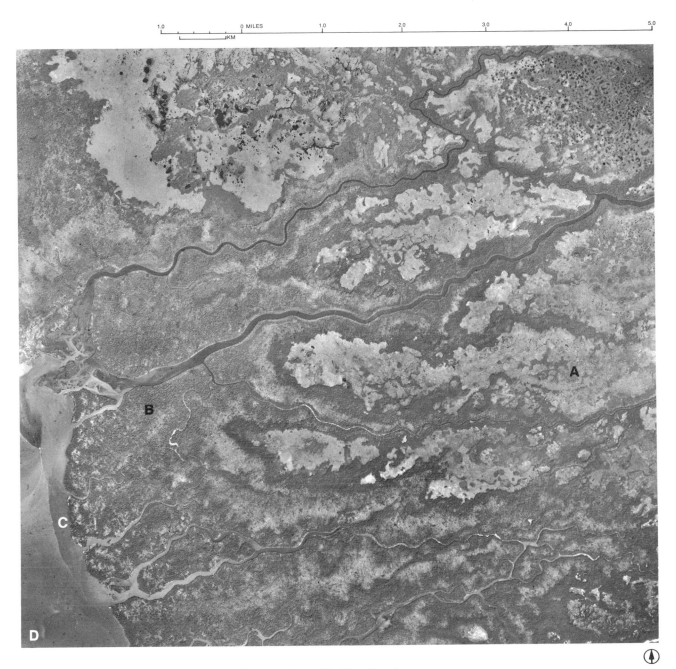

7.5 Broad River area north of Ponce de Leon Bay, Florida, showing saw-grass swamp (A) inland along stream divides; black mangrove swamps (B) bordering rivers, inland from the coast; and red mangroves (C) along the present coastline. Saw-grass peat is formed in fresh water, black mangroves are tolerant to brackish water, while red mangroves grow in normal sea water. From color aerial photograph by U.S. Coast and Geodetic Survey, 1964.

stretch of coastline called the Ten Thousand Islands. The mainland coast has the drowned mouths of several small creeks draining the Everglades area and includes the town of Everglade. Adjoining this shore is the shallow Chokoloskee Bay (B), with brown organic-rich sediment brought in by the rivers. In the bay, a series of very narrow chainlike and branching islands formed as oyster reefs and now support

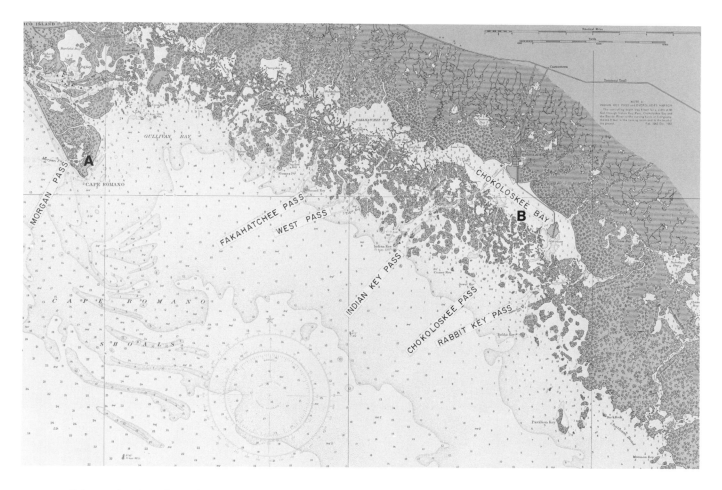

7.6 Navigation chart showing Ten Thousand Islands and Cape Romano, Florida. U.S. Coast and Geodetic Survey Chart 1254, 1965.

mangroves. Seaward from the bay is a series of irregularly shaped mangrove-covered islands, which are segmented by a number of dismembered drowned stream courses passing through Chokoloskee Bay to the outer bays and then into the Gulf of Mexico. In the open Gulf are several small mangrove-covered islands with very narrow quartz sand beaches, derived from Cape Romano to the west.

Scholl has suggested that the shoreline 4,000 years ago was at least as far seaward as the outermost islands. The streams draining the adjoining Everglades were lined with mangroves, behind which were saw-grass marshes. As sea level gradually rose, mangroves in some areas kept building upward, rooted in their own peat. Elsewhere, the mangroves were drowned by the 4- to 5-mile transgression, resulting in the dismembered stream patterns, the latter being

caused in part by tidal currents and river currents from Everglades streams. Organic reef growth, consisting of oysters in the bays and vermitoid gastropods along the open Gulf of Mexico, built small reefs, which, in turn, supported mangrove trees, thus developing the present coastal configuration. The intermittent sand beaches were probably piled up at times of hurricanes.

CAPE ROMANO, FLORIDA [Fig. 7.6]   The Cape Romano area is described by William Tanner and others as a low-energy coast with normal wave heights of only 4 inches. The cape is the southern tip of a 50-mile chain of sandy beaches and barriers originating at the mouth of the Caloosahatchie River. Quartz sand was introduced into the sea by one of the northern rivers and shifted southward by littoral

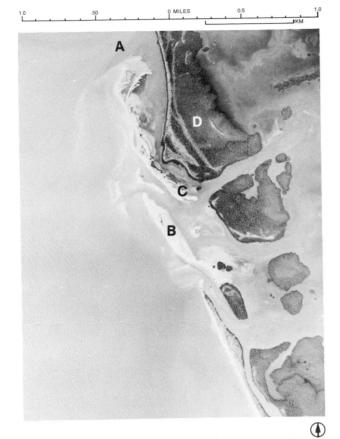

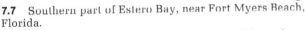

7.7 Southern part of Estero Bay, near Fort Myers Beach, Florida.

a April 13, 1944. Narrow sandy barriers offshore from mangrove islands. Black Island (D) has one offshore barrier. U.S. Department of Agriculture vertical aerial photograph.

b March 7, 1951. A second sandy barrier (A) has developed offshore from Black Island (B). The inner barrier has grown and become vegetated. Photo by D. L. Inman.

currents as far as Cape Romano. Shell hash of local origin is mixed with quartz sand.

At Cape Romano, the coast makes a sharp bend; but sand drifting southward past the cape continues seaward for 10 miles, forming the Romano Shoals, 12 feet or less in depth. These are counterparts of the shoals off the North Carolina capes. An arcuate hook partly overgrown by mangroves has been built at Cape Romano. Some sand has evidently drifted eastward around the cape toward the Ten Thousand Islands.

Morgan Pass, a mile north of Cape Romano, is the inlet to a small lagoon. A lunate bar (not shown) had formed on the Gulf front of the inlet by 1951, the result of sediment brought into the open Gulf by the ebb tidal currents and shifted slightly southward by littoral currents.

Tanner estimated that Hurricane Donna in 1960 accomplished about as much change in this area as normal shore processes would produce in 100 years.

ESTERO BAY, FLORIDA [Figs. 7.7a and b]
Estero Bay, an amusing name because *estero* in Spanish means "bay," is a shallow body of water located 10 miles east of Sanibel Island. The bay is protected on the north by the broad barrier Estero Island, where the resort Fort Myers Beach is situated. To the south of Big Carlos Pass (A in Fig. 7.7a), a series of barrier beaches backed by mangrove islands extends to the southern end of Estero Bay. The barrier beaches on the open Gulf side are apparently a recent development. The southern (B) clearly overlaps the northern (C). The latter has two hooks at its north end. This configuration points to a northward drift, in contrast to the indicated southward drift at Cape Romano, 40 miles to the south of Estero Bay.

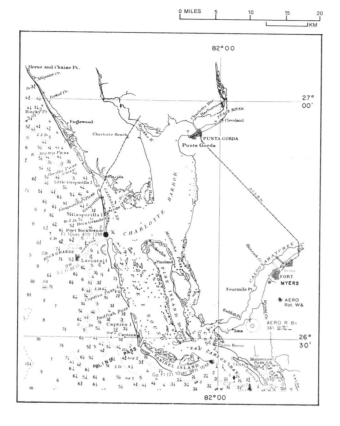

7.8 A location map for Charlotte Harbor area, Florida, showing Blind, Redfish, Captiva, and Boca Grande Passes. From U.S. Coast and Geodetic Survey Chart 1255, 1961.

Comparison of Figure 7.7*a* (1944) and the photo of the same area in 1951 (Fig. 7.7*b*) shows the addition of a sandy barrier (A in Fig. 7.7*b*) off Black Island (B). This key had built up from an offshore shoal in the seven-year period. In 1951, the new barrier already supported a little vegetation. Florida was hit by several hurricanes between 1944 and 1951, and the new barrier may have been built during one of them.

SANIBEL ISLAND TO CHARLOTTE HARBOR, WEST FLORIDA[1] [Figs. 7.8 through 7.13]   To the north of Estero Bay, the mainland coast continues the northerly trend; but a group of barriers including Sanibel, the shell collectors' island, bend westward, extending the outer coast for 20 miles beyond the mainland (Fig. 7.8). The waterways inside the chain of barriers continue north to Charlotte Harbor, the

[1] Much information on this area is derived from a report by Mohamed T. El-Ashry, prepared in 1966.

latter being a combination lagoon and estuary with a channel that shoals gradually to 9 feet at Punta Gorda, 30 miles up from Boca Grande Pass.

The river drainage entering the inland waterways exceeds in volume the flood tidal inflow, so the ebb tide has the stronger current, and more sediment is carried out through the passes into the Gulf than into the sounds. The Caloosahatchie River, to the south, coming from Lake Okeechobee, debouches into San Carlos Bay, the southern outlet between Sanibel and Estero Islands. To the north, the Peace and Myakka Rivers enter the two heads of Charlotte Harbor, and this river water drains largely through Boca Grande Pass between Gasparilla and Lacosta Islands. The southern part of Charlotte Harbor is mostly less than 7 feet deep; and the inlets separating Lacosta, North Captiva, Captiva, and Sanibel Islands have only small excess river drainage to add to the ebb tides.

Sanibel Island (Fig. 7.9) is about 10 miles long and 2 miles wide at the widest point. Its beaches are

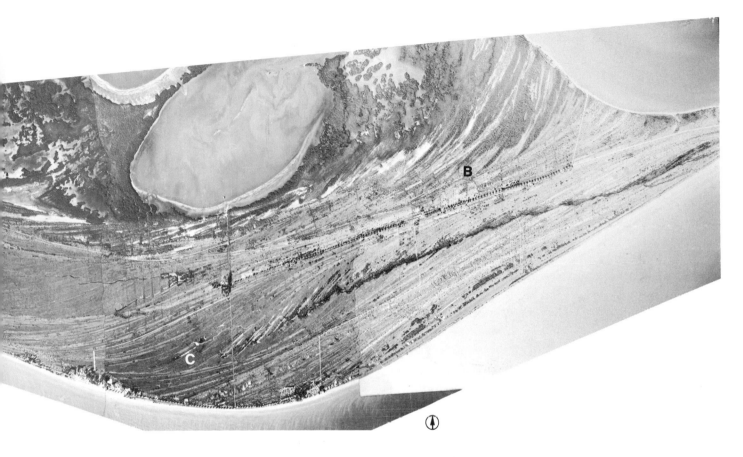

7.9 Sanibel Island, Florida, has a remarkable display of successive sets of beach ridges, formed as the island was prograding into the Gulf. At A to E, sets of older beach ridges are truncated by newer ridges. These truncations presumably resulted from erosion during tropical hurricanes. U.S. Department of Agriculture, 1944.

among the best known in the United States for collectors because of a large variety of molluscan shells. The island probably grew over a period of several hundred years as a lengthening hook curving southeast and east to enclose Charlotte Harbor. The outlines of a spectacular display of closely spaced beach (or dune) ridges tell the story of the growth of the island. At five or more positions (A, B, C, D, E, in Fig. 7.9) older ridges are truncated, and a newer set is developed at an angle to the older. The ridges must have been truncated by major hurricanes and a new series developed parallel to the eroded shoreline. The present shore is in general diagonal to the beach ridges, showing that truncation has been more recent

than any new progradation. Sanibel Island has approximately the same form now as shown in a chart made in 1859, so the storms which eroded it deeply from time to time must be of earlier dates.

The northwestern end of Sanibel Island is separated from Captiva by Blind Pass, so called because it is usually invisible from offshore because of the overlap of the south end of Captiva Island. Prior to 1859, spits must have been built to the north (A in Fig. 7.10); but since then the predominant direction of beach drifting here has been south and southeast, as shown by this overlap. However, the south spit of Captiva is truncated from time to time during storms. Examination of charts and aerial photos dating back

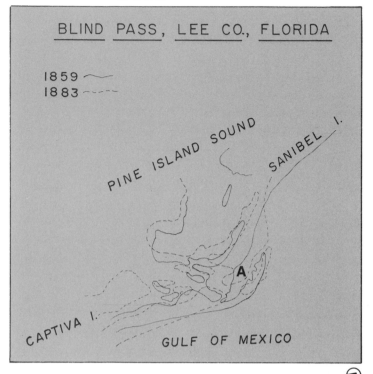

7.10 Outline maps showing configurations of shoreline near Blind Pass, Florida, in 1859, 1883, and 1961. Prepared by Mohamed T. El-Ashry.

7.11 Changes in shore outlines near Blind Pass shown by aerial photographs.
a February 17, 1944. U.S. Department of Agriculture.

as far as 1859 has indicated some of these sequences. In 1859 (Fig. 7.10), the overlap existed; but by 1883 the spit had been cut, allowing direct passage through the inlet. By 1938 (not shown), the Captiva spit had been reconnected and extended well south of Sanibel. In 1944 (Fig. 7.11a), the spit was somewhat shorter than it was in 1938 but still present. In 1948 (not shown), the eastern part of the spit had been breached; but part of the overlap remained. By 1958 (not shown), the gap was filled and the spit slightly extended; but in 1960 (not shown), a new gap developed as the result of Hurricane Donna, and again there was an opening directly off the inner pass. In 1961 (Fig. 7.11b), the gap had been closed and finally, in 1965, when the area was visited by Wanless, Blind Pass was completely closed.

An 1880 chart (not included) shows Captiva

Island as 9 miles in length but narrow in the middle portion. At this narrow place, a new inlet, Redfish Pass, was opened by the 1926 hurricane, the storm that proved to be the worst in the history of the Miami area. Tidal currents have now cut a channel through Redfish Pass to a depth of 12 feet. Little river water reaches this pass, so the flood and ebb tidal currents had formed a double tidal delta in 1944 (Fig. 7.12), of which the larger part is built into Charlotte Harbor. In 1960, Hurricane Donna opened five temporary sluiceways across North Captiva Island 0.5 and 0.7 mile north of the pass. Washovers were also conspicuous in 1961. The 1960 photograph shows that some sand has shifted northward on the seaward side of Redfish Pass, as compared with 1944.

Captiva Pass separates North Captiva from Lacosta Island. Because some of the excess water

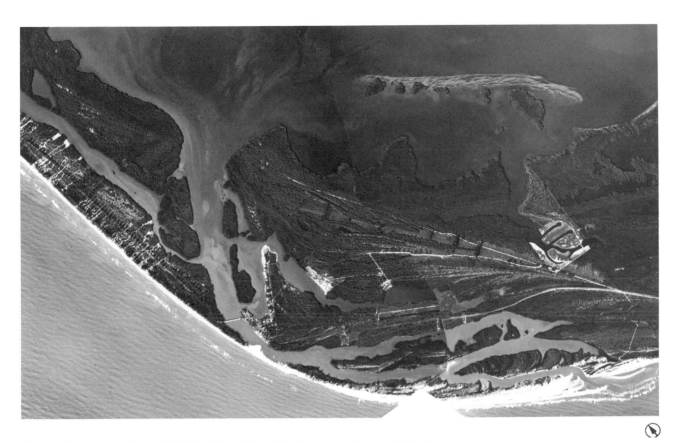

b   March 18, 1961. From U.S. Coast and Geodetic Survey color aerial photograph.

brought in by the Peace and Myakka Rivers flows out through this pass, the tidal delta forms only on the Gulf side of the pass. Outside, a strong littoral current deflects the sand southward, forming a shoal 1 or 2 feet deep a little offshore and extending about 1.5 miles south from the inlet. At Captiva Pass, with an ebb tidal current strengthened by river water, sand is transported into the Gulf and then drifted southward. In Redfish Pass, with little river discharge, a large delta has been built into the bay, and some sand is drifting northward from the inlet.

According to T. C. Huang and H. G. Goodell, Boca Grande Pass, between Lacosta (A in Fig. 7.13a)

7.12   Redfish Pass, between Captiva and Little Captiva Islands, Florida, opened by a 1926 hurricane, has a double tidal delta, the larger growth in Charlotte Harbor. U.S. Department of Agriculture, 1944.

WHITE BEACHES AND SWAMPS: FLORIDA TO MISSISSIPPI SOUND

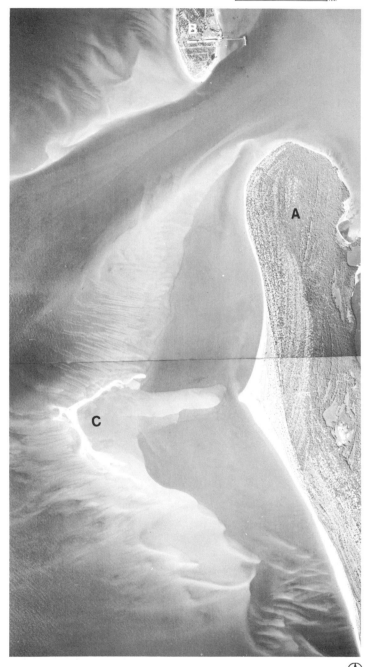

7.13 Boca Grande Pass, between Lacosta and Gasparilla Islands. This pass carries gulfward most of the drainage from the rivers feeding Charlotte Harbor. The channel is locally 47 feet deep.

a 1944. Sand drifted southward by a littoral current has formed an offshore cuspate sandkey. In the protected water behind this key, a small cuspate foreland has developed, and a shoal partly connects the two. U.S. Department of Agriculture.

b 1960. The cuspate sandkey has been breached by a hurricane and driven inshore, and the shoals have disappeared. The cuspate foreland has changed shape. U.S. Coast and Geodetic Survey.

and Gasparilla (B), 6 miles north of Captiva Pass, carries most of the discharge of the Peace and Myakka Rivers into the Gulf and has a discharge larger than the Charlotte Harbor outlet adjoining Sanibel Island. The inlet channel has been cut by tides to a maximum depth of 51 feet, but elsewhere depth is maintained for ships by dredging. Outside the pass, it continues its direct southwestward course for about 4 miles seaward from the inlet. Shoals have formed on each side of this channel, but littoral currents have been drifting most of the sand to the south. Probably during a major storm between 1929 and 1944, a lunate sandkey was developed from the shoal 1.5 miles south of the inlet and 1.5 miles offshore (C in Fig. 7.13*a*). As this built slightly above sea level it protected the shore from erosion, and another shoal extended shoreward from the center of the arc of the sandkey. The beach, protected by the sandkey, had build out about 1,500 feet by 1944, forming a cus-

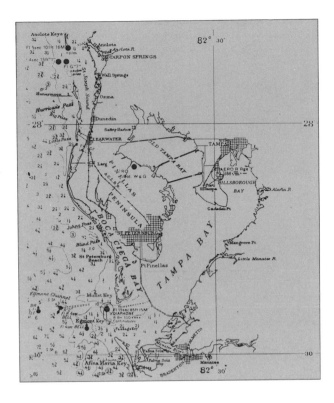

7.14 Tampa Bay and barriers along the Pinellas Peninsula. U.S. Coast and Geodetic Survey Chart 1114, 1959.

pate foreland. Between 1944 and 1950, the sandkey had been split, leaving a remnant on each flank. In 1951 (Fig. 2.23b), the cuspate foreland had been reduced to 1,000 feet. By 1960 (Fig. 7.13b), the remnants of the sandkey had migrated landward about 0.2 mile. Also, the shoal shoreward from the center of the sandkey had disappeared, and the cuspate foreland on the beach had been modified in shape to form an asymmetrical point.

TAMPA BAY AND PINELLAS PENINSULA, FLORIDA [Figs. 7.14 and 7.15] Tampa Bay, the largest body of inland water in Florida, covers an area of 350 square miles (Fig. 7.14). It is protected from the open Gulf by a string of keys and Pinellas Peninsula, a north-south land mass on which are the large cities of St. Petersburg, to the south, and Clearwater, to the north. Tampa is located along the north side of the inner bay. Tampa Bay receives

the drainage of five small rivers of west-central Florida. According to H. G. Goodell and Donn Gorsline, none of the rivers form deltas where they enter the estuary, because their drainage areas are almost wholly in Cenozoic limestones, which yield little detritus. Water depths in the bays are predominantly 15 feet or less, but tidally scoured channels are locally 25 feet or slightly deeper. North of the bay entrance, littoral currents appear to be from the north, and south of the entrance, from the south.

Barrier spits and barrier islands built from both directions partially close the harbor entrance. From south to north, these include Anna Maria and Passage Keys; Egmont Key in the center of the entrance; and Mullet (A in Fig. 7.15), Tierra Verde (B), and St. Petersburg Beach (C). Egmont and Passage Keys lie at either end of a submerged lunate bar that has formed outside the entrance to the bay. Mullet Key has a V-shape with one arm extending as a hook (D) into Tampa Bay. Mangroves grow along the bay sides of these protecting barriers and even on the Gulf side where protected by shoals. The lower end of Tampa Bay is now crossed by the Sunshine Skyway bridge connecting St. Petersburg with Bradenton and the south coast. There are three relatively deep channels at the bay mouth. The one between Passage Key and Anna Marie Key is more than 30 feet deep just north of Anna Maria. This channel was probably deepened by tidal currents.

A series of barrier islands extend for 45 miles all along the west side of Pinellas Peninsula (Fig. 7.14). These include the resort beaches of St. Petersburg and Clearwater. Boca Ciega Bay, a 12-mile lagoon behind the southern barrier islands, has several dendritic tributaries coming from the peninsula on the east. The 1951 aerial photo of the southern barrier (Fig. 7.15) shows a series of cuspate keys and shoals. On either side of Bunces Pass (E) there are only cuspate shoals (F and G); but, in the 1965 edition of the chart, the one to the north was shown as a key. The cuspate key (H) just south of the entrance to Boca Ciega Bay (I) has shown some growth, according to the 1965 chart. In Boca Ciega Bay, islands elongate in a north-south direction and represent barriers older than the present series of islands. The Pinellas Bayway, a road constructed between 1951 and 1965, follows the series of older barriers to the tip of Mullet Key, where Tampa Bay waters join the Gulf of Mexico.

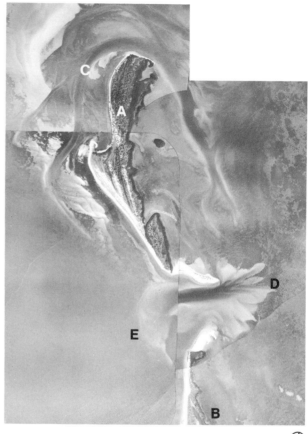

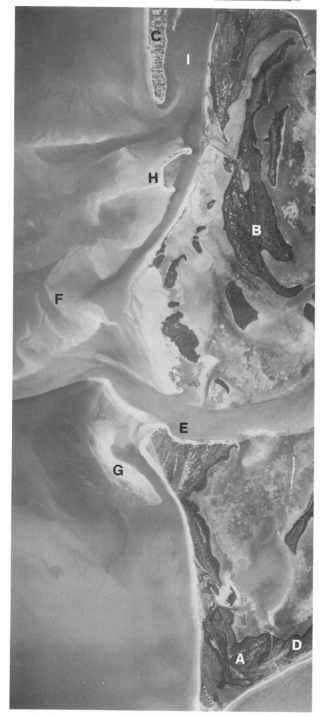

7.16 Honeymoon (A) and Caladesi (B) Islands and Hurricane Pass (E) near Dunedin, Florida. A large tidal delta has been built into St. Joseph Sound. Just north of Honeymoon Island a horseshoe-shaped channel (C) connects St. Joseph Sound with the Gulf of Mexico. U.S. Department of Agriculture, 1951.

7.15 Gulf Coast between the entrance to Tampa Bay and the southern end of St. Petersburg beaches (C), Florida. One lunate sandkey (H) and two lunate sand bars (E and F) are shown. U.S. Department of Agriculture, 1951.

HONEYMOON ISLAND AND HURRICANE PASS, FLORIDA [Fig. 7.16]

The chain of barrier islands continues north past the resort towns of Clearwater and Dunedin, but a 6-mile break in the chain occurs north of Honeymoon Island (Fig. 7.14). North of Dunedin, there is no local source of sand because of the low marshy coast and the limestone bedrock of the interior. The small barriers off Tarpon Springs must have received their sand supply from the south, due to longshore currents.

Honeymoon Island (A in Fig. 7.16) was formerly joined with Caladesi Island (B) to the south; but the hurricane of 1921 breached the island at a narrow point, forming the new Hurricane Pass, which

7.17 Homosassa Bay, Florida, about 50 miles north of Tarpon Springs, has a flat limestone coast with no sandy barriers. When sea level was lowered during the Pleistocene glacial stages, the limestone surface was extensively pitted by sinkholes. With a rise in sea level, the coast has become very irregular. U.S. Geological Survey, 1951.

The tidal channel (C) is horseshoe-shaped around the northern part of Honeymoon Island. Tidal deltas (D and E) have been formed by tidal currents on both the Gulf and lagoon sides of the same island. According to the 1965 chart, the water was only 1 to 5 feet deep for about 3 miles north of Honeymoon Island, so that hurricane winds at some future date may pile this up into a new barrier island, extending the chain farther in this direction.

HOMOSASSA BAY AREA, FLORIDA [Fig. 7.17] The Homosassa River (A) enters the Gulf of Mexico about 50 miles north of Tarpon Springs. The streams in this vicinity are largely fed by strong artesian springs discharging from solution cavities in limestone, developed when sea level was lowered by Pleistocene glaciation. A very flat surface here has been gradually inundated by the sea. The rivers carry very little sediment, although some have large discharges of clear water. Mangroves are present here; but because of the cooler climate of the more northern latitude, they are less abundant than in the Ten Thousand Islands and the Everglades of southwestern Florida. The Gulf is 5 feet or less in depth for 7 miles offshore from the area that is illustrated in Figure 7.17. The highly irregular coast and the lack of barrier islands show that sand is unavailable to produce barriers. A short distance west of the area shown in Figure 7.17, the drowned channel of Homosassa River is 7 to 13 feet deep, having been eroded before it was drowned. A few oyster reefs may be present, but they are less conspicuous than near the mouth of Suwannee River, about 30 miles farther northwest. In the near future, the coast should suffer little damage, because the many small islands are stabilized by growing vegetation and because of very low wave energy and a very shallow sea where occasional large waves break some distance seaward from the islands. These characteristics have prevented this part of the Florida coast from developing as a winter resort.

has remained open since that date. Between the photos of 1941 (not shown) and 1951 (Fig. 7.16), the inlet broadened from 2,000 to 3,000 feet, and by 1957 (not shown), to about 3,700 feet. The inlet was widened by erosion of the tips of both Honeymoon and Caladesi Islands. As one result of this erosion, hooked spits 1,300 and 1,700 feet long had been developed eastward into the bay between 1941 and 1957. Also, a large double tidal delta had been built with most of the growth to the east into the shallow lagoon. The deeper part of the tidal channel through the inlet is about 10 feet. Recently a causeway from the mainland has been built to the southern tip of Honeymoon Island to make the beaches available for swimming.

CEDAR KEYS–SUWANNEE RIVER AREA, FLORIDA [Figs. 7.18, 7.19, and 7.20] Cedar Keys (A in Fig. 7.18), a fishing town on the Gulf of Mexico, lies about 70 miles northwest of Tarpon Springs and 10 miles southeast of the mouth of Suwannee River. This area probably shows the finest development of oyster reefs in the United States. At

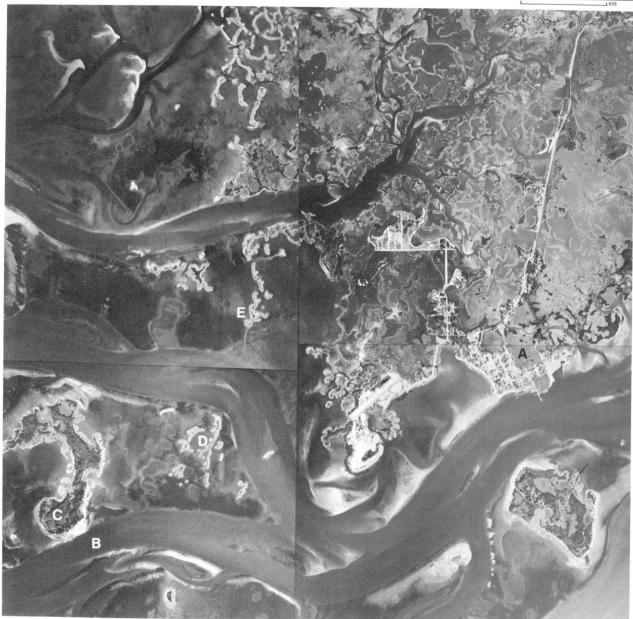

7.18 Cedar Keys area, Florida. A series of small stream valleys drowned by post-glacial rise in sea level have left interstream flats and inland bays as the growth sites of many small oyster reefs (D and E), most of which are barely below high tide level. U.S. Department of Agriculture, 1961.

Cedar Keys, there is a sharp angle in the coast with an archipelago of limestone islands. The mainland is extremely flat and marshy for 10 or more miles inland. Numerous drowned creeks are seen along the coast, but, unlike the equally marshy Homosassa Bay area, there is no maze of offshore islets. This portion of the Florida coast was classified as a zero-energy coast by William Tanner, meaning that the waves have virtually no effect. It seems to the present authors, however, that whereas the partially cemented

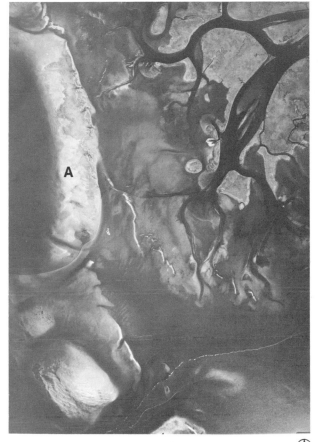

7.19 The small delta of the Suwannee River, Florida, fronted by the Suwannee Oyster Reef (A). U.S. Department of Agriculture, 1961.

carbonate rock, some of which may be as old as the last interglacial stage of the Pleistocene, is difficult to dislodge by any ordinary waves, hurricanes and other violent storms may produce occasional changes.

The Cedar Keys museum has an excellent display of coastal features and of the marine life of the area. This is a favorite locale for shell collectors. The water is 5 feet or less deep from 3 to 7 miles offshore, except for the three deeper channels (Fig. 7.18), which have 10-foot depths; and Deadmans Channel (B) to the south is deep enough for fishing boats to come into the Cedar Keys wharf. The channels do not appear to connect with streams on land but may represent the drowned courses of coastal streams several thousand years old, cut before sea level had reached its present position. The offshore islands, such as North Key (C) in the vicinity of Cedar Keys,

appear to be slightly more elevated parts of the coastal belt located between stream valleys prior to drowning. Fringing oyster reefs (D) (shown by white curving lines) have formed all around the margins of these islands. They are also found on shoals 1 to 2 feet deep on the interchannel flats and in even greater abundance in the bays, notably in the bay traversed by the highway that enters Cedar Keys from the north.

The Suwannee River, famed in song and story, drains much of the northwestern part of the Florida Peninsula and heads in the Okefenokee Swamp of southeastern Georgia. Along most of its course it traverses low marshy country, underlain by limestone bedrock, so it also carries little detrital sediment to the Gulf. Figure 7.19 shows the small delta of the Suwannee River. About a mile offshore from the delta is the Suwannee Oyster Reef, which extends as a barrier for nearly 12 miles. At high tide it is almost wholly inundated, but it shows prominently as a continuous barrier island at low tide (A in Fig. 7.19).

In Suwannee Sound, between Cedar Keys and the Suwannee River, two oyster reefs rise nearly to the sea surface as barriers (Fig. 7.20). Lone Cabbage Reef (A), 2 miles offshore, is 3.5 miles long and is bordered by Suwannee Reef (B), 1.5 miles farther seaward. Suwannee Reef, the more massive of the two, is probably the older, and the Lone Cabbage Reef probably developed after the rise in sea level had drowned much of the flat coast. Both reefs have been breached at many places by hurricanes. These storms are reported to have struck the Cedar Keys coast in 1880, 1886, 1888, 1889, 1896, 1920, 1924, 1932, and 1941. All were minor except the 1896 storm, in which 100 persons were killed. Each storm has probably contributed new cuts across the oyster reefs. Small double tidal deltas have formed in many of the breaches (C).

FENHOLLOWAY RIVER, FLORIDA   The mouth of the Fenholloway River is about 70 miles northwest of Cedar Keys, near the northern end of the Gulf Coast of the Florida Peninsula. From the present shoreline inland for 1 to 1.5 miles, a marshy coast is drained by many small drowned creeks. Behind this narrow coastal strip is a marshy flat with numerous very small round sinkhole ponds and with nearly complete lack of stream drainage. The Fenholloway is one of a very few streams that maintain

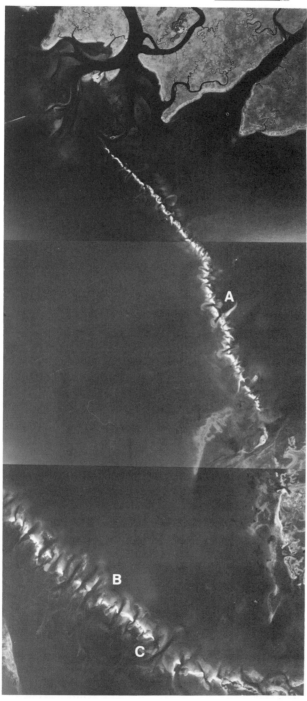

surface channels a few miles into this marshy lime-stone flat. Offshore, the drowned valley of the Fen-holloway River can be traced for about 4 miles, where its base is 16 feet below sea level, while the benches on each side average 4 feet deep. The Gulf, for about 3 miles offshore, is generally 5 feet or less in depth and deepens gradually to 20 feet about 9 miles off-shore. There are very few offshore islets in compari-son with the Homosassa Bay and Cedar Keys areas. No habitation is evident along this coast, no sandy beaches, and virtually no indication of contemporary shore erosion.

OCHLOCKONEE BAY, FLORIDA [Fig. 7.21] Eighty miles northwest of the Suwannee River, the coast of Florida undergoes a radical change of direc-tion; and the Panhandle begins, with its general westerly trend. A few miles from the turn, we en-counter the first of the numerous lagoons and bays that characterize the Gulf Coast as far as the Missis-sippi Delta. Ochlockonee Bay extends into the coast for 5 miles, but because of the deposition of sediment from the Ochlockonee, the easternmost river in the Panhandle, the water is too shallow to allow more than small craft.

The Ochlockonee River drains an area of pre-dominant sands and clays. Beyond its delta, sediment is carried through the estuary to its mouth and there is redistributed by beach drifting. The predominant littoral current in this area is southwestward, so more sand is carried south and west from the entrance to the estuary than north and east. A tidal delta (A) has formed at the north entrance to the bay. A narrow sandy beach and hooked spit have been built north of the bay entrance (B); but a broader beach has been built along the marshland south of the entrance for about 3.5 miles to Lighthouse Point (D) and then westward, where a sand spit has been extended for 5 miles (C). The 1959 chart shows a shoal running almost due south for 5 miles from the spit west of Lighthouse Point, with depths of 5 to 10 feet, while depths east and west of the shoal are about 20 feet. A curved oyster reef partly blocks the entrance to Ochlockonee Bay (E), and small fringing oyster reefs can be observed along the northern shore of the lagoon enclosed by the spit west of Lighthouse Point. Hurricanes struck this coast in 1899 and 1941. At the later date, the beach a short distance north of Lighthouse Point was largely destroyed.

7.20 The linear oyster reefs, the Lone Cabbage (A), and Suwannee Reef (B), offshore from a low marshy coast, are broken by many narrow sluiceways formed during hurricanes. Note small double tidal deltas at each end of the sluiceways (C). U.S. Department of Agriculture, 1961.

7.21 Ochlockonee River delta and bay, Peninsula Pt. (G), and Alligator Harbor (F). Just west of the Florida limestone coast, rivers introduce sand and mud, permitting development of sandy beaches and barrier spits. U.S. Geological Survey, 1942.

DOG ISLAND AND DOG ISLAND "REEF," FLORIDA [Fig. 7.22]

Dog Island, about 20 miles west-southwest of the entrance to Ochlockonee Bay, is the first of a series of barrier islands that extend westward along most of the Florida, Alabama, and Mississippi coasts. Dog Island is about 4 miles offshore from the Florida mainland at Carabelle. It is separated from St. George Island by an inlet at its western end (not shown). Hooks bend toward the coastal lagoon at each end of the island. Shoals trend east and then northeast for a total of 10 miles out from Dog Island. The water on these shoals for the first 2 miles from the island is about 10 feet deep, but the white streaks shown in the photo indicate the shallow sand waves farther east, where depths are only 3 to 4 feet. Five miles east of the island, a series

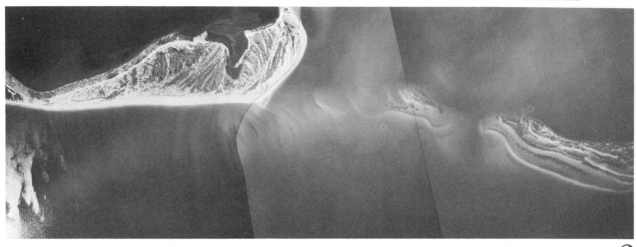

7.22 Dog Island, the easternmost coastal barrier of the west Florida Panhandle, adjoined to the east by two subaqueous bars. These appear to represent early stages in the formation of coastal barrier islands. U.S. Geological Survey, 1942.

7.23 Delta of Apalachicola River built into Apalachicola Bay. This river introduces much red mud from the red soils of Georgia and Alabama. U.S. Geological Survey, 1942.

of sand waves can be seen. Two potential tidal inlets are indicated between these sand waves.

Dog Island "Reef" and a shorter shoal to the west appear to mark early stages in the building of new barrier islands, which may eventually extend the chain eastward from Dog Island for about 10 miles. As the prevalent direction of littoral currents is westward here, it should require many years to build the shoals to sea level, unless a major hurricane stirs up the sand in the vicinity and accelerates the process.

APALACHICOLA–ST. VINCENT ISLAND AREA, FLORIDA [Figs. 7.23 and 7.24]

Just north of Apalachicola, the river of the same name carries the drainage of the Chattahoochee and Flint Rivers of Georgia into Apalachicola Bay. These rivers drain most of western Georgia and part of the Florida Panhandle. The Apalachicola has built a large delta into the bay, a part of which is shown in Figure 7.23. A 5-mile highway bridge crosses East Bay just south of the delta. When visited by Wanless, the bay water under the bridge was brick red, due to the quantity of suspended sediment derived from the red clay soils of Georgia. The mud-laden water pours out through Indian Pass (A in Fig. 7.24) and West Pass (B) and is recognizable at least 3 miles out into the Gulf of Mexico. At the outer margins of these turbid masses of water, much of the mud has been flocculated and settled out.

To the east, Apalachicola Bay is protected from the Gulf by a long narrow island. St. George. To the west, St. Vincent Island (Fig. 7.24), 9 miles long and 4 across, is a remarkably wide segment of the barrier island chain. This photograph shows at least

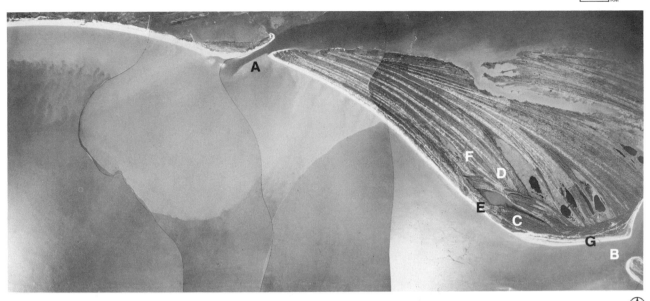

7.24 St. Vincent Island (F) and Indian (A) and West (B) Passes. St. Vincent Island displays a long series of beach ridges truncated at times by erosion. The red mud of Apalachicola Bay enters the Gulf through Indian and West Passes. Outlines of the front of the mud-laden waters against the relatively clear waters of the Gulf can be seen. U.S. Geological Survey, 1942.

twenty-five beach-dune ridges on the barrier, separated by either sand flats or shallow ponds. William Tanner has reported that there are about fifty ridges on St. Vincent Island and the mainland shore north of it; and, because all are at approximately the same level, he thinks they have developed since sea level reached its present elevation. He suggested that new beach ridges might have formed at intervals of about 100 years. However, such a rate would have to be supported by some carbon-14 dates. In view of the probable history of sea level (Fig. 2.1), the present authors suggest that the beach ridges have developed more rapidly. According to most current thinking, sea level has been relatively stable for only one to two thousand years.

From a study of the shapes of the beach ridges, they seem to merge westward toward Indian Pass (A). The oldest ridges extend nearly straight to the east, but most of them curve southward toward the eastern end of the island. As the distance between the ridges increases, the shoreline curves more and more southeastward. The island was developed by long continued progradation. Near the southern end, two sets of beach ridges do not parallel the shoreline; and each set truncates older ridges. The western

of these two sets (C) is older because it is truncated by the eastern (D). Presumably, these anomalous directions followed rapid beach erosion during a hurricane; and the new ridges were subsequently built parallel to the eroded shoreline. After the interruption of accelerated erosion and a new beach ridge orientation, the spit (E) resumed growth in its original direction. The modern beach (G) is built on the truncated end of all these ridges.

CAPE SAN BLAS AND ST. JOSEPH SPIT AREA, FLORIDA [Fig. 7.25]   Cape San Blas (A) is the most prominent cuspate foreland in the Gulf of Mexico. At its extreme point it extends seaward 50 miles south of the general east-west trend of the Gulf Coast in this vicinity (see Fig. 7.1). To the south-southwest of the cape, shoals can be traced seaward for an additional 15 miles, so that here again we find the same relationship between shoals and cuspate capes. The two arms leading to the cape are of unequal length, as is true also of the Hatteras group of cuspate forelands. The short east arm measures 4 miles, whereas the north arm, St. Joseph Spit, is 17 miles long. On the mainland side of the bay, Port St. Joe (B) is the chief center of population.

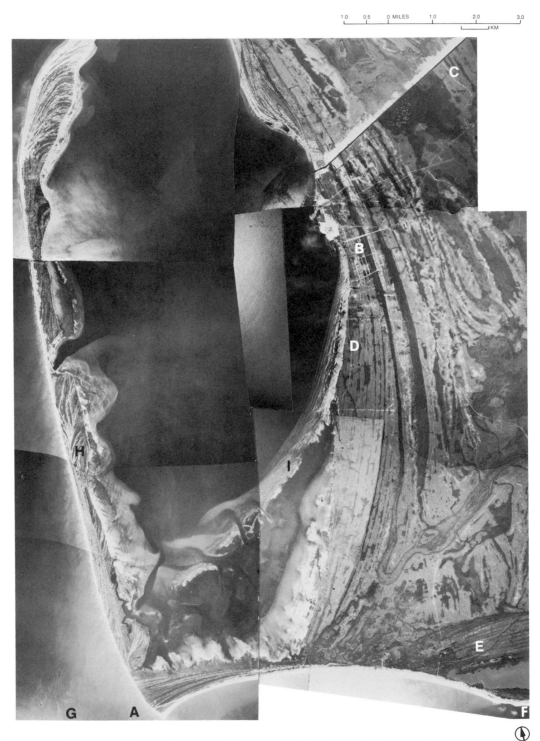

7.25 Cape San Blas, St. Joseph Spit, and St. Joseph Bay, western Florida. Cape San Blas, the largest cuspate foreland in western Florida, formed from sand drifting southward and westward along the margins of the Apalachicola River Delta. The history of growth and shifting locations of the cape are well displayed by beach ridge patterns. A new sand ridge (I) appears to be in the process of formation as a result of a gyrol flow in the southern part of St. Joseph Bay. U.S. Geological Survey, 1942.

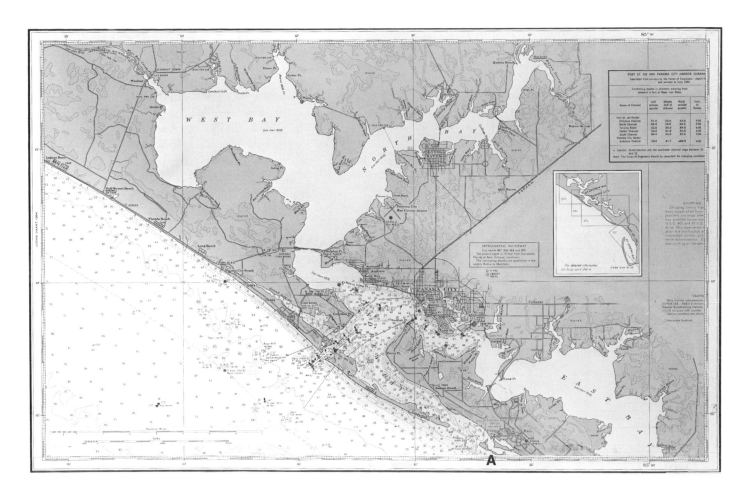

7.26 Chart of the three arms of the bay at Panama City, Florida. U.S. Coast and Geodetic Survey Chart 1263, 1966.

Marshy lowlands occupy much of the area between the Apalachicola River Delta (shown in part), to the east, and the sandy shore areas of St. Joseph Bay and Cape San Blas. A few faint sand ridges, probably old beaches (C), can be seen in the delta marshes northeast of Port St. Joe. These earliest sandy beach ridges seem to have grown southeastward, flanking the marsh and terminating about 6 miles north of the present shoreline. Successive ridges have overlapped the older ones, developing trends more to the south and then to the southwest. The latest of the series of ridges form the eastern shore of St. Joseph Bay (D) and are truncated to the south. Another series of ten ridges (E) extend west-southwest, forming the north shore of Apalachicola Bay west of Indian Pass (F). This series is truncated by the present shoreline but may have joined the ridges southwest from Port St. Joe to form an earlier Cape San Blas, a mile south of the southeast corner of St. Joseph Bay. Following truncation of the old cape, sand drifted both east toward Indian Pass and St. Vincent Island and west to the present cape. This beach drifting evidently established a new cape (G) a little west of the present one, from which a spit began to grow northward. The beach ridges (H) on the spit nearly all curve eastward toward St. Joseph Bay. As the terminal portion of St. Joseph Spit grew northward, the older southern part suffered erosion, as shown by the truncation of old ridges at the present Gulf shore. At the north end, a series of overlapping hooks have developed.

Evidently there is a rotary current in St. Joseph

7.27 Lunate sandkey about 6 miles southeast of Panama City, Florida. Fourteen years after the photography, a new eastern prong of the sandkey had been added. See also A in Figure 7.26. Photo by D. L. Inman, 1951.

Bay, for sandy shoals in the southern part of the bay (I) curve more sharply southwestward than does the bay shore. Four breaks in these underwater sand ridges may be tidal channels.

Thus, Cape San Blas, originating as arcuate ridges flanking the western and southern margins of the Apalachicola River Delta, has had a history remarkably well recorded by a series of beach ridges, chronicling growth interrupted from time to time by substantial truncations. If carbon-14 dates were available for several of the old beach ridges, this history might be documented even better.

PANAMA CITY AREA, FLORIDA [Figs. 7.26 and 7.27]   The harbor of Panama City, in Panhandle Florida, 30 miles northwest of Port St. Joe, was formed originally by a 2-mile-wide natural inlet through a barrier, outside of which a spit 11 miles long had developed, leaving only a shoal narrow entrance. An artificial inlet was opened in the spit opposite the natural inlet, and this is protected by short jetties on the Gulf side. Lands End, the terminus of the outer spit, has a succession of five hooks sharply recurved northward and westward toward the natural inlet. The bay, along the shore of which Panama City is located, has three arms—East Bay with a length of 20 miles; North Bay, 12 miles; and

West Bay, 14 miles. These bays are a combination of lagoons behind old barriers and drowned river valleys. North Bay is entirely the latter, while the others are primarily lagoons.

Three miles southeast of Lands End, where there is no outer barrier, a large lunate sandkey had formed in 1951 (Fig. 7.27). This key had been only a cuspate shoal, according to a chart published in 1950. A cuspate spit that developed in the sheltered area behind the eastern part of the sandkey had extended seaward 900 feet when photographed in 1951. According to the 1965 chart (Fig. 7.26), the lunate sandkey has added an eastern prong since photographed in 1951; and the cuspate spit is nearly opposite the center of the double lunate sandkey. The beach drifting is apparently southeastward in this area, accounting for the spit outside the harbor and the growth of the sandkey.

CHOCTAWHATCHEE BAY AND SANTA ROSA ISLAND, FLORIDA   As can be seen on Figure 7.1, the coastal barriers have only one break in the 100 miles between Panama City and Pensacola. This inlet, Choctawhatchee Bay, located halfway along the otherwise unbroken arc, is only 0.5 mile wide; but the bay on the inside extends as a wide lagoon for almost 30 miles east and west. At the eastern end of Choctawhatchee Bay, a delta is being built by the Choctawhatchee River. Probably this same river has filled in most of the lagoons that formerly existed inside the barriers all the way to the Panama City embayments. The land is largely marsh in this area. East of Choctawhatchee Bay, a narrow coastal barrier bordered a previously narrow lagoon, which is now represented only by a series of small lakes.

West of Choctawhatchee Bay, the 50-mile-long Santa Rosa Island terminates at the entrance to Pensacola Bay. This island is a narrow barrier rarely more than 0.5 mile wide. The beach of the island is remarkable for its whiteness, consisting of almost 100 percent quartz sand that is derived from the Appalachians to the north. Back of the beach is a narrow dune ridge that is almost continuous the entire length of the island. The lagoon on the inside, Santa Rosa Sound, is also narrow, about the same width as the island near Choctawhatchee Bay, but increases to 2 miles nearing the entrance to Pensacola Bay. On the island side of the lagoon, twenty or more cuspate spits project for 1,000 feet or more

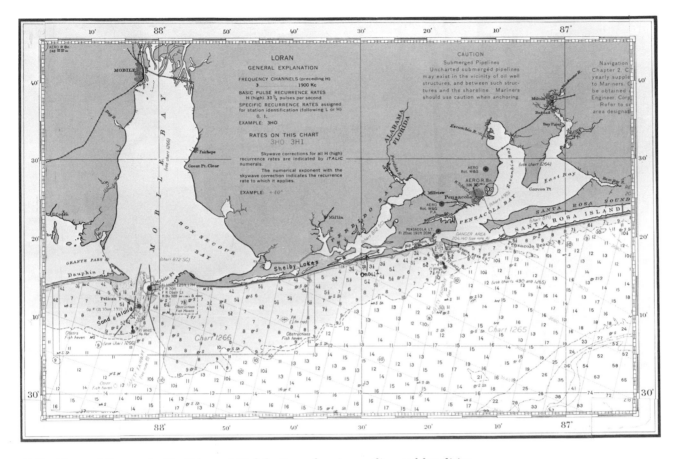

7.28 Chart of Pensacola, Perdido, and Mobile Bays showing outline and localities described. U.S. Coast and Geodetic Survey Chart 1115, 1967.

into the lagoon; and, on the mainland side, there are four or more similar features. Some of these are shown in Figure 7.34, but they differ from the cuspate spits inside Nantucket Harbor (Fig. 3.20) in being irregularly spaced.

PENSACOLA BAY, FLORIDA [Fig. 7.28]   Pensacola Bay resembles the bays at Panama City in being protected by two barriers. The outer of these is Santa Rosa Island; and the inner is considerably wider, mostly 1 to 2 miles, and has a natural opening 3 miles wide, similar to that through the inner barrier in the entrance to Panama City. In this case, however, the outer Santa Rosa Island has apparently built west past the natural opening, instead of east as at Panama City. On the inside, Pensacola Bay extends as a lagoon for 20 miles but has two large

estuaries, East and Escambia Bays, penetrating deeply into the mainland. The city of Pensacola is located directly inside the large natural opening in the barrier.

PERDIDO BAY, FLORIDA AND ALABAMA [Figs. 7.28, 7.29, and 7.30]   Thirteen miles west-southwest of Pensacola, Perdido Bay (Fig. 7.28), the estuary of the Perdido River, forms the state line between Florida and Alabama. The long axis of the bay trends obliquely northeastward for 16 miles. Subaqueous sand ridges with water 5 feet or less in depth are conspicuous on aerial photographs along most of the margins of the bay (Fig. 7.29). Since the bay is largely floored with mud, the sand appears to have been introduced from the Gulf of Mexico and distributed along the shallow margins of the bay by

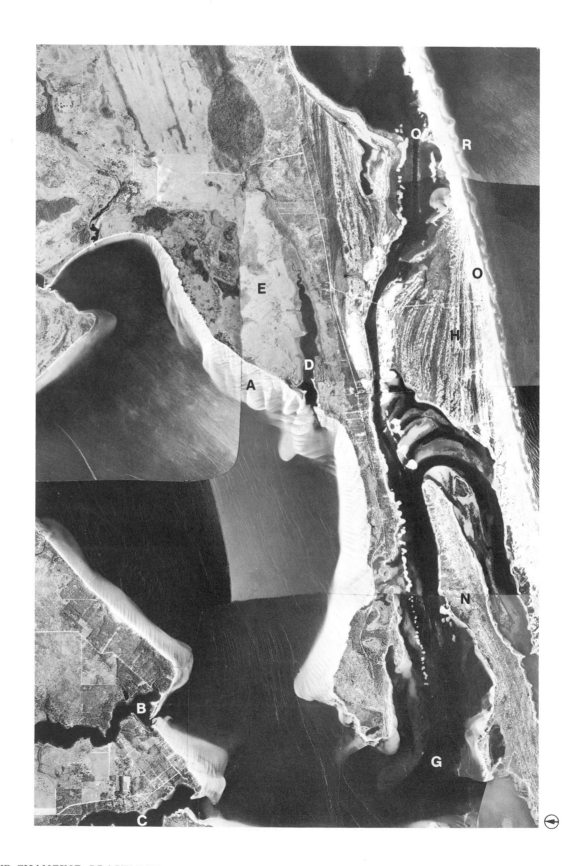

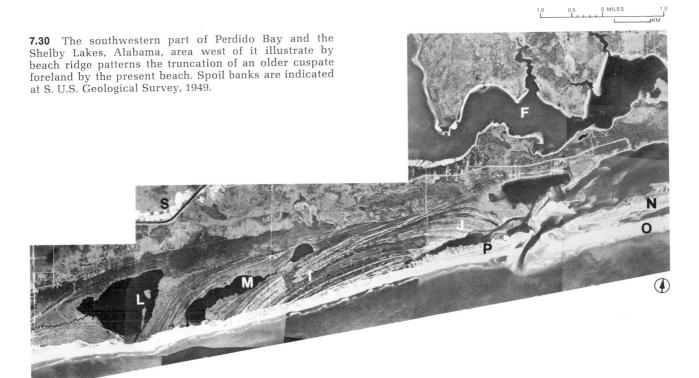

7.30 The southwestern part of Perdido Bay and the Shelby Lakes, Alabama, area west of it illustrate by beach ridge patterns the truncation of an older cuspate foreland by the present beach. Spoil banks are indicated at S. U.S. Geological Survey, 1949.

relatively weak littoral currents. The underwater sand ridges are wider in the lower bay than near its head and are particularly wide along the southeastern shore. These ridges seem to show two preferred directions of orientation, predominantly north-south and east-west (A), probably resulting from two prevailing wind directions.

Perdido Bay has several tributary estuaries. Baymouth spits (B) have formed, partly closing the entrances to some of them. Cuspate spits (C) are also present in two of these tributaries.

The southern end of the bay represents an alternation of remnants of partly filled lagoons and partially truncated barriers, with beach and dune ridges diagonal to the general trend. Starting to the north of the barriers, we find remnants of a lagoon in Bayou Garcon (D) and widespread marshes (E). Traced westward, this continues in the main bay and then

7.29 Perdido Bay, western Florida and eastern Alabama, is a drowned valley of Perdido River. Near the coast, a complex succession of barrier spits has been constructed, some formed by littoral currents from the west, and others from the east. Patterns of underwater sand bars in Perdido Bay are well displayed. The patterns of these sand bars indicate two different current directions. U.S. Department of Agriculture, 1949.

in Bay La Launch (F in Fig. 7.30).[2] On the south, these lagoons are bounded by an old barrier 0.5 to 1 mile in width. This is heavily forested except where it has been artificially cleared. The wooded portions show no evidence of beach ridges. The barrier is cut by a mile-wide gap (G) that is offset 4 miles to the east-northeast of the outer inlet that connects with the Gulf. A younger barrier (II and I) developed farther seaward. Only remnants of this are preserved; but it has a prominent sequence of beach ridges, especially to the southwest where the ridges extend diagonal to the general trend of the barrier. The ridges to the northeast of the inlet in the older barrier (Fig. 7.28) seem to have developed hooks (J) in the earlier beach ridges, but later ridges have a trend more nearly parallel to the present shore. Those to the southwest appear to have been formed by beach drifting east and west from a cuspate foreland 7 miles southwest of the present inlet and seaward from the present shore. The large triangular lake (L) now lies inside the angle of this old cuspate foreland. A lagoon trending northeast-southwest (M) divides this series of beach ridges into two sets, the one to the southeast having formed later.

[2] These letters are a continuation of those of Figure 7.29.

7.31 Delta formed by Tensaw and Mobile Rivers at head of Mobile Bay, Alabama.
U.S. Department of Agriculture, 1960.

The next event seems to have been a straightening of the coast by the erosion of projecting cuspate forelands east and west of the Perdido Bay Inlet. Sediment from the eroded forelands to the southwest was redistributed to the northeast by littoral currents and formed a long straight barrier, of which the eastern portion is now called Ono Island (N on Figs. 7.29 and 7.30). The latter extended northeast about 3 miles past the inlet in the older barrier and nearly joined the hooked barriers formed earlier by beach drifting from the northeast. Still later, a breach a mile wide, constituting the modern inlet, was cut into the southwestern part of the Ono Island barrier,

leaving the northeastern part as an island.

Probably within the past century, another new barrier seaward from Ono Island (O in Figs. 7.29 and 7.30) has been formed, presumably growing southwestward. Near the entrance to Perdido Bay, this barrier merges (P) into the former western connection of the Ono Island barrier. The new barrier supports little or no vegetation, and beach or dune ridges cannot be distinguished on the available aerial photographs. Photographs of this area between 1945 and 1962 show little change except in details around the inlet to Perdido Bay. In 1962 (not shown), a highway bridge was built across the inlet, and the modern barrier shows more vegetation than at earlier dates. The Perdido Bay coast has not been affected by a major hurricane since 1926. With the rather low energy of waves on Gulf of Mexico shores and the infrequency of hurricanes, the area has displayed stability during the period covered by aerial photographs.

A portion of the modern barrier has a series of cuspate spits (Q) along the lagoon side. On the Gulf of Mexico side, a series of breaks in the wave fronts are due to rip currents, with narrow arcuate shoals at the outer ends (R). Each rip current trace is oriented toward the southwest, probably as a result of the littoral currents. No carbon-14 dates are at hand to put the chronology of these changes near the entrance to Perdido Bay into a time scale.

MOBILE BAY, ALABAMA [Figs. 7.28, 7.31 through 7.34]   The rectangular shape of Mobile Bay (Fig. 7.28) makes this estuary unique in its contrast with the usual dendritic branching arms that characterize most drowned valleys of the East and Gulf Coasts. It is also one of the larger estuaries of the Gulf Coast, having a length of 33 miles and a width of 10 miles, except in its lower portion where it bulges to 20 miles in Bon Secour Bay, on the east side. Mobile Bay was formerly twice its present length, but the upper part has been filled by the confluent Tombigbee and Alabama Rivers, which together drain much of the state of Alabama. The lower courses of these rivers have been named respectively Mobile and Tensaw, the latter having several mouths (Fig. 7.31). The rectangular delta formed by the rivers has advanced a total average of 2 miles since the earliest reliable chart made in 1890. The advance is now slowed because of dams constructed in the upper reaches of both rivers.

Except for the shoal margins, Mobile Bay has a very consistent depth of 9 to 11 feet. A shipping channel, 40 feet deep, has been dredged along the length of the bay up to Mobile, located at the head of the bay on the west side.

The mouth of the bay is protected by an 18-mile spit built out from the east side and on the west by the cuspate east end of Dauphin Island. A natural gap of 4 miles separates these two barriers; and the channel, which is cut through the eastern side of this gap, is kept open by the tides coming into the bay. Beyond the bay mouth, an arcuate shoal extends 4

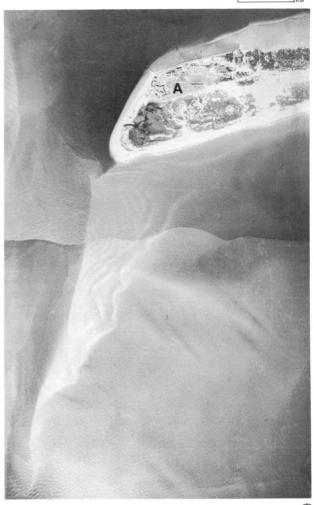

7.32 Fort Morgan (A) at eastern side of entrance to Mobile Bay and shoals on each side of navigation channel. U.S. Department of Agriculture, 1949.

miles into the Gulf. Figure 7.32 shows the deep entrance channel with a darker shade of gray, having a series of about twelve wavy discontinuous sand ridges elongate in a north-south direction. West of the shipping channel, two islands, Sand and Pelican, rise above the shoal southeast of Dauphin Island. Fort Morgan (A in Fig. 7.32) is at the end of the spit on the east side of the bay entrance, and Fort Gaines (not illustrated) lies at the east end of Dauphin Island.

From 5 to 7 miles east of Fort Morgan, the present spit displays more than fifty beach ridges, which spread out like a fan (Fig. 7.33) to the northwest. Here, the barrier spit widens to about 2.3 miles at

7.33 Little Point Clear, an old hooked spit built partly across the southern end of Mobile Bay by littoral currents from the east. It is truncated by the present shore. Underwater sand bars have been formed by modern currents. Shows reticulate bars. U.S. Department of Agriculture, 1949.

Little Point Clear (A). This appears to have begun as a hook that formed as the spit grew westward toward the present entrance to Mobile Bay. More recently, some of the ridges trending south-southwest have been truncated by beach erosion (B). After the building of the Little Point Clear series of hooks, the beach was lengthened westward an additional 4 miles without any more hook development.

Currents drifting northeastward from Little Point Clear have formed a prominent shoal (C). Although the shoal has a southwest-northeast elongation, the majority of the sand ridges composing it trend north-south.

At the eastern end of the long spit separating southeastern Mobile Bay from the Gulf of Mexico, a lagoon 6 miles long and 0.6 mile wide lies between an older barrier to the north and the modern beach to the south. In the part of the lagoon illustrated in Figure 7.34, there are eight or more cuspate spits on the south side and five on the north.

The Soviet geologist, V. P. Zenkovich, illustrated a very similar series from the Chuckchi Sea north of Siberia. In describing the development of such cuspate spits, Zenkovich proposed that they are constructed by wind-induced currents when the wind is parallel to the lagoon axes. Because the lagoon illustrated here trends nearly east-west, according to his idea, the dominant cause of spit building in the western part of the lagoon would have been an east wind, while in the eastern part, a west wind would have been dominant. Later in the evolution of the cuspate spits, according to Zenkovich, they tend to be nearly opposite one another and extend nearly perpendicular to the long axis of their lagoon. Ultimately, spits from opposite sides of these lagoons join, dividing the lagoons into smaller segments. Two such segments occur at the narrow west end of the lagoon (A). It will be observed that some of the beach ridges are truncated by oval segments of the lagoon, indicating that the development of cusps has involved ero-

7.34 Large cuspate spits formed on both sides of the coastal lagoon east of the entrance to Mobile Bay, Alabama. Underwater sand bars in bay (B) illustrate the directions of currents at different times. The broader and older sand bars trend northwest-southeast. U.S. Department of Agriculture, 1960.

sion and redistribution of older beach sands during shaping of the lagoon. This also favors the Zenkovich idea.

HORN ISLAND, MISSISSIPPI [Fig. 7.35]   West of Mobile Bay, the mainland is separated from a row of islands by Mississippi Sound, a lagoon averaging 10 miles in width. The narrow barrier island chain from east to west includes Dauphin (in Alabama), Petite Bois, Horn, Ship, and Cat Islands. The last adjoins the outer arc of the barrier islands of the Mississippi Delta.

Horn Island (Fig. 7.35), representative of the narrow barriers, is 15 miles long, ranges from 0.3 to 1 mile in width, and is located offshore from the delta of Pascagoula River. Sandy beaches are found along both sides of the island but are broader on the open Gulf side. A low line of coastal dunes lies behind the Gulf beach, and the older dunes of the interior of the island are partly wooded.

Off the easternmost 3 miles of Horn Island, in a single longshore bar there are seventeen loops (A), called *cuspate bars*. The first ten are connected to beach cusps and extend about 500 feet offshore between the cusps. To the west, the last seven loops are longer, less curved, and do not make contact with the shore. Still farther west, a longshore bar (B) runs straight for about 3 miles, gradually fading. Here, it has a maximum distance of 0.4 mile offshore. Inside the straight stretch of the longshore ridge 4.5 miles west of the eastern end of the island, another longshore ridge (C) diverges westward from the beach and shows a series of cuspate bars for about 4 miles, then straightens (D). Farther west along Horn Island, a third longshore ridge separates from the beach, has a looped section, and again straightens. Although these cuspate bars have been observed off other islands in this area and in some other places, particularly in the Mediterranean, the cause for loops is not well understood. They appear to be related to

7.35 Horn Island, a barrier about 10 miles south of Pascagoula, Mississippi, displays two sets of longshore bars which, at the east, are attached to the shore with a series of loops for several miles before straightening and disappearing. U.S. Coast and Geodetic Survey, 1962.

seas with small tides, but an exception occurs off Cape Cod (Fig. 3.14c).

GULFPORT, SHIP ISLAND, AND HURRICANE CAMILLE   Farther west along the Gulf Coast, we come to the cities of Biloxi and Gulfport, which received the brunt of Hurricane Camille on August 19, 1969. As this is being written, it is too early to evaluate this storm, which may have been the greatest to hit the coasts of the United States in history. Barometric pressure was at least as low as 26.61 inches and possibly 26.31, according to early accounts. If the latter is correct, this is the second lowest ever recorded during storms in any part of the world. Winds of more than 200 miles an hour were thought to have developed. Tremendous damage, probably amounting to several hundred million dollars, was inflicted on the coastal area along with the loss of at least 130 lives, not including 70 to 80 still missing a few weeks later. The water rose about 30 feet on the coast around Gulfport and Biloxi. Even large buildings were toppled and huge steamers were washed up onto the beach. The narrow beaches characterizing this coast must have all been washed into the interior or the sand carried seaward.

In the offshore area, damage to the oil platforms and other installations is said to have reached $100 million. This is an area of extensive drilling in the shallow sea floor. The islands were considerably changed. The east end of Ship Island was washed away completely. The remaining portion was thickened, apparently by overwashes. Farther west, a breakthrough has occurred and a new tidal delta has been built on the lagoon side. The beach on the Gulf side has evidently disappeared.

CAT ISLAND, MISSISSIPPI [Fig. 7.36]   Cat Island, 8 miles offshore from Gulfport, Mississippi, is the westernmost of the chain of Mississippi barrier islands. It is shaped like an anchor and consists of two east-west barriers, West Point to the north and Middle Spit, respectively 4 and 2 miles long. These are in line with the other Mississippi barriers to the east. However, at the eastern end of these two spits, they are cut off by South Spit, another slightly curved barrier 6.5 miles long and oriented northeast-southwest. Aerial photos (not illustrated) show that West Point and Middle Spit are vegetated and are obviously older, since they are cut off by the northeast-southwest barrier. The latter is largely a sand beach without vegetation and is evidently quite young. South

7.36 Cat Island consists of two parts, an east-west barrier of the Horn Island series and a northeast-southwest barrier formed near the margins of an abandoned subdelta of the Mississippi. U.S. Coast and Geodetic Survey Chart 1267, 1967 and Chart 1268, 1965.

A

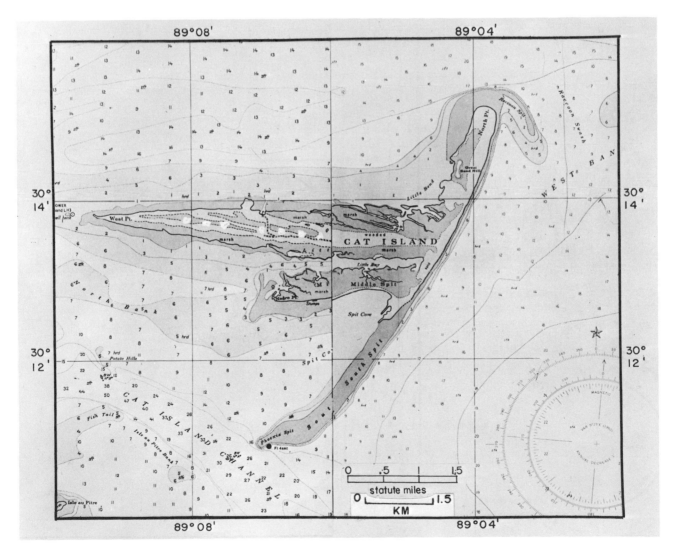

Spit is virtually in line with Isle au Pitre, a small island to the southwest, the northeast outlier of the Mississippi Delta. A channel separates the two, but a small shoal gives evidence of a former connection.

Apparently the newer portion of Cat Island is a part of a frontal arc of barrier islands, formed marginal to the abandoned and sinking St. Bernard sub-delta of the Mississippi. The Cat Island and Isle au Pitre arc is several miles inside the Chandeleur Island arc.

REFERENCES

Brenneman, Lionel, and William F. Tanner, 1958. Possible abandoned barrier islands in Panhandle Florida. *Jour. Sed. Petrology*, vol. 28, no. 3, pp. 342–344.

Carlson, Charles W., 1950. Pleistocene history of coastal Alabama. *Geol. Soc. Amer. Bull.*, vol. 61, pt. 4, pp. 1119–1130.

Corps of Engineers, U.S. Army, 1948. *Anna Marie and Longboat Keys, Florida, Beach Erosion Study*. House of Representatives, 80th Congr. 2d Sess., Document 760.

————, 1948. *Harrison County, Mississippi, Beach Erosion Control Study*. House of Representatives, 80th Congr., 2d Sess., Document 682.

Davis, J. H., Jr., 1946. The peat deposits of Florida. *Florida Geol. Survey Bull. 30*.

Dunn, G. E., and B. I. Miller, 1964. *Atlantic Hurricanes*, rev. ed. Louisiana State University Press, Baton Rouge.

El-Ashry, Mohamed T., 1966. Photointerpretation of shoreline changes in selected areas along the Atlantic and Gulf coasts of the United States. Univ. Illinois Ph.D., thesis in geology, pp. 73–87.

Goodell, H. G., and D. S. Gorsline, 1960. A sedimentologic study of Tampa Bay. *Internat. Geol. Congr., 21st Sess.*, Norden, pt. 23, pp. 75–88.

Huang, Ter-Chien, and H. G. Goodell, 1967. Sediments of Charlotte Harbor, southwestern Florida. *Jour. Sed. Petrology*, vol. 37, pp. 449–474.

Kofoed, J. W., and D. S. Gorsline, 1963. Sedimentary environments in Apalachicola Bay and vicinity, Florida. *Jour. Sed. Petrology*, vol. 33. pp. 205–233.

Martens, J. H. C., 1936. Beaches of Florida. *Florida State Geol. Survey, 21st-22nd Ann. Rept.*, pp. 67–119.

Scholl, D. W., 1963. Sedimentation in modern coastal swamps, southwestern Florida. *Amer. Assoc. Petrol. Geologists Bull.*, vol. 47, pp. 1581–1603.

————, 1964. Recent sedimentary record in mangrove swamps and rise in sea level over the southwestern coast of Florida. *Marine Geol.*, vol. 1, pp. 344–366; vol. 2, pp. 343–364.

————, and M. Stuiver, 1967. Recent submergence of southern Florida: a comparison with adjacent coasts and other eustatic data. *Geol. Soc. Amer. Bull.*, vol. 78, pp. 437–454.

Spackman, W., D. W. Scholl, and W. H. Taft, 1964. *Field Guidebook to Environments of Coal Formation in Southern Florida.* Geol. Soc. Amer., pre-convention field trip guide.

Tanner, W. F., 1959. Near-shore studies in sedimentology and morphology along the Florida panhandle coast. *Jour. Sed. Petrology*, vol. 29, pp. 564–574.

————, 1960. Florida coastal classification. *Gulf Coast Assoc. Geol. Soc. Trans.*, vol. 10, pp. 259–266.

————, 1961. Offshore shoals in area of energy deficit. *Jour. Sed. Petrology,* vol. 31, pp. 87–95.

Warnke, D. A., V. Goldsmith, P. Grose, and J. J. Holt, 1966. Drastic beach changes in a low-energy environment caused by Hurricane Betsy. *Jour. Geophys. Res.*, vol. 71, no. 8, pp. 2013–2016.

Zenkovich, V. P., 1967. *Processes of Coastal Development.* Interscience Publishers, New York, especially pp. 514–526.

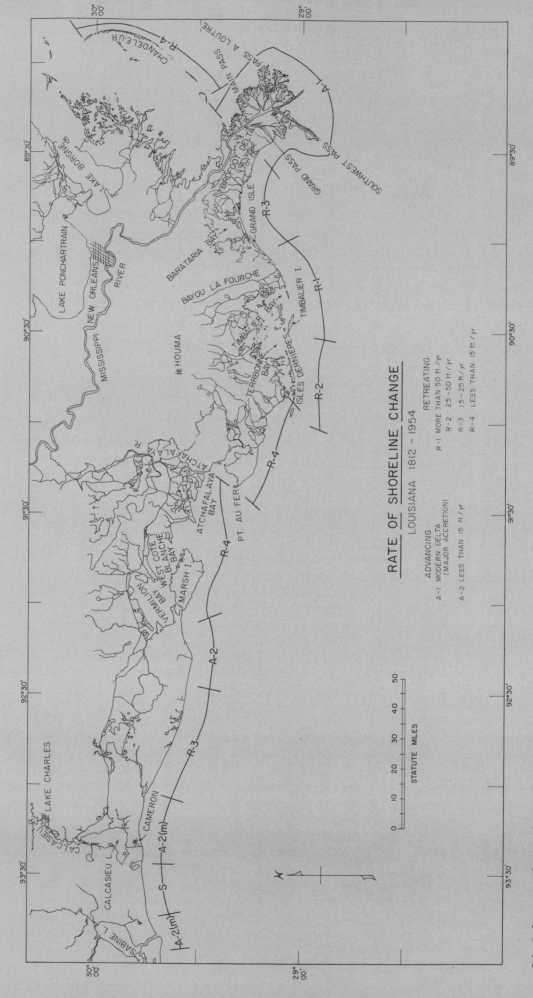

RATE OF SHORELINE CHANGE
LOUISIANA 1812 - 1954

ADVANCING   RETREATING

A-1 MODERN DELTA   R-1 MORE THAN 50 ft./yr.
     (MAJOR ACCRETION)   R-2 25 – 50 ft./yr.
A-2 LESS THAN 15 ft./yr. R-3 15 – 25 ft./yr.
                           R-4 LESS THAN 15 ft./yr.

```
         0   10   20   30   40   50
STATUTE MILES
```

8.1 Index map of coastal Louisiana showing localities described and rates of shoreline change, 1912 to 1954. From Morgan (1963).

Deltaic Coasts

Louisiana

8 Of all the coasts of the United States, the one with the greatest changes in outline during historical times is that of the Mississippi Delta. Although one thinks of a delta as increasing the land mass and even though the Mississippi Delta has added large tracts of land to Louisiana since the first charts were made, the loss of land has been quantitatively greater than the additions. This has been well documented by James P. Morgan and others of the Geology Department and Coastal Studies Institute of the Louisiana State University. The apparent inconsistency can be explained by reference to Figure 8.1. Here, the entire delta coast is shown; and the only advancing shoreline, which is largely at the present river mouths, is seen to be much smaller in coastal area than all the abandoned and retreating deltas that had been built in the past on either side of the modern delta.

The modern delta projects into the Gulf of Mexico beyond the general coast. The old deltas on either side are deeply embayed, and sand barrier islands have formed along a part of their margins. Vast marshy and swampy areas cover much of the coast, particularly to the west of the modern delta.

In addition to the old and new deltas of the Mississippi, coastal Louisiana includes 75 miles of smooth, gently curving shoreline west of the deltaic complex, where a broad coastal plain is characterized by many low ridges that run roughly parallel to the shore. These are covered by low scrubby live oak trees and hence are called *cheniers*, from the French *chêne*, meaning "oak." These ridges contain a mixture of shells and sand, which have yielded important evidence concerning the history of the area.

NATURE OF DELTA BUILDING   Deltas form where a river is carrying more sediment into a standing body of water than can be carried away by the waves and currents. The Mississippi is one of the world's largest systems,

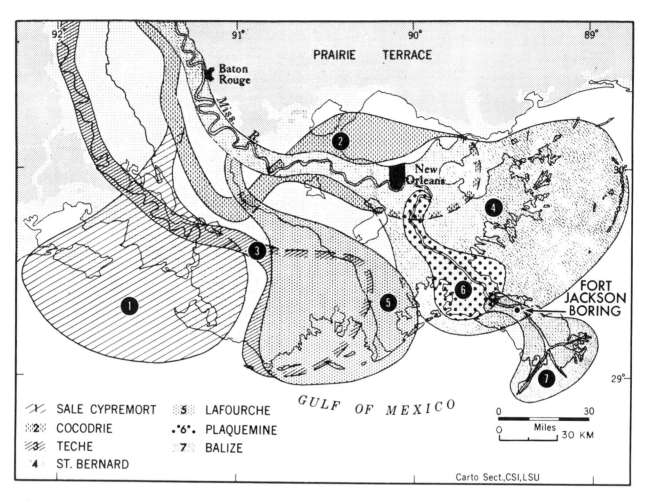

8.2 Outlines and names of seven successive subdeltas of the Mississippi River. From C. R. Kolb and J. R. van Lopik. U.S. Army Engineers Waterways Experiment Station, Corps of Engineers, Vicksburg, Mississippi.

draining an area of 1,240,000 square miles and having a length, including the Missouri River, of 3,800 miles. Where this huge river comes to the Gulf of Mexico it loses its velocity, and most of the sediments that were being carried along the bottom and in suspension are deposited. Much of this deposition takes place in the form of a bar at the mouth of the river. A channel with relatively shallow water goes through the bar. During times of flood, the bar is breached and a new bar develops farther seaward. In this way the channel is elongated. Also, during floods, the river surface grows higher and the water piles over the sides. In the shoaler water, there is increased friction and deposition takes place, developing what are called *natural levees* or embankments that build to several feet above sea level. In

addition to forming the levees, the chief effect of the flood is to build up the shallow sea floor on either side of the channel. In this way, broad marshes are formed that are seen extending for miles away from the river levees.

If an advancing river system, with its seaward-moving bars, natural levees, and marshes is not interfered with by man it will ordinarily develop bifurcations or distributaries, due to flood waters breaking gaps in the levees or to the formation of bars at the river mouth. These *crevasses*[1] enlarge rapidly and start new channels across the marshes. Before the

[1] The term *crevasse* is also applied to vertical cracks in glacial ice, resulting from strains from different rates of movement of adjoining parts of a glacier (Fig. 13.16).

development of the relatively high artificial levees, the Mississippi Delta had bifurcated many times. This is particularly well shown about 12 miles upstream from the mouths of the three principal distributaries (Fig. 8.1). Here, at what is called "Head of Passes," the river divides into Southwest Pass, South Pass, and Pass a Loutre. The first two are used for deep-draft ships plying to and from New Orleans; therefore, a deep channel is maintained through their bars. Pass a Loutre has a shallow bar at the channel mouth, so it can be used only for small boats or shallow-draft barges. The same is true of Main Pass and Batiste Collette, which break off the main channel respectively 4 and 10 miles upstream from Head of Passes. Locally, however, these east-draining passes have had channels dredged in them, permitting petroleum company supply ships to enter.

HISTORY OF THE MISSISSIPPI DELTA   To understand best what is happening to the part of the Louisiana coast that includes the old and new Mississippi Delta, we will review briefly the history of these deltas. This has been intensively studied by the geologists at Louisiana State University and by the U.S. Army Corps of Engineers. Especially notable contributions have been made by R. J. Russell, C. R. Kolb, J. P. Morgan, S. M. Gagliano, David Frazier, and the late H. N. Fisk. With the help of many carbon-14 dates, it has been possible to reconstruct the building of the delta during the past 5,000 years, the period during which sea level rise became greatly diminished. This history is portrayed in Figure 8.2 where we see a series of seven deltaic lobes that have been built forward at different times. The oldest, the Sale-Cypremont, developed about 5,000 years ago and is farthest to the west. This delta was succeeded by the Cocodrie, an easterly trending lobe, and then by the Teche with an intermediate location. The St. Bernard, the largest lobe of all, next built far to the east, and then the Lafourche, with two deltaic lobes, had a middle location. The Plaquemine, farthest east, was a precursor to the last lobe, called the Balize or Birdfoot Delta. This is the only one now actively building into the ocean, although slow forward growth is taking place at the far west border in a small area west of Marsh Island (Fig. 8.1). For some years, the Atchafalaya has threatened to develop a shortcut to the Gulf of Mexico. The Army Corps of Engineers has been controlling this diversion

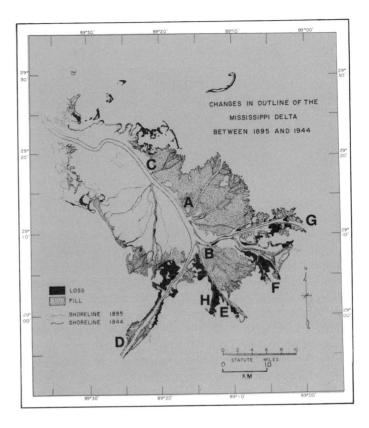

8.3 Changes in outline of the Mississippi Delta between 1895 and 1944. Prepared by Shepard and J. R. Moriarty.

and will probably continue to do so for a long time. Further discussion of these deltas is included in the rest of this chapter.

THE MODERN DELTA   All of the Balize or Birdfoot Delta is very recent. According to the late Harold Fisk, the growth beyond Head of Passes must have started about A.D. 1500. The growth of the various eastern and southern distributaries is well documented since 1838, when the Coast and Geodetic Survey made their first detailed chart; but the chart of 1895 was much more exact and complete. Virtually all these extensions between 1838 and the present took place from 1895 to 1944, and are illustrated in Figure 8.3. The principal changes in this period are large additions of land built into shallow water resulting from crevasses. These breaks were mostly cut as ditches by early settlers: one on the west side in 1839 and three on the east between

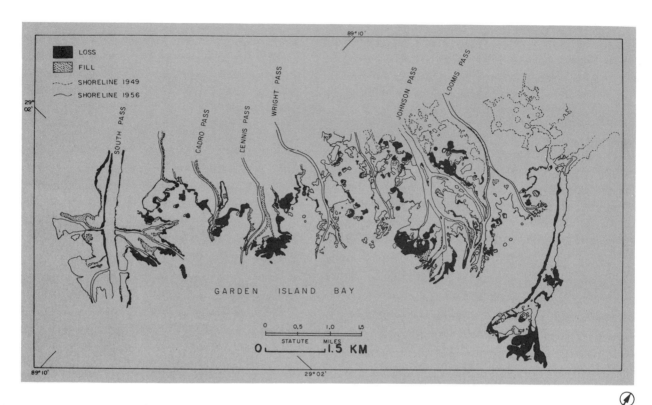

8.4 Changes in delta distributaries in Garden Island Bay between 1949 and 1956, prepared by Shepard from a comparison of aerial photographs.

1860 and 1891. The 10-mile growth of Main Pass since Cubits Gap (A) was opened in 1860 and 8 miles in Garden Island Bay since Johnson Pass (B) was cut in 1891, are particularly impressive. Batiste Collette (C), cut through in 1874, has advanced 5 miles in 60 years. In 100 years, Southwest Pass (D) has also advanced about 5 miles; but the land area has actually decreased because the artificial levees have prevented overflow, and part of the old marshes has sunk below sea level. Less extension has occurred at South Pass (E). Here, growth has been very slow because this pass is being built into deep water; and the growth of Southwest Pass is gradually decreasing, as it has also grown across the continental shelf, and further advance has to build out the slope. Southeast Pass (F) had reached the edge of the shelf before it became inactive in about 1900. Pass a Loutre (G) is now approaching the slope and actually building it forward beyond the 2-mile-wide shallow platform at its two mouths.

Comparison of the shape of the Birdfoot Delta in 1838 with its present shape (Fig. 8.3) indicates that the projecting prongs, which gave it its name, are becoming much less conspicuous and that the delta is developing a more lobate shape, like most other large deltas. This rounding effect is taking place especially between South Pass and Batiste Collette. However, East Bay, between South Pass and Southwest Pass, has had no fill; in fact, it is becoming more of a cleft, because the jetties along these two passes prevent fill and have resulted in considerable loss due to sinking of the old distributaries on the west side of South Pass, including old Grand Pass (H). Although Garden Island Bay, the large bight between South Pass and Southeast Pass, was largely eliminated between 1890 and 1944, it appears to have essentially stopped its growth since that time (Fig. 8.4), and only slight adjustments have taken place.

Most large deltas are known to be subsiding. The

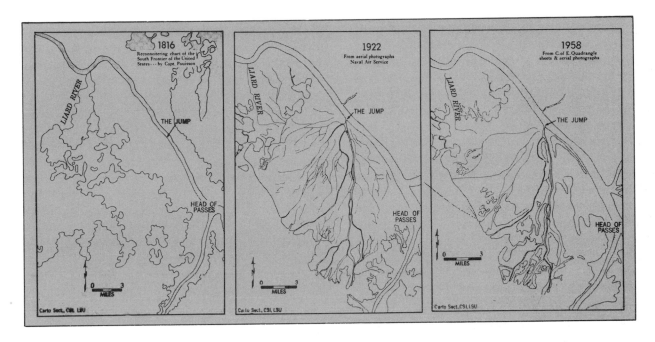

8.5 Development of a new subdelta, called The Jump, between 1816 and 1958. From Morgan (1967).

subsidence is partly explained by compaction of the muds, particularly in the swamp areas on either side of actively growing channels. Almost certainly the sinking is also the result of earth movements. At the mouths of some large rivers, notably the Amazon, sinking is so rapid that the delta has not yet filled the resulting embayment. Where active growth associated with the channels and levees is progressing, the land stays above sea level; but as soon as a break-through diverts the main flow into another channel, the old channel becomes clogged and the adjoining shoreline starts to recede. As evidence of this recession in the Mississippi Delta we can see old abandoned lighthouses that once marked the entrances to formerly active passes but are now surrounded by water.

One fast rate of retreat is shown between 1922 and 1958, when The Jump (Fig. 8.5), the distributary on the west side of the delta above Head of Passes, became inactive following 100 years of fill. An embayment spread back into the delta a total of 12 miles in the 36-year interval. The nature of this change is well illustrated by the contrast in the aerial photos along the new Grand Pass in 1947 and 1958

(Figs. 8.6a and b). In the earlier photo, the distributaries to the southeast (Fig 8.6a), are clearly shown, but they are partly covered with water in the later photo (Fig. 8.6b). Also, several bodies of water (A in Fig. 8.6a) are largely choked with vegetation at their southern ends, indicating that the rising water in 1949 was disrupting the peat marshes. In 1958, this same area is seen to be entirely inundated. The masses of vegetation (B in Fig. 8.6a) are illustrative of the way floating islands are developed. These are often carried downstream and even out into the open ocean, transporting various types of animal life. This process often results in the spreading of species beyond their usual habitats, and may even lead to populating outlying islands.

There is a curious feature about the relation of gain and loss to the passes between Pass a Loutre and Southwest Pass (Fig. 8.3). In each case most of the loss has occurred on the right bank. This is particularly surprising because it is true of the natural Pass a Loutre and Southeast Pass, as well as of the levee-controlled South and Southwest Passes. Apparently, this is some form of downwarp of an arcuate character.

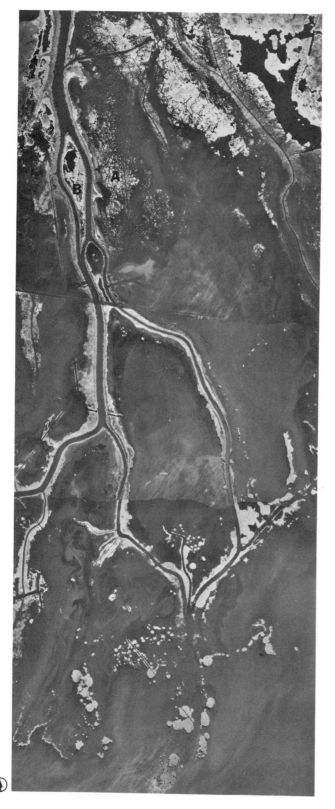

8.6 Aerial photographs showing changes in the new Grand Pass between 1947 and 1958.

a December 7, 1947. Distributary channels are flanked by narrow natural levees adjoining marshland. In several ponds, as at A, masses of marsh vegetation have become detached and floated south until trapped near the end of the pond (B). U.S. Army Corps of Engineers.

b October 11, 1958. Marsh tracts between natural levees have largely disappeared due to subsidence. A few distributary channels have been dismembered by drowning. U.S. Coast and Geodetic Survey.

8.7 Mud lumps near the South Pass. Photo by James P. Morgan.

DELTA MARGINAL DEPRESSIONS   To the northeast of the Mississippi Delta, a series of marginal depressions (Fig. 8.1) all connect with the Gulf of Mexico. These include the western part of the Mississippi Sound, Lake Borgne, and Lake Ponchartrain, the last just north of New Orleans. Lake Maurepas lies farther west and is not connected with the Gulf. Such depressions are characteristic of the large deltas of the world, being found on one side of the Ganges, Indus, Irrawaddy, Yangtze-Kiang, Po, Danube, and Orinoco. According to Morgan, the depression in Lake Borgne is now shown to be due to nondeposition, rather than to downwarping, as had been suspected. The drowned mouth of the Kuskokwim River (Fig. 14.6), which formerly served as the mouth of the Yukon River, is another example of delta marginal depression. The fact that the depressions are more pronounced on one side of deltas than the other suggests that the sinking is accompanied by tilting.

MUD LUMP ISLANDS   Features that are reported only from the Mississippi Delta are the mud lump islands. These small land masses are found directly off Pass a Loutre, Southeast Pass, and South Pass (Fig. 8.7). They are pushed up from below and have been seen to come above sea level in a period of a few hours. They consist of mud that was buried deeply by subsequent delta deposits and has later been squeezed up, like toothpaste, through the overlying formations until the mud lumps reach the surface. Fossils found in the mud of these islands show that some of the mud was deposited in water several hundred feet deep. The formations in the exposed

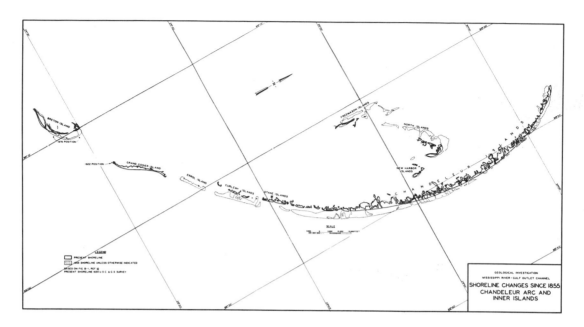

8.8 Changing locations of the Chandeleur Island arc east of the St. Bernard sub-delta between 1855 and 1965. From U.S. Army Corps of Engineers.

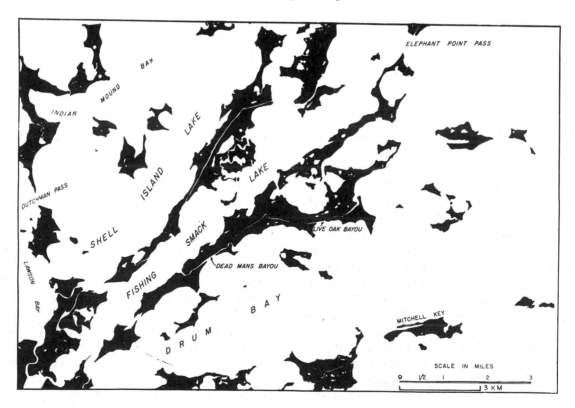

8.9 Partly dismembered distributary channels of the abandoned St. Bernard sub-delta. From R. J. Russell (1936).

OUR CHANGING COASTLINES

islands are often highly tilted, showing the deformation they have undergone. The islands are of short duration. They are so soft that even the small waves of the Gulf cut them away, usually in a few years.

DROWNED ST. BERNARD DELTA   The St. Bernard Delta extended somewhat beyond the present Chandeleur Islands some 3,000 years ago. The remnants of this delta are now found more than 20 miles to the west (Fig. 8.8). The average rate of retreat, according to Morgan, has been 13.7 feet a year. Remnants of the delta that are above water are found along Bayou la Loutre and Bayou Terre aux Boeuf, which were used for shallow-draft boats until the construction of the Mississippi River Gulf outlet (about 1967). In approaching Chandeleur Sound, only relics of the natural levees remain as sand ridges above the sea. These old passes are illustrated in Figure 8.9. This compilation by R. J. Russell comes from a 1932 survey. Comparisons with aerial photographs taken in 1948 show that most of the channels have widened and indentations have largely increased in size, indicating the continued subsidence of the area. According to the U.S. Army Corps of Engineers, the old delta in Chandeleur Sound is covered with 10 feet of water, and borings show another 10 feet of shallow marine deposits.

CHANDELEUR ISLANDS   As soon as a delta lobe has been abandoned it is attacked by the waves. The result is the washing away of the mud from the deposits, leaving a concentration of the sand. The latter is built up in the form of beaches. These are well represented around most of the old delta lobes. The Chandeleur Islands (Fig. 8.8), off the east side of the Mississippi Delta, and their southwestward continuation in Breton Island, form a curving bank 40 miles long. According to the U.S. Army Corps of Engineers, since 1855 these islands have gradually been driven to the west before the easterly storm waves. Most of the islands have moved about a mile in that direction, and a few have disappeared. A comparison of photography of the southern part of the Chandeleur Island arc on May 11, 1955, and October 18, 1965 (not illustrated), shows that Stake and Curlew Islands had migrated westward about 600 feet, and that 5,835 feet of the length of these islands had disappeared during the 10-year period. In the same interval, Grand Gosier Island had mi-

grated about 200 feet. Because the 1965 photographs were taken one month after Hurricane Betsy struck the area, most of the changes seen in the 1965 photographs were presumably accomplished by this one storm. However, the islands inside the Chandeleur arc have either been eliminated or have been moved to the southeast, apparently by strong northers.

BARATARIA BAY, LOUISIANA [Figs. 8.10 and 8.11]   Just west of the modern Mississippi Delta, there is a north-south depressed zone with a series of lakes (Fig. 8.10). The south end of this depression includes Barataria Bay, a very irregular body of water having a width of about 20 miles, including the interlocking bays on the side. The main bay extends in from the string of barrier islands for about 10 miles. On the west, Barataria Bay is bordered by the old Lafourche Delta (Fig. 8.2), which, according to carbon-14 dates, was formed between approximately A.D. 800 and 1400. This is an extremely important area economically, because Grand Isle (Fig. 8.10), the principal barrier protecting the bay, is the center and home port of a booming offshore oil industry. Looking out into the Gulf from Grand Isle at night, the myriads of lights on the oil platforms give the impression of a large city in the sea (Λ).

The western side of the bay is partially filled with paired islands that adjoin the old Lafourche Delta. These are partly drowned natural levees of old distributaries. North from Barataria Pass, a string of marshy islands (Fig. 8.11) with portions of dismembered tidal streams are evidently partially drowned segments of a former delta distributary that extended north for 16 miles. According to Fisk, the Barataria depression is separated from the rest of the Lafourche Delta by a fault with northwest-southeast trends, so that the dismembered delta remnants in the depression are of the same age as the exposed Lafourche Delta remnants southwest of the fault.

In the 600 to 700 years since the active growth of the Lafourche Delta ended, the portions of the delta fronting on the Gulf of Mexico have been eroded; and the whole delta has been settling due to compaction of its sediments, whether or not it was depressed by downfaulting. As subsidence and erosion progressed, frontal barrier islands developed, like the Chandeleur Island arc outside the St. Bernard Delta. In the Barataria Bay area, islands shifted landward as erosion progressed; and in the Grand Terre Islands

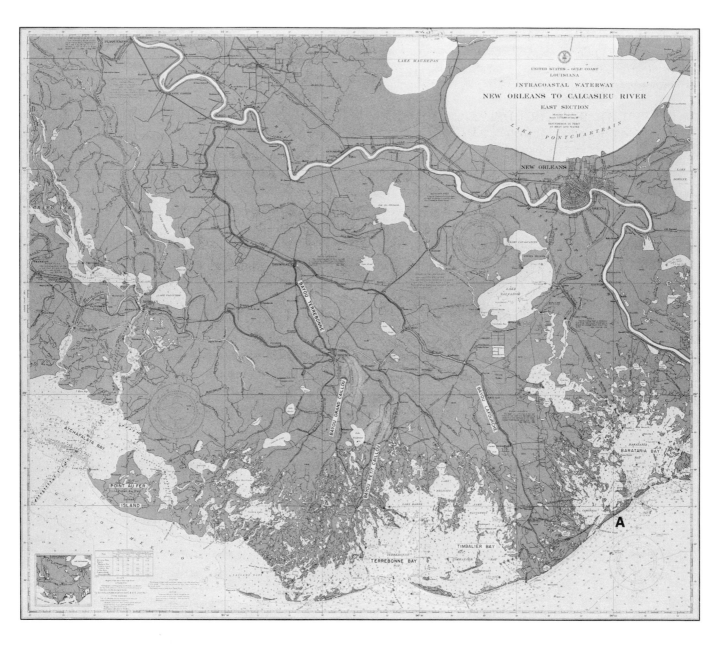

8.10 Barataria Bay to Atchafalaya Bay, showing two arms of old Lafourche sub-delta. U.S. Coast and Geodetic Survey Chart 1050, 1959.

(Fig. 8.11), these barriers are in contact with deltaic sediments and four round lakes, as well as dismembered tidal streams. Strong tidal currents that enter and leave Barataria Bay had deepened Barataria Pass (B in Fig. 8.11) as much as 165 feet by 1949, but depths change constantly in the entrance. Quatre Bayous Pass (C) has depths to 34 feet. Pass Able, east of Barataria Pass, has developed a double tidal delta (D); and the two small islands to the right of Pass Able seem to be exposed washover deltas.

8.11 Barataria Bay (A) and the Grand Terre Islands. A portion of the old Lafourche Delta (F), including round lakes, adjoins a chain of barrier islands. A prominent double tidal delta (D) has formed at Pass Abel. Aerial photography by Ammann International, San Antonio, Texas.

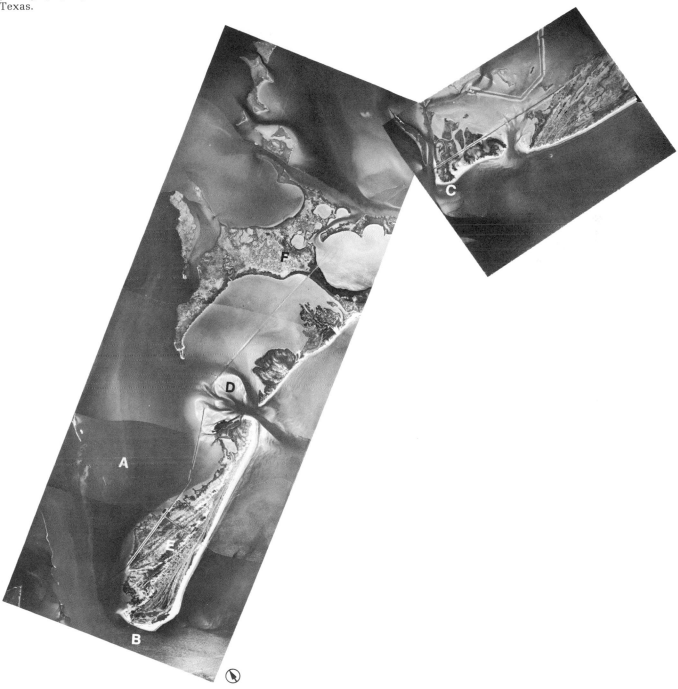

Beach ridges (E) of the chenier type on the west end of Grand Terre Island and Chenier Ronquille are at an angle to the present shoreline, suggesting a former cuspate projection now truncated by coastal erosion.

Morgan showed that in the Barataria reentrant between the Lafourche and modern deltas, erosion of the barrier islands has been progressing at the rate of 16 feet per year. If this rate has been maintained for 700 years, the time since the delta was abandoned, the outer 2 miles of the delta would have been destroyed and overridden by the barrier islands. A comparison of aerial photographs of Grand Terre Island in 1945 (not shown) with those from 1954 (Fig. 8.11) shows coastal erosion of about 300 feet, twice the rate given by Morgan.

Grand Isle, 7.5 miles long, just west of Barataria Pass, was settled about 1800 by Jean Lafitte and was used as headquarters for smuggling and piracy. Later, sugar plantations were located on this island until the Civil War and, still later, truck gardening, shrimp and oyster fishing, a seaside resort, and finally oil and sulphur development. During an 8-year period, prior to 1934, 348 acres, 13 percent of the island area, were lost by erosion, as reported by the U.S. Army Corps of Engineers. Between 1878 and 1935, the 6-foot and 12-foot depth contours offshore each shifted landward about 1,500 feet along the western part of the island, while advancing seaward along the eastern part. This may have been the result of differential subsidence along the axis or, conversely, may be due to an eddy in surface currents causing an easterly set along this coastal sector. Prior to 1933, the Gulf shore was reported to have been covered with driftwood, but because of complaints of inconvenience to swimmers, it was removed. Erosion became accelerated after the driftwood was gone from the beach, especially during major storms.

LAFOURCHE, TIMBALIER, TERREBONNE AREA, LOUISIANA [Figs. 8.10, 8.12, 8.13, and 8.14]

The Lafourche Delta, which began form-ing about 1,200 years ago, spread from the west side of Barataria Bay to the west side of Terrebonne Bay. This delta was developed after the abandonment of the east-draining St. Bernard Delta (Fig. 8.2). The Lafourche lobe branched south from the course of the present Mississippi at Donaldsonville, 30 miles below Baton Rouge. About 25 miles farther downstream, near the town of Thibodaux, the river subdivided. For the first 30 miles, Bayou Black actually flows in the reverse direction from the old course of the main channel of the Teche Delta of 3,000 to 3,800 years ago. Beyond the 30 miles, it turns into its predominant southwest course and discharges into the Gulf south of Morgan City. Each of the three main distributaries divided repeatedly, so that a multitude of channels, spreading out in fan shape, carried the Lafourche drainage to the Gulf of Mexico. Some 600 to 700 years ago, when the Mississippi became diverted eastward from the site of the modern town of Donaldsonville toward present-day New Orleans, the Bayou Lafourche persisted as a minor distributory. It was closed artificially in 1903.

The Lafourche Delta (Figs. 8.2 and 8.10) is less modified by subsidence, erosion, or burial by younger delta deposits than any other abandoned delta. The natural levees along the distributaries are actually higher than those along the modern delta. The southeastern prong formed by Bayou Lafourche and the southern prong built by Bayou Terrebonne and its distributaries extend into the Gulf about 15 miles farther than the small distributaries in between. A large indentation between the two prongs includes Timbalier Bay and Terrebonne Bay and a series of inner lakes. Barrier islands partially close off these bays and lakes from the open Gulf. The principal barriers of an earlier stage include Isles Dernieres (Fig. 8.10), to the west and several islands to the east. Timbalier and East Timbalier Islands (Fig. 8.14) form an outer chain 1 to 3 miles seaward of the older barriers.

The history of development of the southeastern part of the Lafourche Delta is suggested by the features shown on the composite aerial photo (Fig. 8.12). From the apex (A) of a fan of chenier beach ridges they multiply and spread out to the southwest. Directly north of this fan, one can see the limit of the Lafourche Delta (B) with a major distributary crossing it in a southeasterly direction until it reaches the belt of cheniers. At this point (C), the channel

8.12 The abandoned Lafourche Delta adjoined by a broad barrier consisting of beach ridges fanning out toward the southwest. A narrow modern beach truncates the ends of older beach ridges. U.S. Department of Agriculture, 1953.

8.13 Adjoins west side of Figure 8.12. West margin of
the east lobe of the old Lafourche Delta. A modern beach
truncates round lakes at C and D. The encroachment of
the beach on the lake remnant has aided in measuring
present-day shore erosion. At E, the delta adjoins the
Timbalier Barrier Island Chain. U.S. Department of Agriculture, 1953.

divides into three distributaries. The large one (D) bends west and flows between the beach ridges for a short distance until it encounters a pond. The smaller branch (E) takes a circuitous course to the southeast where it subdivides; and one branch extends northeast along the northern limit of the cheniers, while the other winds its way across the cheniers, finally entering a sizable lake near the coast.

The interpretation of this contact between the old delta and the cheniers has led to a difference of opinion between two of the delta experts. Richard J. Russell has considered that the Lafourche Delta formerly extended about 30 miles farther into the Gulf and was then eroded back to the present contact between delta and chenier ridges. He believed that the ridges were added later to the eroded remnant, producing the present conditions. Harold N. Fisk, on the other hand, suggested that the beach ridges were formed at the terminus of the delta and were essentially contemporaneous. Fisk referred to the interpenetration of some of the channels into the depressions between the ridges as evidence for his contention.

We have not studied the area extensively, so feel hesitant in offering an opinion as to which hypothesis is correct. However, we note that the chenier belt appears to originate to the east of the Lafourche Delta, suggesting that it had a source other than from the distributaries coming down the delta. Also, the Lafourche Delta seems to be sharply truncated by the ridges in much the same manner that the chenier ridges themselves are truncated by the present shoreline and beach. James P. Morgan's map, showing the retreat of old delta coasts, gives an annual retreat of 62 feet per year for this old Lafourche Delta, which gives further indication of the credibility of an earlier epoch when the delta extended much farther into the Gulf. Therefore we are inclined to think that the Russell interpretation is more likely correct.

Figure 8.13 (a western extension of Fig. 8.12) shows the contact (E) of the Timbalier barriers with the western side of the Bayou Lafourche prong of

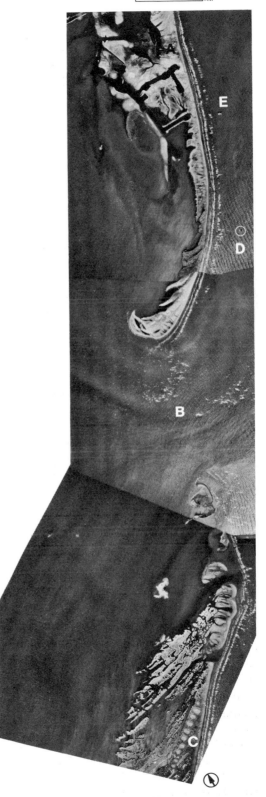

8.14 Timbalier (C) and East Timbalier (A) Islands. A lighthouse (D) built on East Timbalier many years ago, by 1957 stood out in the Gulf 1,800 feet south of the island. This is a measure of the northward migration of this barrier. At point E, offshore oil drilling platforms are shown. U.S. Coast and Geodetic Survey, 1957.

the old Lafourche Delta (A). Here, the deltaic deposits have buried the barrier and are therefore younger. The same delta lobe also buried the chenier ridges (B), which are a continuation of the cheniers shown in Figure 8.12. Thus the delta lobe is relatively young. However, there is clear evidence that active growth of this lobe has ceased, although a moderate discharge continued through the Bayou Lafourche Channel until it was closed in 1903. Examination of Figure 8.13 shows one large round lake (C) with a bight taken from its seaward end. To the west, the small remnant of another large lake (D) can be seen. A thin barrier of sand separates both truncated lakes from the Gulf. Russell has shown that the old delta front at this point has receded 1,500 feet in a 20-year period.

The Timbalier Islands (Fig. 8.10) form a barrier chain gulfward from an older barrier in the eastern part of the Terrebonne-Timbalier Bay complex. Figure 8.14 shows the western part of East Timbalier Island (A), Little Pass Timbalier (B), and the eastern part of Timbalier Island (C). Tidal-current scour has cut the channel between these islands to a maximum depth of 25 feet, while depths surrounding the channel are 5 feet or less. Timbalier Island is made up of a series of beach ridges or cheniers at an angle to the present shoreline, another example of erosional truncation. East Timbalier Island has a succession of eight hooks, several of the outer ones being sharply recurved. South of the narrow neck of East Timbalier Island, a dark object in the water (D) is a lighthouse originally built on East Timbalier Island; but by the time of the 1957 photo, it was left out in the Gulf of Mexico 1,800 feet offshore. Wave erosion had caused the island to migrate northward to that extent since the lighthouse was constructed. Figure 8.14 also shows drilling platforms for offshore oil exploration (E), both in the bay to the north of the islands and in the Gulf of Mexico. According to Coast and Geodetic Survey Chart 1274 (1963), centering 4 miles south of East Timbalier Island is an oil field that had forty-seven drilling platforms.

West of Timbalier Island, a 7-mile-wide inlet, Cat Island Pass (Fig. 8.10), is the main entrance to Terrebonne Bay. Here, the depths reach 24 feet. Beyond this pass, the Isles Dernieres, another chain of barrier islands, apparently belong to an older series than the Timbalier Islands. Borings on one of the Isles Dernieres have shown that it overlies the deep valley occupied by the Mississippi during low sea level of the climax of the last glaciation. The floor of this valley was at about 600 feet where penetrated in the Isles Dernieres, but rivers are capable of cutting well below sea level. Also, the delta has been sinking. Isles Dernieres are situated offshore from the part of the Lafourche Delta formed by the deeply embayed Terrebonne Bay complex. The barrier islands have not yet migrated landward far enough to encroach against the delta front, as has happened east of the Timbalier Islands (Fig. 8.10). However, near Coupe Nouvelle, where the Dernieres are closest to the mainland, small drowned and dismembered parts of the Terrebonne complex are bordered by a narrow coastal barrier.

ATCHAFALAYA BAY–MARSH ISLAND AREA, LOUISIANA [Figs. 8.15 and 8.16]   The area in central coastal Louisiana (Fig. 8.15) includes the western margin of the old Mississippi River Delta. The Sale-Cypremont (or Maringouin), dating from approximately 3000 to 2000 B.C., was the first of seven postglacial deltas that discharged into the Gulf of Mexico (see Fig. 8.2). More than half of the deposits of this delta are now inundated by the Gulf of Mexico, because of a combination of a slight eustatic rise in sea level, compaction of the deltaic sediments, and subsidence under load of the delta deposits of the region. During the building of all later deltas, the Mississippi River entered the Gulf of Mexico east of this area. Because of the antiquity and present low level of the Sale-Cypremont Delta, the coast has a major indentation in the Atchafalaya Bay–Marsh Island area, amounting locally to 20 miles. This includes Vermilion, East and West Cote Blanche, and Atchafalaya Bays. Marsh Island largely protects Vermilion and West Cote Blanche Bays from the waves of the open Gulf of Mexico.

The postglacial geological history of this embayed area was described by James Coleman in 1966. When the Mississippi discharged here, some of the mud and silt introduced into the Gulf was redistributed by shore currents westward along the shore beyond the limit of delta sedimentation, resulting in progradation of coastal areas to the southwest. When the Mississippi discharged into the Gulf 50 miles or more to the east of this area, as it did during all except the Sale-Cypremont, Teche, and Lafourche delta stages, little sediment was supplied to central Lou-

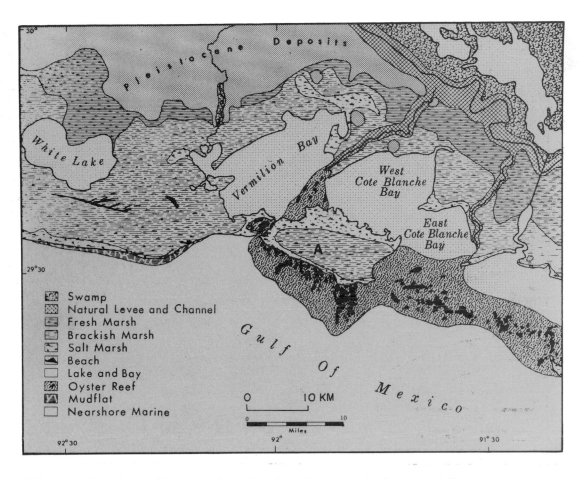

8.15 Map of surface sedimentary depositional environments in the area of Vermilion and Cote Blanche Bays and Marsh Island (A). From Coleman (1966).

isiana; and mud plains developed previously became the sites of widespread marshes—salty at their gulf-ward limit and brackish to fresh water farther inland. Figure 8.15 shows the vast extent of these marshes as surface deposits, whereas beaches are nearly lacking along these coasts. However, after prolonged periods of erosion, the coarsest detritus, made of shell and a little sand, has been concentrated locally, forming narrow beaches.

Seaward from the marshy shore, shallow-water marine invertebrates flourished and formed many oyster reefs (Fig. 8.15), some of which are elongate normal to the shoreline. According to Coleman, the reefs formed on hard surfaces of the natural levees of the old stream courses and in other shallow areas. Some of the shoals were probably on interstream divides, developed when sea level was a little lower than now. Oyster reefs are plentiful on the south side

of Marsh Island, and they form a series of reef shoals that protect Atchafalaya and East Cote Blanche Bays from the open Gulf of Mexico.

The history of the Mississippi Delta shows that whenever one of the deltas had grown well south of the "common head of deltas," which is near the mouth of Red River (north of Fig. 8.1), a new delta was initiated. A breach in the natural levees along the river was developed during a flood, and eventually most of the water drained through it wherever the new course had a gradient advantage in its route to the Gulf. The outer margin of the modern delta is about 200 miles southeast of this apex of postglacial deltas, whereas the outlet of the Atchafalaya River (Fig. 8.1), heading near the apex, is only 110 miles to the south. In 1915, about 10 percent of the Mississippi River water reached the Gulf through the Atchafalaya, but by 1950, the proportion had in-

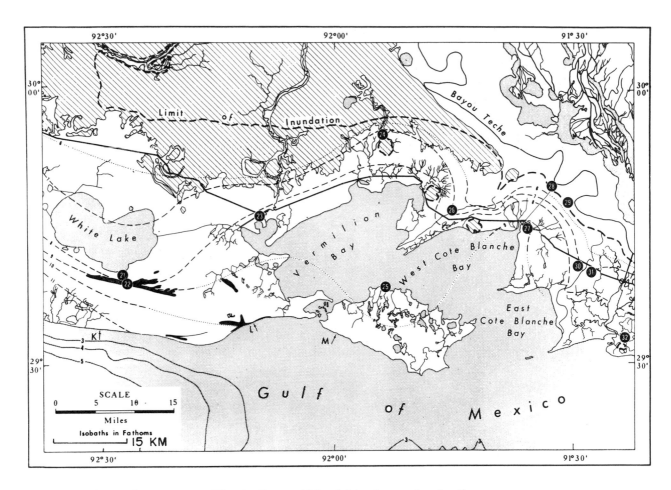

8.16 Map of Vermilion Bay, Cote Blanche Bay, and Marsh Island area, showing the extent of inundation of this central Louisiana coast by Hurricane Audrey in June 1957. Note that the western part of the coast was inundated to a depth of 11 feet. From Morgan, Nichols, and Wright (1958).

creased to 30 percent. It was predicted that the amount of water thus derived would continue to increase, and that before the end of the twentieth century the modern delta would be abandoned and replaced by a new delta building into Atchafalaya Bay. However, to prevent the Mississippi from bypassing the port cities of New Orleans and Baton Rouge and its present lower channel, the U.S. Army Corps of Engineers has completed a control structure that stops continued diversion. Sediment carried to the Gulf through the new outlet has been drifted westward by shore currents, causing part of the shore west of Marsh Island to advance at the rate of 60 feet per year between 1927 and 1951.

Occasionally this flat coast of central Louisiana has been struck by hurricanes. The first reported was

in 1766. In June 1957, Hurricane Audrey, coming from the south, struck the Louisiana coast; and its center passed a little east of the Texas-Louisiana line. The greatest effects of this hurricane were caused by the waves during abnormally high tides. The tidal level in the Atchafalaya Bay–Marsh Island area ranged from 7 to 9 feet above normal sea level, a height greater than any elevation on this flat coast. As a result, every part of the area within 15 to 25 miles of the coast was inundated, much of it by water as deep as 12 feet. James Morgan, Lewis Nichols, and Martin Wright studied the effects of the hurricane on this coast and prepared an inundation map, part of which is shown in Figure 8.16. Other features of coastal change resulting from Hurricane Audrey are described later in this chapter.

CHENIER PLAIN, VERMILION PARISH, LOUISIANA [Figs. 8.17 through 8.20] To the west of the area occupied by the various lobes of the postglacial Mississippi Delta, the coast loses its embayments and follows a smooth curve along the edge of a broad coastal plain. This is referred to as the *chenier plain,* which is defined by W. Armstrong Price as "a belted marsh and ridge plain." The chenier beach ridges with their high shell content, according to Price, "rest on clay along a marshy or swampy seaward-facing tidal shore." Other areas of this type of coastal lowland are Surinam, French Guiana, and Venezuela, in South America, and near the deltas of the Rhone and Po Rivers in southern Europe.

The Louisiana Coastal Studies group consider that requisite conditions for the development of a chenier plain include (1) proximity to a large delta where great quantities of clay and silt are introduced into the ocean or gulf; (2) littoral currents that distribute much of the clay along the coast in a direction downcurrent from the delta; and (3) interruptions in the progradation of a mud coast, during which the frontal margin suffers erosion, allowing the coarser particles of shell or sand to accumulate at the shoreline and be piled up into a ridge, augmented by shell and sand brought to the beach from the shallow sea bottom. Cheniers are commonly 3 to 10 feet high and average 600 feet wide.

The southwestern Louisiana chenier belt covers the southern parts of Vermilion and Cameron Parishes, and extends a short distance into eastern coastal Texas. Features of this belt have been described by Price in 1954; by Howard Gould and E. McFarlan, Jr. in 1959; and by J. V. Byrne, D. O. LeRoy, and C. M. Riley also in 1959. Figure 8.17, showing the distribution of the cheniers, is based on studies by these writers.

In Vermilion Parish, the eastern part of the chenier plain, clay and marsh flats predominate over ridges; but, to the west, in Cameron Parish (described in the following section), ridges are much more prominent. The Vermilion Parish area received accretions of mud during the times of the Teche Delta (2,800 and 3,800 years ago) and again while the Lafourche Delta was growing (1,200 to 600 years ago). There was a gap in mud accretion from about A.D. 1400 until early in the present century when the Atchafalaya River began to introduce large quantities of clay into the Gulf. Since then, the eastern part of Vermilion Parish again has become the site of progradation of the shore.

Cheniers can be recognized on aerial photos (Figs. 8.18 and 8.21) by the lines of dark dots representing trees or by the white streaks showing the light-colored soil where trees are missing on the ridges. Figure 8.18 shows the coastal plain west of Mud Island and includes three sets of cheniers. The continuous east-west ridge (A) is Chenier au Tigre. This truncates several ridges coming down from the north-northwest (B). Others with a northeast-southwest (C) trend lap up on the south side of Chenier au Tigre. Gould and McFarlan date the northeast-southwest cheniers as 800 B.C to A.D. 200 corresponding to the period following the abandonment of the Teche Delta. Chenier au Tigre probably formed about A.D. 900, following a long hiatus in which the shoreline had changed drastically in outline. The three cheniers with northeast-southwest orientation, belonging to what is called the Mulberry Island Series, are dated as ranging from 225 to 675 years old. These younger cheniers are nearly parallel to the coast. They formed after the abandonment of the Lafourche Delta. The marshes and mudflats between the youngest cheniers and the Gulf of Mexico are the products of mud accretion from the Atchafalaya River during the twentieth century.

Recent erosion (E) has truncated the older cheniers, as well as the Chenier au Tigre, and perhaps one of the younger Mulberry Island cheniers. To the east of the cheniers, a very narrow beach was built against the clays that were deposited during the growth of the Teche Delta. Black areas (F) in the marshes are sites of grass fires just prior to when the photo was taken.

One of the extraordinary results of Hurricane Audrey on this mud coast was the transportation as a unit of a mass of gelatinous mud from the shallow waters of the Gulf to the immediate shore and beach. Figure 8.19, prepared by Morgan, Nichols, and Wright, illustrates the eastern of the two mud arcs thus moved. It was 11,350 feet long, 1,000 feet wide, arcuate in shape, concave landward, and breached in the center. The ends (horns) of the arc overlapped the marsh, the prestorm shell-sand beach, and an older chenier belonging to the Mulberry Island Series. Although the clay was very fluid and gelatinous at the time of deposition, six months later it was dry and suncracked. Nine months after the

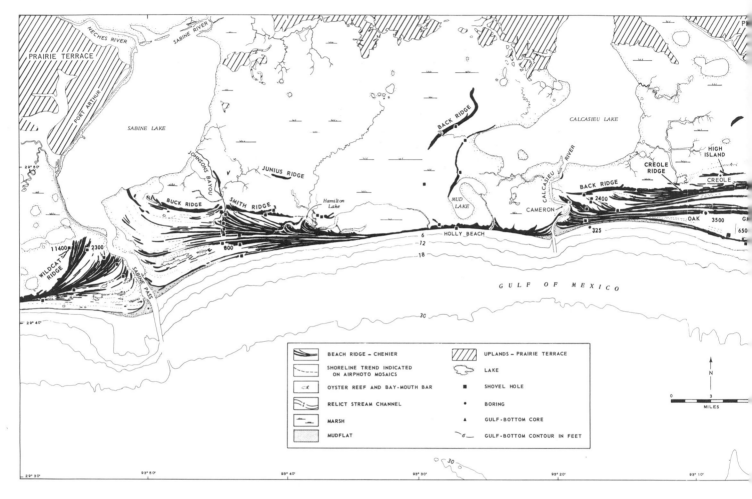

8.17 Map showing the distribution of chenier ridges in southwestern Louisiana. From Gould and McFarlan (1959).

hurricane, the mud arc was further breached, probably by runoff channels, and a new shell-sand beach began forming at its outer border.

Erosion of the muddy coast of an area in western Vermilion Parish including Flat Lake, is illustrated in Figures 8.20a and b. East Constance Bayou (A), which carries overflow water from Flat and Rollover Lakes, as well as from the adjoining marsh, was photographed in December 1950 (Fig. 8.20a) and then in March 1958 (Fig. 8.20b), the latter photo taken nine months after Hurricane Audrey. The 1950 photograph shows the lower end of East Constance Bayou with its four bends between the natural outlet to Flat Lake and its entrance into the Gulf of

Mexico. In 1958, after the hurricane, the two bends closest to the Gulf shore had been nearly cut off by shore erosion, a recession of about 600 feet. The 1950 photo also shows that tidal waters evidently entered Flat Lake through the natural outlet and through an artificial cut farther west. Small tidal deltas had been built into the lake at each inlet. In 1958, after Hurricane Audrey, sand carried in from the shore had blocked the natural outlet along one meander loop, and the tidal delta built into the lake by the natural channel was no longer visible. Additional evidence of dismemberment of winding streams in the marsh was found near Tolan and Little Constance Lakes, west of Flat Lake.

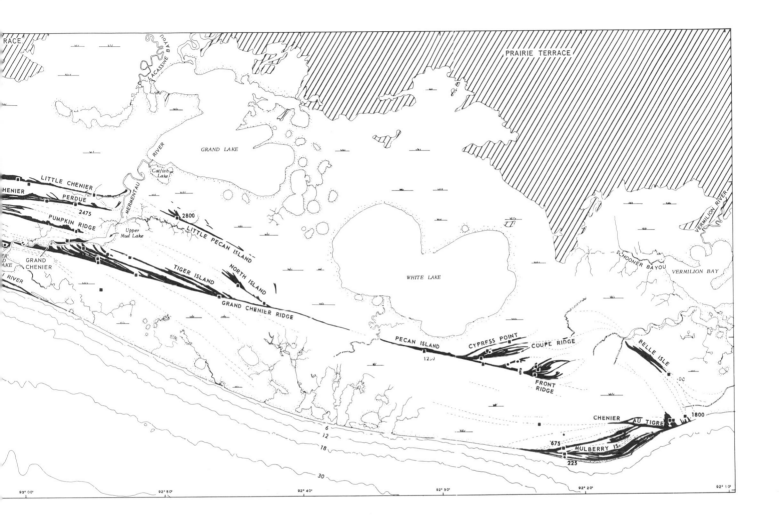

CHENIER PLAIN, CAMERON PARISH, LOUISIANA [Figs. 8.17, 8.21, and 8.22]

In eastern Cameron Parish, the chenier plain extends as much as 11 miles inland from the Gulf Coast (Fig. 8.17); but near the center of the parish, the mud plain south of the main chenier ridges diminishes in width, and the rather closely spaced ridges cover a belt of only 3 to 7 miles. Since the central part of the Cameron Parish shore is 120 miles west of the long-since abandoned Teche Delta and 140 miles from the also abandoned Lafourche Delta, the closer spacing indicates that the contributions of mud carried westward along the Gulf from these deltas must have diminished considerably.

Three rivers draining coastal plain lakes and inland areas of western Louisiana enter the Gulf in Cameron Parish. From the east, these include the Mermenteau, Calcasieu, and Sabine, the latter forming the boundary between Louisiana and Texas. As the distance from deltas of the Mississippi increases, contributions of mud from these other rivers become more important.

The longest chenier ridge in southwestern Louisiana (Fig. 8.17)—called respectively, Front Ridge and Pecan Island, in Vermilion Parish; Grand Chenier, east of the Mermenteau River; and finally Oak Grove Ridge, between the Mermenteau and Calcasieu Rivers—is about 60 miles in length. It has not been

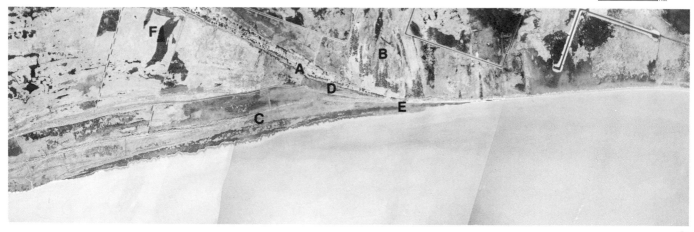

8.18 A portion of the chenier plain southwest of Vermilion Bay, showing chenier ridges of three ages, the oldest (B) trending nearly north-south, the second (D) trending nearly east-west, and the youngest (C) trending northeast-southwest. Black areas are portions of the marsh blackened by fires shortly before photography. U.S. Department of Agriculture, 1964.

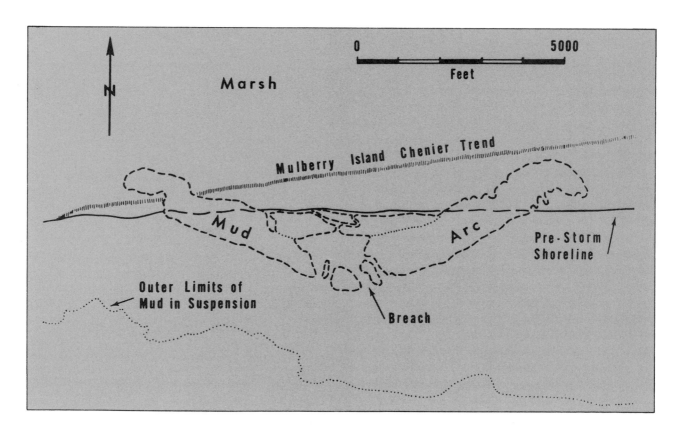

8.19 Sketch map of a mass of mud 11,350 feet long and 1,000 feet wide, which was pushed up as a unit on the shore by Hurricane Audrey. One end of the arc-shaped mass crossed a chenier ridge. From Morgan, Nichols, and Wright (1958).

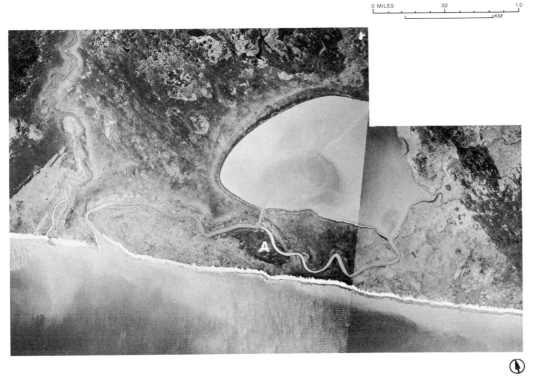

8.20 Coastal erosion at East Constance Bayou (A) near Flat Lake, Louisiana.

a 1950. Flat Lake drains through East Constance Bayou to the Gulf. U.S. Department of Agriculture.

b 1958. The shore had cut back so as to touch and block the stream at two meanders, and the lake now drains through an artificial channel west of East Constance Bayou. U.S. Department of Agriculture.

8.21 Three successive groups of chenier ridges 8 to 16 miles east of the Texas-Louisiana line. The innermost group shows hooked ridges (A). The middle group is nearly straight, and the outermost ridges have numerous notches cut by Hurricane Audrey, five months before photography. U.S. Department of Agriculture, November 9, 1957.

identified between the Calcasieu and Sabine Rivers.

East of the Calcasieu River, about twenty-seven cheniers, including separate hooks, can be recognized in an aerial photo (not illustrated). Several hooks near the western curve of the river appear to merge into a single chenier. Radiocarbon age determination correlates this ridge with the Grand and Oak Ridge cheniers farther east, which have been dated as 1,100 to 1,250 years old. The younger chenier gulfward from Oak Grove Ridge is dated as 600 to 800 years old. The older cheniers to the north, including those in the town of Cameron, are considered 1,800 to 2,000 years old. Thus, within a belt of only about 2 miles, there are twenty to twenty-seven cheniers covering a time span of about 1,400 years. West of the Calcasieu River, three cheniers are dated as covering a time span of A.D. 700 to 1350. Older cheniers

have not been observed in the mile-wide delta immediately west of this river.

Figure 8.21 illustrates a portion of the chenier belt in western Cameron Parish, 8 to 16 miles east of the Texas line. Johnson Bayou, a former outlet of Sabine Lake, is visible at the upper left. Two sets of cheniers appear in this area; the one to the north is sharply hooked toward Johnson Bayou, and also displays two sets of hooks (A, B) near Old Bayou. The curious pattern of these two hooked cheniers resembles the profile of large breaking waves. The dates of these older cheniers are probably 1,200 to 2,200 years ago. Radiocarbon ages from ridges in this area include several anomalous dates as old as 1300 B.C. The latter were probably derived from old shells redeposited in younger beach cheniers.

The second set are nearly straight cheniers, largely

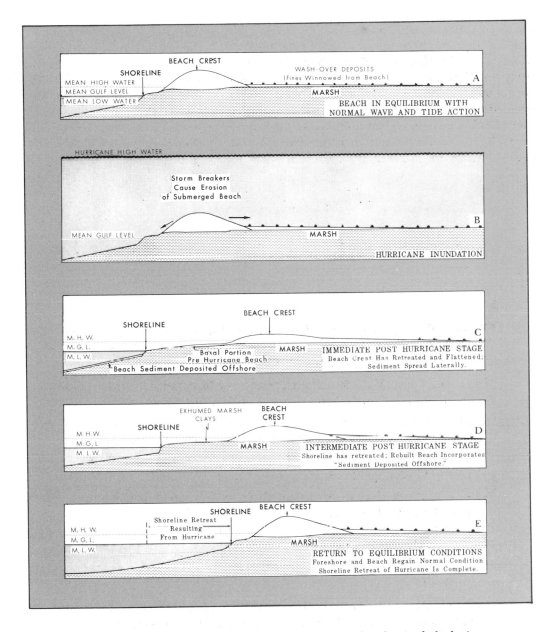

8.22 Sketches illustrating processes of shoreline retreat in the chenier belt during and after a hurricane. From Morgan, Nichols, and Wright (1958).

south of the east-west road, and probably date from about A.D. 750 to 1350 but also include one anomalous date as old as 1900 B.C., the latter from a coastal ridge.

Near the shore, numerous short stream cuts extend perpendicular to the shoreline, as well as narrow sluiceways cut by the June 1957 Hurricane Audrey.

This hurricane had maximum tides of 9.5 feet above mean high water at the town of Johnsons Bayou. The photographs of Figure 8.21 were taken in November 1957, five months after the hurricane.

Morgan, Nichols, and Wright have prepared a series of eight cross-sectional diagrams showing the nature of the recession of a chenier coast following a major hurricane, such as Audrey. Five of the sections are reproduced as Figure 8.22. Before the hurricane (A), a beach crest or chenier had been formed, rising 4 or 5 feet above mean Gulf level; and a stable underwater profile had developed gulfward from a small scarp between mean water level and mean low-water level. The area is then inundated by the hurricane (B) to depths greater than the chenier crest. During the storm, much of the chenier is swept inland and spread over a broader area. This uncovers the marsh clay below the displaced chenier, and soon after the storm (C) a notch is cut in the clay. The water recedes rapidly (D) until it reaches the place protected by the chenier in its posthurricane location. Then, for a period of a year or two, the underwater profile is modified until it returns into equilibrium with the new shape of the shoreline and chenier ridge (E).

REFERENCES

Byrne, John V., Duane O. LeRoy, and Charles M. Riley, 1959. The chenier plain and its stratigraphy, southwestern Louisiana. *Gulf Coast Assn. Geol. Soc., Trans.*, vol. 9, pp. 1–23.

Coleman, James M., 1966. Recent coastal sedimentation: central Louisiana coast. *Louisiana State Univ., Coastal Studies Inst., Tech. Rept.* 29.

Corps of Engineers, U.S. Army, 1936. *Beach Erosion of Grand Isle, Louisiana.* House of Representatives, 75th Congr., 1st Sess., Document 92.

Fisk, Harold N., 1944. Geological investigation of the alluvial valley of the Lower Mississippi River. *Miss. River Comm., U.S. Army Corps Engrs.*

————, 1960. Recent Mississippi River sedimentation and peat accumulation. *Compte Rendu quatrième Congrès pour l'avancement études stratigraphie et géol. du carbonifère*, 1958, Heerlen, pp. 187–199.

Gould, H. E., and E. McFarlan, Jr., 1959. Geologic history of the chenier plain, southwestern Louisiana. *Gulf Coast Assn. Geol. Soc., Trans.*, vol. 9, pp. 1–10.

Kolb, C. R., 1958. Geological investigations of the Mississippi River–Gulf outlet channel. *U.S. Army Engr. Waterway Experimental Sta., Corps of Engrs. Misc. Paper* 3–259.

————, and J. R. van Lopik, 1958. Geology of the Mississippi River deltaic plain. *U.S. Army Engrs. Waterways Experiment Sta., Corps of Engrs. Tech. Rept.* 3.

McFarlan, E., Jr., 1961. Radiocarbon dating of late Quaternary deposits, south Louisiana. *Geol. Soc. Amer. Bull.*, vol. 72, pp. 129–158.

Morgan, James P., 1963. Louisiana's changing shoreline. *Louisiana State Univ., Coastal Studies Inst., Contrib.* 63–5, pp. 66–78.

————, 1967. Ephemeral estuaries of the deltaic environment. *Coastal Studies Inst., Louisiana State Univ. Tech. Rept.* 46.

————, J. M. Coleman, and S. M. Gagliano, 1963. Mudlumps at the mouth of South Pass, Mississippi River; sedimentology, paleontology, structures, origin, and relation to deltaic processes. *Louisiana State Univ. Studies, Coastal Studies Ser., no.* 10.

————, L. G. Nichols, and Martin Wright, 1958. Morphological effects of hurricane Audrey on the Louisiana coast. *Louisiana State Univ., Coastal Studies Inst., Tech. Rept.* 10.

Price, W. Armstrong, 1954. Environment and formation of the chenier plain. *Texas A. & M. Res. Found., Project* 63.

Russell, R. J., 1936. Physiography of Lower Mississippi River Delta. *Louisiana Geol. Surv. Bull.* 8, pp. 3–193 (also biblio. on delta, pp. 279–320, and list of maps, pp. 321–338).

————, 1940. Quaternary history of Louisiana. *Geol. Soc. Amer. Bull.,* vol. 51, pp. 1199–1234.

————, 1953. Coastal advance and retreat in Louisiana. *Congress Geol. Intl., 19th Sess., Comptes Rendus.,* vol. 4, pp. 108–118.

Scruton, P. S., 1956. Oceanography of Mississippi Delta sedimentary environments. *Bull. Amer. Assoc. Petrol. Geologists,* vol. 40, no. 12, pp. 2864–2952.

Shepard, F. P., 1956. Marginal sediments of Mississippi Delta. *Bull. Amer. Assoc. Petrol. Geologists,* vol. 40, no. 11, pp. 2537–2623.

Trowbridge, A. C., 1930. Building of Mississippi Delta. *Bull. Amer. Assoc. Petrol. Geologists,* vol. 14, no. 7, pp. 867–901.

Welder, Frank A., 1959. Processes of deltaic sedimentation in the Lower Mississippi River. *Louisiana State Univ., Coastal Studies Inst. Tech. Rept.* 12.

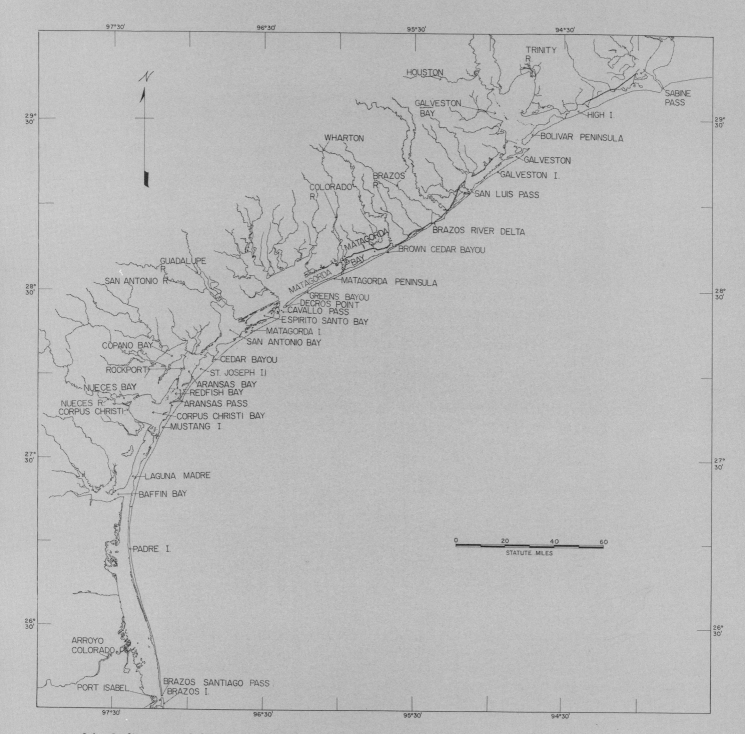

9.1 Outline map of the Texas coast showing localities described.

Barrier Island Coast

Texas

9 The broad arc-shaped Texas coast (Fig. 9.1) is remarkably smooth. Of the 400-mile length of the outer coast, there are barrier islands along 320 miles. Of these, Padre Island joined to Mustang Island (except during storm tides) has a combined length of 130 miles, one of the longest barriers in the world. Most of the Texas barriers are also wider than those along the other coasts, having widths of 5 miles or more in several of the northern and central portions. An 80-mile zone without barriers is found mostly east of Galveston Bay, where there is a continuation of a plain with low ridges, like that of the Louisiana chenier coast. Near the Louisiana line, the bulge at Sabine Pass is suggestive of a cuspate foreland and is reflected seaward as a shoal.

The Texas bays include long lagoons inside the barriers and a few large estuaries. Of the former, Laguna Madre, which extends along most of Padre Island, is particularly interesting as it is one of the few embayments along the United States coasts that have salinity well above that of the open ocean. Also, in one large area, it is so shallow that a change in the wind direction causes the water to disappear, leaving a broad mud flat. Of the estuaries, Galveston Bay is the largest and the most important because it reaches almost to Houston, the largest city in the South. Farther south, Corpus Christi Bay indents the land up to the large city of the same name. Most of the Texas rivers enter the heads of estuaries where they are building deltas; but two of the largest rivers, the Rio Grande and the Brazos, have filled their former estuaries into which they once drained.

The climate along the Texas coast changes gradually from humid in the north to semiarid at the south end. This accounts for the increase in unvegetated dunes to the south. Most of the dunes are on the barrier islands, and they are ordinarily covered with growth to the north. Dunes also extend inland

9.2 High Island, a salt dome and a producing oil field, along the Texas coast. U.S. Department of Agriculture, 1958.

in the semiarid areas landward of the Laguna Madre. The high salinity of this lagoon is a product of heavy evaporation, as well as of the scarcity of streams entering all except its southern end, where distributaries of the Rio Grande flow into the lagoon at times of high water.

Hurricanes have had significant effects on the development of the Texas coast. The greatest hurricane disaster in United States history occurred at Galveston in 1900. The coastal changes produced by more recent hurricanes are well illustrated by aerial photos.

The Texas coast has been studied for years by geologists of many oil companies. Notable among these are R. J. LeBlanc, H. A. Bernard, and especially the late Harold Fisk. It was also the main locus of the work on recent marine sediments in the American Petroleum Institute Project 51 directed by Shepard. Numerous scientific studies have been made of Laguna Madre and Padre Island. Noteworthy are

the contributions by W. Armstrong Price, Edwin McKee, and G. A. Rusnak.

HIGH ISLAND, TEXAS [Fig. 9.2]   High Island, a circular hill along the Texas coast 30 miles east-northeast of Galveston, would not have been given such a name by a Californian because its maximum height is only 20 feet. This is a region in which there are numerous salt domes, injections of salt squeezed upward from deeply buried salt beds through adjacent younger sediments toward or to the surface. Surrounding sediments are dragged upward around the margins of the salt. Oil and gas migrate up along the deformed sediments and are trapped near the junction with the impermeable salt. Thus very rich oil fields have been discovered by locating the positions of salt domes. If the salt rises within a few hundred feet of the surface, the ground is slightly elevated above its surroundings, so that a round knoll on a plain may be a clue to a buried salt dome and a potentially rich oil field.

High Island (A in Fig. 9.2) was formed by such a salt intrusion. Found in 1901, it was one of the first oil-bearing salt domes to be discovered; and production began in 1922. By 1936, 9 million barrels of oil had been produced. The top of the salt is about 1,200 feet below sea level, but a hard cap of anhydrite (calcium sulphate) extends to within 350 feet of the surface. The geology of the High Island salt dome was described by Michael Halbouty in 1936.

The margins of the dome are clearly outlined by a circle of drilling sites. Storage tanks and loading facilities for barges on the Intracoastal Waterway northeast of High Island show that oil production was still in progress when the area was photographed in 1958. Proximity to the shore indicates that High Island installations, which are mostly around the low rim, would be subject to serious damage by waves and floods if a hurricane should strike this relatively flat coast.

GALVESTON ISLAND AND BAY, TEXAS [Figs. 9.3, 9.4, and 9.5]   Galveston, the largest bay on the Texas coast, differs from Mobile Bay in having two principal arms (Fig. 9.3), each related to a large river, the San Jacinto and the Trinity, that discharge into the two heads of the bay. Another large branch, East Bay, extends as a lagoon to the east of the lower bay, and West Galveston Bay is a narrower lagoon on the southwest side. The bay is protected from the open Gulf by a long spit on the east, Bolivar Peninsula, and on the west by Galveston Island, a barrier.

According to state of Texas reports, the two principal rivers are contributing 463,000 acre-feet of sediment to the bay per year, most of this sediment coming from the Trinity River, which provides more sediment to a Texas bay than any other river. Another source of fill for Galveston Bay comes from the erosion of Red Bluff (A in Fig. 9.3), on the west side of the bay near the entrance to the Houston ship canal. According to the U.S. Army Corps of Engineers, this cliff is retreating 6.5 feet a year, yielding sediment to the bay floor. The result of the total fill is very evident from a comparison of sounding surveys separated by 80 years. These show that the bay has had a total average shoaling of 1.15 feet. Since the average depth of the bay is approximately 8 feet, in a few centuries the bay may become a marsh. Fill

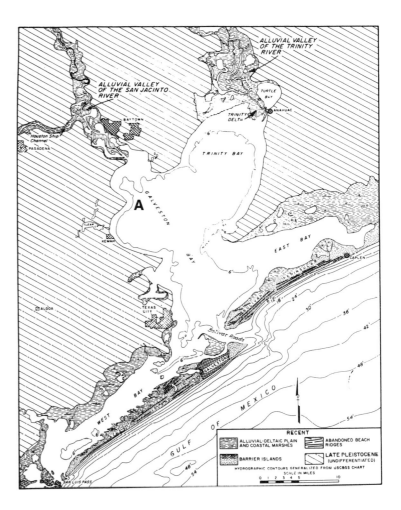

9.3 Pleistocene geology of the Galveston Bay area. Note how Turtle Bay has been blocked by the delta of the Trinity River. From Bernard, LeBlanc, and Major (1962).

in a bay of this sort, however, is not uniform. The chief fill in Galveston Bay takes place at the head of Trinity arm where the Trinity River has built a delta, which has closed off Turtle Bay completely in recent years, and has advanced about a mile to the south since the chart of 1855. Directly beyond the delta, the water has shoaled much more than the average. The lower bay has changed depth very little, and West Galveston Bay is slightly deeper than at the time of the older survey. The local deepening is in part due to the general sea-level rise of about 0.4 foot during the past century, but is probably also due to local sinking. Some of the sinking is the result of the withdrawal of water and oil from under the sea. Also, local faulting may have contributed. Resurvey-

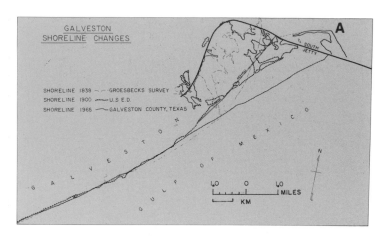

9.4 Changes in the Galveston shoreline between 1838 and 1966. Most changes followed reconstruction of the 6-mile South Jetty between 1884 and 1894. Compiled from maps of the U.S. Army Corps of Engineers.

ing of bench marks around Texas City, on the mainland just north of Galveston, has shown that there has been local sinking of as much as 2.5 feet. These lowerings of surface are probably related to petroleum operations. If the area directly seaward of Texas City had been dropping from natural causes at any such rate, the bay depths in the interval between surveys would have increased markedly; but near Texas City, the soundings show that there had been no appreciable change in the 80 years before the 1935 surveys. Most of the petroleum operations have been subsequent to that survey.

The Army Corps of Engineers have sketched the shoreline of the city of Galveston for nine dates from 1838 to 1934, based on a succession of surveys. Figure 9.4 shows these outlines for 1838, 1900, and 1966. Between 1884 and 1894, the 6-mile South Jetty was built, curving around the north end of the city and then 3.5 miles seaward.

On September 8, 1900, Galveston was struck by a ferocious hurricane with tides 15 feet high and winds estimated at 120 miles per hour. This flooded all parts of the island, destroyed many buildings, killed 6,000 residents, and caused property damage in excess of $20 million. This was before modern hurricane-tracking programs had been developed, and, except for a low wall, the city was completely unprepared for the storm. The hurricane cut the Gulf side shoreline back several hundred feet, as is shown by a comparison of 1899 and 1900 surveys

by the Army Corps of Engineers. Much of the eroded sand formed massive bars offshore but was shifted back to the beach within a year following the hurricane, restoring the shoreline in 1901 nearly to its prehurricane position.

A solid concrete seawall 17 feet high was completed by 1905 and later was raised to 21 feet. Thus Galveston was the first city in the Western Hemisphere to be properly protected from destructive hurricanes. It had experienced previous hurricanes; the first occurred in 1818 when it was the headquarters of the pirate Jean LaFitte, who lost four ships at that time. Prior to the destructive 1900 hurricane were those of 1835, 1837, 1842, 1866, 1867, two in 1871, 1888, and 1895. Since 1900, Galveston has been struck by severe hurricanes in 1909, 1915 (extremely strong), and 1949, but the seawall spared the city any tragic repetition of the destructiveness of the 1900 storm.

Evidently the prevailing littoral current is northeastward here, because the construction of the South Jetty has extended the shore on that side 3,000 feet. Galveston Island now projects gulfward about 2.5 miles beyond the shore of Bolivar Peninsula, compared to 1.7 miles before the jetty was built.

The eastern end of Galveston Island has long, even ridges (probably dunes) parallel to the shore of the peninsula; but, in the City of Galveston, the urban development has largely obscured the ridges on the eastern end of the island. All of the land against the south side of South Jetty is sand that has been trapped there since 1894 when the jetty was completed. A small sand bar (A in Fig. 9.4) with a lunate outline has formed on the north side of South Jetty, evidently where sand drifted around the end.

SAN LUIS PASS, TEXAS [Fig. 9.5]   The southwestern third of Galveston Island does not display ridges like those that dominate the island for several miles southwest of Galveston. Instead, the island is quite low and somewhat marshy. Several transverse furrows (A) are evidently the sites of sluiceways across which the waters of hurricane tides have swept. Visible, also, are many small ponds, some elongate parallel to the transverse furrows, especially on the lagoon side of the island.

In 1952, the southwest end of Galveston Island was nearly a point (Fig. 9.5) but had been lengthened by the addition of a hook at San Luis Pass. The

9.5 San Luis Pass separating Galveston and Folleis Islands. Both have been cut by sluiceways during hurricanes. Note numerous small rounded lakes on the bay sides of the islands. A bridge was constructed across the San Luis Pass in 1966. U.S. Department of Agriculture, 1962.

angle between the barrier and hook was nearly 90 degrees in 1952, but it had been rounded by erosion of the end of the spit by 1958 (not illustrated). A bridge across the inlet was constructed in 1966. Tidal scour has deepened the pass between the two islands to 25 feet, but there are 10-foot shoals on both sides. Inside the inlet, a tidal delta has grown about 2 miles into the bay, and the water is shoal for about a mile into the Gulf off the ends of both islands. Southwest of the pass, Folletts Island (B) has a broad beach extending as a hook along the inlet. The beach rapidly narrows along the Gulf shore. The interior of the island appears to be low and marshy with numerous small ponds. Inside these marshes is a large tidal delta (C) built by an overflow into Christmas Bay (D) through a pass that is now closed.

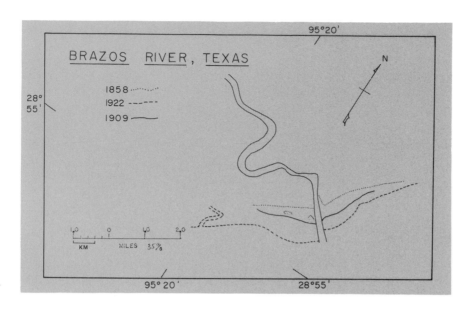

9.6 Outlines of the coast at the old outlet of the Brazos River, in 1858, 1909, and 1922. Prepared by Mohamed T. El-Ashry.

FREEPORT–BRAZOS RIVER DELTA AREA, TEXAS[1] [Figs. 9.6 through 9.9]   Aside from the Mississippi, the Brazos is the only river in continental United States (excluding Alaska) that is actively building a delta out into an unobstructed gulf or ocean. All the other large rivers have their deltas in estuaries or lagoons or are entering straight coasts where the marine currents are sufficient to keep the sediments from building seaward.

There are no barrier islands for about 20 miles along the Texas coast in the area in which the Brazos River now discharges. Geologists believe that until a few hundred years ago the Colorado River also discharged into this 40-mile belt. Measurements of the Army Corps of Engineers indicate that the Brazos River carries more than 30 million tons of silt to the Gulf of Mexico annually, far exceeding the load of other Texas rivers.

The Brazos River originally discharged into an estuary; and a barrier island and lagoon had formed in line with Galveston Island and West Bay, which separated the mainland from the Gulf of Mexico. Since sea level arrived at approximately its present position a few thousand years ago, the Brazos has

[1] Much of the material on the Brazos River Delta is derived from a 1966 manuscript by Mohamed T. El-Ashry.

filled its estuary and lagoon with sediment. In 1858 (Fig. 9.6), the shoreline was nearly straight at the river mouth. By 1881, an arcuate delta had built 2,000 feet into the Gulf of Mexico; and, by 1938, the arc extended out 4,000 feet. The addition of silt to this delta required frequent dredging to maintain a channel to the important city of Freeport (A in Fig. 9.7). Jetties were constructed to discharge much of the sediment into deeper water offshore.

Between 1922 and 1936, the Army Corps of Engineers dredged a new outlet for the Brazos River (B) 6 miles southwest of its natural outlet (C) and blocked off the entrance to the old channel northwest of Freeport. Here, as at Galveston, there were substantial additions to the southwest side of the old delta in the form of three arcuate sand ridges growing northeastward (D). Thus some of the sediment introduced into the Gulf from the new outlet was drifted northeastward toward the old delta.

After the delta growth had become well established at the new outlet, the old delta began to be cut back. Hurricanes struck the coast at Freeport in 1942, 1949, 1959, and 1961. Following Hurricane Carla of 1961, reported to be the largest, most intense, and destructive to strike the Gulf Coast, the old Brazos River Delta had been cut back about 0.5 mile (not illustrated). The delta had been virtually destroyed

9.7 Aerial photo composite showing new and old outlets of the Brazos River, near Freeport (A). The natural outlet of the river had formed a delta projecting into the Gulf of Mexico, which impeded navigation to Freeport, so a new channel was dug and the old outlet channel blocked. Later, shore erosion destroyed most of the old delta, and a new delta developed at the new outlet. U.S. Department of Agriculture, 1938.

9.8. The site of the old Brazos River outlet about 30 years after the river flow had been diverted. Note that the coastline is nearly straight, and most of the former delta has been eroded. U.S. Coast and Geodetic Survey, 1962.

by 1962, and the shore at the old Brazos River mouth was nearly as straight (Fig. 9.8) as it had been in 1858.

When the new river outlet first began to transport sediment into the Gulf, littoral currents distributed

9.9 Development of the delta at the new outlet of the Brazos River. The earliest stage, 1938, 6 years after the diversion of the river, shown in Figure 9.7.

a May 13, 1952. Since 1938, natural levees have developed along the sides of the new outlet channel. The delta has been extended about a mile farther into the Gulf, and two additional arcuate frontal islands have formed. U.S. Department of Agriculture.

most of the sand along the straight shore. By 1938 (Fig. 9.7), however, a pair of arcuate islands had formed a bulge of the shoreline about 0.5 mile into the Gulf, enclosing a small lagoon in which silt was accumulating and discharging into the Gulf through a channel between the two islands. By 1952 (Fig. 9.9a), natural levees extended above water level, and two new sets of arcuate islands had formed in front of the ends of the natural levees. By 1958 (not shown), much of the lagoon enclosed by the arcuate islands was filled with deltaic sediment, some derived from the river and some introduced as tidal delta deposits through breaches in the arcuate sand islands. In 1960 (not illustrated), a new barrier ridge had emerged on the southwest flank of the delta. The very destructive Hurricane Carla completely demolished this new arcuate barrier (Fig. 9.9b) and cut back the front of the natural levees flanking the channel. By September 1962, a year after Hurricane Carla, a new arcuate barrier had formed, enclosing the uneroded outer margins of the

remnants of the southwest side of the delta, which had escaped erosion by the hurricane. In 1954, W. Armstrong Price reported that a bar marginal to the new delta formed but remained submerged until the high tides of a hurricane built it above water. When the tide returned to normal level, the bar was left as an emergent feature. If this is a common origin of arcuate barriers, the three shown in the 1952 photographs (Fig. 9.9a) may be the result of hurricanes in 1938, 1942, and 1949. The new barrier in 1960 (not illustrated) could be the result of the 1959 Hurricane Debra; and the new barrier in 1962 (Fig. 9.9c), a product of Hurricane Carla. Also, the eight remnants of arcuate barrier spits on the old delta in front of Freeport (E in Fig. 9.7) may be due to eight hurricanes during the growth of this delta prior to December 1938.

The outlet of the Brazos River provides an opportunity not matched elsewhere in the United States to follow the yearly changes involved in the destruction of an old delta and the growth of a new one.

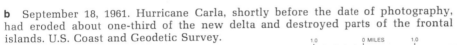

b September 18, 1961. Hurricane Carla, shortly before the date of photography, had eroded about one-third of the new delta and destroyed parts of the frontal islands. U.S. Coast and Geodetic Survey.

c June 1, 1962. Nearly a year after Hurricane Carla, a new arcuate island has formed at the margin of the remaining portion of the delta, U.S. Coast and Geodetic Survey.

BARRIER ISLAND COAST: TEXAS

COLORADO RIVER DELTA, TEXAS [Fig. 9.10] The mouth of the Colorado River of Texas (Fig. 9.10) is now about 50 miles southwest of the Brazos River Delta. Until a few hundred years ago, according to R. J. LeBlanc and W. D. Hodgson, the Colorado River drained southeastward from the town of Wharton, 50 miles from the coast. Prior to that time, it contributed its sediment load to the construction of the 40-mile-wide composite Brazos-Colorado delta plain, filling the old estuaries and the lagoon inside an old barrier. Then the Colorado River abandoned its lower valley and followed a new course almost due south from Wharton, discharging into Matagorda Bay, a 4-mile-wide lagoon that separates Matagorda Peninsula from the mainland. According to A. W. Weeks, about 1831, a "raft" of logs formed in the river just above the town of Matagorda (B in Fig. 9.10), on the north shore of the bay. This resulted in deposition of sediment in the river valley upstream from the logjam. Between 1925 and 1929, the logs and newly deposited silt were dredged; and, in 1929, much of the "raft" was swept away by a flood. At this time, delta growth into the bay began to be rapid, so that in 1930 the delta (shown by line in Fig. 9.10) covered 1,780 acres, as compared with 45 acres in 1908. The delta not only was built southward across the bay but also had been widened by distributaries. By 1941, the delta had built clear across the lagoon to the Matagorda Peninsula and covered 7,098 acres. In 1936, a channel was dredged through the delta, and an artificial cut was made through the Matagorda Peninsula to the Gulf. In 1940, the Intracoastal Canal was dug, crossing the Colorado River just south of the town of Matagorda (A), but most of the new flow continued to the Gulf. By 1943, an automobile road had been built from the mainland to Matagorda Peninsula on the delta over an area which had been part of the bay 15 years earlier. A spit formed partly across the new river mouth from 1943 to 1952 but had been mostly eroded by 1958, as shown in Figure 9.10.

9.10 Delta of the Colorado River, near Matagorda (B). The delta extends across Matagorda Bay (C) and enters the Gulf of Mexico through an artificial channel across Matagorda Peninsula. The building of the delta started in the early 1920s. The approximate outline in 1930 is shown by the black line. It had built across Matagorda Bay by the late 1950s. In 1940, the Intracoastal Waterway was constructed and crosses the Colorado River at A. U.S. Department of Agriculture, 1958.

1.0 .50 0 MILES 1.0
KM

9.11 Coastal changes in a portion of Matagorda Peninsula 5 to 10 miles southwest of the Colorado River Delta following a hurricane in 1942, and before and after Hurricane Carla, 1961.

a October, 1943. The peninsula has been shredded by many sluiceways and five broader breaches made by the 1942 hurricane have been nearly closed by spits from the northeast. U.S. Department of Agriculture.

Since 1941, there has been little widening of the delta in the bay, and beach drifting has been able to redistribute almost all the sediment brought into the Gulf. The annual silt load of the Colorado River is only about 9 million tons per year, as compared with 30 million tons for the Brazos. This probably explains why a delta has not yet been formed into the Gulf at the mouth of the Colorado River.

MATAGORDA PENINSULA, TEXAS[2] [Figs. 9.11 and 9.12] Originally, Matagorda Peninsula was a barrier spit extending for 35 miles west-southwest of the mouth of Caney Creek to Cavallo, the entrance to Matagorda Bay. In addition to the artificial cut in the peninsula made by engineers to allow the passage of the Colorado River, several breaches have been the result of hurricanes. These other inlets have been transitory but, along with the artificial cut, have at times converted the peninsula into a group of barrier islands.

The existence of old channels across the barrier, now filled, can be attested by the low swampy divides with tidal deltas on the inside. One of these old cuts is at the eastern inner end of the peninsula. Four miles farther along the peninsula, Brown Cedar Cut has had an interesting history. It was missing on the 1922 chart and appeared first in the 1931 edition, with a width of 360 feet. This was increased to 510

[2] Much information on Matagorda Peninsula was derived from an unpublished paper prepared by Mohamed T. El-Ashry in 1966.

feet in the 1940 edition. In 1943, the first aerial photos show that a tidal delta had formed on the inside of the cut, and the width had increased to 1,950 feet. Between 1943 and 1960, the tidal delta had grown extensively; but the cut had narrowed to 450 feet.

In the middle portion of Matagorda Peninsula, southwest of the artificial Colorado River entrance, sluiceways have developed as the result of the frequent hurricanes that have crossed this area. A major hurricane occurred in August 1942; and, in September 1961, Hurricane Carla passed inland with its center across lower Matagorda Peninsula. Earlier hurricanes in 1921 and 1929 had similar courses.

Photographs were taken in October 1943, a year after the 1942 hurricane; in 1957 and 1960, a period during which the beach had been partially rebuilt; and on September 17, 1961, six days after Hurricane Carla.

The 1943 aerial photos of the Long Bayou area show four sluiceways (A, B, C, and D in Fig. 9.11a). These are probably the result of the 1942 hurricane. Five other sluiceways in the area appear to have been closed just prior to the photographs and may have been opened by the storm. Some of these cuts may have originated during the 1921, 1929, and earlier hurricanes, but accurate maps and photographs of these earlier dates are not available. In the 1943 photograph (E in Fig. 9.11a), at the ends of the longer sluiceways about a mile back from the modern beach, there are oval or V-shaped islands that repre-

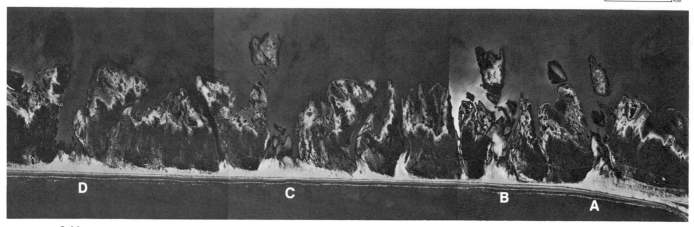

9.11
b September 16, 1960. All sluiceways had been closed, forming a continuous beach.
U.S. Coast and Geodetic Survey.

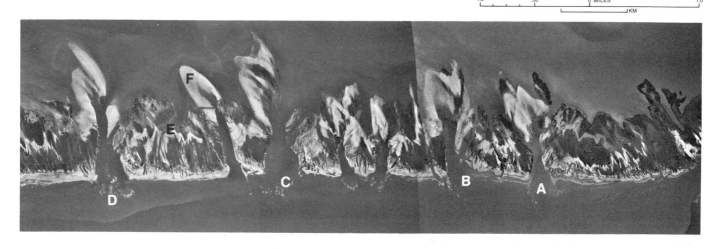

c September 17, 1961. Photography six days after Hurricane Carla shows seven major newly opened sluiceways with washover deltas (light-colored areas) (F) in Matagorda Bay. U.S. Coast and Geodetic Survey.

sent washover deposits. In the year between the 1942 hurricane and the time of the photography, spits had been extended from the northeast margin of each sluiceway, with hooks curving northward into the sluiceways. This direction of growth suggests that currents were from the northeast, contrary to the general direction of drift shown by sedimentation against most of the jetties along the Texas coast. These reversals are the same as found along much of the southeast coast of the United States and are apparently due to local back eddies.

By 1952, as shown by a topographic map of that date, all sluiceways along the coast in the Long Bayou area had been closed, and they remained closed until 1960 (A, B, C, and D in Fig. 9.11*b*). At this time, sand had blocked the larger sluiceways inland for about 0.3 mile; and a coastal road, interrupted at many places by the 1942 hurricane, had been rebuilt, crossing the newly formed flats.

The eye of the 1961 Hurricane Carla, as reported by Miles Hayes, crossed the Texas coast about 20 miles southwest of the Long Bayou area with maximum winds of 175 miles per hour; and, at one Matagorda Bay locality, tides were reported as 22 feet above normal. At the height of the storm, wind velocities of 75 miles per hour or more were recorded for 300 miles along the coast from Brownsville, Texas, to the Texas-Louisiana border. This unusually wide hurricane reopened most sluiceways of the 1942 storm (A, B, C, and D in Fig. 9.11c). The largest of these new sluiceways was 1,700 feet wide at the Gulf end. On the bay side, U-shaped washover deltas (F in Fig. 9.11c) had formed, some extending 0.5 mile or more in from the barrier. Between the major sluiceways, many smaller washovers had carried beach sand inland about 0.6 mile to form U-shaped washover fans (E) on the island. Measurements of the width of the island before and after Hurricane Carla showed that the beach along the peninsula was cut back uniformly for about 800 feet. Several years should be required to close the many sluiceways opened by this hurricane.

Greens Bayou (Fig. 9.12), about 11 miles northeast of Decros Point, the southwest end of Matagorda Peninsula, is the most persistent inlet on the peninsula. According to a U.S. Coast and Geodetic Survey field sketch dated 1872 (not shown), there was no inlet at Greens Bayou; but blocked sluiceways showed evidence that an inlet had been opened by an earlier hurricane and later closed. The 1929 field sketch shows Greens Bayou and Cotton Bayou as opened, probably by a hurricane. Both were closed in the 1939 field sketch. Greens Bayou was reopened by a hurricane in August 1940, at a location 1,200 feet southwest of its 1929 location. The August 1942 hurricane opened Cotton Bayou (B in Fig. 9.12a) and widened Greens Bayou (A) to about 0.5 mile; but, by the time of the 1943 aerial photos (Fig. 9.12a), a recurved spit had grown southwestward toward Greens Bayou, narrowing the inlet to 1,200 feet. A road (C) on the southwest side terminated near the lagoon end of the inlet.

When rephotographed in 1955 (not illustrated), lengthening of the recurved spit had further narrowed the inlet to 600 feet. The road was only 400 feet back from the shore, indicating 200 feet of beach erosion since the 1943 photos. The inlet had shifted 1,000 feet southwest of its 1943 position, destroying the part of the road that had formerly curved north toward the inlet. This erosion probably was the result of a hurricane in August 1945. A large tidal delta formed since 1943 extended into the bay more than a mile beyond the inlet.

In 1957 (Fig. 9.12b), Greens Bayou (A) was nearly closed and Cotton Bayou (B) was blocked by sand on the Gulf side. A series of hooks marked the lengthening of the spit toward the southwest end,

9.12 History of coastal changes at and near Greens Bayou, southwestern Matagorda Peninsula, from 1943 to 1961.

a October 16, 1943. Greens Bayou (A) had been widened recently, and Cotton Bayou (B) opened by the 1942 hurricane, but spits growing from the northeast have nearly closed Cotton Bayou and partly closed Greens Bayou. Note road southwest of Greens Bayou for comparison with later photographs. U.S. Department of Agriculture.

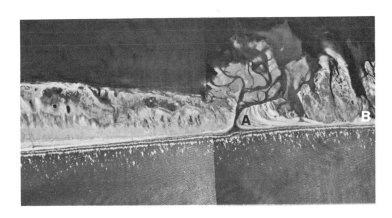

b April 6, 1957. Cotton Bayou is closed, Greens Bayou nearly closed, and a large tidal delta has formed in Matagorda Bay, northwest of Greens Bayou. A portion of the road southwest of the inlet has been cut away. U.S. Coast and Geodetic Survey.

and much of the tidal delta lay east of the remnant inlet. The south side of the inlet had been cut back further, leaving it entirely southwest of its 1953 position.

By 1960 (Fig. 9.12c), the former Greens Bayou inlet (A) was entirely closed by a 2,000-foot-wide barrier. The tidal delta had ceased to grow. However, by September 17, 1961, as a result of Hurricane Carla, Cotton Bayou (B in Fig. 9.12d) was reopened and widened to 1,000 feet, while Greens Bayou developed a mile cut (A in Fig. 9.12d). All of the bar-

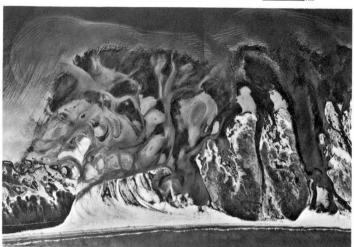

9.12

c September 16, 1960. Greens Bayou is closed and growth of the tidal delta has ceased. U.S. Coast and Geodetic Survey.

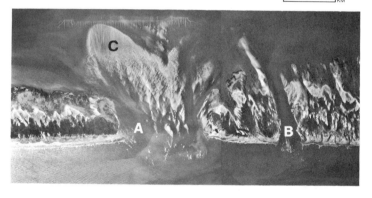

d September 17, 1961. Hurricane Carla has reopened Cotton Bayou to a width of 1,000 feet, and Greens Bayou to a width of a mile. The shore was cut back nearly to the coastal road, and a large washover delta has formed in Matagorda Bay. U.S. Coast and Geodetic Survey.

rier formed between 1942 and 1961 was swept away; and a large U-shaped shoal (C), extending nearly 2 miles into the lagoon, resulted from the redistribution of the sand of the Greens Bayou hooked spit. Since the Greens Bayou inlet, widened by the 1942 hurricane to 0.5 mile, required about 17 years to close, the new inlet, twice as wide after Hurricane Carla, may require at least 30 years to close, provided no other destructive hurricanes occur here within that period. As another result of Carla, the remnants of the road southwest of Greens Bayou appeared at the inner margin of the beach, showing erosion of nearly 400 feet.

Greens Bayou illustrates the history of the opening of an inlet by a major hurricane, closing it by spit extension between hurricanes, and reopening by another storm. Because much beach sediment drifting southwestward at Greens Bayou is swept into the bay to form the tidal delta, the southwest side of the inlet and the beach farther southwest, thus impoverished for sand, suffer erosion, so that the inlet shifts southwestward, and the beach downcurrent from the inlet recedes.

ROCKPORT, TEXAS, AREA [Figs. 9.13 through 9.18]   The area described in this section (Fig. 9.13) comprises two closely joined islands, Matagorda (not to be confused with the peninsula) and St. Joseph. Inside these barriers are four lagoonal bays; from east to west: Espiritu Santo, Mesquite, Aransas, and Redfish. In addition, two estuaries, San Antonio and St. Charles Bays, penetrate the mainland. Somewhat on the dividing line between an estuary and a lagoon is Copano Bay with its small tributary, Mission Bay, which is a largely filled estuary. This Rockport area is treated as a unit because it was one of the two principal centers of investigation in a seven-year project of the American Petroleum Institute. During this work, headquarters were maintained in Rockport at the Texas Fish and Game Commission. All these bays and the two barrier islands were studied intensively.

Perhaps the most interesting thing about the Rockport area is the remarkable development of the barrier islands. Several large ranches are located on these islands, including the fabulous Richardson estate. Both Matagorda and St. Joseph Islands are the widest barriers along the United States coasts. The unusual width is due to a combination of relatively wide beaches, even wider dune belts, and miles of swamps and barrier flats on the inside (Fig. 9.14). The dunes consist of ridges with a cover of vegetation and irregularly shaped masses, which spread widely over the inner barrier flats. These latter dunes are U-shaped or blowout type, indicating prevailing southeast winds. The parallel ridges have often been interpreted as beach ridges, but the investigation made by Shepard produced clues that appear to establish that they are the typical low dune ridges that form directly inside many beaches. Their height

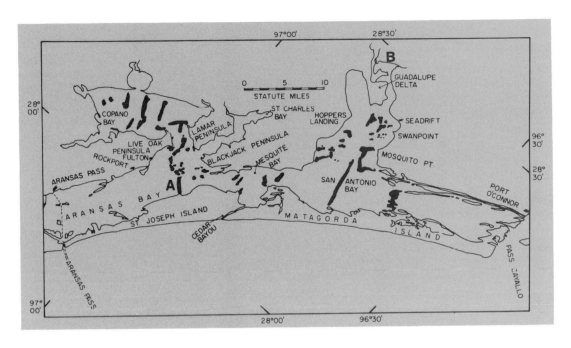

9.13 Index map of Rockport, showing locations described and distribution of oyster reefs.

above sea level is greater than that of beach ridges made of fine-textured sand found in this area. Furthermore, the sand grains are distinctly rounder than beach sands from the vicinity but comparable to dune sands. Other more technical characteristics confirm this diagnosis. Apparently, during the development of these ridges the beach was growing seaward intermittently. When it advanced into the Gulf, widening the berm, the east winds began building ridges on the inner edge of the broad beach. Presently these ridges became covered with grass and were thus stabilized. Then as the beaches grew farther seaward, new dune ridges formed parallel to those on the inside.

The result of building a sequence of dune ridges in this fashion produces an appearance from the air that is similar to that of beach ridges (see Fig. 8.21). The beach ridges in the chenier area west of the Mississippi Delta were built by storms to heights as great above present sea level as are the dune ridges in the Rockport area; but the material in the cheniers is largely shells, which are coarse enough to allow the formation of these wave-elevated ridges.

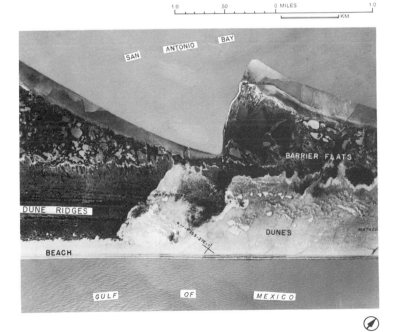

9.14 A portion of Matagorda Island near Panther Point, showing dunes, dune ridges, barrier flats, and round lakes. Aerial photo mosaic by Edgar Tobin Aerial Surveys, 1937.

BARRIER ISLAND COAST: TEXAS

241

9.15 Oblique aerial photograph of St. Joseph Island near Cedar Bayou, showing barrier flat with washover delta pattern. Aransas Bay is in foreground and Gulf of Mexico in background. Photo by D. L. Inman, 1951.

The barrier flats, illustrated in Figures 9.14, 9.15, and 9.16, are low marshy surfaces with channels that form as washover deltas during inundations, such as accompany hurricanes. Unlike typical tidal deltas, these marshes and channels are often built above sea level. Figure 9.15 shows an example of a barrier flat at the north end of St. Joseph Island, with fanlike distributaries diverging from point A. However, in Figures 9.14 and 9.16, the deltaic distributary pattern is missing. It seems likely that we have in these two areas the results of a gradual change that affects the overwash deltas when they are not disturbed by further flooding for a number of years. The sediments compact, tending to increase the area of water; and the action of wind gradually develops rounded lakes in place of the elongate channels. However, if sediment is introduced, the area may be built up and the lakes filled. Also, the growth of marsh grass and peat deposits gradually fill many of the lakes.

A sequence of development in the barrier flats of western Matagorda Island is shown by comparison of aerial photographs taken in 1929 (Fig. 9.16*a*, vertical) and in 1951 (Fig. 9.16*b*, oblique). The same lakes can be recognized in both photos, and it will be seen that in the 1951 photo their rims (A) have expanded so that they tend to overlap each other. From the ground, these lakes (Fig. 9.17) are seen to have rims of grassy turf.

Another change is found on the inside of the barrier islands. The gradual erosion of overwash deltas leads to the formation of sand spits. These are shown in Figure 9.17. Sand bars can also be seen in the shallow water along the inner margins of the islands in many places (see Fig. 9.15). These may build up above the surface due to wave action. One example of an elongate spit (A) is seen in Figure 9.18. Breaking waves on the outside of this spit indicate submerged sand bars. A marshy surface is located in the interior and another submerged bar (B) is shown next to the narrow lagoon.

The depths of the bays in the Rockport area (Fig. 9.13) are greater to the southwest. Aransas Bay is mostly 8 to 12 feet deep; Copano, 6 to 8 feet; Mesquite, only 3 to 4 feet; and San Antonio 4 to 6 feet. Between the surveys of 1875 and 1935, all of the bays had shoaled:[3] Aransas, 0.84 feet; Copano, 0.52 feet; Mesquite, 0.58 feet; and San Antonio, 0.76 feet. As would be expected, the greatest shoaling has taken place at the head of San Antonio Bay near the Guadalupe Delta. The two surveys show a more significant difference in Cedar Bayou, which connects Mesquite Bay with the Gulf. It has shoaled about 5 feet in this 60-year interval.

The bays in the Rockport area have some striking contrasts to those farther north. Oyster reefs, although present to the north, become much more common near Rockport. The intermediate salinity conditions along this part of the Texas coast are most favorable for oyster growth. The reefs develop best in parts of the bays away from the high salinity at the mouths and away from the fresh water where rivers enter. The result of oyster reefs has been the shoaling of the Rockport bays. Oysters, like corals, build reefs up to low tide, but waves are capable of throwing the dead shells up on top of the reefs so that they may emerge. The best example of emerged shell ridges is Long Reef (A in Fig. 9.13), which extends north from St. Joseph Island and forms a natural block across Aransas Bay, which had to be severed for the Intracoastal Waterway. Most of the oyster reefs in the Rockport bays are elongated at right angles to the general trend of the lagoons on the inside of the barrier islands (Fig. 9.13). This direction is at right angles to the prevailing currents

[3] Based on hundreds of comparisons by Shepard with original data of the charts and averaging of depth contrasts.

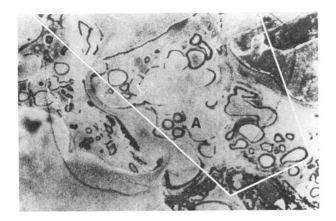

9.16 Development of round lakes on St. Joseph Island barrier flats.

a 1929 photograph (vertical aerial). White line indicates area included in Figure 9.16b. Note three small round lakes near center of photo. Edgar Tobin photography.

b 1951 oblique aerial photograph, showing expansion of the three lakes noted in Figure 9.16a, so that the rims connect. Photo by Shepard.

in the bays. This trend is best exemplified in Copano Bay where three north-south reefs cross the long direction of the bay.

Oyster reefs also grow near channels because of the food provided by circulation along the channels. The central part of San Antonio Bay appears to have particularly widespread reefs without definite pattern. The work of the American Petroleum Institute sedimentary project involved much sampling in San Antonio Bay; and the irregular pattern of the reefs made this very difficult, because accurate navigation was impossible and the boats were constantly running aground. It was decided that what the boatmen meant when they said that they knew every reef in this bay was that they had run aground on them all.

The pattern of bays in the Rockport area is related both to present-day barrier islands and to ancient barriers that existed farther landward. The latter, now considerably modified, can be recognized by the low ridges in Live Oak Peninsula, which includes the cities of Rockport and Aransas Pass (Fig. 9.13), and by the ridges of Black Jack Peninsula, farther to the northwest. Copano Bay and the upper part of St. Charles Bay are the remnants of lagoons inside the old barriers, and Redfish, Aransas, Mesquite, lower San Antonio, and Espiritu Santo are the lagoons inside the present barriers. This last group may have had much more uniform width when the barriers first formed and may have been similar to West and East

9.17 Ground view of a circular pond, showing rim of grassy turf, Matagorda Island. Photo by Shepard, 1952.

Matagorda Bays. Irregularities in the outer lagoons of the Rockport area are apparently due principally to overwash deltas and tidal inlets, which have considerably decreased lagoonal width, particularly in Redfish Bay and on either side of Mesquite Bay.

San Antonio Bay is the best example in the area of a drowned river valley. This estuary is somewhat

9.18 Mud Island (A), a sand spit that formed inside Aransas Bay. St. Joseph Island, the coastal sand barrier with active sand dunes (C). U.S. Coast and Geodetic Survey, December 9, 1948.

comparable in shape to Mobile Bay, as it has relatively straight sides and no large tributary bay enters it. A large delta has been built into the head of the bay by the Guadalupe River. This delta has not filled all the head of the bay but left two bodies of shallow water on either side, Hynes Bay to the west and Mission Lake (B in Fig. 9.13, almost cut off) on the northeast. The outline of this delta has scarcely changed at all during the 60 years between surveys. However, comparison of 1929 and 1951 aerial photos shows that a small subdelta had been built in the interim in one indentation in Mission Lake.

The outlets through the barriers in the northern Texas bays are opposite the principal estuaries. In the Rockport area, on the other hand, the outlets have no relation to the estuaries. Thus the outlet for most of the rest of the bays is at the south end of St. Joseph Island through Aransas Pass. However, Mesquite Bay does have its own outlet, Cedar Bayou, which is evidently an old arm of one of the distributaries of a large overwash. At the mouth of Aransas Pass, jetties have been built to allow large ships to come into Corpus Christi Bay (Fig. 9.19). On the outside, the buildup of sediment is considerably greater on the south jetty than on the north, again indicating that

the predominant drift of sediment is to the north. The outlets for Espiritu Santo Bay are through several shallow passages in the tidal delta built on the west side of Pass Cavallo that leads into Matagorda Bay. This pass compares somewhat with the entrance to Galveston Bay. The southwest side of the pass protrudes into the Gulf more than 2 miles beyond Matagorda Peninsula, indicative of northwestward drift.

CORPUS CHRISTI BAY AND MUSTANG ISLAND [Fig. 9.19]   Corpus Christi, the deepest bay on the Texas coast, resembles San Antonio Bay in being blocked by a barrier island with no direct pass into the Gulf and having only one entering river. Nueces Bay, at the northwest end of Corpus Christi, is nearly cut off by spits built out from both sides of the mainland. The Nueces River is building a delta into the bay of the same name; and the chart shows that in the 66 years between 1868 and 1934 the delta has advanced about a mile into a cove, considerably decreasing the size and shoaling Nueces Bay to such an extent that it is navigable only for small craft. The main Corpus Christi Bay, on the other hand, has large areas between 12 and 14 feet deep; and the 10-foot contour hugs the shore of most of the lower bay. Unlike San Antonio Bay, Corpus Christi Bay has relatively few oyster reefs. The depths in the bay had changed between 1868 and 1943 with an average shoaling of 1.03 feet.

Mustang Island, which cuts off direct approach to Corpus Christi Bay, was separated from Padre Island by a narrow pass until about 1930 when they became connected. Rise in the water levels, such as accompany even rather distant hurricanes, cause a temporary reopening of the pass between these two islands. Shepard saw such a rise September 2, 1954, when a hurricane damaged Vera Cruz, 400 miles to the south. The water came up, completely covering the beach along the front of Mustang Island, and began attacking the adjacent dunes, then spilled over the old pass into Corpus Christi Bay. A shallow boring was being drilled in Mustang Island at the time, and baffles had to be built to protect it from being inundated. The boring showed that the old pass was formerly 20 feet deep.

Mustang Island is similar to St. Joseph Island to the northeast but does not have as wide washover deltas; and the dunes are mostly covered with vegetation. One large spit (A) extends out into Corpus

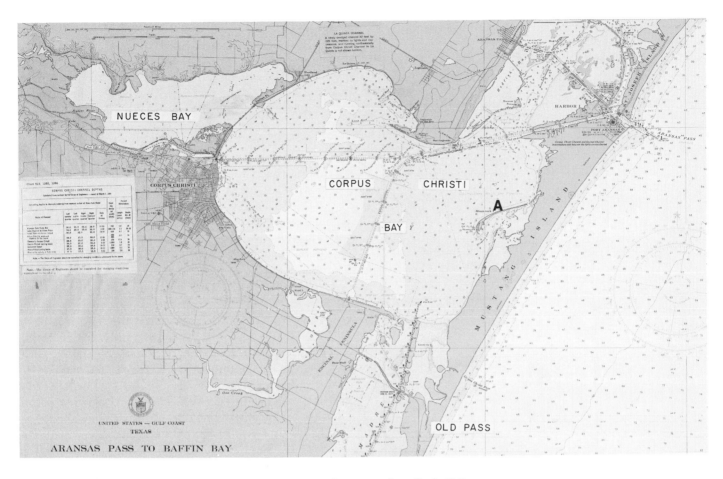

9.19 Index map of Corpus Christi area, Texas, showing locations described. U.S. Coast and Geodetic Survey Navigation Chart 1286, 1966.

Christi Bay, apparently the result of concentration of the sediment from an old washover fan into a ridge, like the spits adjacent to St. Joseph and Matagorda Islands.

The city of Corpus Christi is mostly located on a low Pleistocene terrace. Along the bay on the south side of town, the soft formations constituting this terrace are being attacked by wave erosion; and sea-walls have had to be built to prevent serious loss of land.

PADRE ISLAND AND LAGUNA MADRE, TEXAS [Figs. 9.20 through 9.23]   If you take a trip along the 130-mile beach between Aransas Pass, at the north end of Mustang Island, and the new National Seashore, at the south end of Padre Island, you

had better be equipped with a jeep and a four-wheel drive because of zones of soft sand; and you should have plenty of extra gas, because the allure of side trips into the beautiful dunes are so great that you may find your tank is empty. That happened to Shepard and G. A. Rusnak. Before the building of the Intracoastal Canal, if you made this trip by boat, following the Laguna Madre on the inside of the tremendous barrier island, you would have had an equally serious problem. You would have run out of water. A central section of Laguna Madre is ordinarily dry. In order to cross this dry area, away from the canal, it is necessary to use air boats that skim over the mud and sand flats.

Despite its great uninterrupted length, Padre Island (Fig. 9.20) is much narrower than the bar-

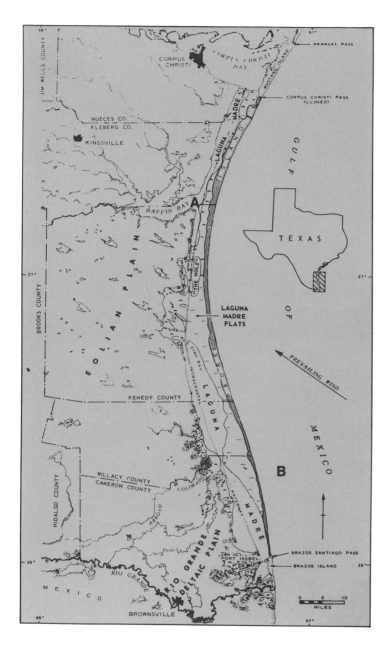

9.20 Padre Island, Laguna Madre, and other coastal features of south Texas. Prepared by Harold N. Fisk.

belong. Twenty miles south of Baffin Bay (A), Padre Island has a series of filled channels that cross the island and rise only slightly above sea level. The cuts are the result of hurricanes. About 20 miles from Brazos Santiago Pass (B in Fig. 9.20), the island is reduced locally to narrow beaches built as barriers across a series of closely spaced blocked inlets that cross the 0.25-mile-wide island. Farther south, the island widens to about 0.5 mile, but in this southernmost stretch there are also occasional blocked channels.

The Padre Island barrier differs from those farther north in having extensive sections of shifting dunes. Locally, these reach elevations of 40 feet and are more than a mile wide (Fig. 9.21). These shifting dunes are an indication of the low rainfall on this part of the coast. They continue most of the way to Brazos Santiago Pass but terminate near the north end of the road that extends for 4 miles north along the island. Figure 9.22 shows the character of the narrow part of the island with a broad washover flat. The dunes in this area are narrow and parallel to the predominant summer east or southeast winds. Because of the shifting dunes and the low passes crossed by hurricane tides, the island changes freqently in appearance.

The effects of Hurricane Beulah, September 1967, on the narrow southern part of the island is shown in Figure 9.23. The water of the Gulf crossed the low beaches and swept into Laguna Madre, cutting channels through the low flats. These breaks heal rapidly after each hurricane. Erosion of Padre Island dunes by the hurricane nearly doubled the width of the beach.

A trip by jeep along the Padre Island beach shows a gradual change in the character of the sand. About 20 miles south of the old Corpus Christi Inlet, the beach is covered with shells. These are derived from older formations that are exposed in hills along the shore. The high shell content continues for another 20 miles to the south. Still farther south, the sand is distinctly coarser than at the north end of the island. This coarser sand is comparable with the sediment of the Rio Grande River. Shore currents flow north most of the time along the island and have transported sand in that direction.

The Laguna Madre was a continuous lagoon in the early days of exploration, but a large dry area in the central section called The Flats (Fig. 9.20) has

riers to the north. Along the northern 30 miles, the average width is about 2 miles, comparable with that of Mustang Island. Farther south, Padre Island narrows appreciably, unless one includes the low flats of Laguna Madre, which are rarely flooded in this intermediate area. Here, we shall refer to these flats as part of the Laguna Madre, to which they genetically

9.21 Shifting dune belts of northern Padre Island, Texas. Laguna Madre in the distance. Light streaks are spoil banks along the Intracoastal Waterway. Photo by D. L. Inman, 1951.

existed for a century. Here, water covers the area only during times of exceptional south winds. The largest body of permanent water is in the southern half and extends north for about 45 miles; but it is almost cut in two where there has been deposition by the Arroyo Colorado, a distributory of the Rio Grande that flows only during flood stages. The northern end of the southern basin is called Redfish Bay because of the unusually good fishing there. The high salinity of the waters, due to evaporation, causes a luxuriant growth of blue-green algae on the bottom, which serves as food for the bottom-living fish. Because of high salinity, the invertebrates are very impoverished and only half their normal size in the lagoon waters.

To the north, a 30-mile basin extends south from Corpus Christi Bay and terminates on the west side of the Laguna flats, 6 miles south of Baffin Bay. A small isolated basin called The Hole lies a few miles south of the northern basin but often connects with it when north winds have driven the waters south from Corpus Christi Bay. The bays have depths to 10 feet in both large bodies of water, but much of the area is only 1 to 4 feet deep, particularly on the side toward Padre Island and in the narrow zone adjacent to Arroyo Colorado.

The broad exposed flats that cover much of the Laguna are underlain by mud on the western side and by sand along the eastern margin. The flats in general are covered with a mat of algae, which changes color from brown, when the algae are in a dormant condition, to red, when the flats become covered with water and the algae are revived.

One result of the high salinity of the Laguna Madre waters, which is three times as much as the

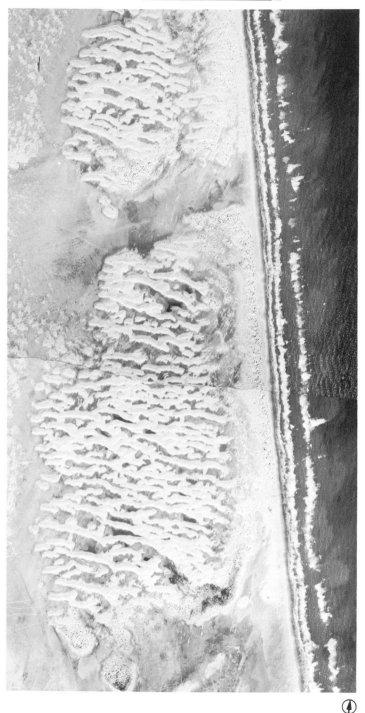

0 MILES   1.0
KM

9.22 Coastal sand dunes, Padre Island. The dunes are elongate parallel to the wind direction, which is a little south of east. Gaps in the sand dune belt mark the positions of sluiceways at times of major storms. U.S. Department of Agriculture, 1955.

open Gulf, is to introduce a deposit on some of the beaches consisting of round grains of calcium carbonate, known as *oölites*. These are apparently caused by lime precipitation due to evaporation of the water in the surf zone. Under the exposed flats on the western side of the Laguna, a zone of black mud is high in hydrogen sulphide. In some places, gypsum crystals have developed from the brine under the flats. These are often exposed in the spoil banks on the sides of the Intracoastal Canal.

The future of the Laguna Madre is somewhat uncertain as it will depend greatly on climatic fluctuations. However, it seems likely that washovers from the Gulf will gradually fill the shallow bodies of water, so that in another century it should become largely a broad exposed flat. The shifting dunes on Padre Island could become stabilized if the park becomes further developed and dune planting is undertaken. These Padre Island dunes are sufficiently high so that, if stabilized, they could be used for home sites above the level of storm tides. The shortage of beach property will probably lead to some such development.

RIO GRANDE DELTA AREA [Figs. 9.24 and 9.25] The Rio Grande heads in the San Juan Mountains of Colorado, more than 1,400 miles from its mouth. It enters the Gulf of Mexico (A in Fig. 9.25) at the United States–Mexico border, about 14 miles east of Brownsville (B). Except for the Mississippi, the Rio Grande drainage basin exceeds in area all other stream systems discharging into the Gulf of Mexico. The small Rio Grande Delta has an apex at Harlingen, about 70 miles in from the Gulf.

Like the Mississippi, the Rio Grande built a series of subdeltas beginning in the very late Pleistocene. The oldest was formed by the Arroyo Colorado (not shown), which leaves the Rio Grande about 12 miles west of Harlingen and now terminates in the Laguna Madre, 25 miles northwest of the parent river. After the abandonment of this delta in early postglacial time, the outer part of the delta subsided and was partly drowned in the Gulf of Mexico and partly eroded by storms.

During postglacial time, the Colorado River abandoned the Arroyo Colorado subdelta; and three successive subdeltas developed. These are the Los Cuates, Del Tigre, and Boca Chica (Fig. 9.24). The Los Cuates Delta spread through distributaries a distance

9.23 Brazos Santiago Pass, the entrance to the Brownsville ship canal, taken shortly after Hurricane Beulah. The hurricane opened a new breach a short distance south of the pass at A. From color photograph, U.S. Coast and Geodetic Survey, November 1, 1967.

of about 20 miles, principally north of the present river mouth. After the delta had extended some distance beyond the present shoreline, the river mouth shifted southward, forming the Del Tigre subdelta and reaching nearly 50 miles into modern Mexico. A reentrant of the shoreline, which has been named Cameron Bay, lay between the central parts of the Los Cuates and Del Tigre subdeltas. When the Del Tigre was abandoned, the Boca Chica subdelta was built into Cameron Bay between the two earlier ones. Together they filled the bay. The present mouth of the river is 4 miles south of the now-abandoned Boca Chica outlet and may be considered as still a part of the Boca Chica subdelta system. The present outer border of the delta appears to be dismembered, indicating that it once extended farther gulfward.

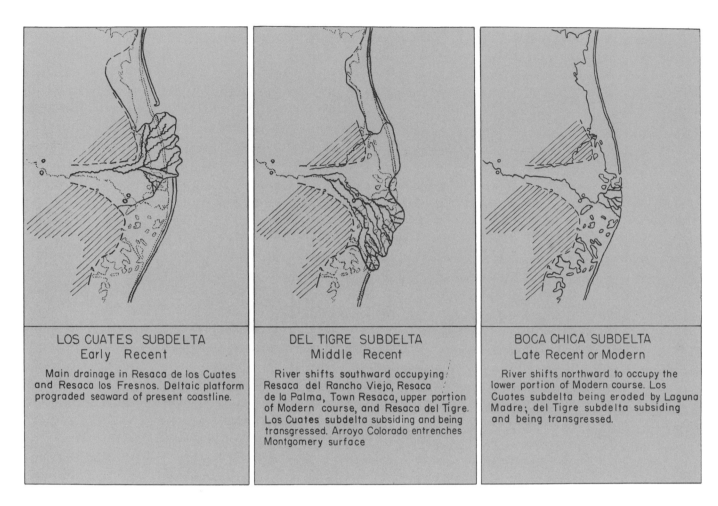

LOS CUATES SUBDELTA Early Recent	DEL TIGRE SUBDELTA Middle Recent	BOCA CHICA SUBDELTA Late Recent or Modern
Main drainage in Resaca de los Cuates and Resaca los Fresnos. Deltaic platform prograded seaward of present coastline.	River shifts southward occupying Resaca del Rancho Viejo, Resaca de la Palma, Town Resaca, upper portion of Modern course, and Resaca del Tigre. Los Cuates subdelta subsiding and being transgressed. Arroyo Colorado entrenches Montgomery surface	River shifts northward to occupy the lower portion of Modern course. Los Cuates subdelta being eroded by Laguna Madre; del Tigre subdelta subsiding and being transgressed.

9.24 Sketch maps of three successive subdeltas of the Rio Grande River. From Lohse and Cook (1958).

The delta of the Rio Grande has been controlled by a combination of factors that are unique to this area because of features not found in other deltas of the United States. Although the river has a long valley and heads in well-watered mountains, most of its course is through alluvium-filled valleys with a dry climate where much water disappears into permeable sediments. Also, large amounts of river water have been diverted to irrigate the fertile bottomlands along its course. As a result, the mouth of the river ordinarily has a small flow. Occasionally the lower Rio Grande dries up completely. Because of fertile soils and mild climate, the delta area or "lower valley," as it is locally called, has been changed by irrigation from a desert to a rich agricultural area.

The coast at and near the mouth of the Rio Grande has northeast winds from October to January, east winds in March and September, and southeast in February and from April to August. The net effect has been a northward drifting of sediment from the delta toward the great Laguna Madre sand plain. Thus, the Rio Grande transports a small load of sediment to the Gulf. Littoral currents transport it northward from the river mouth almost as fast as it reaches the Gulf, and the sand is later blown inland. As a result, there is virtually no gulfward bulge at the delta.

The complex forms of the lower part of the Rio Grande Delta from the southern end of the Laguna Madre to the river and from the Gulf Coast inland about 18 miles are illustrated by high-altitude photography in Figure 9.25.

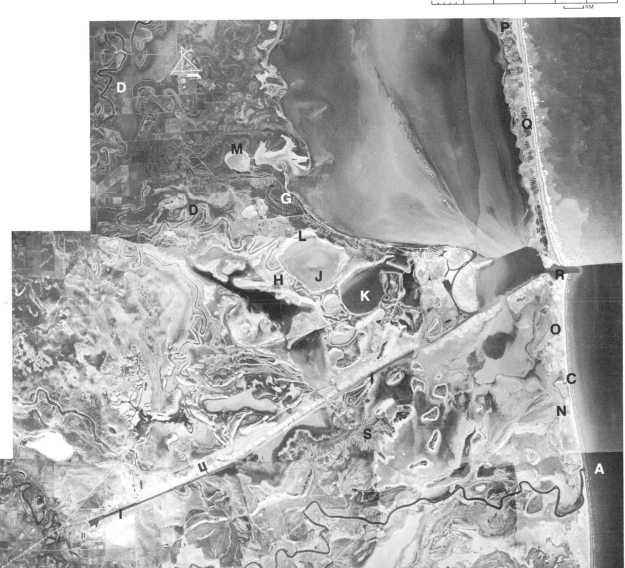

9.25 Composite high-altitude aerial photography of the Rio Grande deltaic plain, from Brownsville (B) to the river mouth (A) at the Texas-Mexico border. Locations C through S are described in the text. U.S. Army Map Service, 1955.

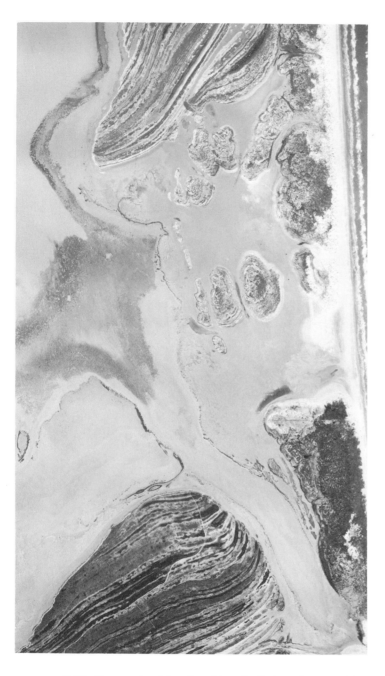

9.26 Remnants of barrier ridges built into Cameron Bay and washarounds, Brazos Island, Rio Grande Delta. U.S. Department of Agriculture, 1962.

A large number of abandoned channels of the Rio Grande are visible. The Spanish term *resaca* is applied to abandoned distributaries of this delta. Some geologists consider that the delta channels are always straight but many of these channels are extremely meandering, as is the present Rio Grande clear to its mouth.

A group of resacas north of the present channel and north of Brownsville evidently represent the subdelta stage of Los Cuates. Some of these (D) terminate at the shore of the Laguna Madre, one (G) at the town of Laguna Vista. Originally this subdelta extended seaward of the present shore, but subsidence and erosion of the Laguna Madre shores during hurricanes have destroyed the outer parts of these channels. Segments of a dismembered channel (H) terminate at two large subround lakes, which were formed after the abandonment of the channels.

On the Mexican side of the river, another group of abandoned distributaries (E), most of which were meandering streams, represent the Del Tigre substage. About 3 miles north of the present river outlet, the Boca Chica (C) was the former mouth of the river during the third subdelta stage. Abandoned distributaries of this stage are marked F and include some straight channels, like that at S, south of the Brownsville ship channel (I).

The destruction of sections of the abandoned resacas results from two causes: (1) winter storms or northers sweeping down through the Laguna Madre erode the weak clays and sands at the southern end of the lagoon, including the abandoned channels of distributaries; and (2) during the long dry season, portions of the very shallow lagoon entirely evaporate, and fine clays from the floor are blown away, leaving circular depressions (J and K). The basins thus excavated usually fill with water during the rainy season.

The muds of the dry beds of the lagoon contain precipitated salts, such as gypsum. Clay particles are stuck together by the salts, and small aggregates are blown like sand grains and accumulate as clay dunes at the borders of the basins. Clay dunes (L, M) are at the northwestern borders of scoured basins. Thus they probably formed during April to August, when the wind was blowing from the southeast. Each of the clay dunes is 30 to 35 feet high. The light color in the photograph along the margins of the scour basins is due to white incrustation of gypsum. Numerous other clay dunes or their erosional remnants are seen throughout the area and may be recognized by the darker color of their vegetation. Some clay dunes show parallel light and dark bands, probably ridges and troughs due to periodic accretion.

Two prominent ridges near the coast (N and O in Fig. 9.25; Fig. 9.26) are characterized by very regular light and dark bands, which represent periodic dune ridge accretions. These ridges are only about 10 feet high and have the appearance of successive bands of dune ridges, formed behind the beach when Cameron Bay indented the coast. Parts of the ridges were destroyed during the construction of the Boca Chica subdelta. No doubt both sand and gypsum-cemented clay aggregates have contributed to these banded coastal dunes.

The Gulf shore of the Rio Grande Delta is a barrier 500 to 750 feet wide, with small dunes locally 5 to 10 feet high. The barrier is nearly straight, trending a few degrees west of north. Just behind it in the mud flats, periodically covered by the waters of the southern Laguna Madre, are numerous small rounded hills, generally 5 feet or less in height, with concentric light and dark bands (P, Q), as in the Mesa del Gavilan. These are also shown on a larger scale in Figures 9.26 and 9.27. They are remnants of beach-dune ridges that have been breached by hurricane floods and have been added to by wind deposits during subsequent dry periods. The origin of these mounds is similar to that of the washarounds on Assateague Island, Maryland, described in Chapter 4 (see Fig. 4.16). However, accretion bands in the Texas washarounds are better developed on the side from which the storm waves approached.

The Brazos Santiago Pass (Fig. 9.23; R in Fig. 9.25), which separates Padre Island to the north from Brazos Island, has been improved as the entrance to the Brownsville ship channel. The dredged channel extends about 18 miles inland to Port Brownsville, where agricultural produce of the lower valley is loaded for shipment. Jetties about a mile long protect the entrances to the channel. Sand has accumulated against both jetties, but the south side has been built out 0.33 mile farther than that on the north, showing again the dominance of northward beach drifting.

The flat Gulf Coast of the Rio Grande Delta has been struck frequently by violent hurricanes. The most recent such storm (at this writing) was Hurricane Beulah, September 20, 1967. This storm had wind velocities of 150 miles per hour; and, at Brownsville, about 25 inches of rain fell within a short time. The combination of hurricane winds and tides and flooded rivers opened many new inlets in

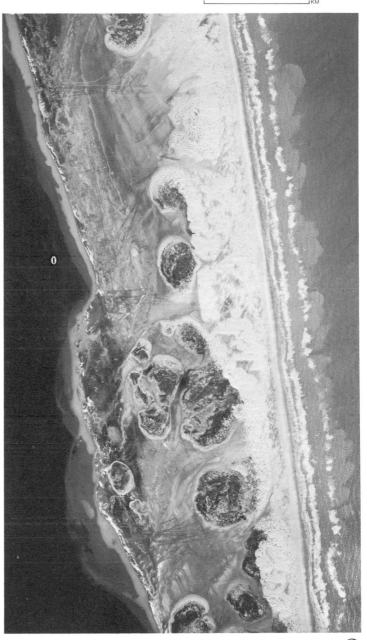

9.27 Washarounds near the southern end of Padre Island. U.S. Department of Agriculture, 1955.

the Padre–Brazos Island barrier. Figure 9.23, a photograph taken November 1, 1967, shows an old inlet (A) that had reopened about 0.5 mile south of Brazos Santiago Pass. It also shows the destroyed remnants of buildings on Padre Island, about a mile north of the pass (B).

REFERENCES

Bernard, H. A., R. J. LeBlanc, and C. F. Major, Jr., 1962. *Recent and Pleistocene Geology of Southeast Texas*. Geol. Soc. Amer., Excursion Guidebook. Geol. of Gulf Coast and Central Texas, 1962 Ann. meeting, pp. 175–224.

Bullard, Fred M., 1942. Source of beach and river sands of Gulf Coast of Texas. *Geol. Soc. Amer. Bull.*, vol. 53, pp. 1021–1044.

Corps of Engineers, U.S. Army, 1934. *Beach Erosion at Galveston, Texas*. House of Representatives, 73d Congr., 2d Sess., Document 400.

Curry, W. H., 1940. Recent shoreline process, Brazoria County, Texas. *Bull. Amer. Assoc. Petroleum Geologists*, vol. 24, pt. 1, pp. 731–735.

El-Ashry, Mohamed T., 1966. Photointerpretation of shoreline changes in selected areas along the Atlantic and Gulf coasts of the United States. Univ. Illinois Ph.D. thesis in geology, pp. 88–132.

Fisk, Harold N., 1959. Padre Island and the Laguna Madre Flats, coastal south Texas. *Nat. Acad. Sci., Nat. Res. Council, 2d Coastal Geogr. Conf.*, pp. 103–151.

Getzendaner, F. M., 1930. Geologic section of Rio Grande embayment, Texas, and implied history. *Bull. Amer. Assoc. Petroleum Geologists*, vol. 14, no. 11, pp. 1425–1437.

Halbouty, M. T., 1936. Geology and geophysics showing cap rock and salt overhang of High Island dome, Galveston County, Texas. *Bull. Amer. Assoc. Petroleum Geologists*, vol. 20, pp. 560–561.

Hayes, Miles O., 1967. Hurricanes as geological agents: case studies of Hurricanes Carla, 1961, and Cindy, 1963. *Bur. Econ. Geol., Univ. Texas, Rept. Inves. 71.*

Henry, V. J., 1956. Investigation of shoreline-like features in the Galveston Bay region, Texas. *Texas A & M Res. Found., Project 24, Office Naval Res., Tech. Rept.*

LeBlanc, R. J., and W. D. Hodgson, 1959. Origin and development of the Texas shorelines. *Gulf Coast Assn. Geol. Soc., Trans.*, vol. 9, pp. 197–220.

Lohse, E. Alan, and T. D. Cook, 1958. Development of the recent Rio Grande deltaic plain. In *Sedimentology of South Texas*, Field Trip Guidebook, Gulf Coast Assn. Geol. Soc., Corpus Christi, Texas, pp. 55–60.

McKee, Edwin D., 1950. Report on studies of stratification in modern sediments and in laboratory experiments. *Office of Naval Res. (Project Nonr 164(00), NR 081 123).*

Norris, R. M., 1953. Buried oyster reefs in some Texas bays. *Jour. Paleont.*, vol. 27, no. 4, pp. 569–576.

Price, W. A., 1954. Shorelines and coasts of the Gulf of Mexico. *U.S. Fish and Wildlife Service, Fishery Bull.* 89, pp. 39–65.

————, 1956. Hurricanes affecting the coast of Texas from Galveston to the Rio Grande. *Beach Erosion Board, Corps Engrs., U.S. Army, Tech. Memo.* 78.

————, 1958. Sedimentology and Quaternary geomorphology of South Texas. *Gulf Coast Assn. Geol. Soc., Trans.*, vol. 8, pp. 41–75.

————, and L. S. Kornicker, 1961. Marine and lagoonal deposits in clay dunes, Gulf Coast, Texas. *Jour. Sed. Petrology*, vol. 31, no. 2, pp. 245–255.

Rusnak, G. A., 1960. Sediments of Laguna Madre, Texas. In *Recent Sediments, Northwest Gulf of Mexico, 1951–1958.* Amer. Assoc. Petroleum Geologists, pp. 153–196.

Shepard, F. P., 1956. Late Pleistocene and Recent history of the central Texas coast. *Jour. Geol.*, vol. 64, no. 1, pp. 56–69.

————, 1960. Rise of sea level along Northwest Gulf of Mexico. In *Recent Sediments, Northwest Gulf of Mexico, 1951–1958.* Amer. Assoc. Petroleum Geologists, pp. 338–344.

————, and D. G. Moore, 1955. Central Texas coast sedimentation: characteristics of sedimentary environment, recent history and diagenesis. *Amer. Assoc. Petroleum Geologists Bull.*, vol. 39, pt. 2, no. 8, pp. 1463–1493.

————, and D. G. Moore, 1960. Bays of central Texas coast. In *Recent Sediments, Northwest Gulf of Mexico, 1951–1958.* Amer. Assoc. Petroleum Geologists, pp. 117–152.

Weeks, A. W., 1945. Quaternary deposits of Texas coastal plain between Brazos River and Rio Grande. *Amer. Assoc. Petroleum Geologists Bull.*, vol. 29, pp. 1693–1720.

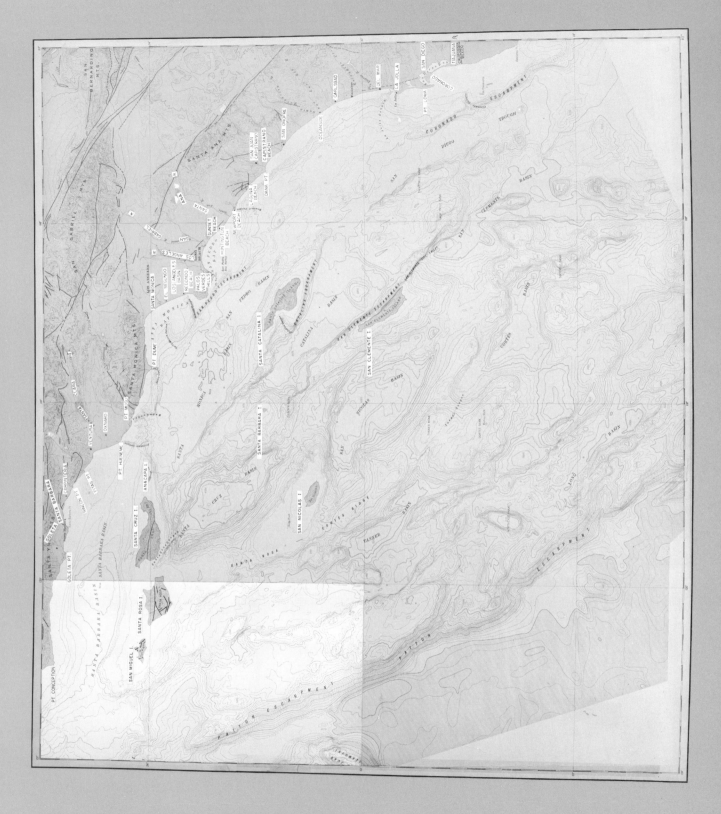

10.1 The coast of Southern California from the Mexican border to Pt. Conception, showing localities described. Includes offshore islands and sea floor topography by depth contours to the Patton Escarpment, about 100 miles offshore. From Shepard and Emery.

Island-Sheltered Coasts

Southern California

10   In discussing the coastal changes along the West Coast of the United States, we are confronted with problems unlike those that are dominant along the Gulf Coast and most of the East Coast. Beginning with Southern California, we encounter mostly cliffed coasts with rocky promontories. Even the intermittent coastal plains differ from those we have already described in having steeper seaward slopes, because they are largely fans built out from the adjacent high mountains. The problems of shifting barriers, which were so much in the forefront of the discussions in preceding chapters, will be given less emphasis during the West Coast descriptions, because, except in southwestern Washington and northwestern Oregon, barriers are rare in the West. Also, there is little evidence about their history, except where jetties have been built. However, cliff erosion that was of importance in only a few localities in the East and the South, becomes of major importance in the West. On the other hand, one problem that the West has in common with the other coasts is the beach changes that result from man-made structures.

Southern California (Fig. 10.1) is characterized by relatively straight cliffed coasts, mostly cut in soft rocks. Somewhat harder rocks are responsible for some of the small promontories, while others protrude because they are fault blocks that have been pushed up from the sea floor. Two relatively low coastal belts in Southern California are both the result of deltaic fans built out from mountain ranges into bordering troughs and basins. One of these, the lowland around Los Angeles, has the center of greatest population in the state, and here the comparatively straight coasts have been greatly controlled by the activities of man. The other large coastal lowland, centering east of Ventura and related to the Santa Clara Delta, is less populous and more of a farming region. Unlike the Los Angeles lowland, the Santa Clara Plain has a deltaic

10.2 San Diego Bay and surrounding areas including False Bay (now Mission Bay). From Imray (1868).

A group of eight off-lying islands are separated from the mainland by deep water. These give some protection to the mainland coasts and effectively reduce storm waves, especially in the area extending along the east-west coast on either side of Santa Barbara. These islands have predominantly rocky coasts with a few cove beaches. Most of the island rocks consist of lavas, intrusives such as granite, and relatively hard sedimentaries. Coves on the leeward sides of the islands are ordinarily sheltered enough for anchoring; and one small natural harbor is located at Santa Catalina, the most populous island.

SAN DIEGO AREA [Figs. 10.2 through 10.16] San Diego Harbor was discovered by Juan Rodríguez Cabrillo in 1542; and San Diego (Fig. 10.2), the oldest city of the West Coast, was founded by Father Junípero Serra in 1769. Because of the tidal currents that come into the harbor and keep the entrance open, except for a bar that has to be dredged occasionally to maintain depths for deep-draft vessels, it is the best protected natural harbor on the California coast. As a result of the protected water and the good flushing by the tides, the U.S. Navy keeps a larger concentration of ships based in San Diego than in any other harbor in the country. The character of the harbor in 1868, before dredging and before the jetty was built out from North Island, is shown in Figure 10.2.

San Diego has gradually grown along the coast to the north and west until its urban area includes most of the elevated promontory of Point Loma, and to the north, the Mission Bay area, Pacific Beach, and La Jolla (Figs. 10.3 and 10.4). A large urban area has also developed on the spit called the Coronado Strand. This spit grew northward from the Tijuana River because of a countercurrent that developed in the lee of Point Loma. In prehistoric times, North Island and Coronado were islands, although connected by a spit in the earliest maps. According to the late Max Miller, in the early days, sailing vessels used to obtain fresh water from a spring on North Island. Miller and an aviator stationed on North Island in the 1920s discovered the spring under a mass of brambles. The juncture between North Island and Coronado is now complete, the fill having been accomplished by man during World War II. The spit and former islands protect the harbor from southerly storms. Originally, the harbor was a combination of a drowned valley

bulge, although no river now enters at Hueneme, the apex of the bulge.

There is only one natural harbor on the Southern California coast, San Diego; but storms are rare and projecting points protect a few other areas, so that in the days before the artificial harbors were built, the old sailing vessels used to anchor in the lee of the points. Embayments were much more open a few thousand years ago, when the Indians were the only people living on this coast. Even in the relatively short time since the white man has taken over, the estuaries have been extensively filled by river deposits brought down from the mountains during the occasional floods.

The Southern California coast has another difference from the other coasts we have been studying.

10.4 Oblique aerial photo taken during unusually large wave conditions, showing Point Loma (A), Mission Bay (C), Pacific Beach (D), and La Jolla (E). Photographer unknown; about 1950.

and a coastal indentation formed by the growth of the Tijuana and Otay River Deltas (just south of the area in Fig. 10.2).

When the construction of the jetty was started in 1900 at the harbor entrance south of the western tip of North Island, the currents caused a change in the beaches such as usually accompanies these artificial developments. The sand built out along the east side of the jetty, and the beach at Coronado was cut back (Fig. 10.5). Because this threatened the popular beach as well as the already famous Hotel del Coronado, sand and rocks have been dumped along the shore repeatedly to preserve the strand. Also, as a result of harbor dredging during World War II, large amounts of fill were deposited in shallow water near the beach, and this seems to have corrected the situation. Very likely more trouble is in store, however, since there is a plan to cut a second entrance into the harbor well south of Coronado, which, if implemented, will cut off most of the supply of sand from the south that maintains the beach.

10.3 Aerial photo composite of the northern part of the San Diego coastline, showing Ocean Beach (D), Mission Bay (A), Pacific Beach (I), La Jolla (J), Mt. Soledad (B), and Scripps Institution of Oceanography (H). U.S. Army Map Service.

10.5 Shore erosion just north of Hotel del Coronado as a result of building San Diego Harbor jetty. Photographer unknown; 1901.

10.7 Destruction of a coastal arch at Sunset Cliffs. Photos by Shepard.

a July 1946.

10.6 Slumping at Sunset Cliffs, Pt. Loma, endangering the coastal road as a result of an earthquake in March 1968. Photo by Shepard, April 1968.

b May 1968. Note that only a small pedestal remains to mark the site of the arch. The isolated rock near the cliff (A in Fig. 10.7*a*) has also disappeared.

Point Loma (Fig. 10.2 and A in Fig. 10.4) is a rock ridge rising to 400 feet near its southern end and sloping off to the north until it is lost under the adjacent beaches and embayments. Cretaceous and Eocene rocks are exposed along both sides of Point Loma. These rocks have a considerable amount of shale, which is easily eroded by the waves. The soft rock cliffs on the west side are exposed to the large swell of the open Pacific, with only a minor protection from the 60-mile distant San Clemente Island. As a result, the coast is retreating, although very un-evenly. The shaly parts of Sunset Cliffs on Point Loma are having real trouble because of undermining that causes occasional slides, threatening the coastal highway and cliffside residences (Fig. 10.6). Most of the stacks and natural bridges adjacent to the shale cliffs have shown conspicuous changes in recent years (Fig. 10.7). However, at the north end of Sunset Cliffs, we have an example where sandstone cliffs have had only very minor changes since photo-graphed in 1887 (Fig. 10.8). Such contrasts in erosion are characteristic of the entire West Coast.

10.8 Coastal sandstone cliffs at the south end of Ocean Beach. The lower part of the bluff (A in Fig. 10.8a) is a massive sandstone overlain by weaker shale.

a 1887. Note isolated rock stack (B) and indentation of coast (C). Photographer unknown.

10.9 Aerial photo of entrance to Mission Bay in 1944, before building of jetties to maintain the boat channel. Compare with Fig. 10.3. U.S. Air Force photo.

b April 1968. There has been little change in the sandstone bluffs in foreground, but the stack has disappeared, and rockslide has reached the shore at the indentation (A). The house at B appears to be in danger of being damaged by slumping of the shale on which it was built. Photo by Neil Marshall.

It is often very hard to see why one area has retreated and another has shown no change, especially where the rock is essentially the same.

North of Point Loma, there is another embayment, formerly called False Bay (Fig. 10.2) but renamed Mission Bay (A in Fig. 10.3). This was a drowned valley of the San Diego River (Mission Valley) and Rose Canyon. The San Diego River had built a large delta into the southern arm of the bay and then spilled over to the south, so that during the time of the early settlements, it was flowing into San Diego Harbor.

Engineers diverted it back to Mission Bay in about 1870. The embayment probably represents a transverse fault that cuts off the north side of the Loma ridge. On the other side of the bay, the formations in Mount Soledad (B in Fig. 10.3) dip to the south. The San Diego River cut its valley at the juncture of these two structures and then was flooded by the postglacial rise in sea level, like most other coastal valleys.

The embayment was protected first by a gravel bar built from the north by the south-flowing currents. These characterize the California coast, except where a countercurrent is set up by a protruding point. The gravel was subsequently covered with fine sand, forming the extensive Mission and Pacific Beaches. The relatively small size of Mission Bay did not produce

10.10 Destruction of Cathedral Rock, La Jolla.
a 1900. Shows large natural arch in sandstone. Photographer unknown.

b October 1963. Only a small remnant of pedestal (A) remained. By 1968 remnant had disappeared. Photo by Shepard.

enough tidal effect at the inlet to maintain more than a shallow entrance (Fig. 10.9) until jetties were constructed in 1950 and dredging operations established a 15-foot navigable channel. This soon became partially blocked by sand coming around the north jetty; and, under storm conditions, the waves broke across the entrance (B in Fig. 10.4). The channel had to be closed until the jetties were lengthened,

and more dredging was necessary to deepen the entrance to 20 feet. A third jetty (C in Fig. 10.3) was built to the south to allow the passage of floodwaters from the usually dry San Diego River. Further difficulties have come from the gradual loss of sand on the south side of the jetties. Sand has to be dredged from Mission Bay and dumped on the shore at Ocean Beach (D). As of this writing, no appreciable flood has taken place in the San Diego River to make the channel necessary; but in the past a number of floods have carried enormous quantities of sediment down this valley, and the material had largely been deposited in Mission Bay, developing a considerable delta since the survey for the 1868 chart (Fig. 10.2). The worst flood was in 1916. There had been a long drought so the city employed Hatfield, "The Rainmaker," to use his magic, hoping to restore the water supply. The success, of course a coincidence, was overwhelming; and the torrent of rain caused a dam to break, the river to overflow its banks, and much property was carried out to sea. Hatfield was never paid; instead he was almost lynched.

North of Mission Bay, the coast bends west around the rocky La Jolla headland, which extends for 4 miles, turning abruptly east at Point La Jolla (E in Fig. 10.3). This headland is protected by relatively firm Cretaceous sandstone similar to that of Point Loma.

Erosion of the coast at La Jolla is quite variable. Old arches, like Cathedral Rock of the late 1890s (Fig. 10.10*a*), have disappeared completely so that not even the small remnant shown in Figure 10.10*b* (1963) was visible in 1968. However, the popular La Jolla Cove at the turn in the coast has remained almost exactly the same as it was in the last century (Fig. 10.11). About the only change is that the proper bathing suits of the Nineties have gradually become briefer until bikinis give new enjoyment to those who come to watch rather than to swim. The most surprising feature of the lack of erosion here is that boulders or concretions protruding from the 20-foot terrace east of the cove have not been altered during this period of 70 years, even though large waves during the occasional northwest storms of winter sweep violently over this platform. The arch on the west side of the Cove has been strengthened by concrete; otherwise it is quite possible that this would have disappeared, like Cathedral Rock 0.5 mile to the south. The La Jolla Caves, which extend

10.11 La Jolla Cove. The small sandy cove is a favored swimming spot.

a 1906. Two buildings were on the bluffs behind the cove. Photographer unknown.

10.12 Tilted rocks adjoining fault that forms north slope of Mt. Soledad. These strata have been planed off to form a wave-cut platform exposed at extremely low tide. East of La Jolla Cove. Photo by Shepard.

b April 1968. Note that sandstone rocks in foreground show almost no change in 62 years, although the 1906 buildings have been replaced, and the cove area is now a city park. Photo by Shepard.

10.13 A small barrier (A) blocking off a small lagoon north of Mt. Soledad. This is directly landward of La Jolla Submarine Canyon (B). Scripps Institution of Oceanography (C) had just been started. This area had been almost entirely built up as La Jolla Shores by 1968, and the lagoon had been filled. Photographer unknown; 1912.

for 50 feet or more into the sandstone just east of the Cove, are practically the same as in 1897, although one mass of rock fell in the early 1900s, causing a retreat of the cliffs of about 30 feet in one small section.

The bend in the coast north of the caves is apparently due to a fault that extends down the north side of Mt. Soledad and comes to the coast. This has had the interesting effect of changing the slope adjacent to the cliffs from a steep rock ledge to a broad platform, which is exposed at low tide (Fig. 10.12).

This is the widest present-day wave-cut terrace in the San Diego area. The extreme low tide bares the surface for 700 feet out from the shale and sandstone cliffs. Because of the tilted nature of the formation, ridges a few inches high protrude above the general surface representing the more resistant beds.

Farther north, a straight barrier beach formerly enclosed a lagoon (Fig. 10.13), but now the lagoon has been almost entirely filled and is covered with houses and apartment buildings. Seaward of this barrier beach is the southernmost of the submarine can-

10.14 Boomer Beach, west of La Jolla Cove, showing seasonal change resulting from different direction of wave approach and heavier winter surf. Photos by Shepard.

a Summer condition when waves from the south have built a beach at the north end, but have taken away sand from the south.

b Winter conditions when heavy surf from northwest has removed the beach shown in Figure 10.14a, and has carried sand to the south, causing another but smaller beach to the right of photo.

yons (F in Fig. 10.3) that come in virtually to the shore at a number of points along the California coast. The effect of La Jolla Canyon, very evident during periods of large swell, is the result of converging wave crests between La Jolla Canyon and Scripps Canyon,

about 1.5 miles north, and the very low waves at the head of La Jolla Canyon due to the divergence of the waves moving in over the deep canyon head (Fig. 2.12). Wave crests are slowed by shoaling water, so the crests over the canyons outrun those on either side and spread laterally. This "canyon effect" allows the launching of small boats at the La Jolla Canyon head, except during periods of the largest waves. The same effect has resulted in the growth of fishing villages at canyon heads in many places, notably the picturesque Nazare, north of Lisbon on the Portuguese coast; Cap Breton in southwestern France; and in Cayar, Senegal, of west Africa.

The extensive scuba-diving investigations in the La Jolla area by R. F. Dill and many others have produced evidence concerning the early history of this lagoon. In the head of La Jolla Canyon, at a depth of 80 feet, Dill found lagoonal sediments with a tree root that has been dated as being a little more than 8,000 years old. This agrees well with the sea-level curve for stable areas (Fig. 2.1), suggesting that this has been a stable coast in recent millenia. The ancient Indians are known to have occupied La Jolla about 5500 B.C., and at that time many of them were living well outside of the present shoreline because of the lowered sea level. As evidence of this Indian occupation, hundreds of stone grinding bowls (metates) and other Indian implements are found out to depths of about 55 feet below the present sea level in the La Jolla area. Also, Indian burials found on the mesa about 300 feet above sea level had skeletons with necklaces of shells, dated as 5500 B.C., of a type indigenous to estuaries. Probably the head of La Jolla Canyon was in an estuary at that time.

An interesting contrast exists between the beach sand around the La Jolla projection and the beach extending for a mile north of La Jolla Canyon. In the coves around the sandstone cliffs of Point La Jolla, there is a medium to coarse sand that is clearly derived from the rock cliffs. However, the sand is fine to very fine on the long beach in north La Jolla adjacent to the barrier. This fine sand is derived indirectly from the mountains to the east and more directly from the wet-weather streams that occasionally flow down the small canyons coming from the 300-foot mesa. Changes in the beaches are partly related to seasons. Thus, Boomer Beach, just southwest of Point La Jolla, is built up each summer, then the sand is cut away each fall by the first large waves from the northwest until only boulders are exposed (Fig. 10.14). Some of the sand moves south and apparently returns when the waves have an approach from the south during the late spring and summer.

One effect of this shifting of sand along the coast of Point La Jolla is illustrated by what is now called "the Children's Pool" or "Casa Pool" south of the cove (G in Fig. 10.3). Here, a short seawall was constructed in an arc, opening to the north to provide a protected place for swimmers. During the first winter after completion, sand was swept into the protected area and failed to go through the small openings in the wall that had been provided for the purpose. As a result, the enclosure has become largely a beach with only a small zone to the north left for swimmers.

The extensive fine sand beach of North La Jolla has had an interesting history. As far back as we know—that is, about 1900—and continuing until 1947, the northern part of this beach was cut away each winter until cobbles were uncovered along much of its length (Fig. 10.15b). In places, even the cobbles were removed and old formations were exposed underneath. Then, in late spring, the sand beach came back and built higher and higher during the summer. Shepard made the mistake of predicting to a class in the fall of 1947 that the cobbles would be visible in a few months. Showing the folly of predictions, the beach was not cut away again sufficiently to expose those cobbles until 1953, and we have seen only scattered cobbles since then.

The low cliffs cut in alluvium, exposed in the background of Figure 10.15, have had a history parallel to that of the beach. Prior to 1947, each year when the sand was cut away, the waves attacked these cliffs; and the average retreat from 1918 until 1946 was very nearly a foot a year. When excessive beach erosion in winter ceased, the active cutting by the waves also stopped; and, in 1968, the cliffs were nearly in the same position as in 1946. The retreat was stopped in part by a virtual extermination of the ground squirrels, which were burrowing actively into the cliffs in the earlier years before construction of the houses.

North of Scripps Institution of Oceanography (H in Fig. 10.3), the cliffs rise to heights of as much as 350 feet and consist of sandstones, conglomerates, and shales of Eocene age (Fig. 10.16). These cliffs are receding very slowly as a combined result of wave

10.15 Beach directly south of Scripps Institution of Oceanography, showing typical seasonal changes that prevailed until 1947. Photos by U.S. Grant IV, 1936.
a Summer condition with broad sand berm.

b Winter condition with most of sand removed exposing cobbles, which have rarely appeared since 1947.

10.16 Coastal cliffs north of Scripps Institution composed of sandstone conglomerates and shales, which are retreating at a relatively slow rate. Photo taken at low tide shows exposed rip current channels. Wave pattern due to submarine canyon heads, which cause more rapid advance of wave fronts up the deep channels. Photo by Shepard, 1960.

erosion, landslides, and weathering. By a study of initials carved in the cliffs, K. O. Emery found that due to weathering alone the cliffs in this area were retreating about a foot in 600 years. Retaking of photographs after an interval of about 30 years has shown us that sufficient changes have occurred to reveal the quite different character of the bedding. This does not give any actual measurement of rate of retreat but shows that it is much faster than weathering alone would produce. Houses built at the edge of these cliffs may not be endangered for a long time, perhaps 100 years; but eventually they will collapse unless measures are taken, such as reinforcing the cliffs and diverting drainage. According to George Moore, of the U.S. Geological Survey at La Jolla, the federal building at the north end of Scripps Institution, constructed in 1964, is located directly over the

trace of a slowly rotating slide block that is causing sagging in the center of the building and may produce some bad cracks before many years, but does not pose any immediate threat.

Elevated wave-cut terraces are found all along the California coast. They are particularly impressive in the La Jolla area where they extend up to more than 800 feet on the top of Mt. Soledad. Too few shells have been found in these elevated terraces to allow their dating. However, in the cliffs north of La Jolla, a 50-foot terrace is covered with a beach deposit containing abundant shells. Carbon-14 determinations showed that these were too old to date by this method. No one has made a thorough study of the terraces in the area, but they appear to be deformed and are apparently the result of earth movements combined with the sea-level changes of the glacial period. The

300- to 400-foot Linda Vista terrace, of unknown age but probably pre-Pleistocene, extends east from La Jolla to the base of the mountains.

The area around La Jolla appears to have had no vertical movement of significance, at least during the past 10,000 years. This is in keeping with the lack of any appreciable earthquake epicenters around San Diego. The faults, such as that of the north face of Mt. Soledad, have apparently become inactive; but some of the supposedly inactive faults farther north, as in Santa Barbara, have come to life.

DEL MAR–OCEANSIDE–SAN ONOFRE AREA

[Figs. 10.17 and 10.18]   Northward for 37 miles from the city limit of San Diego, the shore bends gradually from north-northwest to northwest. Sandy beaches are virtually continuous along this coast, except where cut away temporarily by winter storms. The towns, including Del Mar (A in Fig. 10.18), Solana Beach (B), Cardiff, Encinitas, Carlsbad, Oceanside, and San Onofre, are mostly built along elevated wave-cut terraces, ranging from 50 to 150 feet above sea level. At Solana Beach, the terrace ranges in height from 80 to 110 feet. The sea cliff, however, reveals that the top of the rock terrace is only about 30 feet above sea level where it is covered by recent or Pleistocene alluvium (Fig. 10.17). Many caves have been cut in the underlying rock. Near Oceanside and Carlsbad, the sea cliff has a distinct terrace at 50 to 75 feet. Near San Onofre, a remarkably level terrace rises from about 120 feet at the top of the shore cliffs to about 200 feet at the base of the eroded foothills (see Fig. 2.14). Each terrace is a sloping plain rising toward a break in slope, showing the position of the shoreline at the time of terrace cutting. After sea level had lowered or the land had risen, a new sea cliff or steepened slope was cut at the seaward limit of most terraces. Some of the lower terraces very likely correspond with interglacial stages when the sea was higher because of less glacial ice than at present, but such terraces are probably no higher than about 150 feet above present sea level. Terraces with greater elevation must be due to differential uplift of the land. Because these land movments were not uniform for long distances along the coast, a careful mapping of the variation in level of a particular terrace should provide a record of the warping of the area. This type of survey has not yet been made for most of the California coast.

10.17 Coastal cliff at Solana Beach. Many caves have developed along vertical joints in soft calcareous sandstone. The upper part of the cliff, retreating more rapidly, is in Pleistocene alluvium. Photo by Shepard, 1968.

Furthermore, where tested, most raised beaches were found to be too old to be dated by carbon-14.

Along the coast from Del Mar to San Onofre, the sea cliffs range in height from about 30 to 120 feet. Thin Pleistocene marine sands on terrace surfaces commonly overlie Eocene and Miocene sandstones and shales. These rocks vary considerably in resistance to erosion. Many sandstones are weakly cemented and crumble readily. Most shales have slumped blocks where the sea cliff is nearly vertical. The sandy beaches are relatively wide during summer, but waves break directly against the cliffs mostly during the storm season when the beaches have been largely cut away. Erosion at the south side of Encinitas caused a well-known restaurant with a gold dome to fall over the cliff.

The cliffs along the Del Mar to San Onofre coast are interrupted by eight partly filled estuaries at the mouths of the larger wet-weather streams. Almost all of the estuaries of the Southern California coast are found here. These estuaries, like those of the East and Gulf Coasts of the United States, are primarily the result of recent rise in sea level following the lowered sea levels of the glacial period, when the larger rivers of that time could cut below the present strand line. The estuaries, as can be seen in Figure 10.18, are now much more filled than those of the East and South Coasts and lack the dendritic tributary estuaries of the Chesapeake Bay type. The greater

10.18 Aerial photo of coast at Del Mar (A) and Solana Beach (B). The Del Mar Race Track (C) and County Fairground are located in the filled estuary of San Dieguito River. San Elijo estuary (D) is largely a marsh. U.S. Department of Agriculture, 1939.

fill is the result of the large source of sediment derived during floods from the nearby mountains. A predominance of southward beach drifting along the coast causes barrier spits to form across the estuaries from the north. Most of the estuaries are now connected with the sea only through temporary channels opened artificially after each serious flood. The upper ends of the estuaries are filling with delta deposits and have been converted largely to marshes. The Del Mar Race Track (C in Fig. 10.18) was constructed on the site of a former estuary. The San Elijo Lagoon (D) is mostly filled with marsh downstream from a delta. Agua Hedionda, near Carlsbad, has the largest unfilled estuary, although it was entirely blocked by a bay-mouth barrier until opened artificially by the San Diego Gas & Electric Company for their new nuclear plant.

CAPISTRANO TO CORONA DEL MAR [Figs. 10.19 and 10.20]   Northwest from San Onofre, a coastal belt about 25 miles long has a prominent wave-cut terrace ranging in height from 80 to 180 feet. Along this coast the communities of San Clemente, Capistrano, Dana Point, Laguna Beach, and Corona del Mar are located. This area differs from that of Oceanside in having conglomerates with greater resistance to wave erosion than the sandstones and shales farther south. This has resulted in a moderately irregular coast with headlands or points projecting seaward and coves or bays cutting more deeply into the terrace. This irregularity is particularly well displayed at Laguna Beach (Fig. 10.19), which has become a well-known seaside resort, partly because of its combination of picturesque rocky cliffs, like those of the Riviera, and its sandy cove beaches. Some offshore rock stacks, detached from the headlands by erosion, are gradually being pounded to pieces by wave attack.

The largest stream entering the sea in this belt is San Juan Creek, along which the famous San Juan Capistrano Mission is situated, about 4 miles upstream. Crowds gather there each year on St. Joseph's Day to watch "The Swallows Come Back to Capistrano." The outlet of San Juan Creek (A in Fig. 10.20) is illustrated in the 1944 aerial photo. Since that date, jetties have been built and a harbor has been formed just north of the outlet, extending to Dana Point (B). The intermittent San Juan Creek is a braided stream overloaded with sand. A sandy

10.19 Very irregular coast at Laguna Beach with projecting headlands and small sandy coves. The headlands are in hard, resistant conglomerates. Emerald Bay and Crescent Bay at right. Photo by R. E. Stevenson, 1952.

barrier about 0.5 mile long encloses the lower end of the creek, except during floods.

NEWPORT BAY [Figs. 10.21, 10.22, and 10.23] The natural harbor at Newport and Balboa Beaches (Fig. 10.21) was the result of the development of spits to the southeast from the sediment supplied at the Santa Ana River mouth (F). These spits were built out seaward of the low cliffs at Newport (G) and across the mouth of a large slough that has no river at present. The entrance to the harbor was formerly shallow and could be used only at high tide,

but the Army Corps of Engineers built jetties (not shown) and dredged the channel so that it can now be used by boats of 20-foot draft. As a result of the nearness to Los Angeles, it has become one of the great yachting centers of the United States.

Newport Harbor somewhat resembles St. Andrew Bay at Panama City, Florida. In both cases, a spit has built eastward across a slough, and there is an older barrier on the inside that is now discontinuous. At Newport, the inner barrier is represented by Lido (A) and Balboa (B) Islands, which are separated by the main channel that leads to the inner harbor. This

10.20 Aerial photo of Capistrano Beach. San Juan Creek enters the ocean here, about 4 miles downstream from the San Juan Capistrano Mission. A narrow barrier blocks the outlet of the former estuary, now mostly filled with sediment. A new boat harbor (C) was completed in 1968. Jetties are superimposed. U.S. Air Force photo, 1944.

old barrier has been modified so much by man that it would be difficult to recognize its origin at present.

At the end of Newport pier (C), where the spit bends more to the east, the head of a small submarine canyon comes in so close to the coast that it is actually possible to throw a stone from the pier into the center of the canyon. Within 600 feet of the pier

10.21 Newport Beach (I), the south end of Huntington Beach (H), and the alluvial plain of the Santa Ana River (E). A submarine canyon (C) heads just offshore. Shore erosion during summers has been very serious at D. U.S. Department of Agriculture photos, 1951.

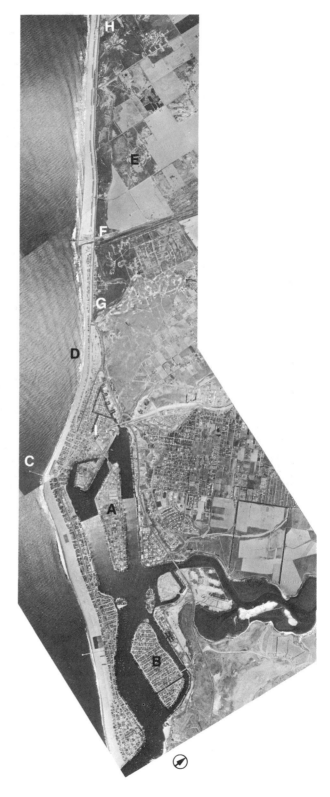

OUR CHANGING COASTLINES

depths of 100 feet occur. This would appear to pose a problem relative to the stability of the pier, although the authors have not heard of any damage from slumping along this steep slope. However, the canyon must catch much of the sediment that is being carried along the shore by the dominant easterly currents, which are responsible for the growth and maintenance of the spit. Probably the reason that, even before the jetties were built, the spit did not close the pass into the lagoon is that only a small amount of sediment bypasses the canyon head; and the tides from the lagoon were able to cope with this.

Newport Beach is a remarkable example of the effects of seasonal changes in direction of approaching waves. During the winter, the westerlies cause waves to approach the beach in a direction that causes currents to move downcoast along the spit. In summer, this is reversed and the southerly swell takes over (as in Fig. 10.21), causing drift to the northwest. The result of this change is that in summer, erosion takes place to the north, as can be seen by the narrowness of the beach (D) 1.5 miles northwest of the pier. Particularly severe erosion occurs when heavy swells come from tropical disturbances to the south, as occurred in the summer of 1939. At this time, beach erosion left many beach houses standing in the water on wooden pilings or badly undermined (Fig. 10.22). During most of the year these houses had had substantial beach in front of them.

Contributing causes for erosion here may be (1) recent building of debris storage basins along the Santa Ana River, which enters the ocean 2 miles northwest of Newport Beach (F); (2) short jetties at the mouth of the Santa Ana River, which have trapped sand against the northwest jetty; and (3) loss of sand into the Newport Submarine Canyon. In July 1968, further erosion resulted from large southerly swells. Sandbags protected shore buildings temporarily. The construction of a 250-foot steel groin stopped erosion and caused deposition to the southeast; but, a month later, high waves originating from a storm off Baja California caused further erosion to the northwest of the jetty, and waves soon cut away the sand around the landward end of the groin (Fig. 10.23).

During 1969, one steel groin four blocks northwest of the one in Figure 10.23 and three additional rock-supported groins were under construction to retain as much sand as possible on the part of the

10.22 Oblique aerial photo of Newport Beach in 1939, showing severe beach erosion and undermining of cottages, about 1.5 miles northwest of the Newport Beach pier. Note accretion on each side of pier. This same area was again severely eroded in winter of 1968. Fairchild Aerial Photos.

10.23 New steel jetty constructed in March 1968 has trapped sand on its southeast (left) side, and the beach on the other side has been seriously eroded. Photo by Shepard, August 1968.

10.24 Long Beach (C), the Port of Los Angeles (D), San Pedro (E), and Wilmington (F). Los Angeles Harbor is artificial and is protected by the long breakwater (B). The artificial outlet of the Los Angeles River is at A. In the Wilmington area (near F) subsidence of the ground has been due to the removal of oil. U.S. Coast and Geodetic Survey photography, 1967.

beach subject to erosion. During the winter of 1968–1969, some moderate waves with an approach from the north eroded the southeast side of the groin; but there were no winter storms sufficiently intense to cause serious beach erosion. Because the coast trends northwest-southeast, the beach is somewhat protected from northwest storms. Robert Reed, director of marine safety at Newport Beach, has kept annual curves of beach erosion and progradation for several years. These show that the beach is built out farthest in March and is most seriously eroded in late November and early December (compare with south Boomer Beach, p. 264).

In February 1969, the first major floods since 1943 in the Southern California mountains brought large amounts of sand through the Santa Ana River to the adjoining Newport Beach, where a small deltaic bulge was formed (F in Fig. 10.21). During 1969, beach drifting from the southeast had developed a new barrier in front of a narrow lagoon at the mouth of the Santa Ana River. Plans call for the removal of excess sand deposits from the river alluvial plain a few miles up the river and its transfer to the Newport Beach areas.

SANTA ANA RIVER TO LOS ANGELES HARBOR [Figs. 10.24 and 10.25]   Northeast of Newport Beach is a long stretch of low coast that forms part of the Los Angeles Basin. This lowland is separated into two parts by the Palos Verdes Hills (see Fig. 10.1). The coast along the southeastern part extends from the Santa Ana River to San Pedro, a distance of 25 miles. The basin is essentially a confluent alluvial plain formed by the delta fans of the Santa Ana, San Gabriel, and Los Angeles Rivers, which drain the San Bernardino and San Gabriel Mountains southward to the sea. Most of this plain has become urbanized as Los Angeles has spread southward. Between San Pedro and Long Beach is the huge man-made harbor of the City of Los Angeles (Fig. 10.24).

The mountains at the headwaters of the Los Angeles and San Gabriel Rivers are about 30 miles from the coast and 45 miles in from the mouth of the Santa Ana River. The latter crosses the low north end of the Santa Ana Mountains in a canyon only about 20 miles from its mouth. The gradients of the rivers as they cross the plain are: Los Angeles, 15 feet per mile; San Gabriel, 20 feet; and Santa Ana,

10.25   The coast at the mouth of the Santa Ana River during the great Southern California flood of 1938. The entire alluvial plain was inundated. Note houses surrounded by water. Compare with F in Figure 10.21 showing normal conditions. Huntington Beach (A), a structural uplift, with a large number of oil derricks, was an island during the flood. Oblique photo by Fairchild Aerial Photos, March 3, 1938.

17 feet. This compares with gradients of inches per mile, rather than feet, for most rivers crossing the coastal plain in eastern and southern United States.

Southern California has a six-month dry season, centering in summer, but occasionally during winter months is subject to torrential rains. In 1825, 1861–1862, 1867, 1909, and 1938, great storms with rainfall up to 20 inches within a week produced flood conditions in the rivers that cross the lowlands. Harold C. Troxell and others have described some of these floods, particularly that of 1938. Because at the beginning of the rains the ground surface is not densely covered with vegetation, torrential winter rains dislodge vast quantities of soil and surface sediment. The larger blocks, boulders, and cobbles build up alluvial cones or fans along the mountain fronts where the slopes are 100 to 250 feet per mile. Much of the rainfall of normal years sinks into the permeable sediments of these fans, so that the rivers carry little sediment to the sea except at times of torrential rainfall. The fans have developed long graded slopes diminishing in magnitude as distance from the mountains increases. During great floods, the streams often shift their courses into shallow natural depressions, but may also use road or railroad cuts and other artificial excavations. During the 1825 flood, the Santa Ana River shifted its outlet from the west to the east side of the Huntington Beach uplift, a distance of 3 miles. Again, after the 1884 flood, the mouth was shifted southeastward another 3 miles,

10.26 Oblique aerial photo of the Palos Verdes Hills, showing six or more elevated marine terraces. Photo by R. C. Frampton.

near its present position. The San Gabriel River developed a new channel during the 1887 flood. The Los Angeles River flowed west into Santa Monica Bay before the 1825 flood, when its mouth was deflected to San Pedro Bay, about 18 miles southeast of its earlier outlet and on the other side of the Palos Verdes Hills. It now enters Long Beach (A in Fig. 10.24).

Sediment that reaches the sea during these floods is largely sand and silt. This is spread across the broad alluvial plain at the time of great floods, as in the Santa Ana River in 1938 (Fig. 10.25), when the flooded area was 3 miles wide, and the bed of the channel was deepened 7 feet at the mouth of the river. Much of the fine silt is swept out to sea, where most of it eventually accumulates beyond the continental shelf; but sand is deposited in shallow water and provides a supply for the beaches of the area. To prevent the continued loss of soil and sediment from Southern California and the burial of urban areas with flood debris, cement-lined channels have been constructed for the principal rivers (see A in

Fig. 10.24). Also, reservoirs have been built in tributary streams to retain the sediment near its source, and debris catchment basins have been excavated along the sides of the stream channels. Plans have been made to remove the accumulated debris from these basins after each future major flood.

After the 1938 floods, it was found that the reservoirs and storage basins had lost 13 percent of their capacity. At the same time, an estimated 10 million to 12 million cubic yards of sediment were swept into the ocean by the Los Angeles River, more than half of which was probably silt and clay. The ultimate effect of storing debris in reservoirs and catchment basins will be to diminish the amount of sand introduced into the ocean, and thus reduce the supply available to replenish beaches. This loss has been partially and temporarily avoided in the Los Angeles River. Warren E. Darrow reported that before 1938, the river discharged into an estuary at Wilmington, so that it provided almost no sediment for beach replenishment; but, after 1938, the outlet was dredged in the development of the Los Angeles inner harbor (Fig. 10.24), and a new outlet (A) was excavated to allow future floods to discharge sediment into the ocean.

The most common direction of beach drifting was southeastward in the Long Beach to Huntington Beach area, but this drifting has been largely arrested by the building of a jetty and breakwater (B), extending 11 miles along the coast to protect the outer Los Angeles Harbor. Also, to the east, the jetties at the mouth of the San Gabriel River and at the entrance to Anaheim Bay interfere with the normal drift. In 1956, Joseph M. Caldwell, of the U.S. Army Corps of Engineers, reported that following the construction of the Anaheim Bay jetties in 1944, the sand supply was cut off for Surfside and Sunset Beach, southeast of the jetties. Erosion of 1,500 feet of beach at Surfside necessitated the dredging of 1.2 million cubic yards of sand and silt from the channel between the Anaheim Bay jetties, and this was used to replenish the beaches. This remedy was expected to protect the shoreline for about 3 to 5 years, then it will have to be repeated. Caldwell also reported that following the 1944 construction of flood-control reservoirs and debris basins along the headwaters of the Los Angeles and San Gabriel Rivers, these streams could no longer be considered significant sources of beach replenishment.

The flat coast is locally interrupted by a series of late Pleistocene or postglacial uplifts trending northwest-southeast, which have been called the Newport-Inglewood uplift. Hills 50 to 100 feet high along or near the coast rise above the plain at Newport, Huntington Beach, Sunset Beach, Seal Beach, and Long Beach (Signal Hill). All these hills have proved to be structural domes, which are prolific sources of petroleum. Many of the wells along the coast at Huntington Beach have been drilled slanting out to positions under the ocean floor, and closely spaced wells are being pumped just behind the beach.

Another factor affecting coasts has become a major problem in the Los Angeles Harbor area. Since the discovery of oil in the Wilmington Pool, near Long Beach, careful surveys have shown that between 1921 and 1948, areas with the largest production of oil have subsided between 0.5 and 8.0 feet. A critical analysis of this subsidence problem by James Gilluly and U. S. Grant IV, in 1949, convinced them that the subsidence was the result of pressure decline in the oil sands following intensive withdrawal of oil.

They estimated that the rate of subsidence would diminish as production declines, with a possible maximum subsidence of about 14 feet. However, injections of fluids into the oil sands has now stopped the sinking. Other coastal areas where subsidence has been associated with oil production include Goose Creek Field of San Jacinto Bay, Texas; Lake Maracaibo, Venezuela, where subsidence of 1 to 2 feet per year has been recorded; and Huntington Beach, California, which has had a subsidence of 0.85 foot.

PALOS VERDES HILLS [Figs. 10.26, 10.27, and 10.28]   The Palos Verdes Hills interrupt the continuity of the low coast of the Los Angeles Basin between San Pedro, at the southeast, and Redondo Beach, at the northwest. Their maximum length is 9.5 miles; the width ranges from 4 to 5 miles; and the highest elevation is San Pedro Hill, 1,480 feet above sea level. The geology, structural development, and Pleistocene and postglacial history of the area has been described by W. P. Woodring, M. N. Bramlette, and W. S. W. Kew.

During much of the Pleistocene, the Palos Verdes Hills area was an isolated island, probably slightly larger than the present hills, and similar to the Southern California islands. The uplift of the hills was matched by subsidence of the Los Angeles Basin to the north. During later Pleistocene, a series of thirteen elevated marine terraces were developed on all sides of the hills to a maximum of 1,300 feet above sea level (Fig. 10.26). There is no place along the entire coast of the United States where the record of successive elevation of a land mass is better displayed and more carefully studied. The most extensive terrace, which is also the latest and lowest, is bounded by sea cliffs 50 feet high on the south coast but rising to as much as 300 feet on the northwest coast.

Each terrace is a wave-cut surface extending seaward from a cliff. Thin covers of beach and shallow-water marine sediment on the terraces were often buried by nonmarine talus fans and alluvial sediments derived from stream and rain erosion of higher and older wave-cut cliffs. In some places, the nonmarine sediments on the terraces are as thick as 100 feet, and these deposits may entirely bury the cliff and rock bench of the next lower terrace. Further complicating the tracing of terraces around the hills is the fact that some terrace surfaces have been de-

10.27 Point Ferman, Palos Verdes Peninsula, an outcrop of Miocene siliceous shale.

a 1898. U.S. Geological Survey photo.

10.28 South side of Palos Verdes Hills near Portuguese Bend. This coastal slope, cut into poorly consolidated weathered volcanic tuffs, has had such extensive damage by landslides that a large exclusive residential subdivision had to be abandoned. Note buckling of pier where slides have advanced into Pacific Ocean. Photo by R. R. Benedict, about 1960.

b April 1968. Note that almost no erosion has occurred in seventy years. Photo by Wanless.

formed by folding or broken by faults. The northwestern margin of the hills locally shows the latest terrace to be tilted as much as 30 degrees. Attempts have been made to relate some of the terraces to glacial and interglacial stages, because the marine sediments on some of the benches contain shells of

mollusks indigenous to waters warmer than those found today in this latitude, while other deposits yield forms found in colder water. Even the latest (lowest) terrace deposits are too old to be dated by radiocarbon.

Some of the early Pleistocene sediments of the Palos Verdes Hills contain fossils of mollusks and foraminifera that must have inhabited water more than 600 feet deep. Thus the maximum emergence of this area during the Pleistocene may have been considerably more than 1,480 feet, the height of the highest summit.

The former Palos Verdes island became attached to the mainland coast as a result of the growth of alluvial aprons across the Los Angeles Basin from the Santa Monica Mountains to the north.

Rocks exposed on the coastal cliffs are largely of Miocene age, including sandstones, mudstones, marly limestones, basalt sills (flat igneous intrusions), diatomites (sediments composed mainly of the siliceous coatings of microscopic marine plants called diatoms), and volcanic tuffs. These varieties of rocks vary considerably in resistance to erosion; the basalt, siliceous shales, and some well-indurated sandstones being most resistant. Coastal cliffs at

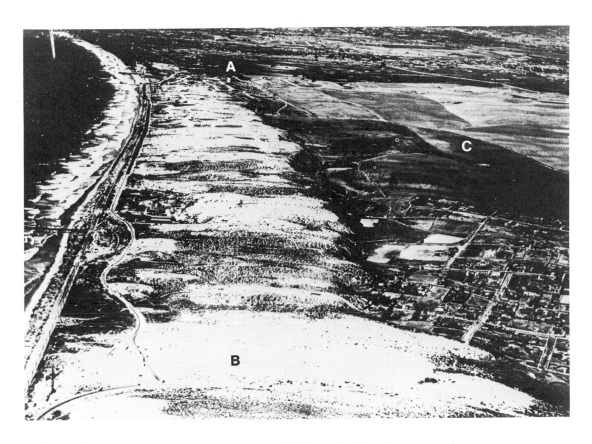

10.29 Oblique aerial photo along coast north of El Segundo, Hyperion pier in foreground. In background is a 3-mile break in the coastal bluffs (A) at the former outlet of the Los Angeles River. In the foreground are active longitudinal sand dunes (B), consisting of sand blown in from the beach. Older dunes inland from the modern dunes are stabilized with vegetation. The present site of the vast Los Angeles International Airport centers around C, and the entire surrounding area has been urbanized. Spence Air Photos, about 1930.

Point Fermin, near the southeastern margin of the Palos Verdes Peninsula, are cut into tilted Miocene siliceous shales. They are shown in photographs taken in 1898 and 1968 (Fig. 10.27). The beach at the base of the cliffs suffered erosion, and slumping has damaged or eliminated trails from the rock terrace to the beach that were present until recently, but otherwise the cliffs show only minor changes.

On the south coast, near Portuguese Bend, the cliffs have volcanic tuffs altered to bentonite interbedded with other sediments. Bentonitic clays swell greatly when moistened, and the bedding surfaces become soft and plastic. Because these tuff beds slope seaward, several large landslides have occurred. The largest (Fig. 10.28) affected a belt more than a mile wide. The slide originated about 600 feet above sea level and extended to the shore. Many houses were destroyed by continued movements along part of this slide. Although much of the Palos Verdes Hills is being converted into homesites, the Portuguese Bend and other slide areas along the south coast are now being avoided because of landslide hazards. The coastal highway along the slide area is subject to damage due to slumping.

REDONDO BEACH TO SANTA MONICA AREA [Figs. 10.29 through 10.32]   Northwest from the Palos Verdes Hills, the coast is very straight for 18 miles. This area includes Redondo, Hermosa, Venice, and finally, Santa Monica, where the coast curves westward along the base of the Santa Monica Mountains. Along most of this area, uplands 100 to 225

10.30 Boat harbor (B) at Redondo Beach and the breakwater that only partly enclosed it but has since been extended. Note accumulation of sand beyond break-water and erosion on inside next to jetty (C). The pier is at the head of a submarine canyon (D). Oblique aerial photo, May 1957. Later, the breakwater was extended to check shore erosion.

10.31 Santa Monica Harbor is protected by a breakwater. Sand has accumulated on each side of a recreational pier. The Santa Monica Mountains, sources of the sand, are seen in background. U.S. Coast and Geodetic Survey, 1934.

feet above sea level are separated from the beach by wave-cut cliffs. Between Playa del Rey and Venice there is a 3-mile gap in the coastal cliffs through which Ballona Creek drains. Prior to 1851, this was the outlet for the Los Angeles River, now at Long Beach. A part of the valley flat has been excavated as a small boat harbor.

South of the Ballona Creek gap, the upland is composed of sand dunes, and cliffs have been cut into these dunes. North of the town of El Segundo, much of the plain is the present site of the Los Angeles International Airport (C in Fig. 10.29). This is now surrounded by a highly urbanized area. Many of the sand dunes illustrated are U-shaped, having been swept 0.5 mile inland through blowout gaps. Farther east for a distance of 2 or 3 miles, the plain is composed of older dunes now almost completely covered with vegetation or houses. North of the gap, the Santa Monica–Venice area is located on a composite alluvial fan, built by streams emerging from the Santa Monica Mountains. This fan rises gradually to an elevation of 400 feet at the base of the mountains. The coastal cliffs cut in this alluvium have many gravel layers interspersed with sand.

The sand beaches are continuous between the Palos Verdes Hills and the turn in the coast at the Santa Monica Mountains, and the area is largely devoted to beach resorts for the immense population of metropolitan Los Angeles. Therefore, the continued maintenance of the beaches is very important. Among others, John W. Handin has investigated sources of sand, the nature of beach drifting, and the effects of human interference on beach erosion or accretion in this region.

At Redondo, just north of the Palos Verdes Hills, a submarine canyon comes in virtually to the coast. Because of smaller waves at the canyon head (D), this was chosen as a locus for pier construction (Fig. 10.30). Soon after it was built, the city engineer became concerned because the water was getting so shoal that it was difficult for the fishing boats to use the pier. Dredging operations were considered, but one day some fishermen at the end of the pier were surprised to find that they had to let out continually more and more line before their sinkers hit the bottom. The city engineer was notified and found that the water had deepened 20 feet, apparently in about two hours. The pier became very unstable and threatened to collapse. What had happened was that the accumulated sand had flowed out into the nearby submarine canyon, making the water along the pier deeper than when it was built. Fortunately, more sand introduced by waves from the northwest was deposited around the pilings, preventing the collapse of the pier.

Somewhat later, a clamor started for constructing a harbor in the Redondo area. A breakwater (A in Fig. 10.30) was built out in an arc from near the town line between Redondo and Hermosa Beaches. This produced a shelter, particularly from the northwest wave approach, but new difficulties soon developed. Because of the breakwater, the source of sand that had formerly produced the beach at the Redondo area was cut off, and sand started to build out on the north side of the jetty. Another difficulty came from the wave convergence north of Redondo Canyon. This began driving the sand northward and started to fill the harbor. Furthermore, it exposed the coastal boardwalk north of the Redondo jetty, and the first large waves undermined it. Despite the dumping of great quantities of huge rocks to stop erosion, the boardwalk was soon cut away and the buildings beyond presently began falling into the ocean. A whole block was destroyed. Finally, in desperation, the Army Corps of Engineers greatly extended the breakwater to the southeast and built a short jetty on the other side, so the harbor was at last stabilized but at far greater expense than had been originally anticipated.

The beach and the cliffs to the south of the harbor are still being eroded. Between the Redondo Beach Canyon and the northern end of the Palos Verdes Hills, there is active erosion of Miocene shales; and the beach is composed of shingle, consisting of shale detritus from the cliffs, but without appreciable sand.

Since the diversion of the Los Angeles River, the chief natural source of sand for beach replenishment along Santa Monica Bay is the wash from the canyons at the base of the Santa Monica Mountains. The Santa Monica shoreline and harbor are illustrated in Figures 10.31 and 10.32, which also show the mountains and the mouths of some of the canyons in the distance. Beach drifting is southeastward in the area. Behind the beach are cliffs cut into the piedmont fan deposits, which are called *palisades* (A in Fig. 10.32). These decline in height southward, as distance from the mountain front increases.

The beach at Santa Monica has been appreciably

10.32 Oblique aerial photo looking southeastward at coastal cliffs near Santa Monica. The coastal cliffs are cut in unconsolidated gravels and sands formed as alluvial fans from the Santa Monica Mountains. Note that sand drifting eastward is trapped against the groins and jetties and that the beach beyond the jetties is very much narrower. Spence Air Photos, 1932.

changed as the result of the 1933 building of a break-water parallel to the shore (Fig. 10.31). This produced a wave shadow in the lee of the breakwater; and the sediment that was formerly moved southeast along the shore, due to the diagonal approach of the waves, is now deposited in the harbor. As can be seen from the 1934 photograph, a considerable part of the harbor had already been filled. Deposition was gradually extended to the northwest, widening the beach. However, after several years, the beach downcurrent from the breakwater grew narrower until it had all but disappeared. To correct this, 14 million cubic yards of sand were pumped from the fill behind the Santa Monica breakwater and deposited along the

shore, widening most of the beach to about 600 feet. In the Venice area and farther south, the beach has also been in need of sand, because the supplies formerly introduced by the floods of the Los Angeles River were no longer available after that river shifted its course to Long Beach. This has required scooping sand from the dunes around El Segundo.

Thus the beach system, which had developed stable equilibrium before human settlement in the region, has been greatly altered by the construction of piers and breakwaters and by flood-control measures, resulting in serious beach erosion from Santa Monica Harbor to the Palos Verdes Hills, except on the upcurrent sides of the jetties and breakwaters.

10.33 A large earthslide near Pacific Palisades, which buried the coastal highway following a period of heavy rains in 1958. U.S. Geological Survey photo.

SANTA MONICA MOUNTAINS COAST [Figs. 10.33 and 10.34]   From Santa Monica west to Point Mugu, the coast hugs the southern flank of the Santa Monica Mountains. The coast is rugged with spectacular cliffs, especially to the west, and all are visible from the highway.

In 1958, near the junction of the coast and the mountain front at Pacific Palisades, a great landslide flowed out from the cliffs below the Pleistocene terrace deposits (Fig. 10.33). The slide killed a state highway engineer who was about to reopen the temporarily closed highway. According to J. T. McGill, of the U.S. Geological Survey, the slide with 600,000 cubic yards of debris buried the road and extended slightly out into the sea. At this place, the bedrock below the alluvial deposits is Miocene shale, which is particularly unstable. Almost this entire section of coastal cliffs is subject to frequent landslides; K. O. Emery mapped twenty-one of them in a 5-mile belt.

Wherever the highway follows the coast west of the large landslide, many indications of coastal erosion are seen. Periodically the highway has to be strengthened or the shoulders rebuilt. However, locally there are outcrops of lava, as at Point Dume, or hard sandstone; and at such places, erosion is very slow. Comparison of new and old photographs shows only minor changes.

The Pleistocene and postglacial evolution of this

10.34 Point Dume, a promontory formed because of basaltic lava at the point. Two former shorelines, bordering coastal terraces, are marked by dashed lines, as mapped by the late William Morris Davis. Oblique aerial photo by D. L. Inman, May 1957.

coast was studied by the late William Morris Davis. He presented evidence of two interglacial stages of higher sea level, which he called the Malibu (older) and Dume. During each of these high-water stands, rock benches were left sloping seaward from the base of low wave-cut cliffs. A thin layer of wave-worn pebbles and marine shells accumulated on the rock floor.

The relation of the fan deposits was explained by Davis as follows: After the high-level benches had been cut, sea level dropped here as elsewhere with the return of the glaciers on the continents. During the low sea-level stages, which were also times of higher rainfall in the Santa Monica Mountains, fans were built out at the mountain base, covering the high wave-cut terraces with 80 to 100 feet of alluvial debris. The last rise in sea level did not get as high

as those of the interglacial stages, but the waves acting at the present levels have started to erode the fans and expose the old terraces. Because of a tilting of the Santa Monica Mountains, the terraces are not now at the same level along the coast, but slope down to the west.

Point Dume (Fig. 10.34), the only major projecting point on the Santa Monica coast, owes its existence to a mass of basaltic lava about 0.25 mile in diameter and rising to 215 feet above sea level. This has protected a triangular area of weak Miocene shale and diatomite, which forms the low plain behind the point. Davis found well-preserved traces of the benches of the two interglacial stages of higher sea level. The younger of them, the Dume shoreline (line marked A in Fig. 10.34), is now at about 150 feet elevation. The basaltic hill (B) at that time was

10.35 Tidal lagoon and inlet just west of Point Mugu (A). The cycle of inlet migration, closing and reopening once every 6 months, is described in text. U.S. Navy photo, 1965.

an offshore island and was later connected with the mainland as a tombolo. The older Malibu shoreline (C), now followed in part by the coastal highway, stood at about 250 feet above present sea level. At that time, the basalt hill at the end of the point may have been entirely inundated.

On the west side of Point Dume, sand brought in by small streams from the mountains has formed a broad beach, now available to the public as a state park. Sand is trapped west of the basaltic cliffs of the point. When visited by the authors in June 1968, wave erosion had partly undermined the road along the narrow inner part of the beach (D). Comparatively little sand is drifted around the point, partly because it falls into a submarine canyon on the west side (E). As would be expected, the beach along the east side of the triangle is much narrower.

Although Davis was one of the greatest physiographers of his generation and was actively engaged in a study of the Santa Monica Mountain coast, especially in the Point Dume area, he was never given permission to visit this point by the owners of the large estate that included Point Dume. In 1968, the present authors were also denied admission to some other coastal areas, which they had photographed many years earlier, and were therefore unable to observe changes in shore configuration for this reason. Fortunately, many fine coastal tracts have been purchased by the state or nation and hopefully will continue to be available to the public.

Westward from Point Dume to Point Mugu, the coast is more rugged because of the superior resistance to erosion of massive sandstones. The headlands descend directly to the sea in some places.

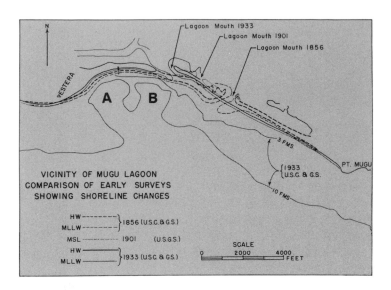

10.36 Coastal changes in the vicinity of Mugu Lagoon between 1856 and 1933. The two heads (A and B) of the Mugu Submarine Canyon are indicated. From Inman (1950).

Fortunately, the coastal highway makes all of this spectacular area accessible. Davis reported that workmen constructing this highway had to be lowered to the coast from above. At one point about 2 miles east of Point Mugu, a sand dune nearly 100 feet high has been formed from sand blown in from the shore and piled up against the cliff. There are narrow pocket beaches here. Recent changes in coastal configuration are very slight.

SANTA CLARA AND VENTURA RIVER DELTA PLAINS [Figs. 10.35, 10.36, and 10.37]   Northwest from Point Mugu, the Santa Monica Mountains terminate abruptly and are adjoined by a flat coastal plain extending 22 miles to Ventura. The plain, formed largely by the delta of the Santa Clara River, has been called the Oxnard Plain, named for the principal town of this area. Much of the region is covered with citrus groves. Inland, the plain rises gradually to the base of the Santa Ynez Mountains.

Heading in the San Gabriel Mountains north of Los Angeles, the Santa Clara River flows westward, draining an area of 1,605 square miles. Because of the permeability of the sediments composing the plain, the river bed is dry except at times of major rainstorms. Thus sediment is transported to the beaches intermittently. Between 1933 and 1938,

7,303,000 cubic yards of sediment accumulated between the mouth of the Santa Clara River (A in Fig. 10.37) and a depth of 30 feet. Most of this was introduced at the time of the 1938 flood. A flood in February 1969 built a delta into the ocean and destroyed a marina (C in Fig. 10.37).

Under the surface of the plain, postglacial sediments are more than 500 feet thick. William Morris Davis noted that the Pleistocene shore benches, which are high above sea level in the Point Dume area, have been so tilted as to be below the level of the plain along the western edge of the Santa Monica Mountains. Davis also considered that the delta plain deposits fill indentations in the western front of the Santa Monica Mountains. Presumably this was a deep estuary before the building of the modern delta.

At the eastern margin of the plain, just west of Point Mugu, a 4-mile lagoon lies behind a barrier spit, which is now a part of the Vandenberg Guided Missile Test Center. The lagoon was studied by D. L. Inman in 1950 and in 1966 by J. E. Warme. A 1965 aerial photo of the inlet and the eastern part of the lagoon indicates its relation to Point Mugu (Fig. 10.35) .The lagoon is connected with the small estuary of Calleguas Creek, which drains the eastern border of the Oxnard Plain. The shore near Mugu Inlet is partly protected from northwest storms by Point Hueneme, 8 miles to the west. The Santa Clara and Ventura River Deltas supply sand to the area. The predominant direction of beach drifting is southeastward. Following the construction of harbor jetties at Point Hueneme in 1938, much less sand has reached the Mugu Inlet area; and the spit separating the lagoon from the ocean has been narrowed by erosion.

Figure 10.36 shows the changes in shoreline near Mugu Inlet between 1856 and 1933 and also the closeness of the head of Mugu Submarine Canyon to the inlet. During the 77 years, the shore had retreated about 250 feet at the canyon head but had advanced an almost equal amount in the mile east of the canyon. During the past century, the eastern end of the lagoon has become largely filled with sediment. Although beach drifting is predominantly from the northwest, occasional storms from the southeast temporarily reverse this trend. Longshore currents have lower velocities in the vicinity of the two heads of Mugu Canyon because of decreased wave heights. Under some directions of wave front approach, sub-

10.37 Aerial photo showing coast near Ventura. Mouth of Santa Clara River (A) and Ventura Delta (B) are indicated. The Santa Clara River has not built any recent delta, but the Ventura River, with its higher gradient and entering at a more protected place, has been able to build a recent delta. The sediment introduced at the mouth of the Santa Clara River is carried south by longshore currents. U.S. Department of Agriculture photo, 1955.

stantial quantities of beach sand spill into the canyon heads. Studies reported by Inman and Warme show that when large storm peaks correspond with the highest spring tides, a new opening is cut into the spit west of the lagoon inlet and is rapidly widened. With a return to normal wave heights, the spit is again extended seaward. The inlet tends to close after it has migrated east to the filled section. Then, in the absence of a storm, a new western inlet is opened artificially, and the inlet again begins to shift eastward. Warme reports that this cycle of inlet migration—closing and artificial reopening—was repeated about every six months in the 1960s. Because of diminished supply of sand for the spit since the 1938 construction of the Hueneme jetties, beach erosion has become serious. To offset this loss, sand has been dredged from the lagoon and spread onto the beach.

The 1904 topographic map of the area between Mugu Lagoon and Point Hueneme shows seven small blocked estuaries, but later editions of the map show that these have been filled by coastal sand drift.

Point Hueneme is located at a pronounced bend in the flat coast of the Oxnard Plain. Large quantities of sand from the mouth of Santa Clara River drift eastward along the shore to this point. In 1938, a small harbor was constructed at the Point Hueneme naval installation by opening a cut through the blocked outlet of a small estuary. The entrance to the harbor was protected by short jetties. The entrance is immediately adjacent to the Hueneme Submarine Canyon, which extends south-southwest and is 600 feet deep a mile beyond the ends of the jetties. Prior to the construction of the jetties, the canyon had intercepted substantial amounts of sand but enough had gone around the point to supply the beaches on the east side. Now very little sand gets beyond the canyon, and shore erosion to the east has become serious. In 1940, to stabilize the shore, a seawall was constructed for 3,000 feet east of the jetties; but just east of the end of this seawall, between 1938 and 1948, the shore was cut back 700 feet. Here, the beach and part of the adjacent dune belt have been eroded.

The sediment near shore adjacent to the Oxnard Plain is predominantly sand. The gradient across the plain, 50 feet in 4 miles, is too low to transport gravel, and the finer muds are largely carried beyond the 30-foot depth. There is no bulge in the shoreline at the mouth of the Santa Clara River, because after major floods most of the new sediment is drifted southeastward along the shore. A delta temporarily resulting from the 1938 flood was depleted at the rate of 475,000 cubic yards per year during the decade from 1938 to 1948. The shore between the Santa Clara River mouth and Point Hueneme advanced 500 feet between 1856 and 1938, but at a much more rapid rate at the time of the 1938 flood (Fig. 10.37). The beach averages 100 to 300 feet in width but widens to 700 feet as the jetty is approached. A belt of dunes extends inland 0.5 mile at the river mouth but narrows to 0.25 mile at Point Hueneme.

The Ventura River has a drainage basin of only 228 square miles, but flows south through a very mountainous terrain to discharge at Ventura, about 4 miles northwest of the outlet of the Santa Clara. The Ventura River has a steeper gradient than the Santa Clara River (150 feet in 4 miles), a more nearly continuous flow, and has built a delta (B in Fig. 10.37) at its mouth about a mile across, which extends seaward 0.25 mile from the adjacent beaches. This is the only active delta on the West Coast that is advancing into the open ocean.

According to estimates by J. W. Handin, the average annual increment of sand coming from the Ventura River to replenish the beaches is 300,000 cubic yards, compared with 1 million cubic yards for the Santa Clara River. There is a wide beach at the mouth of the Ventura River, but it is considerably narrowed at a rock outcrop 0.5 mile east of the Ventura pier. At this pier the beach was widened by 580 feet between 1855 and 1933.

The adjacent deltas of the Ventura and Santa Clara Rivers are important sand sources for beach replenishment in this part of the California coast.

VENTURA–CARPINTERIA AREA   For about 12 miles to the west of the Ventura River, the coast is mountainous. The area has been described by the late William C. Putnam. The mountains are very young, having been elevated in the middle of the Pleistocene from what was a deep basin filled with 47,000 feet of Tertiary and Pleistocene sediments. After the mountains were built, an erosion interval reduced the range to a rolling surface of low relief, but later, the area was elevated vertically about 1,000 to 1,200 feet. At intervals during this uplift, there

10.38 Aerial photo of the Santa Barbara coast, showing boat harbor. Note accumulations of sand behind jetty (B) and near entrance to harbor (A). Base of the Santa Ynez Mountains (C) is north of the city. U.S. Department of Agriculture photo, 1967.

were stillstands, during which marine benches were cut by waves and later raised above the sea. These terraces have been deformed by both warping and faulting. At Rincon Mountain, 7 miles east of Carpinteria, marine terraces are found at the following average elevations: 500, 800, 1,100, and 1,300 feet. The 500-foot terrace is the broadest, from 0.33 to 0.5 mile wide. Putnam traced the 200-foot terrace on the side of Rincon Mountain to the west, finding that it reaches sea level near Carpinteria. Just east of Carpinteria, asphalt deposits have formed on this terrace. They contain marine shells and the bones of carnivorous birds and mammals, along with logs. This assortment somewhat resembles the fauna in the famous La Brea tar pits in the Los Angeles area. Kitchen middens of early man are also found on this terrace. The Carpinteria fauna seems to indicate a cooler climate than that of the present, suggesting deposition at the end of the last glacial stage of the Pleistocene.

This part of the coast, as elsewhere, was subject to effects of the eustatic changes in sea level that accompanied the waxing and waning of the ice sheet during the Pleistocene. However, so much independent warping has occurred here that it is impossible to tell which of the terraces are the result of the high

10.39 Coastal promontory 10 miles west of Santa Barbara at the campus of the University of California, Santa Barbara (C). The Santa Barbara Airport (B), a filled estuary, is blocked off from the sea by a sandy barrier. Coastal bluffs near the campus are composed of relatively weak siltstones and shales. The cliffs have suffered erosion at D. U.S. Department of Agriculture photo, 1967.

sea level stands during the interglacial stages. Despite this warping, the outer edge of the continental shelf lies about 350 feet below sea level, which is normal for Southern California. Also, the continental shelf is relatively broad, about 10 miles in this area. This suggests either that the warping had stopped after the last glacial lowering, about 19,000 years ago when the sea was approximately 350 feet lower, or that the shelf was not involved in any of the subsequent movements.

The outline of the coast shows three prominent projecting points—from east to west: Pitas Point, Punta Gorda, and Rincon Point. Each extends seaward about a half to two-thirds of a mile from the intervening concave coast. Each point is at the mouth of a small stream, with a gradient of at least 200 feet per mile. These points originated as alluvial delta fans at the mouths of streams. Each point is asymmetrical with a long northwest and a short east side. The wave fronts are parallel to the longer stretches of coast northwest of the points and strike the short segments east of the points at angles of 20 to 30 degrees. The eastern side of each point is being actively eroded, and seawalls have been built to check shore loss. A thin sand beach following the northwestern side of each point increases in width at the point, but the sand gives out to the east.

SANTA BARBARA AREA: SANDYLAND TO GOLETA [Figs. 10.38 through 10.42]   At the base of the high Santa Ynez Range between Carpinteria and Goleta, there is a relatively flat piedmont area with complicated topography. The coast for 3 miles west of Carpinteria, including Sandyland and Serena, is a low swampy region bordered seaward by a sand barrier. Farther west, the cliffed edge of the piedmont fan forms the coast; and, between Summerland and Santa Barbara, the low cliffs are fringed by beaches of variable width (Fig. 10.38). Bordering the piedmont fan on the west side of Santa Barbara, hills of recently deformed Miocene and Pliocene formations rise as high as 620 feet above sea level. About 4 miles west of Santa Barbara, the coast has a well-developed terrace somewhat more than 100 feet high. This lowers to the west and is cut by a marshy tract, Goleta Slough (A in Fig. 10.39), near the Santa Barbara Airport. This marsh is bordered by a barrier beach. Farther west, at Goleta Point, the Santa Barbara campus of the University of California (C) is located on top of a 50-foot coastal terrace. A low plain on the north is the westerly continuation of the Goleta Slough.

After investigating the Santa Barbara area, Joseph Upson, of the U.S. Geological Survey, suggested that it has been relatively stable, at least since the last interglacial epoch when the terraces, now about 100 feet above present sea level, were cut by high stands of the sea. As substantiating evidence, he refers to the continental shelf, which here has a margin around 300 feet below sea level, roughly conforming with the rest of the shelves along the Southern California coast. Also, Upson refers to the approximate 200 feet of stream fill in the valleys near the coast, showing that they were cut by that amount below present sea level during the last glacial lowering.

The city of Santa Barbara (Fig. 10.38), with its picturesque location between the sea and the rugged Santa Ynez Mountains to the north, has become an important agricultural, educational, and recreational center. In the late nineteenth century, the people of Santa Barbara began to promote the building of a harbor capable of accommodating deep-water vessels. The U.S. Army Corps of Engineers prepared five reports between 1873 and 1921, all somewhat unfavorable to the project. Finally, in 1925, $750,000 was raised locally, and an L-shaped 1,500-foot breakwater was constructed from 1927 to 1929, in spite of the unfavorable reports. At first, the breakwater was not quite tied to the shore on the west side of the harbor, but almost immediately sand began to pour through the gap and fill the harbor, necessitating continuing the wall to the coast. On the east side of the harbor, a pier extended out from near the center of town, leaving only a small gap for boat traffic.

This coast has a strong east-flowing longshore current, which is active in transporting the sand supplied by the small streams entering the coast between Santa Barbara and Point Conception, 45 miles to the west. It has been estimated that new sand reaches the shores of that area at a rate of 775 cubic yards per day, or about 280,000 cubic yards annually. The littoral current is so strong that several boulders averaging two feet in diameter, dumped on the beach in 1917, were found 20 years later 2,500 feet to the east. A large boiler that broke through a wharf and fell on the beach west of Santa Barbara in 1931 was filled with stones to prevent it from drifting. In spite of this, it moved east 900 feet in six years.

10.40 Miramar Beach, 3 miles east of Santa Barbara Harbor. Photos by U.S. Grant IV.
a 1927. A broad sandy beach with a line of cottages well in from the shoreline.

b 1936. Seven years after the construction of the Santa Barbara breakwater nearly all of the sand was eroded, leaving coarse rubble and the beach cottages supported on pilings.

Because of this large drift along the shore, the L-shaped breakwater began to trap sand on the west side. Between the completion of the breakwater, in 1929, and 1936, accretion behind the shore-connected arm took place at the rate of 275,000 cubic yards per year, nearly equal to the estimate of sand

10.41 Sandyland, 10 miles east of the Santa Barbara Harbor.

a Seven years after construction of the Santa Barbara Harbor and jetty, beach cottages were undermined by erosion and were toppling into the sea. Eleven years after the harbor completion, the Sandyland beach had been cut back 245 feet. Photo by U.S. Grant IV, 1936.

b June 1968. The relocated and rebuilt beach cottages were protected by huge blocks. Photo by Shepard.

supplied by all streams in the 45 miles of coast west of Santa Barbara. The fill built out a wedge along the west end of the breakwater, filling the angle between it and the original shore. It then moved along the south side of the breakwater to its end, and accumulated a sand island on the inside (A). Effects of this deposition were twofold: the harbor became so filled with sand that it was usable only for shallow-draft boats, and beaches east of the harbor began to be seriously eroded.

At Miramar Beach in Montecito, 4 miles east of the Santa Barbara Harbor, a photograph was taken in 1927 (Fig. 10.40a), which shows great contrast with a 1936 photograph (Fig. 10.40b). A wide sand beach in front of the line of cottages in 1927 had been largely destroyed by 1936, exposing the coarse cobbles beneath and theatening the homes.

At Sandyland, 10 miles east of the Santa Barbara Harbor, a series of beach cottages had been constructed on the narrow sandy barrier between the marshy lagoon and the ocean. By 1936, 7 years after the completion of the Santa Barbara breakwater, the beach at Sandyland had retreated so far that the cottages were being undermined and toppling into the sea (Fig. 10.41a). Property damage amounted to $2 million. By 1940, the beach had been cut back 245 feet.

To try to resolve the dilemma, a government dredge removed 200,000 cubic yards of the fill from shoals in the Santa Barbara Harbor and deposited it in 20 feet of water a mile east of the harbor. It was expected that this sand would distribute itself eastward along the shore, but this did not happen. Several years later, the sand was still where it had been dumped, and erosion of the beaches was continuing.

Following these catastrophic results of the construction of the Santa Barbara Harbor, the Army Corps of Engineers investigated the whole problem of this beach erosion and harbor shoaling and proposed several solutions. As a result, in June 1938, a hydraulic pipeline-dredge pumped about 600,000 cubic yards of sand from shoals in the harbor to a shrunken beach about a mile east of the Santa Barbara pier. Consequently, all of the beaches for many miles to the east have been partially replenished. Dredging has been repeated at 2- or 3-year intervals, and the process has been reasonably satisfactory. The cost has exceeded $30,000 per year; and, during the intervals between dredgings, the harbor has been extensively filled with sand. The authors visited Sandyland in June 1968, and found that the shore is now protected by a rubble seawall (Fig. 10.41b). Nearer the harbor, at Miramar, a narrow sand beach has developed, and the cottages are apparently no longer threatened.

Another cause for alarm to the Santa Barbara beaches comes from oil leakage in the Santa Barbara Channel. The most serious leak came in late January 1969, when a Union Oil Company drilling operation penetrated a high pressure zone in an oil sand, resulting in a leakage of 500 barrels per day into the surrounding waters. This eventually washed ashore, polluting the beaches and killing many marine animals along the beaches and rocky shores. Rigorous beach cleaning helped solve the situation. The effects appear not to have been as serious as those caused by the wreckage of the oil tanker *Torrey Canyon* in the English Channel in 1968; but, at this writing, the leaks have not been entirely stopped and oil slicks continue to invade the shore at irregular intervals. The most serious ecological effect has been the loss of life among the seabirds. A point of argument by authorities is whether continued removal of oil from the offshore wells will increase the leakage due to further breaks, or decrease it, due to relieving the pressure that causes oil to escape. The fault pattern on the sea floor is not well known, and it is always possible that drilling may allow oil to escape along some of the faults.

Along large parts of the coast at Santa Barbara, nearly vertical cliffs have been cut into weak shales and siltstones beneath the late Pleistocene terrace. In some locations, such as near the new Santa Barbara campus of the University of California at Goleta, homes have been built in rows just back of the cliff edge (D in Fig. 10.39). The authors visited this community in June 1968 and found that the edge of the cliff was about 15 feet nearer a large tree than when photographed in 1960. Slump scars were seen along the top of the cliff. An earthquake with the intensity of 5.3 on the Richter scale affected the area in early July 1968. Wanless returned to that locality a few days after the earthquake and observed freshly fallen talus blocks at the base of the cliffs, but no major changes were seen or reported by the local residents despite the earthquake. Nevertheless, it appears to be courting disaster to build a house on the edge of a vertical cliff, or even cantilevered out

10.42 Coastal shale cliffs (D in Fig. 10.39) just west of the University of California, Santa Barbara. Residences have been built right along the top of the cliff, and one home is cantilevered out beyond the cliffs, although this coast is subject to winter storms and earthquakes. Photo by Wanless, July 1968.

over cliffs of nonresistant rock (Fig. 10.42), particularly where subject to earthquakes.

GAVIOTA TO POINT CONCEPTION [Figs. 10.43 and 10.44]   West of the broad coastal lowland in the Goleta area, the piedmont narrows to less than 0.5 mile for a 30-mile zone extending to Point Conception. In this zone, narrow elevated terraces and narrow fans flank the slopes of the Santa Ynez Mountains, which rise 2,500 to 3,000 feet within 2 to 4 miles of the coast.

Near Point Conception, where the coast bends to the north, the terrace averages about 100 feet above sea level and widens to about a mile. The Santa Ynez Mountain chain terminates abruptly a short distance north of the point.

Numerous streams flow south to the coast from the Santa Ynez Mountains. The gradients of the longer valleys average about 150 feet per mile in their lower 2 miles. Most of the streams move cobbles or even small boulders to the seacoast during times of flood. Many cobbles on the beach are of rock types known only high in the mountains. Abundant cobbles are strewn along the mouths of delta fans and adjoining

10.43 Coast just west of Arroyo Hondo, showing sandstone dipping about 60 degrees toward the narrow beach. Erosion proceeds slowly except where the sandstone has been cut away. Photo by Shepard, 1968.

10.44 A bluff of shale and thin-bedded siltstone at Refugio State Park.
a 1950. Photo by Joseph Upson, U.S. Geological Survey.

b June 1968. Sandstone ledges in the foreground show little erosion, but shale bluffs behind have retreated and the notch eliminated. Photo by Shepard.

beaches. Between the mouths of streams, sand beaches are generally narrow and include cobbles of rock types exposed in adjacent cliffs. Many of the wet-weather small streams have "hanging valleys," dropping 50 feet or more vertically at the shore. This indicates that wave erosion of the cliffs has progressed faster than downcutting by the small streams.

The rocks exposed in the shore cliffs are largely Middle Miocene shales, diatomites, and thin-bedded sandstones. The dip of the rocks at many beaches is toward the shore at angles from 10 degrees to nearly vertical (Fig. 10.43). Where the lower slope is cut into one of the more resistant layers, erosion is retarded; but where the slope is in weak shale, erosion progresses much more rapidly. Evidence of fast retreat comes from the abundant angular chips or flakes of shale on the beach, which are quickly ground up by the waves. Also, one of the shaly points shows distinct changes in the 18 years since photographed by Upson (Figs. 10.44a and b). A notch was eliminated during the interval.

To the east of the Santa Barbara area, several of the points of land are related to fans built out at the mouths of streams. An example of the same type of projection is found at El Capitan Beach State Park, 12 miles west of Goleta, where the stream has built

out the land a third of a mile. Farther west, the coast is quite straight, and has only two minor bulges, both related to stream fans. This suggests that most of the sediment carried to the sea by the streams is shifted eastward by longshore currents. These currents become stronger in approaching Point Conception.

The coastal terraces in the Gaviota quadrangle, the central part of the area, have been studied by

10.45   A succession of ten or more marine terraces on the southwest side of San Clemente Island. Photo from helicopter by John Shelton, 1960.

Joseph E. Upson. He has tentatively recognized twenty-two levels of marine shore benches ranging in elevation from 5 to 1,660 feet, with the possibility of others at still greater heights. Three of the seven terraces below the 200-foot level are traced rather easily for 14 miles along the coast. The lowest terrace at 5 or 6 feet above sea level is indicated at several places by benches truncating tilted rocks and by wave-cut notches in weak overlying rocks. These might imply that postglacial sea level had been a few feet higher than at present, but there is a possibility that these benches and notches were cut by the high waves of great storms at the present sea level.

CALIFORNIA ISLANDS [Figs. 10.45 through 10.54]   The islands off the Southern California coast are all related to the structural pattern of the mainland and to the basins and ranges of the adjacent sea floor (Fig. 10.1). The most northern are called the Channel Islands because they protect the Santa Barbara Channel from the open sea. They are clearly a continuation of the east-west Santa Monica Mountains. To the southeast, Santa Catalina Island (generally called Catalina) rises from a northwest-southeast submarine ridge along the west side of the Santa Monica and San Pedro Basins. Santa Catalina Basin, to the southwest of the island, is bordered by another submarine ridge with San Clemente and Santa Barbara Islands rising above it. San Nicolas Island tops a third ridge that extends southeast from Santa Rosa Island. It may be just a coincidence, but San Clemente, Catalina, and Palos Verdes Hills are all in a line and each pair is separated by about the same distance, 30 miles. The finding of submarine highs farther south on the same line, the first also 30 miles distant, adds some credence to the possible signifi-

10.46 Spectacular cliffs cut in crystalline rocks on the south side of Santa Catalina Island. Although the straight cliffs resemble a fault scarp, they are due to wave erosion. U.S. Navy Electronics Laboratory photo, 1948.

San Clemente (Figs. 10.45 and 2.8) is a rectangular island 20 miles long. It is 4 miles across at the southern end, but tapers to 2 miles at the north. The two sides of the island are quite different in appearance, although both have relatively straight coasts. The precipitous northeast side is the result of faulting, and the fault scarp continues to the deep floor of Catalina Basin. The seaward (southwest) side is more gently sloping, and has a series of well-developed wave-cut terraces rising to the 1,800-foot summit (Fig. 10.45). Apparently the island was intermittently lifted as a fault block, and the terraces were cut by wave action on the exposed southwest side. The only island beaches are in coves; the chief one, Pyramid Cove, is at the southeast end. This was used extensively by whalers in the nineteenth century.

In recent years, San Clemente has become entirely a military reservation; but before World War II, there were some ranches and only a small Navy post was located to the north at Wilson Cove. Scientists from Scripps Institution used to wander around the island studying the geology. One time Shepard and others were investigating an area near the northwest end of the island when they were startled to hear shells from Navy ships exploding on the northeast of the island and occasionally coming across to the side where they were collecting rocks. Since they had to return to the northeast side to get back on their ship, they decided against their first plan, which was to skirt the north end. This was just as well because they would have passed a target area at about the time when destroyers started another heavy bombardment. After that, more caution was taken in studying the geology of the island.

Santa Catalina (Fig. 10.46), one of the California islands that the military has failed to take over, except for a short occupation during the Civil War, was acquired by its present owners as a result of the excessive gum-chewing habits of Americans. The island is now owned by the Wrigley family. Catalina is about 21 miles long and 8 miles across at the widest part. It differs from San Clemente in having an irregular shape with conspicuous embayments at the north end. At Avalon, on the southeast end, a sizable resort has been established. There is no all-weather harbor at Avalon, only a cove unprotected from northeast winds. Since strong winds from that direction develop only on rare occasions, the anchor-

cance of this relationship between the islands and the Palos Verdes Hills. However, the rock formations of San Clemente, Catalina, and Palos Verdes are quite different. San Clemente is predominantly built of a series of lava flows of Miocene age with small interbedded outcrops of Middle Miocene sedimentary rocks. Catalina has principally very old intrusive rocks, such as quartz diorite and metamorphic schists, along with lavas; whereas Palos Verdes, as we have seen, is predominantly sedimentary.

The California islands have an interesting mammalian fauna. Some of it no doubt was introduced by the Indians; but the presence of endemic foxes, which are different on each island and different from those of the mainland, suggests that they may have been there prior to the time of Indian occupation. These may indicate former land connections. Also, the mammoths of Pleistocene age of Santa Cruz and Santa Rosa clearly suggest former land bridges. Other animals, such as the wild boar and wild goats of Catalina and San Clemente were introduced by early Spanish explorers and have survived, especially in the unpopulated areas.

age is usually safe. During northeasters, the boats have to upanchor and hasten around to the southwest side. At the narrow isthmus, near the north end of the island, a landlocked harbor indents the seaward side. On the other side of the isthmus, a cove is also used extensively by yachts; but, like Avalon, it is not protected from the occasional northeast winds.

The northeast side of Catalina offers excellent cruising for yachtmen in Southern California. The southerly swell that predominates in summer is cut off by the island, allowing cruising along the entire northeast side without exposure to the waves of the open sea. Also, numerous small coves have convenient anchorages, provided one goes in close to the land, because of the steeply sloping sea floor. The water is usually clearer than along the mainland, making it a favored place for skindiving and observation of the beautiful fish and marine plants.

The outer rough-water side has spectacular cliffs cut by waves into the crystalline rocks (Fig. 10.46). The late revered but argumentative geologist Andrew Lawson first called attention to the absence of terraces on the slopes of Catalina. He contrasted this with the terraced seaward slopes of San Clemente (Fig. 10.45) and Palos Verdes Hills (Fig. 10.26). This led Lawson to suggest that Catalina has had a very different history from its neighbors, although he recognized the existence of a fault scarp 2 miles seaward of the cliffs on the south side. However, W. S. Tangier Smith, another early-day California geologist, visited Catalina and came to the conclusion that the lack of terraces was due to its more resistant rocks. Smith claimed that he had found shells near the summit of Mt. Orizaba, 1,400 feet above sea level, and thought these were Pleistocene, which would indicate a relatively recent uplift of the type experienced by San Clemente.

Shepard, U. S. Grant IV, and R. S. Dietz attempted to solve the problem. They visited the area where Smith found the shells and discovered that actually two types of shells are present. One consists of Miocene fossils from a sedimentary formation 30 million years old and the other contains modern abalone shells, probably introduced by the aboriginal Indians who lived on the island in the early days and could have carried the shells up to the peak, perhaps for ceremonial purposes. There may be some elevated terraces that really are indicative of recent uplifts on the island, but an examination of the slopes all around

10.47 Two coastal terraces (A and B) on the northeast side of San Nicolas Island. Note extensive gullying of upper terrace margin. U.S. Navy Electronics Laboratory photo, 1945.

the island shows a general absence of terracing. The difference may be partly due to Catalina having more resistant rocks, but the good development of a shelf and wave-cut cliffs along the south coast, formed in what was presumably a relatively brief period, suggests either that the uplift of Catalina was so remote, perhaps Late Miocene, that the terraces have largely disappeared or that the uplift was too rapid and continuous to allow terracing of the type so common along most of the California coast and offshore islands.

San Nicolas Island (Figs. 10.47, 10.48, and 10.49), 65 miles from the California mainland, is the most remote of the islands. The geology is well described by J. D. Vedder and R. M. Norris. The island extends like Catalina and San Clemente in a northwest-southeast direction, typical for California islands and ranges. The length is 9 miles and the width is 3. San Nicolas is less mountainous than the others we have described, having a summit of about 900 feet. The rocks of the island are almost entirely sedimentary, consisting of alternating sandstones and shales of Eocene age. These rocks are well exposed

10.48 Sand spit and shoal at southeast end of San Nicolas Island. Compare with Figure 10.53, sand spit at east end of San Miguel Island. U.S. Navy Electronics Laboratory photo, 1948.

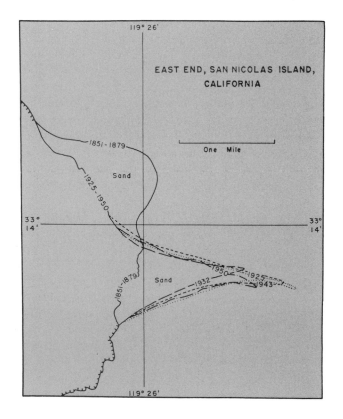

10.49 Changes in configuration of the sand spit on San Nicolas Island between 1851 and 1950. Note that there was no spit until after 1879. From Norris (1952).

in the canyons of the steep south side and in some of the shorter canyons on the northeast, but are largely covered elsewhere. The center of the island has a mantle of terrace deposits that are spread well down the north slope in many places. The terraces are best developed on the northeast (Fig. 10.47). This is on the opposite side from the terraces of San Clemente, but San Nicolas has a more westerly trend, and there is heavy surf on its north side. The northwest end of the island is almost entirely blanketed by wind-blown sand. This is derived from the strong northwest winds that blow almost continuously in this area and bring the sand, washed ashore during storms, up onto the terraces. Streamers of dune sand extend to the middle of the island.

Another conspicuous sand deposit occurs in a spit projecting out for almost a mile from the southeast end of San Nicolas (Fig. 10.48). A long shoal is a submerged continuation of this spit. The sand supply for the spit and shoal, according to Norris, has moved principally along the northeast side, apparently being moved during the stormy northwesters of winter. Spits of this kind at the leeward end of islands are relatively common where longshore currents carry sand along a straight coast. Another has been built at San Miguel Island (Fig. 10.53). Similar spits in the Caspian and Black Seas are described by V. P. Zenkovich. The San Nicolas spit is unstable in shape and position. Norris has shown that between 1851 and 1879 the spit was located farther north than it is now (Fig. 10.49). It has also changed considerably in more recent years.

San Nicolas was missed by Cabrillo during his expedition in 1542–1543, although he saw and named most of the other California islands. The first landing by white man was made on the island in 1602 when Vizcaíno came ashore on a fete day for Saint Nicholas and gave the island its name. The Spaniards found a well-organized Indian community. Recent archaeology has shown that the Indian culture had numerous implements, and apparently a large population lived there long before the Spaniards visited the island. Subsequently, the island was taken over by American ranchers, who raised sheep and

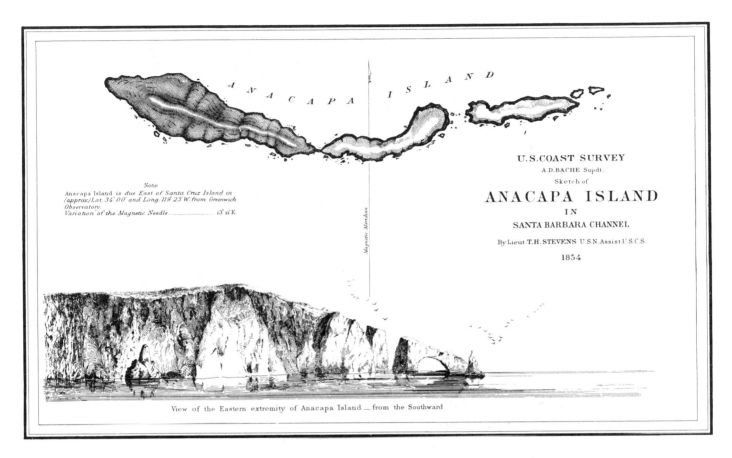

Note
Anacapa Island *is due East of Santa Cruz Island in*
(approx.)Lat.34°00' and Long.119°23'W.from Greenwich
Observatory.
Variation of the Magnetic Needle............13°21'E.

Magnetic Meridian

U.S.COAST SURVEY
A.D.BACHE Supdt.
Sketch of
ANACAPA ISLAND
IN
SANTA BARBARA CHANNEL
By Lieut.T.H.STEVENS U.S.N.Assist.U.S.C.S.
1854

View of the Eastern extremity of Anacapa Island — from the Southward

10.50 Map and sketch of Anacapa Island, Santa Barbara Channel. U.S. Coast and Geodetic Survey, 1854. The island sketch at lower left was by the famous nineteenth-century artist James A. M. Whistler.

cattle. Overgrazing by the sheep destroyed much of the sparse vegetation, allowing the dunes to spread. Like San Clemente, the island was taken over by the military, first as a Navy gunnery range and later for the development of the guided missiles program of the Vandenberg base.

Santa Barbara Island should not be confused with the group of islands that protect Santa Barbara Channel and are often called the Santa Barbara Islands. This small isolated island lies a little north of a midway point between Catalina and San Nicolas. It is only 1.5 miles long and is shield-shaped with the greatest width at the north end. The island is so small that it is often referred to as simply Santa Barbara Rock. The highest part of the island is at the southwest end where it rises abruptly from the shore to 635 feet and is being actively eroded, as is all of the southwest coast. The island is very barren, having

largely bare rock of Middle Miocene volcanics, similar to those of San Clemente. The only landing place is on the east side where a small Coast Guard installation is located on top of the steep high cliff. There are terraces well above sea level, but they are not proven to be wave-cut benches.

The Channel Islands extend for 60 miles east and west along the Santa Barbara coast at an average distance of 30 miles from the mainland. These islands were all discovered by Cabrillo in 1542–1543. He is said to have died from blood poisoning (attributed to a broken arm by some and to a broken leg by others) on San Miguel, the westernmost island of the group, and was buried by his shipmates in a grave that has never been discovered. Possibly it may have been covered or undermined by the migrating dunes.

Anacapa (Fig. 10.50), a group of three small slightly separated islands, extends for 5 miles as an

10.51 High-altitude aerial photograhs of Santa Cruz Island. A longitudinal valley (B) follows a fault. Note the rugged topograhy and the scarcity of beaches except at C. U.S. Army Map Service, 1955.

arc at the eastern end of the Channel Islands. The rocks are Miocene volcanics. The cliffs of these islands are so steep on all sides that landings are difficult. Max Miller referred to the curious fact that sheepherders formerly owned the islands and kept their flocks out there despite the virtual absence of any drinking water. However, a seasonally filled natural rock tank on the flat provided some water. The sheep, no doubt, helped remove the vegetation from the relatively flat 28-foot terrace. Also, the introduction of rabbits in 1935 was an experiment that boomeranged and certainly helped to make these islands barren. The only residents now are men of the Coast Guard, which is appropriate because there have been many wrecks on the islands in this foggy area.

The famous James Whistler sketch of Arch Rock, at the east end of Anacapa (Fig. 10.50), was made in 1854 when he was a member of the Coast and Geodetic Survey. His survey was made to determine if it were feasible for a lighthouse to be built on the island. A recent photograph shows this arch still standing, although it has become considerably thinner than indicated in the sketch, and the separation between the Arch Rock and the easternmost island has apparently increased. Also, the modern chart shows an appreciable decrease in the size of the rocks from that shown in the Whistler sketch.

Santa Cruz (Fig. 10.51), the largest of all the California islands, somewhat resembles Catalina. Santa Cruz has a rugged coastline with almost no coastal plain. Its rock formations include intrusive granites, metamorphic schists, and volcanics, along with a few sedimentary rocks. Like Catalina, the island has two main parts; but the divide (A) be-

10.52 Northern shore of Santa Rosa Island showing two coastal terraces (A and B), resembling those on San Nicolas Island (Fig. 10.47). U.S. Navy Electronics Laboratory photo, 1948.

tween them is not so pronounced as is the Catalina Isthmus. Another distinctive feature of Santa Cruz is the relatively broad longitudinal valley (B). The main buildings of a large cattle ranch are located in this valley. The eucalyptus trees here include the best stand on the West Coast and grow to unusual heights.

Fossil pygmy mammoths were first discovered by Phil Orr, of the Santa Barbara Museum of Natural History, on Santa Rosa Island. Since the original discovery, these fossil animals have been found also on both Santa Cruz and San Miguel. Evidence that the islands were once connected to the mainland thus receives additional support from these mammoths, because one could scarcely expect even these small elephants to be brought from the mainland on a natural raft of vegetation or expect them to swim for

such a distance. As Phil Orr has said, Santa Cruz had the smallest elephants in the world as well as the largest rats. The present connection with the mainland is far too deep to have developed a land bridge during the Pleistocene low sea levels. Apparently a former connection has sunk, separating the islands from the mainland.

The longitudinal valley has a fault that can be traced west to Santa Rosa Island, and is believed to have a displacement along it in a horizontal direction, which is opposite to that found along the well-known San Andreas Fault. The formations on the north side of the valley have been displaced many miles to the west. The sedimentary rocks of Santa Cruz include Cretaceous, Paleocene, Eocene, Miocene, and Pleistocene.

A few elevated terraces are found on Santa Cruz,

10.53 San Miguel Island, the westernmost of the Santa Barbara Channel Islands. The climate is semiarid, and the sand sweeps clear across the island from northwest to southeast. The dunes are shown as parallel light bands. Note sand spit at east end of island. Headlands, coves, and stacks are conspicuous at west end and along the north central coast. U.S. Department of Agriculture, 1940.

but they are in general quite inconspicuous (Fig. 10.51), and in this respect the island also resembles Catalina. Yachtsmen describe the north side of Santa Cruz as a paradise. Numerous small coves indent the coast, allowing safe anchorage except during northers. Many interesting grottoes and caves are found, especially west of the island isthmus. Near the northwest end, Painted Cave is one of the largest and

deepest sea grottoes in the world. It was explored and sounded by K. O. Emery. The entrance room is 80 feet high and the water 40 feet deep. It is possible to proceed in for more than 500 feet in small craft; but it is so dark on the inside that an ordinary flashlight is ineffective, and large flares are necessary to see the huge domelike roof and walls. Emery found that the cave had been cut in volcanic flows along an

OUR CHANGING COASTLINES

the more barren landscape on Santa Rosa, the good development of raised terraces, the softer character of the rock, which is perhaps the reason for the wider terraces, and the large areas on the northeast and northwest covered by dunes. Thus, Santa Rosa compares rather well with San Nicolas. They have a somewhat similar shape, but Santa Rosa is larger—13 miles east to west and 8 miles north to south. It is not exposed to the violent northwest winds as is San Nicolas but shows some of the bleakness, and both islands have extensive dunes.

Santa Rosa has predominantly sedimentary rocks, covering a large range in age, as in Santa Cruz. The terraces provide good grazing areas for the cattle on the island. Also like Santa Cruz, Santa Rosa is privately owned ranchland. Phil Orr found the dwarf mammoth fossils in the terraces. In addition, he found extensive charcoal deposits, which he thinks were left by early Indians, because the charcoal was found in circular formations, not easily explained by fires due to lightning. These charcoal deposits have been dated back to about 14,700 B.C. Perhaps this is the oldest sign of human occupation along the California coasts. Poorly preserved human bones were found in a Santa Rosa deposit dated as 8200 B.C., but they may be much older. Another interesting feature of Santa Rosa is the finding of living Torrey Pines, a relict flora that used to be widespread in California but now is confined to Santa Rosa and to Torrey Pines Park and its vicinity north of La Jolla.

San Miguel (Figs. 10.53 and 10.54) is the most barren of the islands. Being located out beyond the protection of Point Conception, it is hit by the full fury of winds and waves from the northwest. The island is 8 miles long and about 4 miles wide at the widest part. It has very little vegetation left on it, mainly because of former droughts and intensive sheep grazing. A large part of the island is covered with dunes (Fig. 10.53). Archaelogists have found San Miguel a treasure house. The winds blowing away the sand expose many old burial grounds, showing that the island probably had a large Indian population some centuries ago.

The view of San Miguel from the air is quite amazing. A series of streaks can be seen that all extend in the direction of the wind and represent alternating dunes and bare rock surfaces or areas with a thin cover of vegetation (Fig. 10.53). These streaks look so much like stratified tilted sedimentary

old fault. Some of the inner rooms have shelves that have been smoothed by the bodies of generations of sea lions that inhabit this cavern in great numbers. The barking of the sea lions combined with the sound of the water against the walls is almost deafening, especially in the inner part of the cave.

Santa Rosa (Fig. 10.52) differs strikingly from Santa Cruz in appearance. The differences include

10.54 Oblique aerial photo of San Miguel Island showing nearly complete cover of drifting sand along the high central island and along the steep slope to the shore in the foreground. Apparently an increase of sand since 1940 (Fig. 10.53). For location, see C and D here and on Figure 10.53. U.S. Navy Electronics Laboratory photo, 1948.

rocks that they are somewhat confusing to a geologist seeing them from the air. The sedimentary rocks that comprise most of San Miguel Island include Cretaceous, Paleocene, Eocene, and Miocene. Geologists have measured very thick sections of rocks, which indicate that a deep basin existed here that kept subsiding and being filled with sediments prior to the deformations that developed a mountain range, of which the island is a remnant.

The dunes cascade over the cliffs on the south side of the island and are actually building out the coast in some places, although the forward building is offset by wave erosion, as can be seen in Figure 10.54. According to Max Miller, the remains of a schooner wrecked in 1898 at Point Bennett (A), just in the lee of the west end, had by 1958 been covered by the forward building of the sand blown across the point. The sand is also carried along the island at the east end, where it forms a point very much like that of San Nicolas (Fig. 10.48).

On the north side of the island, Cuyler Harbor (B) makes a rather large indentation into the land, and nearby is a freshwater spring, the only one on the island except for a cave that drips fresh water from the ceiling. The harbor once had a wharf, but now it has been wrecked by the waves.

REFERENCES

Caldwell, Joseph M., 1956. Wave action and sand movement near Anaheim Bay, California. *U.S. Army Corps Engrs., Beach Erosion Board Tech. Memo.* 68.

Corps of Engineers, U.S. Army, 1938. *Beach Erosion at Santa Barbara, California.* House of Representatives, 75th Congr., 3d Sess., Document 552.

———, 1948. *Santa Barbara, California, Beach Erosion Control Study.* House of Representatives, 80th Congr., 2d Sess., Document 761.

———, 1950. Accretion of beach sand behind a detached breakwater. *Beach Erosion Board, Corps Engr. Tech. Memo.* 16.

Darrow, Warren E., 1942. The hydrologic aspects of beach-material supply, with specific reference to the shoreline at Long Beach, California. *Amer. Geophys. Union, Trans. for 1942*, pp. 644–652 (with discussion by C. B. Brown).

Davis, W. M., 1933. Glacial epochs of the Santa Monica Mountains, California. *Geol. Soc. Amer. Bull.*, vol. 44, pp. 1041–1133.

Dill, Robert F., 1964. Sedimentation and erosion in Scripps Submarine Canyon head. In *Papers in Marine Geology*, Shepard Comm. Vol., Macmillan Company, New York, pp. 23–41.

Ellis, A. J., and C. H. Lee, 1919. Geology and ground waters of the western part of San Diego County, California. *U.S. Geol. Survey Water Supply Paper* 446.

Emery, K. O., 1941. Rate of surface retreat of sea cliffs based on dated inscriptions. *Science*, N. S., vol. 93, pp. 617–618.

————, 1954. The Painted Cave, Santa Cruz Island. *Sea and Pacific Motorboat*, vol. 46, pp. 37–39, 91–92.

————, 1960. *The Sea off Southern California*. John Wiley & Sons, New York.

————, 1967. The activity of coastal landslides related to sea level. *Rev. géographie physique et de géologie dynamique*, vol. 9, no. 3, pp. 177–180.

Gilluly, James, and U. S. Grant IV, 1949. Subsidence in the Long Beach Harbor area, California. *Geol. Soc. Amer. Bull.*, vol. 60, pp. 461–529.

Handin, J. W., 1951. The source, transportation, and deposition of beach sediment in southern California. *U.S. Army Corps of Engrs., Beach Erosion Board, Tech. Memo.* 22.

Hanna, M. A., 1926. Geology of the La Jolla quadrangle, California. *Univ. Calif. Dept. Geol. Sci. Bull.*, vol. 16, pp. 187–246.

Imray, James F., 1868. *Sailing Directions for the West Coast of North America Between Panama and Queen Charlotte Islands*, 2d ed., F.R.G.S., London.

Inman, D. L., 1950. Report on beach study in the vicinity of Mugu Lagoon, California. *U.S. Army Corps of Engrs., Beach Erosion Board Tech. Memo.* 14.

Lawson, A. C., 1897. Post Pliocene diastrophism of the coast of Southern California. *Bull. Dept. Geol., Univ. Calif.*, vol. 1, pp. 115–160.

Miller, Max, 1940. *Harbor of the Sun*. Doubleday & Company, Garden City, N.Y.

————, 1959. *. . . And Bring All Your Folks*. Doubleday & Company, Garden City, N.Y.

Moore, George W., 1968. Geologic observations at the Fishery-Oceanography Center. *U.S. Geol. Survey Memo.*, mimeo.

Norris, R. M., 1952. Recent history of a sand spit at San Nicolas Island, California. *Jour. Sed. Petrology*, vol. 22, pp. 224–228.

Orr, Phil C., 1960. Radiocarbon dates from Santa Rosa Island, I. *Santa Barbara Mus. Nat. History Bull.* 2 (also Bull. 3).

———, 1968. *Prehistory of Santa Rosa Island.* Santa Barbara Mus. Nat. History.

Putnam, W. C., 1937. The marine cycle of erosion for a steeply sloping shoreline of emergence. *Jour. Geol.*, vol. 45, pp. 844–850.

Scholl, D. W., 1960. Relationship of the insular shelf sediments to the sedimentary environments and geology of Anacapa Island, California. *Jour. Sed. Petrology*, vol. 30, no. 1, pp. 123–139.

Shepard, F. P., 1943. Shoreline erosion at La Jolla, California. *Civil Engr.*, vol. 13, no. 2, pp. 80–82.

———, and R. F. Dill, 1966. *Submarine Canyons and Other Sea Valleys.* Rand McNally & Company, Chicago.

———, and K. O. Emery, 1941. Submarine topography off the California coast: canyons and tectonic interpretation. *Geol. Soc. Amer. Spec. Paper* 31.

———, and U. S. Grant IV, 1947. Wave erosion along the southern California coast. *Geol. Soc. Amer. Bull.*, vol. 58, pt. 4, pp. 919–926.

———, U. S. Grant IV, and R. S. Dietz, 1939. The emergence of (Santa) Catalina Island. *Amer. Jour. Sci.*, vol. 287, pp. 651–655.

———, and D. L. Inman, 1950. Nearshore water circulation related to bottom topography and wave refraction. *Trans. Amer. Geophys. Union*, vol. 31, no. 2. pp. 196–212.

———, and D. L. Inman, 1951. Nearshore circulation. *Proc. 1st Conf. Coastal Engr.*, Long Beach, California, 1950, pp. 50–59.

———, and E. C. LaFond, 1940. Sand movements along the Scripps Institution pier. *Amer. Jour. Sci.*, vol. 238, pp. 272–285.

Smith, W. S. T., 1933. Marine terraces on Santa Catalina Island. *Amer. Jour. Sci.*, vol. 25, pp. 123–136.

Troxell, H. C., and others, 1942. Floods of March, 1938, in Southern California. *U.S. Geol. Survey Water Supply Paper* 844.

Upson, J. E., 1949. Late Pleistocene and Recent changes of sea level along the coast of Santa Barbara County, California. *Amer. Jour. Sci.*, vol. 247, pp. 94–115.

———, 1951. Former marine shore lines of the Gaviota quadrangle, Santa Barbara County, California. *Jour. Geol.*, vol. 59, pp. 415–446.

Vaughan, T. Wayland, 1932. Rate of sea cliff recession on the property of the Scripps Institution of Oceanography at La Jolla, California. *Science,* vol. 75, no. 1939, p. 250.

Vedder, J. G., and Robert M. Norris, 1963. Geology of San Nicolas Island, California, *U.S. Geol. Survey Prof. Paper* 369.

Warme, J. E., 1966. Paleoecologic aspects of the recent ecology of the Mugu Lagoon, California. Univ. Calif. at Los Angeles, Dept. of Geol. Ph.D. thesis.

Wiegel, R. L., D. A. Patrick, and H. L. Kimberley, 1954. Wave, longshore current, and beach profile records for Santa Margarita River beach, Oceanside, California, 1949. *Amer. Geophys. Union Trans.*, vol. 35, no. 6, pp. 887–896.

Woodring, W. P., M. N. Bramlette, and W. S. W. Kew, 1946. Geology and paleontology of Palos Verdes Hills, California. *U.S. Geol. Survey Prof. Paper* 207.

Zenkovich, V. P., 1967. *Processes of Coastal Development*, J. A. Steers (ed.). Interscience Publishers (Div. of John Wiley & Sons), New York.

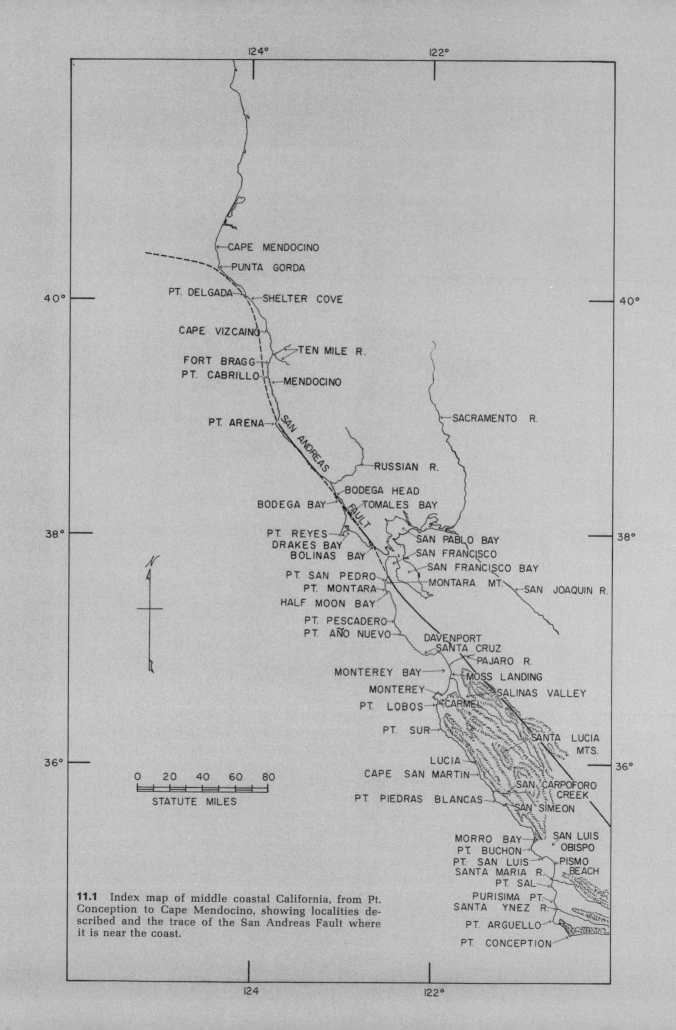

11.1 Index map of middle coastal California, from Pt.
Conception to Cape Mendocino, showing localities described and the trace of the San Andreas Fault where
it is near the coast.

Rugged California Coast

Point Conception to Cape Mendocino

11 The grandest scenery on the California coast is found in the area between Point Conception and Cape Mendocino (Fig. 11.1). The San Simeon Highway, which extends along the 3,000-foot coastal range for 70 miles south of Carmel, is certainly no place for a timid driver, particularly if he is hugging the edge of the south-bound side of the highway, with drops of 1,000 feet or more next to him. Even more precipitous is the area south of Cape Mendocino, which is mostly without roads. However, one can cover the portion from Shelter Cove to Punta Gorda on foot, principally along a narrow beach.

To the south of the San Simeon Highway, the coast is less mountainous, and three large intermontane valleys come to the sea in this region. Each has abundant sand dunes in its lower stretches and a broad gently curving embayment. The Santa Maria Valley is the largest of the three and is bordered by a long sandy coast with broad beaches. As in Southern California, the rivers in these valleys virtually dry up in summer.

North of the San Simeon Highway, there are two major embayments, one at Carmel and one north of Monterey. The latter is much the larger, comparable in size and shape with Santa Monica Bay. Carmel Bay is more of an estuary, but does not extend deeply into the land because it has been partly filled by a river delta. Bordering Monterey Bay, a broad coastal lowland contains one of several large structural valleys that enter the California coast.

Between Point Conception and San Francisco, the structural trends and the mountain ranges enter the coast diagonally from the south and are apparently chopped off, suggesting that faulting has broken the trend. This tendency terminates at San Francisco where the San Andreas Fault comes to the coast (see Fig. 11.1), but is resumed again where the San Andreas finally heads out to sea just south of Cape Mendocino. This fault, one of the greatest

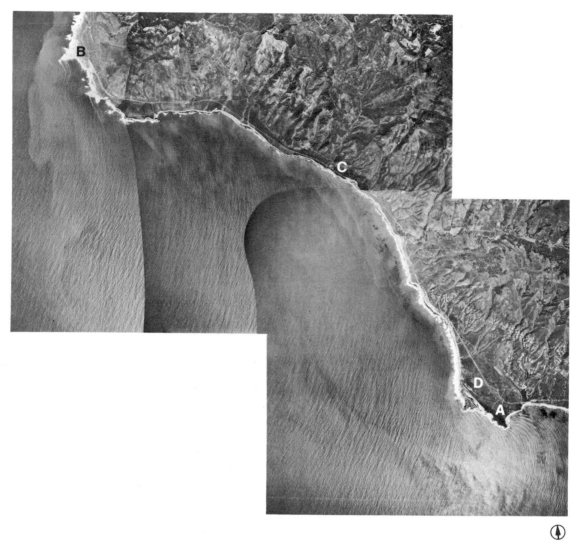

11.2 Aerial photo composite of coast between Pt. Conception and Pt. Arguello. Note that beaches are absent or narrow throughout this coastal section. The climate is semiarid and trees are limited to stream valleys. Much of the shore is along cliffs below an elevated coastal terrace as at C. Sand dunes (D) cross Pt. Conception in parallel bands northwest to southeast. U.S. Department of Agriculture, 1965.

structural features in the world, is located close to the California coast for 220 miles. The horizontal displacement along it is not known exactly; but, in recent years, geologists and geophysicists have concluded that it is measured in scores, perhaps hundreds, of miles. It has a definite effect on the coast,

although the influence is not nearly so clear as it is on the relief of the sea floor, where it finally is traced out to sea at Punta Gorda.

San Francisco Bay is by far the largest enclosed bay on the West Coast south of the glaciated area, where the Strait of Juan de Fuca cuts deeply into the north coast of Washington. San Francisco Bay is a structural depression fed by the two longest rivers in California, the Sacramento and San Joaquin. The bay is connected to the ocean through a drowned river valley. Drakes Estero, however, is the only good example of a dendritic estuary along the West Coast between Point Conception and Cape Mendocino.

Northward from Point Conception, the coastal rainfall increases, producing a gradual change in vegetation, especially pronounced north of San Francisco Bay. Most of the main valleys to the north have permanent streams, although the summer dry season continues to be important as far as the Oregon line.

POINT CONCEPTION TO PISMO BEACH [Figs. 11.2 and 11.3]   The major change in trend of the California coast from its westerly direction along the Santa Barbara Channel begins at Point Conception (A in Fig. 11.2), but it is another 12 miles before a northerly direction is initiated at Point Arguello (B). The frequent fogs and the sudden change in vessel course near these points have often led to maritime disasters. On September 8, 1923, a squadron of American destroyers was steaming south in line at 20 knots along this coast. The navigators of the flagship *Delphy* decided that they were south of Point Arguello, so the commanding officer changed course to the east to run along the Santa Barbara Channel. Immediately they were in a thick fog bank, and minutes later the *Delphy* hit the rocks at Devil's Jaw near Point Arguello, then eight other following destroyers also piled up on the rocks; all within 10 minutes. However, the remaining five destroyers in line changed course at the last minute and were saved. Twenty-two men were killed, and seven vessels were total losses; more U.S. Navy combat vessels were lost than during action in all of World War I. This was our worst peacetime naval disaster.

Between Point Conception and Pismo Beach, there are three prominent points: Arguello, Purisima, and Sal. These are respectively 11 and 12 miles apart and separate, in each case, coasts that run first in a general northwest and then in a northeasterly direction. Point Arguello is at the westerly termination of the Santa Ynez Mountains. Point Purisima adjoins the Purisima Hills; and Point Sal, the Casmalia Hills (A in Fig. 11.3). The coast between Point Conception and Point Sal is very rocky with numerous stacks and has cliffs, mostly less than 100 feet high, and

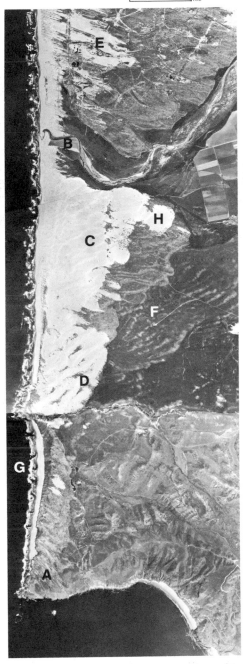

11.3 Straight coast north of Pt. Sal (A) at the western end of the Casmalia Hills. Sand dunes extend east-southeast from beaches and include a large dune field lacking vegetation (C), a narrow belt of sand elongate in the prevailing wind direction (E), and older vegetation-covered dunes (F). Note small scallops along the beach (G) that are related to the rip currents, which form the wave pattern (see Fig. 2.12). U.S. Department of Agriculture photos, 1967.

11.4 Stacks cut in diatomite cliff at Shell Beach. Stacks mostly eroded by 1970. Photo by Shepard, 1965.

very discontinuous narrow beaches bordered by relatively narrow terraces. This coast has little civilian habitation and is largely controlled by the military.

Although the coast north of Point Arguello is almost all rocky, there are broad valleys farther north that are filled with alluvial gravels, sands, and clays. From south to north, the Santa Ynez and Santa Maria Rivers occupy the two largest valleys. Because the summer climate is dry for many months and the sediments in the lowlands are porous, very little water enters the ocean at these river mouths except during major winter storms. At the northern end, Oso Flaco and Berros Creeks, when flowing, drain into lakes that are remnants of small estuaries. Comparisons between new and older topographic maps show that these lakes have been considerably filled with sediment in recent years.

Along each of the northerly trending stretches of coast, sand brought to the shore by streams during floods and sand washed in from the shallow sea floor has formed a nearly continuous beach. From these beaches the sand has been blown inland. Along the Santa Maria Valley (B in Fig. 11.3), the dunes extend in for a distance up to 10 miles (beyond edge of photo). Wendell P. Woodring and M. N. Bramlette, who have mapped the northern part of the area, and T. W. Dibblee, Jr., who mapped the southern end, have described the dunes as belonging to at least

two series. The older dunes are much farther inland (F) and have been stabilized by vegetation. These dunes may date back to an interglacial time of higher sea level.

The younger (postglacial) sand dunes (H) spread inland at some places as far as 2 miles from the beach. They are predominantly of the type called U-shaped or parabolic (D). Straight dune ridges are elongate in the direction of the prevailing wind (E). These dunes are still active, although partially grass-covered. Widths of dune belts diminish on the slopes of the uplands, and directions of dune ridges are influenced by local topography. Although they are derived from the beaches, younger dunes extend up to an elevation of 120 feet and older dunes to nearly 400 feet. Alluvial deposits in the stream valleys and the dunes have effectively buried the coastal terraces in the lowland areas between the rocky promontories.

Although the seaward fronts of the alluvial fan-deltas of the several streams may have formed deltaic bulges at one time, so little sand reaches the sea today that the southward-flowing longshore currents prevent any projections at the present river mouths, such as the Santa Maria (B). The sand is drifted southward and accumulates next to the rock promontories, building out the shore, similar to deposition on the upcurrent side of a man-made jetty.

The late Parker Trask, by a study of the mineralogy of beach sands in this coastal stretch, has shown that some sand is drifted around each point, even Point Conception, and that a small portion of the sand that builds against the Santa Barbara breakwater has come from the Pismo Beach area, 100 miles distant.

Photographs are not at hand to measure recent amounts of erosion or progradation of the shore. Because there are no jetties between Point Conception and Pismo Beach, there has been no human interference with the natural processes of beach drifting, and the beach is probably in equilibrium with sand supply and rate of beach drifting.

SAN LUIS OBISPO–MORRO BAY AREA [Figs. 11.4, 11.5, and 11.6]   The inland city of San Luis Obispo has two nearby ports, Port San Luis to the south and Morro Bay to the west. North of Pismo Beach, the coast becomes rocky and is bordered by a terrace, mostly about 100 feet above the ocean. Shell Beach, 4 miles north, has striking cliffs cut into the folded rocks at the margin of the 100-foot terrace. Stacks stand out from the shore (Fig. 11.4) and must be undergoing erosion, although we have no old pictures to establish such changes. Farther north, photographs taken by G. W. Stose in 1898 show cliffs which apparently had not changed by 1945 (Fig. 11.5). However, we found one of the localities was impossible to visit on our 1968 trip, so that here we do not have any photographs since 1945. The area shown in Figure 11.5 would seem to be the place where erosion should be fairly rapid because it is exposed to the full force of the open sea. The stacks shown at the present coast and also rising above the elevated wave-cut terrace certainly suggest rapid erosion. Nevertheless, we should recall that many of the late nineteenth-century photographs of the San Diego area show no appreciable change in the rock cliffs, but others have clear evidence of erosion. Therefore, the few available old photographs along this more northerly part of the coast may not be representative.

Port San Luis has a natural protection in Point San Luis, which cuts off the surf from the west and northwest. A breakwater provides further protection. Morro Bay, 15 miles northwest, has an artificial harbor, a necessity here because the natural harbor behind the long barrier ridge of sand dunes (Fig. 11.6) and in the largely filled estuary of Chorro Creek (A) was so shallow that only small craft could enter, and these only when the sea was calm. Originally, Morro Rock (B) was an island lying a short distance offshore. Because of this island, a counter-current flows to the north, resulting in deposition of a sand spit all along the coast north of Pt. Buchon, terminating directly southeast of Morro Rock. Dunes 50 feet or more in height developed on the spit, with a steep front toward the lagoon. The landward-blowing winds had partly filled the lagoon with sand.

The area seaward of Morro Bay was known to be excellent for fishing. Also, the possibilities were good for building industries at this point. Accordingly, a jetty (C) was built in 1930 between the rock and the mainland. It was hoped that this would sufficiently intensify the tidal currents coming into the bay to maintain the entrance channel. However, the tides proved to be ineffective. Also, sand built rapidly out along the north side of the jetty, completely filling in the angle between the mainland and the rock (C). Soon the wind began to blow sand over the jetty, forming shoals at the bay entrance. Also,

11.5 Cove about 5 miles north of Pt. San Luis, an elevated wave-cut bench including rock stacks.
a 1898. Photo by G. W. Stose.

b 1945. Showing very little erosion during 47 years. Photo by U.S. Grant IV.

the north end of the sand spit began to migrate landward. Much more elaborate steps were called for by the rapidly deteriorating situation at the harbor entrance. Two extra breakwaters (D, E) were built. One extends south from the outer edge of Morro Rock and the other west from near the end of the spit. These keep the harbor open. However, the channel has to be maintained somewhat by dredging; and,

11.6 Morro Bay and Morro Rock (B), a tombolo, and the delta of Chorro Creek (A). The bay is partially closed by a barrier spit with high longitudinal sand dunes. Jetty (C, E) attached to Morro Rock and (D) to the barrier have formed an artificial harbor. U.S. Department of Agriculture photo, 1956.

during periods of unusually large swell, we are told, the waves occasionally break across the entrance.

Apparently Chorro Creek is slowly building a delta (A) into the bay; but, judging from the 1956 aerial photo, it has not advanced much since the 1900 chart, so it does not appear to constitute much of a menace to the harbor.

North of Morro Bay, the low coast has an extensive beach, partly the result of the jetty. Farther

north, where the coast is relatively straight, terraces appear, again with heights of about 50 feet.

SANTA LUCIA MOUNTAIN COAST, SAN SIMEON TO CARMEL [Figs. 11.7, 11.8, 11.9, and 2.15]   The coastal highway (California Route 1) between San Simeon and Carmel is often described as the most spectacular coastal road in the United States. For about 120 miles it follows either raised coastal terraces (Figs. 11.7 and 2.15) or is blasted out of cliffs on the southwestern slopes of the Santa Lucia Mountains at elevations between 400 and 1,000 feet above the sea. When the trip can be made on a clear sunny day rather than in fog, the scenery is comparable with the finest on the Mediterranean Coast of southern Europe, such as the Corniche Coast near Monaco and even the Amalfi Drive near Naples; and it lacks the wild horn-tooting Italian drivers. Sandy beaches are generally limited to small pockets between rocky headlands; some can be seen hundreds of feet below the highway. In the southern part of this coast, the climate is semiarid, with grass and shrub vegetation. Northward, as the rainfall increases, trees become more prevalent, and on the northern slopes of the canyons, the coastal redwoods have their southernmost groves.

The Santa Lucia Range has a northwest trend. From Point Estero, near Morro Bay, northwest to San Carpoforo Creek, the main Santa Lucia Range lies several miles inland, and much of the highway traverses elevated coastal terraces 100 feet or less above sea level (A in Fig. 11.7). The terraces are bordered by wave-cut cliffs, and arch rocks and stacks (Fig. 11.8) are seen at many places. North of Carpoforo Creek, the southwest slopes of the mountains come right to the coast, and, within 3 miles, the highway climbs from near sea level to about 750 feet, the beginning of the spectacular coastal scenery. Figure 11.7 is a view southeast looking back from the mountainous coast to the lower terraces.

Parts of the area were described by Parker Trask and others and by Parry Reiche. The rocks forming the mountains include old metamorphics of undetermined age, intruded by granitclike quartz diorite and overlain by Jurassic (Franciscan) sedimentary rocks of probable deep-sea origin. Other patches include Cretaceous, Eocene, Oligocene, Miocene, and Pliocene sediments. During the early Pleistocene, the sediments were deformed by faulting; then, after being elevated, the newly formed mountains were reduced to gentle relief. In the middle or late Pleistocene, the area was again elevated 1,500 feet or more. During pauses in the uplift, several narrow wave-cut terraces were formed (Figs. 11.7 and 11.9). Still later, the streams cut deep canyons, and wave erosion formed coastal cliffs locally 400 feet or more in height. Active erosion is still in progress.

11.7 View looking south along San Simeon Highway (California Route 1), with a low coastal terrace (A) in the distance and a higher terrace (B) in the foreground. The Santa Lucia Mountains along the coast in this area provide spectacular scenery. Photo by Shepard, 1968.

In places, the narrow coastal terraces have been cut away, and elsewhere they have been buried by alluvial or talus sediments; but wherever possible the coastal highway follows one of the benches. Narrow terrace remnants have been reported up to about 1,000 feet above sea level, but the more extensive terraces range from 40 to 200 feet, comparable with those along most other parts of the California coast.

The Santa Lucia Mountains are cut by a series of faults, generally at an angle of 10 to 15 degrees to the trend of the coastline but partly parallel to it. For the area about 16 miles northwest from the small town of Lucia toward Point Sur, Reiche has suggested that one fault lies parallel to the coast but just offshore. In this same area, the continental shelf is less than a mile wide, the narrowest along the entire California coast, suggesting that this is essentially a fault coast (p. 12) controlled by Pleistocene faulting.

At the mouth of Partington Canyon, about 12 miles southeast of Point Sur along the fault coast, Partington Submarine Canyon, heading within 0.5 mile of the shore, trends for about a mile southeastward parallel to the coast, then curves seaward, attaining a depth of 3,000 feet only 8 miles from shore.

11.8 Cape San Martin, on the San Simeon Highway, and an offshore bird island discolored white by bird guano. Photo by Shepard, 1968.

From the many lookout points along the mountain highway, one can see numerous offshore rock stacks coated with white guano from seabird rookeries (Fig. 11.8) and occasionally sea lions or even sea otter, the latter at one time thought to be extinct. During California's colonial period, sea otters were hunted extensively by the Russians, Spanish, English, and Yankees, because of the great value of their beautiful fur. There was even a so-called battle over the hides in San Diego Harbor in 1803. Finally, the sea otter were seen no more until comparatively recent times. In 1934, when Shepard visited Point Sur, the light-house keeper pointed out some of the surviving sea otters that were living on the adjacent rocks and in the sea. Rigid game control has now allowed these rare mammals to increase, so that now they live all along this part of the coast.

Point Sur (A in Fig. 11.9), about 30 miles south-east of Carmel, is a tombolo composed of ancient metamorphosed highly colored lava flows. A little farther north, at the mouth of Little Sur River (B), there is a small barrier spit; and sand blown from the flat has formed a dune reaching up the slope to about 400 feet (C) above sea level.

The rocks exposed along the Santa Lucia Mountain coast include wave-resistant granites, gneisses, quartzites, and marbles, along with smaller areas of more easily eroded shales and sandstones and various rocks sheared by the displacements along the faults. Rock stacks and coastal cliffs are subject to nearly constant wave pounding, and eventually the cliffs wear back and the stacks disappear. Comparative photographs with intervals of 20 or 30 years show that changes take place at a slow rate. Aerial photos, such as Figure 11.9, indicate little if any visible differences in a 10- to 20-year period. Ground photographs of segments of the coast would be more likely to show effects of erosion during a 20-year period. When the authors visited this coast in June 1968, they observed that some of Shepard's 1950 pictures must have been taken from the top of a shale cliff when it extended 15 to 30 feet farther seaward than in 1968, so that it was impossible to take exactly matching photographs. However, at a point 12 miles south of Carmel, a photograph retaken after 22 years showed identical cliffs and stacks.

CARMEL–MONTEREY BAY AREA [Figs. 11.10, 11.11, and 11.12]   The relatively straight mountainous coast of the San Simeon Highway terminates at Point Lobos, the beautiful peninsula projecting seaward on the south side of Carmel Bay. Despite its bay, Carmel does not have a well-protected harbor (Fig. 11.10). However, on the north side of the bay,

11.9 Pt. Sur (A), a tombolo. Sand dunes cross the plain behind Pt. Sur, and dunes are also near the mouth of Little Sur River (B), some extending several hundred feet above the highway. There are no clearly indicated coastal terraces. U.S. Department of Agriculture, 1956.

11.10 Carmel Bay and Monterey Peninsula. Point Lobos to the south. Submarine canyon heads (B, C) extend close to the shoreline. Coves and points along Monterey Peninsula are due to wave erosion. U.S. Department of Agriculture, 1956.

11.11 Granite coast at Pt. Lobos State Park on a day of high waves. This coast shows very little change due to the resistance of the granite cliffs. Photo by Shepard, 1968.

two small coves form a good protection from all but southerly gales. These coves are used for small yachts by the residents of what is known as the Seventeen-Mile Drive, another beauty spot.

Carmel Bay (Fig. 11.10) is unusual in having a submarine canyon with arms (B, C) coming into its indentations. All other California submarine canyons are located off relatively straight coasts. The southern arm of Carmel Canyon comes so close to the cove at Carmelite Missions that one can easily throw a stone into the canyon head. In 1934, Shepard made a detailed chart of this submarine canyon, using a skiff that was anchored at night in a little protected cove on the north side of Point Lobos Park. After rowing out 0.5 mile from the cove it was actually possible to lower a sounding weight to a depth of over 1,000 feet.

Carmel Bay is separated from Monterey Bay by a hilly peninsula with bold rocky shores (D in Fig. 11.10). The rocks are predominantly granite, both in this peninsula and in Point Lobos (E). However, Monterey diatomites of Miocene age constitute most of the rock in the broad Carmel Valley (F). The hard rock on both flanks of Carmel Bay is very stable. Old

photographs show that no particular change has taken place, despite the violent wave attack, which is particularly noticeable on Point Lobos (Fig. 11.11) and on the outside of Monterey Peninsula at Midway Point (Fig. 11.12), Point Joe, and Point Pinos.

The sand dunes at the north end of the Monterey Peninsula (G in Fig. 11.10) are being quarried extensively, but the sand blown in from the beach replaces the quarried sand with a constant supply. The source of this sand is somewhat uncertain. The wide beaches northeast of Monterey have abundant sand, but it is certainly rare that any currents flow northwest past Monterey and Pacific Grove against the predominant northerly wave approach. Thus, the only reasonable source appears to be the continental shelf. One can imagine that such a source is very limited, because the water deepens to 180 feet only 0.5 mile off Point Pinos (H), and it is doubtful if waves would bring sand in from greater depths.

Monterey (A) was chosen by the early Spanish settlers as their second port after San Diego, and later it became their capital. This, of course, was long before the building of the breakwaters for this important fishing center, so Monterey evidently has considerable natural protection. The swell coming into Monterey Bay from the violent northwesters is deflected by the coastal projection on the north side of the bay, and therefore has a westerly approach, giving Monterey a lee under most circumstances. It always seems amazing to leave the tremendous swell outside the peninsula and find smooth water almost immediately after rounding Point Pinos. The general lack of high waves along the coast at Pacific Grove has been important in its development as a resort, and Stanford University's Hopkins Marine Laboratory has certainly benefited because the staff and students are able to launch small boats along this part of the shore except during northwest blows.

Almost the entire 30 miles along the gently curving eastern shore of Monterey Bay is bordered by a wide, relatively coarse sand beach. The southern half of this beach is adjoined to the east by a wide belt of sand dunes (Fig. 11.13) rising commonly to more than 100 feet above sea level. Beyond the dunes is the broad Salinas Valley, which comes to the coast (A) from the southeast. From here, a coastal lowland is virtually continuous past Elkhorn Slough to the broad Pajaro Valley, where it meets the coast near Watsonville. The broad beaches and sand dunes are

11.12 Midway Pt., along the Seventeen-Mile Drive of Monterey Peninsula. The rock is granite. Photo by Wanless, 1939.

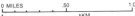

the result of the enormous quantities of sand brought to the sea by the Salinas and Pajaro Rivers. In general, this sand is carried south along the shore and blown inland to form the dunes. These dunes do not extend as far up the Salinas Valley as those of the Santa Maria Valley to the south. This is probably due to the higher precipitation that helps in stabilizing the dunes by growth of vegetation. Nevertheless, this is the longest tract of dunes along the California coast.

Between the mouths of the Salinas (A) and the Pajaro Rivers, there is a series of lagoons (called *sloughs*) that are remnants of old estuaries, mostly blocked by sand barriers and largely filled by stream deposits, so now they are predominantly marshes. These lowlands are the only features along this part of the coast that are equivalent to the deltas of the Gulf Coast. In spite of considerable runoff during winter rains, these streams have not had sufficient sediment to build out the coast against the influence of waves and longshore currents that tend to distribute the sediment along the shore.

Perhaps the most surprising feature of the Monterey area is the submarine canyon that extends in

11.13 Straight coast northeast of Monterey near the Salinas River mouth (A). Coastal dunes extend for many miles along this shore. The cultivated land behind the dunes is largely developed in a filled estuary. U.S. Department of Agriculture, 1956.

11.14 Head of Monterey Submarine Canyon (A) at Moss Landing, the mouth of Elkhorn Slough. The position of the canyon head can be recognized by the breach in the belt of large waves. U.S. Army Corps of Engineers photo, March 1947.

so close to shore off Elkhorn Slough that it has had an important influence on the development of the community at Moss Landing and Castroville. Here, as shoreward of other submarine canyon heads, the wave pattern is related to the submarine topography. The canyon head is easily spotted from the air (Fig. 11.14) by noticing the zone of small waves and the wave convergence on either side. At Moss Landing (B), a pier was built out into the quiet water at one of three branches at the canyon head. At one time, this pier was partly destroyed when a slide occurred at the canyon head, but it has since been stabilized. Harbor jetties were built at another branch to allow shipping to come into Elkhorn Slough because of its importance to the oil industry. One of these jetties collapsed into the canyon head, but the tides serve to keep open the channel into the lagoon. Monterey Canyon is one of the deepest in the world. Most other submarine canyons are located off large rivers, but Monterey Canyon is an exception in being off a slough with no appreciable entering stream. However,

at some time in the past, the Great Valley of California may have come to the sea at this point. In any case, G. W. Starke and A. D. Howard have found from studying oil-well logs that during the Miocene there was an east-west trending canyon, now filled, with a floor 4,000 feet below sea level, and this old canyon heads directly toward the present-day Monterey Canyon.

North of the Pajaro Valley lowland, the coast has more relief, but the beach continues along the shore as far as the turn in the coast at Soquel Cove. The typical 100-foot terrace is found again along this northern arm of the bow-shaped Monterey Bay.

SANTA CRUZ [Fig. 11.15]   The city of Santa Cruz is situated at the north margin of Monterey Bay. From Santa Cruz the coast extends northwest and then north toward San Francisco. Its regularity is interrupted by a series of points projecting seaward 1 or 2 miles. Nearly all of the coast has sandstone or shale cliffs capped by elevated marine terraces, generally 50 to 100 feet above sea level, and up to 2 miles wide. South of San Pedro Point, an exception is the 4-mile Montara Mountain section, composed of granite with coastal cliffs rising to 1,000 feet above the sea.

The cliffs at Santa Cruz are cut into nonresistant Miocene sandstone, and in places are vertical or overhanging, with narrow discontinuous sandy beaches at their base. The site of an overhanging sandstone, photographed in 1950 (not illustrated), was rephotographed by the authors in 1968, and no change was observed. Detached sections of the sandstone cliffs have formed stacks offshore, and natural arches have been cut in several places. One of these arches, in the western part of Santa Cruz, collapsed between 1950 and 1968 (Figs. 11.15*a* and *b*). Another arch at Natural Bridges State Park, on the northern outskirts of Santa Cruz, will probably collapse in the near future.

DAVENPORT TO SOUTH SAN FRANCISCO [Figs. 11.16 through 11.21]   At Davenport, 10 miles northwest of Santa Cruz, a pier was built out for 0.5 mile from shore. In June 1968, when visited by the authors, the pier had been seriously damaged by storms and abandoned. Also, a 100-foot vertical cliff had receded so much that there was no longer any access to the pier from the town. A short distance

11.15 Arch Rock cut in sandstone in the western part of Santa Cruz. Photos by Shepard.

a June 22, 1950.

b June 1968. The arch has collapsed, and the rock (A in Fig. 11.15*a*) has been eroded. Most other features show no change.

east of Davenport is a small cove where a sand beach had formed against a small projecting headland. This was photographed in 1950 and again in 1968. Other than slight erosion at the top of a stack, no obvious changes were observed. However, the shale cliff from which the early photograph was taken had receded from about 20 to 50 feet.

West of Davenport, near Waddell Creek, the coastal highway runs for about a mile along the base of the shore cliffs, here composed of shale (Fig. 11.16). Erosion and slumping have been sufficiently rapid to necessitate dumping large boulders along the shore side of the highway.

At Point Año Nuevo (Fig. 11.17), the trend in the coast changes at nearly right angles. Año Nuevo Island (A), about a mile offshore from the point, is composed of sandstone similar to that forming the coast of the landward side. The cleared area shown behind the point and extending to the forested slopes, is a broad elevated coastal terrace. Evidently the island was formerly connected with the mainland. The photograph illustrates the manner in which waves refract around an obstruction, such as an island, and meeting on the lee side, deposit sediment. Eventually this process may form a tombolo, as at Point Sur (Fig. 11.9). The wind is reported to sweep across Point Año Nuevo with such force that it is very annoying to people on the beach on the lee side. The aerial photo shows straight lines of sand dunes reaching across the point from northwest to southeast. These lie between straight bands of vegetation (dark in photo).

Six miles to the northwest of Point Año Nuevo, Franklin Point (not shown) is very similar in shape and size and is also crossed by longitudinal dunes, but with a somewhat more northerly trend.

Half Moon Bay and Pillar Point (A in Fig. 11.18) are about 30 miles northwest of Año Nuevo. A fault with uplift on the west side trends parallel to but landward of the coast road (B). The west side of the

11.16 Coastal highway near Waddell Creek east of Pt. Año Nuevo. The coastal bluffs of shale have eroded rapidly. The coastal highway is protected from destruction by coarse rubble. Photo by Shepard, 1968.

11.17 Pt. Año Nuevo formed because of resistance of hard rock island offshore (A). Note wave refraction patterns, illustrating both refraction and interference of wave fronts. Strong northwest winds drift sand across the point. U.S. Department of Agriculture, 1956.

11.19 The Montara Mountain coast, south of San Francisco, offered a challenge to highway engineers. The coastal highway is frequently damaged at Devil's Slide (A). U.S. Department of Agriculture, 1956.

11.18 Half Moon Bay. The rounded shore of the bay was cut in weaker shales, which are faulted against hard sandstone at Pillar Pt. The new jetty and breakwater are shown by black line (D). U.S. Department of Agriculture, 1958.

fault exposes more resistant sandstone, so that sheer cliffs more than 100 feet high front the sea. Landward of the fault, an alluvial plain is cut in shales. The shore of Half Moon Bay has a broad beach of coarse sand. It is said to be the only safe swimming beach along this part of the California coast. Pillar

Point protects the beach from the waves of the strong northwest winds.

In 1959 and 1960, a jetty was constructed from Pillar Point, and another breakwater was extended from the shore at El Granada (shown in Fig. 11.18 by black line) to develop a small-boat harbor. This was followed by serious erosion of the coastal road (C) and a bridge was destroyed. Waves from the west strike the shore directly south of the breakwater, and eroded sand is shifted southeastward, but now there is no replenishment because of the jetty and breakwater. Waves reflected from the jetty add to the erosion.

11.20 View from coastal highway in the Montara Mountains near Devil's Slide. Photo by Shepard, 1958.

11.21 North of San Pedro Pt. (B in Fig. 11.19), the terminus of the Montara Mountains is flanked by a low coastal terrace along which a railroad was formerly operated. Erosion has removed several parts of the terrace, and the railroad was abandoned. Photo by Shepard, 1968.

From 8 to 12 miles north of Half Moon Bay, the coastal highway presents a spectacular display of highway engineering. As the highway crosses the Montara Mountains, there are steep-sided road cuts and a climb to more than 700 feet above sea level (Figs. 11.19 and 11.20). Rock slides on the precipitous

sea cliffs have frequently endangered the highway. Devil's Slide, descending abruptly 500 feet to the sea, is the most unstable section (A in Fig. 11.19).

At one time, a railroad was operated in a notch cut into the cliffs of this precipitous coast, but slides and wave erosion have destroyed much of the old roadbed. A mile north of San Pedro Point are remnants of the bench on which the railroad was located (Fig. 11.21). The sandy beach (foreground of photo) has formed at the seaward end of the flood plain of a small stream.

SAN FRANCISCO BAY AND THE GOLDEN GATE [Figs. 11.22 through 11.26] San Francisco Bay (Fig. 11.22), the largest indentation on the California coast, has a maximum northwest-southeast length of 55 miles, and a northeast-southwest width of about 10 miles, with an arm at the north extending 25 miles up Suisun Bay. San Francisco Bay receives the drainage of most of California through the San Joaquin and Sacramento Rivers. These rivers together drain all the Sierra Nevada Range (excluding aqueducts) through the Great Valley of California. They join near the head of the south arm of Suisun Bay. Farther west, Napa River and Petaluma Creek bring drainage into San Pablo Bay from the north. The long south segment of San Francisco Bay has much less drainage, only that of the lower Santa Clara Valley and the ranges on either side.

Around the relatively low borders of the bay are the homes of about 2.5 million people, along with great centers of industry, commerce, and education. In contrast, the open Pacific Coast north and south of the Golden Gate is almost entirely cliffed, and densely populated only for about 10 miles south of the Golden Gate and nowhere to the north.

To understand the origin of this embayment, it is necessary to review briefly the geological history of the area. Slow subsidence continued for a long time during the Tertiary, with many thousand feet of sediment accumulating in what is now the Great Valley of California. During this period, bordering areas were elevated periodically by warping or faulting. These included the Sierra Nevada on the east and the Coast Ranges on the west. The latter appeared first as coastal islands in a large sea. In the early Pleistocene, about 2 million years ago, the prehistoric Sacramento River was located near what is

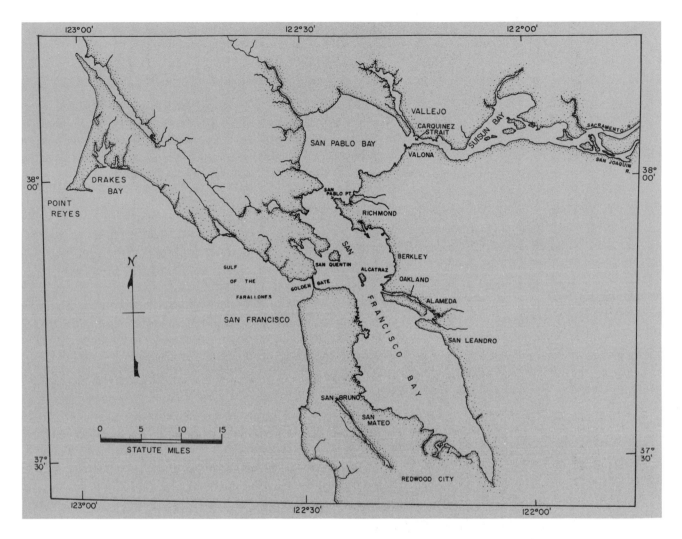

11.22 Map of San Francisco Bay region showing areas described in text. Shaded area (−12 ft.) shows how bay could be reduced from 400 to 187 square miles by filling to 12-foot depth.

now San Francisco Bay and drained the Great Valley westward across a series of parallel coastal ranges. Because these ranges generally were parallel to the modern coast, trending northwest-southeast, the intermontane valleys joined this prehistoric Sacramento River from the north and south. Continued mountain building during the mid-Pleistocene diverted the mouth of the ancient Sacramento River southward about 20 miles to its present outlet at the Golden Gate.

Changes in level in the San Francisco region in relation to the end of the glacial epoch have not yet been placed in accurate sequence. Until quite re-

cently, the outlets of the rivers that joined to flow through the Golden Gate were at least 350 feet below present sea level. This might have resulted either from recent subsidence of the Golden Gate area, from eustatic rise in sea level at the end of the latest glaciation, or from a combination of these causes. The attainment of the present bay shoreline was so recent that wave-cut cliffs have not developed along the borders of the bay, and there are only a few short gravel beaches.

The subsidence that formed the bay was rather localized near San Francisco, because the rivers that enter the open coast to the north and to the south do

11.23 Along the east side of San Francisco Bay. San Pablo Pt., the site of oil storage tanks and docks for ocean-going vessels, is the end of a range of hills extending into San Pablo Bay. Tidal marsh deposits (A) have filled part of the bay. U.S. Department of Agriculture, 1968.

not have drowned mouths. The greatest inundations within the bay are at the lower ends of rather small valleys, Coyote Creek to the south, Napa and Petaluma Creeks to the north.

The lower ends of the principal rivers, the Sacramento and San Joaquin, enter a relatively narrow bulbous bay with deltaic islands. Both rivers have jointly built a large deltaic plain in their lower

courses at the eastern end of Suisun Bay (Fig. 11.22). Here, the distributary streams are flanked by natural levees, often surmounted by artificial levees, allowing the use of the delta for agricultural purposes. At several places, the flats behind the levees are 2 to 4 feet below sea level, suggesting that subsidence may still be in progress. Much fine sediment must have accumulated in the bay, because the abandoned deep channels are largely filled. Eighty percent of San Francisco Bay is less than 30 feet deep. The bay will probably be largely filled within a few hundred years unless subsidence is resumed.

San Francisco Bay has a very complex shoreline. Eight or nine spurs of mountain chains project into the bay. San Pablo Point (Fig. 11.23), in the northeastern part of the bay, is the site of oil tanks, a refinery, and dockage for ocean-going vessels. San Quentin, a promontory nearly opposite, is where the California State Prison is located. Alcatraz, the top of a largely drowned rock hill out in the bay, was until recently the site of a highly secure federal prison.

At this writing, the bay is crossed by six major bridges, the shortest at Carquinez Strait (Fig. 11.24), the bottleneck lower end of Suisun Bay. The water in this strait, coming from the Sacramento and San Joaquin Rivers, is more turbid than that in San Pablo Bay. A long jetty was built into the latter to prevent the river mud from settling and blocking the shipping channel. Much silt has accumulated in San Pablo Bay and is responsible for its shallow depth. During the early history of California, a large source of this detritus was the debris from hydraulic mining of gold-bearing deposits along the rivers of the Sierra Nevada. This method of mining was prohibited by law in the early twentieth century, because gold-mine tailings buried much rich agricultural land.

In the Golden Gate narrows, the greatest channel depth is 382 feet, a short distance west of the center of the Golden Gate Bridge. The channel is maintained by a tidal current that reaches 6 knots during maximum ebb. Five or six miles seaward from the ocean terminus of Golden Gate, there is a large lunate bar resembling those formed at the mouths of streams along the southern Atlantic and eastern Gulf of Mexico Coasts. The bar is 25 to 35 feet deep, and waves break heavily on it during large wave periods. A 0.5-mile-wide channel has been cut through the center of this bar, and a natural channel, also 0.5-mile-wide, lies at the north end.

11.24 Carquinez Strait was a water gap along the combined Sacramento and San Joaquin Rivers in their crossing of the coast ranges until it was drowned by subsidence and by postglacial rise in sea level. It is crossed by one of the six San Francisco Bay bridges. U.S. Department of Agriculture, 1958.

An unusual mineral industry has been developed at the southern end of San Francisco Bay in a tidal marsh area near the delta plain of Coyote Creek. This area, locally 3 miles wide and exposed at low tide, was formerly traversed by an intricate maze of tidal channels (Fig. 11.25). It has now been partitioned into a series of plots bounded by dikes (Fig. 11.26). Bay water is introduced, then the borders of the plots are sealed and the water allowed to evaporate, precipitating its salt. The south end of San Francisco Bay is in a rain shadow in the lee of the Montara Mountains, and has about 6 months with little or no rainfall, during which the salt is precipitated.

The lack of change in San Francisco Bay by wave current activity is partly explained by the small width of the bay, giving a short fetch for the winds adequate to build up large waves. Silting of the bay from rivers entering it is the dominant natural process. Man-made changes, such as newly built land in the bay margins, causeways, jetties, breakwaters, bridge abut-

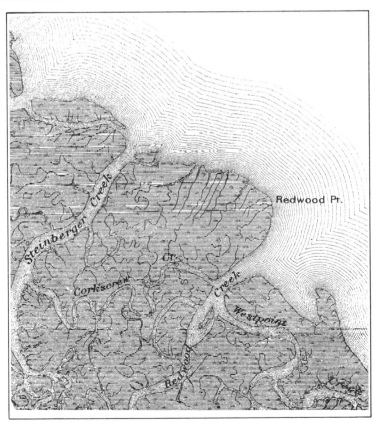

11.25 Tidal marshes and streams near the southern end of San Francisco Bay. From U.S. Coast and Geodetic Survey topographic map of Hayward quadrangle, 1915.

11.26 The area illustrated in Figure 11.25, now the site of a salt recovery industry, is in the rain shadow of the Montara Mountains. The tidal marshes have been divided into tracts that are filled with seawater, where the water is evaporated and the salt recovered. U.S. Department of Agriculture, 1956.

ments, and dockage for international trade, predominate over natural changes.

The shrinking size of San Francisco Bay, more than 40 percent since 1850, is a matter of great concern to conservationists, such as the Sierra Club. The U.S. Army Corps of Engineers consider depths less than 12 feet as "susceptible to reclamation." If all the areas less than 12 feet deep in San Francisco Bay were filled—and this might happen with present private and county ownership of these shoal areas— the size of the bay would be reduced from its 400 square miles to 187 (see Fig. 11.22). Hopefully, the state legislature will act to prevent this tragedy, but the real estate and industrial lobbies will certainly do what they can to reclaim the new land.

11.27 South of San Francisco, the San Andreas Fault (dashed line) reaches the coast. Another parallel fault comes to the coast (A). There is virtually no offset of the shore along the San Andreas Fault, because both sides are in easily eroded shale. Active erosion has destroyed most of a former highway along the coastal cliffs, as at B illustrated in Figure 11.28. Note proximity of many homes to fault line. By 1968, the entire area had been covered with houses. U.S. Department of Agriculture, 1956.

SAN ANDREAS FAULT COAST, SAN FRANCISCO TO PUNTA GORDA [Figs. 11.27 through 11.44]   The San Andreas Fault became world famous after the 1906 San Francisco earthquake. At this time, the earth's crust shifted horizontally along a northwest-southeast trending fault that runs through the south side of the San Francisco urban complex. This resulted in the displacement of fences and roads to a maximum of 20 feet. The violence of the sudden shift set up a major earthquake that caused great destruction of property and life and started terrible fires that destroyed much of San Francisco. Along the coast, bad landslides were one of the principal effects. The famous Cliff House restaurant fell into the sea at Golden Gate.

The San Andreas Fault is shown on geological maps as extending from Imperial Valley in south-central California to Point Arena, where it leaves the coast. To the south of Imperial Valley, it certainly continues, perhaps as a group of parallel faults, down into the Gulf of California. To the north, it has been traced by the new sonic profiling method as continuing near the coast all the way to Punta Gorda (Fig. 11.1). In this northern section, it probably also consists of several parallel faults; one certainly comes ashore near Shelter Cove.

The 20-foot offset that caused the 1906 San Francisco earthquake was what is called "a right lateral fault," meaning that if you were walking east or northeast along a road after the earthquake and came to the fault, you would find the road continuation to the right. In other words, the displacement moves the area on the southwest side of the fault to the northwest. This is important because it has been found that over the course of the past 60 million years (plus or minus), the western side of California has been moved many miles—perhaps hundreds of miles—to the northwest. The displacement of stream valleys at the fault is one of the phenomena by which this movement is demonstrated. This shifting of the surface raises the question of what has happened to the coast where the fault comes to the sea. In the 200 miles north of San Francisco, the fault clearly does leave the land at seven places (see Fig. 11.1) and finally is traced along the inner shelf close to the land until it bends seaward near Punta Gorda. One might expect to see large displacements of the coast at each of these junctures, but in most places there is little evident effect. Much more important are the elongate

11.28   Photograph at B in Figure 11.27, where slumping and erosion have destroyed a coastal highway, leaving a severed end (A). Photo by Shepard, June 1968.

depressions that characterize the San Andreas Fault. These account for indentations at Bolinas Bay, Bodega Bay, and the long arm of the sea at Tomales Bay. The displacements are not of the type that would push California into the sea in the foreseeable future, as was predicted by a crank in 1969.

SAN FRANCISCO PENINSULA AND THE SAN ANDREAS RIFT   South of San Francisco, an elongate valley with intermittent lakes extends to the northwest towards the seacoast, but this valley dies out before reaching the ocean (Fig. 11.27). The valley is apparently due to a rifting action along the San Andreas Fault. However, the coast is straight where the fault goes to sea. Except for Mussel Rock (A), where another fault comes to the coast just south of the San Andreas, there is no sign of any effect of the 1906 faulting. Either the wave erosion has been so rapid as to eliminate the displacements that have occurred in the past few thousand years since sea level virtually stabilized, or there had not been much displacement in the San Francisco area prior to the big earthquake. Marine erosion is active here in the soft rock cliffs (B). The old coastal highway (first a railroad bed) is largely destroyed, leaving many broken

0 MILES   .50   1.0
KM

11.29 Bolinas Lagoon, north of San Francisco, is a rift valley along the San Andreas Fault (straight line). The lagoon has been largely blocked by a sand spit, which is the site of a popular bathing beach. The perfectly rounded shoreline from Duxbury Pt. (B), including the spit, resembles Half Moon Bay south of San Francisco. U.S. Department of Agriculture, 1943.

remnants (Fig. 11.28). Much of the coast where the San Andreas extends out into the water has been so greatly modified by the bulldozing activities related to housing construction in the southern San Francisco metropolitan area that it is difficult to determine the natural terrain. One cannot help but wonder what the effect of another San Francisco earthquake would be on these hillsides covered with boxlike houses.

BOLINAS BAY [A in Fig. 11.29]   Ten miles north of the Golden Gate, the San Andreas first comes back onto the land at Bolinas Bay. The shallow lagoon, about a mile across, was clearly formed by the fault. It was originally one of the rift valleys, like the lakes of the San Andreas rift valley of the San Francisco Peninsula; but it has probably been widened somewhat by erosion and drowned by the sea level rise. The effect of Duxbury Point (B) has been to develop a countercurrent, and the resulting north flow has caused the building of a spit across all but the narrow entrance to the lagoon, leaving a gap so shoal that only small boats can enter.

Less than a mile northwest of the head of Bolinas Lagoon, the valley has a divide beyond which the waters flow northwest along a rift that can be traced for 30 miles (see Fig. 11.22). Tomales Bay occupies the northern part of this rift valley with Inverness, a resort town, at its head on the southwest side and Dillon Beach at the mouth of the bay on the northeast side. The earthquake fault extends down the center of Tomales Bay, except at the north end where it crosses two land projections. The rock formations on the southwest side of the rift are entirely different from those on the northeast, giving confirming evidence of the large displacement along the San Andreas Fault. On the southwest side of the bay, Tomales Point is a mass of granite hills up to 540 feet high and contrasts greatly with the gentle slopes and low sandy points on the Dillon Beach side of the bay. A comparison of the 1860 chart of the north end of Tomales Bay with that of 1957 (Fig. 11.30) shows an extensive buildup of sand on the north side of Sand Point. Also, the sand flats exposed at low water south of the point have been considerably modified. The study by C. C. Daetwyler of the sediments of Tomales Bay has shown that they are virtually undisturbed, as if there had not been much faulting other than that of the San Francisco earthquake rifts.

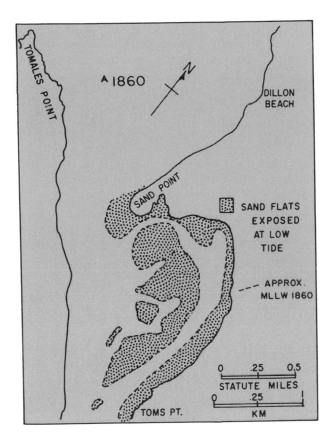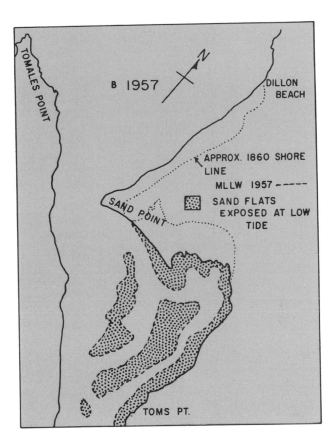

11.30 Tomales Bay, a rift valley northwest of Bolinas Bay. A sand spit was built part way across the bay near its northern end. The configuration of Sand Pt. in 1860 (A) and in 1957 (B). From Daetwyler (1965).

POINT REYES PENINSULA [Fig. 11.31]   One of the strange features of this peninsula 10 miles southwest of the rift valley in the Tomales Bay area, is Drakes Bay (A). According to one story, Sir Francis Drake anchored in the lee of Point Reyes (B) after missing San Francisco Bay. A metal seal, believed to have belonged to Drake, was found at Drakes Beach (C) and led to this story but, according to one account, this seal was picked up in the Oakland area of San Francisco Bay by a chauffeur and inadvertently dropped at Drakes Beach. Drakes Estero (D), whether or not a misnomer, is the only good estuary of the Chesapeake Bay type along the California coast and gives the impression of having once had a large drainage area both to the northwest and to the southeast. The relatively large drowned valley with its various branches must have had a larger drainage area during a low sea-level stage when it was eroded.

Probably the coast to the northwest has retreated for a long distance. This is indicated by the straight cliffs cut by waves into the dunes (E), which are seen along the coast northeast of the seaward end of Point Reyes. Further evidence of erosion is found in the curving cliffs that extend north and then east from the Coast Guard Station on the east side of Point Reyes toward Drakes Estero (Fig. 11.32). This erosion has cut off some of the southern part of the drainage pattern, as can be seen from the stub end of the bays west of Drakes Estero. After the erosion of the cliffs on the south side of the Point Reyes Peninsula, deposition has built a 3-mile spit across the eastern bays toward the entrance of Drakes Estero. The 1943 photos (Fig. 11.31) show a spit built eastward across the mouth of Drakes Estero; but the 1957 photos (Fig. 11.33) show this spit removed, and the spit from the east considerably lengthened.

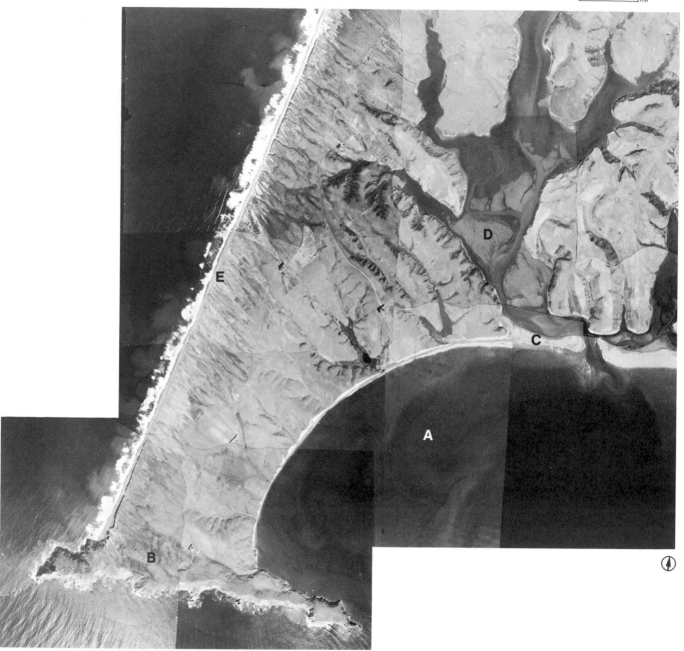

11.31 Pt. Reyes Peninsula (B) is a high east-west ridge of granite connected with the mainland block west of Bolinas Lagoon by a lower area of flat-lying sedimentary rock. The latter was dissected by a number of streams which were drowned, forming Drakes Estero (D). The entrance to the barrier is partially blocked by barrier spits. In producing the rounded outline of Drakes Bay, high bluffs have been cut in interstream divides, and small drowned streams have been blocked and filled with marsh vegetation (See Fig. 11.32). U.S. Department of Agriculture, 1943.

OUR CHANGING COASTLINES

11.32 Coastal bluffs on the north side of Drakes Bay, showing rapid cutting of weakly consolidated sediments by gullying and wave erosion. Note small cusps along beach. Photo by Shepard, 1968.

11.34 Bodega Bay and Harbor, a segment of the San Andreas Rift northwest of Tomales Bay. The harbor is partially closed by a barrier spit (A) resembling that in Bolinas Lagoon (Fig. 11.29). Bodega Head (C) is bordered landward by the southwestern of three parallel faults of the San Andreas system; two are shown by lines. Bodega Head is a tombolo tied to the shore by a broad sand plain on which modern dunes are active. U.S. Department of Agriculture, 1941.

11.33 Entrance to Drakes Estero (compare with C in Fig. 11.31). Note that the barrier spit west of the entrance has been destroyed; and the barrier spit to the east has been lengthened, occupying some of the area covered by the western spit of 1943. U.S. Coast and Geodetic Survey, 1957.

At the end of Point Reyes (B), there is an east-west ridge of granite rock that rises to 552 feet. Wave erosion has cut irregular coves into the south side and left many stacks. The view from the lighthouse on the west end of the point is spectacular, because the entire Point Reyes Peninsula can be seen, including Drakes Estero and the straight cliffs on the seaward side. Unfortunately, in 1968, the public access to the lighthouse had been closed because the narrow road was inadequate for the heavy traffic.

11.36 Coastal photographs at point B in Figure 11.35. Photos by Shepard.

a 1950. Tilted sandstone ledges along low coast.

b 1968. Almost no change is apparent in the coastal form in 18 years.

11.35 Pt. Arena. The San Andreas Rift crosses the coast a short distance north of the point. The rocks are tilted along the road southeast of Pt. Arena. U.S. Department of Agriculture, 1963.

BODEGA BAY [Fig. 11.34]   Five miles north of Tomales Bay, Bodega Bay is also along the San Andreas Rift. The outer bay is only slightly protected from the open ocean by discontinuous shoals along its seaward margin. Inside the shoals, the rift has depths to 72 feet. A hooked spit (A) extends from the east across most of Bodega Harbor. At the north end of Bodega Bay, the granitic Bodega Rock (B) and Bodega Head (C) form a protection from the waves. A broad belt of sand dunes connects Bodega Head with the mainland. The point has the same

granite rock as Tomales Point. Bodega Head was proposed as the site of an atomic power plant. The close proximity to the San Andreas Rift was apparently overlooked in these plans. Fortunately, the scientists of neighboring laboratories, under the leadership of Joel Hedgepeth, aroused so much opposition that the plan was dropped. The University of California at Berkeley has established a marine laboratory at Bodega Head, where they should be in a good position to report any new movements along the adjacent San Andreas Fault.

SALMON CREEK TO POINT ARENA AREA

The trace of the 1906 fissure crosses Salmon Creek north of Bodega Harbor, and the fault system leaves the coast again, but follows close to the land for 12 miles until it returns near Fort Ross. From that point for 44 miles, the fault extends along a series of inland valleys with a few lakes and finally goes out to sea 5 miles northeast of Point Arena. Here, as in the San Francisco Peninsula, the coast is not displaced where crossed by the fault. This is less surprising near Point Arena, however, because the coast is low and has a wide sand beach. Presumably it has been straightened subsequent to any offset movements along the fault. Again we seem to have evidence that, aside from the 1906 faulting, displacements may not have been very great in recent centuries.

The coast between Bodega Head and Point Arena is relatively straight with small projecting points and small indentations; the latter are the type produced by wave erosion rather than by drowning of river valleys. Along most of this coast, a terrace, again about 100 feet high, is the locus for the coast highway.

At Point Arena (Fig. 11.35), highly folded marine formations of Miocene age form the coast. Photographs taken from the same places in 1950 and 1968 show that erosion is not very rapid, because the arches and stacks look almost the same after 18 years (Figs. 11.36a and b). At the end of the point, however, photographs show that one mass of limestone has collapsed (Figs. 11.37a and b), and we are told by the lighthouse keepers that an arch had existed at this point until it disappeared in the spring of 1968. This arch does not show in the 1950 picture, so apparently it was formed between the two dates of photography. The comparisons of old and new photos taken at Point Arena appear to confirm the general indication found along the California coast that rock cliffs are for the most part quite stable, with little change during the past few decades. The exception all along the coast is where the cliffs are of soft shale or where soft shale layers weaken the structure, allowing collapse.

ELK TO FORT BRAGG, A WAVE EROSION COAST [Figs. 11.38 and 11.39]

Two miles north of the point where the San Andreas Fault goes out to sea near Point Arena, the character of the coast changes from relatively straight to highly irregular.

11.37 Point Arena near A in Figure 11.35. Photos by Shepard.
a 1950.

b 1968. Block in center has fallen; an arch was reported to have collapsed in the spring of 1968 before photo was taken.

The irregularities increase to the north, and are especially pronounced near the town of Mendocino (Fig. 11.38) and at Fort Bragg. Along here, the coast is cut into comparatively soft Pleistocene marine formations. It will be recalled that coasts can be made ir-

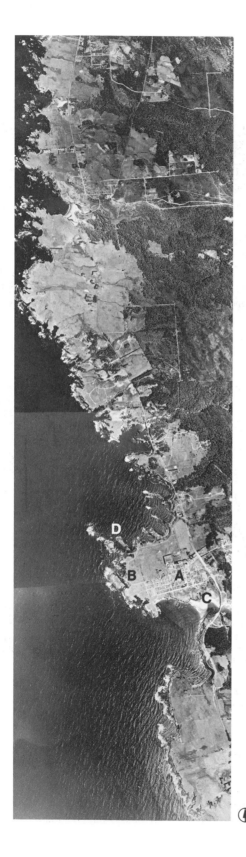

regular by drowning (Fig. 11.31), but the irregularities of this Northern California area are strikingly different in shape from typical drowned valleys. The Mendocino coast has none of the maple-leaf pattern estuaries. Scoop-shaped indentations characterize the coast with cliffed shorelines instead of low valleys at the heads of embayments. This is particularly evident around the Mendocino headland (B in Fig. 11.38). The major cause of these irregularities is certainly wave erosion. The general rise in sea level after the last glaciation tended to drown the valleys, but this may have been offset by a general upwarping of the coast. This differential movement is suggested by the higher level of the coastal terraces in this area, although no careful study has been made of this speculation. There is a slight indication of drowning at the mouths of some of the larger rivers, such as Big River (C) just south of the headland on which Mendocino is located; but the virtual absence of broad floodplains in their lower courses testifies against any appreciable fill.

Joe W. Johnson, of the University of California at Berkeley, discovered a group of photographs taken in 1860 near Mendocino and Fort Bragg. He visited the area in 1960 and took photographs from the same points. The differences are noticeable in all cases, indicating that this coast is being cut back by the waves. Figure 11.39 shows one of Johnson's comparisons at the location of D in Figure 11.38. This is an example of significant erosion of stacks and jutting points.

Another opportunity to investigate recent erosion along this coast came from comparing the present configuration with old pictures taken at St. Anthony Point, near Elk. These showed almost no change in the past 18 years. As far as could be seen from the brief inspection, the coast does not appear to be retreating sufficiently to endanger coastal highways or residences built along the coastal cliffs.

Just north of Fort Bragg, the irregular wave erosion coast comes to an end. The rocky points continue for 2 miles, terminating at MacKerricher State Park. For about 5 miles north of this park, there is a straight sand dune coast with the usual north-northeasterly

11.38 Very uneven coast near and north of Mendocino (A), due to wave erosion, has abundant rock stacks and coves. Big River enters the ocean at C, but has formed no delta. U.S. Department of Agriculture, 1963.

11.39 Coastal erosion 1860–1960 (at D in Fig. 11.38). Provided by J. W. Johnson.

a 1860. Note arch at A and rock at B.

b 1960. The arch (A) has partially collapsed, and the dark colored rock has been eroded.

11.40 Point Delgada (A) is in the midst of a steeply cliffed coast. Shelter Cove (B) can be reached by a narrow mountain road. Fault movement occurred just east of Shelter Cove during the 1906 earthquake. One of the faults of the San Andreas system crosses a few miles of land in this area. Redwood forests lie just inland from the coastal cliffs. U.S. Department of Agriculture, 1954.

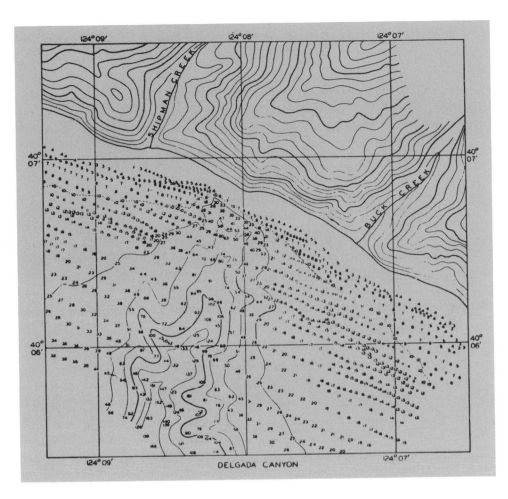

11.41 Seven miles northwest of Pt. Delgada, a submarine canyon heads 1,000 feet offshore opposite a high cliff and midway between two stream valleys. The San Andreas Fault probably parallels the coast and displaced the canyon head, which originally connected with one of the coastal streams. From Shepard and Dill (1966).

trend typical of Central California dune coasts. The sand has come to the sea from Tenmile River and, being moved to the south, has built out the coast with a wide beach backed by dunes.

MOUNTAIN WALL COAST—CAPE VIZCAINO TO PUNTA GORDA [Figs. 11.40 and 11.41] North of the mouth of Tenmile River, the coast becomes more mountainous. Narrow raised terraces, cut into a fringe of Pleistocene deposits, continue for about 7 miles, and then at Cape Vizcaino, the steep mountain slope comes to the shore. This mountain coast is virtually continuous to the northeast for 50 miles. The coast highway is forced inland, crossing

the mountains to the northeast to meet the Redwood Highway. Because of the absence of a coastal highway for the southern 25 miles, little can be reported about this part of the coast. At Point Delgada (A in Fig. 11.40), however, a good road leads down to Shelter Cove (B). This is the only anchorage along this mountain coast, and even it is not protected from occasional south winds. Also, the *williwaws* that frequently blow down from the mountains are very violent; and, even though they are offshore winds, they are a danger to ships, causing anchors to drag.

According to the late Francois Matthes, of the U.S. Geological Survey, in 1906 at the time of the

San Francisco earthquake, a displacement occurred and a large crack opened in the cliffs to the east of Shelter Cove. This is the only indication that the San Andreas Fault zone comes ashore along this coast. As at other places where the fault, or a branch of it, extends across the land-sea boundary, there is no displacement of the coast to indicate a large horizontal shift. Fifteen miles to the south, J. R. Curray, using the reflection profile method, discovered the San Andreas Fault apparently headed toward Point Delgada. The fault that was displaced in 1906 at Point Delgada can be traced to the northwest for 2 miles, where it goes again into the sea. Shepard, on trips along the beach from Point Delgada to Punta Gorda, found that the rocks in the southern half of the area are greatly disturbed. They have all the structural indications of the violent movements that should accompany a displacement of many miles along the San Andreas Fault zone.

The most interesting feature is found 7 miles northwest of Point Delgada. Here there is a straight mountain wall not interrupted by canyons (Fig. 11.41), but directly offshore a submarine canyon heads into the coast and is apparently chopped off about 800 feet from the shore. An escarpment with a 45-degree slope leads down from depths of 40 to 200 feet. It seems highly probable that the head of the canyon formerly connected with one of the land valleys, and the horizontal shift, typical of the San Andreas Fault, has separated the canyon from its head, leaving the uneroded mountain wall directly inside the sea floor valley. Unfortunately, it is impossible to decide which land valley, if any, connected with the submarine canyon.

Evidence of the effects of the San Andreas Fault farther to the northwest is clearly provided by the submarine topography. About 5 miles south of Punta Gorda, the continental shelf has some elongate depressions running northwest-southeast that appear to be comparable to the rift valleys along many mainland portions of the San Andreas Fault. Directly seaward of Punta Gorda, there is an escarpment sloping to the north and running first in a west-northwesterly direction and then west. To the north of this escarp-

11.42 The coast between Punta Gorda and Cape Mendocino has broader beaches than areas farther south. The Mattole River (C) has filled an estuary and comes to the sea near the head of a large submarine canyon (D). U.S. Department of Agriculture, 1959.

ment, the 6,000-foot curve is displaced landward about 40 miles. This is what would be expected if movement along the San Andreas had caused a shift of 40 miles. Thus we have evidence at this point of the amount of displacement along this great fault. How long a period of movement was necessary for such a shift is entirely unknown. Probably many millions of years.

We have no comparative pictures along this mountain-front coast, so we find it impossible to estimate how fast it is receding under wave erosion. Projections, like Delgada, are subject to more concentrated attack than the straight portions. Figure 11.40 shows the indentations indicative of wave erosion in the exposed areas of Point Delgada. Most of the rest of this mountain coast is quite straight; but a scattering of small stacks stand out beyond the sea cliffs, suggesting that the coast may formerly have been more irregular and was straightened by wave erosion. Beaches are generally missing along the mountain coast south of Point Delgada but are sufficiently continuous to the north of this point to allow easy access on foot or horseback. At Big Flat Creek, 10 miles north of Point Delgada, a protruding delta fan extends out about 0.33 mile beyond the cliffs. Here, also, there may be a filled estuary. The only other possible example of a filled estuary along this mountain coast is seen at Usal, near the southern end of the mountain-front coast, where some remnants of an estuary are shown on the topographic map of the area.

PUNTA GORDA–CAPE MENDOCINO AREA [Figs. 11.42 and 11.43]   North of the coast influenced by the San Andreas Fault, coastal characteristics change somewhat. The aerial photo compilation (Fig. 11.42) shows broad sand flats (A, B), especially in the bight between Punta Gorda and Cape Mendocino. These sand flats are a type of berm but, unlike most berms, they have rocks or stacks at their outer margins. Apparently they are topped by occasional high waves introducing sand. Another feature that contrasts with most of the area to the south is the alluvial valley with a width of about 0.5 mile, which extends well up the Mattole River (C). This remnant of a long estuary can be seen in the photograph. The Mattole River mouth is nearly inside the head of a large submarine canyon. The stack just north of the river mouth (D) is at the canyon head.

0 MILES 1.0 2.0 3.0 4.0 5.0

11.43 Cape Mendocino (A), the westernmost point of the Pacific Coast of the United States, excluding Alaska. U.S. Department of Agriculture, 1954.

Here we return to the more normal relation between submarine canyons and large land valleys, since one branch of the canyon points directly in toward the Mattole River. In the aerial photo, the spit built part way across the mouth of Mattole River seems to indicate a north drift; but the U.S. Geological Survey topographic map, made a few years earlier, shows a continuation of the spit south across the river mouth. Evidently the current flows alternately in either direction.

According to Robert Nason (personal communication), there are notches in the cliffs and flat-topped stacks that vary from 10 to 20 feet above sea level all along the coast from Punta Gorda to Cape Mendocino. Exact levels have not been determined, so there is no assurance that these terrace levels have not been warped. Nor is there any evidence of their age.

Cape Mendocino (Fig. 11.43) is of special interest in being the westernmost point along the Pacific coast of the conterminous United States. The road maps show that this cape can be reached on an unimproved road leading to the Coast Guard Station. All around the cape are myriads of rock stacks extending almost a mile out from the cliffs.

REFERENCES

Cooper, W. S., 1960. Coastal dunes of Monterey Bay, California. *Geol. Soc. Amer. Bull.*, vol. 71, p. 1845.

Curray, J. R., 1966. Geologic structure on the continental margin, from sub-bottom profiles, Northern and Central California. In E. H. Bailey (ed.), Geology of Northern California. *Calif. Div. Mines and Geol. Bull.* 190, pp. 337–342.

Daetwyler, C. C., 1965. Marine geology of Tomales Bay, Central California. Univ. Calif., Scripps Inst. of Oceanography, Ph.D. thesis.

Dibblee, T. W., Jr., 1950. Geology of southwestern Santa Barbara County, California. *Calif. Dept. Natural Resources, Div. Mines Bull.* 150.

Dickinson, W. R., and Arthur Grantz, 1968. *Proceedings on Conference on Geologic Problems of San Andreas Fault System.* Stanford Univ. Publ., Geol. Sci., vol. 11.

Hinds, N. E. A., 1952. *Evolution of the California Landscape.* Calif. Div. Mines Bull. 158.

Howard, A. D., 1951. *In* Development of the landscape of the San Francisco Bay counties. *Calif. Div. Mines Bull.* 154, pp. 95–106.

Jenkins, O. P., and others, 1951. Geologic guidebook of the San Francisco Bay counties—history, landscape, geology, fossils, minerals, and routes of travel. *Calif. Div. Mines Bull.* 154, pp. 95–106.

Johnson, J. W., 1961. Historical photographs and the coastal engineer. *Shore and Beach*, April (no pp.).

Lawson, A. C., and others, 1908. The California earthquake of April 18, 1906. *Rept. State Earthquake Inv. Comm., Carnegie Inst., Washington Publ.* 87.

Matthes, F. E., 1907. (Quoted by) A. C. Lawson, The California earthquake of April 18, 1906. *State Earthquake Inv. Comm. Rept., Carnegie Inst., Washington Publ.* 87, vol. 1, pt. 1, pp. 54–58.

Reiche, Parry, 1937. Geology of the Lucia quadrangle, California. *Univ. Calif. Dept. Geol. Sci. Bull.*, vol. 24, no. 7, pp. 115–168.

Rice, S. J., 1961. Geologic sketch of the northern Coast Ranges. *Calif. Div. Mineral Info. Service*, vol. 14, no. 1, pp. 1–9.

Shepard, F. P., and R. F. Dill, 1966. *Submarine Canyons and Other Sea Valleys.* Rand McNally & Company, Chicago.

Starke, G. W., and A. D. Howard, 1968. Polygenetic origin of Monterey Submarine Canyon. *Geol. Soc. Amer. Bull.*, vol. 79, no. 7, pp. 813–826.

Trask, P. D., Jr., 1926. Geology of Point Sur quadrangle, California. *Univ. Calif. Dept. Geol. Sci. Bull.*, vol. 16, no. 6, pp. 119–186.

————, 1952. Source of beach sand at Santa Barbara, California, as indicated by mineral and grain studies. *Beach Erosion Board, Dept. Army Corps Engrs., Tech Memo.* 28.

Ver Planck, W. E., 1951. Salines in the Bay area. *Calif. Div. Mines, Bull.* 154, pp. 219–222.

Weaver, C. E., 1949. Geology of the Coast Ranges immediately north of San Francisco Bay region. *Geol. Soc. Amer., Memo.* 35.

Woodring, W. P., and M. N. Bramlette, 1950. Geology and paleontology of the Santa Maria District, California. *U.S. Geol. Surv. Paper* 222.

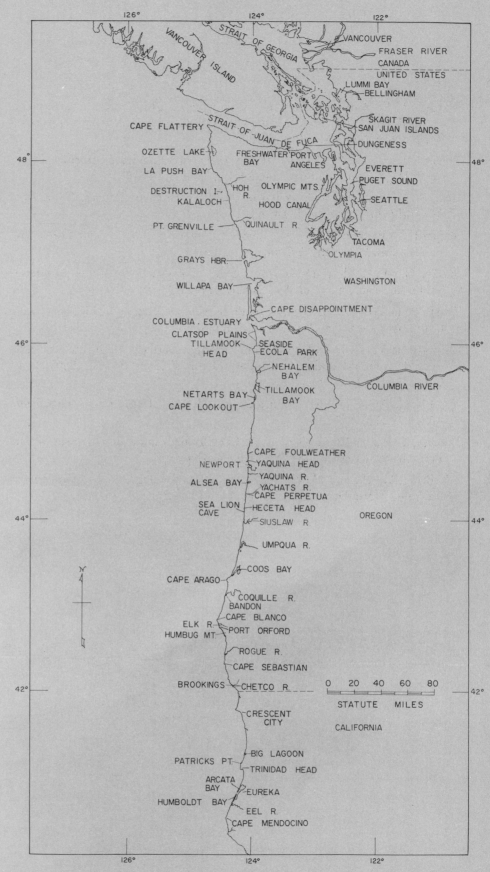

12.1 Index map of the coast of Northern California, Oregon, and Washington, showing localities described.

Storm-Exposed Open Coasts to Deeply Indented Glaciated Coasts

Northernmost California to Canada

12
A few miles north of Cape Mendocino, the rugged mountainous coast of Northern California comes to an end. The remainder of the relatively straight West Coast (Fig. 12.1) that continues up to the Strait of Juan de Fuca alternates between lowlands associated with the large rivers and mountainous tracts of comparatively short extent. The lowlands are mostly bordered by long barrier spits with partly filled lagoons on the landward side. In northernmost California, these barriers trend in a north-northeasterly direction, as do most of the barrier coasts farther south (described in Chap. 11). In Oregon, the barrier trends are mostly north; and, finally, in Washington, the direction is somewhat west of north. The mountain tracts that intervene between lowlands are bordered by a rugged coast with many prominent points and with myriads of off-lying stacks and small islands.

The climate continues to change going north from California. The long dry summers come to an end; and the annual rainfall increases until it reaches a high of more than 100 inches in portions of the Olympic Mountains in northern Washington, ten times as much as falls at San Diego. With higher rainfall, all the principal valleys have permanent streams, and the mountainous coasts are covered with a heavy growth of trees.

The winds are somewhat different in this northern area from those off Southern and Central California. Off Oregon, according to Samuel N. Dicken, of the University of Oregon, winter storms have a preponderance of southerly winds, whereas northwest winds are predominant in summer. As a result, the winter storms drive the sand north along the beaches, and the smaller waves of summer return it to the south. This produces a net transport to the north.

Help in revising this chapter was given by J. S. Creager, of the University of Washington.

343

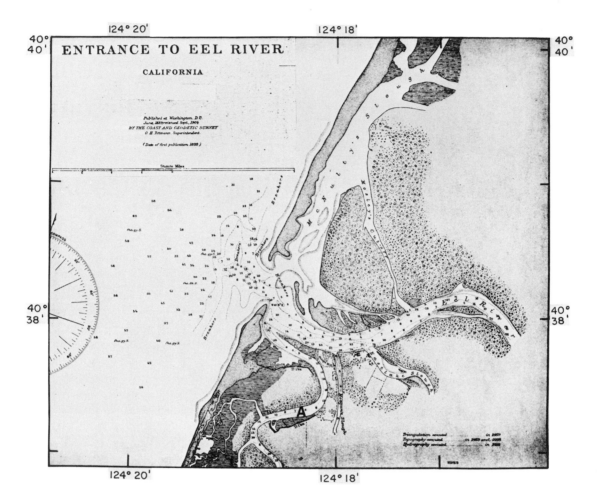

12.2 Changes in the entrance to Eel River estuary.
a 1899, U.S. Coast and Geodetic Survey.

Comparing sand accumulation along north and south jetties at harbor mouths, one finds that in general there is somewhat more deposition on the south side.

Embayments along the northern part of the West Coast virtually lack the branching pattern that is so common on the South and East Coasts of the United States. However, there are a number of deeply penetrating estuaries without tributaries. The three largest estuaries are in a restricted area from the mouth of the Columbia to Grays Harbor. Farther south, smaller embayments are found at the mouths of most of the larger rivers. The entrances to most of these embayments are considerably restricted by large barriers; and, in most cases, jetties have been built to maintain channels for navigation.

A complete change in coastal character begins where the powerful lobe of Pleistocene ice moved out to sea through the Strait of Juan de Fuca. This strait is the southernmost of the deep glacial troughs that continue north along the coasts of British Columbia and southern Alaska. The effects of glaciation are also very marked in the inner reaches of the Strait of Juan de Fuca, where such intricate embayments as Puget Sound and the numerous passageways between the San Juan Islands produce a coast even more irregular than that we have described for northern Maine. Instead of the woeful lack of natural harbors, such as characterize most of the West Coast south of Juan de Fuca, the glaciated area has myriads of shelters for boats of all sizes.

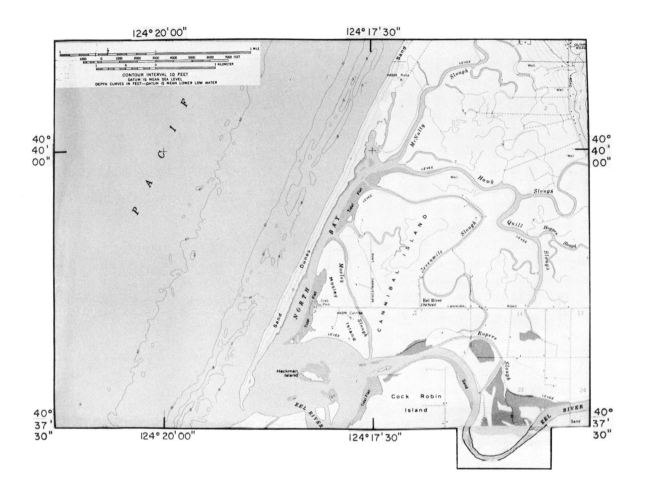

b 1959, U.S. Geological Survey topographic map, Cannibal Island quadrangle. Note that the entrance to Eel River has widened since 1899, while tidal inlet has narrowed.

The coastal modifications along the northwestern United States are not as well documented as those along most of the East and South Coasts. However, we have a few good sources of information. Dicken has made a considerable study of the recent changes of the Oregon coast. Reports from the University of Washington's Department of Oceanography discuss the bays and other areas along the coast of Washington. The old harbor charts of the Coast and Geodetic Survey show some modification of shorelines. The changes at the mouth of the Columbia are particularly well documented from the studies of the U.S. Army Corps of Engineers. In general, the effects of jetties and breakwaters along this northern coast are as great as along the California coast, to the south.

EEL RIVER, CALIFORNIA [Fig. 12.2]   Eight miles north of Cape Mendocino, the mountainous coast terminates and a relatively narrow coastal plain extends for about 30 miles in a north-northeasterly direction. The straight coast along this section includes a large sand barrier with a partly filled lagoon on the inside. To the south of the Eel River mouth, the only remnant of the lagoon is a twisting slough running through the marshes. The Eel River, named for the graceful loops (Fig. 12.2b) along its lower course, is the largest of the rivers coming to the California coast from the northern Coast Ranges. The river has filled most of the estuary that extended some 15 miles into the coast a few thousand years ago when postglacial sea level rise had neared its end.

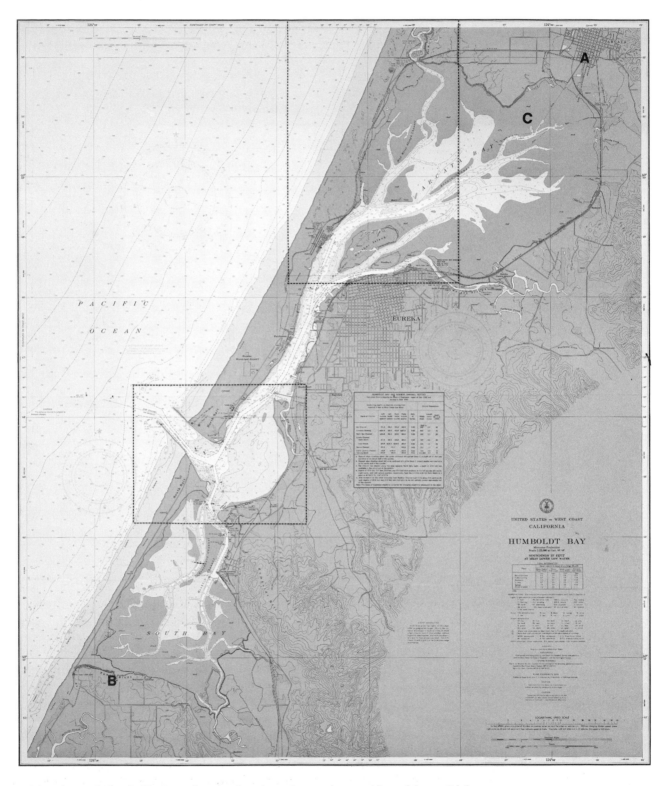

12.3 Chart of Humboldt Bay, showing barrier spits on the outside and large tidal deltas in Arcata and South Bays. Channels are also indicated. Dashed lines show location of Figures 12.4 and 12.5. U.S. Coast and Geodetic Survey Chart 5832, 1965.

However, comparing the 1899 chart (Fig. 12.2a) with a recent topographic survey (Fig. 12.2b), we find that the mouth of the Eel River is farther from the barrier than it was 55 years ago. In the earlier survey, the levees at the river mouth were longer. On the other hand, more land has been added to the south, where sediment has filled the lagoon on the inside of the barrier. Also, the channels in the island on the north side of the river mouth have been filled. Another indication of deposition is that the channels, which formerly allowed small boats to ply the river mouth, have now become so shallow that the Coast and Geodetic Survey no longer issues the chart that showed the depths for 4 miles up the Salt River (A in Fig. 12.2a) and the lower 2.5 miles of the Eel River.

The barriers at the river mouth have changed, but these changes may be seasonal and do not appear to be drastic.

HUMBOLDT BAY [Figs. 12.3, 12.4, and 12.5] Eureka is the only California port city north of San Francisco where large ships can enter. Humboldt Bay (Fig. 12.3) is a lagoon 13 miles long inside a wide barrier island with a natural gap near the south end that is stabilized by jetties. The channels in the bay are maintained artificially and extend both north to Eureka and south to Fields Landing.

Humboldt Bay was first entered in 1806, by a Russian ship under an American captain. In 1849, the bay was visited by a scientist, Dr. Josiah Gregg, with an American party who were investigating possibilities of developing a port. Shortly afterward, Arcata (A) at the northern end of the bay, was founded, but the broad mud flats made this an unsatisfactory port, and Eureka was established as the port a few years later because it offered better shipping capabilities. In 1859, this westernmost city of the conterminous United States became the county seat. Because of trouble with the Indians during the 1850s, a fort was established at Humboldt Heights (B), next to the south end of the bay. The chief historical interest of this fort is that a trouble-prone subaltern, who was second in command of the fort in the early days, later became our most famous Civil War general, U. S. Grant.

As shown in Figure 12.3, the barrier spit at the north end of the bay is wider than that to the south. At the north, the wide beach is bordered by an ex-

12.4 Portion of barrier at north end of Humboldt Bay with old vegetated dunes and north-south active longitudinal dunes. Note giant cusps and rip currents on seaward side of barrier. Delta of Mud River to north. U.S. Department of Agriculture, 1954.

tensive dune tract (Fig. 12.4) with older dunes covered with vegetation (A) and younger active dunes (B) trending north-south. This barrier is about 4,000 feet wide, whereas the south spit averages only about 1,400 feet and has much smaller dune tracts. Deposition has been somewhat greater along the north jetty, indicating the predominance of south-flowing currents. However, a comparison of the 1929 survey (Fig. 12.5a) with the 1965 chart and the 1954 aerial photographs shows that during the past few decades no further growth has occurred, and actually there has been a slight loss of sediment next to the north jetty. The older survey indicates that the south barrier has been growing in width with an increase of about 300 feet, but the north barrier has scarcely changed.

The lagoon inside the barriers is mostly very shallow. As indicated on the 1929 chart, natural channels that were maintained by the tides extend about 7 miles to the north past Eureka and almost to Arcata. On the south, two channels wind for about 4 miles

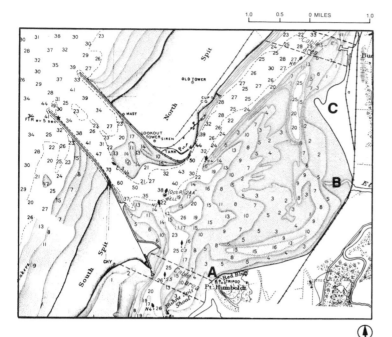

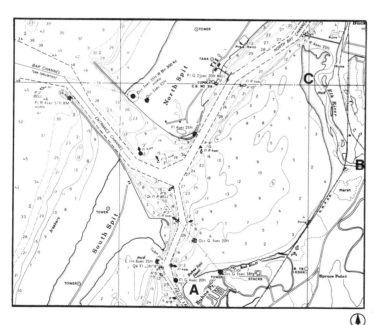

12.5 Changes of depositional features near entrance to Humboldt Bay during a 36-year interval. From U.S. Coast and Geodetic Survey charts.

a 1929 survey. Note that Elk River (B) enters directly into the bay. A spit (C) north of the river. Another spit extends south of Red Bluff (A).

b 1965 survey. Elk River (B) has now shifted its entrance and flows along the enlarged spit (C). The spit south of Red Bluff has grown into a low promontory.

nearly to the south end of the bay. These channels have been modified by dredging, so that they are slightly different in the 1965 chart from that of 1929 (Fig. 12.3).

The pattern of shoals at the north end of the bay is very much the same in the charts of the two dates and suggests that a large tidal delta had been built into Arcata Bay by incoming tides. Deposition had also occurred along the north end of the bay as the result of entering streams. This deposition is a combination of subaerial deltas (C) and mud flats exposed at low tide. The south end of the bay also has a combination of stream deltas and a tidal delta, but the latter is less developed at this end. Deposition at the bay ends between the 1929 and 1965 surveys has been far less than at the mouth of the Eel, as expected from the smaller entering streams.

Directly inside the pass, the east side of the bay has a large concavity, evidently due to a combination of waves coming through the opening and to tidal currents on the inside. This concavity has grown larger since the 1929 survey (Fig. 12.5) by about 1,000 feet. Part of this increase is due to the growth of the sand spit (C) north of the concavity. By 1965, this had lengthened 0.33 mile over that in 1929; and the mouth of the Elk River (B) had shifted to the right shortly after the 1929 survey, flowing along the newly developed spit.

TRINIDAD HEAD–PATRICKS POINT AREA, CALIFORNIA [Fig. 12.6]   The low barrier coast comes to an end just south of Trinidad Head. Six miles of cliffed rocky coast with protruding capes follow. At the southern end of this coast, just north of Moonstone Beach (A), there is a hole in the rocks 50 feet back from the edge of the cliffs, which connects with a submarine cave. During periods of high waves, geysers of water are sent up through this hole, making fountains that are comparable with the Spouting Horn, near Honolulu.

Trinidad Head is the most spectacular point among the coastal projections. It has a circular hill that rises like a volcano to a height of 380 feet (Fig. 12.6). The coast conforms to the base of this hill, but the rock is an old metamorphic type and has nothing to do with vulcanism. The headland forms a protection for boats from all but large southerly waves. Despite this protection, the harbor is not very satisfacory because of the shallow water inside the point; and kelp

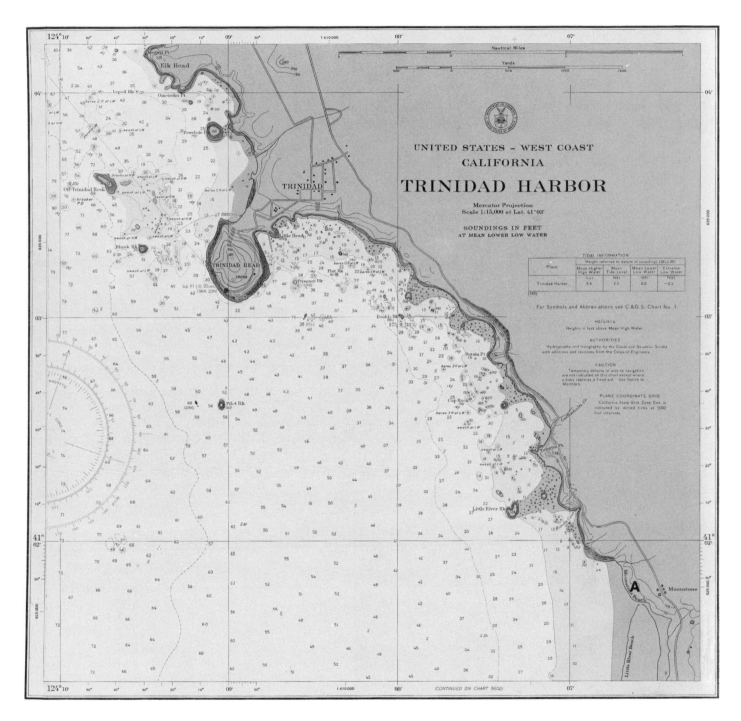

12.6 Trinidad Head, a tombolo on the northern California coast. U.S. Coast and Geodetic Survey Chart 5846, 1938.

12.7 Big Lagoon, an estuary closed off by a narrow barrier. A delta (A) has formed at the mouth of Maple Creek. U.S. Department of Agriculture, 1954.

and numerous stacks make it dangerous to enter during a fog. The bay was discovered in 1775 by the Spaniard Bruno de Hezeta. The town of Trinidad has had an interesting history. It is now only a village; but in the gold rush days, according to Aubrey Drury, it had a roaring camp with a population of 3,000.

Patricks Point, at the northern end of the 6-mile rocky promontory, has a very scenic state park with small rock-walled canyons. One trail leads down to a beach where agates and opals are abundant in the coarse sand. The park is famous for its spring wild-flowers and its fine growth of redwoods.

BIG LAGOON AND ADJACENT BARRIER COASTS [Fig. 12.7]   North of Patricks Point, a straight barrier coast stretches for 20 miles with the usual north-northeasterly trend. The barriers largely border Pleistocene and postglacial sands, but rocky tracts intervene that cause minor coastal projections. In the southern 8 miles of this straight coast, three lagoons have all been cut off from the ocean by barriers. The southernmost of these, Big Lagoon (Fig. 12.7), is bordered by a 4-mile beach. According to an 1870 chart, there was an opening at the north end of the barrier, but now it is closed. The stream that enters the lagoon at the south has extended its delta since the old chart was made. The lagoons farther north have, as far as we know, been completely barred since the earliest surveys. All these lagoons have estuaries to the southeast that have been partly filled.

CRESCENT CITY, CALIFORNIA, AND ITS TSUNAMI (TIDAL WAVE) [Figs. 12.8, 12.9, and 12.10]   Crescent City, 15 miles south of the Oregon line, is unique for the West Coast of the United States (except Alaska) in having had the only very serious damage from the great sea waves that spread from submarine earthquake centers. These tsunamis (popularly called tidal waves) are caused by sudden movements on the sea floor. Oscillations set up in the sea over an area where the sea floor has had a vertical displacement send out trains of waves for thousands of miles without losing much of their power. In recent years, a series of disastrous waves have hit the Hawaiian Islands (Chap. 15) and parts of southern Alaska (Chap. 13); but the West Coast of the contiguous United States had little damage from such

12.8 Effects of 1964 tsunami in Crescent City Harbor.
a Wrecked fishing fleet at Crescent City, California, following 1964 tsunami. Harris Studio, Crescent City, 1964.

waves until 1964, when the huge Alaskan earthquake made an exception. The fourth and fifth waves, each 12 feet high, seriously damaged the waterfront at Crescent City. Twenty-nine blocks of the business district were largely destroyed, with an estimated loss of $27 million. Twenty-one boats of the fishing fleet in the harbor were greatly damaged (Fig. 12.8*a*). The same tsunami caused $250,000 loss of property at Seaside and Cannon Beach, Oregon, and four people were drowned at DePoe Bay, also in Oregon.

Comparative aerial photos (Figs. 12.9*a* and *b*), taken respectively 13 years before the tsunami and a few days after, show some of the effects, although extensive building during the 13 years makes comparison difficult. Also, the small scale of the buildings in the photos fails to show much of the damage along the waterfront. Points where changes are evident have been labeled with the same letters (A to E in Figs. 12.9*a* and *b*). At E, however, the swimming

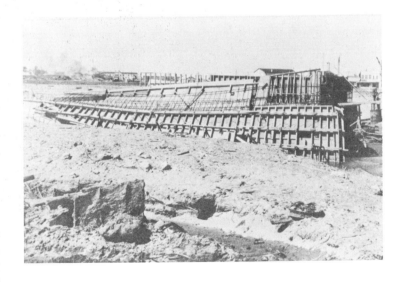

b Swimming pool at Crescent City, California, destroyed by tsunami. Harris Studio, Crescent City, 1964.

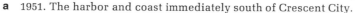

12.9 Shore near Crescent City, California, before and after 1964 tsunami. A to E are same locations on both photos. U.S. Coast and Geodetic Survey.

a 1951. The harbor and coast immediately south of Crescent City.

b April 6, 1964. Crescent City and adjoining coast. The buildings (D) were seriously damaged or destroyed, and new gullies (C) were cut across the beach. There was much damage to the long jetty (G).

pool had not been built at the time of the 1951 photographs. The results of the waves on the pool are shown in Figure 12.8*b*.

One of the surprising features of the damage at Crescent City is that the locality is apparently protected from the north-approaching waves by Point St. George (F in Fig. 12.9*b*) and a series of small off-lying islands and reefs. Also, the long jetty (G) that protects the harbor from ordinary wind waves was evidently quite ineffective. Furthermore, several other tsunamis had previously swept down from Alaska and caused great devastation in the Hawaiian Islands, which are approximately the same distance from Alaska as is Crescent City; but these earlier waves did not produce any appreciable damage here nor at any other place along the West Coast. Conversely, the 1964 waves that originated in Alaska did not damage Hawaii. At the time of the 1946 Aleutian earthquake, the largest waves on the West Coast of the contiguous United States occurred at Half Moon Bay, California (Fig. 11.18), and at the city of Santa Cruz. At both of these places, the water rose 11 feet above normal compared to 6 feet at Crescent City. It is interesting that all these locations are on the south sides of projecting points. In the

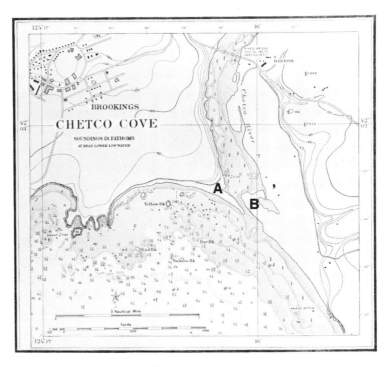

12.10 Chetco Cove, Brookings, Oregon.
a 1933. Mouth of Chetco River. Note spits (A and B) at mouth of river. U.S. Coast and Geodetic Survey Chart 5896.

b 1952. One spit (A) has been greatly reduced in size, while the other (B) has lengthened, overlapping A. Oregon State Highway Department photo.

12.10

c 1965. After jetties had been built on both sides of the river entrance, eliminating the west spit. The lagoon behind the southeast spit (B in Figs. 12.10a and b) has been filled. Note the numerous headlands and stacks and the round cove (B) with the pocket beach. Brookings has now grown to occupy most of the coastal land. U.S. Department of Agriculture.

Hawaiian Islands, large waves approaching from the north have also caused damage south of projecting points. Probably the waves rose even higher north of the points; but towns were located in the lee, and this is where the damage was evident. In any case, it is clear that land projections do not serve as much protection from this special type of wave.

The explanation for Point St. George, north of Crescent City, is that outcrops of hard rock at the edge of the land have inhibited erosion. After this fringe of hard rock is finally removed, the coast should retreat rapidly because only unconsolidated alluvium is found on the inside of this rocky fringe.

BROOKINGS AREA, OREGON [Figs. 12.10, 12.11, and 12.12]   Brookings is the first city north of the California-Oregon line. It is in the midst of a hilly to mountainous coast, although the shore is relatively smooth south of the city. The Chetco River

enters just south of Brookings and has a small estuary at its mouth. In 1957, jetties were constructed to provide a harbor (Fig. 12.10c). Before the jetties were built, the beach consisted of two spits of variable length. In 1933 (Fig. 12.10a), they were nearly the same length, and the north spit overlapped the south. By 1952 (Fig. 12.10b), the south spit was far longer and overlapped the short stubby north spit. In 1965, after the jetties were built, the spits had disappeared (A in Fig. 12.10c) because of the jetties; the south beach had widened greatly since 1952, due to extensive fill against the south jetty. This fill made it necessary to lengthen the jetties to prevent sand from blocking the harbor entrance. The greater deposition on the south is a result of the strong south winds in winter. Samuel Dicken described the sand on the south beach as mostly fine-grained; whereas on the small beach next to the north jetty, the beach is predominantly gravel resting on bedrock.

The town of Brookings is located on a 60-foot terrace. The coast north of Brookings is very irregular with numerous wave-eroded coves (Fig. 12.10c). Remnants of this erosion stand out as stacks all along this part of the coast, some with arches (Fig. 12.11). Nine miles north of Brookings, the bluffs are interrupted by the mile-long Whalehead Beach (Fig. 12.12), composed of fine- to medium-grained sand. Above the sea cliff bordering this beach, there is a terrace (A) 125 feet high. A small building at the edge of the terrace was built in 1923 in connection with an attempt to reclaim gold from the black beach sands. This building has served to indicate the rate of retreat of the sea cliff, which Dicken reports to have been 20 feet in 38 years.

ROGUE RIVER AND VICINITY, OREGON [Figs. 12.13 and 12.14]   The coast from Crook Point to Euchre Creek is much smoother than to the south and includes three long beaches respectively at the mouths of the Pistol, Rogue, and Euchre Rivers. The beach at Pistol River is 4 miles long. The 1873 chart shows that the north end formerly was more than a hundred feet narrower than at present. Since 1873, the stacks adjacent to the beach have been eroded about 35 feet, although this erosion may be due in part to the cutting of the Pistol River, which has shifted its course along much of the length of the beach. Except during high water, the mouth of the river is blocked by a barrier.

12.11 Natural arch in rock stack north of Brookings, Oregon. Photo by Wanless, 1968.

12.12 The northern end of Whalehead Beach, 8 miles north of Brookings, Oregon. Note the elevated marine terrace (A) 125 feet above present sea level, and rugged coast to the north. Oregon State Highway Department oblique aerial photo, 1958.

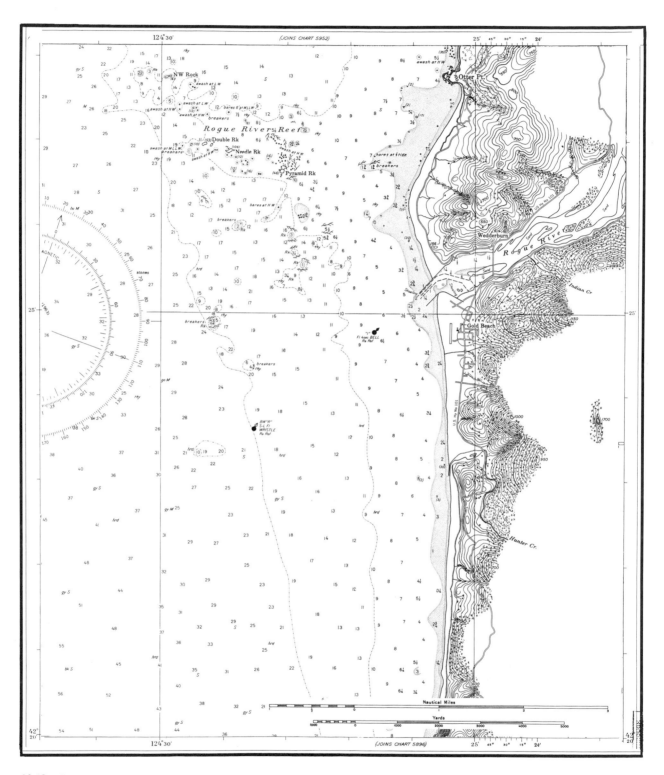

12.13 Oregon coast at the mouth of Rogue River and Gold Beach. Note convex beach to the north related to offshore reefs. U.S. Coast and Geodetic Survey Chart 5702, 1948.

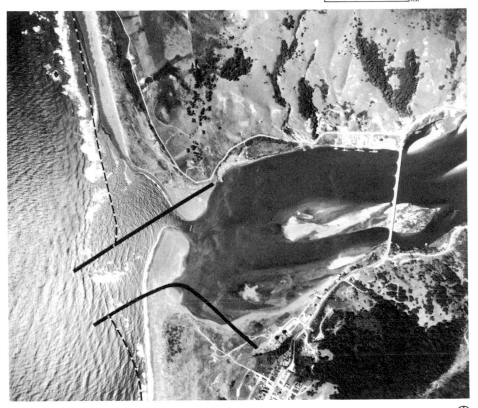

12.14 Rogue River entrance, showing spits which were later modified by jetty construction in 1957 and 1960. The accumulation of sand against the jetties through 1960 is shown by dashed line. Oregon State Highway Department photo, 1952. Jetty outlines and beach modification from Dicken (1961).

Gold Beach, which owes its sand to the large Rogue River, is about 7 miles long (Fig. 12.13). It extends well south of the river mouth and of the town of Gold Beach. Although it is slightly drowned, the Rogue River has enough flow to keep open all year, and the tide flowing up the river for a few miles adds to the river current during ebbs. The mouth formerly changed its position on frequent occasions; but jetties (lines on Fig. 12.14) were built in 1959 and have now stabilized the mouth, as well as allowing access to the small port. As shown in Figure 12.14, the buildup of sand against the south jetty is somewhat in excess of that on the north jetty. As at the mouth of the Chetco, the effect of the southerly winter storms appears to be the predominant influence.

North of the Rogue River mouth, the beach is unusual in having a convex shape (Fig. 12.13), in contrast to the usual concavity that characterizes almost all West Coast beaches between rocky points. According to Dicken, the local convexity is due to the resistance of the rock inland from the beach and to the Rogue River reefs that protect the area. A convergence of the waves caused by the reefs brings sediment in to the coast from both sides, resulting in the development of a giant cusp at this point.

Euchre Creek Beach is also lengthy, being almost 6 miles long. As at Gold Beach, the stream supplying sand enters near the north end of the beach. Euchre Creek enters the coast only during high water. It changes its point of entrance from side to side and erodes the bluff, thus undercutting the highway that extends along the shore adjacent to the beach. It has been necessary to construct groins to stop this erosion. Euchre Creek Beach has a preponderance of medium-grained sand, coarser than that of Gold Beach. Considerable slumping of the cliffs at the north end of the beach accounts for many of the offshore stacks.

12.15 Humbug Mountain, 5 miles south of Port Orford, Oregon. A great rock slide has extended into the ocean. University of California Hydraulic Engineering Laboratory, 1948.

12.16 Cape Blanco, north of Port Orford, is composed of hard rock adjoining shale and weak sandstone to the east, which has been eroded from both sides, forming a narrow neck with sand beaches. There are many rock stacks offshore. Oregon State Highway Department photo, 1958.

HUMBUG MOUNTAIN, PORT ORFORD, AND CAPE BLANCO, OREGON [Figs. 12.15 and 12.16]

For the next 10 miles to the north, the coast has greater irregularities, with three major land projections. The first of these is formed by a large landslide on the southwest flank of Humbug Mountain (Fig. 12.15). The slide, according to Dicken, has such a quantity of large resistant rock fragments that it has not been worn back by the waves to the old rock cliff.

Port Orford developed because of the very irregular point called The Heads, where vessels can anchor except during southerly storms. The area was settled in 1851 by Captain William Tichenor and eight other men. They were attacked by the local Indians but managed to defend their lives from atop a large rock. They had to leave the area and await reinforcements before returning and establishing a permanent settlement. The modern town has not developed commercially. The scenic beauty makes the point highly desirable for a summer resort. Also, one of the University of Oregon marine laboratories and a Coast Guard Station are located there. The 2-mile-long beach south of Port Orford is bordered by an unstable slope from which landslides frequently carry material out across the beach.

The longest beach in the vicinity of Port Orford is to the north, where the Elk River has developed a 7-mile beach all the way north to Cape Blanco. This is the southernmost of the large beaches along the West Coast that has a trend west of north. The beach is bordered by a 200-foot terrace that is higher than most of the main terraces to the south. However, the terrace is warped downward to the north, getting more in line with the typical 100-foot terraces.

Cape Blanco (Fig. 12.16) is one of several points along the Oregon coast that juts well beyond the otherwise straight shoreline. This point stands out because of the hard rock at the tip. The neck has a steeper slope on the south side than on the north, although the same rock outcrops on both sides. This is due to the strong attack of the southerly storms in winter. Numerous rock reefs are found outside Cape Blanco and to the south-southwest. Small islands rise above these reefs in several places.

BANDON, CAPE ARAGO, AND COOS BAY, OREGON [Figs. 12.17 through 12.20]

North of Cape Blanco, the Oregon coast is remarkably straight for 120 miles. In the first 40 miles, the straight

12.17 Mouth of Coquille River at Bandon, Oregon. The entrance to the Port of Bandon is protected by jetties, which have trapped sand on both sides, widening the beach. North of the entrance is a sand spit with dunes inside the beach. U.S. Department of Agriculture, 1967.

beaches are interrupted only by a small rocky point south of Bandon and a large irregular promontory at Cape Arago, south of the entrance to Coos Bay. Except for these rocky points, the coast is largely sand covered, and dune belts border the beaches on low terraces. South of Bandon, the beach is 15 miles long and includes small barriers with narrow lagoons on the inside. Old maps show that the mouths of streams along this beach have been shifted from time to time.

The two principal ports along this coast are at Bandon (Fig. 12.17) and Coos Bay (Figs. 12.18 and 12.19). Both of these harbors are in lagoons at the drowned mouths of rivers; and, in both cases a spit has built south, probably due to a current in the lee of a point. It will be recalled that San Diego Harbor and Morro Bay had a similar origin, except that the currents in California are predominantly to the south, so that eddies develop on the south sides of points; whereas in Oregon, the predominant northerly currents develop eddies on the north sides of points. The effect of the building of jetties at the entrance to Coos Bay between 1891 and 1931 has been to cause deposition on the south side, and the rocky coast has been flanked by a wide beach. At the south side of the entrance to Coos Bay, the rocky coast was irregular (A in Fig. 12.18), but has been straightened by the building of the beach. The north jetty at Coos Bay was built adjacent to a shoal, and the deposition of the southerly countercurrent has brought this shoal up to the surface (Fig. 12.19).

The rocky coast just south of the city of Bandon has projections and many off-lying stacks and islands

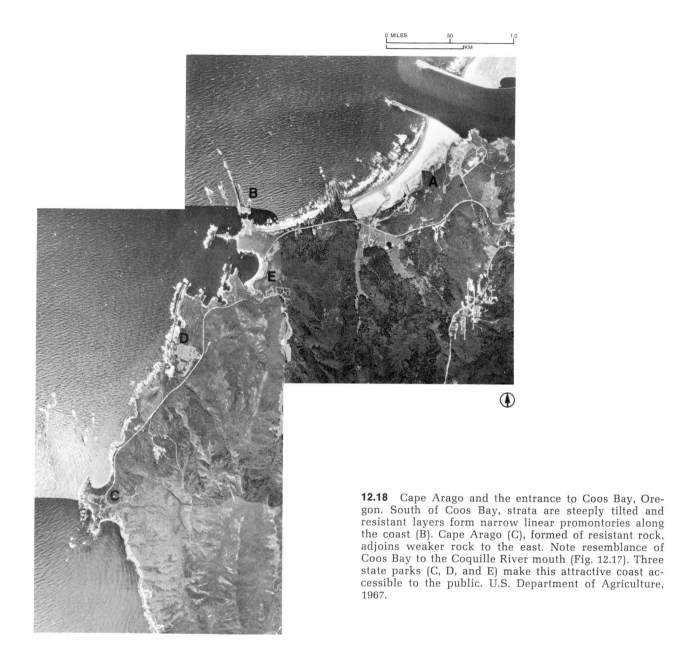

12.18 Cape Arago and the entrance to Coos Bay, Oregon. South of Coos Bay, strata are steeply tilted and resistant layers form narrow linear promontories along the coast (B). Cape Arago (C), formed of resistant rock, adjoins weaker rock to the east. Note resemblance of Coos Bay to the Coquille River mouth (Fig. 12.17). Three state parks (C, D, and E) make this attractive coast accessible to the public. U.S. Department of Agriculture, 1967.

(Fig. 12.17). From the entrance to Coos Bay south to Cape Arago (C in Fig. 12.18), there is an even more spectacular series of points, narrow promontories, stacks, and coves, which are eroded into the tilted sedimentary rocks (Fig. 12.20) that trend out into the Pacific. This is one of the most dramatic scenic areas of the entire West Coast. The rocks are hard enough to prevent rapid erosion. A terrace about 50 feet high extends back from the cliffs.

Coos Bay, shaped like an inverted U, is a combined lagoon and estuary. To the south, a drowned valley

(Fig. 12.19) has tributaries like those of Chesapeake Bay. Apparently the coast has sunk here in relation to the area to the south. Possibly the lower elevation of terrace levels is evidence of this sinking.

12.19 Chart of Coos Bay, Oregon. Shows dendritic pattern of some of the tributary bays and the inverted U-shape of the estuary. Changes in the north spit (dashed line) developed when the north jetty was built. A delta is building at the mouth of the Coos River 11 miles inside the mouth of the bay. From U.S. Coast and Geodetic Survey Chart 5984, 1950 edition, and from Dicken (1961) (dashed line).

12.20 Tilted rock formations truncated by uplifted terrace at Shore Acres State Park (D in Fig. 12.18). Photo by Shepard, 1968.

SAND DUNE COAST NORTH OF COOS BAY AND UMPQUA RIVER, OREGON [Figs. 12.21 and 12.22]   The best development of sand dunes along the Oregon coast is seen inside the barriers north of Coos Bay. According to W. S. Cooper, these dunes have blocked the mouths of a group of estuaries, and this has produced the lakes that can be seen along the coast highway (A and B in Fig. 12.21). A 22-mile beach of fine sand extends continuously from the north jetty of Coos Bay to the south jetty of the entrance to the Umpqua River. Barriers and narrow lagoons occur along much of this coast. The dunes have ridges that trend in a west-northwesterly direction. These are transverse dunes,

due to the southerly winds of winter. Fingers of sand (C) are shown where the dunes are advancing north into a forest that is growing on older dunes.

Winchester Bay, at the mouth of the Umpqua River, is a narrow estuary similar in shape to Coos Bay. The changes resulting from the jetty construction are illustrated in Figure 12.22. Previously the spit north of the entrance terminated a mile farther north, but a shoal in the entrance had pushed the natural channel farther south than at present. The sand coast south of the entrance protruded slightly beyond the spit. Now the north spit has built out to the jetty, covering most of the old shoal; and the channel lies farther north. Since 1948, the south

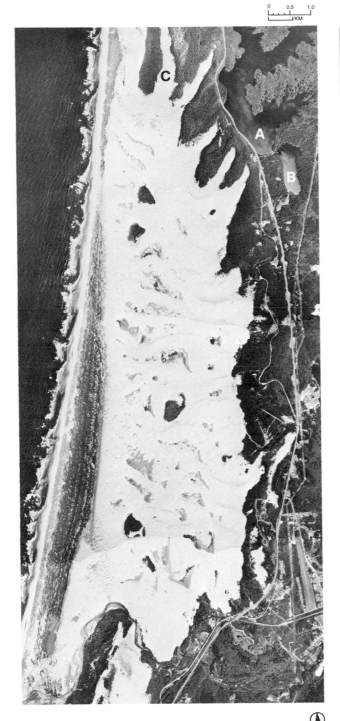

12.21 Behind the beach between Coos Bay and the Umpqua River estuary is a belt of active dunes extending 2 miles from the beach and flanked by older dunes fixed by vegetation. Some of the sand dunes blocked streams (A), forming lakes. Sand dunes are as much as 100 feet high and are accessible by dune buggies. U.S. Department of Agriculture, 1967.

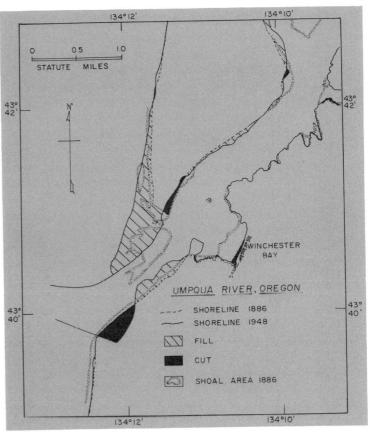

12.22 Changes in shore configuration at the entrance to Umpqua River estuary between 1886 and 1948. The north jetty was constructed from 1917 to 1919; the south in 1934 and extended in 1951. Sand has accumulated against the north jetty. A cut has formed, presumably by incoming tides. The eroded sediment was deposited next to the cut. The main channel is now where there was a shoal area in 1886. From Dicken (1961).

jetty has been lengthened seaward and sand has been building out against this jetty. The cut on the north side of the south jetty has been stopped by building a seawall along the south side of the channel. The southward growth of the spit at the mouth of the Umpqua River cannot be explained by a projecting rock point, as was the case in the embayments to the south.

To the north of the Umpqua, a long straight beach stretches for 30 miles, virtually to the Sea Lion Caves and Heceta Head, although it is breached by several small creeks and the Siuslaw River. Sand dunes continue all along this straight beach, but they do not reach as far inland as those between Coos Bay and the Umpqua River. This 50-mile-long dune tract is

12.23 Heceta Head as viewed from Sea Lion Cave. At A are seen large numbers of seabirds that produce guano deposits. Photo by Wanless, 1968.

SEA LION CAVES, HECETA HEAD, AND CAPE PERPETUA   North of the 50 miles of sand dunes and straight beaches, the Oregon coast becomes rugged and has rock cliffs of basalt several hundred feet high. At the Sea Lion Caves, 1.5 miles north of the northern end of the dunes, the cliffs are bordered by a low terrace on which hundreds of sea lions can be seen. A large cave cut into the cliffs is also a resting place for the sea lions. Tourists can go down in an elevator along a rock tunnel and look at them. A view through an opening on the north side of the cave (Fig. 12.23) shows the vertical wall and a northward continuation of the terrace at a somewhat higher level than where it is occupied by the sea lions. This higher terrace is partly covered with a landslide and is a seabird rookery coated with white guano.

Just north of the Sea Lion Caves, Heceta Head is the only appreciable promontory along this part of the coast. The low terrace continues past this headland, and at Cape Perpetua it is a rock bench cut in basalt about 3 feet above sea level.

Just north of the town of Yachats, there is much evidence of recent coastal erosion. Dicken calls attention to the retreat of the 20-foot coastal terrace with the loss of the county road. Retreat of 0.5 foot per year has been observed in some places. Here the coves are being enlarged, but farther north the projections are retreating.

NEWPORT, YAQUINA HEAD, AND CAPE FOULWEATHER, OREGON [Figs. 12.24, 12.25, and 12.26]   North of Cape Perpetua, the coast again resumes its straight course with another long beach. The Alsea River mouth is embayed; and at Newport, 10 miles farther north, another estuary is located at the mouth of the Yaquina River. Both of these estuaries have small tributary bays and represent a continuation of the dendritic drowned coast found first at Coos Bay, 80 miles farther south.

At the entrance to Yaquina Bay, the long jetties (A in Fig. 12.24), built in 1897 but later greatly extended, have trapped large quantities of sand on the south and very little on the north. This return to indications of predominant north drift may be in part the result of the southwesterly trend of the jetties, which would allow sand to move past the north jetty during south drift; whereas north drift would trap it against the south jetty. Between 1952, when the aerial photos were taken, and our 1968 field trip,

the most extensive mass of dunes along the ocean coasts of the United States. The dunes interfere with navigation up the Siuslaw River because the southerly winds blow sand into the river and develop shoals.

The Siuslaw River represents a change in pattern from that to the south. The river mouth has been pushed northward by a spit that grew in that direction, instead of to the south as at Umpqua River and Coos Bay. However, the building of jetties at the Siuslaw River caused rapid deposition on the north side, filling a previous indentation. The coast had built out 0.5 mile by 1950. At the same time, there was erosion on the south side. Thus we have indications of a south-flowing current along this part of the coast.

12.24 The coast from the entrance to Yaquina Bay (A) north past Newport (B) to Yaquina Head (D). Much sand has been trapped against the south jetty, constructed in 1897. North of Newport (C), several sections of an elevated coastal terrace have slumped into the sea during the past century. Yaquina Head affords spectacular views of the Oregon coastline. U.S. Department of Agriculture, 1952.

12.25 Photographs of Jumpoff Joe, a projection with a natural arch near Newport, in 1880, 1910, and 1930, showing considerable erosion of the point, but little change in the arch in 50 years. The arch had collapsed in 1960. Photos from W. D. Smith, as published in Byrne (1964).

sand deposition had built the beach to the end of the south jetty and to the elbow of the north jetty, showing that there has been some deposition on each side.

The fine sand beach at Newport (B) is interspersed with outcrops of sandstone and mudstone. The backshore of this beach has been extensively changed during the past 100 years by a combination of slumping and faulting. This movement produced

12.26 Coastal erosion near the Devil's Punchbowl, showing suggestions of two elevated coastal terraces (A and B). Photo by Wanless, 1968.

numerous curving scarps, which, according to Dicken, have greatly changed since the survey for the 1868 chart. Many houses built along the edge of the terrace have been destroyed. Some of the remaining old houses are tilted to the northeast as a result of the slump faults. Dicken reports that 25 feet of the outer scarp have been eroded by waves in 10 years.

At Jumpoff Joe (C), just north of the city of Newport, a headland of Miocene sandstone had been considerably eroded in the 50 years between 1880 and 1930 (Fig. 12.25). A small cave in the point became an arch and then was disconnected, forming a stack. According to J. V. Byrne, of Oregon State University, the arch has now collapsed and the ter-

race edge in 1960 was 167 feet back from its position in 1880. This would make an erosion rate of about 2 feet annually, a surprisingly rapid rate for rock. Such rates have been observed elsewhere only on projecting headlands where a thin mass protrudes seaward.

Four miles north of the Yaquina Bay entrance, Yaquina Head (D in Fig. 12.24), with its hard lava rock, projects for a mile out beyond the north end of Newport Beach. Erosion appears to be greater on the south side of this point. Sand has built out on the north so that the point does not protrude far on this side.

The 5-mile beach north of Yaquina Head is terminated by a small headland, the Devil's Punchbowl, where well-exposed terraces truncate the silty sandstone beds. Photographs taken by the Oregon State Highway Commission in 1958 are so similar to ours of 1968 that there had been no appreciable erosion of these points in the 10-year period.

Otter Crest and Cape Foulweather, just north of the Devil's Punchbowl, represent another return of volcanic rocks to the coast and much more rugged topography (Fig. 12.26). This is one of the beauty spots of the Oregon coast.

TILLAMOOK AND OTHER RECTANGULAR SPIT-PROTECTED BAYS, OREGON [Figs. 12.27 through 12.30]   North of Cape Foulweather, the Oregon coast is characterized by a succession of seven bays that are nearly or completely cut off from the ocean by barriers. Three are shown in Figure 12.27. Of the seven bays, four are protected by spits that have grown to the south and two by spits that have grown to the north. The seventh, Sand Lake, has spits of nearly the same length on both sides. It is difficult to determine the relationship of these spits to the predominant current, nor is there any clear evidence of the effect of headlands in producing countercurrents, like those of California. However, it may be significant that all but one of the principal rivers enter the side of the bay where the spit is tied to the land. This suggests that the introduced sediment is an important factor in building the spits.

Tillamook, the largest of the bays, is 4 miles long and 2.5 miles wide. In spite of its rectangular shape, it is an estuary partly filled by deltas at its southeast end. A spit has grown across the bay from the south. Dunes were built on top of the spit with heights up to almost 100 feet. The spit is called Bayocean Beach but its northern end is referred to as Kincheloe Point. A summer resort was formerly located on top of the dunes near the southern end of the tract. In 1917, a jetty was constructed at the north entrance of Tillamook Bay. At first there was little change, but the jetty was considerably lengthened in 1931, and soon after this lengthening there were extensive changes in the barrier to the south. Dicken has shown the nature of these alterations up until 1957 (Fig. 12.28). Great erosion has taken place in the area where the resort was built. Also, the ocean broke through the south end of the spit, but this break was healed by constructing a dike across the gap. Shepard saw the remnants of the old resort in 1950; but when

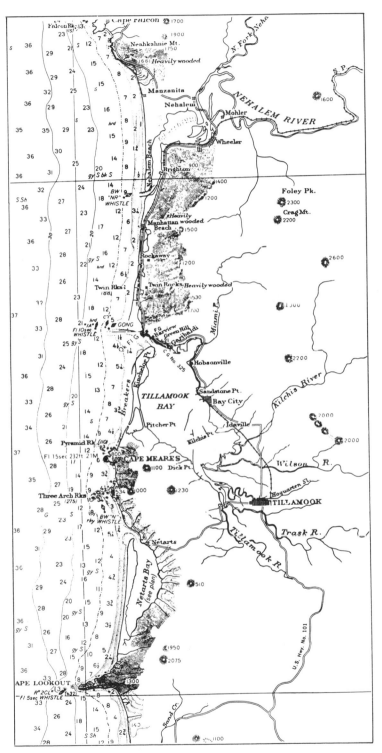

12.27 Chart of coastal northwestern Oregon, showing Netarts, Tillamook, and Nehalem Bays. Note different direction of spit growth. U.S. Coast and Geodetic Survey Chart 5902, 1965.

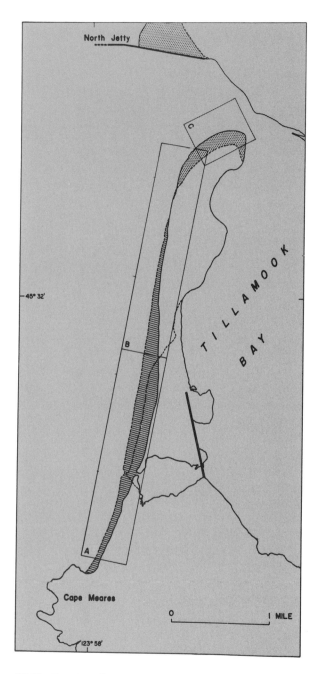

12.28 Erosion (lines) and progradation (stipples) of Bayocean spit following construction of the north jetty at Tillamook in 1917. From Dicken (1961).

12.29 Erosion of sand dunes behind beach at Bayocean spit. This erosion has destroyed all buildings of a coast resort. Photo by Shepard, 1968.

both writers returned in 1968 the old abandoned buildings had gone over the seaward cliff, and the dunes had been deeply eroded (Fig. 12.29). The erosion from 1939 up to 1960 had amounted to 1,200 feet. During the same interval, the north end of the spit had been prograding, and the point had narrowed the entrance to Tillamook Bay. Also, extensive deposition was taking place against the jetty on the north side of the harbor, building out the shoreline for 0.5 mile.

Nehalem Bay, 10 miles north of Tillamook, is protected by a spit that has grown southward from the north side of the bay. This bay is being filled slowly by the delta of the Nehalem River, but the changes in recent years have been very slow. The jetties built at the mouth of Nehalem Bay in 1916 have not had as much effect on the shoreline as have the jetties at most other bay entrances along the Oregon coast. This, according to Dicken, is because shortly after their construction, the jetties at Nehalem suffered storm damage and settling so that the sand has washed over them. They were never repaired. Extensive shifts in the inner channel occur but the entrance to Nehalem Bay has been stabilized by the damaged jetties. Between 1939 and 1960, a growth of 140 feet had occurred against the remnant of the south jetty.

12.30 Cape Lookout, Oregon, a narrow promontory just south of Netarts Bay (A). University of California Hydraulic Engineering Laboratory, 1948. From Dicken (1961).

12.31 Ecola State Park, north of Cannon Beach, Oregon, showing result of the 1961 landslide, 3,000 feet long (at A in Fig. 12.32). The rocks at Ecola Point (B) are volcanic. Oregon State Highway Department. From Dicken (1961).

Nehalem Beach, north of the river entrance, is more than 11 miles long. At its north end, slumping has taken place at the town of Neahkahnie Beach, with some retreat of the bluffs.

The barrier-protected bays and long beaches of this part of the Oregon coast are interspersed by some spectacular headlands, mostly of lava rock. Cape Lookout, just south of Netarts Bay (Fig. 12.30), is the most striking of these. It extends out for 2 miles from the straight coast on either side. Erosion of this point is greatest on the south side, as elsewhere along the Oregon coast.

NEAHKAHNIE MOUNTAIN TO TILLAMOOK HEAD, OREGON [Figs. 12.31, 12.32, and 12.33]

Beyond the seven bays, the Oregon coast becomes more mountainous for a distance of about 17 miles. Just north of Nehalem Bay, the coast highway encounters another mass of lava at Neahkahnie Mountain. The road is cut into a south-facing cliff that rises from the shoreline almost vertically for 600 feet. In this area, Oregon has a series of state parks,

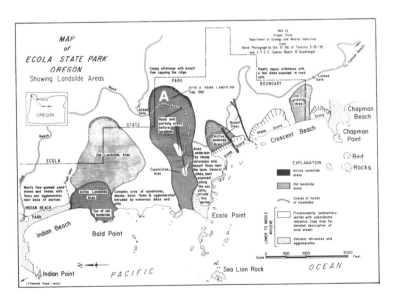

12.32 Map of recent and older landslides in Ecola State Park. The slide (A) is shown in Figure 12.31. Oregon State Department of Geology and Mineral Industries, 1961.

12.33 Haystack Rock near Cannon Beach, Oregon, a tombolo at low tide. When revisited in 1968, the rock had suffered little erosion, but the bluff from which the 1950 photo was taken had receded 25 to 30 feet. Photo by Shepard, 1950.

which are effectively preserving the scenic beauty.

Ecola State Park, at Tillamook Head, has had an interesting history. The entire cape is subject to landslides. In February 1961, the park headquarters and picnic grounds were largely covered by an active slide (Fig. 12.31) coming from the cirquelike head of a valley just north of Ecola Point. The picnic area has now been restored. This slide extended the coast seaward and a new beach has now developed at the toe of the slide. Other slides have occurred previously in the area (Fig. 12.32). Some of the numerous stacks that are seen out in the ocean are probably in part the erosion remnants of still older slides.

Evidence of wave erosion can be seen along various parts of this coast. The old roads on the top of low terraces have had to be moved. At Haystack Rock, which becomes a tombolo at low tide (Fig. 12.33), a photograph was taken from the edge of one of these terraces in 1950. Trying to retake the photograph in 1968, the authors found that the bluff had retreated at least 25 feet and the foreground had disappeared, making it impossible to get into the same position.

12.34 The Clatsop Plain averages 1.5 miles wide and widening northward, and separates eroded highlands (B) from the ocean. The plain consists of a sequence of fifteen or more parallel beach or dune ridges separated by linear swales or narrow ponds. Most or all of these ridges are believed to have developed during the past century. Note that the sand deposits on the estuary side of the south jetty (A) extend well beyond the deposit on the ocean side. This indicates recent recession on the ocean side. U.S. Coast and Geodetic Survey, 1967.

12.35 Delta of the Columbia River built into its estuary 20 miles above the entrance. The construction of a series of dams, such as the Grand Coulee Dam, has probably decreased the rate of delta growth. U.S. Coast and Geodetic Survey, 1955.

CLATSOP PLAIN [Fig. 12.34]   North of Tillamook Head, Clatsop Plain, bordered by a beach, extends 17 miles to the Columbia River. At the southern end of the plain, Seaside, a beach resort, is built on a spit that grew northward, like those of Netarts and Tillamook Bays. The plain is about a mile wide and has a series of beach and dune ridges. Elongate lakes lie between the ridges in many places. The extreme southern end of the beach has a steep cobble slope; but just to the north these cobbles are covered with fine sand and do not appear along the rest of the beach. According to Dicken, 50 years ago the cobbles were exposed farther north but have since been covered.

COLUMBIA RIVER ESTUARY AND JETTIES, OREGON AND WASHINGTON [Figs. 12.35 through 12.39]   The Columbia is the largest United States river entering the Pacific. Its headwaters are in British Columbia 1,210 miles above its mouth. The Columbia is known as a low sediment river, relatively clear of suspended load along much of its course, although large volumes of sand are drifted along the river bed. The U.S. Army Corps of Engineers report that in 1922 the river carried 120 parts of suspended load per million near Portland. At times of major flood the load is much larger.

The Columbia experienced devastating floods in 1848, 1876, 1894, and 1948. Of these, the greatest was in 1894, when the maximum discharge at The Dalles, Oregon, was more than 1,220,000 cubic feet per second. In 1948, flood conditions persisted at Portland for 15 days. During such floods, large quantities of sediment are moved through the estuary to its mouth.

Large volumes of sand are moved along the river bed in a series of sand waves up to 14 feet high near Portland, decreasing in height downstream. Much of this sand is eventually carried to the ocean, where it accumulates temporarily in a bar 3 to 5 miles seaward of the estuary mouth. From here, the sand is distributed north and south by littoral currents. The construction of a series of dams in the Columbia River, of which the Grand Coulee is the best known, has resulted in storing more sand in the reservoirs, and cutting off much of the supply of sand to the sand bars in the estuary. As a result, the beaches adjoining the Columbia Estuary may be expected to lose part of the sand necessary to maintain equilibrium.

Tidal range at the mouth of the Columbia is from 6.5 feet to an extreme of 14 feet. The river is affected by tides as far as the Bonneville Dam, 145 miles upriver. The Columbia is the upstream migration route of myriads of salmon. To permit the continuance of this migration, fish ladders were constructed at the Bonneville Dam.

Sand bars and sand islands (Fig. 12.35) are common in the estuary between Portland and the river mouth, forming a special kind of delta. These sand deposits are shifted in location at times of major

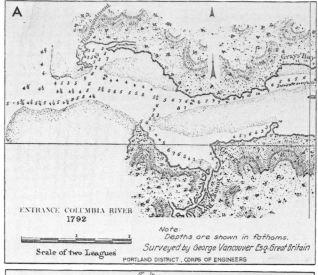

ENTRANCE COLUMBIA RIVER
1792

Note:
Depths are shown in fathoms.
Surveyed by George Vancouver Esq. Great Britain

Scale of two Leagues

PORTLAND DISTRICT, CORPS OF ENGINEERS

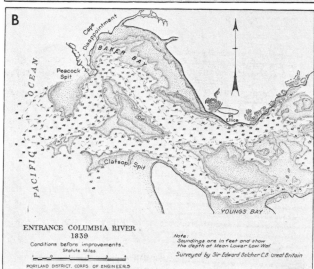

ENTRANCE COLUMBIA RIVER.
1839

Conditions before improvements.
Statute Miles

Note:
Soundings are in feet and show
the depth at Mean Lower Low Wat

Surveyed by Sir Edward Belcher C.B. Great Britain

PORTLAND DISTRICT, CORPS OF ENGINEERS

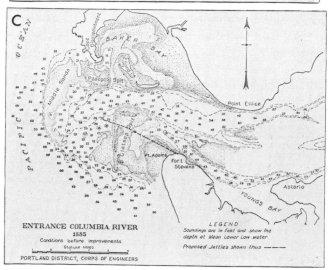

ENTRANCE COLUMBIA RIVER
1885

Conditions before improvements
Statute Miles

LEGEND
Soundings are in feet and show the
depth at Mean Lower Low water

Proposed Jetties shown thus

PORTLAND DISTRICT, CORPS OF ENGINEERS

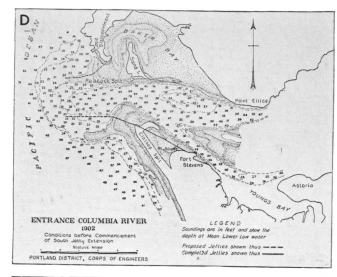

ENTRANCE COLUMBIA RIVER
1902

Conditions before Commencement
of South Jetty Extension
Statute Miles

LEGEND
Soundings are in feet and show the
depth at Mean Lower Low water

Proposed Jetties shown thus
Completed Jetties shown thus

PORTLAND DISTRICT, CORPS OF ENGINEERS

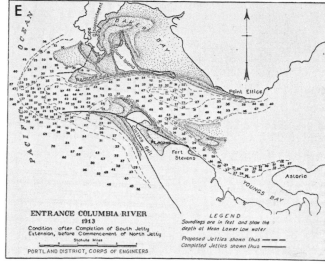

ENTRANCE COLUMBIA RIVER
1913

Condition after Completion of South Jetty
Extension, before Commencement of North Jetty
Statute Miles

LEGEND
Soundings are in feet and show the
depth at Mean Lower Low water

Proposed Jetties shown thus
Completed Jetties shown thus

PORTLAND DISTRICT, CORPS OF ENGINEERS

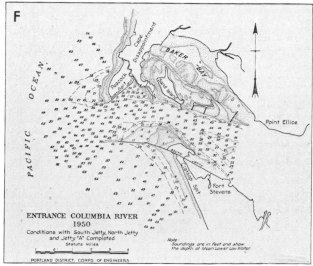

ENTRANCE COLUMBIA RIVER
1950

Conditions with South Jetty, North Jetty
and Jetty "A" Completed
Statute Miles

Note:
Soundings are in feet and show
the depth at Mean Lower Low Water.

PORTLAND DISTRICT, CORPS OF ENGINEERS

OUR CHANGING COASTLINES

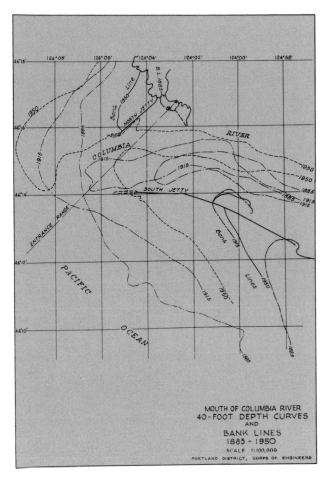

12.37 Sketch showing changes in position of the 40-foot depth contour between 1885 and 1950. Showing also a lunate bar in 1950, the Clatsop Spit, and the retreat of the coast after the building of the south jetty of the Columbia River. From Hickson and Rodolf, U.S. Army Corps of Engineers, 1950.

floods and become an obstruction to river navigation. Comparison of recent aerial photographs with old navigation charts shows that parts of the shoals on the older charts have later become islands.

Changes at the mouth of the estuary from 1792 to 1950 are described by R. E. Hickson and F. W. Rodolf, of the U.S. Army Corps of Engineers. Their series of maps (Fig. 12.36) go back to a 1792 survey by Captain George Vancouver of Great Britain (Fig.

12.36 Changes in coastal configuration at the entrance to Columbia River at six dates from 1792 to 1950. The south jetty was constructed shortly after 1885 and lengthened after 1902. The north jetty was constructed after 1902. From Hickson and Rodolf (1950).

12.36*a*). In 1839, a much more accurate survey was made by Sir Edward Belcher (Fig. 12.36*b*). At this time, the natural mouth of the Columbia consisted of the Clatsop Plain, south from Point Adams, and a rocky promontory called Cape Disappointment, on the north. The survey shows a large offshore shoal, the Clatsop "Spit," which extended 4 miles seaward from Point Adams, and a sand shoal, Peacock "Spit," 3 miles southeast of Cape Disappointment. A shifting sand shoal 5 miles long lay southeastward from Cape Disappointment for 5 miles toward Point Adams (Fig. 12.36*b*). The channels were north and south of this shoal.

Because the shifting shoal was a hazard to navigation in the lower Columbia, between 1885 and 1889, a jetty 5 miles long was constructed on the south side of the river mouth, then lengthened by 2 miles between 1903 and 1913 (Fig. 12.36*e*). This jetty cut across the shoal that blocked the entrance to the estuary and cut off the northern end of Clatsop Spit. A part of this northern remnant migrated north to form Sand Island (Figs. 12.36*d* and 12.36*e*). After construction of the jetty, sand at first accumulated on the south side, changing Clatsop Spit from a shoal to a sandy promontory; but after a time the jetty cut off sand supplies from the river to the south, and, by 1950, the shore just south of the jetty had receded 2,000 feet, while 2 miles to the south the recession had been 1,000 feet. The 40-foot depth contour had migrated landward 2 miles up to 1950 (Fig. 12.37).

In 1913, the north jetty was built across the slightly submerged Peacock "Spit." After the jetty was completed (A in Fig. 12.38) in 1917, the shoal was filled to the surface in some places. Since jetty construction, a land area a mile across has been added next to the jetty. Deposition has also taken place all along Cape Disappointment and on the north side of North Head (C in Fig. 12.38) until the point has virtually ceased to be a protuberance. Extensive northward beach drifting of sand has occurred since the jetty was built, so that the beach has been widened by about 0.25 mile near Long Beach, Washington, deceasing to 0.1 mile near the south entrance to Grays Harbor, 31 miles north of the Columbia Estuary.

One result of the deposition north of the north jetty has been that less sand is carried into the entrance; and some erosion has taken place at Sand

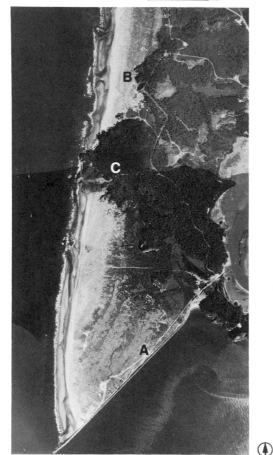

Island (C in Fig. 12.39), which fronts Baker Bay. Since 1839, this island has shifted northward a mile and now adjoins the navigation channel east of Cape Disappointment. To stabilize the position of the channel and the islands, six short jetties were constructed south from the tip of Cape Disappointment (D), Sand Island (E, F), and an unnamed island and shoal to the east (G). South of Sand Island, the channel is between 70 and 80 feet deep.

COAST OF SOUTHWESTERN WASHINGTON

[Figs. 12.40, 12.41, and 12.42]   The Columbia River Estuary is the first of the three largest bays of the Pacific Coast between San Francisco Bay and Puget Sound. Willapa Bay has an entrance 25 miles north of the Columbia River mouth, and Grays Harbor is 12 miles farther north.

It is perhaps significant that the most deeply embayed portion of the unglaciated East Coast and West Coast both lie within 150 miles of the southern glacial boundaries. This may be explained as resulting from the bulging of the territory outside the glacial margin, causing rivers to incise themselves more

12.38 Sand fill behind the north jetty (A) of the Columbia River mouth. In 1792 (Fig. 12.36a) and until 1885 (Fig. 12.36c) there was no sand beach adjoining North Head (C). Note numerous rip current channels (B) exposed by low tide. U.S. Department of Agriculture, 1963.

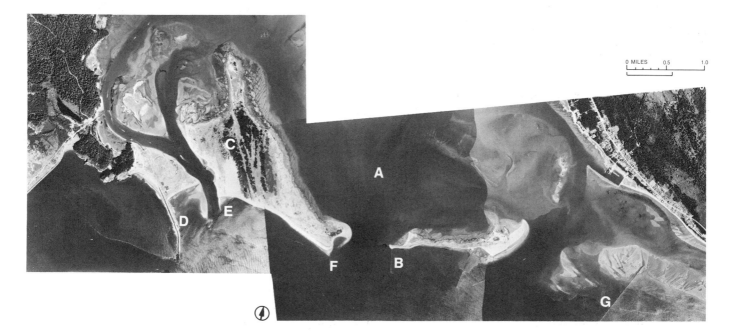

deeply into this bulge than into adjacent areas, so that when the glaciers melted and the bulge subsided, the returning sea would extend farther into the bulged area. Although both Willapa Bay and Grays Harbor have estuary reentrants into the coast, including the drowned valleys of several rivers, Willapa Bay has a north-south elongation of 25 miles, and its southern extremity is only 5 miles north of the Columbia River. This arm is a coastal lagoon; whereas Grays Harbor, with a maximum north-south length of 13 miles and east-west length of 15 miles, is primarily an estuary.

The history and development of this coast has been interpreted by William S. Cooper. Southwestern Washington is largely underlain by easily eroded marine Miocene and Oligocene shales and sandstones, with intervening patches of resistant Eocene volcanic rocks. The coast had been worn down to a gently rolling plain before the Pleistocene period. When the sea level was lowered about 300 to 500 feet during the glacial maxima, the shoreline shifted about 15 miles westward, and the seaward part of the rolling plain was further leveled by marine planation. As sea level gradually rose after the last ice stage, a relatively straight shoreline migrated eastward until encountering the resistant volcanic rocks of Cape Disappointment, just north of the Columbia River mouth, and the Eocene volcanic rocks on the present divide between Willapa Bay and Grays Harbor. Here, eastward migration was checked, and the hard rock developed headlands. The coast became irregular as the rising sea level flooded the lowlands of the Willapa and its tributary rivers, forming Willapa Bay; and the lowlands of the Chehalis River formed Grays Harbor.

The Columbia River transports a vast quantity of sand to the sea; and, due to strong southwest winter winds, much of this sand is carried northward by littoral currents. Hence, a spit was built northward from near Cape Disappointment, largely cutting off Willapa Bay from the sea. During the past 3,000 years of approximately stable sea level, this spit grew

12.39 A series of sand islands and shoals east of Cape Disappointment, which separates Baker Bay (A) from the Columbia River. Sand Island (C) was formerly a part of the Clatsop Spit at the river mouth before the south jetty was constructed. Jetties (B, D, E, F, G) built to prevent shifts of the channel or the chain of islands. U.S. Department of Agriculture, 1965.

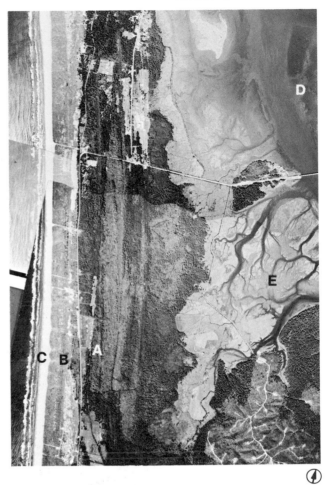

12.40 Prograding beach separating southern Grays Harbor (D) from the Pacific, and delta of Elk River (E). The outer beach (C) and shrub-covered area (B) have formed since the completion of the Columbia River jetties. U.S. Department of Agriculture, 1964.

in width and the length increased to 22 miles. The construction of the Columbia River north jetty in 1913 decreased the amount of sand free to drift northward from the river mouth; but the straight beach has continued to widen, probably because sediment bypasses the jetty in large quantities.

During this same period, sediment introduced into Willapa Bay and Grays Harbor by rivers has formed the substantial deltas of the Noselle and Bear Rivers into the south end of Willapa Bay and of Elk River into Grays Harbor (Fig. 12.40). River flow and tidal currents have maintained channels through the bays to a maximum depth of slightly more than 100 feet just inside the entrance to Willapa Bay. Some sand

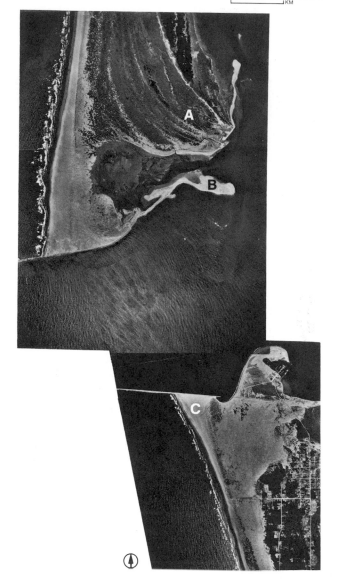

12.41 Entrance to Grays Harbor, Washington.

a 1950. Jetties protect the northern and southern harbor entrances. On the north side, a series of prejetty beach ridges (A) hook toward the entrance. After jetty construction the straight beach extended to the jetty, and a spit (B) had been built into the bay beyond the inner end of the jetty. The south jetty has also trapped much new sand (C). U.S. Coast and Geodetic Survey.

b August 1967. The old beach ridges hooking toward the bay entrance have been developed as a new beach resort (A). Spit (B) has lengthened and sand has been eroded from the south jetty (C). U.S. Coast and Geodetic Survey, from color photo.

is swept out of the bay entrances through these channels; and, like the sediment introduced by the Columbia, more is drifted along the coast northward than southward. The straight shorelines are offset westward about 2 miles on the north sides of both bay entrances, although, according to J. S. Creager,

the beach at Tokeland, on the north entrance to Willapa Bay, is undergoing rapid erosion.

A series of barrier beach ridges that border both Willapa Bay and Grays Harbor include (1) old inner sediments with many nearly parallel sand ridges separated by vegetated marshes or linear lakes, the latter representing interruptions in the progradation of the shore; (2) a relatively barren dune ridge and trough belt without trees, but with grasses and small shrubs, and generally without habitation; and (3) a belt of bare beach and dune sand without vegetation, forming the outer coast. These three belts (A to C) are displayed in Figure 12.40, showing the south side of Grays Harbor. These belts are about 2 miles wide at the southern end of Willapa Bay; and they narrow northward with increasing distance from the source of sand, which is largely the Columbia River, according to R. S. Andrews. Most habitation is on the oldest tree-covered dune ridges. The beach-dune ridges curve toward the inlets. On the north side of Grays Harbor entrance, a new beach resort has been developed since 1950 (A in Fig. 12.41b) on the older dune ridges.

Strong tidal currents enter the inlets to Willapa Bay and Grays Harbor. They have scoured deeper channels in the inlets and directly inside than the channels of drowned rivers that enter the bays. The entrance to Grays Harbor (Figs. 12.41a and b) is less than 2 miles wide and is protected by jetties. Much sand has accumulated as backfill behind both Grays Harbor jetties. In 1950, a spit (B in Fig. 12.41a) 0.7 mile long had been built into the bay on the north side of Grays Harbor entrance. By 1967, the spit (B in Fig. 12.41b) had grown to 1.3 miles. The entrance to Willapa Bay is 4 miles wide and is not protected by jetties. According to Andrews, the predominant drift at the entrance is to the north, accounting for the development of the broad shoal north of Leadbetter Point and for the erosion on the north side of the entrance. An arcuate shoal with water less than 20 feet deep has formed on the seaward side of the bay entrance. In 1956, there was a triangular shoal with a circular island (A) south of the middle of the bay entrance; but, by 1965, this had developed into a crescent-shaped island (not shown). Willapa Bay is notable as one of the few examples of large embayments on the United States coasts that are free from the pollution of industrial wastes.

Although the southwestern Washington coast may suffer some beach erosion after major storms, progradation should be the principal change because of the large supplies that continue to be introduced by the Columbia River and other small streams to the north.

12.42 The entrance to Willapa Bay, southwestern Washington, is divided by a triangular island (A). By 1965, this had developed into a crescent-shaped island. U.S. Coast and Geodetic Survey, 1950.

12.43 Western coast of Olympic Peninsula, near La Push, showing stacks and cobble beaches. Photo by Shepard, 1950.

12.44 Shore at Kalaloch, Olympic National Park, showing masses of driftwood piled on beach against shore bluffs, providing battering ram during heavy surf. Discoidal pebbles compose the landward side of the beach. Photo by Wanless, 1968.

WEST SIDE OF OLYMPIC PENINSULA, WASH-INGTON [Figs. 12.43 and 12.44]   For 60 miles north from Grays Harbor, the coast is almost straight, trending 10 degrees west of north. Midway along this stretch, two small projections are the only irregularities. This straightness represents an amazing change from the three large estuaries to the south.

Probably there are two or more explanations for the contrast. It seems likely that estuaries may have existed in this stretch but have been filled by sediment introduced by the high gradient streams coming from the Olympic Mountains. Also the indentations to the south, particularly the Columbia Estuary, suggests that this coast has undergone subsidence that did not extend north of Grays Harbor. Farther north, the coast is more irregular with small coves and narrow beaches between rocky headlands. One small estuary is found at La Push and two others near Cape Flattery. The bedrock along this northwest coast is Miocene marine sandstones and shales except at Cape Flattery, where the rocky promontory 400 feet high is composed of Eocene volcanic rocks.

Glaciation of the Olympic Mountains east of this coastal belt produced a series of valley glaciers, which advanced to or nearly to the coast along the Quinault, Queets, and Hoh River valleys in the southern half of this coastal belt. The Grays Harbor lowland received glacial outwash from the north through the Humptulips River valley and from the east and northeast through the Chehalis River valley. The northern 30 miles of the coast from the Soleduck and Quillayute Rivers to Cape Flattery, was covered with a spillover from the tongue of ice moving into the ocean along the Strait of Juan de Fuca. This ice did not come from the mountain glaciers of the Olympics but was part of the Cordilleran ice sheet, a true continental glacier.

The rainfall along this coastal belt is the heaviest in the United States except Hawaii, ranging up to 115 inches at Forks, in the Hoh River valley. In consequence of this heavy rainfall and high humidity, the area is densely covered with a temperate rain forest, largely Douglas fir and Sitka spruce, with many trees 200 feet high. Although travel along parts of this coast is difficult, there is a coastal highway in the southern 20 miles from Grays Harbor to the Quinault River, and U.S. Highway 101 follows the coast for 12 miles between the Queets and Hoh Rivers. A stretch of 45 miles north from the Queets River is a detached portion of Olympic National Park, with headquarters at Kalaloch.

The plain behind the beach rises gradually from about 40 feet, just north of Grays Harbor, to 100 feet about 7 miles farther north. Beyond this point, a coastal cliff extends continuously to Cape Flattery except at the mouths of rivers. An uninterrupted beach lies at the base of the cliff for 16 miles from Grays Harbor to Point Grenville, decreasing in width northward from 0.5 to less than 0.1 mile. North of Point Grenville, the beach is virtually continuous as far as Hoh River. Farther north, cove beaches are separated by rocky headlands. North from the Quinault River, a prominent coastal terrace averages 160 feet above sea level as far as the Hoh River. North from there, the coastal terrace, if present, is obscured; and at many places coastal cliffs are 300 feet or more in height. Starting 20 miles south of Cape Flattery, a somewhat uneven coastal terrace is indicated on the topographic maps. In this area, the 8-mile-long Ozette Lake extends parallel to the coast and 1 to 2 miles inland. The lake basin was probably gouged out by the ice sheet, which had advanced westward along the Strait of Juan de Fuca. Otherwise, the coast between the Quillayute River and Cape Flattery shows surprisingly little evidence of glacial erosion. The lack of fiords and other glacial troughs is most unusual for a glaciated area and suggests that the ice was relatively stagnant.

From Point Grenville north, there are hundreds of rock stacks (Fig. 12.43), some as far as 3 miles offshore. One of the stacks, Destruction Island, nearly a mile long and 3 miles offshore, was so named because, in 1776, the Spanish explorer Juan Francisco Bodega y Quadra (for whom Bodega Bay in Northern California was named) anchored in the lee of the island and sent men ashore for food and water. All were killed by the Indians who inhabited the island. Eleven years later, Captain Charles William Barkley of the *Imperial Eagle* anchored landward of the same island near the mouth of a river and sent six men ashore, all of whom were also killed by Indians. He named the river Destruction River, but it has since been renamed Hoh River for the Hoh tribe of Indians who presumably were responsible for these massacres.

The coastal cliffs and rock stacks are largely composed of sandstones and shales, which erode quite rapidly, as shown by the steep coastal cliffs along this shoreline. Evidently erosion has been extensive since sea level approached its present position some 3,000 years ago. One factor in this erosion may be the great numbers of large Douglas fir logs that float down the rivers and wash ashore, piling up against the base of the shore cliffs, along with beach cobbles, mostly worn to a discoidal shape (Fig. 12.44). Even on some of the National Park trails at Kalaloch it is necessary to climb over eight or ten huge logs to reach the water. Under ordinary wave conditions these logs protect the cliffs; but during times of heavy surf and storm tides, the waves hurl the trunks against the cliffs like battering rams, and the beach cobbles also play an important role.

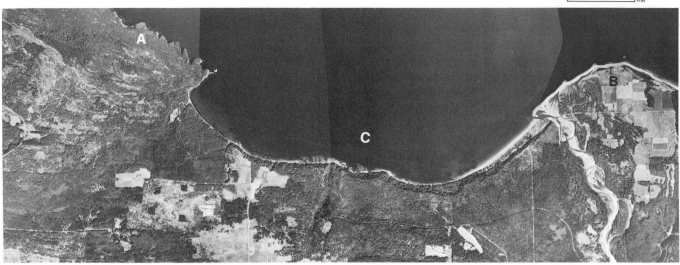

12.45 Two projecting points along the south shore of the Strait of Juan de Fuca separated by Freshwater Bay. The serrate projection (A) is due to the outcrop of resistant Eocene volcanic rocks. The curving point (B) has been formed by the Elwha River Delta. U.S. Department of Agriculture, 1963.

SOUTH SHORE OF STRAIT OF JUAN DE FUCA, WASHINGTON [Figs. 12.45 and 12.46] The east-west trending Strait of Juan de Fuca separates northwestern Washington from Vancouver Island. For the first 50 miles in from the open Pacific, the Strait has a remarkably even width of about 12 miles but widens farther east to 20 miles in the vicinity of Port Angeles, on the mainland side, and Victoria on Vancouver Island. Farther east, the inland waterway spreads out in both directions and is complicated by large sounds and numerous islands to the north and to the south.

Late in the sixteenth century, both British and Spanish explorers were attempting to locate a northwest passage by which they could reach the Pacific Ocean. The Viceroy of Mexico, learning that the Englishman Francis Drake had been seen along the northwest coast, felt sure that Drake had secretly discovered such a passage. The Viceroy authorized an expedition in 1592, with a Greek, Apostolos Valerianus, in command, to explore and fortify this passage in order to keep out the English. The Greek invented the name Juan de Fuca to please his Mexican employers. He reported upon his return that he had found such a passage between 47° and 48°, and had sailed it for 20 days, reaching the North Sea (Atlantic). This Ananias aroused considerable in-

terest in renewed exploration. Later, a strait south of Vancouver Island, which is often fogbound, was discovered somewhat north of the place Juan de Fuca had described, although this may have been pure coincidence. Two centuries later, it was named in his honor, even though he may never have seen the strait; and obviously it is not a passage to the Atlantic.

The Strait of Juan de Fuca is clearly an example of glacial erosion, being comparable to the Bay of Fundy and the Gulf of St. Lawrence on the glaciated East Coast. Juan de Fuca is the southernmost of a whole series of these glacial troughs that extend all along the coast of British Columbia and southern Alaska. Like most of these troughs, Juan de Fuca has quite straight walls, and the water depths descend rapidly away from the shore. The 100-fathom curve reaches up the Strait for almost 40 miles, and basins greater than that depth continue along the Vancouver Island side for another 10 miles. The deep trough also continues southwest of Cape Flattery across the entire continental shelf.

The tongue of ice that moved along the Strait, coming from the Cordilleran continental ice mass, overlapped the south shore and spread 10 miles inland at the east end of the Strait but had widened to 30 miles in the vicinity of Cape Flattery. The maximum glacial extent in this area is thought to have

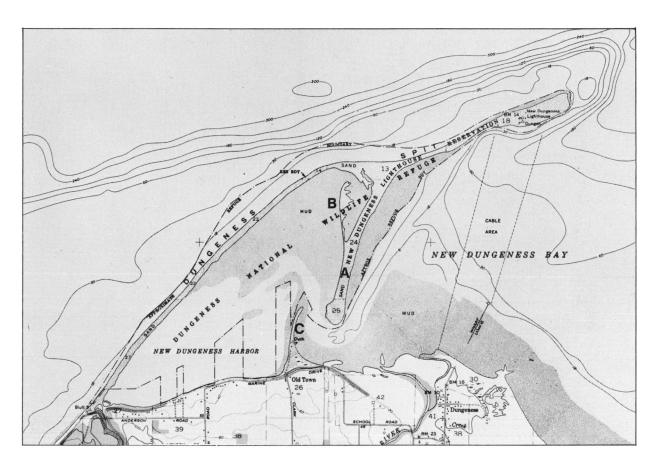

12.46 Dungeness Spit, along the southern shore of the Strait of Juan de Fuca, with a long south arm (A). Note two small northward extending arms (B and C). U.S. Geological Survey, Dungeness quadrangle, 1956.

occurred more than 30,000 years ago. The work of F. E. Anderson shows that the later Wisconsin ice lobe, which carved out the Strait and spread out onto the continental shelf, did not have much effect on the topography along the south side of the entrance. However, boulders were carried by the ice from Vancouver Island and dumped on Cape Flattery. This is known because there is no granite along the south side of the Strait.

The Strait of Juan de Fuca is nearly parallel with the strike of the rocks on both sides and was evidently excavated along the less resistant formations that underlie the trough. Rocks exposed along the south side of the Strait are Eocene, Oligocene, and Miocene sedimentaries, except at Cape Flattery, Pillar Point, and the points between Agate, Crescent, and Freshwater Bays (C in Fig. 12.45). At each of these points, Eocene volcanic rocks are exposed except at

Pillar Point, which is massive Middle Miocene conglomerate and sandstone. The volcanic rocks are more resistant than the sedimentary rocks and project into the Strait about 0.5 mile farther than adjoining areas with sedimentary rocks. At and just west of Port Angeles, the sea cliffs are cut entirely in glacial drift. This was a lowland before glaciation. There are no prominent coastal terraces along this Juan de Fuca coast.

Rivers that enter the Strait from the south have steep gradients and come from a high rainfall area. As a result, they have formed alluvial fans or relatively small deltas where they discharge into the Strait. Because littoral currents are weaker than on the exposed Pacific Coast, even the fans form projections into the Strait. The deltaic mouth of the Elwha River, about 4 miles west of Port Angeles, projects 1.3 miles farther than the cliffed coasts on each side

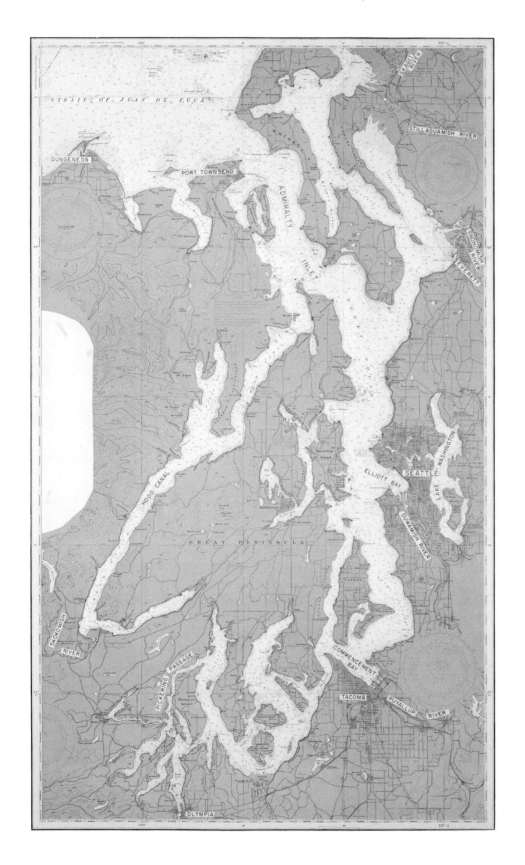

(B in Fig. 12.45). Smaller projections are found at the mouths of other streams.

Port Angeles is situated at an angle in the coast and is largely protected from wave erosion by Ediz Hook, a spit 3.5 miles long, built eastward from the angle in the coast. An air strip, boat dock, and Coast Guard station are located on the spit. Fifteen miles farther east, a similar point, Dungeness Spit (Fig. 12.46), is 5 miles long and has a southward extension (A) a mile in length. This nearly encloses the shallow New Dungeness Harbor. The name comes from the Dungeness in southeastern England, which is a large cuspate foreland. Dungeness Spit is even more comparable with Presque Isle along the south shore of Lake Erie. In each of these cases, the spit has grown eastward and the shoreward projection has come from a countercurrent.

Beaches are narrow and quite discontinuous along this shore. The largest form crescents at Neah Bay near Cape Flattery, Clallam Bay, and Crescent and Agate Bays farther east. All of these have coastal resorts. Collecting agates from the beach gravels at Agate Bay is a great attraction. It seems likely that when the glaciers retreated, the Juan de Fuca coast was much straighter but that postglacial wave erosion caused cliff recession up to 0.5 mile at some places along this heavily forested shore, and elsewhere, deltas built out into the Strait.

PUGET SOUND LOWLAND, WASHINGTON
[Figs. 12.47 through 12.52]   East of Dungeness Spit, the comparatively smooth southern shore of the Strait of Juan de Fuca is interrupted by small southward-trending glacial troughs (Fig. 12.47), including, from west to east, Sequim Bay, Port Discovery, and Port Townsend. These bays are the first indication of a change in direction of ice movement from east to west, as along Juan de Fuca Trough, to north to south, which is clearly indicated in the large inlets of the Puget Sound Lowland.

These north-south trending inlets were discovered on May 2, 1792, by the English explorer, George Vancouver. He named Port Discovery for his sloop *Discovery*; and, after anchoring here, he sailed farther east in a small boat, coming into the nearby inlet

12.47 Chart showing the fiord coast of the Puget Sound Lowland. U.S. Coast and Geodetic Survey Chart 6401, published 1965.

which he called Port Townsend in honor of the Marquis of Townsend. Then he moved his ship into the longer fiord, Admiralty Inlet, and into its narrow tributary, which he named Hood's Channel in honor of Lord Hood. Later the name was changed to Hood Canal, although it is not a canal. Although at times valley glaciers from the high Cascade Mountains to the east formed piedmont glaciers along the eastern border of the Lowland, the effect of these local glaciers was masked by the southward advance of the Cordilleran ice sheet, from the coastal mountains of British Columbia, as a series of narrow lobes or tongues moving through preexisting river valleys in the Puget Sound Lowland to terminal positions a little south of Olympia but north of Chehalis River. The narrow tongues of ice, as they thickened, occupied the intervalley divides, covering the whole Lowland with glacial ice.

The glacier that last occupied the Lowland reached its terminal stand between 15,000 and 13,500 years ago. The complex of narrow fiordlike sounds separated by narrow peninsulas or islands (Fig. 12.47) provides a pattern of coastal irregularity comparable to the northern Maine coast and southeastern Alaska. The longest of the glacial troughs, a combination of Admiralty Inlet, Puget Sound, and a group of branching inlets to the south, has a total length of about 110 miles. Hood Canal extends for 65 miles. An aerial photograph composite taken near Olympia, at the south end of the fiords (Fig. 12.48) will serve to illustrate the complexity of the glacially eroded shoreline. In the area of the photograph, Pickering Passage (A), the principal drowned valley, is about 0.5 mile wide and 50 to 60 feet deep.

Although in many places the divides between the fiords rise 500 to 700 feet above sea level and the troughs have maximum depths of about 1,100 feet below sea level, the geologic map of the state of Washington shows that the Puget Sound Lowland is glacial drift with no rock. The area was depressed under the weight of glacial ice, which is estimated to have been between 5,000 feet thick in northern Washington and 1,300 feet at the southern extremity of the fiords. Seawater entered the glacially scoured troughs about 13,500 years ago and the area that had been loaded with glacial ice began to rise (*isostatic rebound*) due to glacial melting. Meanwhile, the return of meltwater to the oceans caused eustatic rise in sea level. These opposing forces had varying effects between the southern limit of glaciation in the Puget Sound Lowland and the international boundary in northwestern Washington. In northern Washington, where the glacial ice was thicker, the rebound resulted in a far greater elevation of the land than occurred near the southern end of the ice sheet. The developments here are comparable with those along the New England coast between Long Island and the Canadian line.

Most of the margins of the Puget Sound waterways are bordered with steep bluffs eroded in glacial drift by storm waves. Numerous steep gullies have also dissected the coastal borders, and landslides have locally displaced the seaward margins of the upland plateaus. Here, as adjacent to the Chesapeake Bay islands (p. 101), erosion has continued to depths of 20 or 30 feet below sea level, leaving little or no shallow bench to record the cliff recession.

The streams entering the fiordlike drowned valleys have built deltas into the ends of the narrow glacial troughs. The delta of the Skokomish River (Fig. 12.49) at the south end of Hood Canal, and the Nisqually, 10 miles east of Olympia, are representative of this delta building. The darker water area in the upper part of the photo is 10 feet or less deep, although the trough nearby has depths of 120 to 200 feet. Smaller deltas have been built where streams enter the sides of the glacial troughs.

The eastern shore of the Puget Sound Lowland includes the important port cities of Tacoma, Seattle, and Everett. The port of Tacoma was constructed on the southwest side of Commencement Bay, at the outlet of the Puyallup River, whose tributaries carry meltwater from the glaciers of Mt. Rainier. A delta was building into Commencement Bay before dockage for the port was developed, about 1900. The artificial levees of the port constricted the flow of the Puyallup River to one channel, and the delta front at water level has not been extended appreciably during the past 65 years. During this period, however, the 300-foot depth contour has moved 2,000 feet seaward, indicating that Commencement Bay is being shoaled by the growth of a submarine delta.

12.48 Pickering Passage (A), Hammersley Inlet (B), and Squaxin Island (C), showing typical fiord outlines in the Puget Sound Lowland. Pickering Passage is generally 30 to 60 feet deep, far less than the fiords farther north. U.S. Department of Agriculture, 1957.

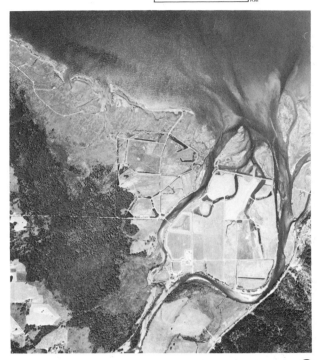

12.49 Delta of Skokomish River built into the south end of Hood Canal, the second longest fiord of the Puget Sound Lowland. U.S. Department of Agriculture, 1958.

Seattle (Fig. 12.50) is on a long, rather narrow upland between Puget Sound and Lake Washington, the latter being a north-south glacially eroded trough with a maximum depth of about 200 feet. A waterway for small boats connects Lake Washington and Puget Sound. Most of Seattle is 250 to 450 feet above sea level, with bluffs rising 200 feet or more, especially along the Puget Sound coast. At the mouth of the Duwamish River (A) in Elliott Bay, the port of Seattle has had a history similar to Tacoma. Like Tacoma, the port structures were built in about 1900. Tributaries of the Duwamish are short swift streams, draining the Cascade Range; and one tributary, the White River, carries glacial silt from the north side of Mt. Rainier. Points protruding into Puget Sound (D, E) are small cuspate spits built out by currents; but another point (F), which looks similar from the air, is an erosion remnant of the retreating bluffs.

Farther north, the port of Everett adjoins the delta of Snohomish River (A in Fig. 12.51), and is protected from wave attack by an artificial spoil bank.

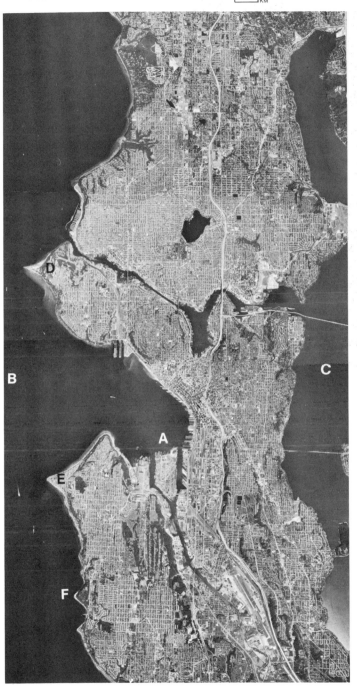

12.50 Seattle, Washington, on a narrow divide between Puget Sound (B) and Lake Washington (C), both of which are glacially eroded troughs. Most of the Seattle upland is composed of glacial till, with the eroded margins forming steep bluffs. Cuspate spits (D and E) as viewed from air resemble other sharp points in the eroded bluffs of glacial till (F). U.S. Geological Survey, 1968.

12.51 The Port of Everett, Washington, just south of the delta of the Snohomish River (A), has an artificial island protecting the waterfront. The underwater part of the delta (B) extends 3 miles offshore with depths of 3 feet or less. U.S. Geological Survey, 1958.

Much of Everett is 300 to 600 feet above sea level, with narrow valleys 200 feet deep extending back from the coastal cliffs.

North of Everett, the Skagit (A in Fig. 12.52), a large river entering from the northeast, drains much of the northern Cascades; and the Stillaguamish River (B), coming from the east, enters Puget Sound near the Skagit. Each has built a relatively large delta (C, D). The northern distributary of the Stillaguamish River discharges at a point where hilly Camano Island (E) approaches the mainland shore. Shoaling of the narrow strait by delta building has practically tied the island to the mainland. Skagit Bay, north of the Strait, is almost entirely less than 6 feet deep because of delta accumulation. Port Susan (F), into which the Stillaguamish discharges, is shallow in the area shown by the lighter tone in Figure 12.52 but, just to the south, deepens abruptly to about 400 feet. Growth of the two large deltas will continue filling

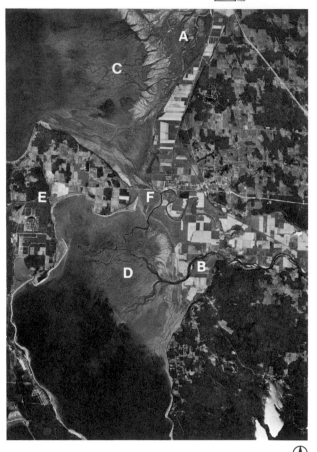

12.52 Deltas of the Skagit (C) and Stillaguamish (D) Rivers. One branch of Stillaguamish (F) goes through a narrow pass between the mainland and Camano Island, discharging into Skagit Bay. The remainder of the discharge enters Port Susan to the south. Large parts of both bays have been filled to depths of 6 feet or less by delta deposits. U.S. Geological Survey, 1968.

the bays; and, since the deltas are not being used for port facilities, the exposed portions of the deltas will grow at the expense of the shallow bays.

DELTAS OF NORTHERN WASHINGTON AND ADJACENT FRASER RIVER [Figs. 12.53, 12.54, and 12.55]   The northernmost extension of the United States coast, like the Puget Sound area, is largely a lowland. It has other bays with sizable deltas. The Nooksack, the largest river south of the Canadian boundary, receives most of the drainage from the northern Cascades and Mt. Baker. It has built a delta into the northern end of Bellingham Bay just west of the city of Bellingham. This delta (Fig. 12.53)

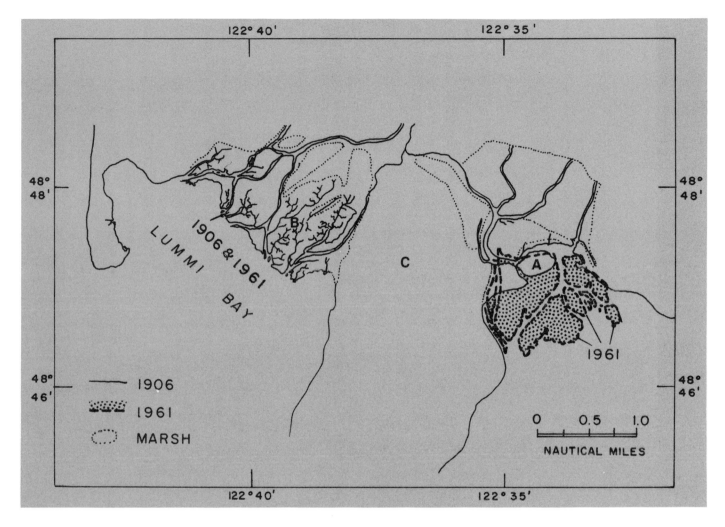

12.53 Nooksack River Delta (A) and the delta of its distributary Lummi River (B). The former is actively building into Bellingham Bay, and has advanced 0.5 mile between the 1906 survey and an undated survey that appears in the 1961 chart. During the same interval, the Lummi River has not built forward probably because of artificial diversion of the water to Bellingham Bay. A hilly peninsula (C) separates the two bays. From U.S. Coast and Geodetic Survey Chart 6378, 1906 and 1961 editions.

has advanced 0.5 mile in about 40 years, as shown by the 1906 Coast and Geodetic Survey Chart 6378 and the 1961 edition. In the same interval, the northern part of the bay has also received considerable sediment. Soundings out to about 70 feet have shoaled approximately 10 feet. However, the large northern distributary of the Nooksack, the Lummi River, has shown no appreciable advance during this same period. This may be because most of the drainage has been diverted to the south. The shallow sea floor in Lummi Bay, off the delta, has a series of rills and bars that trend largely north and south, except close to the delta where they run normal to the shore (Fig. 12.54). The only explanation for these that occurs to the writers is that they are due to north winds that elongate the submerged delta deposits in that direction.

According to D. J. Easterbrook, marine deposits with a date of 10,000 B.C. are found in the vicinity of the Nooksack River at an elevation of 500 to 700 feet above sea level. These deposits were made by glacial meltwater and indicate that the area was much

12.54 Showing the reclaimed land of the Lummi River Delta now used for farming. The striking rill and bar pattern (A), with a north-south orientation, is visible in the shallow water south of the delta. This has developed since the active growth of the delta stopped. U.S. Department of Agriculture, 1966.

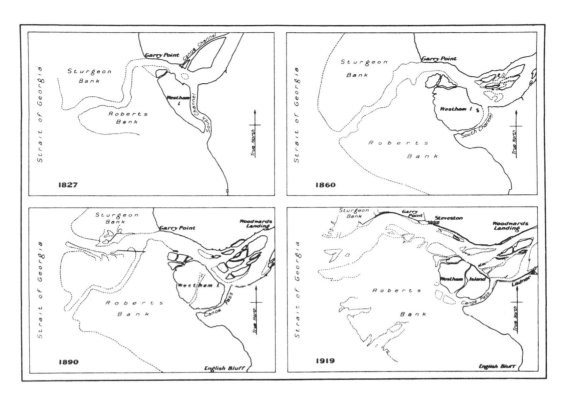

12.55 Diagram of the outlines of the exposed portions (solid line) and submerged portions (dotted line) of the Fraser River Delta, southernmost British Columbia, in 1827, 1860, 1890, and 1919. From Johnston (1921).

more deeply submerged when the ice was retreating than it is now. Easterbrook claims that the present high stand of these marine deposits can be attributed in part to glacial rebound of the land after the 5,000-foot-thick ice melted, but he thinks that some of the uplift was due to earth movements coming from another cause.

The Fraser River, which enters the sea just north of the United States boundary, is the largest in western Canada and drains much of the Canadian Cordillera west of the Rocky Mountain Continental Divide. It is the only river that has filled a fiord; and it has extended its delta out into the wide Strait of Georgia, which separates British Columbia from Vancouver Island. When the glaciers retreated from this area, the sea came in over the entire delta and even covered much of Vancouver to the north; but the recovery of the crust from the weight of the glaciers brought up the land as much as 650 feet, and the river built rapidly into the emerging valleys, forming the present delta. This delta was partly built during

early interglacial stages and can be traced for about 100 miles. The most recent addition is 19 miles wide and is mostly below high tide level but is diked to keep out the tidewaters.

The Fraser Delta was studied extensively by W. A. Johnston. His report shows some of the changes in the distributaries of the main channel between 1827 and 1919 (Fig. 12.55). The principal change is in the shape of Westham Island, which has enlarged since 1827, but had not advanced far into the Strait of Georgia. A more recent study by W. H. Mathews and Shepard showed that between a 1929 survey and their work in 1959, when the delta was revisited, the edge of Roberts Bank, a shoal, had advanced at a rate of 7.5 feet per year; but the delta front at a depth of 300 feet had advanced in the same period 28 feet per year. This faster advance below the water level is the same as reported for the Puyallup Delta at Tacoma. It contrasts with the advance of the Mississippi Delta that occurs both at sea level and below at about the same rate. As a result,

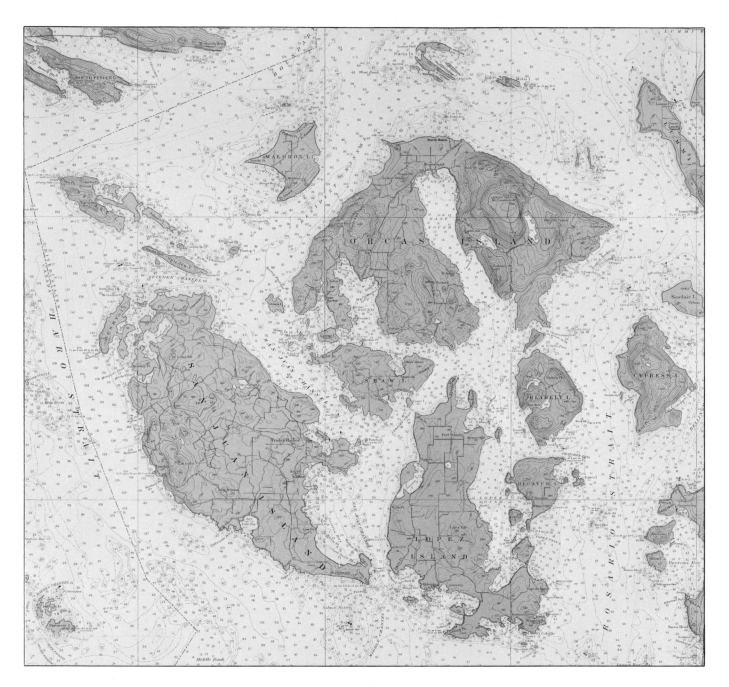

12.56 Chart showing San Juan Islands, Washington. U.S. Coast and Geodetic Survey Chart 6300, 1966.

the slope off the Fraser and Puyallup is decreasing, while it is remaining the same off the Mississippi.

SAN JUAN ISLANDS [Fig. 12.56]   Between the wide Juan de Fuca Strait on the south and the equally wide Strait of Georgia on the north, the passageway between Vancouver and the Washington mainland is almost filled with a group of irregularly shaped islands, known collectively as the San Juans. These rugged islands, with mountains up to 2,400 feet, and the intricate sounds that separate them, constitute one of the beauty spots of America and provide a paradise for yachtsmen and summer vacationists. The large islands include Orcas to the north, San Juan to the west, and Lopez to the south. According to R. D. McLellan, the group contains 457 islands standing above high tide (786, if one includes the rocks and shoals exposed at low tide). The San Juan Islands are bounded on the west by Haro Strait and on the northwest by Boundary Strait, both constituting the international boundary with Canada. Rosario Strait forms the eastern boundary of the islands.

The history of the San Juans includes a serious dispute between the United States and Great Britain in 1859, which almost led to war and was often referred to as the "Pig War." Prior to this, in 1846, a treaty had been signed that placed the boundary as the channel between Vancouver Island and the mainland. This overlooked the great mass of intervening islands. Both countries claimed the islands and gradually started to settle portions of them. After a few skirmishes, it was decided pro tem that San Juan Island would be neutral, so a fort was erected by the United States at the southeast corner, and the British erected another near the northwest corner. These forts are still well preserved. Finally, in 1872, the disputed territory came up for arbitration; and William I of Germany, the arbitrator, awarded all of the islands up to Haro Strait to the United States.

The climate of the San Juan Islands is a surprise to visitors who are familiar with the cloudy and rainy climate of Seattle and western Washington. The San Juans are in the rain shadow of rugged Vancouver Island and actually have an annual rainfall of only about 25 inches, with almost no rain in summer. As a result, some parts of the islands have little forest cover, and cactus grows locally. Elsewhere, particularly in Shaw Island in the middle of the group, the islands are heavily forested with many conifers. Wind storms are very severe during the winter season.

The rock formations are a mixture of sedimentaries ranging in age from Paleozoic to early Tertiary and igneous intrusives, which cut the sedimentary rocks and have caused local metamorphism. The older sedimentaries are highly folded and faulted.

The effects of glaciation are well preserved on the San Juans. The passageways between the islands and the deep embayments are glacial fiords, many of them with steep walls and most of them with relatively deep water that characterize fiords. One fiord, East Sound, almost cuts Orcas Island in two equal halves.

Because the Strait of Georgia is supplied by tidal water coming almost entirely from the Strait of Juan de Fuca, very strong tidal currents run through the passageways between the islands. One of the effects of these strong currents, according to R. D. McClellan, is that the storm waves do not produce much erosion while the tides are running. As a result, the chief wave erosion occurs during the slack current at high tide. This has produced wave-cut benches at the high tide level that are well exposed when the tide is down.

REFERENCES

Anderson, F. E., 1968. Seaward terminus of the Vashon continental glacier in the Strait of Juan de Fuca. *Mar. Geol.*, vol. 6, no. 6, pp. 419–438.

Andrews, R. S., 1965. Modern sediments of Willapa Bay, Washington: a coastal plain estuary. Univ. Washington, M.S. thesis *Tech. Rept.* 118.

Bretz, J. H., 1913. Glaciation of the Puget Sound region. *Washington Geol. Survey Bull.* 8.

————, 1920. The Juan de Fuca lobe of the Cordilleran ice sheet. *Jour. Geol.*, vol. 28, pp. 333–339.

Brown, R. D., Jr., H. D. Gower, and P. D. Snavely, Jr., 1960. Geology of the Port Angeles–Crescent Lake area, Clallam County, Washington, *U.S. Geol. Survey, Oil and Gas Investigations Map* OM–203.

Byrne, J. V., 1964. An erosional classification for the northern Oregon coast. *Assoc. Amer. Geographers, Annals*, vol. 54, pp. 329–335.

Cooper, W. S., 1958. Coastal sand dunes of Oregon and Washington. *Geol. Soc. Amer. Memo.* 72, 169 pp.

Crandell, D. R., 1965. The glacial history of western Washington and Oregon. In H. E. Wright, Jr., and D. G. Frey (eds.), *The Quaternary of the United States.* Princeton University Press, Princeton, N.J., pp. 341–353.

Danner, W. R., 1955. *Geology of Olympic National Park.* Univ. Washington Press, Seattle, Wash.

Dicken, Samuel N., 1961. *Some Recent Physical Changes of the Oregon Coast.* Rept. on Invest. Project NR 388–062 between Univ. Oregon and Office of Naval Research.

Drury, Aubrey, 1947. *California, an Intimate Guide.* Harper & Row, New York, p. 352.

Easterbrook, D. J., 1963. Late Pleistocene glacial events and relative sea level changes in the northern Puget Sound Lowland, Washington. *Geol. Soc. Amer. Bull.*, vol. 74, pp. 1465–1483.

Fagerlund, G. O., and Frances I. Fagerlund, 1954. Olympic National Park. *U.S. Nat. Park Service, Nat. Hist. Handbook Ser., no. 1.*

Gower, H. D., 1960. Geology of the Pysht quadrangle, Washington. *U.S. Geol. Survey, Geol. Map* GQ–129.

Hands, E. B., 1968. Inner continental shelf sediments in the vicinity of Cape Flattery, Washington. *Univ. Washington Spec. Rept.* 40.

Hickson, R. E., and F. W. Rodolf, 1950. History of the Columbia River jetties. In J. W. Johnson (ed.), *Proceedings of First Conference on Coastal Engineering.* Council on Wave Res., Engr. Found. Publ., pp. 283–298.

Johnston, W. A., 1921. Sedimentation of Fraser River Delta. *Geol. Survey Canada, Memo.* 125.

Lowry, W. D., 1952. Late Cenozoic course of the Columbia River. *Geol. Soc. Amer. Bull.*, vol. 63, pp. 1–24.

Mathews, W. H., and F. P. Shepard, 1962. Sedimentation of Fraser River Delta, British Columbia. *Bull. Amer. Assoc. Petroleum Geologists*, vol. 46, no. 8, pp. 1416–1438.

McLellan, R. D., 1927. The Geology of the San Juan Islands. *Univ. Washington, Publ. in Geol.*, vol. 2.

Paulsen, C. G., S. E. Rantz, and H. C. Riggs, 1949. Floods of May–June, 1948 in Columbia River Basin. *Geol. Survey Water Supply Paper* 1080.

Strum, C. G., and W. B. Strum, 1964. *Good Friday Nightmare.* Strum Publishing Co., Crescent City, Calif.

Waldron, H. H., B. O. Liesch, D. R. Mullineaux, and D. R. Crandell, 1962. Preliminary geologic map of Seattle and vicinity, Washington. *U.S. Geol. Survey, Misc. Geol. Investigations, Map* I–345.

Willis, B., 1899. Description of the Tacoma quadrangle. *U.S. Geol. Survey, Geol. Atlas, Folio* 54.

13.1 Relief map of Alaska showing some of the
localities described in Chapters 13 and 14.

Glaciers, Earthquakes, and Volcanoes

Mountainous Southern Alaska Coast

13 The coast of Alaska (Fig. 13.1) has a length of about 25,000 miles, more than the circumference of the earth at the equator. Even omitting the many small bays and fiords, it is about 6,800 miles, as compared with 5,100 miles for the Atlantic, Gulf, and Pacific coasts of the forty-eight conterminous states measured in the same way. Although the northern tip of Alaska, at 71°20' N. Lat., lies well within the Arctic Circle, the southernmost point of the Aleutian Islands is only 50°, and the south end of the Panhandle 55°. From east to west, Alaska extends from 130° west longitude in the southeastern part to 170° east longitude at Attu Island, the United States terminus of the Aleutian chain. Climatically, its southern borders lie in the cool temperate zone, while the Arctic coasts of Chukchi and Beaufort Seas are in the boreal (frigid, arctic) belt.

On May 29, 1867, papers transferring Alaska to the United States for a purchase price of $7.2 million were signed by Secretary of State William H. Seward and the Russian ambassador. Americans at this time knew little about Alaska; and many were bitter about wasting all that money on an "arctic wasteland," calling it "Seward's Folly." In later years, annual new wealth derived from a single mine has often exceeded this purchase price. The 1969 oil leases on the North Slope netted the forty-ninth state $900 million.

Only a few old maps of the Alaska coasts dating prior to 1867 are available, but these show amazing changes in the glaciers. Alaska is now well covered by modern U.S. Coast and Geodetic Survey charts and U.S. Geological Survey topographic maps. During the 1950s, the Geological Survey photographed

Help in revision of this chapter has been provided by the various members of the U.S. Geological Survey at Menlo Park and La Jolla, California, especially G. W. Moore and Erk Reimnitz.

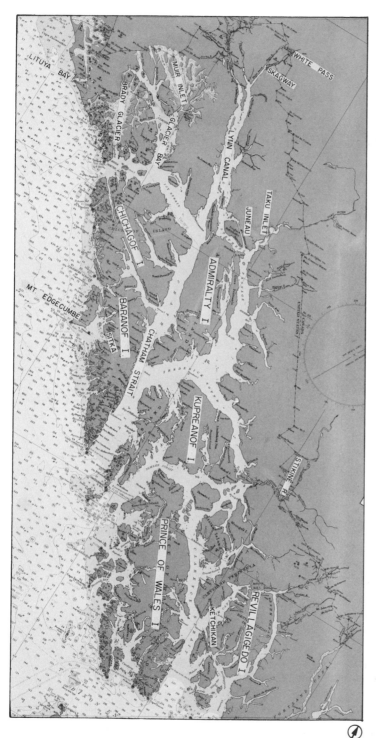

13.2 Southeastern Alaska, showing inland passages and islands. From U.S. Coast and Geodetic Survey Chart 8002, 1966.

from the air most of the Alaskan coast, and a vast number of photographs of south-central Alaska were taken after the disastrous earthquake of March 27, 1964 by the U.S. Coast and Geodetic Survey, the U.S. armed services, and other governmental agencies. These aerial photos help illustrate the changes produced by this catastrophe.

In this chapter, we will discuss only the southern coast of Alaska, from the British Columbia border to the west end of the Aleutian Islands. This coast forms a large concave sweeping arc. To the southeast, the Panhandle consists of 350 miles of elongate islands and fiords, which represent the northwestward continuation of the islands and passageways of northwestern Washington and the entire coast of British Columbia. Beyond the island-protected Panhandle, the coast bends to the west and for 400 miles is relatively straight, following the margin of a lowland at the base of a series of very high mountain ranges. The cruise ships mostly stop before getting to this open water, where the full force of the waves of the North Pacific contrast greatly with the quiet sailing through the island passageways.

Beyond the coastal lowlands, the mountains again come to the sea; and the coast becomes deeply indented for another 400 miles, first with the many-armed Prince William Sound and the smaller indentation of the Kenai Peninsula and then with a return to the Inland Passage, consisting here of the elongate Cook Inlet and Shelikof Strait that separates the mainland from Kodiak Island. Again, an open coast with short ragged embayments takes over and extends along the southeastern side of the Alaska Peninsula for 450 miles. Beyond this, the Aleutian Islands continue for 1,300 miles.

This curving coast of southern Alaska has many features that form a great contrast to those of the conterminous forty-eight states (called the "Lower Forty-eight" by Alaskans). The overlapping belts of the Pacific Mountain system, which follow the general curve of the coast and extend inland for 150 to 200 miles, include the highest mountains in North America, crowned by Mt. McKinley with its 20,300-foot summit and the St. Elias Range, almost as high. These mountains are still growing, which accounts for the numerous severe earthquakes that cause great catastrophes along this coast and have on occasions radically changed the coastal configuration. Unlike the horizontal shifting that characterizes the California faults, the movements in Alaska are mostly vertical. Two of these Alaskan earthquakes (1899 and 1964) were accompanied by uplifts of land greater than any ever recorded in other parts of the world. The earthquakes are particularly severe in the central and western sections. Vulcanism has also been important in the Pacific Mountain system. Only a few old volcanoes are found in the southeast; and there are some inland volcanoes in the Wrangell Range, west of the St. Elias Mountains. Volcanoes are very important in the Alaska Peninsula and the Aleutian Islands where they have had a predominant part in shaping the coast. In some places, lava has built out the coast, as have the mudflows accompanying eruptions. On the other hand, some small islands have been largely destroyed by volcanic explosions.

In southern Alaska, we see the effects of Pleistocene glaciation in the Inland Passage and islands, which dominate the southeastern Panhandle, and in the numerous fiords that are found indenting the coast in the upper part of the arc, as well as along the Alaska Peninsula. These are comparable to the fiord coasts we have already described for Washington and Maine, but on the Alaskan coast, glaciation takes on a further significance as it is still in operation. The mountains have the largest glaciers in North America, and some of them extend down to the coast where their ends break off as icebergs that float out to sea. Since the glacial termini are very changeable, we find here an important cause of coastline alteration. Since first mapped by early explorers, some of the glaciers have retreated as much as 60 miles, opening up lengthy embayments that were filled with glacial ice when first discovered. Elsewhere, the glaciers have advanced, but these advances have been mostly of a temporary nature. In another way the glaciation of the Alaskan coast differs from those we have described previously. The effect of ice sculpture on some of the low mountainous islands of southern Alaska has left amphitheater-headed embayments that are comparable with the *cirque* heads of formerly glaciated valleys, which we find only in the lofty mountain ranges in lower latitudes.

SOUTHEASTERN ALASKA [Figs. 13.2 through 13.9]   The Alaska Panhandle is a fiordland bordered by a belt of rugged islands 100 miles wide. It greatly resembles other glaciated coasts, notably southern Chile and Norway. Although its mountains are for the most part only a few thousand feet high, the humid climate nourishes many glaciers, especially to the north; and some of them come down to sea level. One of the effects of present-day glaciers is observable as one sails north through the Inland Passage. The relatively clear water of the fiords of British Columbia and southernmost Alaska changes to the cloudy, milky appearance that characterizes streams coming out of the snouts of glaciers.

The coastal islands, known as the Alexander Archipelago, trend mostly in a northwest or northerly direction, which permits ships to traverse this 350 miles of coast with scarcely any exposure to the open sea. The names of the islands are a combination of Russian (Baranof and Chichagof), British (Prince of Wales, Admiralty), Spanish (Revillagigedo), and Indian, which is true of most of the rest of Alaska. The names represent the influence of early explorers, British and Spanish, and early colonization by the Russians. The longest island, Prince of Wales, has a length of 125 miles.

Among the fiords, Chatham Strait, with its northward continuation in Lynn Canal and Taiya Inlet, is the longest fiord in the world, 240 miles, with a width of 6 miles and depths mostly 1,000 to 2,500 feet. It is flanked by mountains rising as high as 4,000 to 5,000 feet. The straightness of this long fiord is the result of glacial excavation along a great fault, which has strikingly different rock character on the two sides. East of this fault is the Coast Range batholith, one of the largest masses of granitic rock in the world. It was formed during the later part of the Mesozoic era and, according to the commonly held idea, was due to intrusion of molten rock into a thick mass of country rock but without breaking through to the surface. It cooled slowly, developing the coarsely crystalline textures. To the south of the batholith, the rocks are mostly metamorphic with some sedimentaries. On the west of the great fault, the Glacier Bay area has sedimentary rocks with some volcanics, and, to the south, greenstones (old altered lavas), and *graywackes* (dark-colored rocks composed of slightly weathered mineral and rock fragments) of Mesozoic age.

During the Pleistocene stages of glaciation, the Cordilleran ice sheet covered virtually all of southeastern Alaska, including the outlying islands, and even extended across most of the narrow bordering continental shelf. The only points that stood above

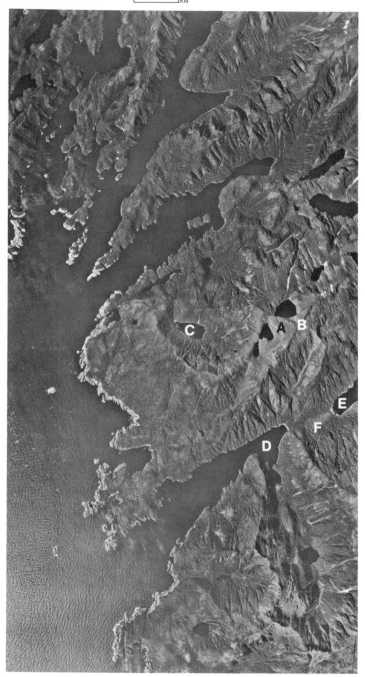

13.3 Southern Baranof Island. The small lakes (A) located on an upland plain on which the Pleistocene ice sheets rested. Note glacial cirque with a small lake (C). The drowned U-shaped valleys of major glaciers form Puffin Bay (D) and Port Lucy (E) with a low divide between them (F). Because the glacier removed most weak material, there has been little erosion since its disappearance. U.S. Geological Survey, 1948.

the general ice cap were a few peaks in the Coast Range. The glaciers followed preglacial valleys, cutting many of them below sea level and widening them to form the present-day fiords.

An example of the effects of glaciation on the islands is seen in Figure 13.3. This aerial compilation shows the southern end of Baranof Island, an area exposed on the west side to the open Pacific. The indented coast is typical of glaciation. A series of small lakes with elevations of 1,800 to 2,000 feet (A) marks the former land surface on which the Cordilleran ice sheet rested. Sharp crested hills (B) rise above the level of the lakes. Numerous narrow valleys in amphitheaters, many of them filled with lakes (C), are glacially excavated cirques formed by small valley glaciers that headed on this island after the ice sheet retreated. The most prominent glacial troughs, Puffin Bay (D) and Port Lucy (E), head opposite each other where the glaciers that formerly filled them have worn the island divide down to a low pass or *col* (F) less than 200 feet above sea level. Many such low passes, cut to or below sea level, have segmented this area into separate islands. According to A. T. Ovenshine, of the U.S. Geological Survey, the light strips on the photographs along the outer coast are bare rock cliffs 10 to 50 feet high, which are the result of storm waves, the high tidal range (10 to 25 feet), and perhaps a relatively recent uplift. Since the glaciers had stripped away much of the soil and weathered rock, there is now little left for the waves to shift, and hence no beaches, bars, or spits are in evidence.

Ketchikan (Fig. 13.4) is the southernmost city in Alaska and the first point of stop of northward-bound excursion steamers and planes. It is located on Revillagigedo Island along Tongass Narrows, 50 miles north of the British Columbia boundary. There is no flat ground here, so the city has been built either on the steep mountain slopes or on a platform supported by pilings that were driven into a narrow shelf, which borders this relatively shallow fiord. Despite the sheltered position of the waterfront and the jetties, the violent storms that are encountered here are a source of danger. On Thanksgiving Day, 1968, winds of 125 miles per hour caused considerable damage to the town and to the fishing boats that were docked there, although the pilings held. Ketchikan is the principal salmon-fishing port in Alaska and has a large cannery (B). Because the mountain slopes

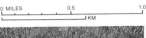

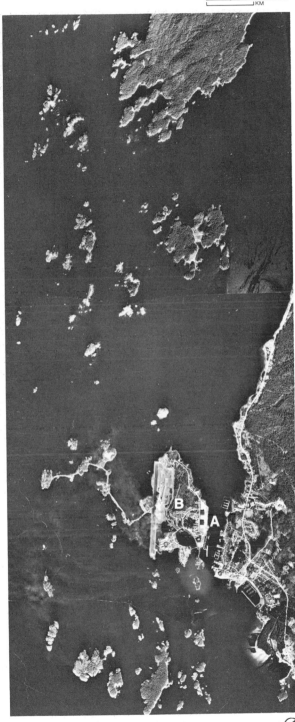

13.4 Ketchikan, the southernmost Alaskan city, is on the northeast side of a fiord, Tongass Narrows. Pennock Island (A) divides the fiord into two parts. Landslides descending the precipitous slopes above the town should be the principal cause of future coastal changes. U.S. Coast and Geodetic Survey, 1962.

are heavily forested, wood products, especially pulp wood, constitute another important industry. In addition, much copper ore has been mined in the Ketchikan area.

Sitka (Fig. 13.5) along the west coast of Baranof Island, was the principal Russian settlement. This is the only major Alaskan city virtually fronting on

13.5 Sitka, the former Russian capital of Alaska, is on Sitka Sound, a broad arm of the Pacific Ocean. The harbor is protected by Japonski Island (B). Many small glaciated rocks form tiny islands in the sound. U.S. Coast and Geodetic Survey, 1967.

13.6 Juneau, the capital of Alaska, is along the narrow fiord, Gastineau Channel. The remains of the Alaska-Juneau Mine (A) are south of the city. A large rock slide (B), at the mouth of Salmon Creek, extends into the fiord. U.S. Geological Survey, 1948.

the Pacific Ocean. Russian interest in northwestern North America was almost entirely as a source of valuable furs, such as the seal and sea otter. The Russians used native Indians, Eskimos, and Aleuts as slaves to harvest the annual fur crops, and large numbers of the natives were slaughtered. Although Russian colonists were aware of the presence of such valuable metals as gold and copper, they never undertook mining. Fort Archangel Gabriel was established in 1799 on Baranof Island, 7 miles north of Sitka. The fortress was demolished by the Thlinket Indians in 1802. Alexander Baranof, a Russian leader, drove the Indians out of their own native fort in 1804 and took possession. He called his capital New Archangel, but this was later changed to Sitka.

The harbor of Sitka (A in Fig. 13.5), mostly 30 to 60 feet deep, is protected by Japonski Island (B), on which is located the Sitka airport and the Mt. Edgecumbe School for Alaskan natives, maintained by the Bureau of Indian Affairs. A chain of small islands west of Japonski is interconnected by sand spits, forming a complex tombolo. Twelve miles west of Sitka, on Kruzof Island, the 3,200-foot Mt. Edgecumbe is the most conspicuous example of relatively recent volcanic activity in southeastern Alaska. Eruptions have not occurred since colonization of Alaska but are referred to in native legends. Ash falls coming from the volcano cover some of the glacial moraines and hence are presumably not more than a few thousand years old. The many small low rock islands west of Sitka may be the remnants of a plain of low relief, like the *strandflat* of Norway.

Juneau (Fig. 13.6), the capital of Alaska, was built on the northeast side of the shallow end of Gastineau Channel, a location similar to that of Ketchikan, except that there is more flat land because of a delta at the mouth of Gold Creek. The Juneau airport, 8 miles to the east of town, is also built on a delta, the latter having its source of sediment from the outwash of Mendenhall Glacier, which terminates 3 miles inland from the bay shore. The mountains rise abruptly above Juneau, reaching 3,600 feet a mile from the city.

The history of Juneau dates back to 1880, when two prospectors, Joseph Juneau and Richard Harris, discovered gold in the vicinity. A gold rush followed, and the new settlement was named after one of the prospectors. About 1887, work was started on two mines, one the Alaska Juneau near the town and the other across the channel on Douglas Island, which, before they were abandoned, had produced $70 million worth of gold. Juneau, in spite of its government activities, has not had much growth in recent years. The terrain is not well suited for road building; and, like Sitka and Ketchikan, it has no roads connecting it with the outer world. All transportation is by boat or air.

Taku Inlet, around the corner to the southeast of Juneau, has at its head one of the few tidewater glaciers descending from the Coast Range. Taku Glacier (A in Fig. 13.7) and its neighbor Norris Glacier (B), both coming from the Juneau Ice Field, are located only 25 miles from Juneau. Taku Glacier has been advancing recently, while Norris Glacier has been retreating and thinning, according to G. F. Jordan. In 70 years, Taku Glacier advanced 4 miles. To determine the earlier history of these glaciers, the tree-growth rings of the adjacent forests were studied by A. P. Muntz. When a glacier advances, the forest in its path is pushed over, but the trees on either side may continue to develop tree rings. Later, if the glacier retreats, seedlings soon begin to grow again on the exposed ground. Years later, cores cut respectively through the old growth and the new along the *trimline* will serve to tell the difference in ages and hence the length of time that the glacier had covered the area. The result of using this method has been to show that Norris Glacier advanced during the late 1800s and early 1900s until it reached a position

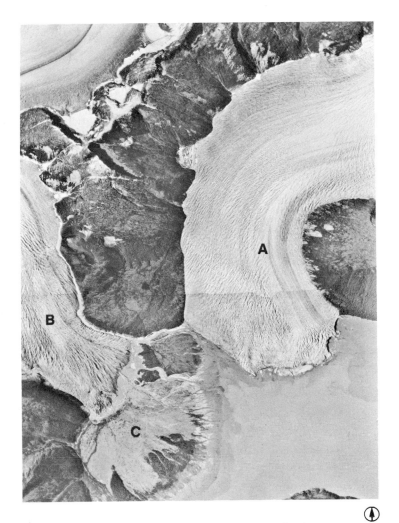

13.7 Taku Glacier (A) and Norris Glacier (B) discharge into Taku Inlet from the same ice field. Norris Glacier had a maximum advance in 1910, and has receded nearly 0.5 mile since 1890, whereas Taku Glacier had advanced 3.5 miles by 1950. An outwash fan and delta have been deposited by Norris Glacier into Taku Inlet. U.S. Geological Survey, 1948.

equal to where it had been about A.D. 1200. Since then, it has retreated between 0.25 and 0.5 mile. On the other hand, the Taku Glacier had a maximum advance in the mid-1700s, reaching a position that may have formed a dam across Taku Inlet. The glacier then retreated until about 1890, when the 4-mile advance got underway.

The outwash streams from both Taku and Norris Glaciers have contributed sediment to Taku Inlet. Norris Glacier has built a delta (C) more than 2 miles long. The delta building of Taku River, which

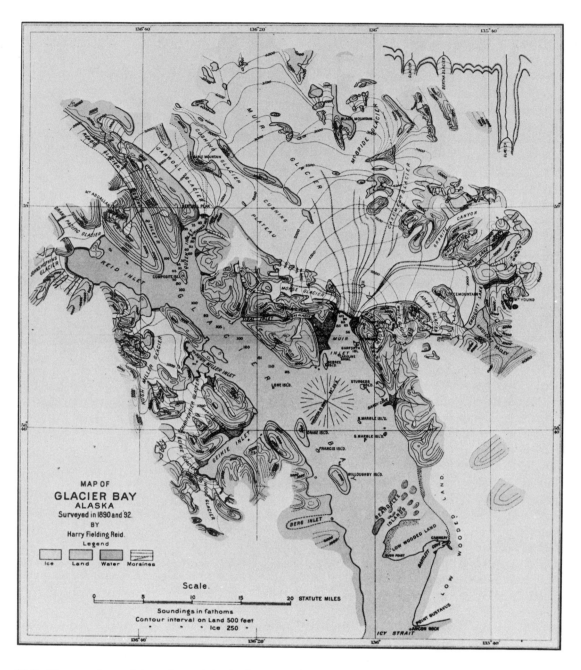

13.8 Changes in position of termini of tidewater glaciers in Glacier Bay, 1892 to 1937.

a 1892. Note that Tarr Inlet and Johns Hopkins Fiords (shown in Fig. 13.8*b*) are entirely ice filled. H. F. Reid (1895).

enters from the east, has also contributed toward filling the inlet. The water in the inlet is more than 600 feet deep at the lower end, but all of the upper part of the inlet is only a few feet deep, allowing only small boats to come up to the Taku Glacier. Jordan has compared surveys of Taku Inlet between 1890 and 1960 and found that, near the head of the bay, some places now built to sea level had depths of as much as 160 feet in 1890. Taku River is one of two that flow all the way across the Coast Range.

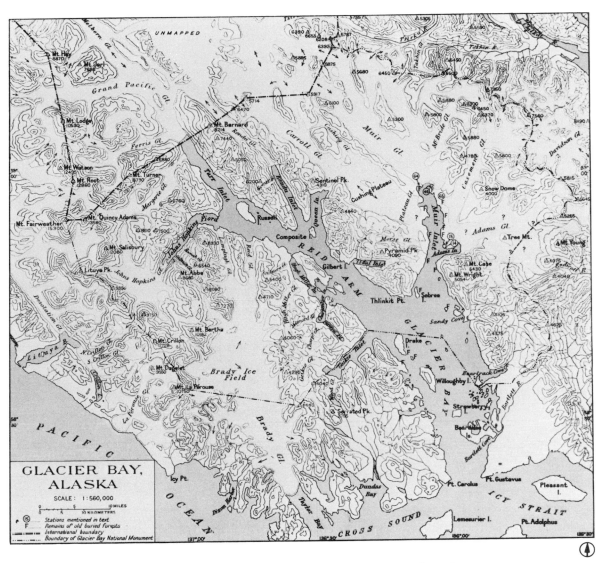

b 1937. Note that Johns Hopkins Glacier has retreated 10 miles, and Grand Pacific Glacier 16 miles (see also Fig. 2.3). From Cooper (1937).

Skagway, near the head of Taiya Inlet, an offshoot of Lynn Canal, is at the northern end of the Inland Passage. The city is built on the delta of the Skagway River. High mountain walls flank the city on both sides. A mile beyond the front of the delta, the 600-foot-deep fiord makes one somewhat apprehensive of the stability of the delta front. The area is close enough to the earthquake belt that slides of the end of the delta might develop, like those at Valdez (p. 425) during the 1964 earthquake. When gold was discovered in the Klondike in 1896, Skagway be-

came an important staging area for the hordes of prospectors who disembarked here to start the climb over the 3,000-foot White Pass and thence down to the Yukon. Prior to the building of the narrow-gauge railroad over the pass in 1900, some 30,000 people had walked over the narrow dangerous trail with their heavily laden mules.

Glacier Bay (Figs. 13.8 and 2.3), 50 miles west of Skagway and Juneau, branches from Icy Strait and extends north and then northwest for 70 miles. This bay and its many branches has the finest display

13.9 Brady Glacier, which discharges into Taylor Bay, is the southern terminus of an ice field 37 miles long between Glacier and Taylor Bays. The southward-flowing ice has pushed into a tributary valley (F). Note contorted flow lines (B). Two small tributaries have formed ice-dammed lakes (A). The dark bands (C) along the axis of the glacier are medial moraines. Delta deposits (D) at the head of the valley train are rapidly being built forward into Taylor Bay. The glacier advanced 5 miles after 1794 but was retreating slowly between 1908 and 1913. It has been relatively static since then. U.S. Geological Survey, 1948.

of tidewater glaciers in Alaska. It is included in Glacier Bay National Monument. Here, we find the greatest change in shoreline of any place in the United States during historical times. When Vancouver visited Glacier Bay in 1794, he found an ice wall about 6 miles north from Icy Strait. Thus there has been more than 60 miles of lengthening of the bay due to the retreat of the glaciers, which almost filled it in the late eighteenth century. Our first good map of the bay, by Harry Fielding Reid (Fig. 13.8a), shows that most of the retreat had taken place by 1892, but many of the arms were still filled with ice. The situation in 1937 is shown on the map by W. S. Cooper (Fig. 13.8b). As the glacier retreated, it opened up fiords as deep as 1,500 feet. These are now rapidly filling with sediment coming from the melting glaciers.

An acceleration in the glacier flow took place as the result of the great earthquake of 1899, centering in nearby Yakutat Bay. Great quantities of ice were disrupted from the ends of the glaciers, choking the fiords and making navigation impossible. Four years later, when the ice had cleared sufficiently to allow access to the end of Muir Glacier, the north tributary of Glacier Bay, it was found that this glacier had retreated 3.5 miles.

Carbon-14 dates provide an earlier history of the ice in Glacier Bay. As summarized by R. P. Goldthwait, this includes a retreat of 7,500 years ago to a position farther back than today's glaciers, followed by a large advance about 2,700 years ago. The ice reached its maximum extent near the mouth of Glacier Bay, according to Goldthwait, about 300 years ago and had retreated very little by the time it was observed by Vancouver in 1794.

Tide-gauge records of the U.S. Coast and Geodetic Survey appear to show that the land centering around the east side of Glacier Bay is rising at a rate that is exceeded in very few other places in the world. At Bartlett Cove, the uplift is nearly 2 inches per year. According to S. D. Hicks and William Shofnos, this appears to be the rebound from the localized deglaciation that removed a heavy weight from the area. The possibility exists that some of the uplift may be due to movements of the earth's crust, such as are responsible for the nearby earthquake belts. However, the uplift curves shown on the tide gauges do not reveal any relationship to the times of the earthquakes.

Johns Hopkins Fiord (Fig. 2.3), a tributary on the west side and near the head of Glacier Bay, was filled with ice until 1899, when Johns Hopkins Glacier became separated from Lamplugh Glacier at the time of the Yakutat Bay earthquake. It is now 10 miles long and was lengthened 8.5 miles between 1907 and 1929. The aerial photographs (Fig. 2.3) show the series of small glaciers that descend the steep walls of the newly uncovered fiord. Johns Hopkins Glacier enters the head of the fiord and is supplying an abundance of icebergs that break off from its steep front.

Taylor Bay (Fig. 13.9) is a north tributary of the western extension of Icy Strait. Brady Glacier, a huge ice field to the north, contributes much of the ice that heads toward John Hopkins Fiord and the west arms of Glacier Bay. The main drainage from the ice field is directed south, and a tongue approaches Taylor Bay (Fig. 13.9). The outwash is now rapidly filling the deep waters of this bay. When seen by Vancouver in 1794, this tongue was apparently about 5 miles farther back than at present, so that he found Taylor Bay was about the same length as Glacier Bay. The advance of Brady Glacier stopped in the late eighteenth century, and it has remained stable since that time.

The mountains through which Lower Brady Glacier passes are not high enough to support valley glaciers, therefore the advancing glacier blocked the outlets of two of the valleys (A). These filled with water, forming North and South Trick Lakes. Some of the glacial ice pushed into another blocked valley a little farther north (not shown), nearly filling it. The parallel dark bands on the glacier (C) are medial moraines formed by the junction of the lateral moraines, which have coalesced and moved downvalley together. The darker appearance of the glacier near its terminus is caused by the accumulation of debris from the melted surface of the glacier.

At the front of the glacier, many sand and gravel bars are visible (D), consisting of sediment carried from the glacial front by meltwater. These extend nearly to the south end of the photograph, although a chart dated 1942 (6 years before the photograph) shows water depths of 19 fathoms (114 feet) adjacent to the projecting point on the east shore (E). Comparison with the 1948 photos suggests that the front of the delta was built southward more than a mile in 6 years.

13.10 Lituya Bay is 8 miles long from the mountain front (M) to the Gulf of Alaska in the foreground. The low hills on each side of the bay entrance are an end moraine of a late glacial advance. Trimlines made by a giant wave in 1936 (G) and an 1853 wave (K) were still visible in this 1954 photo. From D. J. Miller (1960).

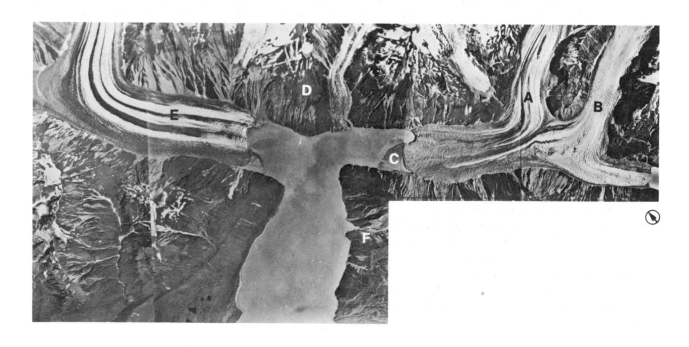

LITUYA BAY, GLACIERS, EARTHQUAKES, AND GIANT WAVES [Figs. 13.10 through 13.14] Lituya Bay (Fig. 13.10) enters the open Pacific on the west side of the Fairweather Range directly opposite Johns Hopkins Fiord but separated from it by 17 miles of high mountains covered by huge glaciers. The bay extends back normal to the coast for 8 miles but has a T-shaped head (Fig. 13.11) into which Lituya Glacier enters on the north and North Crillon Glacier on the south. These two and other glaciers occupy much of the 120-mile northwest-southeast-trending valley, which follows Fairweather Fault and has a width of approximately 2 miles along this great distance. The reason for this lineation is that the rocks adjacent to the fault are so shattered that erosive processes, mostly glacial, have produced a lowland in the fault zone.

Lituya Bay was discovered in 1786 by a French expedition under La Pérouse. He spent about a month at the bay and wrote a good description of it and also made a map of the area. Two years later, a Russian trading vessel landed on the coast. At the times of these early visits, an Indian village adjoined the bay.

Don J. Miller, of the U.S. Geological Survey, presented evidence that sometime during the past 1,000 years, Lituya and North Crillon Glaciers joined and turned southwestward along Lituya Bay as a small piedmont glacier similar to, but smaller than, the Malaspina Glacier (see p. 410). The narrow entrance to Lituya Bay, only 1,000 feet across (Figs. 13.10 and 13.13), cuts the abandoned end moraine of this piedmont glacier, breached and kept open by strong tidal currents.

North Crillon Glacier (A in Fig. 13.11) is closely adjoined to the southeast by South Crillon Glacier (B). Both descend the mountain front steeply until they reach the Fairweather Fault Valley, where North Crillon Glacier bends northwest, and a stream coming from the ice has built a small delta (C) into Crillon Inlet, an arm of Lituya Bay. South Crillon Glacier divides upon reaching the fault valley, one part joining North Crillon Glacier (A), while the other part veers southeastward and discharges into the ice-dammed Crillon Lake, about 300 feet above sea level. The sides of the fault valley were oversteepened by glacial erosion, and the rocks forming the walls are greatly shattered by faulting.

13.12 Trimline caused by giant wave of July 9, 1958, which cut off all vegetation on the cliff opposite the giant rockslide up to 1,740 feet. The front of Lituya Glacier (right) was cut back 1,800 feet by the slide (compare Fig. 13.11). From D. J. Miller (1960).

Lituya Bay is unique in having a record of the highest waves recorded in human history. At 10:16 P.M. on July 9, 1958, a major earthquake centered near Lituya Bay. At one point, the southwest side of the Fairweather Fault moved northwestward 21.5 feet and had a relative rise of 35 feet. The effects of this earthquake with an ensuing rockslide and a giant wave were described by Miller, who flew over the area in a helicopter the following day. The earthquake triggered the rockslide on the northeast side of Gilbert Inlet (D), heading at 3,000 feet above sea level, and causing 40 million cubic yards (about 90 million tons) of rock to fall into the bay. This generated a wave that swept across the inlet and up the opposite cliff, where it destroyed all vegetation and uprooted all trees to a maximum height of 1,740 feet above the bay (Fig. 13.12). The wave continued

13.11 The T-shaped head of Lituya Bay and the valley that has been cut partly by glaciers along the Fairweather Fault. North Crillon (A) and South Crillon (B) Glaciers follow the fault valley in their lower courses, and the latter divides, partly flowing into Crillon Lake (on the right of the photo). Note dark color of the lower part of North Crillon Glacier due to accumulation of debris as it is thinned by melting. Lituya Glacier (E) follows part of the Fairweather Fault zone. A gigantic rockslide (D) coming from a height of 3,000 feet occurred after the earthquake of July 9, 1958, and generated a giant wave. U.S. Geological Survey.

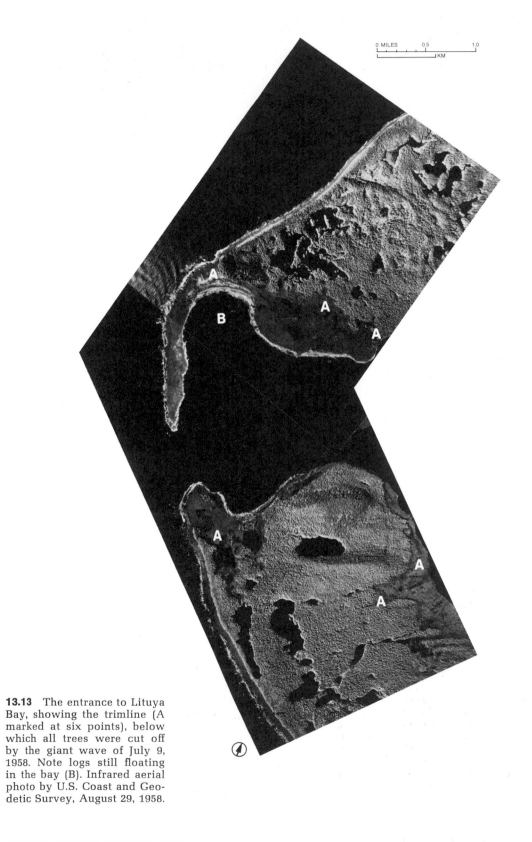

13.13 The entrance to Lituya Bay, showing the trimline (A marked at six points), below which all trees were cut off by the giant wave of July 9, 1958. Note logs still floating in the bay (B). Infrared aerial photo by U.S. Coast and Geodetic Survey, August 29, 1958.

through the bay and inlet, making a swath up to 100 feet near the coast.

At this time (still daylight at this high latitude), three fishing boats were in Lituya Bay. One boat and its two passengers were lost, but this spectacular event was reported by the fishermen in the two other boats. About two and a half minutes after feeling the tremors of the earthquake, the boatmen heard a deafening crash at the head of the bay, presumably from the great rockslide. Shortly afterward a wave was seen advancing rapidly down the bay. About three minutes after the crash, the wave arrived near the boats, and it looked like a wall of water 100 feet high. One boat's anchor line snapped, and the boat rose with the wave and was swept diagonally over the south shore of the bay, but the backwash quickly returned it toward the center of the bay where it remained afloat. The occupants reported some later waves which they estimated to be as high as 20 feet.

The second boat with a man and his wife was picked up by the wave and carried completely over the spit at the lower end of the bay. Looking down from the boat as it passed over the spit, they estimated that it was about 80 feet down to the trees growing on the spit (Fig. 13.13). The boat foundered on the ocean side of the spit, but the passengers escaped in their dinghy and were picked up two hours later, having miraculously survived an experience probably unparalleled in history.

The following day when Miller flew over the bay, it was evident that all trees, even as large as 4 feet in diameter, below the level affected by the wave had been sliced off as if cut by a saw. This trimline, cut by water waves, was as sharp as the trimline produced by an advancing glacier. Where trees were in soil, they were completely carried away. Where rooted in rock, they were twisted and snapped off near the ground. In many places just above the trimline, bark was stripped from the trees. The sharp trimline in the lower bay is clearly evident on an aerial photograph taken August 29, 1958 (A in Fig. 13.13), 51 days after the wave. In contrast, the photograph taken before the wave (Fig. 13.10) shows the trees growing close to the shore.

Although little had been reported about giant waves in Lituya Bay until 1958, largely because the area was sparsely populated or uninhabited, Miller found evidence of earlier great waves in 1853 or 1854, height 395 feet; in 1874, 80 feet; in 1899,

about 200 feet (possibly associated with Yakutat Bay earthquake); and on October 27, 1936, 490 feet.

The area was probably uninhabited in 1853 and 1854, but the approximate date of a major wave was worked out by tree rings just below the trimline (K in Fig. 13.10). The giant wave may have obliterated the Indian village of earlier days. Miller thought it was caused by a rockslide from the south wall of Mudslide Creek (F in Fig. 13.11). There was no major earthquake in Alaska in 1853 or 1854.

Four persons at Lituya Bay on October 27, 1936, two in a cabin on Cenotaph Island near the center of the bay and two in a boat, gave eyewitness descriptions of the events. Three waves swept down the middle of the bay, each higher than the preceding, all in the range of 50 to 100 feet. Trimlines resulting from this wave were plainly visible (G in Fig. 13.10) until destroyed by the greater wave in 1958. The exact location of a rockslide, if one occurred in 1936, has not been found. There is no record of a major earthquake at that time. Although it has been proposed that glacial melting might suddenly have opened a subglacial channel which drained Crillon Lake (Fig. 13.11), no disturbance of the delta or terminal face of the North Crillon Glacier was observed. Another suggestion has been that an underwater toe of the North Crillon Glacier may have slid off into Lituya Bay, but no trace of such a slide was detected. The cause of the 1936 great waves remains a mystery.

Because this small bay has experienced five of the highest waves ever recorded, it seems likely that occasional rockslides, snow avalanches, or the drainage of Crillon Lake may cause other great waves.

G. F. Jordan has compared soundings in Lituya Bay made by the Coast and Geodetic Survey in 1926 with those of 1959. He found that the axial depths of the bay had been reduced on an average of about 100 feet. He noted that some of this was no doubt the result of sediment washed from the glaciers but suggested that a large part of it was due to the huge amount of material carried into the bay by the rockslides and distributed along the bay by the great waves of 1936 and 1958.

COASTAL LOWLANDS ADJOINING ST. ELIAS AND CHUGACH RANGES   The only appreciable lowlands along the great southern arc of Alaska are found at the base of the massive and lofty St.

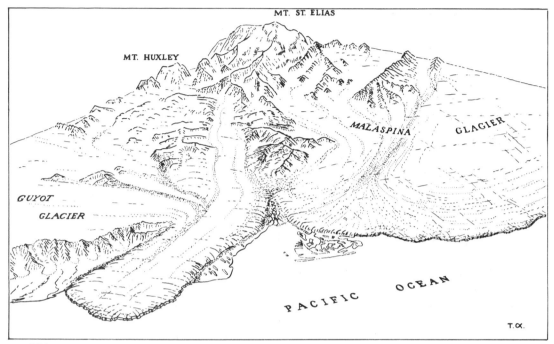

a 1794

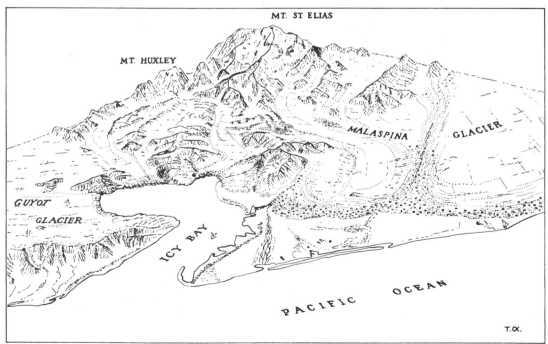

b 1964

13.14 Block diagram showing the great change in the glaciers at Icy Bay since first observed by Captain Vancouver in 1794. Shows the growth of a delta and sand barriers on the east side of Icy Bay. Diagram by Tau Rho Alpha, U.S. Geological Survey.

Elias Range and along the eastern portion of the Chugach Mountains. The lowlands are somewhat broken by small uplifts, notably the Robinson Mountains that extend almost to the shore. The coastal plain, with an average width of 30 miles, has a relatively straight shoreline with local development of barriers and sand plains. Two large embayments reach far into the lowland, Yakutat and Icy Bays. Between these embayments, the coastal plain is almost covered by a great piedmont glacier, the Malaspina, the largest glacier in North America. West of the Robinson Mountains, the Bering Glacier also spreads over much of the continuation of the coastal plain. At present, neither of these piedmont glaciers comes to the sea; but the Malaspina Glacier fronted on the coast along much of its length when observed by Vancouver in 1794 (Fig. 13.14a) and, according to the U.S. Geological Survey, still came to the coast at one point in 1951. The St. Elias Range, aside from the Andes, is the highest coastal mountain system on earth and includes Mt. St. Elias, 18,008 feet, and Mt. Logan, 19,850 feet, in the Canadian part of the range. A large system of ice fields covers much of the range and feeds long valley glaciers. The Hubbard Glacier, with a length of 70 miles, heads on the eastern slope of Mt. Logan but after a circuitous course empties into Disenchantment Bay (Figs. 13.15 and 13.16). The 42-mile Seward Glacier is fed by ice fields on the flanks of St. Elias and Logan Mts., and is the principal feeder of the Malaspina Glacier.

Yakutat Bay (Fig. 13.17) extends inland for 40 miles, with the outer 30 miles having a width of 15 miles; but the northern arm, which enters Disenchantment Bay, narrows to 3 miles. This narrow inner bay, with depth to 1,000 feet, is much deeper than the broad bay outside. Part of the shoaling outside is due to the presence of a glacial moraine that dates back to the ice age when the entire bay was filled with glaciers.

On September 10, 1899, Yakutat Bay was the epicenter of one of the greatest earthquakes of all

13.15 Western side of the terminus of the 7-mile-wide Hubbard Glacier (A) into Disenchantment Bay, at the head of Yakutat Bay. Hubbard and Turner (D) Glaciers discharged icebergs into the fiord, but Miller (B) and Haenke (C) Glaciers were stagnant and appear dark because covered by debris. U.S. Coast and Geodetic Survey, August 1958.

13.16 The east side of the terminus of Hubbard Glacier. Near A in 1899, eight prospectors panning for gold on an alluvial fan experienced in rapid succession the Yakutat Bay earthquake, a flood resulting from the sudden draining of a lake upstream, and a tsunami advancing up the bay—and survived to tell the story. Variegated glacier (B) is stagnant and debris covered. U.S. Coast and Geodetic Survey, 1958.

time. This was thoroughly studied by Ralph Tarr and Lawrence Martin. The only persons who witnessed the earthquake at Yakutat Bay were eight prospectors washing sand for placer gold on an alluvial fan about 5 miles east of the front of Hubbard Glacier (A in Fig. 13.16). They reported a heavy shock, followed by fifty-two minor shocks during 4 hours; and then the principal earthquake, during which the ground moved up and down like the waves of the sea. The men could not stand without holding onto their tent pole. Just after the shock, a lake described as 2 acres in extent broke its dam; and water and debris rushed down on the camp, carrying away or burying all of the equipment, but the men all escaped to high ground. The ice wall at the front of Hubbard Glacier "ran" out into the bay 0.5 mile, filling this area with what was apparently a multitude of shattered ice blocks. This action was described as taking place in about 5 minutes. Almost immediately afterwards, a terrible roar came from the bay, and a wall of water 20 feet high rushed up onto the shore. This has been considered a tsunami due to faulting rather than a rock fall, as in Lituya Bay. Because the area where the men were caught was near the center of faulting, the waves followed the earthquake shocks and the flood from the lake after only a short interval.

After the tremors had subsided, geologists investigating the area found that the west side of Disenchantment Bay had been elevated at different places varying from 17 to 47 feet. This meant that all beach materials and intertidal marine life were suddenly raised above reach of even high tide. Figure 13.18 shows the west shore of Disenchantment Bay near the Turner Glacier where the 47-foot uplift was measured. This change in level during the earthquake is the largest that has ever been recorded on land.

Near the head of Disenchantment Bay, the glaciers have fluctuated but have had no great changes since 1899. Hubbard Glacier, with a frontal wall of ice about 7 miles wide (A in Fig. 13.15), discharges icebergs into the bay. Miller, Haenke, and Turner Glaciers (respectively B, C, D) have also at times discharged into the bay. Turner Glacier extended to tidewater when photographed in 1946 (not illustrated) as well as in 1958 (D); but Haenke Glacier (C) was relatively inactive in 1958, its front deeply covered with detritus and its terminus on land. The contrast between Turner and Haenke Glaciers is typical of the difference between an active glacier,

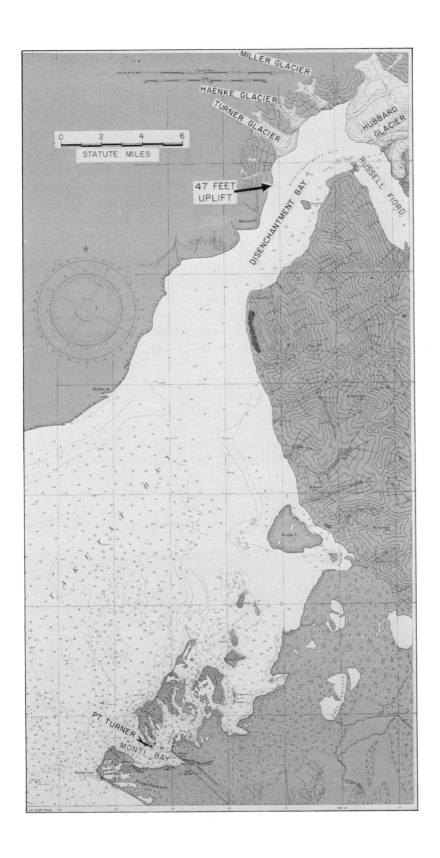

13.17 Yakutat Bay on the east side of the Malaspina Glacier. Shows the area along Disenchantment Bay where an uplift of 47 feet occurred at the time of the 1899 earthquake, exceeding any other sudden change of level. The glaciers at the head of the bay have oscillated in position, but remained essentially the same since first observed. Monti Bay to the south has shown considerable depth changes (see text). From U.S. Coast and Geodetic Survey Chart 8455, 1962.

13.18 The west shore of Disenchantment Bay, which was elevated 47 feet during the 1899 earthquake at a locality south of Turner Glacier. The prequake shore is at A. From Tarr and Martin (1912).

movement being shown by open crevasses, and a stagnant glacier, the terminus deeply buried by detritus.

Tarr and Martin, who studied the history of the glaciers at Yakutat Bay, reported that in 1906 Haenke Glacier was advancing rapidly, eventually burying its outwash fan and extending into Disenchantment Bay, where it merged with Turner Glacier. This activity continued for 10 months, after which Haenke Glacier again became stagnant. Tarr and Martin noticed that in 1906 many other glaciers in the Yakutat Bay region and some as far as 100 miles distant, suddenly became active, crevasses formed, the terminal faces advanced, and trees growing near the margins of the glaciers were overturned. Observers who were near the Yakutat Bay glaciers at the time of the earthquake heard the roar of ice falls and rockslides. Tarr and Martin suggested that the additional mass of ice and rock added to the glaciers would, after a period of years, lead to accelerated flow; and, in the Yakutat Bay area, after about seven years, the glaciers did begin to advance. A year or so later, this extra energy had been expended, and the glaciers returned to their preearthquake condition.

Maynard Miller studied the short-time early twentieth-century advances of Alaskan glaciers and noted that some of them were more than 200 miles from the epicenter of the Yakutat Bay earthquake. Weather records for southeastern Alaska show that in the late 1870s and early 1880s, precipitation was unusually high. In the rugged areas this would be largely in the form of snow. Therefore, Miller suggested that the advance of numerous glaciers in about 1906 was mostly a result of greater snowfall which occurred at least 25 years earlier, rather than due to avalanches and rockslides caused by the earthquake about seven years earlier, as Tarr and Martin had suggested.

G. F. Jordan compared Coast and Geodetic Survey soundings in Monti Bay, at the southeast entrance of Yakutat Bay, from surveys made in 1892, 1941, and 1958. He found that between the first two surveys the bay showed a shoaling to an average amount of 70 feet. If this had continued, the bay would have been largely eliminated sometime in the twenty-first century. However, the 1958 survey, made after the great earthquake of that year, showed that there had been considerable reversal of the trend. At the entrance to the bay the bottom had deepened as much as 95 feet and about 90 feet off Point Turner. This point had grown to the south by 1941. At the time of the 1958 earthquake, a slide occurred at the end of the point and caused a land recession of about 200 feet, drowning three people. Some of the slumped sediment produced knolls on the bottom of the bay.

Malaspina Glacier covers an area of 850 square miles; and its surface altitude ranges from 2,500 feet, where the Seward Glacier enters from the St. Elias Range, to about 75 feet near the outer margin. Sound reflection studies by R. P. Sharp have shown that the floor of the glacier a few miles inland is 800 to 1,000 feet below sea level. However, the base of the glacier at its frontal margin is near sea level, so that the lower part moves uphill while the upper surface slopes continually seaward. The surface slope of Seward Glacier, in the St. Elias Range, is much higher than that of the Malaspina, resulting in a slower rate of flow in the latter. The surface of the Malaspina Glacier is thinned by ablation; and the sediment collected on the surface of the nearly stagnant ice supports a rich growth of forest vegetation, with some trees almost 200 years old. Hence, Sharp claims that the glacier attained its maximum postglacial extent about 200 years ago and has experienced only minor retreat since then.

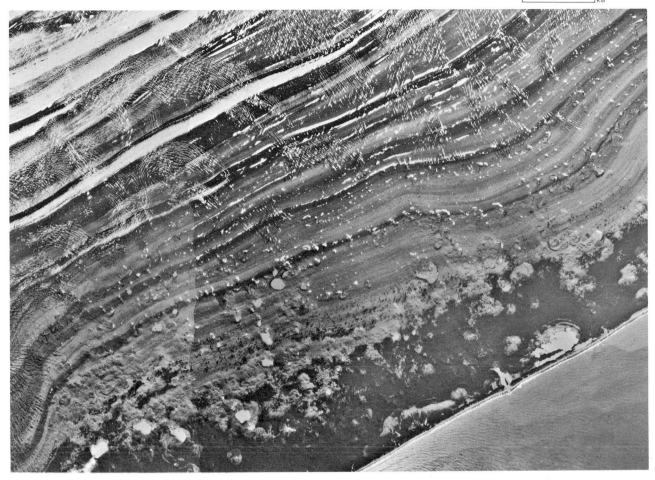

13.19 The central part of the terminus of the Malaspina piedmont glacier, where stagnant glacial ice forms the coast. Many ponds fill kettle holes, due to uneven melting of glacial ice and the collapse of sand and gravel into the resulting depressions. The regular parallel bands with low ridges and troughs are eroded ice folds and shearing plates near the terminus of the glaciers. U.S. Geological Survey, 1948.

Several years after the Yakutat earthquake, the frontal area of the Malaspina Glacier developed crevasses, indicating renewed motion; and the glacier advanced over the forest, toppling trees. After a few years, during which the front advanced slightly, the glacier again became stagnant. Figure 13.19, showing the seaward margin of the central part of the glacier, indicates many small ponds filling kettle holes on or just outside of the glacier. These were formed by the melting of ice blocks after being buried with debris or covered with vegetation. The many striking ridges and troughs parallel to the ice front in Figure 13.19 are believed by Sharp to be accordion-type

folds, and shearing forms as the base of the glacier is shoved uphill toward its frontal margin.

Icy Bay (Figs. 13.14 through 13.20) indents the coast about 19 miles on the western side of the Malaspina Glacier. This bay is narrower than Yakutat Bay, only 6 miles across its mouth and 3 miles in the upper part where it is bordered by Guyot and Yahtse Glaciers. Like Glacier Bay, Icy Bay has been the site of large-scale retreat of the ice front. When it was first visited by Vancouver in 1794 (Fig. 13.14*a*), the combined glaciers extended beyond the present mouth of the bay, although Vancouver's sketch shows an indentation somewhat to the east of the present

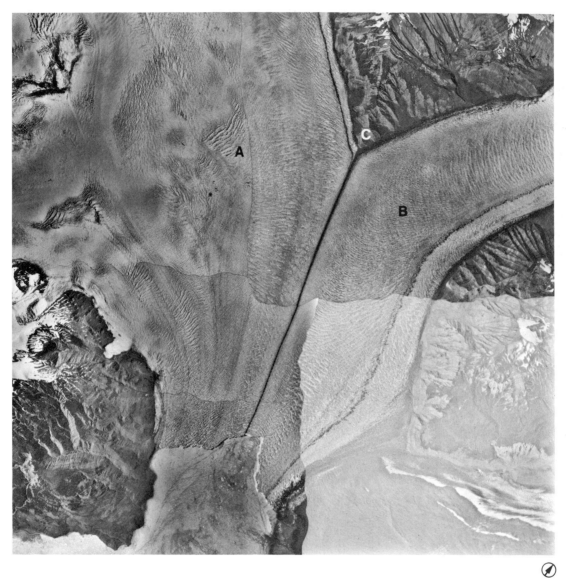

13.20

a 1948 aerial photo of the frontal portion of Guyot (A) and Yahtse (B) Glaciers. Note the prominent medial moraine that extends from the junction of the glaciers to the terminus. U.S. Geological Survey, 1952.

bay where deposition from the glacial outwash combined with spit building has now formed a low marsh at the east entrance to the bay (Fig. 13.14*b*). In 1891, a map drawn by I. C. Russell shows that there was still no Icy Bay; but in 1913, Tarr and Martin found that the glaciers had retreated from 3 to 9 miles, leaving a body of water, which was named Icy Bay. The front of Guyot Glacier was photographed in 1948 (Fig. 13.20*a*) and again in 1957;

the latter was used as a basis for a map (Fig. 13.20*b*). During this interval, the glacier had retreated about 7.5 miles, separating Guyot and Yahtse Glaciers. The total retreat up to 1957 appears to have been about 25 miles.

ALASKA EARTHQUAKE OF 1964 [Figs. 13.21 and 13.22]   On Good Friday, March 27, 1964, at 5:36 P.M., a vast area in southern Alaska was

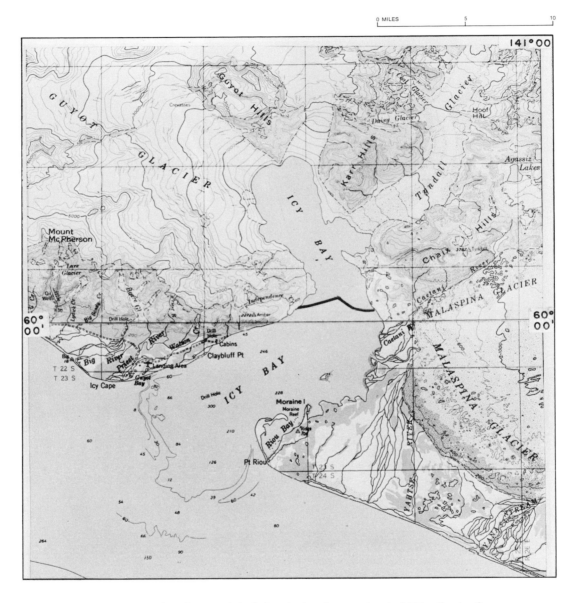

b 1957 map showing that the termini of the glaciers have retreated 7.5 miles to the sharp point (C in Fig. 13.20*a*) at the junction of the two glaciers. U.S. Geological Survey, topographic maps of Icy Bay and Bering Glacier quadrangles.

shaken by the most intense earthquake ever recorded in North America. It was rated 8.4 to 8.6 on the Richter scale (the San Francisco earthquake of 1906 rated 8.25) and crippled the industry and economy of most of southern Alaska. The epicenter was on the west side of Unakwik Inlet in Prince William Sound (Fig. 13.21). According to George Plafker, areas seriously affected extended 450 miles from Yakataga, east of the Copper River Delta, to Kodiak Island at the southwest. The width of the stricken belt is at least 200 miles.

Nearly half the population of Alaska lives within the area of extensive damage. Property destroyed amounted to about $750 million, more than 100 times the purchase price of Alaska 97 years earlier. One hundred and fourteen people lost their lives. Anchorage, at the center of the most populous area in Alaska, was seriously damaged. Other towns or

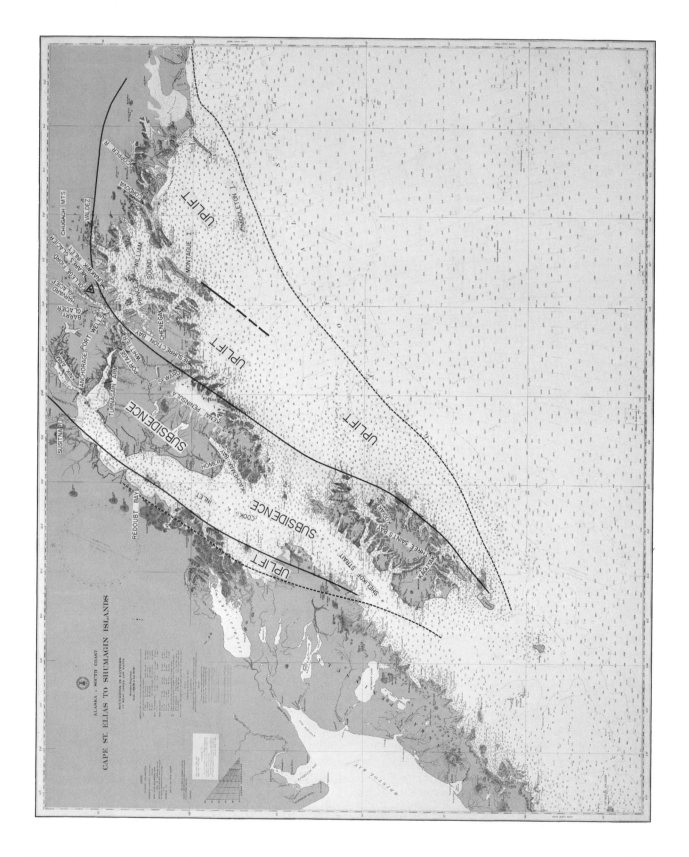

ALASKA - SOUTH COAST

CAPE ST. ELIAS TO SHUMAGIN ISLANDS

13.22 The southern end of Montague Island, showing the former submerged terrace 0.25 mile wide, which was elevated 33 feet during the 1964 Alaska earthquake. From Hansen *et al.* (1966). Photo courtesy George Plafker.

cities affected by the quake were Seward, Valdez, Kodiak, Whittier, Homer, and Cordova. Cordova was built on resistant rock, so suffered much less destruction than the other towns, which were built largely on unconsolidated sediments. As a result, although its port facilities were destroyed, Cordova served as a temporary refuge for many who were made homeless by the quake.

13.21 Chart showing area affected by 1964 Alaska earthquake. Extends from Kodiak Island to Bering Glacier and gives place names discussed in text. Areas of uplift and depression are indicated with hinge lines (solid) and boundaries of information (dashed). Earthquake fault passing through Montague Island shown by heavy line, and earthquake epicenter by triangle. Earthquake data from Plafker (1969) and hydrography from U.S. Coast and Geodetic Survey Chart 8502, 1960 edition.

The most widespread and permanent result of the quake was the changes in elevation of most of the affected area. A hinge line, or axis, of change of level (Fig. 13.21) reaches from near Valdez southwestward across Prince William Sound and the Kenai Peninsula to the southeastern tip of Kodiak Island. Northwest of the hinge line, an area of at least 70,000 square miles was lowered to a maximum of 7.5 feet. Southeast of the line, an area of 25,000 square miles was uplifted. The maximum rise of 33 feet was on Montague Island (Fig. 13.22). Middleton Island, in the Gulf of Alaska 60 miles southeast of Montague Island, was elevated as much as 12 feet, increasing its land area and exposing ledges of tilted resistant rock, which now extends 0.5 mile seaward from the old shoreline.

The earthquake also caused earth and rock slides. Some port facilities, which were built on deltas and

fans, slid off into the adjacent fiords. Another source of damage was tsunamis that moved out in a wide quadrant from the center of the quake, producing inundations as far as Crescent City, California (p. 350). In southern Alaska, vast quantities of marine and plant life were destroyed, either from being uplifted out of the marine habitat or from salt water invasion of lakes and lagoons. Portions of the city of Anchorage had to be abandoned, and the town of Valdez was moved to an entirely new location.

Areas affected by the earthquake ranged from rugged mountains, such as the Chugach and Kenai Ranges with many ice fields and tidewater glaciers, to fiords, like Resurrection Bay (Seward), Knik and Turnagain Arms (Anchorage), and Port Valdez. Severe damage occurred to the Cook Inlet region and nearby continental shelf islands. Much movement took place beneath the waters of the Gulf of Alaska. Ten thousand miles of shoreline were depressed, elevated, or otherwise modified.

COPPER RIVER DELTA [Figs. 13.23, 13.24, and 13.25]   The Copper River drains a large interior lowland area and its surrounding mountains. It flows to the sea through a canyon that crosses the lofty Chugach Range. The canyon was filled with ice during the Pleistocene; and, according to O. J. Ferrians, Jr. and H. R. Schmoll, a large lake existed in the interior lowland prior to about 7000 B.C. because of the ice dam in the canyon. When the dam broke, a flood of water came down the valley and began to fill a glacial fiord at the river mouth, forming the Copper River Delta. Erk Reimnitz states that the glaciers past which the Copper River flows in crossing the Chugach have occasionally advanced and produced temporary blocking of the river, followed by violent floods. Tarr and Martin call attention to such a flood in 1909. According to Reimnitz, since the draining of the large interior lake, approximately 180 cubic miles of delta sediment have accumulated in the lower valley; and the delta has built a protruding bulge onto the inner continental shelf (Fig.

13.23 Outline map of the Copper River Delta, showing flats filled to a tidal condition, the river discharge draining west through the Pete Dahl and Alaganik Sloughs, then through Orca Inlet to Cordova and Hawkins Island Cutoff, and finally into Prince William Sound. From Reimnitz (1966).

13.23). The delta has also grown along the coast to the west, due to the westerly currents, accounting for the shoal water along much of Orca Inlet; and sediment has even been carried through the passageway between Hawkins and Hinchinbrook Islands and deposited as a tidal delta into the east margin of Prince William Sound. Thus the front of the delta extends for at least 50 miles.

The delta includes three zones parallel to the coast: the inner marsh, the tidal flat, and the barrier islands on the outside. At right angles to these are the floodplain in the mouth of the river and a dune tract on the low islands outside. A north-northeasterly lineation (D in Fig. 13.24) can be seen on some of the larger islands of the delta. These lineations are longitudinal sand dunes formed by very strong northerly winds, called *williwaws*, which sweep down the Copper River Valley from the glaciers in the Chugach Mountains. Winds of 60 to 100 miles an hour develop suddenly for short periods and transport great quantities of sand.

The marshland is traversed by a series of channels, through which the predominant flow from the river discharges in a southwesterly direction. Prior to the 1964 earthquake, the Pete Dahl and Alaganik Sloughs carried the bulk of the drainage; but, according to recent information provided to us by Reimnitz, Castle Island Slough and its distributaries now have the main discharge. One might have expected the main channels to be more in line with the general southerly direction of the Copper River, but the westerly flowing currents have evidently played an important part in diverting them to the west.

The sand and silt from the Copper River meltwater, augmented by that from the Martin River, an easterly tributary of the delta, have been deposited in what was a lagoon inside the barrier islands but is now largely a tidal flat with surface sediment of sand.

Orca Inlet, leading up to Cordova, was formerly a fiord but is now also mainly a tidal flat because of the fill from the Copper River sediment. The Army Corps of Engineers dredge one side of it to keep it open for fishing vessels. A deeper channel extends to Cordova around the north end of Hawkins Island.

The history of the Copper River Delta has been complicated by earth movements. According to Reimnitz, gradual subsidence has been active for at least the past 1,700 years but has been interrupted

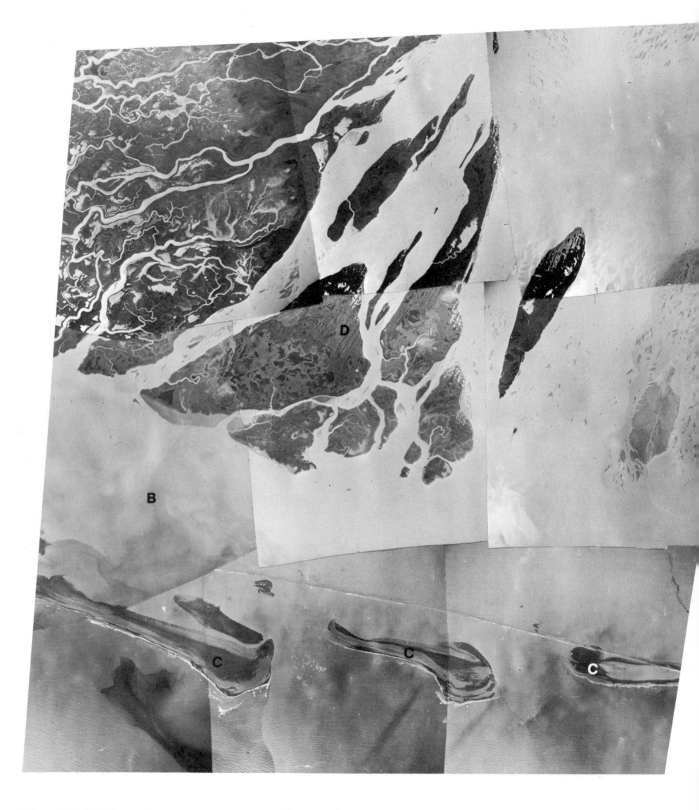

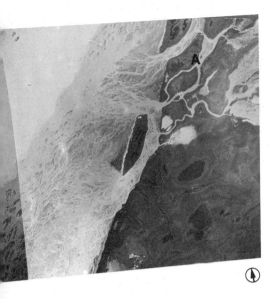

13.24 Aerial photo composite of the Copper River Delta. The Copper River is joined almost at right angles by Martin River (A). The offshore lagoon (B) has been so nearly filled that it is essentially a tidal flat above which the barrier islands (C) rise a few feet. Most of the Copper River drainage follows channels cut through the delta marshes westward along a continuation of the trend of the Martin River. U.S. Geological Survey, 1952.

from time to time by occasional uplifts, during which forests covered the present salt marshes and tidal flats.

The Copper River Delta is near the eastern end of the area affected by the 1964 Alaska earthquake. The most complete descriptions of the effects of the quake are those by Erk Reimnitz and Neil Marshall, who visited the area three weeks afterward. They found considerable alterations from what they had observed in previous field work. The most striking change resulted from an uplift of about 6 feet that brought many of the tidal flats above high water. This caused immediate erosion at the margins of the channels, producing small waterfalls at various places. During the earthquake, sand or mud spouts were reported by the local inhabitants. The spouts were said to have been as high as 30 or 40 feet. Reimnitz and Marshall found craters left by these geysers and determined that some of them brought up sand from deeper than 20 feet below the surface. Cracks developed in many places on the tidal flats; and sand squeezed out from below had filled many of them, forming sand dikes.

Another strange phenomenon was the development of mud cracks after the earthquake on some uplifted mud flats. Generally, mud cracks are the result of drying, which causes shrinking of the mud; but here there had been almost continuous precipitation between the time of the uplift and the visit by Reimnitz and Marshall. They think that the cracks may be the combined result of shrinkage due to loss of salt content, denser packing of the elevated sediments, and less saturation with water.

The water waves accompanying the earthquake had important effects on the delta but are best described by observers at Orca Inlet where considerable wave damage was inflicted on Cordova. The waves were described by Reimnitz and Marshall and later discussed by B. W. Wilson and Alf Tørum. The waves came along the inlet with velocities of 30 to 40 knots, moving large Coast Guard buoys for miles from where they were anchored and wrecking many boats. The wave periods were from 30 to 60 minutes, and the waves rose high enough to inundate the 20-foot-high dock at Cordova, despite the fact that it had been elevated 6 feet by the earth movements. One effect of the waves moving along the inlet was to scour off the mud cover from the bars, exposing great quantities of clams that were living in a sand

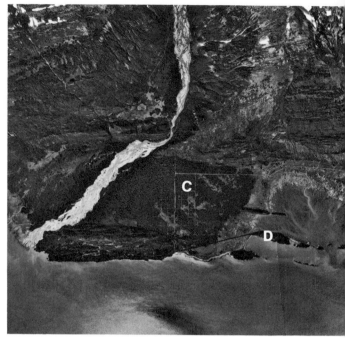

13.25 Rockslide on Sherman Glacier (see Fig. 13.23), resulting from the Alaska earthquake of March 27, 1964. Copper River Delta is seen in background. From Post (1968).

layer underneath the mud, and many invertebrates were killed by the combination of scour and uplift. Soundings taken after the earthquake in the channel north of Cordova showed that there had been shoaling of as much as 33 feet as the result of the seiches, but shortly afterward the normal tides caused some deepening.

On land, the Copper River Highway, which had been constructed on the old roadbed of a railroad connecting Cordova and the mines in the Copper River basin, had fifty-two bridges destroyed and fourteen seriously damaged. In the neighboring Chugach Mountains, many rockslides occurred, the largest on Sherman Glacier (Fig. 13.25) consisting of 700 million cubic feet of shattered rock debris mixed with ice and snow.

PRINCE WILLIAM SOUND [Figs. 13.26, 13.27, and 13.28]   This partly enclosed bay lies south of the end of the Chugach Mountains and east of the Kenai Peninsula (Fig. 13.21). It is largely separated from the Gulf of Alaska by Hawkins, Hinchinbrook, and Montague Islands. Much of Prince William Sound and the Kenai Peninsula coast to the southwest, although partly elevated in 1964, had evidently had a previous long history of subsidence, so that only the summits and upper slopes of glacially eroded mountains stand above water level. The open part of the sound is about 35 miles across.

The margins of the bay are deeply indented with fiords, several of which have tidewater glaciers. The Prince William Sound glaciers were described in detail by U. S. Grant (no relation to the general) and D. F. Higgins in 1913, and by Tarr and Martin in 1914.

The sound contains many mountainous islands, which have been intensely glaciated, along with valleys excavated by glaciers and drowned when the glaciers melted. Most water depths in the sound are greater than 1,000 feet and range to 2,430 feet. These great depths are largely the result of glacial excavation during the Pleistocene.

Valdez (A in Fig. 13.26), an important fishing and transportation center, was located at the head of a deep northeast reentrant of Prince William Sound. The town was built on the outwash delta of Valdez

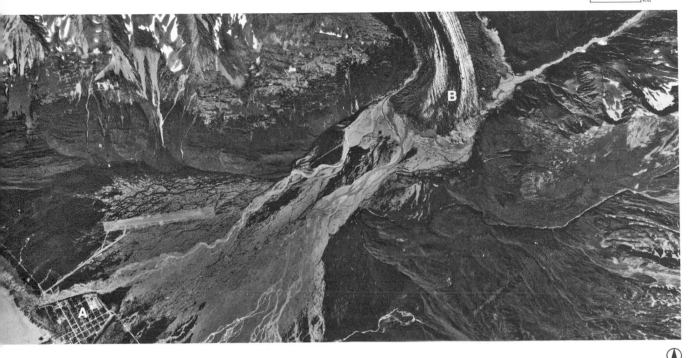

13.26 Valdez before the 1964 earthquake. Also shows location of the new town (C) 4 miles west of the now-abandoned port. The old town was on a delta at the end of a valley train at the foot of Valdez Glacier. U.S. Coast and Geodetic Survey.

Glacier (B), which terminates 4 miles to the northeast. During the Klondike gold rush, Valdez was the closest deep-water port to the gold area; and prospectors actually walked up over the entire Valdez Glacier to reach the gold fields. Later, a military trail was constructed up the valley of Lowe River, southwest of the town, and then north to the Yukon. Valdez is now the southern terminus of the Richardson Highway leading to Fairbanks and will also be the terminus of the pipeline carrying oil from the North Slope. The merged deltas of the Valdez Glacier and Lowe River have built forward into the fiord with slopes as steep as 12 degrees. The water is 360 feet deep a short distance offshore and deepens westward to more than 800 feet in Port Valdez fiord.

Valdez was only 45 miles from the 1964 earthquake epicenter. Vivid eyewitness accounts from local residents and from the master of the S. S. *Chena*, which was anchored at the dock in Valdez at the time of the earthquake, were presented by Wilson and Tôrum, of the U.S. Army Corps of Engineers, who described the earthquake vibrations, the slides that destroyed the waterfront, the fires that were ignited in oil storage tanks, and the tsunami waves.

During the earthquake, violent shaking of the soft ground of the delta resulted in visible ground waves 3 to 4 feet high and 400 feet apart. As the delta compacted, these waves squeezed water from the silts, which sprayed into the air as fountains, like those on the Copper River Delta. The strong earth waves cracked the ground; and, within about a minute, sections of the delta began sliding off into the fiord. Much of the pier with its warehouses disappeared suddenly, carrying many people to their deaths. Figure 13.27 shows a vivid illustration of the nature of the slump and accompanying waves. The latter deluged the waterfront to heights of about 20 feet above normal water. Buildings were displaced to the east and many collapsed. At Valdez, thirty-one people were killed and property damage amounted to $12 million. Most of the destruction occurred within the first few minutes. About two hours after the quake, a series of water waves developed at intervals of 40 minutes and with amplitudes of about 20 feet. These were generated by the slides in the delta and traversed the 12-mile length of the Port Valdez fiord,

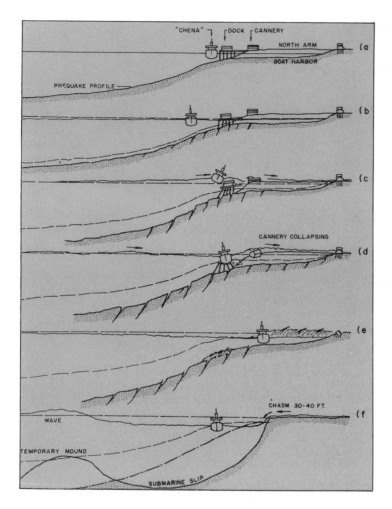

13.27 Schematic diagram illustrating the sequence of events at the front of the delta at Valdez. The S. S. *Chena*, shown in the diagram, was tied up at the dock when the earthquake of March 27, 1964, hit the area. From Wilson and Alf Tørum (1968).

then were reflected back to the starting point. Six and eight hours later, other sets of waves rose still higher but advanced more slowly, so they did little damage. These late arrivals were probably the tsunamis from distant areas where the ocean floor had undergone movements.

After studying the situation, it was decided that because Valdez was located near the unstable frontal margin of a delta extending into a deep fiord and had also been subject to periodic flooding from the Valdez glacial stream, the town could not adequately be protected against future catastrophic damage. Therefore, the entire town was relocated 4 miles west on a flat

formed by the delta of Mineral Creek but protected along the sea front by bedrock ledges (D in Fig. 13.26). The new town, although safe from delta-front slides, is only a few feet above high tide; therefore, it could be destroyed or badly damaged by tsunamis accompanying future earthquakes. Most of the relocation has now been accomplished.

At the entrance of Unakwik Inlet, 12 miles south of the epicenter and 45 miles west of Port Valdez, the occupants of two fishing vessels reported that the water sloshed back and forth across the bay, running up the sides of the mountains as high as 100 feet in some places, then withdrawing to expose the sea bottom 24 to 30 feet below low tide level. After the earthquake ended, the water receded for two and a half hours, but a half-hour later, water had risen higher than the former high-tide stage. Meares Glacier, at the head of Unakwik Bay, has a frontal ice cliff about 1.5 miles wide. The cliff was photographed in 1913 and from the same position in 1950. At the later date, abundant icebergs were seen at the head of the bay, and these were probably still more numerous just after the 1964 earthquake.

Harvard Glacier terminates in College Fiord, a large glacial trough 15 miles west of Unakwik Inlet. The frontal face of this 35-mile-long glacier is 2 miles wide and breaks off into water 700 feet deep. The tidewater Yale Glacier enters an arm of College Fiord. This glacier provides southwest drainage from the same interior ice field that supplies the huge Columbia Glacier to the east. There were no eyewitnesses of the earthquake in College Fiord. Tributaries to Harvard Glacier along College Fiord include Wellesley, Vassar, Bryn Mawr, Smith, and Radcliffe, all small glaciers named after women's colleges, while the trunk glaciers, Yale, Harvard, and Columbia show some favoritism to the male sex. Where College Fiord terminates in another fiord, called Port Wells, Barry Arm branches north and leads to a series of tidewater glaciers (Fig. 13.28) a few miles up from the juncture. In 1913, when the map of Figure 13.28a was made, a single glacier front extended 1.2 miles from just below Cascade Glacier across to the east wall of Barry Arm. In 1964, after the Alaska earthquake, there had been little recession of Cascade Glacier (A), but the eastern side of Barry Glacier (D) had retreated 1.6 miles to the rock divide between Barry and Coxe Glaciers. As viewed from the air by Shepard in 1969, there appeared to be

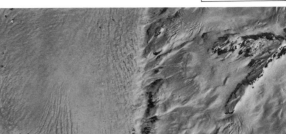

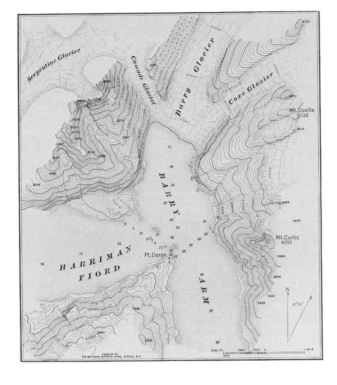

13.28 Changes in the termini of Barry and Coxe Glaciers, which enter Barry Arm.

a 1913. Cascade, Barry, and Coxe Glaciers join above their entrance to Barry Arm. From Tarr and Martin (1912).

little further change. The extensive glacial mapping by Tarr and Martin and others in Prince William Sound shows that except for Barry Glacier, the glaciers, including those discussed and the large Columbia Glacier, aside from minor fluctuations, have hardly changed at all since 1913.

During the 1964 earthquake, in Port Wells, just south of Barry Arm, the water receded, exposing bottom normally below lowest tide. During the later part of the earthquake, the water rose to 4 feet above high tide. Then a succession of small waves came in at intervals of 2 or 3 minutes. Three hours after the earthquake, the water rose to 9 feet above high tide in the first of three waves that came in during a 2-hour period.

At the village of Chenega, on Chenega Island, in the southwest corner of Prince William Sound, there was a huge tsunami 60 to 90 minutes after the end of the quake. It was caused by a submarine slide. The water ran up onto the shore 52 feet above sea level.

b May 1964. There has been very little recession of Cascade Glacier (A) and of the west side of Barry Glacier (B), but Coxe Glacier (C) and the east side of Barry Glacier have retreated about 1.5 miles beyond the ridge dividing them. U.S. Coast and Geodetic Survey.

GLACIERS, EARTHQUAKES, VOLCANOES: SOUTHERN ALASKA

13.29 Cape Puget, a part of the very rugged south coast of the Kenai Peninsula. Oblique aerial photo, U.S. Air Force, date unknown.

The wave came in like a fast-rising tide. A minute later, the water receded 50 feet, carrying with it some houses. Four minutes after that, a second wave arrived with a roar and swept away all remaining houses of the village. A total of twenty-five persons were drowned.

KENAI PENINSULA [Figs. 13.29 through 13.32] This area includes a southwest continuation of the Chugach Mountains and is a part of the Coast Range of southern Alaska. The peninsula (Fig. 13.21), 150 miles long with a maximum width of about 100 miles, is almost severed from the mainland at the north end by two fiords, Turnagain Arm and Passage Canal, which are separated only by a 10-mile glacier-covered isthmus. The peninsula is bounded on the southeast by the open Gulf of Alaska and on the northwest by Cook Inlet. The southeastern two-thirds of the peninsula consists of the rugged Kenai Mountains, with large ice fields and a few tidewater glaciers. Due to glaciation, the mountainous southeast coast is deeply indented with fiords separated by wave-eroded promontories (Fig. 13.29). The northwestern third of the peninsula has low reliefs, mostly under a thousand

feet. Oil has been discovered recently in the Tertiary rocks of the western peninsula.

Seward (Fig. 13.30), the largest city on the peninsula, is near the head of Resurrection Bay, which indents the coast 20 miles. In contrast to Anchorage, Seward is an ice-free port throughout the year and is the southern terminus of the Alaska Railroad and the Seward-Anchorage Highway. Seward is located on a fan-delta at the mouth of Lowell Creek. The front of this delta has a sharp dropoff to the deep floor of Resurrection Bay. The larger delta of Resurrection River at the head of the fiord, also within the Seward urban area, resembles the delta on which Valdez had been located before the 1964 earthquake. Mountains on each side of the fiord rise to more than 4,000 feet above the city.

In 1964, like Valdez, Seward experienced violent earth shocks followed almost immediately by large water waves. Because the adjoining terrain is even more rugged than that near Valdez, snow and rock-slides were triggered on the slopes and in the canyons above the city. Also, the delta deposits on the bayward side of the waterfront broke off in slices and partly slid into the bay. Within 30 seconds, this ruptured area spread from the Standard Oil Company dock to the San Juan dock (Fig. 13.30a), completely destroying the port facilities. A strip of town from 50 to 500 feet wide was lost. Muddy water was spewed from some of the open cracks. Waves generated from slides of the Lowell Creek fan interfered with other sets of waves coming from the slides in the delta at the head of the fiord. Boats in the small-boat harbor were lifted and carried over the break-water.

When the Standard Oil Company dock started to go, tank cars spilled oil, which ignited, creating an inferno that persisted much of the night. At one time, a wave with burning oil surged shoreward onto the railroad tracks where a train with 40 oil tank cars was starting to move. One car exploded, setting off a chain reaction, which ignited all the rest.

Some people left town by road just after the quake ended and escaped just in time, because the first tsunami arrived about 25 minutes later. It spanned the width of the bay and was 30 to 40 feet high. Much of its surface was covered with burning oil. The wave carried boats, houses, and railroad cars inland, completely blocking the exit road. At the airport, a wall of water rushed up the airstrip at what was estimated

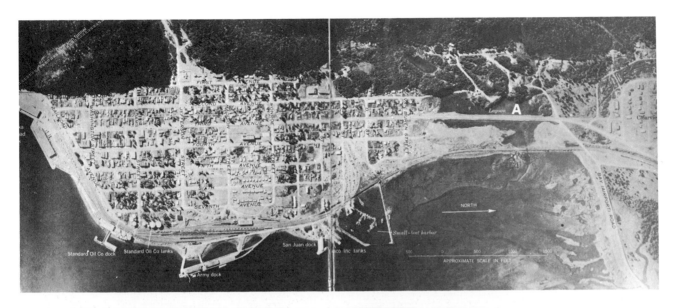

13.30 Destruction at Seward caused by the earthquake and tsunami of 1964. From Lemke (1968).

a (Top) Before the earthquake. Note docks, pier, boat harbor, and lagoon area (A).

b (Bottom) March 28, 1964, one day after the earthquake. All piers, docks, and boat harbors are destroyed. Subsidence of 3.5 feet has submerged much of the land at the lagoon where the road and railroad connected Seward with the rest of Alaska.

to be 50 or 60 miles per hour. Later, high waves kept arriving at intervals until 4:20 A.M., nearly 12 hours after the quake.

The land at Seward subsided 3.5 feet, and the west side of the Resurrection River Valley moved 5 feet north with respect to the east side. Most of the ground cracks above the area inundated by the waves are believed to have resulted from landslides. Unlike Valdez, there was no alternative site for the town. The city of Seward is being rebuilt except for the waterfront. It will continue to serve as an important transportation center. After the disaster, a new gov-

ernment dock was constructed at the head of the bay, although this location might be subject to damage by another large earthquake.

In Seward, thirteen people were killed, eighty-six homes totally destroyed, and reconstruction costs were more than $22 million.

In the southwest part of the Kenai Peninsula, there are extensive ice caps, mostly limited to areas 3,000 feet or more above sea level. In an area 35 miles southwest of Seward, at least four of the valley glaciers shown in Figure 13.31 once extended to sea level and occupied North Arm, but large parts of the

13.31 Head of north arm of Nuka Bay. The rugged uplands, part of the Kenai Mountains, and Split Glacier (B). A delta (C) is built into the head of the arm by meltwater of the glacier. A fault (A–A') trends northwest-southeast. U.S. Geological Survey, 1952.

valleys are now free of ice. The same photograph indicates the north-northeast trend (D) of the Kenai Mountain structures. The only level lands are small fan-deltas built into the head of the fiord. A prominent line reaching from one valley to another (A–A') is probably a fault, therefore a line of potential earthquake displacement.

Homer and Homer Spit (Fig. 13.32), on Kachemak Bay, a tributary of Cook Inlet, on the north side of Kenai Peninsula, show another type of earthquake modification. The residential district in the town of Homer is on the mainland near its junction with the spit, which projects 4 miles into the bay, but much of the industrial, commercial, and recreational part of the town was on the spit. Submarine slides are

believed to have occurred at the end of the spit. Waves up to 9 feet high were observed a short time after the quake. A 20-foot tsunami arrived at 9:30 P.M., 4 hours after the shock.

The next day, it was found that Homer Spit had subsided about 6 feet, partly due to closer packing of the gravel. Because the preearthquake spit was only a few feet above sea level, this sudden subsidence had catastrophic effects on the spit and its use as a port and industrial and recreational center (Figs. 13.32a and b). The total damage here was more than $1 million, mostly to the small-boat harbor near the end of the spit. No lives were lost.

Due to subsidence along the coast near Homer, accelerated bluff erosion was noted within a year.

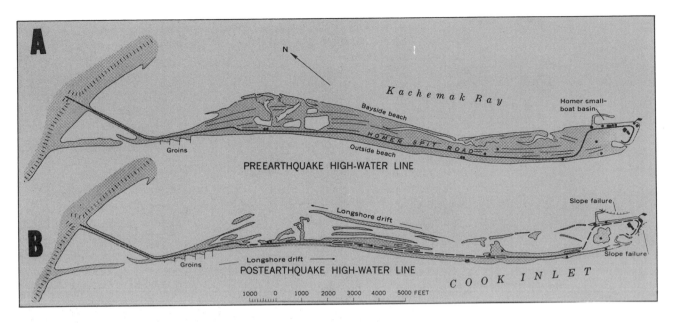

13.32 Sketch maps showing changes in Homer Spit, which extends halfway across Kachemak Bay. From Waller and Stanley (1966).

a Before earthquake.

b After earthquake. The spit was completely submerged by waves 20 feet high. The area subsided 6 feet after the quake, covering much of the road that connected with the mainland. A part of the jetty protecting the boat basin slumped into the bay.

This increased the quantity of sediment drifting along the shore, which should rebuild the spit by natural processes within a few years.

COOK INLET, INCLUDING THE ANCHORAGE AREA   Cook Inlet occupies a large structural depression between the Alaska Range on the west and the Chugach-Kenai Ranges on the east (Fig. 13.21). The Inlet is 180 miles long and the width varies from 80 miles near its mouth to 20 miles near the north end, where it subdivides into Knik and Turnagain Arms. The structural depression extends north of Cook Inlet but is filled by the delta of the Susitna and the broad Matanuska Valley lowland, which continues north from the head of the Inlet for 100 miles. This structural depression is partly filled with Tertiary sedimentary formations, including coal beds and some indications of petroleum. After deposition of these sediments, a large south-flowing stream developed a river valley along the depression. This was subsequently modified by glaciers that extended along the entire length and helped develop a very broad trough. The depths along Cook Inlet, rarely more

than 250 feet, are very small compared to those in most other fiords, notably Prince William Sound. The shoal depths may indicate that there have been thick and widespread deposits of glacial outwash from the receding glaciers. This seems likely in view of the hundreds of feet of postglacial deposits in Turnagain and Knik Arms, which have almost filled formerly deep fiords, leaving broad mud flats that are widely exposed at low tide. Extensive mud flats are found also at the mouth of the Susitna River.

Captain James Cook sailed up the Inlet named after him, looking for the Northwest Passage. He even explored Knik and Turnagain Arms for the same purpose. The latter received its name because Cook had to "turn again" after following it until the water became too shallow to proceed further.

Anchorage, the largest city in Alaska, is located on the lower end of Knik Arm near the mouth of Turnagain Arm. The population of greater Anchorage was estimated to be 150,000 in 1969. The city is built on a gently sloping plain of largely glacial outwash deposits and is separated from Knik Arm by a bluff 50 to 100 feet high, which saved the city

13.33 The eastern portion of Anchorage, showing the immense Turnagain Heights slide (A), and another slide area (B). U.S. Coast and Geodetic Survey, 1964, five months after the earthquake.

from the tsunami flooding of Valdez, Seward, and other towns in the earthquake belt. The city is the center of air transport for Alaska, having become an important center in World War II. It is the gateway of the largest agricultural development in Alaska, the Matanuska Valley.

Anchorage is located 80 miles west of the epicenter of the 1964 earthquake; and, despite its being above the effect of the waves, it was severely damaged during the catastrophe. The chief reason for destruction at Anchorage was the layer of finely laminated clay deposit underlying the outwash gravels on the top of the terrace. This clay has a property that allows it to flow like a liquid when violently shaken. As a result of the flowage of the clay, large blocks of the surface began to break away along the bluffs and slide toward the bay or toward the river valley north of the center of the city. When one block had slipped away another inland from it became loosened and began to slide. In the heart of the city, a drop in ground level of 20 feet occurred, destroying much of the business center. This area has been converted into a parking lot. Along a front of 1.5 miles, a slide moved forward 0.5 mile, carrying

many homes into Knik Arm and breaking apart many others[1] (Fig. 13.33).

The effects of the earthquake included (1) a nearly completed six-story apartment collapsed and was a total loss; (2) a thirty-block area in the business district was almost completely leveled; (3) most buildings in Anchorage suffered serious structural damage, if not total loss; (4) cracks opened in the soil to 12-foot-depths; (5) 200 miles of overhead telephone wires were destroyed; (6) the Anchorage area subsided on an average of about 2.5 feet; (7) property damage amounted to $200 million; and (8) nine persons were killed.

After the quake, parts of Turnagain by the Sea (also called Turnagain Heights) and some other badly damaged slide areas were classified as unsuitable for business or residential use. One part of the slide area was set aside as an earthquake park. Most of the business section was rebuilt, with greater em-

---

[1] The harrowing experience of a home owner with two small children in the sliding area was described by Mrs. Lowell Thomas, Jr., in the *National Geographic Magazine* for July 1964.

phasis on earthquake-resistant structures; and the city now continues its rapid growth.

Because of the properties of the underlying clay, it is probable that parts of the city nearest the places affected by the 1964 slides will be damaged again by other severe earthquakes.

Turnagain Arm, extending east and west, crosses a lowland at its outer end and then cuts deeply into the Kenai-Chugach Mountains, almost severing the peninsula from the mainland. A railroad along its north side continues by tunnel under the mountains to Whittier on Prince William Sound. The road along the same side of the Arm bends around the head of the inlet at Portage (A in Fig. 13.34) and then goes south to Seward, with a branch of the railroad paralleling it.

Turnagain Arm has an unusual feature, a tidal bore (Fig. 13.35), which runs up the shallow Arm and covers the tidal flats at the head, moving with a speed of about 15 miles per hour. Such tidal bores are found only in narrow inlets where the tide has unusually great range. Here, during spring tides, there is said to be a difference of 42 feet, almost as great as that in the Bay of Fundy where the tidal bores are also developed. The tidal bore makes navigation very dangerous in Turnagain Arm, so boats are prohibited. One can imagine the consternation that such a bore would have caused Captain Cook if he had encountered it. Apparently he did not or it would have been included in his log. Also, probably the Arm had shoaled considerably since Captain Cook sailed up it. Here again we have outwash from a glacier that is carrying enormous quantities of sediment into the head of the bay.

The earthquake in 1964 destroyed many bridges along the north side of Turnagain Arm, including that at Twenty Mile River (B in Fig. 13.34). The latter was first crumpled by compression and then settled. The highway was badly disrupted due to slumping and snow avalanches. Much of the new road has been built on a fill away from the mountain slope. After the earthquake, it was found that the

13.34 The head of Turnagain Arm, with an important road and railroad intersection at Portage (A). The area subsided 5.7 feet as a result of the earthquake, submerging roads, railroads, and the village of Portage. Road relocation was necessary. U.S. Coast and Geodetic Survey, 1966.

13.35 Showing tidal bore which moves up the shallow Turnagain Inlet, as a solitary wave, with the incoming tide during periods of spring tide. This wave advances at about 15 miles per hour and in places extends all the way across the inlet. It is comparable to the tidal bores in the Bay of Fundy and at Mont-Saint-Michel in France. Photo by Shepard.

area near Portage, at the head of the Arm, had subsided 5.7 feet. This caused an inundation of 5 miles of the railroad right of way and submerged the entire village of Portage.

The Susitna River Valley, west of Anchorage, was a fiord until it became filled with glacial drift, glacial outwash, and alluvial sand from the southeast side of the Alaska Range. The Susitna Delta, built into the north end of Cook Inlet (Fig. 13.36), is about 10 miles wide. The surrounding lowlands have myriads of small lakes, which formed in depressions in the thick glacial deposit (not illustrated). The Susitna River is heavily loaded with silt, sand, and gravel carried into it by glacial streams, developing its braided pattern. The winding channels are partly choked with sand and gravel bars.

The 1964 earthquake affected the Susitna Delta; but, since it is very sparsely populated, damage to man-made structures was negligible. Evidently there were no eyewitness reports of the quake. The area subsided 1 to 2 feet, in part due to the compaction of loose delta sediment, following the development of cracks at the time of the earthquake. As elsewhere, a part of the front of the delta slumped into Cook Inlet.

Redoubt Bay is in a gently curving indentation of the west shore of Cook Inlet, 65 miles southwest of

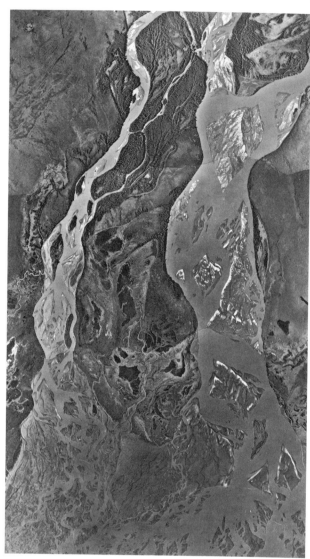

13.36 The 10-mile-wide delta of the Susitna River built into Cook Inlet, 20 miles west of Anchorage. This river drains a large area in south-central Alaska and has filled a former glacial fiord. U.S. Geological Survey, 1950.

Susitna Delta. The strip of lowland between the Alaska Range and Cook Inlet narrows from a 30-mile width near the Susitna River to 10 miles near Redoubt Bay. The 10,192-foot Redoubt Volcano, west of Redoubt Bay, has extensive steeply sloping valley glaciers. Drift River (A in Fig. 13.37), carrying glacial meltwater from the north slope of Redoubt Volcano, is an intensively braided river, which has formed a delta projecting about 2 miles into the very

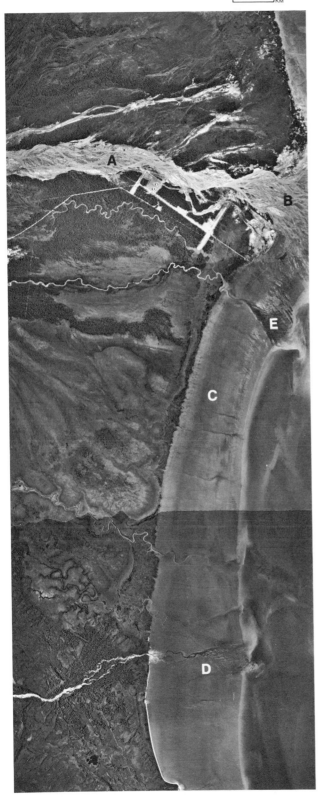

shallow west margin of Cook Inlet. A large outwash fan (B) of the delta extends 4 miles along the shore. South of Drift River, there is a tidal flat 1.5 miles wide (C). Two small streams south of Drift River (D and E) continue as meandering channels across the tidal flat, and arc forming deltas on its outer margin, which is submerged at high tide. This area is near the western border of damage by the 1964 earthquake.

KODIAK ISLAND [Figs. 13.38 and 13.39]   Kodiak Island is at the southwestern end of the North American Coastal Mountain systems. It is a structural continuation of the Kenai Peninsula but separated from it by a 40-mile-wide strait with the rugged Barren Islands in the middle. The 30-mile-wide Shelikof Strait, a southern continuation of Cook Inlet, intervenes between Kodiak Island and the Alaska mainland. Kodiak Island is largely mountainous, with elevations up to 4,470 feet. Even the tiny Barren Islands include mountains as high as 1,980 feet. The coasts of Kodiak Island are deeply embayed by fiords formed during the Pleistocene ice age; and tiny remnants of glaciers remain near the mountain tops.

Three Saints Bay, on the southwest part of Kodiak Island, was the first white settlement in Alaska, established by the Russians in 1792. Eight years later, the settlement was moved to the present site of Kodiak, near the northeast point of the island. Although sparsely populated, Kodiak Island is the center of the king crab industry and processed 17 million pounds in one recent year. Crab, salmon fishing, and processing seafood products constitute the principal occupations. A naval station is located 3 miles south of the main city.

Although Kodiak Island is 250 miles southwest of the epicenter of the 1964 earthquake, there is evidence that movement during the earthquake and in the following weeks was along a fault extending southwest from Montague Island under the waters of the Gulf of Alaska (Fig. 13.21), and exposed only on Montague Island where a scarp 12 feet high de-

13.37 Redoubt Bay, on west side of Cook Inlet. The Drift River (A) carries glacial meltwater from glaciers on Redoubt Volcano, and has formed a delta (B) discharging into the bay. Tidal range here is 18 feet. There is a tidal flat 1.5 miles wide (C). A small stream (E) winds across the tidal flat, and has formed a delta at its outer margin. U.S. Coast and Geodetic Survey, 1966.

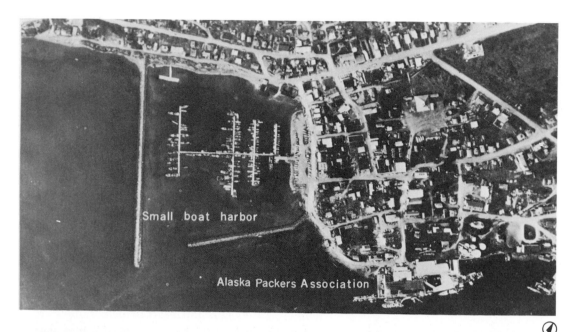

13.38 Changes at Kodiak produced by the Alaska earthquake. From Kachadoorian and Plafker (1967).

a 1962. Kodiak, showing docks and small boat harbor. U.S. Bureau of Land Management.

b April 14, 1964. Note that jetties protecting boat harbor and docks have been destroyed. The ground subsided 6 feet, and the area at A is inundated. Air Photo Tech, Anchorage.

veloped during the earthquake. From a calculation based on the interval of time between the earthquake and the arrival of the first tsunami, the points of origin of the tsunami (not the earthquake epicenter) were determined to be on the continental shelf 17 to 28 miles southeast of Kodiak Island. According to R. J. Malloy, the tsunami originated as the result of the elevation of a portion of the sea floor by as much as 50 feet, which occurred approximately along the fault. This uplift, if correctly interpreted, exceeds the record 47-foot change at Yakutat Bay (p. 414). During the month following the 1964 earthquake, 50 of the 7,500 aftershocks with magnitudes of at least 5.0 on the Richter scale originated in waters southeast of Kodiak Island along a possible continuation of the fault.

At Kodiak, the 1964 earthquake produced violent vibrations that lasted, according to various witnesses, from 2.5 to 7 minutes. The principal result of these vibrations was a series of more than 100 major landslides along the southeast border of the island, largely in areas of weak rock or unconsolidated sediment. Many snow avalances also occurred in the mountains. Fissures opened and spewed out muddy water. Loose heavy objects were moved or overturned.

The ground was tilted so that it subsided 6 feet near the city of Kodiak, with diminishing amounts to the southwest; and a very narrow band along the southeast coast was elevated as much as 2 feet. Where the surface consisted of loose sediment or man-made ground, subsidence was 2 to 10 feet more than in adjoining rock areas. A volcanic ash deposit a foot thick in places had come from Mt. Katmai in 1912 (p. 439). This ash compacted during the quake, contributing to local subsidence.

Thirty-eight minutes after the earthquake, the Kodiak Naval Station received a call reporting a 30-foot tsunami at a Coast Guard Station 15 miles to the southeast. The report was broadcast in Kodiak, but its importance was not fully realized by the inhabitants or the naval personnel. An observer, near the point of first sighting, reported that the sea withdrew a long distance from shore, after which a wall of water surged forward, spreading 0.75 mile across low ground inside the beach. Twenty-five minutes after first being sighted, the tsunami arrived at Kodiak, fortunately at a very low tide stage. Afterward, an abrupt withdrawal of the water carried fishing boats out to sea, drowning some of their occupants. Sixty-

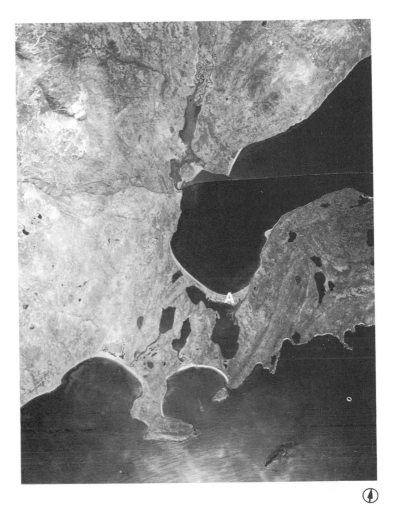

13.39 The village of Kaguyak (A), formerly on a barrier at the head of Kaguyak Bay in the southern part of Kodiak Island, was entirely obliterated by the 28-foot tsunami following the 1964 earthquake. The townsite was abandoned. U.S. Geological Survey, 1951.

five minutes later, a second and higher wave arrived, causing more destruction and loss of life than the first. A third wave an hour later was about as high as the second. Later waves continued until after midnight. Although the waves were diminishing in height by this time, the ocean was at high tide stage; and the midnight waves reached some areas untouched by earlier waves of greater amplitude. Tidal range at Kodiak is about 8 feet. The tsunamis took eighteen lives by drowning, whereas the quake itself killed no one, chiefly because the city is on bedrock. Property damage and losses to the fishing industry totaled $50 million. Damage from the waves (Figs. 13.38a and b) to waterfront canneries, boat harbors, naval instal-

13.40 A large ice field located in the saddle between two volcanoes, Mt. Douglas (E) and Four Peaked Mountain (F). A valley glacier (A) has descended nearly to sea level. An end moraine (B) is separated from the glacial terminus by small lakes. An older moraine (C) has been truncated by shore erosion. U.S. Geological Survey, 1951.

Kaguyak (A in Fig. 13.39), a former village with nine houses and a church on a barrier beach at the head of a fiord on the southeast coast of Kodiak Island, was wiped out. The runup of the tsunami there was 28 feet. A salmon trawler was floated 2 miles upstream where it was stranded. A wooden house was carried for 0.5 mile and deposited intact in a field. Parts of three other villages on Kodiak Island were destroyed or badly damaged.

Although Shelikof Strait, on the west side of Kodiak Island, has a tidal range of 11 to 14 feet (more than that on the east coast of the island), there were no reports of a damaging tsunami on this side. The island shielded Shelikof Strait from the high waves.

Damage to Kodiak had been largely repaired within a year; and, like Anchorage, the city is now enjoying more prosperity than before the quake.

PACIFIC COAST OF THE ALASKA PENINSULA [Figs. 13.40 through 13.44]   The Alaska Range, on the northwest side of Cook Inlet, merges southward with the Aleutian Range, one of the great mountain arcs of the earth. This range forms the Alaska Peninsula, 510 miles long, separating the Pacific Ocean from Bristol Bay and the Bering Sea. The Peninsula is 120 miles wide at the northeast end, narrowing to 20 miles to the southwest. All of the Peninsula was covered by glaciers during the Pleistocene ice age. Now many small glaciers and a few ice caps remain on the slopes of the higher mountains. Along this Peninsula there are sixteen volcanoes, four of them calderas, active in postglacial times. Most of these are spread at irregular intervals along the southeast coast of the Peninsula, and there are a few others to the northeast. Twelve of the volcanoes have erupted since 1762. The southern coast of the Peninsula is very rugged because of the great volcanic cones and the sculpturing by the Pleistocene glaciers. The northern (Bering Sea) coast (discussed in Chap. 14) is a part of the vast lowland belt that occupies much of Alaska north of the Alaska Range.

Mount Katmai, at the northeast end of the Alaska Peninsula, erupted spectacularly in 1912. This region, included in the Katmai National Monument, is unique for the study of volcanic landscapes, having eleven other active volcanoes. Two of these, Douglas and Four Peaked Mountains, are only 9 miles apart. In the saddle between them, there is a large remnant ice field from which a valley glacier (A in Fig.

lations, highways and bridges, was most serious. Freshwater lakes separated from the ocean by barrier beaches were polluted by salt infiltration. Spits were breached by the tsunami. Some of the well water in Kodiak and other coastal locations turned salty. Vegetation was killed in coastal strips throughout the island up to levels inundated by the tsunamis.

13.40) descends to within a mile of the coast. Half a mile seaward of the border of the glacier, an arcuate end moraine has ponded the water, forming a chain of small lakes (B). Meltwater flowing through two gaps in the moraine has built an outwash fan. Part of the older end moraine (C) has been cut away by wave erosion. A smaller glacier (D) ends 300 feet above sea level 2 miles from the coast. A succession of end moraines and an outwash fan are visible outside the terminus of this small glacier, and these are bordered by a narrow beach.

The Mt. Katmai area eruption, 40 miles northwest of Kodiak, beginning June 6, 1912, developed into one of the greatest volcanic manifestations in history. At that time, the region was almost completely uninhabited. Only six people were in the village of Katmai, 16 miles south of the mountain. Violent earthquakes started 5 days before the eruption; and, as a result, the six people abandoned the village on June 4.

The Katmai area was studied by Robert Griggs in summers from 1916 to 1919 and by A. S. Keller and H. N. Reiser in 1954. Although it was four years after the eruption before observers reached the desolated Mt. Katmai area, this is what seems to have happened in 1912. A fissure opened on the west side of Mt. Katmai 6 miles from the peak, and a new volcano, Novarupta, was born. Within a few minutes after a preliminary burst of liquid pumice, an extremely violent eruption from Novarupta shot more than 2.5 cubic miles of ash into the air. Pieces several inches in diameter fell as far away as 10 miles from the opening; and places as distant as Naknek, 80 miles west, and the town of Kodiak, 90 miles east-southeast, were plunged into complete darkness that lasted several days. Some of the erupted material flowed as incandescent sandy ash for 12 miles down a valley northwest of the orifice. After the flow had cooled sufficiently to form a surface crust, superheated steam arose through the fissures, called *fumaroles*; hence the area was called the "Valley of Ten Thousand Smokes." These continued smoking for al-

13.41 During the explosive eruption of Mts. Katmai and Novarupta in 1912, more than 7 cubic miles of rock were blown to pieces, and a layer of ash 10 to 50 feet thick settled in the vicinity of the eruption. Katmai River (A) and Soluka Creek (B) transported vast quantities of loose ash to the seacoast, filling a narrow bay and burying a series of old beach ridges (C). Even the latest beach (G) is partly buried by ash. U.S. Geological Survey, 1951.

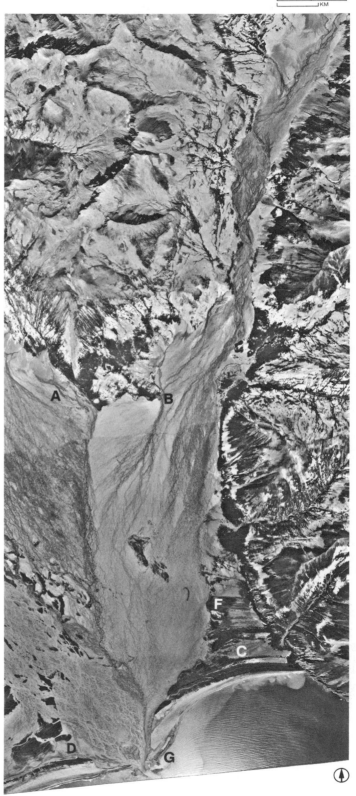

most 10 years and then, like many of us, gave up the bad habit.

Shortly after the eruption from Novarupta, the top of Mt. Katmai collapsed because of the removal of several cubic miles of lava from below its cone. This collapse, producing a central depression or caldera (like Crater Lake, Oregon) 3 miles long by 2 miles wide, resulted in a violent eruption of Mt. Katmai. By the time both eruptions had ceased, 7 cubic miles of pumice and broken rock had been hurled into the air. In the dying stages of the second eruption, a new lava cone formed on the floor of Mt. Katmai caldera. By the 1950s, a lake had developed in the caldera and two small glaciers had formed on the walls. The hot ash and the incandescent ash flow killed all vegetation nearby, and very little new growth has replaced it. The ash accumulated to depths of 50 feet near the two centers of eruption, decreasing to 3 feet along the shores of Shelikof Strait at the abandoned village of Katmai, to 1 foot at the town of Kodiak, and even left a thin film in Seattle. The winds of the upper atmosphere carried the ash around the world, and it was detected within 13 days over the Sahara Desert of North Africa by the sharp diminution of the intensity of the sun's radiation.

Ash from Novarupta and Mt. Katmai contributed to forming vast deposits in Katmai Valley (A in Fig. 13.41) and Soluka Creek (B). Both of these valleys became choked with ash and developed braided streams. Near the mouths of the streams, waves piled up ash and pumice on the beaches at Soluka Creek and Katmai River (C, D). These deposits have largely buried a series of beach ridges, but remnants are seen on the east side of Soluka Creek (F). Drainage of the two streams has formed a deltaic promontory (G).

Mageik Volcano (not illustrated), 10 miles southwest of Mt. Katmai, erupted for 5 days in 1927 and again in 1936 and 1946. The Trident, a volcano 4 miles west of Mt. Katmai (not shown), built a lava cone 300 feet high in 1953, and remained active for a year. During this time, lava flowed south into the valley of Katmai River. Thus the Katmai National Monument is one of the world's best laboratories for the study of volcanic activity.

Wide Bay (Fig. 13.42), 75 miles southwest of Mt. Katmai, is partly separated from the Pacific Ocean by five islands of sandstone (A), all with rock dipping toward the ocean. Elliptical hills, probably drumlins (B), indicate that the ice advanced toward

13.42 Wide Bay is partly separated from the Pacific Ocean by a series of islands (A), composed of resistant sandstone dipping toward the ocean. Glacial drumlins (B) show that Pleistocene glaciers advanced toward the southeast. U.S. Geological Survey, 1951.

the southeast (along their axes) through Big Creek Valley and out into Wide Bay.

To the southwest, 70 and 130 miles from Wide Bay are two of the large Alaskan volcanoes: Aniakchak, with a crater 5 miles across and a cone 1,000 feet high inside the crater, and Veniaminof, nearly 8,000 feet high, with a crater also 5 miles in diameter, which is filled with an ice cap and has ten glaciers extending down the mountain flanks. Veniaminof, despite its present ice cap, was sending up plumes of smoke from 1830 to 1838; had an ash eruption in 1838; was smoking in 1852 and again in 1874; had an ash eruption in 1892, a lava flow in 1930, and another ash eruption in 1939.

Devil's Bay (Fig. 13.43), 35 miles east of Veniaminof Volcano, has rocks composed of Tertiary sedimentaries and volcanics, with the highest divides up to 3,500 feet above sea level. The area was sculptured by valley glaciers during the Pleistocene ice age and was drowned by postglacial rise in sea level so that the valleys became fiords with cirques at their heads. There is no forest vegetation here and beaches are virtually missing along the shore. Solid rock scraped free of soil extends to the water line.

Pavlof Volcano, 8,200 feet high and 100 miles southwest of Veniaminof, was first recorded as erupting in 1762 and has been one of the most active Alaskan volcanoes since that time. Its peak is along a northeast-southwest rift on which a series of cones have been built. These include lava flows forming gently sloping cones, which alternate with steeper cones due to violent eruptions of cinders, blocks, and volcanic ash. Pavlof is the type of volcano represented by Mts. Shasta, Hood, and Rainier in western United States. Between eruptions of Pavlof, occasional plumes of smoke rise from the cone. Historic eruptions have been reported on many occasions from 1762 to 1942. A major earthquake occurred in 1917, the year of one of the eruptions. In 1846 and again in 1914, ash from the volcano fell in large quantities on Unga Island, 45 miles east of Pavlof. In 1911, the top of the volcano is reported to have cracked open. In 1922, incandescent gases rose to 2,000 feet above the mountain. Pavlof thus affords visitors to Alaska one of the best chances of seeing a volcano in eruption.

Bechevin Bay (Fig. 13.44) is the narrow passage dividing Unimak Island (upper) from the western end of the Alaska Peninsula. This bay is the southwest-

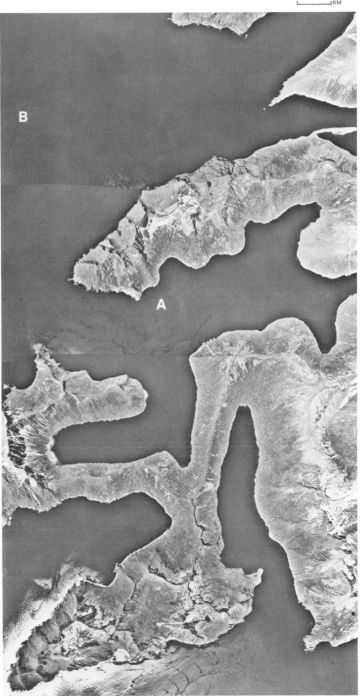

13.43 The Devil's Bay area (A) was sculptured by the now-vanished valley glaciers during the Pleistocene ice ages. The valleys were scoured below sea level, forming spectacular fiords. A small sand spit has developed at B. U.S. Geological Survey, 1957.

ernmost of a series of fiordlike arms of the sea that were formed by valley glaciers from the southeast, which must have grown as ice caps on what is now the continental shelf. As mapped by T. N. V. Karlstrom, the western side of the bay is an end moraine (A), but the central part of the moraine has been drowned or eroded. The frontal moraine of Morzhovoi Bay (B) is 5 miles wide, and displays knob and kettle topography characteristic of end moraines, with hills as high as 100 feet separated by many lakes. The breached morainal front of Bechevin Bay has been partially closed by two hooked spits divided by an inlet 2 miles wide. This shows little change in size and location between photographs taken in 1943 (not shown) and that of 1962 (Fig. 13.44). Spit building along the northern coast of the Alaska Peninsula is straightening the irregularities between the lobate fronts of the end moraines.

THE ALEUTIAN ISLANDS [Figs. 13.45 through 13.51]   The island prolongation of the Alaska Peninsula includes the higher parts of an arcuate ridge 1,300 miles long. The islands are bordered by a shallow platform 20 to 60 miles wide, which was largely exposed and glaciated during the lowered sea levels of the Pleistocene ice age. The Aleutian Ridge rises 9,000 to 13,000 feet above the deeper southern end of Bering Sea and 18,000 to 24,000 feet above the Aleutian Trench to the south. The islands were principally built by volcanoes in Pleistocene and postglacial time on foundations of older rocks, mostly volcanic. Of the fifty-seven volcanoes, twenty-seven have been active within historic times; five of them have calderas. In addition to the intense volcanism, the Aleutian Islands are one of the world's principal earthquake areas. They are also known as one of the most heavily fog-bound regions, and violent winds add to the other dangers encountered by people in this desolate area.

Most of the Aleutians are bounded by cliffs 100 to 1,000 feet high. In some places, lava and ash from

13.44 Entrance to Bechevin Bay between Unimak Island and the southwestern end of the Alaska Peninsula. End moraines of glaciers (A, B), which advanced from the south out of the Gulf of Alaska. Hooked spits from both directions have partially closed the bay entrance. U.S. Coast and Geodetic Survey, 1962.

13.45 Shishaldin Volcano, the highest mountain on the Aleutian Islands, 9,732 feet, resembles Mt. Fujiyama. It is intermittently active, and steam was emerging when photographed. Remnant of an older volcano in foreground. From *Landscapes of Alaska—Their Geological Evolution*, Howel Williams, ed., U.S. Navy photo, 1942.

recent eruptions have built uniform slopes to sea level, but ash erodes rapidly and is soon cut back by waves, forming steep cliffs. Lava erodes more slowly. A small coastal lowland is located on the north shore of Unimak Island. Various geologists report that the islands have wave-cut platforms up to at least 500 feet above present sea level, and at many places a 6- to 10-foot bench extends above the present shore. As many as twenty concentric benches parallel to the coast were found on Umnak Island by F. M. Byers, Jr.

Some of the uneven topography of the submerged Aleutian Ridge is interpreted as moraines drowned by postglacial rise in sea level. Many of the shorelines are indented by fiords with depths to 1,000 feet.

Shishaldin Volcano (A in Fig. 13.45), in the center of Unimak Island, is the highest of the Aleutian mountains, rising 9,372 feet and resembling Mt. Fujiyama. Shishaldin has had frequent eruptions since 1796. Although snow always covers the summit and upper slopes, there is sufficient heat near the summit to prevent enough accumulation to form glaciers. After each winter snowfall, the mountain gradually turns gray because of ash falling on the snow. In 1932, R. H. Finch, while studying Shishal-

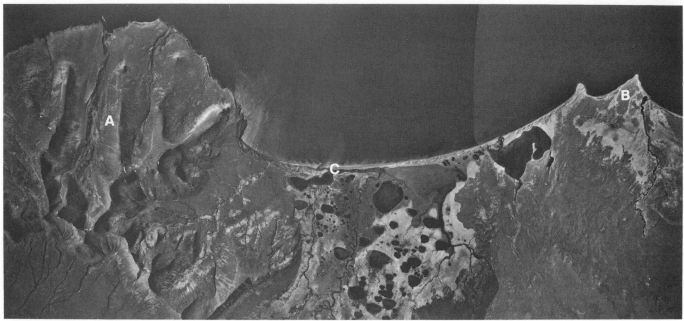

13.46 Tugamak Range (A), showing a volcano deeply eroded by Pleistocene glaciers, and the lower northwest slopes of an earlier Shishaldin Volcano. The two
older volcanoes have been tied together by a narrow barrier (C). A marshy plain has
formed in the lagoon behind. U.S. Coast and Geodetic Survey, 1962.

din Volcano, found remnants of an old volcano (foreground, Fig. 13.45) 6,500 feet high, with a wide
crater (caldera) now almost covered by the modern
cone.

Tugamak (A in Fig. 13.46), on the northwest
side of Unimak Island, is the remnant of a small
older volcano. It has been eroded by glaciers, which
produced U-shaped valleys. At the southwest end of
the island, Pogromni Volcano, 5,500 feet high and
30 miles in diameter, was last active in 1830. Between Tugamak and Pogromni is the remnant of a
still older volcano with a caldera 10 miles wide,
partly occupied by lakes.

The preceding examples illustrate the manner of
growth of many of the Aleutian Islands. Starting with
a single cone rising out of the ocean, successive eruptions form a series of new cones, some of which adjoin older ones but others remain separated by bays
or lakes. Ash blown and washed by rains from the
slopes of the cones is carried to the shore and drifted
by longshore currents to form tombolos, tying the
islands together. Sediment drifts in through the inlets
in the barriers, and they become filled with marsh

vegetation. Cape Lapin (B) is a lava flow built north
from a volcano. This flow is joined to Tugamak Range
by a barrier enclosing Christianson Lagoon (C). Unimak Island was formed by the tying together of seven
major volcanoes and numerous smaller cinder cones.

In 1946, along the southwest coast of Unimak,
the huge tsunami that caused so much damage to
Hawaii (Chap. 15) rose to a height of 115 feet at
Scotch Cap and destroyed a lighthouse.

Unalaska Island is located 70 miles west of Unimak. The important U.S. naval base, Dutch Harbor,
was built on an island in Unalaska Bay at the northeast end of Unalaska. This bay is a fiord, as are numerous other bays that cut deeply into the island.
Beaver Inlet, south of Unalaska Bay, is the deepest
fiord in the Aleutian Islands, with basins of more
than a thousand feet. The only active volcano, Maku-
shin, is in the north projecting lobe of the island,
10 miles west of Dutch Harbor. The southern ridge
of Unalaska is 70 miles long and is composed of
older volcanic rocks, which have been eroded and
have lost the typical volcanic outline. Similar elongate
ridges of older eroded volcanics form Amilia, Atka,

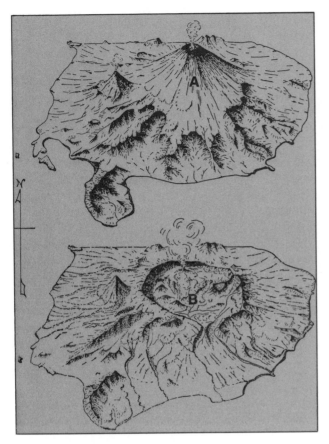

13.47 Two stages in the development of Okmok Caldera, Umnak Island. From Byers (1959).

a Ancestral Okmok Volcano.

b Caldera formed by collapse of the top of a volcano. Cinder cones and younger lava flows have partly filled the caldera.

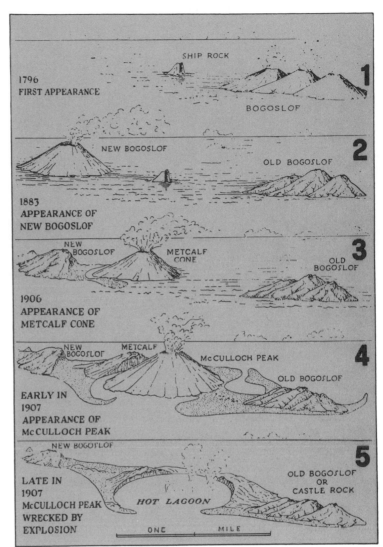

13.48 Volcanic events between 1796 and 1907 of Bogoslof Island, which rises from ocean depths of 7,000 feet, and is 25 miles north of Umnak Island. Note that Metcalf Cone appeared in 1906 and was cut in two early in 1907, when McCulloch Peak was formed. Later in 1907, McCulloch Peak collapsed. For later history, see text. From Jaggar (1908).

Amchitka, and Kiska Islands farther west, two of them with young volcanoes, also built as a north projection. Forest vegetation is almost wholly lacking on Unalaska, as it is in most of the Aleutians. Because glacial erosion had removed nearly all soil and weathered rock, there has been little cliff cutting in the hard country rock, which characterizes the southern ridge. Beach building has also been slight since the retreat of the glaciers.

Okmok Caldera (Fig. 13.47), 90 miles west of Dutch Harbor, occupies the northeastern end of Umnak Island. According to Byers, it formed as a lava cone (A) during the early part of the Pleistocene ice age, with slopes of about 500 feet per mile, which were later grooved and polished by the glacial ice. Near the end of glaciation, a violent gas-charged glowing avalanche, like those of Mt. Pele, Martinique, and the Valley of Ten Thousand Smokes, flowed out from under the basaltic cap, undermining it so that shortly after the flow, the top of the mountain collapsed along a ring fault, forming a caldera 8 miles in diameter (B). This was accompanied by violent explosions, which erupted about a cubic mile of ash. After the eruption, water filled the crater to a maximum depth of about 500 feet. While the caldera was being filled, four lava cones erupted on its floor,[2] two of which rose as islands in the crater lake. When the water level reached about 1,600 feet above sea level, the lake spilled over the northeast rim. Since then, the lake has been drained by the deepening of the outlet channel by more than 500 feet. Four additional volcanic cones have formed in the crater since the lake was drained (Fig. 13.47b). The latest cone formed about 200 years ago and may have been seen in eruption by Russian explorers in the middle 1700s. An eruption in 1945 occurred from one of the cones on the floor of the caldera, only 10 miles northwest of Fort Glenn, an Air Force base located in a precarious position on the lower eastern slopes of Okmok Volcano.

The ash from numerous eruptions has collected as beach sediment along the flanks of Okmok Volcano. Part of the beach sediment has been blown into coastal dunes on the northeast side of the cone near the mouth of Crater Creek, where the north winds of winter frequently attain velocities of 100 miles per hour.

Bogoslof (Fig. 13.48), a tiny island 25 miles north of Umnak, is one of the world's most famous volcanoes. The sea floor on all but the south side of the island is more than 7,000 feet deep. On the south, a sill of 4,500 feet separates it from Umnak Island. These great depths bordering Bogoslof are part of Bering Canyon, the longest submarine canyon in the world.

Bogoslof was first seen by Russians in 1769 when it was only a tiny pinnacle, referred to as Ship Rock. It was also seen by Captain Cook ten years later. In 1796 (Fig. 13.48, 1), lava and explosive debris formed an island 0.25 mile south of Ship Rock, which was called Ioann Bogoslof (Russian name for St. John the Apostle). It continued to steam for eight years. In 1806, lava flowed from the summit into the sea on the north side; and the eruption persisted intermittently until 1823, when the new island was about 400 feet high. This was later called Old Bogoslof or Castle Rock. In 1882 and 1883, eruption was renewed north of Ship Rock, and a violent explosion

[2] This is determined by finding pillow lavas that form only under water.

showered ash on Unalaska, 60 miles to the east. The new cone, which was 500 feet high (Fig. 13.48, 2), was named New Bogoslof. The two Bogoslofs and Ship Rock became connected by barriers of sandy volcanic debris by 1887. At that time, Old Bogoslof was being reduced by erosion, and Ship Rock began to disintegrate and disappeared about 1890. New Bogoslof was steaming violently in 1891 and 1897 but had cooled 2 years later. In 1906 (3), a new volcanic cone, called Metcalf Peak, formed from a lava eruption between Old and New Bogoslof. It had a sheer spine of lava projecting from the summit. In 1907, a severe eruption destroyed the south half of Metcalf Peak, but a new and larger cone, McCulloch Peak (4), was built by this eruption. On September 1, 1907 (5), still another violent eruption entirely destroyed McCulloch Peak, at that time only a few months old. In 1909, a new cone (not shown), Tahoma Peak, was pushed up in the bay where McCulloch Peak had been. Explosions in 1910 formed a deep crater in the new cone. By 1922, explosions, collapse, and marine erosion had destroyed the remnants of Metcalf and McCulloch Peaks. Old Bogoslof had been reduced to two horns, and a wide channel separated the two islands. In 1926, a submarine explosion produced another new cone 200 feet high near the sites of Metcalf, McCulloch, and Tahoma Peaks. Hot lava was still visible 5 years later. Since 1931, wave erosion has reduced the two Bogoslof remnants to less than 200 acres. Bogoslof illustrates the alternate dominance of volcanism building new islands, and marine erosion and volcanic explosions destroying them.

The Islands of the Four Mountains, about 100 miles southwest of Bogoslof, include Carlisle Volcano (A in Fig. 13.49), 5,283 feet high; Cleveland Volcano (B), 5,675 feet; and Herbert Volcano (not shown), 4,235 feet, 7 miles south of Carlisle Volcano. The ocean is 700 feet deep in the glacial trough directly southwest of the mountain. The volcano is a cone formed by a combination of lava flows, which tend to build gentle slopes (C), and ash and cinder falls from explosive eruptions, which build steep slopes (D). All major eruptions seem to have come from a vent at the summit of the mountain and to have extended down the slopes. Many flows are flanked by lava levees, retaining the flow in narrow channels (E) and hardening before reaching sea level. Ash falls are spread more widely, much ash

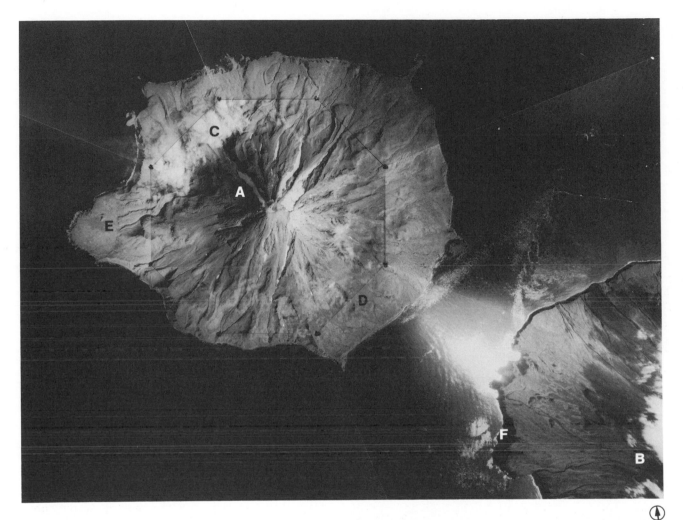

13.49 Carlisle Volcano (A) and Cleveland Volcano (B) in the Aleutian area, known as the Islands of the Four Mountains. Carlisle Volcano is largely composed of cinders and ash (D) but also has lava flows with gentle slopes (C). Mt. Cleveland is bordered by wave-cut cliffs several hundred feet high, as compared with much lower cliffs on Carlisle Volcano, indicating that Cleveland is older. Nine-lens photograph from U.S. Coast and Geodetic Survey.

dropping into the ocean. Carlisle Volcano was active in 1774 and 1828, and smoke plumes rose from it in 1838. Cliffs several hundred feet high can be seen along the margins of Mt. Cleveland (F), indicating that it is much older than Carlisle.

Semisopochnoi Island (Fig. 13.50) is located in the Rat Island group of the western Aleutians, 460 miles west of the Islands of Four Mountains. This 10- by 12-mile island, according to R. R. Coats, is composed wholly of Pleistocene and postglacial volcanic products. The island is at the southern end of

a deep submarine ridge that arcs to the north and then west for a total of 500 miles. The early history of volcanic activity here was marked by the building of a 3,000-foot rounded cone of basaltic lava covering about the same area as the modern island. Later, several smaller but steeper cones of andesitic lava and explosive debris rose above the basalt cone, probably to heights of 5,000 or 6,000 feet. These cones (A) were subsequently glaciated and are now somewhat eroded. Cirques and U-shaped glacial valleys were also carved into the surface. Then, near the end of

the Pleistocene, three new basaltic cones were built. Anvil Peak, the largest of these (B), rises to 3,867 feet, at present the highest point on the island.

A short time after the building of these basaltic cones, a very violent eruption produced great volumes of inflated incandescent pumice and ash, which rushed down the valleys as a flaming avalanche. This was soon followed by the collapse of the center of the island to form an elliptical caldera nearly 5 miles in greatest diameter. The northern and western borders of this caldera (C) are shown on the aerial photographs. Remnant walls on the north are 500 to 700 feet high. After the collapse, a major new volcano, Mt. Cerberus, erupted on the floor of the caldera and now has three prominent craters (D). Lava flows from Cerberus (E and F) have been little changed by erosion. A smaller cone on the northeast side of the caldera, Lakeshore Cone (G), adjoins a lake formed in the caldera where lava flows blocked a stream outlet.

Smoke was seen rising from the island in 1772, 1790, 1792, and 1830, and the volcano was active in 1873, the probable date of one of the fresher lava flows on Mt. Cerberus.

The rounded coast of Anvil Peak (H) has cliffs 100 to 400 feet high, whereas the older cone east of it (I) has a cliff with maximum height of 1,000 feet. These heights are a measure of the amount of wave erosion of lava and ash respectively since the late and early Pleistocene. Sandy beaches and coastal dunes have developed at the mouths of the three larger streams (not shown).

Kiska Island, 100 miles west of Semisopochnoi Island, is at the western end of the Rat Island Group. The island extends about 27 miles from northeast to southwest, but despite this transverse direction, Kiska forms a part of the east-west Aleutian Range. The island was first seen in 1741 by Vitus Bering, a Danish explorer employed by Russia. It was also one of the Aleutian Islands occupied by the Japanese in 1942, but it was recovered by American and Canadian forces the next year. Although it has one of the best harbors in the Aleutians, the island has been uninhabited since 1947.

According to Coats, most of the island is composed of volcanic rocks of Tertiary and Pleistocene age, and erosion has destroyed most of the volcanic land forms. The northern end of the island (Fig. 13.51) includes the 4,004-foot Kiska Volcano (A),

13.50 Semisopochnoi Island was first built by volcanoes as far back as the Pleistocene ice age. Glacial erosion (A) is prevalent. Anvil Peak (B) was formed somewhat after the age of glaciation when, according to R. R. Coats, the mountain was 6,000 feet high. The center collapsed, forming a 5-mile caldera. Borders of the caldera are seen at C. Mt. Cerebrus (D), with three cones, formed in the caldera and also emitted lava flows (E). The oldest part of the island (I) has a coastal cliff 1,000 feet high. U.S. Coast and Geodetic Survey, 1952.

5 miles in diameter at sea level. The north side of the volcano appears to continue its unusually steep seaward slope to a depth of 2,000 feet, 6,000 feet offshore. The volcano is in line with the Haycock marine depression, 1,200 feet deep, and therefore the building of the volcano may have started in relatively deep water. The volcano is composed of an alternation of lavas and fragmental rocks coming from explosive eruptions. Older lavas at the southwest margin (B) show parallel ridges and depressions formed while the lava was hardening. Several of the younger flows (C, D) are darker colored in the photograph than the adjoining older flows. Although the channels that were followed by various flows are plainly visible in the photograph, there are no historic reports of eruptions of Kiska Volcano; however, some of the lava flows appear to be very young. Erosion on the north face has produced coastal cliffs 1,500 feet high.

A series of lakes and lagoons just south of the volcano (E) may have formed in an area depressed during the development of the adjoining deep-sea depression. Beach sediment, principally of pebble size, has drifted northward along the coast, forming a barrier shutting off the lagoons from Bering Sea.

On February 4, 1965, a very heavy earthquake in the Rat Islands, 7.7 on the Richter scale, had its epicenter about 60 miles southeast of Kiska Volcano and 60 miles southwest of Semisopochnoi Island. There were 870 aftershocks within 45 days after the initial earthquake, as compared with 728 in the same period after the Prince William Sound earthquake of 1964. Because the islands near the epicenter are uninhabited, there has been no published report of changes in shoreline, landslides, mudflows, or other modifications due to the earthquake. A tsunami 10 feet high struck the shore of Attu Island, about 290 miles northwest of the epicenter, but no serious damage occurred.

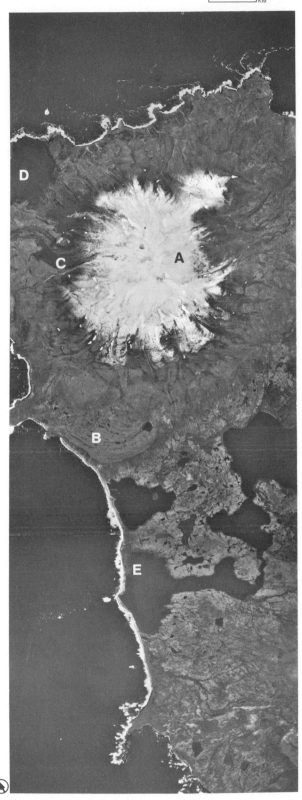

13.51 Kiska Volcano at the northeast end of Kiska Island. Promontories along the north coast are lava flows. Coves with cliffed shorelines have been cut in volcanic ash. Recent lava flows (C and D) form dark-colored zones in the photograph. Parallel ridges and depressions (B) were formed during the hardening of older lavas. Much older volcanic rocks to the south are separated from Kiska Volcano by depressions and tied to the volcano by barriers. U.S. Coast and Geodetic Survey, 1951.

REFERENCES FOR CHAPTERS 13 AND 14

Adams, Ben, 1959. *Alaska, the Big Land.* Hill and Wang, New York.

Brooks, A. H., 1906. Geography and geology of Alaska. *U.S. Geol. Survey Prof. Paper* 45.

Dutro, J. T., Jr., and T. G. Payne, 1957. Geologic map of Alaska. *U.S. Geol. Survey.*

Karlstrom, T. N. V., 1964. Surficial geology of Alaska. *U.S. Geol. Survey Misc. Geol. Inv. Map* I–357, 2 sheets.

Smith, P. S., 1939. Aerial geology of Alaska. *U.S. Geol. Survey Prof. Paper* 192.

Stefansson, Evelyn, 1943. *Here Is Alaska.* Charles Scribner's Sons, New York.

Wahrhaftig, Clyde, 1965. Physiographic divisions of Alaska. *U.S. Geol. Survey Prof. Paper* 482.

Williams, Howel (ed.), 1958. *Landscapes of Alaska—Their Geologic Evolution.* University of California Press, Berkeley, Calif.

REFERENCES FOR CHAPTER 13

Buddington, A. F., and T. Chapin, 1929. Geology and mineral deposits of southeastern Alaska. *U.S. Geol. Survey Bull.* 800.

Byers, F. M., Jr., 1959. Geology of Unmak and Bogoslof Islands, Aleutian Islands, Alaska. *U.S. Geol. Survey Bull.* 1028–L, pp. 267–369.

Coats, R. R., 1959. Geological reconnaissance of Semisopochnoi Island, western Aleutian Islands, Alaska. *U.S. Geol. Survey Bull.* 1028–O, pp. 477–519.

————, W. H. Nelson, R. Q. Lewis, and H. A. Powers, 1961. Geologic reconnaissance of Kiska Island, Aleutian Islands, Alaska. *U.S. Geol. Survey Bull.* 1028–R, pp. 563–581.

Cooper, W. S., 1937. The problem of Glacier Bay, Alaska—A study of glacier variations. *Geogr. Rev.,* vol. 27, pp. 37–62.

Drewes, H., G. D. Fraser, G. L. Synder, and H. Barrett, Jr., 1961. Geology of Unalaska Island and adjacent insular shelf, Aleutian Islands, Alaska. *U.S. Geol. Survey Bull.* 1028–S, pp. 583–676.

Ferrians, O. J., Jr., and H. R. Schmoll, 1957. Extensive proglacial lake of Wisconsin age in the Cooper River Basin, Alaska. Abs., *Geol. Soc. Amer. Bull.*, vol. 68, no. 12, pt. 2, p. 1726.

Field, William O., and Maynard M. Miller, 1951. Studies of the Taku Glacier, Alaska. *Jour. Geol.*, vol. 59, pp. 622–623.

Finch, R. H., 1934. Shishaldin Volcano. *Fifth Pacif. Sci. Congr., Canada, 1933, Proc.*, vol. 3, pp. 2369–2376.

Gibson, W. M., and Haven Nichols, 1953. Configuration of the Aleutian Ridge, Rat Islands–Semisopochnoi Island to west Buldir Island, Alaska. *Geol. Soc. Amer. Bull.*, vol. 64, pp. 1173–1187.

Goldthwait, R. P., 1963. Dating the Little Ice Age in Glacier Bay, Alaska. *Rept. 21st Sess. Intl. Geol. Congr., 1960, Norden*, pt. 27, pp. 37–46.

Grant, U. S., and D. F. Higgins, 1913. Coastal glaciers of Prince William Sound and Kenai Peninsula, Alaska. *U.S. Geol. Survey Bull.* 526.

Grantz, A. P., G. Plafker, and R. Kachadoorian, 1964. Alaska's Good Friday earthquake, March 27, 1964. *U.S. Geol. Survey Circ.* 491.

Graves, W. P. E., M. M. Miller, and Mrs. Lowell Thomas, Jr., 1964. Alaska earthquake. *Nat. Geographic Magazine*, vol. 126, no. 1, pp. 112–156.

Griggs, R. F., 1922. *The Valley of Ten Thousand Smokes*. National Geographic Society, Washington D.C.

Hansen, W. R., 1965. Effects of the earthquake of March 27, 1964 at Anchorage, Alaska. *U.S. Geol. Survey Prof. Paper* 542–A, pp. A1–A68.

————, E. B. Eckel, W. E. Schaem, R. E. Lyle, W. George, and G. Chance, 1966. The Alaska earthquake, March 27, 1964: Field investigations and reconstruction effort. *U.S. Geol. Survey Prof. Paper* 541.

Hicks, S. D., and William Shofnos, 1965. The determination of land emergence from sea level observations in southeast Alaska. *Jour. Geophysical Res.*, vol. 70, no. 14, pp. 3315–3320.

Jaggar, T. A., Jr., 1908. The evolution of Bogoslof Volcano. *Amer. Geogr. Soc. Bull.* 40, pp. 385–400.

Jordan, G. F., 1962. Redistribution of sediments in Alaskan bays and inlets. *Geographical Rev.*, vol. 52, no. 4, pp. 548–558.

Kachadoorian, R., and G. Plafker, 1967. Effects of the earthquake of March 27, 1964, on the communities of Kodiak and nearby islands. *U.S. Geol. Survey Prof. Paper* 542–F, pp. F1–F41.

Karlstrom, Thor N. V., 1964. Surficial geology of Alaska. *U.S. Geol. Survey Misc. Geol. Inv. Map* I–357.

Keller, A. S., and H. N. Reiser, 1959. Geology of the Mt. Katmai area, Alaska. *U.S. Geol. Survey Bull.* 1058–G, pp. 261–298.

Kennedy, G. C., and H. H. Waldron, 1955. Geology of Pavlof Volcano and vicinity, Alaska. *U.S. Geol. Survey Bull.* 1028–A, pp. 1–19.

Knappen, R. S., 1929. Geology and mineral resources of the Aniakchak District. *U.S. Geol. Survey Bull.* 797, pp. 161–223.

Lemke, R. W., 1968. Effects of the Alaska earthquake of March 27, 1964 at Seward, Alaska. *U.S. Geol. Survey Prof. Paper* 542–E, pp. E1–E43.

Malloy, R. J., 1964. Crustal uplift southwest of Montague Island, Alaska. *Science*, vol. 146, no. 3647, pp. 1048–1049.

Martin, G. D., B. L. Johnson, and U. S. Grant, 1915. Geology and mineral resources of the Kenai Peninsula. *U.S. Geol. Survey Bull.* 587.

Mertie, J. B., Jr., 1938. The Nushagak District, Alaska. *U.S. Geol. Survey Bull.* 903.

Miller, Don J., 1960. Giant waves in Lituya Bay, Alaska. *U.S. Geol. Survey Prof. Paper* 354–C, pp. 51–86.

Miller, Maynard M., 1958. The role of diastrophism in the regimen of glaciers in the St. Elias District, Alaska. *Jour. Glaciology*, vol. 3, pp. 293–297.

Muntz, A. P., 1955. Recent glacier activity in the Taku Inlet area, southeastern Alaska. *Arctic*, vol. 8, no. 2, pp. 83–95.

Plafker, George, 1969. The Alaska earthquake, March 27, 1964, regional effects: Tectonics of the March 27, 1964 Alaska earthquake. *U.S. Geol. Survey Prof. Paper* 543–I, pp. I1–I74.

————, and R. Kachadoorian, 1966. Geologic effects of the March, 1964 earthquake and associated seismic sea waves on Kodiak and nearby islands, Alaska. *U.S. Geol. Survey Prof. Paper* 543–D, pp. D1–D46.

Post, Austin S., 1968. Effects of glaciers. *In* The Great Alaska Earthquake of 1964. *Hydrology Vol., Nat. Acad. Sci. Publ.* 1603, pp. 266–308.

Reid, H. F., 1895. Glacier Bay and its glaciers. *U.S. Geol. Survey, 16th Ann. Rept.*, pt. 1, pp. 421–565.

Reimnitz, Erk, 1966. Late Quaternary history and sedimentation of the Copper River and vicinity, Alaska. Univ. California, San Diego, Ph.D. thesis in oceanography.

————, and Neil F. Marshall, 1965. Effects of the Alaska earthquake and tsunami on recent deltaic sediments. *Jour. Geophysical Res.*, vol. 70, pp. 2363–2376.

Robinson, G. D., 1948. Exploring Aleutian volcanoes. *Nat. Geographic Magazine*, vol. 94, no. 4, October, pp. 509–528.

Russell, I. C., 1893. Malaspina Glacier. *Jour. Geol.*, vol. 1, pp. 219–245.

Sharp, R. P., 1958. Malaspina Glacier, Alaska. *Geol. Soc. Amer. Bull.*, vol. 69, no. 6, pp. 617–646.

Stanley, K. W., 1968. Effects of the Alaska earthquake of March 27, 1964, on shore processes and beach morphology. *U.S. Geol. Survey Prof. Paper* 543–J, pp. J1–J21.

Tarr, R. S., and B. S. Butler, 1909. The Yakutat Bay region, Alaska: physiography and glacial geology. *U.S. Geol. Survey Prof. Paper* 64, pp. 11–44.

————, and Lawrence Martin, 1912. The earthquakes at Yakutat Bay, Alaska in September 1899. *U.S. Geol. Survey Prof. Paper* 69.

————, and Lawrence Martin, 1914. *Alaskan Glacier Studies.* National Geographic Society, Washington, D.C.

Twenhofel, W. S., 1952. Recent shoreline changes along the Pacific Coast of Alaska. *Amer. Jour. Sci.*, vol. 250, pp. 523–548.

Waller, R. M., and K. W. Stanley, 1966. Effects of the earthquake of March 27, 1964, in the Homer area, Alaska. *U.S. Geol. Survey Prof. Paper* 542–D, pp. D1–D28.

Wilson, B. W., and Alf Tørum, 1968. The tsunami of the Alaskan earthquake, 1964: Engineering evaluation. *U.S. Army Corps of Engrs., Coastal Engr. Res. Center, Tech. Mem.* 25.

UNITED STATES
DEPARTMENT OF THE INTERIOR
GEOLOGICAL SURVEY

ALASKA
MAP E

COMPILED FROM THE GEOLOGICAL SURVEY ALASKA RECONNAISSANCE
TOPOGRAPHIC SERIES, SCALE 1 : 250,000, AND OTHER OFFICIAL SOURCES

1 INCH APPROXIMATELY 40 MILES

SCALE 1 : 2,500,000

0   120   240

STATUTE MILES

Icy, Unglaciated Lowland Coasts

Bering Sea and Arctic Alaska

14 The Bering Sea and the arctic coasts form a striking contrast to those of southern Alaska. The coastal mountains and the deep fiords end north of the Alaska Peninsula; and coastal plains predominate, traversed by winding streams and dotted with a maze of lakes. Scattered mountain ranges terminate as promontories into the Bering Sea. The interior of Alaska is largely drained by the Yukon River and its many tributaries. The Yukon Delta is exceeded in area along United States coasts only by that of the Mississippi.

The Brooks Range is the north and west continuation of the Rocky Mountains of the United States and Canada. On the arctic side of this range, the broad coastal plains, called the *North Slope*, were formed by alternating marine erosion and by both river and marine deposition that continued through the Pliocene and Pleistocene. Delta building at the mouths of the numerous north-flowing rivers has been the most important recent development.

North of the Alaska Peninsula, permanently frozen ground, called *permafrost*, is found first in scattered areas underlain by muddy sediments; farther north, the permafrost becomes more widespread and attains great thickness, of more than 1,000 feet on the arctic slope. The surface vegetation acts as insulation for the permafrost. However, where the vegetation is denuded either naturally or by man, permafrost tends to melt; and, where the volume of ice is large, as in fine-grained sediments, the melting causes depressions. This accounts for vast numbers of *thaw lakes* that characterize much of the coastal plains. In the northeastern United States during the Pleistocene, the areas bordering the glaciers developed similar ponds; and many are still left or have been filled with marsh deposits.

Extensive help in obtaining information for this chapter has been provided by the U.S. Geological Survey, particularly D. S. McCulloch, George Moore, and J. M. Hoare. Some of their information has not yet appeared in print but was kindly offered for our use.

455

14.1 Entrance to Ugashik Bay. Hooked spits have pro-graded from each side of the inlet, forming successive beach ridges. To the southwest, these ridges (A) lie shoreward from a lake-filled marsh. At the north, more than thirty ridges are seen along a 4-mile belt (B). At C, C′ one ridge truncates several older ones, implying erosion. A marshy shoal (D) is just inside the inlet, and a mud flat (E) outside the north entrance. U.S. Geological Survey, 1951.

Large level areas of central and northern Alaska stand only a few feet above sea level and are floored with marine sands and muds of relatively recent age. Some of these are slowly sinking, perhaps due to the slow sea level rise; whereas others, notably the north slope, have been emerging. The sinking portions are deeply indented by estuaries and bordered by barrier islands, which have a total length of 400 to 500 miles. Where there are no barriers along the north-west coast, wave erosion has been rapid and has left low, straight coastal bluffs.

Bering Strait, which separates Cape Prince of Wales on the Alaska side from Mys Dezhneva (East Cape) on the Siberian side, is of special interest to archeologists. It was across this 56-mile-wide gap that man is believed to have migrated first to North America. One might have supposed that the glacial climate of the late Wisconsin would have stopped such a migration; but actually it was favorable be-cause Bering Strait is only 180 feet deep and the lowered sea level produced a land bridge, perhaps as much as 1,000 miles wide. Man and the higher mammals could travel easily across this bridge because most of Alaska north of the southern ranges was not glaciated. Also, game was apparently plentiful, espe-cially along the seacoast where marine life evidently was fully as abundant as today.

BRISTOL BAY [Figs. 14.1 through 14.4]   North of the Alaska Peninsula, the generally low coast of the Bering Sea is deeply indented by the shallow Bristol Bay. Captain Cook was the first explorer to sail into this long bay, in July of 1778; he named it in honor of the Earl of Bristol. In contrast to the deep fiords of southern Alaska, Bristol Bay has few sound-ings deeper than 250 feet. The shores are relatively straight with only low hills, except for the Ahklun Mountains that border a part of the northwest side of the bay. The estuaries of the Kvichak and the Nushagak Rivers at the head of the bay are both funnel-shaped, and have tides ranging as high as 23 feet. The tides race up these bays somewhat as in the funnel-shaped Bay of Fundy in New Brunswick, where the tide is the highest in the world. Great spawning runs of the king salmon occur in these rivers, and the sparse population of the coastal area is mostly involved in fisheries.

The shores of Bristol Bay are largely bordered by mud and sand flats. The sediment is derived from the outwash plain coming from the glaciers of the Alaska Peninsula and, to the lesser extent, from smaller glaciers of the Ahklun Mountains. Drillings along the coast show that the glacial till and outwash extends down to depths of about 200 to 300 feet below sea level.

Ugashik Bay (Fig. 14.1), on the east side of Bristol Bay, is the combined estuary of Ugashik, Dog Salmon, and King Salmon Rivers. The 16-foot tidal range develops currents that keep the entrance to this bay open with the help of large river drainage. A succession of beach ridges have grown toward the entrance from both sides. On the south side of the entrance, the ridges have been built around the marsh, which has many small lakes. At C and C′ in Figure 14.1, the beach ridges have been truncated, either by a storm or due to change of current direction. The truncations on the two sides may not have been contemporaneous. After the truncation, more beach ridges have built out the two sides of the bay. A large tidal flat is exposed at D, and a sand or mud flat at E extends out beyond the north side of the entrance. This bay entrance resembles Chincoteague Bay in Virginia (Fig. 4.18) and that of Beaufort Inlet of North Carolina (Fig. 5.9). Here, however, the tidal range is much larger.

Kvichak Bay (Figs. 14.2 and 14.3), at the head of Bristol Bay, is still within the province of glaciation, and entering streams are clogged with debris outwash from the nearby glaciers. The braided channel of the Kvichak River (Fig. 14.2) is full of sand bars, and the bordering treeless plain is pitted with lakes interspersed between masses of tundra vegetation. The small village of Koggiung (A) has a well with 300 feet of glacial drift that extends 250 feet below sea level.

The east shore of Kvichak Bay (Fig. 14.3) has morainic topography with larger lakes than at the head of the bay and small strings of lakes (C) that represent kettle holes where blocks of ice have melted after being partly buried in outwash. The north-flowing currents, the product of the west winds and the flood tides coming into the bay, have built out the sand beach (A) and built sand spits for a total of 9 miles to the northeast. At least twenty-five curved beach ridges separated by swales have been built out over the mud flats. Shore cliffs just east of the area shown in the photo rise 50 to 100 feet and were cut into the glacial till but have subsequently

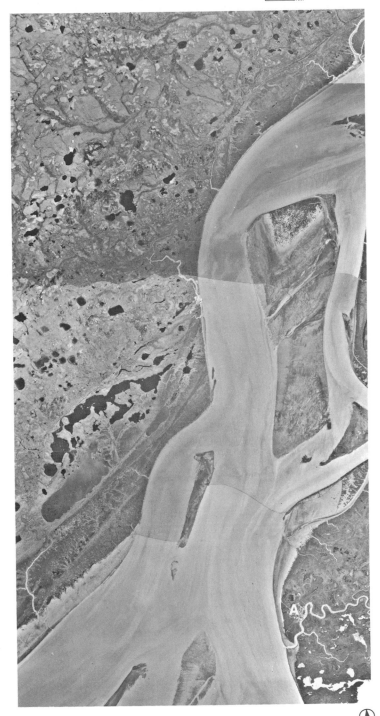

14.2 The Kvichak River estuary at the head of Bristol Bay has a tidal range of 23 feet, and the river is famous for salmon spawning. The adjoining area is a flat treeless outwash plain pitted with small lakes. U.S. Geological Survey, 1951.

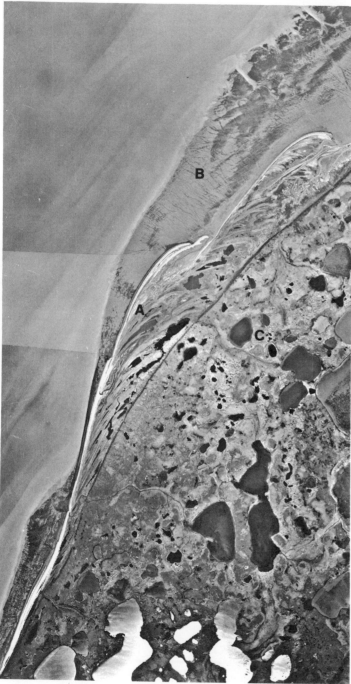

been separated from the sea by the beach building. At this point, Kvichak Bay is 20 miles wide.

Nushagak Bay, west of Kvichak Bay, indents the coast 40 miles. It has a tidal range of 21 feet. The west side of the bay is built of glacial outwash and is overgrown by tundra vegetation. Moraines from the Pleistocene glaciers have dammed eleven of the western tributaries to Nushagak River and have formed elongate lakes that look like the Finger Lakes of New York state. This area is at the southern boundary of permafrost; and, at Clark Point, on the east side of the bay, a well penetrated a 10-foot lens of ice at a depth of 20 feet and several others at greater depths.

Togiak Bay (Fig. 14.4), 90 miles west of Nushagak Bay, has a chevron-shaped shoreline. The Togiak River enters the head of the bay and drains the central part of the Ahklun Mountains. The channel (A) is a distributary of the Togiak, and the photograph suggests that the head of the bay has been filled by a delta; but bedrock is found along the valley, so delta building has not been significant. The elongate hill (B), a mile from the shore on the west side of the bay, is part of a hogback ridge that rises here to 1,000 feet. According to J. M. Hoare, the rocks in this area are highly folded. Narrow spits (C, C') have been built into the estuary at the main mouth of the river. The small lakes are due principally to the melting of buried ice lenses. This bay is 30 miles east of a former glaciated area where the glaciers from the Ahklun Mountains come to the coast. The glaciers left moraines on Hagemeister Island and on the hilly southwest continuation of the Ahklun Mountains. The strait between Hagemeister Island and the mainland has tidal currents up to 4 knots, according to Hoare.

At Cape Newenham, the Ahklun Mountains terminate and the coast changes direction to north. Thirty miles up this north trend we encounter one of the rich ore-mining areas of Alaska. Here is located the largest source of platinum for the United States. The shallow bay, appropriately called Goodnews, is used to lighter out the ore to the cargo ships. The water is so shallow along this coast and to the north around the Yukon deltaic plain that such operations are necessary in many places.

YUKON AND KUSKOKWIM DELTAS [Figs. 14.5 through 14.8]   More than 500 miles of the

14.3 The southeast side of Kvichak Bay, showing a glacial moraine with many ponds and kettle holes (C). A spit extending northward with a series of hooks (A) borders the moraine, and a broad tidal flat (B), averaging 2 miles in width, separates the shore from Kvichak Bay. U.S. Geological Survey, 1951.

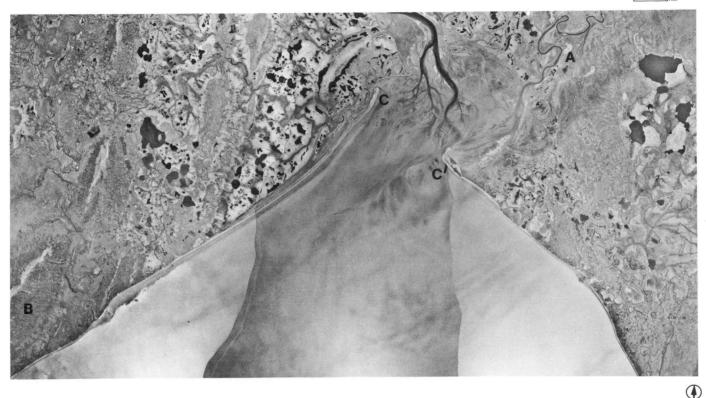

14.4 Togiak Bay, an estuary in the Ahklun Mountain Range. A delta has formed into the head of the estuary. A hogback mountain (B) is about 1,000 feet high. This is near the southern end of areas affected by permafrost, and many of the small lakes were formed by collapse due to the melting of the ice a short distance below the surface. U.S. Geological Survey, 1954.

Bering Sea coast consists of the deltaic lowlands of the Yukon and Kuskokwim Rivers (Fig. 14.5), which cover 21,000 square miles and are generally less than 10 feet above sea level. The Yukon is the largest river in Alaska, with a length of 2,300 miles and a drainage basin of 330,000 square miles, more than half of it in Canada. The Kuskokwim is the second largest river in Alaska, about 600 miles long, and has a drainage area of 50,000 square miles.

The Yukon has a modern arcuate delta at the northern end of the plain, while the Kuskokwim enters Bering Sea through an estuary 60 miles long that indents the southern end of this same deltaic plain. The Kuskokwim is navigable for shallow-draft steamers for 500 miles from its mouth; whereas the Yukon, because of the shifting sand and mud banks of its lower valley, can be entered only by shallow-draft river boats. The Yukon, however, was used extensively in transporting prospectors during the Klondike gold rush of 1898.

The deltaic plain surrounds various uplands, including Nelson Island, 40 miles long; Askinuk Mountains, 30 miles long; and the Kuzilvak Mountains, 11 by 5 miles. The Askinuk and Kuzilvak Mountains include elevations more than 2,000 feet above sea level, and the uplands on Nelson Island are 1,485 feet high. There was local alpine glaciation in the Askinuk Mountains. At many places in the deltaic plain, other hill areas (not shown on Fig. 14.5) have elevations locally as high as 500 feet, which are entirely surrounded by alluvial and deltaic lowlands. Because unconsolidated sediments have been penetrated to depths of 600 and 1,000 feet by deep wells, it seems probable that both the mountains and lower elevations, many of which are volcanic, rise out of and are partly buried beneath the immense plain of alluvial deposits. Elsewhere, the deltaic plain includes bands of hummocky topography where, according to J. M. Hoare, the silty deposits have been windblown, accounting for the hummocks and some of the basins.

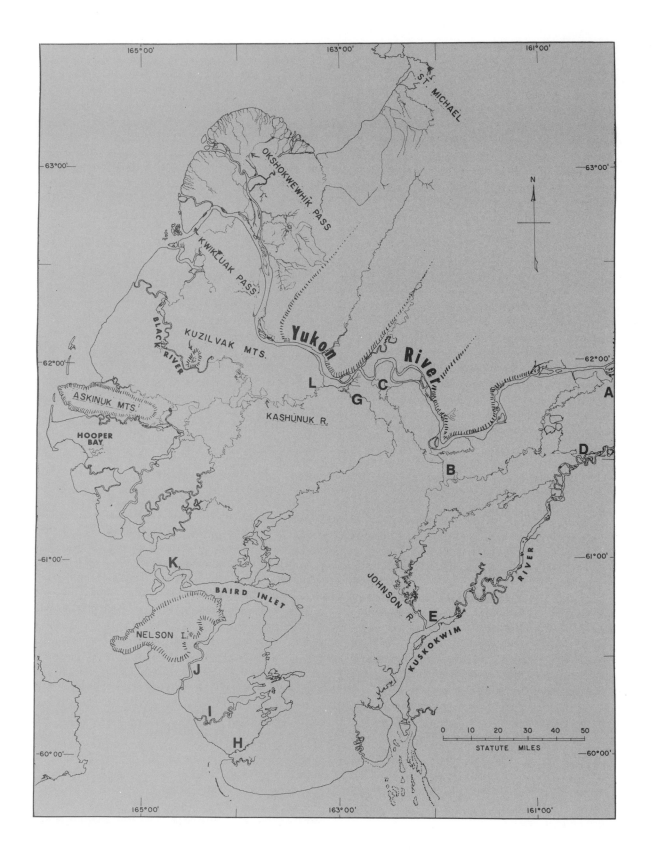

Probably a portion of the plain is due to beach progradation rather than being strictly deltaic. Lakes cover 40 to 50 percent of the plain, and are mostly related to permafrost action.

The Yukon-Kuskokwim deltaic plain has not yet had the thorough study that Louisiana geologists have given the Mississippi Delta. Hoare and W. H. Condon, in 1966 and 1968, published geologic maps and descriptions of the west-central part of the Yukon Delta plain and have identified several sedimentary units that represent successive stages in the growth of the delta. All units are composed of similar silts and sandy silts, but they have been differentiated on the basis of surficial characteristics observed on aerial photos and by erosional scarps cut in older units at their contacts with younger ones. Although the remainder of the delta has not yet been mapped in detail, the west-central part is probably representative of much of the remainder. Hoare and Condon have found bones of the mammoth elephant in surficial sediments, indicating an age greater than 8,000 B.C., because the mammoth became extinct about that date. Wood samples found in well cuttings at a depth of 600 feet are older than 34,000 years and probably date from the Sangamon, the last interglacial stage.

The authors have made some additional speculations based on the study of topographic maps and charts of the Yukon-Kuskokwim deltaic plain. Figure 14.5 shows the positions of a succession of distributaries and their outlets into Bering Sea during the postglacial and since the sea-level rise virtually stopped.

Channels leaving the Yukon River (A, B, C) join the Kuskokwim River at D and E. We consider this evidence that the Yukon River discharged into the Kuskokwim long before it formed its present delta farther northwest. The lower Kuskokwim River is in

14.5 Outline map of the Yukon-Kuskokwim deltaic plain in central-western Alaska. The plain is very level, but includes isolated mountain uplifts, volcanic cones, and many small uplands (not shown). The earliest deltas seem to have discharged southward from the Yukon River into the Kuskokwim by several channels. Later, a southwestward discharge reached the sea through four channels from Baird Inlet. Next, the Kashunuk River built a subdelta with eight or more outlets. The present subdelta is to the north and has an arcuate front with three major outlets. Compiled from U.S. Geological Survey quadrangles by J. R. Moriarty.

a broad estuary (Fig. 14.6), and modern deltaic deposits are found in the estuary but not in the Bering Sea. Elongate sand bars with north-south trend and with tops generally 18 feet or more below sea level (some marked G on Fig. 14.6) extend nearly 100 miles into and beyond the estuary. These seem likely to have formed when the Kuskokwim River carried the Yukon drainage to the sea at a time of substantially lower sea level. However, the tides, which have a larger than average range, may be the cause of these bars, just as the tides of the English Channel have produced a series extending out of Dover Strait in both directions. The bars that lead out of the Kuskokwim estuary are also similar to bars that border the estuary on the east side of the great Ganges Delta in East Pakistan. It may well be that both estuaries represent the early course of the great rivers that have formed these deltas. If the submarine sand bars are indicative of lower sea level, they represent deltaic sedimentation during the postglacial rise of sea level.

On the east side of the Kuskokwim estuary (A in Fig. 14.6), a former shoreline marked by a beach ridge is adjoined by a prograding beach zone with two additional ridges (B). These are abruptly separated from modern estuarine sediments (C, D) by a scarp a few feet high. On the west side of the estuary, a plain (E) of older alluvial deposits, with abundant thaw lakes and an elevation of 13 feet, is separated from estuarine deposits (F) by an erosion scarp at least 10 feet high. The sea level was probably a few feet higher than at present when the beach ridges (B) formed.

A later channel (G in Fig. 14.5) leaving the Yukon River can be traced to Baird Inlet, from which four channels (H, I, J, and K) enter the Bering Sea. These may be distributaries of one subdelta or, alternatively, a succession of subdeltas.

Still later, the Kashunuk River (L) diverged from the Yukon and seems to have discharged into Bering Sea through seven channels, not necessarily contemporaneously, of which Black River is the northernmost. The Hooper Bay–Black River area was geologically mapped by Hoare and Condon, who distinguished the following succession of surficial materials on the deltaic plain: (1) old alluvial deposits (late Pleistocene or early postglacial); (2) glacial and colluvial deposits adjoining highlands (late Pleistocene or early postglacial); (3) old floodplain and delta deposits (postglacial); (4) old beach deposits,

14.6 The estuary of the Kuskokwim River (see Fig. 14.5). The land west of the estuary is a typical delta plain, modified by permafrost which has produced the myriads of lakes. Former shorelines are shown (A, B), and deposits of the modern estuary are at C. U.S. Geological Survey, July 1952.

probably about 3,000 years old; (5) estuarine deposits, less than 3,000 years old; (6) young floodplain deposits, forming in the modern Yukon Delta; and (7) young beach deposits forming on modern beaches and spits. This succession may record the past 40,000 to 50,000 years.

The old alluvial deposits (A in Fig. 14.7) include coarse gravelly sediments that accumulate around the borders of enclosed uplands or mountains and sloped toward the sea as piedmont fan deposits. Only small tracts of old floodplain and delta deposits (B, B′) are recognized. Old beach deposits (C) display at least eight "beach" ridges, or cheniers, as they were called by Hoare and Condon, separated by as much as 0.8 mile. Since these ridges are made of silt, it seems to the authors that they are more likely to be dune ridges than beach, because waves appear to be able to build ridges along the coast only if they are dealing with coarse sediment, otherwise the material is washed inland. The ridges terminate at the modern delta but appear again on the far side, indicating that the ridges were cut away when the river developed its present mouths. Numerous thaw lakes are found in swales between the ridges. The estuarine deposits (D) adjoin Hooper Bay and have tidal channels draining toward the bay. They are separated by a scarp not higher than 3 feet from tidal flat deposits in the modern estuary. This illustrates how the several successive stages of evolution of the Yukon-Kuskokwim deltaic plain can be differentiated on aerial photographs.

The modern Yukon Delta forms a bulge extending northwest about 30 miles from the predelta shoreline. A series of four passes have distributed Yukon sediment throughout the delta. At present, the principal outlet channel is Kwikluak Pass (Fig. 14.8) at the extreme southwestern border of the deltaic arc. The pass is flanked by young alluvial deposits (A, B). South of the pass is a belt of old beach or dune ridges

14.7 The Hooper Bay area. North of Hooper Bay is a typical permafrost region of old alluvial deposits with numerous thaw lakes. South of Hooper Bay, many low interrupted beach ridges (C) rise slightly above the marshes and lakes. These represent an earlier stage of the river delta. Bordering Hooper Bay are estuarine deposits (D). The contacts between these and later deposits are indicated by a black line. Modern tidal flat deposits (E) are forming along the shallow borders of Hooper Bay. U.S. Geological Survey, 1951.

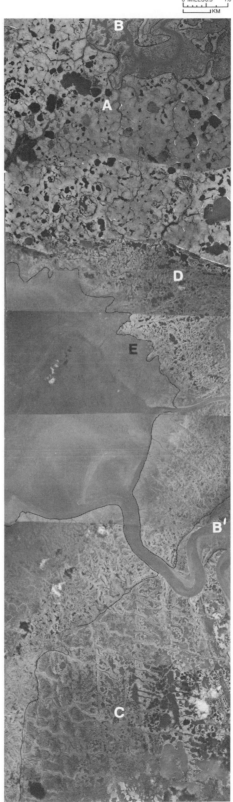

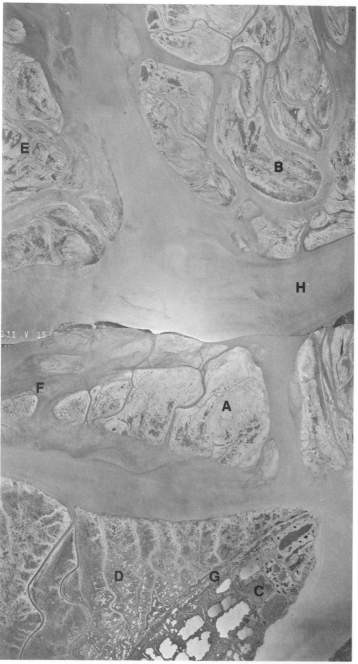

At the top of the image: a scale bar reading "0 MILES 0.5 1.0" and "KM".

(C). West of the ridge belt is a zone mapped by Hoare and Condon as young beaches (D). The young beaches are described as being composed of silt and sandy silt, making it probable that they are dune ridges. Hoare and Condon report that at one place (not shown) a new ridge had formed by 1963, which was not shown on 1951 aerial photos, indicating 0.25 mile of progradation during the twelve years. If the Kwiklauk Pass continues to be the principal outlet, it will build another arcuate bulge seaward.

The distributaries entering the Bering Sea by way of Baird Inlet and all the channels that entered through Kashunuk River, except Black River, have embayed lower courses, of which Hooper Bay (center of Fig. 14.7) is representative. There is no embayment at the mouth of Black River or at the mouths of passes associated with the modern Yukon Delta. This suggests that these outlets have been in use since the present sea level was nearly reached about 3,000 years ago, while the other deltaic lobes are older. An alternative possibility is that the older subdeltas may have continued to subside after they were abandoned, and the lower parts of distributary channels have been drowned.

The modern delta has, in addition to the main channels, a maze of diverging and converging channels separated by sand bars and mud flats. A comparison of Coast and Geodetic Survey charts based on surveys in 1898, 1914, and 1966, a topographic map dated 1952, and aerial photographs of small parts of the delta taken in 1951, suggests that changes in delta morphology between 1898 and 1966 have been minor, in contrast to vast changes displayed in the Mississippi and most other United States deltas during the same period. Some alluvial islands (E, F in Fig. 14.8) have developed since the chart of 1916.

Permafrost is present through much of northern Alaska. During the long winters, temperatures are extremely low; and moisture in the ground freezes to depths of hundreds of feet. During this freezing, water is squeezed into cracks in the soil, so that in drilling wells, layers of clean ice several feet thick may be encountered at various depths. During the summer, with the long hours of sunshine, the ice near the surface melts and the ground settles. Because the amount of melting is not uniform over such a vast tundra area as the Yukon and Kuskokwim Deltas, small depressions develop all over the plain;

14.8 A small part of Kwikluak Pass (H), the largest distributary of the modern Yukon Delta. Young beach deposits join (at G) a series of old beach ridges and swales. U.S. Geological Survey, 1951.

and water collecting in these depressions forms thaw lakes. Many are tiny, but the thaw lakes on the older deltaic sediments are generally 0.5 to several miles in diameter. This is the principal origin of the myriads of lakes on the deltaic plain, such as just west of the Kuskokwim Bay estuary (Fig. 14.6) and north of Hooper Bay (A in Fig. 14.7). Baird Inlet and possibly Dall Lake may be due to subsidence within the delta of the type that produced Lake Pontchartrain and Lake Borgne, near New Orleans in the Mississippi Delta. Some of the lakes in the deltaic plain are mapped as having surfaces as much as 4 feet below sea level. They are separated from the main channel, Kwikluak Pass, by natural levees that have impermeable material.

NORTON SOUND [Figs. 14.9 and 14.10]   Norton Sound is a large embayment between the northern end of the Yukon Delta and Seward Peninsula. The coast adjoining the Yukon Delta along the south and east sides of the bay consists of a broad belt of deformed Cretaceous sedimentary rocks, interrupted by the volcanic St. Michael promontory and adjacent Stuart Island. In this area, there are no large depositional plains of recent age, and the stream mouths show scarcely any embayment. However, on the north side of the bay, where the rocks are largely made up of the older metamorphics with some granite intrusives, there are two considerable embayments, whereas the coast farther west is smoothly curving.

On the north side of St. Michael promontory is the principal port, where ships land supplies for transshipment in small boats to the Yukon River. These boats have to cross 45 miles of rather dangerous open water before getting to the mouth of the river. Norton Sound is also the center of Eskimo habitation, including the towns of Teller, Nome, and Unalakleet.

The mouth of the Shaktolik River is partly protected by Cape Denbigh and the Reindeer Hills (A in Fig. 14.9), a promontory at the south entrance to Norton Sound, with elevations to 640 feet. This upland of quartzite and schist is a land-tied island connected to the mainland by discontinuous sand barriers and intervening peat marshes. Most of the area shown in Figure 14.9 is a reindeer preserve. The marshes, partly deltaic, at the mouths of the Sineak (B) and Shaktolik (C) Rivers are separated from Norton Sound by barrier spits (D, E). The longer spit indi-

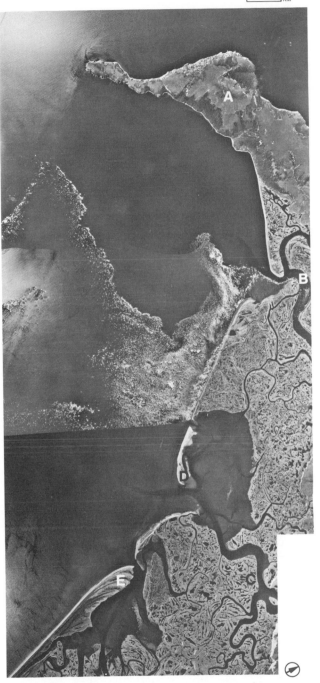

14.9 The Reindeer Hills (A) partially protect a broad marshy tract, including the estuaries of the Sineak (B) and Shaktolik (C) Rivers. Entrances to small bays are partially closed by hooked spits (D, E). The many small lakes are related to permafrost. The western part of the figure, showing drift ice in Norton Sound, was photographed on June 5, while the eastern part, on July 2, shows the sound free of ice. U.S. Geological Survey, 1950.

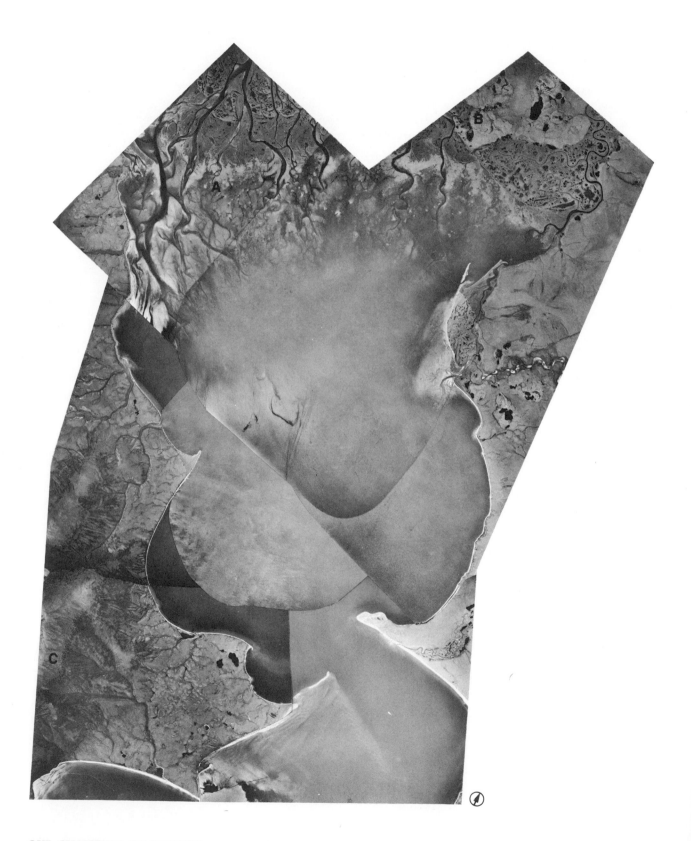

cates that the predominant longshore transport is northwest. The marsh is traversed by a multitude of small tidal streams and is spotted with small lakes. The tidal range here is only 2 to 3 feet, in great contrast to the large tides of southern Bering Sea.

The western portion of Figure 14.9 was taken June 5, 1950, and large numbers of floating ice blocks were still evident; while the eastern part, photographed a month later, shows ice-free conditions. This shows how late in the season ice disappears at these high latitudes.

Golovnin Bay, 45 miles west of Reindeer Hills, is a 20-mile-long estuary, with its mouth flanked by Cape Darby to the east and Rocky Point to the west. The first settlement, other than of Eskimos, was in this bay. At the head of the estuary, Fish River has built a delta 10 miles into the bay (A in Fig. 14.10). The delta has a maze of meandering streams, channels, and interdistributary marshes.

Mountains of the Seward Peninsula, with elevations of more than 4,000 feet, were sculptured by alpine glaciers during the Pleistocene. The Fish River carried outwash deposits from the glaciers, which helped build the delta. Permafrost on the peninsula is now several hundred feet deep. The mountains and ridges of the peninsula are covered with fine to coarse weathered rock and soil. During the summer when the frost in the surface layer melts, the weathered material becomes a sticky mass that flows down the slopes of the mountains as mudflows following tiny channels. This process is well illustrated at White Mountain (B), where the mudflows appear dark colored, and also in a series of hills 400 to 600 feet high between the delta and the open coast of Norton Sound (C). Sediment is also carried to the beach by solifluction, a slow downhill creep due to seasonal freeze and thaw. As a result of both processes, an important source of beach sand is provided, both here and along the hilly arctic coasts farther north.

14.10 The delta of Fish River built into Golovnin Lagoon, an estuary on the north side of Norton Sound. In hilly areas where there is permafrost during the summer thaw season, trains of debris move down the slopes, a process known as solifluction. This is shown by dark bands on White Mountain (B). U.S. Geological Survey, 1951.

NOME [Fig. 14.11]   Located 75 miles west of Golovnin Bay, Nome has been built on a straight coast at the mouth of the Snake River. Nome was at one time the second largest city in Alaska. Between 1898 and 1920, it produced more than $80 million of gold, but Nome has decreased in importance ever since. The city not only lacks any natural harbor but the shallow water is only 20 feet deep 0.6 mile offshore, making it necessary for vessels to anchor as much as a mile from the beach. This same difficulty exists farther south off much of the Yukon Delta. Furthermore, the ships can come to Nome only during 5 months of the year because the approach is frozen over for the rest of the time. There are no railroads, but air transportation is now maintained throughout the year. Another difficulty at Nome is that the permafrost prevents obtaining an adequate supply of water.

Despite these disadvantages, Nome had a meteoric rise at the turn of the century. Gold was first found in the area in 1865 by a party of Russians surveying for a telegraph and cable line to connect Asia with North America, but little attention was given to the discovery. In 1898, a party of prospectors traveling along the south coast of Seward Peninsula were marooned for several days near the future site of Nome. They found signs of gold but did not consider the prospects promising. However, one of them, J. J. Brynteson, returned later the same year and found some rich placer deposits on Anvil Creek (A in Fig. 14.11), 5 miles in from the seacoast. Word of the strike spread rapidly, and by early 1899 many prospectors had arrived and established a town, which they first called Anvil City, but later, due to an error in reading, a cartographer's notation, "Name?" was changed to Nome. In 1900, many disappointed gold seekers were returning from the Klondike but were diverted when they heard of the strike in the Nome area. A large mining camp developed in a short time. Placer claims along the creeks were soon exhausted, but gold was discovered in the beach sand near the camp. During a period of two months, a million dollars worth of gold was recovered from the beach.

Most of the Nome gold was obtained later by dredging along the coastal plain and up the river valleys. This coastal plain can be traced for 25 miles west of Nome to the Sinek River Delta. It forms a gentle surface at the foot of old marine cliffs. An examination of the Nome area continued. It was

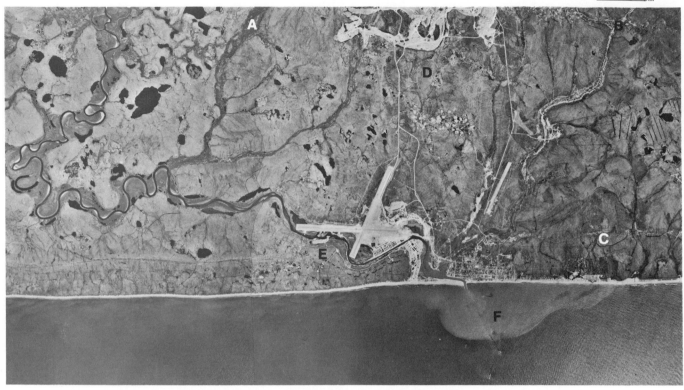

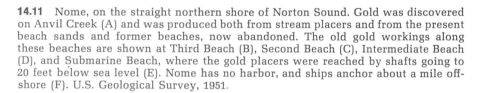

14.11 Nome, on the straight northern shore of Norton Sound. Gold was discovered on Anvil Creek (A) and was produced both from stream placers and from the present beach sands and former beaches, now abandoned. The old gold workings along these beaches are shown at Third Beach (B), Second Beach (C), Intermediate Beach (D), and Submarine Beach, where the gold placers were reached by shafts going to 20 feet below sea level (E). Nome has no harbor, and ships anchor about a mile offshore (F). U.S. Geological Survey, 1951.

found that there are several old sand beaches in from the coast (Fig. 14.11). These have been studied particularly by D. M. Hopkins. The highest, called Third Beach (B), lies 70 to 79 feet above the present sea level, and has yielded the richest deposits of beach placer gold. According to Hopkins, this beach was formed during the high sea-level stand of the first interglacial, making it about a million years old. Second Beach (C) is located about 37 feet above sea level. Hopkins assigned this to the third interglacial (Sangamon). This former shoreline, according to D. S. McCulloch, can be traced along the west coast of Alaska for almost 1,500 miles. In most places, it is found as a sea cliff, partly covered by alluvium, and has a base between 30 and 40 feet above sea level. Intermediate Beach (D) is located

between Second and Third Beaches, and has been interpreted by Hopkins as being nearly equivalent in age to Third Beach. The name First Beach is applied to the modern beach. Just west of Nome but inland from the coast, borings revealed another old beach 20 feet below sea level; and this was appropriately called Submarine Beach. Like the other beaches, this has been worked by shafts. Studies of the fossil fauna indicate that Submarine Beach is the oldest, early Pleistocene in age or even Pliocene.

Various other beaches have recently been found offshore, and these are being investigated by industry and by the U.S. Geological Survey. As in so many other places, the sea floor gives great promise of future economic development. The Nome area can be considered an outstanding example of the accumulation of rich deposits as an indirect result of the changes in sea level that characterized the glacial period.

POINT SPENCER SPIT [Fig. 14.12]   Seventy miles northwest of Nome, the relatively straight coast of the Nome area terminates, and a segmented bay extends into the land for more than 40 miles. The outer bay, Port Clarence, is protected from the open sea by Point Spencer, an elongate north-trending spit with an enlarged multiple hooked terminus. A military airfield was constructed on this north end during World War II and led to special geological studies by R. F. Black. The spit consists of three segments that are very distinct. At the south end, a sand beach encloses swampy land with large thaw lakes that are somewhat segmented. The middle section of the spit has only a narrow beach; whereas the outer part consists of multiple sand ridges with small freshwater ponds in the intervening troughs. Most of these ridges trend east and west and evidently represent the former hooked end of the spit. The ridges become more closely spaced near the north point, and the trend is more to the northeast. The northern ridges are separated by a peaty soil and there are no lakes.

One of the problems of the airfield personnel was the scarcity of water. The permafrost is found 3 to 8 feet below the surface, being lower in the center than on the borders of the spit. The low precipitation, about 11 inches per year, falls mostly as snow. The melting snow forms the ponds in the center and can be used for the water supply, but storms often generate waves that sweep across the outer 10- to 14-foot-high sand ridges and pollute with salt the freshwater ponds. In 1912, the entire spit was inundated by a storm. When wells were drilled through the permafrost, sand and gravel were encountered, but these strata contained saltwater. As a result, a careful conservation of the small freshwater source on top of the permafrost is required.

Another problem was encountered in constructing the runway for the airfield. A dome-shaped mound

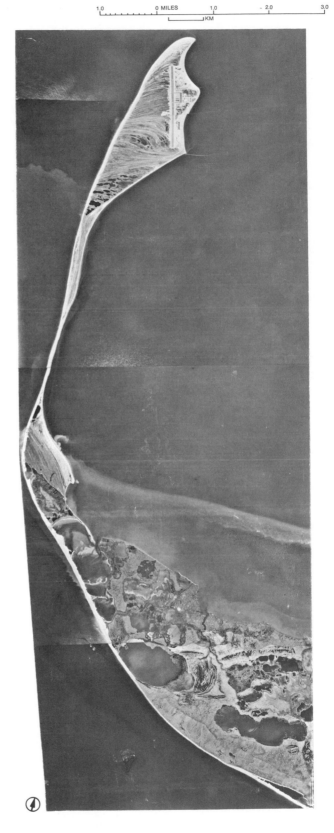

14.12 Point Spencer Spit enclosing Port Clarence. The base of the spit includes large thaw lakes. This adjoins a very narrow middle section and a broad hook on the outer 3.5 miles. In the latter, beach ridges are abundant, along with some thaw lakes, which provide fresh water for the airfield. U.S. Geological Survey, 1950.

of ice 30 feet across and a foot high developed during freezing in the fall. The ground froze from the surface downward, and a lense of soil water was left between the new ice and the permafrost. When this finally froze it formed the low dome.

The terminus of the spit is very unstable. The position of the shoreline near the end has been observed to change as much as 100 feet during one night as the result of wave and current action. This rapid shifting adds difficulties to the building of permanent structures.

BERING STRAIT AND BERING LAND BRIDGE
There are few places in the world from which one can see two oceans. The most accessible is the Cape of Good Hope, but less well known is Cape Mountain (A in Fig. 14.13), along Bering Strait where, on a clear day, one can see the Bering Sea, an arm of the Pacific on the left, and the Chukchi Sea, an arm of the Arctic Ocean, on the right. Also visible is East Cape in Sibera.

Both Bering and Chukchi Seas have unusually broad continental shelves. It is possible to go north from the Aleutians across these shelves for 1,300 miles without encountering water more than 300 feet deep. The flatness of the shelf floor testifies to lack of active warping or faulting in recent times; but actually the basement of these seas has been sinking and has undergone large faulting, although rapid deposition has built up the flat shelves, keeping pace with the sinking. In some places, sound-reflection methods show the deposits are as thick as 10,000 feet.

Hopkins and his associates in the U.S. Geological Survey have made extensive explorations of the Bering Sea Bridge and have cooperated with Soviet geologists in this investigation. They have looked for old beaches below sea level and have dated shells from these beaches by carbon-14 methods. They have also investigated glacial deposits to determine limits to migrations during these stages of lowered sea level.

14.13 Cape Mountain (A), at Cape Prince of Wales (B), provides a distant view of the coast of Siberia, 60 miles away. Northeast of the cape, a barrier about a mile wide extends 150 miles, broken by only one inlet. There is a lagoon behind the barrier at most places. Here the barrier shows at least fifteen beach ridges, modified by thaw lakes in the intervening swales. U.S. Geological Survey, 1950.

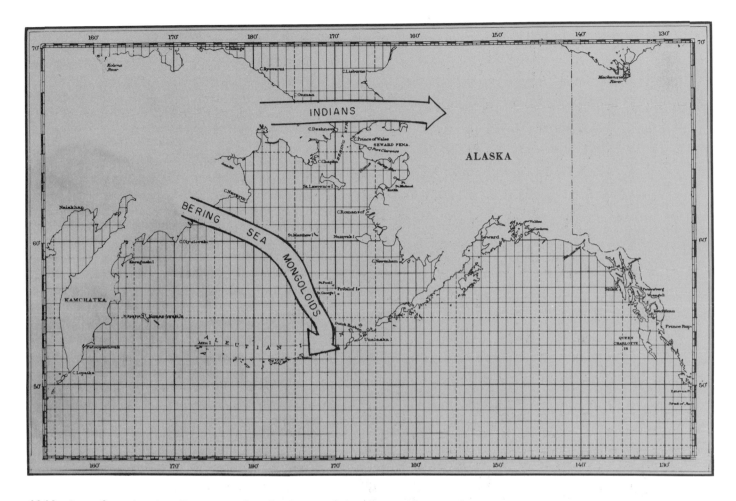

14.14 A northern immigration route taken by ancestral American Indians and a more southern sea route followed by Eskimos and Aleuts.

Many collections of Pleistocene and Tertiary fossils have added to the information on former bridges, and the history of Bering Strait and the Bering Sea has thus been traced back for millions of years.

During most of the Tertiary as well as during the glacial stages of the Pleistocene, vast areas in the Bering Sea were exposed as land. The less resistant portions were reduced to plains by erosion or built up as plains by delta deposition. The more resistant rocks, such as granites, were left standing above the flat surface and now form the islands such as the Diomedes in Bering Strait and St. Lawrence and Nunivak to the south (Fig. 13.1). Volcanic eruptions led to the formation of the Pribilof Islands, which are a breeding ground of fur seals; and the

central part of St. Lawrence Island is also an old volcano.

During glacial stages, the temporarily exposed sea floor in Bering Strait and the adjacent lands supported tundra vegetation; and the winter temperatures were lower than at present. Although migrants could reach Alaska from Asia during the glacial stages, the huge mountain glaciers of southeastern Alaska extended into the sea and probably prevented any southward migration. Also, the Cordilleran continental glaciers lay to the east so that no migration could move in that direction.

Hopkins has shown that with sea level 230 feet lower than at present, the Bering Land Bridge would have been open; and the Pribilof and St. Matthew

14.15 Shishmaref (A), the first inlet in the long barrier northeast of Cape Prince of Wales. Former beaches are indicated (B, C, D). The concentric ridges may represent outlines of hooks formed at old inlets by incoming currents building ridges in from both sides. U.S. Geological Survey, 1950.

Islands would have been attached to the mainland. At −130 feet, the bridge would still have been open, but the islands would have been separated; while at −100 feet, St. Lawrence Island would have been attached to Alaska but separated from Asia.

Although remains and artifacts of early man are rare in easternmost Siberia, Alaska, and the islands, it seems probable that the ancestors of the North American Indians crossed Bering Strait during the last glacial stages, about 25,000 years ago; whereas the Aleuts and Eskimos, with a different culture, came by boats to the Alaska mainland and the Aleutian Islands by a more southerly route, entering near the western end of the Alaska Peninsula about 10,000 years ago (Fig. 14.14). It is also possible that the first humans crossed the strait still earlier in some kind of boats. At the time when the ancestral North American Indians arrived, glacial barriers prevented them from reaching warmer southern lands until about 10,000 B.C. The late arriving Aleuts reached this continent near the end of the last glacial stage but, unlike the Indians, remained in these northern lands.

BARRIER COAST; CAPE PRINCE OF WALES TO CAPE ESPENBERG [Figs. 14.13, 14.15, and 14.16] Extending 150 miles northeast of Cape Prince of Wales, the coast consists of a sand barrier that curves gradually to the east until terminating at Cape Espenberg. For 120 miles, the barrier is separated from a very marshy mainland by a long narrow lagoon; and for the remaining 30 miles, mostly at the northeastern end, the lagoon has been filled with marsh deposits. Here, we have the first of several arctic barrier coasts that can be compared with the barriers of Texas. The arctic barriers trend mostly northeast-southwest, which, by coincidence, is true of much of the Texas barrier coasts, although the ocean is on the opposite side in the two groups.

Two different sources of the sand and gravel that constitute the arctic barriers have been suggested. Based on studies north of Kotzebue Sound, Moore considers that the material is partly wave erosion of the cliffs and partly is carried to the beach as a result of winter freeze that starts downslope movement and mudflows that carry debris to the shore during summer thaws. McCulloch, on the other hand, basing his opinion on the barrier northeast of Cape Prince of Wales, believes that the principal source of sediment is from the continental shelf, much of it brought in during the postglacial sea level rise, and that an important secondary source is the outwash from the small glaciers that formerly extended to the coast between Cape Spencer and Cape Mountain. As evidence against the importance of wave erosion, McCulloch points to the fact that the Sangamon beach mapped by C. L. Sainsbury (Fig. 14.13) has been

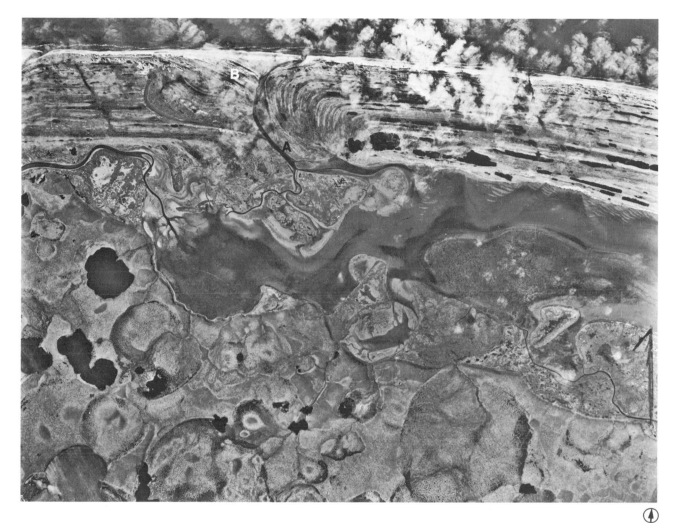

14.16 Part of the barrier 10 miles west of Cape Espenberg, illustrating hooks strongly recurved toward the southwest, opposite the principal direction of beach drifting. An inlet was probably developed here during a storm, and hooks from both sides closed the gap. U.S. Geological Survey, 1950.

preserved for the past 70,000 years or more, suggesting that erosion has been very minor in amount. It seems to us that the barriers are probably due to a combination of all of these processes. The importance of derivation of sediment from the continental shelf has been demonstrated in many other areas. Whatever the source, the sediment has apparently been carried northeast through Bering Strait and along the coast in the Chukchi Sea, then brought shoreward by small wave conditions to form the barriers. However, the decrease in the barrier width to the northeast suggests a southerly source for the sediment.

The extensive barriers northeast of Cape Prince of Wales have a succession of ridges. A total of fifteen are shown in the 2-mile-wide barrier to the south (Fig. 14.13). The intervening troughs have segmented rectilinear lakes, in contrast to the ribbon-shaped lakes in the troughs between beach ridges in temperate climates. The rectilinear type is the result of permafrost. Since permafrost cannot be developed appreciably in less than about 100 years, the finding of permafrost in this barrier indicates that it has been in existence for a long time. Further proof of antiquity comes from the large number of beach ridges

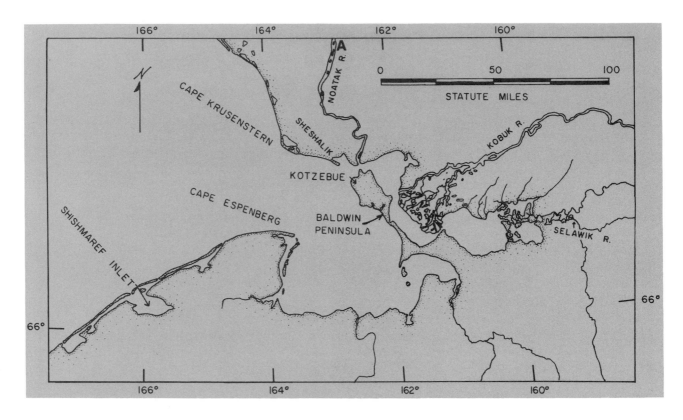

14.17 Location map of Kotzebue Sound flanked by Cape Espenberg on the south and Cape Krusenstern on the north. A glacial lobe from the Selawik lowlands to the east formed an end moraine, Baldwin Peninsula, nearly closing the bay. A glacial lobe from the north formed another end moraine (A) but did not reach the coast. The large delta of the Kobuk River partially fills the sound behind the moraine. The smaller deltas of the Selawik, to the east, and the Noatak River, to the west, are contributing to the filling. From geological map by T. N. V. Karlstrom, U.S. Geological Survey.

and the considerable width along much of the barrier.

Other sections of the barrier are shown in Figures 14.15 and 14.16. At Shishmaref Inlet (A in Fig. 14.15), the southernmost break in the barrier, the beach ridges are very discontinuous and show festoon curves. Our interpretation of these, based only on the aerial photo, is that old inlets have existed at points B, C, and D at different times during the past and that beach ridges have curved around each inlet as it was being filled. Hooks of this nature that are continuations of beach ridges are found in many other places (Fig. 8.21). Tidal deltas built into the lagoon to the southwest of the barrier are seen at C and probably also at B. The new barrier growth that formed after the inlets were filled has not developed appreciable sand ridges. Figure 14.16, a photo taken 10 miles west-southwest of Cape Espenberg, shows

a much better development of beach ridges. Since the ridges can be traced well to the east, the inlet at A, now largely filled, appears to confirm the origin of the curved ridges suggested for Figure 14.15. Fill of the inlet has come from both sides. The curved ridges at B appear to have formed first and then were apparently truncated with a widening of the inlet. Subsequently the ridges on the east formed and now have left only a ribbon that connects the ocean with the lagoon. According to Moore and McCulloch, these inlets are opened by the breakout of the waters shortly after the beginning of the summer thaw. Then the inlet fills rapidly because the small tidal range in this arctic area does not keep inlets open, as do the strong tidal currents farther south in Alaska.

The straight crack shown crossing the barrier diagonally (Fig. 14.16) on the west side is interpreted by McCulloch as a frost crack due to winter freezing. Another feature of the barriers is well illustrated in E of Figure 14.15. Along the shore there are almost continuous submerged bars. McCulloch notes that these bars serve a useful purpose for small-boat operations. A boat can go along the trough keeping just inside the wave that breaks over the bar and starts to reform before breaking again along the shore. This is far safer than following the coast outside where there is the danger of a breaking wave overturning a boat. Survival in the frigid water is very brief, generally much shorter than the time required to right a boat and bail out the water.

Inside the lagoons, the marshy mainland is pockmarked with thaw-depression lakes (Fig. 14.16, 14.18, 14.19). Some of these have been filled with tundra vegetation. Small winding streams carry the overflow of the lakes into the lagoon.

KOTZEBUE SOUND [Figs. 14.17, 14.18, and 14.19]   The largest and most intricate bay on the arctic coast of Alaska, Kotzebue Sound (Fig. 14.17), forms on the north side of Seward Peninsula a counterpart to Norton Sound on the south. It is bounded by cuspate barrier capes, Espenberg on the south and Krusenstern on the north. Like Port Clarence, Kotzebue Sound has segmented bays on the inside. To the south and west, there is a low swampy coast with one or more drowned river valleys. On the east, according to McCulloch, Baldwin Peninsula is a glacial moraine partly due to ice shove. It separates the main bay from the segmented inner bay that extends east for 40 miles. The moraine was formed during the Illinoisan glaciation, more than 100,000 years ago. At that time, the largest valley glaciers in northern Alaska were located east and north of Kotzebue Sound. After the retreat of the glaciers, the moraine was left above water and still forms a partial dam for elongate Hotham Inlet. Deltas of the Noatak and Kobuk Rivers have filled a large portion of this inlet, and some contribution may have been made by the Selawik River; but in this eastern area the deposits are thought to be loess resting on an old moraine.

Several settlements have been built in this area. Kotzebue, at the northwest end of Baldwin Peninsula, is the largest and has a mixed population, partly Eskimo; and Sheshalik, on the spit of the same name across the narrow strait, has a population largely Eskimo and is the summer camping place for the

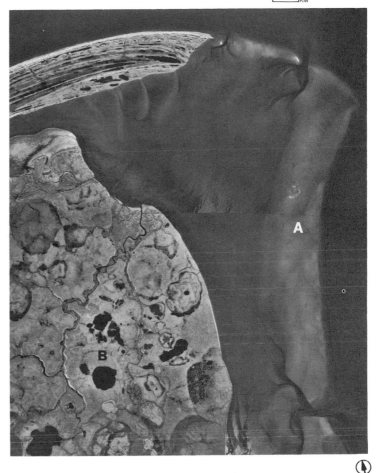

14.18 Cape Espenberg, the southern entrance to Kotzebue Sound, is the end of the 150-mile barrier which extends from Cape Prince of Wales. A shoal (A) indicating a right-angle bend is shown as a row of islands on a 1947 chart. The many thaw lakes (B) and depressions are due to permafrost. U.S. Coast and Geodetic Survey, 1962.

villagers of Noatak. The principal food of inhabitants of the smaller Eskimo settlements in this area is fish, seal, walrus, and whale meat. Many of the natives are occupied by carving ivory, some of which is fossil ivory. During the winter, the natives hunt marine mammals. We are informed that the federal welfare program has unfortunately stopped much of the activity of the natives, and many of them do little to support themselves. Missionary activities of several creeds have led to considerable friction among the natives.

Relics of human culture on Sheshalik spit, according to J. L. Giddings, date back to 3000 B.C. Moore

14.19 Cape Krusenstern (C), at the northern entrance to Kotzebue Sound, was developed during the past several thousand years from sand drifting southward past a narrow spit and developing a series of hooks that eventually connected with the coast to the east. Older beach ridges have large thaw lakes (B), some a mile long. Although all beach sediment was introduced from the west, there have been several episodes of truncation followed by formation of new ridges at an angle to the old. Some of these are marked by lines. The ridges contain archaeological remains of three Eskimo cultures as indicated, dating back to about 5,000 years ago. U.S. Coast and Geodetic Survey nine-lens photograph, 1950.

found that the growth of the spit to the east since that time has added approximately 1.5 square miles, showing the importance of easterly drift along this coast.

The cuspate capes on either side of Kotzebue Sound are somewhat comparable with the Carolina cuspate forelands. Cape Espenberg (Fig. 14.18) had only one emergent arm when photographed in 1962, but the 1947 edition of the Coast and Geodetic Survey chart shows a row of islands along the line of the slightly submerged bar (A) in the 1962 photograph. Apparently, the sediment extending along the adjacent 150-mile barrier is deflected southward into

Kotzebue Sound, forming the other limb of the cuspate cape. According to the effects of the latest storms, this limb is either submerged or emerged.

Cape Krusenstern (Fig. 14.19), on the north side of the sound, also has one limb much better developed than the other, although they are both emergent. Moore believes that the western and narrow arm was built first and was hooked to the east by currents moving into Kotzebue Sound. The history of the growth of the many ridges that have been added to the east limb is now well documented by a combination of the archaeological studies of Giddings and subsequent work of D. Anderson. They found that there are three cultures represented in the artifacts they obtained from the various ridges. The oldest, called Denbigh (Fig. 14.19), dated by carbon-14, is at least 4,200 and possibly 5,000 years old. The Choris, in the middle ridges, has an age of 2,500 to 3,500 years, and the Ipiutak includes artifacts dated at 1,200 to 1,600 years ago. Permafrost lakes (B) have developed just seaward of the oldest Denbigh ridges. Some of the old ridges are truncated, especially near the point of the foreland. These truncations may be due either to changing current directions or to great storms. New ridges grew along the old truncated series.

A difference of opinion exists relative to sea level constancy during the growth of the numerous ridges. Moore considers that there has been a slight rise in sea level since the oldest ridges were built, because of finding the highest, 3 meters (10 feet), in the Ipiutak culture zone. Giddings, however, notes that there are lower ridges outside the 3-meter ridges referred to by Moore and considers that the sea level has been constant. If this has been a stable area and if we can believe the growing evidence that sea level has risen a few meters since 3000 B.C., the stand by Moore is more likely correct; and the outer ridges simply have not been built as high because the relatively recent storms have not been accompanied by waves as high as those of the Ipiutak stage. It is hard to resolve these cases of slight sea level changes by these small height differences.

The straightness of the west arm of the cuspate cape is striking. One might expect that ice shove during winter would have deformed such a narrow barrier; but Moore explains that in October before the sea freezes, a layer of ice is left over the beach gravel by contributions from each large wave that runs up the shore. This develops a bed of ice, including thin layers of gravel, up to about 5 feet thick, and by the time the sea has frozen, this bed is as much as 40 feet wide with a level top. This is called a *kaimoo* by the Eskimos and is their principal route of winter travel along the shore. When wind-blown sea ice in spring exerts its thrust against the shore, it is often only the kaimoo that is deformed and the barrier escapes damage.

POINT HOPE AND WESTERN FOOTHILLS OF BROOKS RANGE [Figs. 14.20 through 14.23] The Brooks Range, a continuation of the Rocky Mountain system, crosses Alaska in a general westerly direction. Approaching the Chukchi Sea, the mountains become foothills, which border the coast northeast from Cape Krusenstern for 70 miles to Cape Thompson. Then a narrow deltaic plain with a cuspate foreland (Fig. 14.20) intervenes for a few miles; but the hilly coast comes in again, extending north for 30 miles to Cape Lisburne (Fig. 14.22), where the north-northwesterly trending Lisburne Hills end abruptly and the coast makes a right-angled turn. From there, the foothill coast continues easterly and then northeasterly for another 85 miles.

The most prominent geographic feature of this foothill coast is Point Hope (Fig. 14.20), which protrudes 15 miles into the Chukchi Sea. The southeastern base of Point Hope is a few miles northwest of Cape Thompson, and the northeastern base adjoins a straight cliffed coast extending to Cape Lisburne. The Kukpuk River, draining mountainous areas inland from the coast, had formed a delta (A) inside the two arms of the cuspate foreland. The water from the Kukpuk now discharges from the lagoon through a narrow inlet in the northern spit.

The important settlement, formerly called Tigara, now Point Hope (B), near the tip of Point Hope, has been intermittently inhabited for 1,600 years by Eskimos and their ancestors, a group with the Ipiutak culture. The present inhabitants hunt the grey whale, the beluga whale, the walrus, and the seal. The Chukchi Sea is solidly frozen from late October until the breakup in late April or May. At that time, grey whales begin their northward migration into the Arctic Ocean, and the whole adult population of Point Hope goes across the ice to the nearest open channel to hunt the whales. One or two whales will provide enough food for the village for a year. Vivid accounts of the annual whale hunt have been given by Claire Fejes and also by the late C. D. Brower. The whaling methods are described by J. V. Vanstone. Whaling boat captains are and long have been the most important members of the Point Hope community. Their crews consist mostly of their families; and usually they have inherited their darting guns, bombs, skin boats, and harpoons. The bombs are needed because of the danger of a wounded whale getting under the ice where it cannot be recovered. The bomb goes off inside the whale and so badly wounds it that the whale is not likely to go far when it dives after being hit.

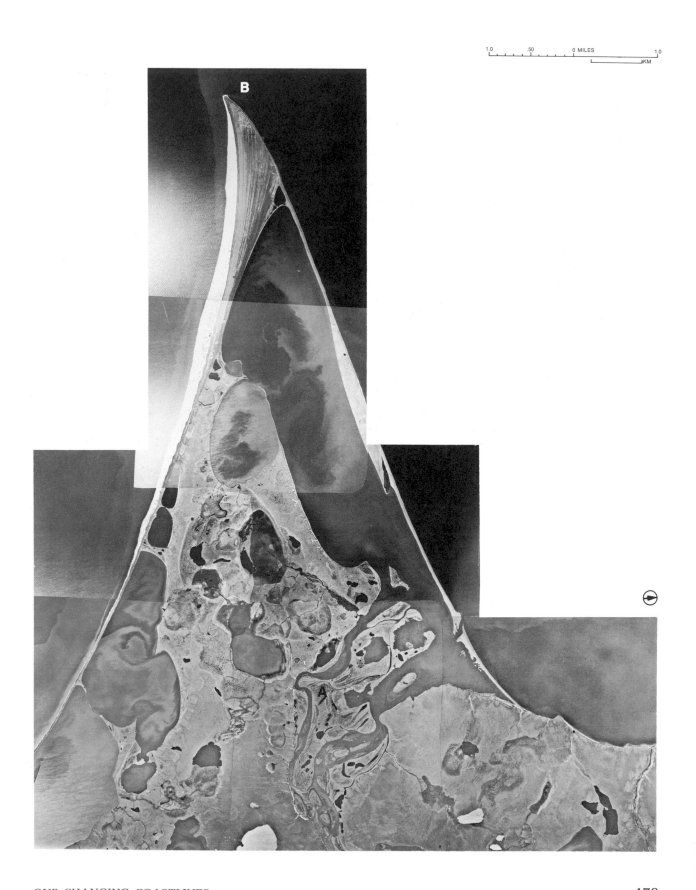

14.21 Diagonal aerial photograph of Point Hope showing bulge on the south side of the foreland that develops in the fall as the result of the north winds. The town of Point Hope is shown near the center of the photo. Courtesy of G. W. Moore, U.S. Geological Survey.

Pack ice offshore may ground in shoal water at depths of about 20 to 30 feet; and, as the summer thaw progresses, an open channel develops between the shore and the grounded pack ice. However, the pack ice may remain until July, leaving an open-water season of only 3 months. The 1952 photographs (Fig. 14.20) were taken on July 11, when the shore was free of ice. The border of the pack ice is rarely more than 100 miles seaward from Point Hope, giving little fetch for the waves.

14.20 Point Hope, a cuspate foreland protruding into the Chukchi Sea. The Kukpuk River built a delta (A) at this point. Many ice polygons are seen in the gravel bars and shallow mud of the delta flats. Sand barriers grew outside the delta, forming the spectacular point. The spit on the south side shows many parallel beach ridges. The narrow north barrier has no conspicuous ridges, but the east-trending point on the lagoon side of the north barrier may be Sangamon in age.

The sediment supply for the Point Hope cuspate spit may come from three sources: the Kukpuk River Delta, which no doubt formed the original coastal projection; the cliffed coasts of Cape Thompson to the southeast; and the cliffs to the north extending to Cape Lisburne. At present, the northern arm of Point Hope is generally only 500 to 1,000 feet wide, while the southern arm near the point is a mile wide. A series of narrow beach ridges at the west end of the southern spit are separated by swales 40 to 100 feet wide, from which the local people obtain their water supply.

Moore called attention to a bulge on the south side of Point Hope at the tip (Fig. 14.21) that forms in the fall as the result of the northerly winds. During the summer, the bulge is smoothed, and the new sediment is spread along the south side. The same bulge was seen in the map made by E. M. Kindle in 1909. The south side has shown a considerable

14.22 Cape Lisburne, a sharp angle in the cliffed coast of the Lisburne Hills. A narrow airstrip (A) is located at the top of cliffs 100 feet high in an area that is foggy most of the time. The steeply dipping rock strata are sharply truncated by the cliffs on both sides of the point. U.S. Navy photo, 1952.

growth. The Ipiutak settlement, about A.D. 300, was on the south side of the spit but now lies over a mile north of the southern shore. The average accretion on the south side of the spit has been 3.4 feet per year. Most of the sand that is added comes around the point from the north side. Southeast winds carry some sand along the point from Cape Lisburne, and this is added to the tip of Point Hope.

The delta of the Kukpuk River displays the ice polygons that characterize many of the arctic deltas and river channel bars. Following the suggestions of E. Leffingwell and A. H. Lachenbruch, David Hopkins describes the origin of the polygons: During the extremely cold winters in this area, the ground contracts and develops cracks; later, as the result of the time lag in conduction of heat from the surface, the cracks remain open during the spring thaw and surface water flows down into the cracks, and freezing forms thin vertical veins of ice; then in summer, the upper parts of the veins thaw, but the veins continue frozen below the permafrost. Repetitions of this process year after year produce ice wedges 5 to 10 feet wide and as much as 15 feet in depth with honeycomblike polygons.

Cape Lisburne (Fig. 14.22), 40 miles north-northeast of the tip of Point Hope, has cliffs 900 feet high that look from the air as if they had been cut by a meat cleaver. One can see the northwest-trending layers of rock cut off clean on both sides of the 100 degree bend in the coast. Ordinarily, the resistant members of the inclined layers would extend out beyond the nonresistant, but this clearly has not happened here. This could be produced by faulting, although the sea floor gives no evidence of such faults. According to Moore, the straight sides have resulted from equal and rapid marine erosion on the two sides; but we know of no other place where such a configuration has developed from diagonally trun-

14.23 A section of Corwin Bluffs, extending 27 to 32 miles east of Cape Lisburne, is a straight cliffed coast with very thick coal beds in the cliffs. When photographed, the winter pack ice had recently broken up, and ice islands up to 0.5 mile in length are still evident. U.S. Geological Survey, 1949.

cated rock formations. Some of the rocks that outcrop on the north side of the cape contain coal seams with thicknesses up to 14 feet. These would be very valuable for mining if near an industrial area. Some attempts were made to develop them, but serious landslides interfered with the work and the mines were abandoned.

Just east of Cape Lisburne, an airstrip (A) is located at the top of a 100-foot cliff. This is commonly in fog and in winter is in darkness most of the time, making it one of the most hazardous landing strips in North America.

A 1949 photograph (Fig. 14.23), taken about 30 miles east of Cape Lisburne, shows more of the sharply truncated inclined layers. This photograph was taken during the late spring breakup of the ice pack, and a remnant of the pack can be seen adjoining the shore to the east; whereas to the west, the sea is partly covered with ice blocks, some of them 0.5

mile long. When strong north winds are blowing at the time of the ice-pack breakup, the blocks are often thrust for several hundred feet up onto the beach and produce vibrations that shake the ground like an earthquake.

BARRIER COAST OF NORTHWESTERN ALASKA [Figs. 14.24, 14.25, and 14.26]   The arctic coastal plain, north of the Brooks Range and its outlying foothills, extends all along the north coast of Alaska and on into the Yukon Territory (Fig. 14.24). The plain first appears north of where the Amatusuk Hills come to the sea; and it widens to a maximum of 110 miles at Point Barrow, the northernmost point of North America, and then narrows until it is only 8 miles wide at the Yukon boundary. This plain is the Alaskan counterpart of the Great Plains east of the Rocky Mountains of Canada and the United States. However, according to McCulloch

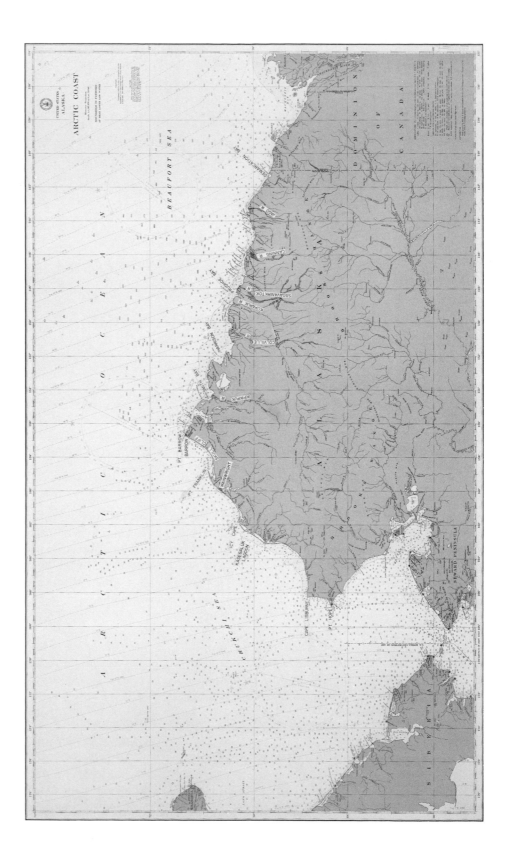

14.24 The northern coast of Alaska, showing locations described. Note succession of three cuspate forelands. Icy Cape, Franklin Point, and Point Barrow in northwestern Alaska, and the many river deltas of northeastern Alaska. Barriers lie outside most of this coastline. Suggested former river courses are indicated by = =. U.S. Coast and Geodetic Survey Chart 9400, 1962 edition.

and others who have investigated the area, the origin is quite different from that of the Great Plains, which are largely built up by the rivers coming down from the Rockies. The North Slope of Alaska is partly due to wave cutting during the Pliocene and Pleistocene incursions of the sea from the north, partly river eroded, and partly river deposited. The most recent development appears to be the formation of river deltas in the area east of Point Barrow.

The coast southwest of Point Barrow is characterized by lengthy barriers. Kasegaluk Lagoon, northeast of Cape Lisburne, extends for 140 miles and is, therefore, the longest lagoon in the United States. Barriers protect it along almost its entire length. The lagoon averages 3 miles in width, whereas the barriers are mostly a little less than a mile wide. The lagoon receives the drainage from the Kukpowruk, Kokolik, and Utukok Rivers, all coming from the Brooks Range. These are large rivers during the melting of the snows, and they carry mostly sand and gravel to the sea with little mud. The passes opposite the entrance of the Kukpowruk and Utukok Rivers are relatively stable, but the other passes through the barriers are often closed by longshore drift. Approaching Point Barrow, the barriers come to an end, then reappear at Point Barrow and extend for 45 miles to the east with a group of islands called the Plovers. Farther east, the barriers are found locally around abandoned deltas.

Another feature that characterizes the northwest coast of Alaska is the three cuspate forelands, Icy Cape, Point Franklin, and Point Barrow, separated from each other by about 80 miles. This is similar to the distances that separate the four cuspate forelands, Capes Hatteras, Lookout, Fear, and Romain, in the Carolinas. Off Icy Cape, a string of shoals can be traced seaward, very much like the shoals off the Carolina capes. There are, however, some differences between the two groups. The barriers are much more continuous along the Carolina coast than off Alaska, where southwest of Point Barrow a 50-mile zone has no barriers at all. The lagoons inside the Carolina barriers are much wider than those in Alaska. The coastal plain in the Carolinas also has a much lower elevation inside the lagoons. In northwestern Alaska, the coast has relief up to a little more than 100 feet; and, directly inside the lagoons, there are coastal cliffs 20 to 50 feet high. Just southwest of Point Barrow, in the zone lacking the barriers, Skull Cliff

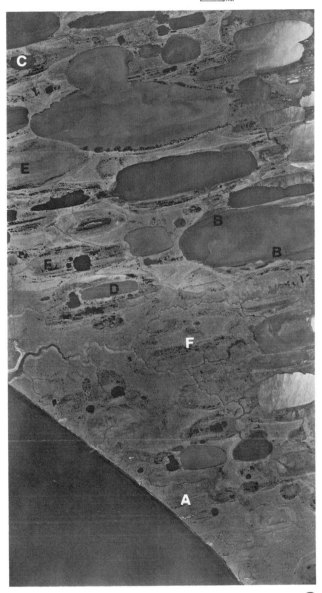

14.25 About 25 miles southwest of Barrow, the flat coastal plain has been truncated by coastal cliffs (A) up to 70 feet high. Almost no beaches adjoin the cliffs. Central-northern Alaska contains thousands of oriented lakes with long axes generally 10° west of north. These lakes somewhat resemble the oval depressions known as the Carolina bays (Fig. 5.15). In northern Alaska, they are generally interpreted as the product of permafrost, thawing, or elongation at right angles to the direction of prevailing winds. Some have benches on east and west sides (B). When a lake is partially drained, it may be confined to the central deeper part (C, D). U.S. Geological Survey, 1955.

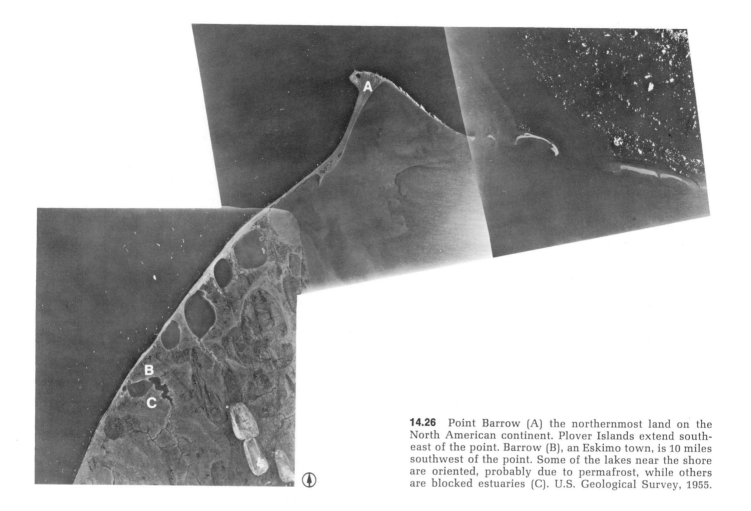

14.26 Point Barrow (A) the northernmost land on the North American continent. Plover Islands extend southeast of the point. Barrow (B), an Eskimo town, is 10 miles southwest of the point. Some of the lakes near the shore are oriented, probably due to permafrost, while others are blocked estuaries (C). U.S. Geological Survey, 1955.

is as much as 70 feet high (A in Fig. 14.25), and the barrier-free coast farther south near Wainwright has cliffs 40 to 50 feet high.

The explanation for the Carolina cuspate forelands (p. 106) is still not very clear, but the finding of similar forelands in the arctic is even more puzzling, because in the arctic we have rather different conditions, including (1) absence of a strong current in the arctic comparable to the Gulf Stream, although McCulloch reports north-flowing currents up to 1 knot; (2) an almost complete lack of tides, except due to wind which raises the sea surface as much as 5 feet; (3) frozen seas during 9 months along the arctic coast; and (4) the small fetch of the waves due to off-lying ice fields at all times of the year. Clearly an unsolved problem of great interest remains concerning the existence in the arctic of not only

these three cuspate forelands but also the much more protruding foreland at Point Hope. According to McCulloch, the Sangamon shoreline shows no forelands, so they have formed during the Wisconsin rise in sea level. The sediment for the forelands was evidently derived from the continental shelf and was carried landward as the sea advanced.

Apparently, wave erosion was interrupted by the building of barriers but continued where there were no barriers. Gerald MacCarthy estimated that the retreat of the unprotected cliffs of soft sediment, south of Pt. Barrow, has averaged as much as 10 feet per year. This retreat is aided by melting of the ground ice during the long summer days, causing extensive undermining and slumping of the cliffs, the material being subsequently washed away by the next major storm during a time of open water.

Settlements are small and widely separated along this barrier coast. A few airfields exist, and the town of Wainwright is located near the mouth of the Kuk River, but by far the most important town is Barrow (B in Fig. 14.26), 11 miles southwest of the cape. This has long been a center for whaling and for hunters of caribou and arctic fox. An old Eskimo village, Nuwuk at Point Barrow (A), is now abandoned because most of the dunes on which it was located have been eroded. The name Nuwuk means "used to be point of land." Recently, a naval station and an arctic research laboratory have been established along the barrier 5 miles northeast of the town of Barrow. The area has also been an important jumping-off place for polar expeditions.

The land inside the barriers and cliffed coasts of northwestern Alaska resembles most other arctic lowlands in having numerous lakes (Figs. 14.25, 14.26) and extensive marshy tracts. Permafrost has penetrated deeper under this lowland than farther south, reaching more than 1,300 feet near Point Barrow. A profusion of soil polygons are shown on the aerial photos, especially in abandoned stream meanders and in thaw lakes that have been drained. Rivers cross the plains, particularly in zones where lakes are relatively scarce. These rivers southwest of Point Barrow have not produced any appreciable deltas, and several of them have estuaries at their mouths. It is possible that this coast has sunk independently, as we have suggested for Chesapeake Bay and the Columbia Estuary. The Kuk River estuary, according to McCulloch, may have had extensive drainage from the east during Wisconsin glaciation, and its continuation seaward into Barrow Submarine Canyon seems probable.

One of the most amazing features of the arctic coastal plains is the abundance of similarly oriented lakes scattered across a zone for about 100 miles east and west of Point Barrow; they are especially well developed near Barrow. It is again noteworthy that the only other place so far discovered in the United States with oriented lakes is in the vicinity of the cuspate forelands of the Carolinas[1] (Fig. 5.15). This may be only a coincidence, but one can scarcely overlook the possibility that both areas have had similar influences despite the great differences in conditions that now exist. The oriented lakes of the Point Bar-

row area were studied by R. F. Black and W. L. Barksdale in 1945 and 1946, R. W. Rex in 1957, and C. E. Carson and K. M. Hussey in 1959 and 1960. The long axes of these lakes are oriented between 10 and 15 degrees west of north (Fig. 14.25), as compared to a more northwesterly trend for the Carolina bays. They differ from the Carolina bays also in lacking any slightly elevated southeast rims and in having many examples of shoal benches on their sides (B in Fig. 14.25). In some cases, the water has been drained from these benches but remains in the rest of the lake (C, D).

Carson and Hussey, following the ideas advanced by Rex, have suggested an origin for the arctic elliptical lakes that also might apply to the Carolina bays, provided the latter were formed during glacial stages of the Pleistocene when the Carolinas may have had the periglacial climate characterizing much of unglaciated Alaska. These authors think that the lakes were originally caused by sags in the tundra plains due to thaw of the permafrost and the development of ice wedges and frost polygons. This would produce somewhat rounded lakes; but thaw continues throughout the year under lakes that are more than 6 feet deep, the depth of ice formed during a typical winter. Beneath one lake near Barrow, the top of the permafrost has been thawed to a depth of 190 feet. This tends to promote permanence and enlargement of the thaw lakes. During the summer thaws, the winds are predominantly northeast and less frequently southwest. Tundra vegetation broken from the lake bottoms and margins is transported by these prevailing winds to the southwest, and sometimes to the northeast sides, and the vegetation grounding on the margin builds up the terraces, which are seen so commonly. These terraces impede wave cutting on the east and west sides; but occasional north and south winds still produce erosion, so the lakes tend to grow in those directions. Some of the lakes subsequently become drained due to extension of channels through the surrounding tundra. This draining first exposes the shallow east and west benches (C, D) and later may drain the entire lake but leaves its outline (E). Also a concentration of ice polygons over the area where the deeper part of the lake formerly existed may show its predrainage outline (F).

The elliptical lake vicinity may become important economically. In 1884, Charles D. Brower and a companion, while hunting a short distance south of

[1] Oriented lakes are also reported in eastern Siberia.

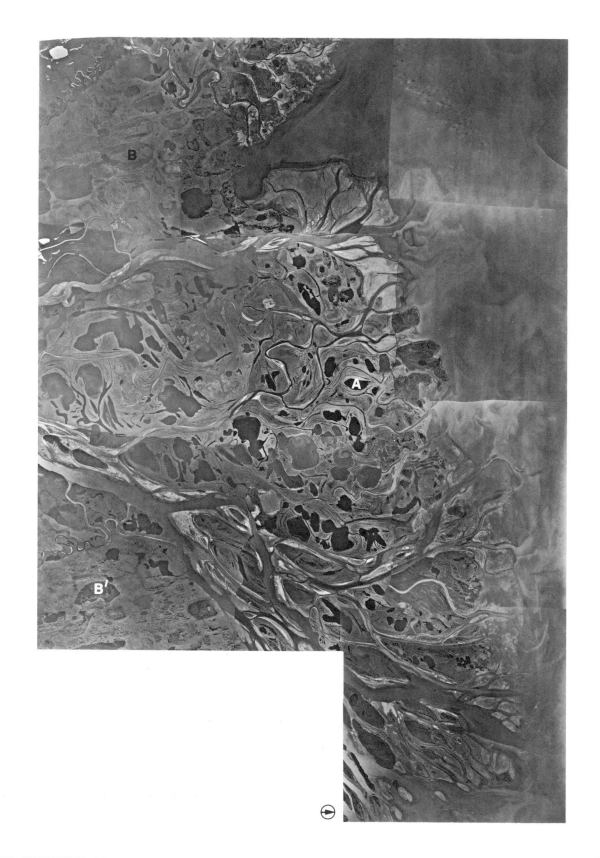

Barrow, discovered two small dark-colored lakes with water in the center but encircled by asphalt. They saw carcasses of caribou in the asphalt of one lake and struggling eider ducks with oil-soaked wings that had landed in the asphalt and were unable to fly. Later, oil seepages were discovered in many parts of the Barrow region; and, after some drilling had shown oil concentrations in the Cretaceous rocks that underlie the plain, the United States established a Naval Petroleum Reserve.

Point Barrow is on a gravel spit that extends 5 miles north of the town of Barrow and then hooks to the southeast with an elongation in that direction of 3 miles. The point, according to T. L. Péwé and R. E. Church, is probably not more than 4,000 years in age, and the northeast portion is younger than 2,000 years. The shoreline at the point has receded southward almost 2,000 feet since 1826, and the recession has been at the rate of 10 feet a year from 1945 to 1961.

DELTAIC COAST OF NORTHEASTERN ALASKA [Figs. 14.24, 14.27 through 14.30]

A profound change takes place in the arctic coastal plain to the east of the barrier coasts. Along with a gradual decrease of the lakes, rivers begin to have greater influence on coastal development. From Harrison Bay to the United States–Canadian border, approximately 280 miles of the coast can be described as deltaic (Fig. 14.24). Except for the greater Mississippi Delta, this is the longest continuous deltaic coast in the United States. The Louisiana coast was developed largely by one river, but the arctic deltaic coast has been built by a series of large rivers coming out of the Brooks Range. The rivers have numerous distributaries in their lower courses and show very much of a braided pattern. The area was well described by Frank Schrader and Ernest Leffingwell, who explored the country in the early part of the century. Both were connected with the U.S. Geologi-

cal Survey, but much of Leffingwell's work was at his own expense. He spent seven summers with a base camp on a small island off this coast and traversed vast areas of the previously unexplored territory.

The westernmost delta is that of the Ikpikpuk River (Fig. 2.5), which is actively building out into Smith Bay. This is an arcuate delta about 12 miles across and has numerous distributaries, some of them abandoned. The aerial photograph shows many permafrost polygons (A) on the sand bars of the abandoned channels. Smith Bay, in front of the delta, is mostly less than 6 feet deep even 10 miles out from shore.

Colville Delta (Fig. 14.27), 100 miles east of Ikpikpuk, was built into Harrison Bay as a large triangular wedge. Judging from the indentations on both sides, the coast had a V-shape before delta building. The Colville is the longest river on the Alaska arctic coastal plain (Fig. 14.24), with a drainage area of 30,000 square miles and a delta front covering 30 miles. Although the adjoining Beaufort Sea is frozen during 8 months of the year, the river water flows continuously seaward under the ice. Sand dunes on the west banks of the larger distributaries are due to the easterly summer winds. Permafrost polygons (looking like mosaics) are common on the edges of the channels (A) and in the partly drained delta lakes.

East of the Colville Delta, the coast bends seaward in the form of another large delta for about 70 miles. Only small streams come into the ocean along most of this arc. A series of barrier islands front this large bow, and on the land there are a mass of lakes, mostly round. Apparently this arc is an abandoned delta, and the barriers are the erosion remnants of a delta similar to the barriers off inactive Mississippi passes. Schrader suggested that some time during the Pleistocene, the north-flowing section of the upper Colville (Fig. 14.24) had continued northeast to the coast, entering through what is now the Kuparuk River on the east side of the abandoned delta. It seems more probable that the Colville and its distributaries and several other rivers built the old delta before developing their present course. Older river courses of the Colville and Sagavanirktok Rivers show that they formerly discharged where the modern Kuparuk River Delta is now located (Fig. 14.24).

The Kuparuk River Delta is very similar to the other arctic deltas. It has numerous distributaries with the flats and lakes in between showing large

14.27 The delta of the Colville, the largest river on Alaska's Arctic Slope. This delta, like that of the Yukon, consists of channels interlaced with sand bars and numerous delta lakes. Because permafrost action is more intense here than in the Yukon Delta, there are abundant ice polygons (A) on the delta flats. Along the landward margins of the delta, oriented lakes (B, B') are visible. U.S. Geological Survey, 1955.

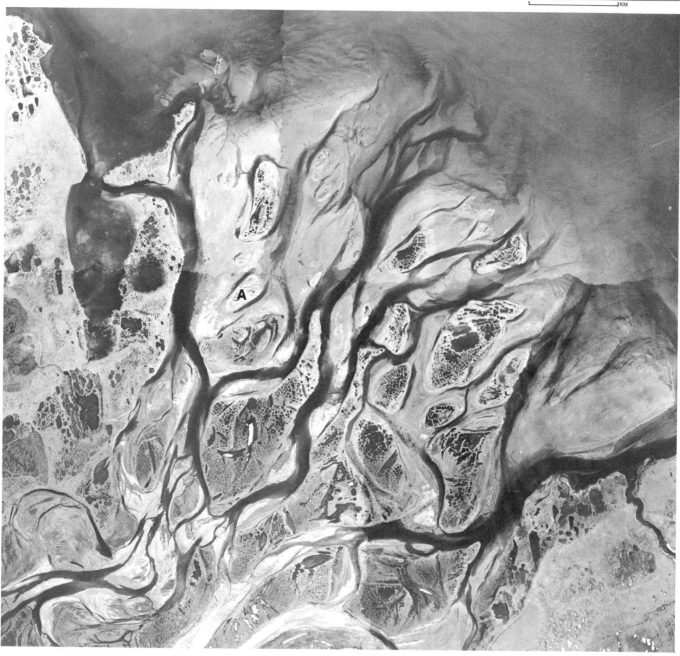

14.28 The Kuparuk River Delta, about 25 miles west of Prudhoe Bay, resembles the Colville Delta but is smaller, and ice polygons are more conspicuous. In permafrost areas, uneven pressure of expanding ground ice may push up the soil into small hills, known as pingos (A). U.S. Geological Survey, 1955.

14.29 A portion of the beach and shallow sea floor thrust by expanding sea ice into a ridge on the north shore of Flaxman Island. From Leffingwell (1919).

permafrost polygons. A 14-foot hill (A) is probably a *pingo* squeezed up during freezing weather as a result of draining of a lake, allowing permafrost to develop underneath. The barrier islands continue eastward 5 miles outside the mouth of the Kuparuk (not shown). Twenty miles farther east, the Saga-vanirktok River has produced another deltaic lobe that may be a part of the same large delta mass.

In this compound delta and on the inner shelf off the coast, intense oil exploration started in 1960; and a field, called Prudhoe Bay, was developed in 1968 that shows promise of having the largest oil reserves in all United States territories, perhaps even com-

parable to those of the Middle East. Recovery of oil here is difficult because of freezing of condensed moisture in the pipes and in the drilling mud; and also the ground pores are filled to great depths with ice, reducing the flow through reservoir sands. Furthermore, the settling of the ground in permafrost areas twists and breaks pipes. Transportation is also a problem, involving icebreakers for oil tankers or pipelines laid on the surface of the tundra for 600 miles to the southern ice-free ports. The heat of the oil flow will melt the top of the permafrost and cause extensive slumping. It may also interfere with game migration, causing considerable opposition from con-

14.30 Demarcation Bay, an indentation of the arctic coast east of the Kongakut River. The bay is partially closed by hooked spits representative of the narrow barrier of the northeastern Alaskan coast. Note blocks of drift ice almost a mile long in the Beaufort Sea. The boundary between the Yukon Territory and Alaska is represented by a dashed line. U.S. Geological Survey, 1959.

servationists. Despite these difficulties, large production in the near future seems assured. The oil pipeline is being initiated; and the *Manhattan*, a large tanker built as an icebreaker, has already demonstrated that it can traverse the Northwest Passage.

Farther east, another deltaic lobe, extending 45 miles along the coast, also lacks present-day streams, although the Canning River with its various distributaries enters on the east side. Here again, we apparently have an abandoned delta, and barrier islands outside the old delta follow the coast east as far as the Canning River mouths. The lagoon inside the islands has a width of 10 miles or more to the west, narrowing as it approaches the Canning River.

Flaxman Island, along this barrier, was the site of the summer camp of the U.S. Geological Survey geologist Leffingwell. He found that the north face of the island apparently had retreated at a rate of 30 feet a year since Sir John Franklin first mapped it in 1826. Some of the promontories, shown in the Franklin map, appeared to have retreated as much as 2 miles during the 80-year period. This gives further evidence of the rapid rate of erosion that may occur along arctic coasts where unconsolidated sediments are attacked by storms during the short season of open water. The photograph by Leffingwell (Fig. 14.29) illustrates the importance of ice shove during the early summer in pushing back the coast.

Still another deltaic arc occurs farther east, with a coastal extent of 90 miles. This differs from the others in having a main stream, the Jago River, entering at the most protruding portion of the arc, although most of the remainder has only minor streams. Again, this arc is bordered by a lagoon and barrier islands. Also, like the others, on the east side of the arc, a series of prominent streams enter with their distributaries. Each of these is beginning to build a new delta.

Approaching the international boundary, Demarcation Bay (Fig. 14.30) has a rectangular 4-mile indentation and is quite different in character from the rest of the arctic coast. Although the west side is part of a deltaic lobe, the origin of the east side is puzzling. Hooked spits have built across the mouth of this bay from both sides. The coast inside this area has far fewer lakes, presumably because of the higher regional slope where the coast is so near the mountains. The photograph was taken on July 24, but it can be seen that even at this late date, many ice blocks were drifting in the Beaufort Sea. The longest of these blocks is about 0.8 mile, and most of the blocks are elongate in one dimension.

In ending the discussion of the deltaic coast at the boundary with the Yukon Territory, it should be noted that 130 miles farther east is the mouth of the Mackenzie, the largest North American river entering the Arctic Ocean. This has also built a large delta (Fig. 14.24). One may wonder if there is any coast in the world that has as great an array of deltas.

REFERENCES

Anderson, Douglas D., 1968. A Stone Age campsite at the gateway to America. *Scientific American*, vol. 218, no. 6, pp. 24–33.

Black, R. F., 1958. Permafrost, water supply, and engineering geology of Point Spencer Spit, Seward Peninsula, Alaska. *Arctic*, vol. 11, no. 2, pp. 102–116.

————, and W. L. Barksdale, 1949. Oriented lakes of northern Alaska. *Jour. Geol.*, vol. 57, pp. 105–118.

Brower, Charles D., 1942. *Fifty Years Below Zero; A Lifetime of Adventure in the Far North.* Dodd, Mead & Company, New York.

Carson, C. E., and K. M. Hussey, 1962. The oriented lakes of northern Alaska. *Jour. Geol.*, vol. 70, pp. 417–439.

Cass, J. T., 1959. Reconnaissance geologic map of the Norton Bay quadrangle, Alaska. *U.S. Geol. Survey Misc. Geol. Inv. Map* I–286.

Fejes, Claire, 1966. *People of the Noatak.* Alfred A. Knopf, New York.

Giddings, J. L., 1966. Cross-dating the archeology of northwestern Alaska. *Science*, vol. 153, no. 3732, pp. 127–135.

Hoare, J. M., 1968. Geologic map of the Hooper Bay quadrangle, Alaska. *U.S. Geol. Survey Misc. Geol. Inv. Map* I–523.

————, and W. H. Condon, 1966. Geologic map of the Kwiguk and Black quadrangles, western Alaska. *U.S. Geol. Survey Misc. Geol. Inv. Map* I–469.

Hopkins, D. M. (ed), 1967. *The Bering Land Bridge.* Stanford University Press, Stanford, Calif.

————, F. S. McNeil, and E. B. Leopold, 1960. The coastal plain of Nome, Alaska. *Internat. Geol. Congr. XXI Sess.*, Pt. 4, pp. 46–57.

Hume, J. D., 1965. Sea-level changes during the last 2000 years at Point Barrow, Alaska. *Science*, vol. 150, no. 3700, pp. 1165–1166.

Kindle, E. M., 1909. Notes on the Point Hope Spit, Alaska. *Jour. Geol.*, vol. 17, pp. 178–189.

Lachenbruch, A. H., 1962. Mechanics of thermal contraction cracks and ice-wedge polygons in permafrost. *Geol. Soc. Amer. Spec. Paper 70.*

Laughton, W. S., 1967. Human migration and permanent occupation in the Bering Sea area. In D. M. Hopkins (ed.), *The Bering Land Bridge.* Stanford University Press, Stanford, Calif., pp. 409–450.

Leffingwell, E. deK., 1919. The Canning River region, northern Alaska. *U.S. Geol. Survey Prof. Paper 109.*

MacCarthy, G. R., 1953. Recent changes in the shoreline near Point Barrow, Alaska. *Arctic*, vol. 6, pp. 44–51.

McCulloch, D. S., 1967. Quaternary geology of the Alaskan shore of Chukchi Sea. In D. M. Hopkins (ed.), *The Bering Land Bridge.* Stanford University Press, Stanford, Calif., pp. 91–120.

Moffit, F. H., 1913. Geology of the Nome and Grand Central quadrangles, Alaska. *U.S. Geol. Survey Bull. 533.*

Moore, G. W., 1966. Arctic beach sedimentation. In *Environment of the Cape Thompson Region, Alaska.* U.S. Atomic Energy Comm., pp. 587–608.

Payne, T. G., and others. Geology of the arctic slope of Alaska. *U.S. Geol. Survey Oil and Gas Inv., Map* OM–126, 3 sheets.

Péwé, T. L., and R. E. Church, 1962. Age of the spit at Barrow, Alaska. *Geol. Soc. Amer. Bull.*, vol. 73, pp. 1287–1292.

Rex, R. W., 1961. Hydrodynamic analysis of circulation and orientation of lakes in northern Alaska. In *Geology of the Arctic*, vol. 2, pp. 1021–1043.

Sainsbury, C. L., 1967. Quaternary geology of western Seward Peninsula, Alaska. In David M. Hopkins (ed.), *The Bering Land Bridge*, Stanford University Press, Stanford, Calif., pp. 121–143.

Scholl, D. W., and C. L. Sainsbury, 1961. Subaerially carved arctic sea valley, under a modern epicontinental sea. *Geol. Soc. Amer. Bull.*, vol. 72, pp. 1433–1435.

Schrader, F. C., 1904. A reconnaissance in northern Alaska. *U.S. Geol. Survey Prof. Paper* 20.

Vanstone, J. W., 1958. Commercial whaling in the Arctic. *Pac. Northwest Quarterly*, vol. 49, no. 1, pp. 1–10.

Walker, H. J., 1962. The Colville River Delta. *First Nat. Coastal and Shallow Water Conf. Proc.*, pp. 472–474.

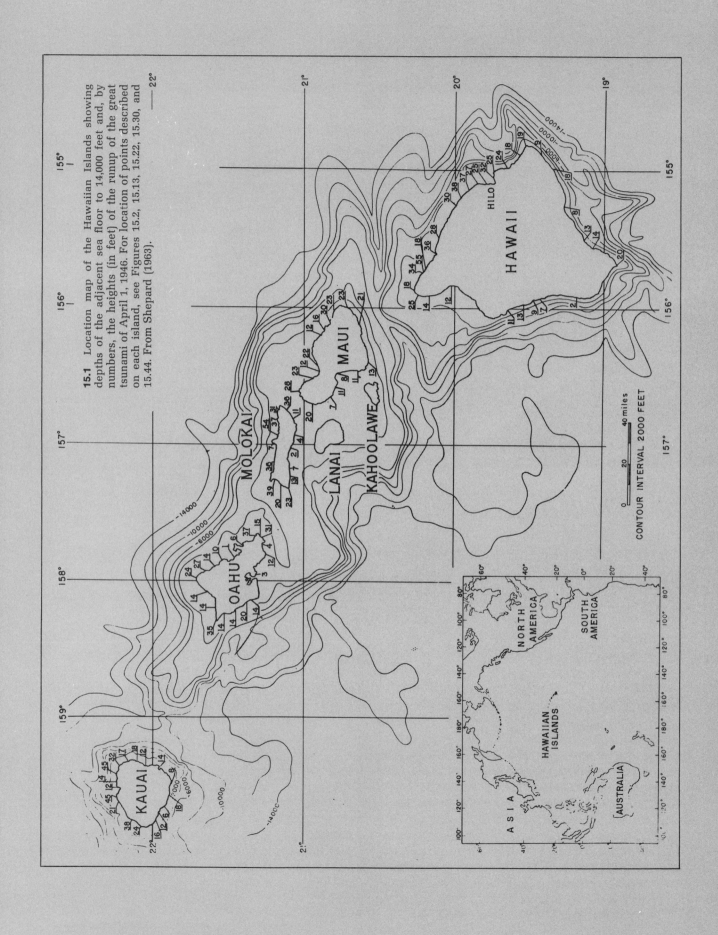

15.1 Location map of the Hawaiian Islands showing depths of the adjacent sea floor to 14,000 feet and, by numbers, the heights (in feet) of the runup of the great tsunami of April 1, 1946. For location of points described on each island, see Figures 15.2, 15.13, 15.22, 15.30, and 15.44. From Shepard (1963).

CONTOUR INTERVAL 2000 FEET

Volcanic Coasts

Hawaii

15 The fiftieth state of the Union differs from all the others in that it consists of a group of oceanic islands thousands of miles from the continent of North America. A map of the largest islands can be seen in Figure 15.1.

The human history of the islands is dramatically told in James A. Michener's *Hawaii*. More authoritive versions are given by Gavan Daws and R. S. Kuykendall (see references). The islands were colonized about A.D. 800 by natives from the Marquesas and Society Islands and by a later wave of colonists from Tahiti in the twelfth and thirteenth centuries. The first white man known to have landed on the islands was Captain James Cook, in 1778. After his death on a return trip a year later, various explorers visited the islands, including Cook's former mate, Captain George Vancouver who, like Cook, did much for the islanders. Fur and sandalwood trade started in 1810 or 1811. The first whalers went ashore in 1819, and that same year the first missionaries left Boston to convert the natives to Christianity. A German named Schaeffer, in Russian employ, made some attempts to gain possession of the islands in 1815, but was expelled in 1817 due to British influence.

Beginning in 1790, during the reign of Kamehameha I, American influence began to be established in the islands; and both the British and French agreed with Americans to respect the sovereignty of the Hawaiian monarchs. However, American business interests grew more and more important, the Hawaiian rule began to sink into second place, and finally, in 1894, a republic was declared that was largely ruled by Americans. This was followed by annexation to the United States in 1898, and statehood was granted in 1959.

The authors are grateful to Doak C. Cox for many suggestions and for updating some of the information given in this chapter.

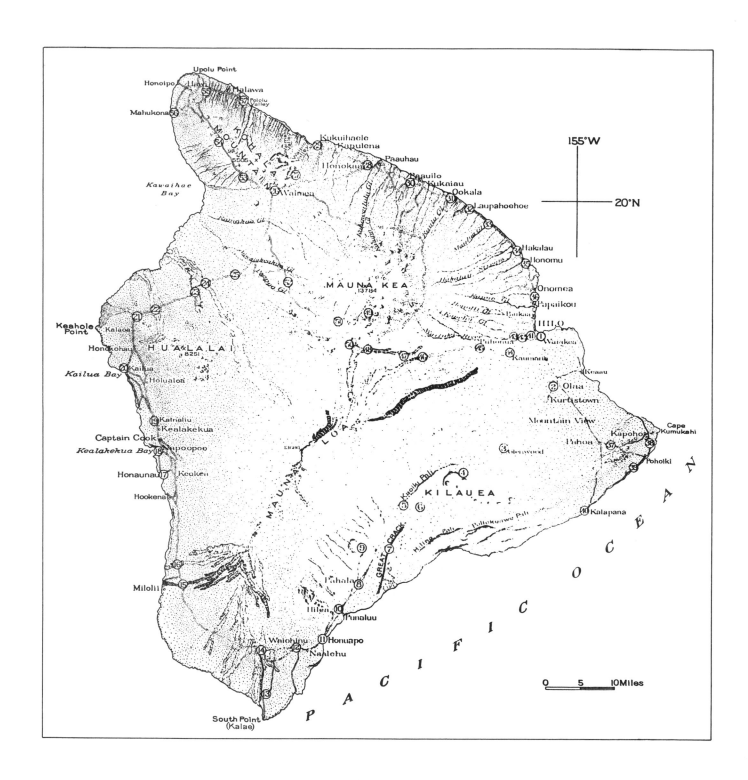

Like most islands rising from the deep ocean, the Hawaiian chain was built by volcanic eruptions, although vulcanism now continues only on the largest island, Hawaii. Maui has a dormant volcano that erupted in such comparatively recent times that native tales of the eruption were still common when the first white settlers came to the island. Perhaps the last eruption occurred in 1790, because the coastal sketches by Vancouver of the area of the eruption (1793) appear quite different from those of La Pérouse made in 1786 (Fig. 15.19). The other islands have much older volcanoes, most of them deeply eroded, although geologists have been able to trace their history and development.

Because of the volcanic origin, a considerable part of the Hawaiian coasts can be described as volcanic. Most of these coasts have been subject to modification by wave erosion and by the building of coral reefs along the margins of old volcanoes. Coastal plains have been built around the base of some of the volcanoes and between others. These plains are partly alluvial and partly raised coral reefs.

The greater part of the Hawaiian coasts consists of sea cliffs, some of them as high as 3,000 feet on the windward sides of the islands. There are also extensive beaches in the Hawaiian Islands, especially on the northernmost island, Kauai. Many of the best beaches in the islands are on the western sides, protected from the waves of the northeast trade winds. The most surprising thing about the beaches is that they are composed primarily of remains of organisms that lived in the sea; volcanic products are much less prevalent. The relatively rare volcanic sand beaches are found principally at the mouths of the larger rivers and along the coast where recent lava flows have killed the coral reefs, which were subsequently broken up by the waves. The white beaches, consisting of organic remains, are often called coral sand beaches but have coral fragments as only their fifth most important constituent. More abundant are foraminifera and fragments of mollusks, red algae, and echinoids.

The character of the Hawaiian coasts is well known, largely from a study of the beaches that was

conducted by the State Department of Planning and Economic Development between 1961 and 1963 and reported by Ralph Moberly, Jr., and others. Shepard spent four months in the initiation of the project and also had the opportunity for an earlier visit to all of the main islands during an investigation (with G. A. Macdonald and Doak Cox) of the wave damage from the 1946 tsunami. Much information concerning the coastal geology has come from the work of the U.S. Geological Survey in conjunction with the Hawaiian Division of Hydrography. The principal contributors to this study have been H. T. Stearns and Macdonald. On the other hand, information is scarce on recent coastal changes. Few maps are available to us that are old enough for comparison with recent maps to detect such changes, and we have had only a few old photos to examine for evidence of recent coastal erosion. The principal changes are to be found along the coasts of Hawaii where modern lava flows have entered the sea. In addition, rather important changes have come from the four large tsunamis that have hit the islands since 1946. Some of these tsunami changes were only temporary, and coasts have later returned essentially to their previous conditions.

The economy of the Hawaiian Islands is closely tied in with tourism. The beaches are one of the great attractions; but, as is the case of the Miami Beach area in Florida, the beaches are subject to serious erosion. The best known of these, Waikiki Beach, is at present largely artificial, and it has been a very serious problem to find enough sources of sand from the north coast of the island and even in adjacent Molokai to replace the losses that occur during storm periods.

In describing the coasts of the Hawaiian Islands, we shall consider only the five largest islands, starting at the southeast with Hawaii, often referred to as the Big Island, then proceeding around each island in a clockwise direction. Special attention will be given to the largest coastal cities and the problems they have faced from tsunamis.

ISLAND OF HAWAII

Hawaii (Fig. 15.2) is at the south end of the chain. It could also be referred to as the "disaster island," as it is here that both volcanic eruptions and tsunamis have produced frequent disasters. Hawaii has been

15.2 The island of Hawaii, showing location of the places described, and of the great volcanoes, Mauna Kea and Mauna Loa, and some recent laval flows. U.S. Geological Survey, Hawaiian Map NE 51, NE 55, 1962.

15.3 The breakwater at Hilo after destruction by the 1946 tsunami. U.S. Navy, 1946.

built by one small and four large volcanoes (Fig. 15.2). Mauna Loa, the huge dome at the southern end of the island, rises to a height of 13,680 feet with a large caldera in the center. A huge underground rift running across the mountain in a northeasterly direction has supplied most of the recent lava flows that have spilled out on both sides and has resulted in building out the southwest end of the island. Along the rift, lava flows have occurred during the past 132 years at an average of one per 7 years. Kilauea, on the southeast side of Mauna Loa, is a low dome rising only a few hundred feet above the Mauna Loa slopes, but it is remarkable for its crater, which has maintained a bubbling lava lake for many years at a time during the past two centuries. It has had eighteen eruptions since 1800 and nine eruptive phases in 1969 up to September. Mauna Kea, the immense dome that dominates northeastern Hawaii, rises to a summit of 13,784 feet. It is often called the highest mountain on earth since it rises an additional 14,000 feet from the sea floor. It is now extinct but has ceased erupting so recently that it is only slightly creased by river valleys. The small glaciers of the Pleistocene smoothed and polished the upper slopes. Hualalai, the 8,251-foot volcano on the west-central side of Hawaii, has had one eruption that occurred in 1801, so it can now

be considered dormant. Kohala, to the north with its 5,505-foot summit, like Mauna Kea, has had no historical eruptions and is apparently older than Mauna Kea, as it has some deep canyons cut into its northeast side, the only appreciable canyons on the island. Elsewhere on the mountain slopes, there are few permanent streams despite the high rainfall on the windward side. The lack of streams is due to high porosity of the lavas. Much of the surface of the island is covered with black lava rock that is almost devoid of vegetation.

HILO AREA, ISLAND OF HAWAII [Figs. 15.3, 15.4, and 15.5]   Hilo, the second largest city in the state, is located at the head of the largest bay, which is open to the northeast, so a jetty is necessary to protect the harbor from the northeast trades. According to Stearns and Macdonald, the bay was caused by prehistoric lava flows from Mauna Loa, flowing northeastward and partially covering wave-cut terraces that had been formed earlier at the margin of Mauna Kea. Two of the rare island rivers, Wailuku and Wailoa, enter the coast here, both with estuaries at their mouths. The city was built in part on a coastal plain (now a park) along the oceanfront but mostly on a Mauna Loa lava flow.

Hilo is unfortunately located because of the continuous threat of being engulfed by lava flows from Mauna Loa, and it was hit four times by destructive tsunamis between 1946 and 1960. The volcanic threat is also very real because lava flows from Mauna Loa in 1852 and 1855 and again in 1881 stopped just short of the Hilo outskirts, and numerous flows have occurred farther south along the coast. Thomas A. Jaggar suggested that a wall or several walls be built that would deflect future flows, but nothing has been done to date. In 1935, one flow was diverted by army bombing; and in 1942, another flow moving toward Hilo, although still far away, was also diverted by bombing.

No severe tsunamis had occurred in the Hawaiian Islands between 1923 and 1946, so when the huge waves swept into the shore on April 1, 1946, few residents had a vivid recollection of earlier experiences. Ninety-six lives were lost during the 1946 tsunami, mostly the result of people running out to the waterfront to see the waves and even going out onto the exposed reef during the wave trough that followed the first appreciable rise. Seeing fish left

high and dry by the withdrawal was a great tempta-
tion to the natives, who are born fishermen.

The 1946 waves knocked down most of the breakwater (Fig. 15.3) and swept over 0.25 mile of the
low coast around the harbor (Fig. 15.4). The water
moved 0.5 mile up the Wailuku River estuary. It rose
as much as 26 feet above normal levels inside the
breakwater and up to 32 feet on a point to the east.
These heights are well below the maximum of 55
feet reached farther north, but because of the heavily
populated lower sections of the city, the waves caused
more damage to Hilo than to any other place in the
islands. A series of waves came into the shores at
intervals of about 15 minutes here as elsewhere in
the islands, and the first was by no means the largest.
At Hilo, some of the later waves were photographed
from the air (Fig. 15.5) and were also photographed
on the ground as they moved up the estuaries. The
waves came in with steep frontal slopes, looking very
much like tidal bores such as occur at the head of
the Bay of Fundy.

Hilo was also damaged in 1952, 1957, and 1960,
but not in 1964 at the time of the great Alaska earthquake. The source of the 1946 waves was the displacement of the sea floor in the Great Trench that
runs along the south side of the Aleutian Islands.
The 1952 tsunami came from a fault movement in
the sea floor off Kamchatka; the 1957 waves, from
the Aleutian Trench; and the 1960 waves, from the
coast of Chile. The fact that they all produced relatively high water levels at Hilo indicates that the sea
floor outside the bay has a form that causes convergence of the waves, and the funnel-shaped bay
adds to this effect. At Hilo, the 1960 waves rose as
high as or higher than those of 1946 and killed sixty-
one people. Significantly, in 1960, despite the siren
warning system that had been installed by the U.S.
Coast and Geodetic Survey here as elsewhere in the
islands, few among the populace moved out of the
danger area. They thought the warning was just another false alarm, such as they had had on several
previous occasions when no appreciable waves developed.

The Hilo area is also subject to serious effects of
wind waves. The seawall at the former Puu Maile
Hospital, east of Hilo, was overtopped by the 1946
tsunami but not damaged, whereas storm waves demolished large sections of it a few months later.
Probably the wall had been weakened by the tsunami.

15.4 Destruction of the Hilo waterfront by the 1946
tsunami. U.S. Navy, 1946.

15.5 Hilo Harbor, showing approach of waves during
a late stage of the 1946 tsunami. Note bridge across the
Wailuku Estuary has been broken by early waves. Army
Transport Command, 1946.

15.6 Lava from Kilauea Volcano flowing over a cliff on the southeast coast of Hawaii, which extended the coast. Photo courtesy of Jerry Eaton, U.S. Geological Survey.

15.7 Kealakekua Bay on the western coast of Hawaii showing the monument (A) at the site where Captain James Cook was killed by natives in 1779. Gravel beach in foreground. Photo by Shepard, 1947.

Finally, added to its other natural disadvantages, Hilo's annual 140 inches of rain is a real handicap to its tourist trade. Some of the tourists also complain of the surprisingly cold water, which results from the huge springs that come up from the sea floor near the shore and locally spread their cool fresh water over the surface. One can dive below this two-foot layer and find the usual warm water beneath.

SOUTHEAST COAST, ISLAND OF HAWAII
The relatively straight southeast coast of the island is mostly a barren rock waste built by many lava flows, including five in historical time. This coast is notable for its black and green sand beaches. The black sand at Kalapana and nearby Kaimu is composed of grains of volcanic glass, probably derived in part from the chilling of the lava flow of 1750 as it entered the sea. The sands here, according to F. W. McCoy, are partly cut away each winter, exposing the underlying gravel. Farther southwest along this coast, there is a desert tract where the rainfall is very low because the area is in the lee of Kilauea. Here, a series of cliffs are due to faulting along the south side of the volcano. No road follows the coast in this section; but, near the southwest end of this long straight stretch, the road comes down to the settlements of Punaluu and Honuapo, where small indentations allow fishing vessels to anchor. There are also volcanic sand beaches here, and the town of Punaluu is built on a wind-blown sand plain directly landward of a beach. A green sand beach is found near the south end of this coast. According to Stearns and Macdonald, the unusual sand color is due to the destruction of a littoral cone of olivene-rich lava that apparently exploded.

The most recent lava flow to come to the shore occurred at the northeast end of this part of the coast. In 1960, the rift near Kapoho was forced open and lava spewed out, flowing down on its way to the sea at Cape Kumukahi and covering the village. Upon reaching the sea, the lava turned south, building out the coast in that direction. After the eruption, 0.54 square mile had been added. In 1955, lava broke from a rift on the side of Kilauea and flowed into the sea (Fig. 15.6), also building out the coast.

KONA COAST, ISLAND OF HAWAII [Figs. 15.7 and 15.8]   On the island of Hawaii, the west side is known as the Kona Coast. In Hawaiian, *kona* means "leeward." On this west side, the waves are considerably reduced because it is in the lee of the predominant northeast winds. Along the Kona Coast, the rainfall generally is low because the trade winds have lost most of their moisture due to the cooling and condensation that results from air rising over the steep sloping land on the other side. Rainfall at the south point of Hawaii is only 13 inches per year and at Kawaihae, in the embayment at the north end of the Kona Coast, only 10 inches per year. However, the long slope of Mauna Loa is warmed each day, causing a special sea-to-land breeze in the afternoon, which results in some condensation and greatly augments the rainfall along the most populated portions of the Kona Coast between Hookena and the resort town of Kailua. Visitors can expect showers during their afternoon siestas. The rain sinks rapidly into the porous volcanic ground, so there are no permanent streams.

The Kona Coast is relatively straight but more indented than the southeast coast. Three bays in the central part of the coast, Honaunau, Kealakekua, and Kailua, provide anchorage for small boats; and Kailua has sufficient depth for small trading ships. All these bays have headlands built by lava flows in prehistoric times. Kealakekua and the adjacent Honaunau are perhaps the most scenic localities along the Kona Coast. On the north side of Kealakekua Bay (Fig. 15.7), Captain James Cook, the British explorer, was killed by the natives in 1779. A small monument marks the spot where the natives, mistaking Cook's motives, attacked him. Only a foot trail leads to this spot, although it can also be approached by boat from the town of Napoopoo, to the south. The coral reef growing outside the rocky shore at Cook's monument is perhaps the most beautiful in the Hawaiian Islands. The water is usually very clear, and a steep slope extends to the south along a fault at the base of a lava flow. The actively growing coral is traced for at least 100 feet down this slope. South of the cliff, there was formerly a black sand beach, but this was destroyed some time during the 1950s, and only volcanic cobbles are left. However, at the south end of the bay, a coarse sand beach is half volcanic and half made of organic remains. This beach gets partly eroded each winter. Just to the south, Honaunau Bay is noted as a former "City of Refuge" (A in Fig. 15.8) where, before the Christianizing of Hawaii, hunted natives could live with-

15.8 South side of Honaunau Bay, west Hawaii, showing a prehistoric lava flow in foreground and ruins of "City of Refuge" at left under palm trees. Photo by Shepard, 1947.

15.9 At the mouth of Pololu Valley, near the north end of Hawaii, where the runup from the 1946 tsunami reached 55 feet (arrow), the greatest height in the Hawaiian Islands. All sand from the beach was removed and the dune ridge deeply eroded. Homes of Hawaiians on the beach were all destroyed. Photo by G. A. Macdonald, 1946.

15.10 Waipio Canyon on the northeastern coast of Hawaii, showing channel cut across the sand dunes (A) by the 1946 tsunami. Waterfall comes from hanging valley of the coastal cliffs to the south. Photo by Shepard, 1946.

15.11 Coast southeast of Waipio Canyon, showing damage to railroad trestle by 1946 tsunami. Photo by G. A. Macdonald, 1946.

out danger of attack by their enemies. Ruins of this settlement, now a state park, are still left on the relatively recent lava flow that constitutes Puuhonua Point on the south side of the bay.

Kailua is the largest tourist resort on the island. Just south of Kailua, a beach called Disappearing

Sands is destroyed each winter by storms from westerly winds. The sand is carried into a pocket offshore and returns in summer.

Tsunamis have caused only minor damage along the Kona Coast; but the 1960 waves rose as high as 16 feet at Napoopoo, the highest on the Kona Coast of any of the four in recent years. A strange development from the 1946 tsunami was found during the investigation by Shepard, Macdonald, and Cox. At Napoopoo and at Hookena, 7 miles to the south, the waves rose highest about 12 hours after the destructive waves along the other parts of the islands had ceased. These waves must have bounced off Asia and then returned to Hawaii after a long voyage, which is reminiscent of a three-corner shot in billiards.

During the twentieth century, volcanic flows coming from eruptions on the side of Mauna Loa have reached the coast south of Hookena on five occasions. One flow in 1950 added 0.5 square mile to the land area. The coastal towns and mountainous ranches in this area are obviously in a dangerous location, and much damage has been inflicted on them. At the south end of the Kona Coast, lava flows came to the sea in 1866 and 1877 but did not cause any damage to habitations. North of Kailua Bay, a lava flow from Hualalai Volcano reached the sea in 1801; and, still farther north, a flow from Mauna Loa veered around Hualalai Volcano and came to the sea in 1859, just north of one of the Hualalai flows. These two flows were responsible for developing Kihola Bay by building out the coast on each side. Still older flows form the coast farther north.

Kawaihae is located in the bight between the northeastern slope of Mauna Loa and Kohala Volcanoes. South of the town, a coral reef extends along the shore and protects it from the open sea, making a popular swimming area. Several hotel resorts are located adjacent to small bays farther south, and these take advantage of the low rainfall of this part of the coast and have clear water for swimming.

WINDWARD COAST NORTH OF HILO, ISLAND OF HAWAII [Figs. 15.9 through 15.12] The windward coast of Hawaii north of Hilo Bay is cliffed most of the way to the northern tip. The relative straightness of this cliffed coast is rather remarkable because the cliffs truncate the slopes of two adjacent volcanoes. Waipio Bay, the largest indentation, is at the juncture of these volcanoes. The cliffs cut into the slopes at the northern part of the Kohala Range are quite low and have terraces, said by Stearns and Macdonald to represent a 25-foot stand of sea level. From Pololu Valley, 10 miles from the north point, to Waipio Valley, a series of deep canyons indent the cliffs; and so far it has not been possible to build a road along this very scenic coast, although a fine view can be obtained from the air during the flight from Honolulu to Hilo. The cliffs along this canyon section rise from 400 to 1,400 feet. In some places, there are hanging canyons with high waterfalls (Fig. 15.10), where the erosion of the sea has been faster than the downcutting of the streams. Pololu Valley, at the northern end of the tract, has a relatively flat floor formed by alluvium that fills a much deeper canyon. The same thing is the case at Waipio Valley. At Pololu, there is a large coastal dune at the mouth of the valley. Here, during the 1946 tsunami, the water rose to a record height of 55 feet (Fig. 15.9), the greatest measured height in all the islands during any of the tsunamis. Waipio Valley, at the south end of this tract, can be visited by a trail leading down from the north end of the coastal road. Spectacular gouges were cut into the dunes at the lower end of this valley during the 1946 tsunami (Fig. 15.10). The water rose at Waipio Valley to 40 feet, considerably higher than during the later tsunamis.

South of Waipio Valley, the slopes of Mauna Kea have cliffs ranging in height from 50 to 350 feet. Small canyons that cut through these cliffs were crossed by trestles of a now-abandoned railroad. Some of the girders were washed away from one of the trestles by the 1946 waves (Fig. 15.11). The girders and huge blocks of rock were carried upstream for hundreds of feet.

Several small low points project along this part of the coast. Laupahoehoe, one of them, is the result of lava delta building, and others are due to landslides. The 1964 waves sweeping north along the coast crossed most of the point, carrying away homes and wrecking a school that was located there. Two boys were swept out into the ocean by these waves, but were seen swimming by an Air Force pilot who dropped them a raft. A photograph of the boys on the raft (A in Fig. 15.12) appears to have been taken as one of the subsequent waves surged along the coast.

15.12 Tsunami wave sweeping along the coast near Laupahoehoe, Hawaii. At A can be seen the raft in which two boys were rescued after being swept into the ocean by earlier 1946 tsunami waves. U.S. Navy, 1946.

MAUI ISLAND

Maui (Fig. 15.13) is the second largest of the Hawaiian Islands and has the third highest peak, Haleakala, 10,025 feet. The island consists of two volcanic masses that have grown together to form the Isthmus. East Maui, which comprises the greater part of the island, has been built up by the eruptions of Haleakala Volcano. Its huge crater is accessible by road, and seeing it is a wonderful if chilling experience, especially at sunrise. East Maui's coast, like that of the island of Hawaii, is greatly influenced by volcanic flows. However, since only one of the flows has occurred within the past few centuries (see p. 508), the waves have had much more opportunity to erode the shore and modify the lavas than around the coast of Mauna Loa. West Maui is an old, deeply eroded volcano. Its coast can be compared with that of Kohala in Hawaii. The canyons cut into the old volcano provide some of the most striking scenery in the islands, such as the Iao Needle west of Wailuku. The canyons along the northeast coast are accessible only by a rather poor road.

The Isthmus has most of the flat land of the island and has the largest centers of population on the north side, including the port city of Kahului. Tourist re-

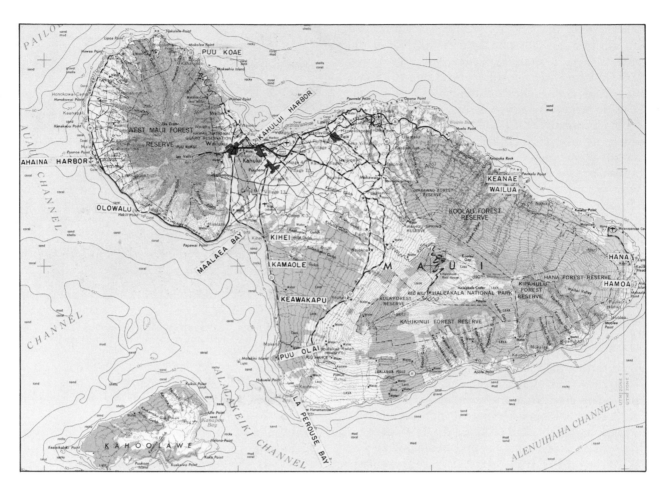

15.13 Outline map of the island of Maui showing locations described. East Maui was built by lavas and ash from Haleakala Volcano, while West Maui was formed by the smaller volcano, Puu Kukui. U.S. Geological Survey, Hawaiian Map NE 4–16, 1966.

sorts are centered around Hana, at the east end of the island, and along the west side of West Maui, north of Lahaina.

As in Hawaii, rainfall in Maui is extremely variable. Along the east coast, the maximum rainfall is in excess of 150 inches per year at the base of the slope of Haleakala (two-thirds of the way between Kahului and Hana) but less than 20 inches per year at Kahului. On the west side, Lahaina is almost a desert with only 13 inches of rain, and Kihei on the south side of the Isthmus has 11 inches. As a counteraction to the pleasantly dry but hot summer climate on the southwest side, the northeast is much cooler due to the trade winds, which also bring more rain.

KAHULUI AREA, MAUI   The port city of Kahului is located on the windward side of the Isthmus. The harbor is protected by two breakwaters, but these were not quite high enough to keep out the 1946 tsunami, although they considerably reduced the height of the waves on the inside. The water rose 17 feet outside and only 7 inside. A small beach inside the harbor has calcareous sand grains from the reef that runs along the coast. A narrow beach east of the harbor (Fig. 15.14) is somewhat discontinuous for about 5 miles, ending near Lower Paia. It is interrupted in many places by beachrock and in a few by lava points. The coral reef along the shore in this area supplies most of the sand. The reef is not continuous enough to prevent the large surf, caused by trade winds, from coming into the beach. The shore was badly cut away by the 1946 tsunami. At Spreckelsville, 3 miles east of Kahului, the water swept as much as 800 feet inland and rose to a height of 28 feet. In addition to the effects of the tsunamis, storm wave erosion in this area has been a serious problem for many years. The beaches and the calcareous sand dunes behind them retreat each winter, and summer fill does not make up for the erosion.

NORTHEAST COAST OF EAST MAUI   To the east of Spreckelsville, the coast runs along the base of Haleakala Volcano, turning gradually to the southeast. This area is generally cliffed, having been made irregular by wave erosion. There are no reefs to protect this part of the coast, and many of the sea cliffs rise to heights of several hundred feet. The projections are the result of relatively recent lava flows. An example is Keanae Point, halfway to Hana

15.14 Narrow beach east of Kahului Harbor, showing beachrock (A). Maui Isthmus in middle ground and West Maui volcano in background. Photo by Shepard, 1962.

15.15 Keanae Point on the northeast coast of Maui, formed by a Pleistocene lava flow that came out of the valley to the left and spread out beyond the old sea cliff. Recent erosion of the end of the point has developed the irregular outline. Photo by Agatin T. Abbott, Hawaii Institute of Geophysics.

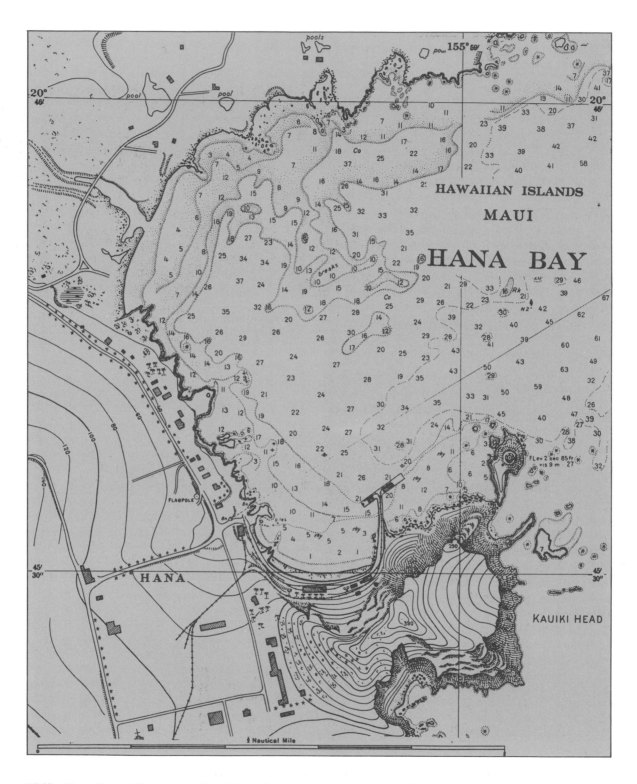

15.16 Hana Bay at the eastern tip of Maui, between two points formed by Pleistocene laval flows. U.S. Coast and Geodetic Survey Chart 4113, 1941 edition.

15.17 Hamoa Bay, south of Hana, showing a house moved 200 feet from its foundation by the 1946 tsunami. Haleakala Volcano in background. Photo by G. A. Macdonald, 1946.

(Fig. 15.15), where a small town has been built. The 1946 tsunami swept over this point, damaging buildings and drowning two people. At Nahiku Landing, 3 miles farther east, the 1946 waves rose 30 feet, the highest on East Maui. The few bays that sharply indent the coast are probably the result of wave erosion working on the soft volcanic ash formations of this area.

The coast highway between the Isthmus and Hana, at the eastern end of the island, is extremely winding as it goes back into each of the small canyons that have cut into the lower slope of this comparatively old volcano.

HANA AREA, EAST MAUI   At Hana, on the north side of the east end of the island, a partly protected bay and a good beach form the basis for a popular resort (Fig. 15.16). The arms of the bay are the consequence of Pleistocene lava flows, and a small coral reef lies on the north side of the bay. The beach sand is predominantly volcanic, due to the erosion of the lava flows. Good surfing beaches are located on the south side of the south headland of the bay and at Hamoa Bay, 2 miles south of Hana. At the latter, in 1946, the surge of the waves rose 23 feet, and some houses built on a terrace about 10 feet

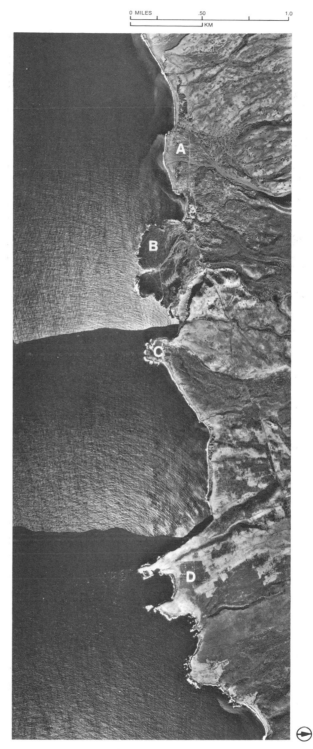

15.18 Southeast coast of East Maui showing a small fan delta (A), two lava flows at Apole Point, which hardened as they entered the ocean (B, C), and a cemented mud flow, breccia (D), forming straight-sided projecting point. U.S. Coast and Geodetic Survey, 1961.

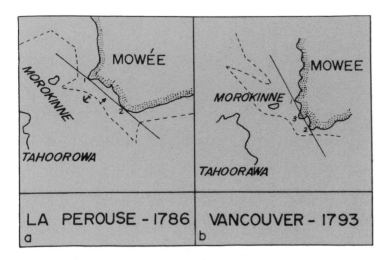

15.19 Sketches of southwest Maui coast by La Perouse in 1786 (*a*) and Vancouver in 1793 (*b*). Projecting point (3) in Vancouver sketch interpreted as being the eighteenth-century lava flow of native legends, from a vent on the side of Haleakala. From Oostdam (1965).

above sea level were destroyed. One house was carried almost intact for 200 feet from its foundation (Fig. 15.17). At Hana, where there is no lowland, the waves were only 13 feet high, and damage was slight.

SOUTH SIDE, EAST MAUI [Figs. 15.18, 15.19, and 2.7]   The steepest slopes of Haleakala are found on the south side of the mountain. The greatest postglacial volcanic activity is also on that side, particularly to the southwest along the great rift which extends in that direction from the summit of Haleakala. The rainfall varies from about 80 inches a year on the east to less than 15 inches on the west. One result of this contrast is that the forested slopes to the east give way to a barren rocky mountainside to the west. Along the well-watered eastern portion, the mountain slopes are cut by beautiful small canyons; and the seacoast is jagged and irregular. The straight-sided point in the aerial photograph (Fig. 15.18) is due to the greater resistance to erosion of a well-cemented mudflow breccia, which comes to the coast at this point.

In 1962, when last visited by Shepard, the western portion of the south coast had only a very poor road and was almost free of habitation. Because of the low rainfall, the mountain slopes are only slightly eroded; and the coastal irregularities are less pronounced than

farther east. Most of the prominent points at the southwest corner of the island were built by Pleistocene or recent lava flows (Fig. 2.7). The relation of these flows to the parasite cones near the base of the mountain is clearly illustrated in the aerial photograph. At the right of this photo, a lava flow is shown that is generally considered to have occurred in the mid-eighteenth century. However, B. L. Oostdam attempted to date the lava flow by comparing charts drawn by the early explorers, La Pérouse in 1786 and Vancouver in 1793 (Fig. 15.19). He thinks these maps show that La Pérouse arrived before the flow occurred, because a new spit (3) appears in the Vancouver chart. The east side of the flow shelters La Perouse Bay from the sea. The recency of lava has prevented the formation of any soil along the mountain slope at this place. The flow lines in each of these relatively recent lava flows are shown in the photograph (Fig. 2.7). Ridges along the sides of the flows are natural levees built by overflow. At La Perouse Bay, studies have been made of the rate of repopulating the adjacent sea floor by coral growth following the lava flow.

WEST COAST OF EAST MAUI   This is a long, comparatively straight coast on the west side of Haleakala. The intermittent white sand beaches are bordered inland by dune sands that are largely vegetated.

At the south end of this coast, there is a wide beach just south of the cinder cone crater, Puu Olai. This usually deserted beach extends for 3,000 feet; and, aside from the beaches at the Isthmus, this is the longest continuous beach on the island. According to Moberly and Chamberlain, the beach was seen to vary from a width of 200 feet in winter to 100 feet in summer. However, a mile to the north, Makena Beach was seen to grow wider in summer. Probably this difference is the result of changing current directions that favor one beach during the winter and the other during summer (see p. 264). At Keawakapu Beach, midway between Puu Olai and the south end of the Isthmus, a 2,000-foot beach is subject to wave erosion during winter storms that threaten the homes built on the sand terrace adjacent to the beach. Kamaole Beach, 4 miles south of the Isthmus, varies little during the winter, probably because of the shallow coral reefs that lie directly outside. At Kihei, next to the Isthmus, the beach has its greatest width in summer, Here, unlike the other beaches along this part of the coast, the sand has a high content of volcanic material introduced by streams flowing down the slopes of Haleakala Volcano.

All along this coast of East Maui the tsunamis had little effect, although the 1946 waves did rise sufficiently to cover the dock at Kihei with a foot of water. It seems likely that Kona storm waves will continue to cause more damage to this coast than will future tsunamis.

MAALAEA BAY, WEST MAUI   The south side of the Maui Isthmus is a low marshy area flanked by a 4-mile-long barrier beach that encloses a partly filled shallow lagoon, Kealia Pond. The town of Maalaea, at the west end of the embayment, has breakwaters enclosing a harbor deep enough only for shallow-draft boats. Studies of the beach at the west end of the barrier showed that it reaches a maximum width at the end of winter, apparently as the result of strong southerly winds that move the sand along the shore in this direction. During the summer, this beach is cut back despite the small waves, suggesting a reversal of currents. Unlike the sand at Kihei to the south, the beach at Maalaea is predominantly calcareous. Locally it is consolidated beachrock. The coast of Maalaca Bay is apparently prograding due to the supply of sediment that is carried down the slope of Haleakala and swept north by longshore currents, forming bars in the shallow water off the Isthmus. These bars are built into barriers, and subsequently the lagoon on the inside becomes filled with overwash and alluvium from the mountain.

LEEWARD COAST, WEST MAUI   The lee coast of West Maui combines an irregularly eroded, rocky shore to the south, where lava spurs from a south-trending rift of the old volcano have built forward into the ocean in the late Tertiary, and a relatively straight coast to the north, where alluvial fans have built out into Auau Channel. The island of Lanai (Fig. 15.22) protects the coast from the occasional westerly storms. A small-boat harbor has been constructed at Lahaina. This prograded shore, both north and south of Lahaina, had been retreating when Shepard last examined it. Trees were being undermined all along the narrow beaches. Coral reefs grow intermittently along the shore, and at depths of about 150 to 200 feet, large masses of black coral

15.20 Oblique aerial view of the irregular windward coast of West Maui at Puu Koae Head (A), showing wave erosion of an old bulbous dome of lava. Photo by Shepard, 1962.

are harvested by local scuba divers. North of Lahaina, some of the small bays are sites of tourist hotels. The 1946 tsunami did little damage along the lee coast of West Maui except at Mala, just north of Lahaina. The wave heights increased progressively to the north of Mala, reaching a maximum of 27 feet at Hawea, the northwest point of the island.

NORTH AND EAST COASTS OF WEST MAUI [Figs. 15.20 and 15.21]   On the exposed north and east margins of the northern volcano, the coast is much more irregular as the result of active marine erosion of the old lavas. Points, such as Puu Koae Head at the north end of the east coast (Fig. 15.20), form promontories due mostly to erosion remnants of local bulbous domes of lava. The road around this north and east coast is narrow and twisty with precipitous flanks leading down into the steep-walled stream-cut canyons that characterize this windward coast. At the base of the slopes near the Isthmus, there is additional evidence of active erosion (Fig. 15.21). Trees are being undermined in many places and falling into the ocean. In fact, Maui appears to have more indications of active coastal erosion than any of the other islands of Hawaii.

15.21 Undermining of trees by wave erosion on the east coast of West Maui. Photo by Shepard, 1962.

MOLOKAI

The island of Molokai (Fig. 15.22) is strikingly different in shape from the other main islands of the Hawaiian group. Its coast forms an elongate rectangle instead of the rounded shores conforming to the outline of volcanoes that characterize the other islands. However, like the others, Molokai was built by vulcanism and, like Maui, is due to the growing together of two main volcanoes, both long extinct on Molokai. As on Maui, the eastern volcano of Molokai is by far

the higher, although it attains an altitude of only 4,080 feet; the western volcano is largely eroded and rises only 1,380 feet. The curve on the southeast side clearly conforms to the East Molokai Dome; and the former leper colony peninsula, Kalaupapa, which protrudes from the straight north side, owes its rounded outline to the relatively recent vulcanism of Kauhako Crater. The dome of East Molokai Volcano has some influence on the south shore, but apparently the activity of this volcano took place so long ago that the waves since then have eliminated most of the original coastal shape. The straight north coast of East Molokai represents a wave-eroded cliff formed largely prior to the volcanic building of the Kalaupapa Peninsula. However, the straightness may also be due to faulting of the north margin, but the fault scarp is now 3 miles seaward of the coastline. The 3-mile shelf probably represents the retreat of the coast under wave attack after the forming of the fault scarp.

Of the five large islands, Molokai is the least developed for tourists. Actually, it has some very attractive areas, notably the Kalaupapa Peninsula at the base of the high cliffs, as well as the beautiful west coast beaches. The former has only recently been opened to the public because it has been a leper colony, which is being gradually phased out. The west coast is part of the property of the Molokai Ranch and up until 1968 was closed to the public. Only small beaches are found on the south side, and

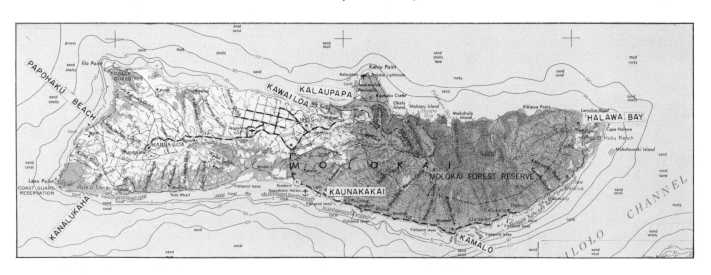

15.22 The island of Molokai, showing locations described. Two old deeply eroded volcanoes joined to form the island. The former leper colony was on the north side of the peninsula. U.S. Geological Survey, Hawaiian Map NE 4–16, 1966.

the north side is almost devoid of beaches except in a few of the coves.

Molokai has much more extensive coral reefs along its coasts than either Maui or Hawaii. The only wide reefs are on the south side. Many of these reefs are now dead, probably due to mud washed on them from the land. Smaller reefs are found on the leeward side of the Kalaupapa Peninsula. Natural breaks in the coral reefs provide most of the harbors.

Molokai has had little damage from the various tsunamis because the coastal habitations are largely on the south side in the lee of the tsunamis, which come mostly from the north. The south side is protected by reefs and by the islands of Lanai and Maui. During the 1946 tsunami, waves rose very high on the north side of the island and swept around both the northeast and northwest corners with little immediate loss of height, but only low waves reached the straight south coast (see Fig. 15.1).

As on the other islands, the climatic belts on Molokai are influenced by the trade winds. The lowest rainfall occurs on the south-central coast, where Kaunakakai has only 12 inches per year compared with 40 to 50 inches per year on the Kalaupapa Peninsula on the north side. The rainfall is also low at the west end of the island, with only 12 to 15 inches per year.

MANGROVE COAST WEST OF KAUNAKAKAI, ISLAND OF MOLOKAI

Kaunakakai, well known because of the ditty about the "Cock-eyed Mayor of Kaunakakai," is the only town of any size on the island. It is the chief outlet for the agricultural products, and a pier 0.5 mile long extends out from shore to the natural channel that cuts into the coral reef. West of Kaunakakai, there is a broad mangrove coastal flat. According to Ralph Moberly, Jr., this plain has been built almost a mile across the reef since the area was first cultivated by man in the middle of the last century. Tilling the soil and the introduction of livestock in this relatively dry region accelerated the erosion of the slopes. A red sediment is being carried down by the occasional rains and is covering the reef. A few narrow short beaches are found in this area; at stream mouths they are largely cobble.

Before the coming of the white man, the Hawaiian natives had many fish ponds along the south shore of Molokai, west of Kaunakakai. They built stone walls

15.23 A high storm beach west of Kolo, on the southern coast of Molokai, with berm being cut back, producing scarp in foreground. The dark masses are beachrock with limonite stain. Photo by Shepard, 1962.

out from the shore in a semicircle and stocked the resulting ponds with fish. Some of these ponds still remain, as at Pakanaka, 5 miles west of Kaunakakai. Others nearer Kaunakakai have been largely covered by the advance of the mangrove coast into the sea.

WEST MOLOKAI [Figs. 15.23, 15.24, and 15.25] West of the lowland that separates the two volcanic masses, the south coast becomes more rugged and has only a narrow discontinuous coastal plain. The intermittent beaches are partly gravel. The sands are almost entirely reef and shell material, in spite of the basalt rocks just landward of the coast. The coral reef pinches out near Kolo (halfway to the southwest point), making it possible for boats to come into the wharf without having to follow a narrow transreef channel, as is necessary to the east. Much of the coast has low cliffs without any appreciable beach. One stretch of sand extends for 2 miles east of Kolo and another discontinuously for 5 miles to the west. Part of the latter is a high storm beach, much of it separated from the shore by beachrock (Fig. 15.23). The beach sands lie landward of the beachrock, and dune belts border the inner beaches. Because of the predominant westward drift, the construction of jetties at Haleolono Point has undoubtedly cut off the sand supply from the beaches to the west. In the spring of 1962, these beaches were being destroyed. The

15.24 Papohaku Beach on the west coast of Molokai is one of the finest beaches in the Hawaiian Islands. Sand here is being mined and used for replenishing Waikiki Beach. Photo by Shepard, 1962.

15.25 Beach escarpment at Kawailoa Bay, northwest Molokai, showing layer of foraminifera (man's hands) exposed by wave erosion. Photo by Shepard, 1962.

only wide beach at that time was at Kanalukaha, 3 miles from the southwest point. It was 150 feet wide, but Moberly and Chamberlain report that in the following winter it was mined and almost disappeared. However, the sand had come back to a slight extent by early fall of 1963. No subsequent information is at hand.

Along the west coast, the 2-mile-long Papohaku Beach is one of the widest in all of the Hawaiian Islands (Fig. 15.24). It lies between a lava point at the south and a cinder cone to the north. The calcareous sand of medium grain size had a steep frontal slope and a wide berm. According to Moberly and Chamberlain, the berm increased in width from 280 feet in the early spring of 1963 to 400 feet in the late summer. The sand source is from the north and is sufficient so that, despite a year-round sand-mining operation at the south end, the sand never disappears. The occasional west winds have carried much of the sand inland, forming broad dunes. One can well imagine how popular this beautiful beach will become now that it is open to the public.

The northwest coast of Molokai is largely cliffs of volcanic material but is fronted in part by eolianite, a consolidated dune sand. Kawailoa Bay, 7 miles from the northwestern point, has a very steep beach scarp (Fig. 15.25) in which a layer of foraminifera was found just below the berm. Foraminifera are relatively common in the Hawaiian beaches but are usually worn and difficult to recognize, so it was surprising to find a concentration of well-preserved tests at this point.

CLIFFED NORTH COAST OF MOLOKAI AND KALAUPAPA PENINSULA [Figs. 15.26, 15.27, and 15.28]   The 25 miles of high canyon-cut cliffs (Fig. 15.26), which extend along the north coast bordering the deeply eroded East Molokai Volcano, provide even more spectacular scenery than that of the cliffed northeast side of Kohala Volcano on the island of Hawaii. Here again, the area can be seen only from the air or the sea, as there are no roads except at the east and west borders. Only one point protrudes well out beyond this straight coast, Kalaupapa Peninsula (Fig. 15.27).

The great cliffs are largely the result of wave erosion. The strong northeast winds cause an almost continuous breaking of large waves against the base of the cliffs. An interesting feature of this coast is that most of the larger land canyons continue seaward as marine canyons. As you steam along the cliffs taking echo-soundings, when you cross a submarine canyon you can usually look in at the coast and see its equivalent directly inside on land. If the idea, suggested previously (p. 510), that the cliffs have been worn back for 3 miles is correct, the sub-

15.26 Cliffed coast and steep canyons along the northwest coast of Molokai. Photo by Shepard, 1962.

15.27 Kalaupapa Peninsula on the north coast of Molokai, where a small volcano (A) built seaward of the wave-cut cliffs. The former leper colony was located here. U.S. Geological Survey, Kaunakakai quadrangle, Molokai.

15.28 Beach outside of Kalaupapa Point showing the driftwood concentrate from the 1946 tsunami as only 8 feet above sea level (A), and logs washed up by a storm of the previous winter at 20 feet (B). Photo by Shepard, 1946.

marine canyons must have been incised by marine processes into the shelf as it was forming. Some of the sea canyons extend in so close to the coast that the surveying ships must approach dangerously near the rocks in order to sound the valley heads.

Kalaupapa Peninsula (Fig. 15.27) must have developed after most of the cliff cutting had been completed, because we can see the continuation of the cliff escarpment inside the peninsula with almost no diminution in steepness and height. One of the submarine canyons outside the point appears to be in line with a land canyon, the lower end of which has been diverted by the growth of the point. The peninsula was built by a Pleistocene volcano with a small crater still evident. According to Stearns and Macdonald, the cone never grew to more than 400 feet above sea level and has been only creased by very small gullies.

The leper colony was established on the peninsula in 1865. Father Damien, a Catholic missionary, gave his life to the development of the colony. After many faithful years of service he finally contracted the disease and died the death of a martyr without ever leaving. Most of the patients have had the disease arrested; but some of them, liking this beautiful fertile area, have used their option that allows them to live

the rest of their lives in the former colony. The place has such scenic beauty that it may soon become a tourist attraction. Small coral reefs and calcareous sand beaches are found on the protected west side of the peninsula. Also on the same side, a volcanic sand beach, which is cut away each winter, lies at the juncture between the cliffed coast and the peninsula. Only a storm beach is located on the east side of Kalaupapa.

The 1946 tsunami rose high all along the cliffed coast, ranging between 28 and 54 feet; but a strange anomaly occurred on Kalaupapa Peninsula. One might have expected wave convergence on the end of the point, as results from the ordinary storm waves breaking on the point. Instead, the tsunami carried driftwood only up to elevations of 7 or 8 feet; whereas the storms of the preceding winter carried the wood to heights of 20 feet (Fig. 15.28). The low tsunami runup was a great contrast to the 54-foot waves in the canyon mouth just east of the peninsula and the 44-foot rise just to the west. The explanation for this contrast along the peninsula is that the end of the point is bordered by a steep slope, so there is no shelf here to cause long-period tsunami waves coming from the north to build up due to the usual friction of a shallow sea floor. The 3-mile-wide shelf on either side allowed the growth of the great waves that hit the coast without interference from any other island, although no life was lost. Residents who saw the waves described them as rising gently, looking like an incoming tide, but returning with considerable violence. In contrast, at Halawa Valley, at the east end of the cliffed coast, the waves came in with great force and developed a smooth bench, cutting away much of one of the few wide island beaches. This beach at Halawa, now rebuilt, is largely volcanic sand.

EAST AND SOUTHEAST MOLOKAI   Along the east end of the island there are no appreciable reefs, and the steep coast is indented with small coves due to wave erosion. Five miles southeast of Cape Halawa, the eastern point, the extensive coral reefs of the south coast begin (Fig. 15.29). They grow to a width of about a mile and are cut by a few natural channels, like those off Kaunakakai, allowing the development of ports for shallow-draft boats. At Pukoo, a wharf leading out to the channel was destroyed by the 1946 tsunami. At the same time, waves rose 39

15.29 Diagonal aerial view along the southeast coast of Molokai, showing the bordering coral reefs and some of the fish ponds (A, B) constructed by the natives for the ancient kings. Photo by Agatin T. Abbott, Hawaii Institute of Geophysics.

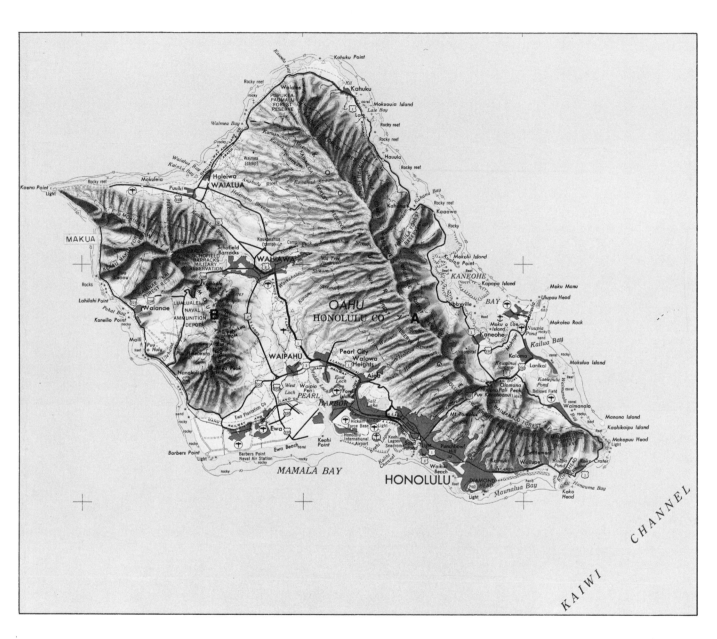

15.30 The island of Oahu formed by two deeply eroded volcanic masses, Koolau Range (A) and Waianae Mountains (B). Honolulu and Pearl Harbor are in the low area between these volcanoes. U.S. Geological Survey, Hawaiian Map NF 4–11, 1961.

feet just south of the east cape of Molokai; but the heights decreased rapidly to the southeast, especially inside the coral reef. It was found that the water rose somewhat higher inside each of the channels that partially cross the reef. As a result, some houses that had been built opposite these channels were damaged.

In the 15 miles of the south coast east of Kaunakakai, there are about fifty partly destroyed fish ponds built by the ancient Hawaiians. At present, most of the fish ponds are being silted rapidly by the deltas of streams coming down the slopes from East Molokai Volcano.

ISLAND OF OAHU

Oahu, (Fig. 15.30), the most populated island of the group, consists of two deeply eroded volcanic masses, Koolau to the east and Waianae to the west, which are elongated in a northwest-southeast direction and are connected by a low plateau that grades into a lowland to the south. Oahu is, therefore, quite similar to Molokai except for the direction and amount of elongation of the ancient volcanoes.

The very active research carried on by Hawaiian geologists Stearns, Macdonald, C. K. Wentworth, and many others, has provided a wealth of information concerning the geological history of Oahu. At first, there were two separate volcanic islands, but these grew together by banking of the lava flows from the Koolau Volcano against the older Waianae lavas. Subsequently, after vulcanism had stopped, alluvial fans were built from the debris eroded from the volcanoes, and these formed lowlands marginal to the intermontane plateau. Coral reefs developed in the shallow bordering waters; and these reefs grew upward as the island sank, making a thick mass of coral at the margins, especially in the southwestern and northernmost points. Alluvium was also deposited inside the reefs, keeping pace with the subsidence.

Several hundred thousand years ago, vulcanism resumed with two important effects. Some of the canyons that had been eroded into the volcanic slopes were partially filled by new lava flows, and some volcanic cones were built along the southeast coast. The latter are principally tuff cones due to explosive eruptions, and include Honolulu's famous Diamond Head.

Changes of level, both uplift and depression, appear to have affected the coasts of the island during the Pleistocene and postglacial. These warping activities are interwoven with the effects of the changing sea levels of the glacial stages. Elevated reefs are far more common on Oahu than on any of the other islands. Also, in Oahu, drowning of river valleys is more clearly indicated. The net result of the level changes and continued erosion has been to leave two mountain masses, with summits up to 4,025 feet in the Waianae Mountains and 3,105 feet in the Koolau Range.

Coral reefs are well developed around most of the coast of Oahu, particularly on the south and east sides. Most of these reefs are dead, but a flourishing live reef exists in Kaneohe Bay.

The climate of Oahu is greatly influenced by the trade winds. The rainfall is high along the northeast coast, amounting to 35 to 50 inches per year, and very low on the west coast, less than 20 inches. The densely populated areas along the coast from Honolulu to Pearl Harbor have low rainfall except for rather frequent light showers. The trade-wind side of the island is almost always comfortably cool, even in summer; whereas the west coast can be unpleasantly hot.

Tsunamis have had only minor effects on the south coast and none at Pearl Harbor. The north coast was severely hit by both the 1946 and 1957 waves, although the coral reefs, especially at Kaneohe Bay, greatly reduced the wave effects.

HONOLULU–PEARL HARBOR AREA, OAHU
[Figs. 15.31 and 15.32]   Before World War II, it was a heart-warming experience to round Diamond Head, look in at the sparkling beaches of Waikiki and up at the precipitous heavily vegetated mountains in the background of the city of Honolulu. Few visitors could leave the lovely place without shedding tears as they sailed past Diamond Head and threw their leis into the sea to guarantee a return visit. Now, visitors whisk by in 600-mile-an-hour jets, and the change is appalling. Instead of a peaceful town, Honolulu has become a metropolis (Fig. 15.31) with scores of high-rise hotels and apartments all along the waterfront. The lovely green slopes above the city are cut up into housing developments, and the traffic on the streets is getting impossible. Even the formerly clear seas that lap onto the shores at Honolulu are becoming murky and polluted.

The lowlands around Honolulu and Pearl Harbor are underlain by coral reefs on the outer borders intermixed with beach sands. Alluvium is found farther inland toward the mountains, and this is mixed with pyroclastics coming from the most recent eruptions. Rising above the lowland is a series of steep-sided volcanic cones, including Diamond Head to the east, the Punch Bowl near the center of Honolulu, and Aliamanu Crater just east of Pearl Harbor. Of these, only Diamond Head comes to the coast. Here, the outward-curving shore (Fig. 15.31) is largely the result of the growth of the cone, slightly modified by wave erosion; but it now is protected due to the growth of a fringing coral reef and local seawalls.

15.31 Honolulu at the southwestern base of the Koolau Range (B), showing Diamond Head, an eroded volcano with a large crater and the famous Waikiki Beach (C). A short distance offshore there are coral reefs. Photo taken during low wave conditions. U.S. Coast and Geodetic Survey, 1960.

Waikiki was originally a barrier beach built at the outer margin of a swampy lagoon by the waves that sweep around Diamond Head and drive reef sand toward the northwest. Various man-made structures were superposed on the beach, including Kalahaua Avenue and the beach hotels, such as the Royal Hawaiian. Seawalls were constructed outside these hotels to protect them. In some cases, these walls were built at times of low waves when the beaches were seasonally prograded. Then later, seasonal cutting began to remove all of the sand beyond portions of the seawalls so that no beach was left along part of the shore. This caused much complaint, and therefore sand has been introduced from other wider beaches, but there are still times when the name "beach" for Waikiki seems inappropriate.

Outside Waikiki Beach, the coral reef, which extends somewhat discontinuously along the shore as far as the entrance to Pearl Harbor, is principally a dead reef. Some of it has been killed in recent years, perhaps in part by water pollution; and many of the remaining live corals have been collected by swimmers. The area is now a poor place for skin divers, although man has not affected the beautiful surf, which comes in almost continuously after being refracted around the east end of the island. When the surf is large well out from shore, it has curling breakers up to 20 feet or more in height but at decreasing heights approaching the beach.

Honolulu Harbor is entered through a natural break in the reef, like Kaunakakai. The break has been enlarged and deepened artificially. On the west side of Honolulu, Sand Island was originally an islet of sand on the old barrier reef but has been greatly changed by the development of Honolulu Harbor. The reef west of the harbor has been similarly channeled, partly for seaplane landings and partly for boats. Considerable ground consists of fill, part of it for the airfields.

Pearl Harbor was so named because a few pearls were found in the bay here in the nineteenth century. It can be compared with Drakes Estero in California (Fig. 11.33). Both are branching drowned river valleys in areas where such features are unusual. The different arms at Pearl Harbor are referred to as West, Middle, and East Loch. According to Stearns, the harbor is one of the results of the great submergence of Oahu, which continued for millions of years. Rivers coming largely from the Koolau Range cut small canyons into the southern part of Schofield Plateau. These canyons were submerged partly by the rise of sea level at the end of the last glacial stage. Fossils show that during the late Pleistocene high sea-level stand (called by Stearns the 25-foot level), oysters up to a foot in diameter were living in what is now Waipio Peninsula, an arm of land extending into Pearl Harbor.

When the report of the April 1, 1946, tsunami reached Pearl Harbor, it was at first thought to be just another April Fool joke. Few saw any effects in the harbor, but tide gauges showed an 18-inch fluctuation. Honolulu did not fare quite so well. The waves swept up the Alawai Canal (A in Fig. 15.31), a modified remnant of the old lagoon, and damaged some of the boats. It also crossed Kalakaua Avenue at Kahio Beach, but the beach was not used much at that time. In 1960, the waves coming from South America rose as much as 9 feet at Waikiki, and water was swept into the basements of many hotels and homes along the shore. In 1946, on the east side of Diamond Head, the water reached as high as 12 feet but came in very gently, causing little damage. The reason why this highly populated area is so free from tsunami destruction is that it is protected from north waves by the headlands to the east and from the South American waves by the intervening islands (Fig. 15.1).

THE WEST SIDE OF OAHU
This coast extends for 23 miles with only broadly curving promontories and indentations. There are no natural harbors; but Waianae, near the middle of the coast, has a jetty that allows small-boat anchorage. To the south, the straight shore borders the coastal plain for 5 miles, then abuts against the southern end of the

15.32 Broad beach flanked by coastal dunes along west coast of Oahu. Photo by Shepard, 1962.

Waianae Range; and, from there north to Kaena Point, there is an alternation of mountain spurs from the Waianae and intervening broad trough-shaped valleys. Some of the widest beaches of Oahu are located along this coast (Fig. 15.32), but elsewhere the sand has become consolidated into beachrock. The sands are predominantly calcareous material and rarely have more than 10 percent of volcanic products, except in a small beach near the north end of this coast. Most of the sand comes from the small offshore coral reef and some from the erosion of raised reefs along the coast. The longest and widest beaches are, as would be expected, adjacent to the trough-shaped valleys of the Waianae Range.

The waves are unusually small along the west coast, as it is protected from the northeast trades. Swimming is generally good along these beaches, but seas occasionally build up when there is a Kona storm with winds from the southwest. Winter storms coming from the north and northwest also cause sizable breakers. This high surf develops, especially near Makua to the north, where the diagonal approach allows long rides, making it popular with surfers.

None of the four recent tsunamis were very destructive to the west coast. The 1946 tsunami had

15.33 Large wind waves entering Waimae Bay, northwest coast of Oahu, one of the best surfing areas in the world. Photo courtesy of Ron Church.

the highest waves but did little damage, although a few houses were wrecked on a low terrace near Waianae. Wave heights were much greater than along the south coast; and 34 feet was measured at the small projection just north of Makua, 4 miles from Kaena Point. After the waves, swimmers at Makua discovered a short distance from shore a shallow bar that had not been there previously.

NORTHWEST COAST, OAHU [Figs. 15.33 through 15.37; 2.10a]   The 23-mile concave coast between Kaena and Kahuka Points, respectively the northwest and north points of the island, include a hilly area at the northwest ends of both Waianae and the Koolau volcanic massifs and the gently sloping northwest terminus of the intermontane lowland. It is notable that no drowned river valley occurs on

the north side of the lowland, like Pearl Harbor on the south side. Instead, the small Kaiaka and Waialua Bays slightly indent the relatively straight coast. Both of these bays have small submarine valleys heading into them. Toward Kahuku Point, there are two other small bays, Waimea and Kawela.

In the center of the lowland, Haleiwa and Waialua are towns supported by small businesses and by sugar plantations. One result of the industries has been to pollute the ocean water. The murkiness is probably due to discharge from the cane washer at the sugar factory. At Waimea Bay and Sunset Beach, 2 miles to the northwest, the winter storms from the Gulf of Alaska provide some of the best surfing in the world. Figure 15.33 shows some large waves coming into Waimea Bay. Surfers ride on the edge of the breaker to the right but have to be careful not to be carried to the left by the strong set shown by foam lines, or they hit the rocks on the far side of the bay. This hazard has caused several deaths.

Coral reefs flank a portion of the northwest coast. The relation between the wave heights during the 1946 tsunami and the coral development between Kaena Point and Waialua Bay is striking (Fig. 15.34). Where the reefs are well developed near Waialua, the heights were only 8 to 11 feet. Where the reefs narrow, 2 miles to the west, the water rose to 16 feet, then dropped farther west with another widening of the reef. The water rose again to 30 feet or more where the reef stops and finally attained 35 feet at Kaena Point, partly due to convergence.

Shepard was living in a rented cottage along the waterfront near Kawela Bay, 2 miles southwest of Kahuku Point, during the 1946 tsunami. The following is a narrative of his experiences:

I was awakened at 6:30 in the morning by a hissing noise that sounded as if hundreds of locomotives were blowing off steam. I looked out in time to see the water lapping up around the edge of our house, rising 14 feet above its normal level. Grabbing my camera instead of clothes, I rushed out to take photographs. My wife and I watched the rapid recession of the water exposing the narrow reef in front of the house and stranding large numbers of fish. A few minutes later, we saw the water build up at the edge of the reef and move shoreward as a great breaking wave (Fig. 15.35). Because the wave looked very threatening, we dashed in back of the house, getting there just in time to hear the water reach the front porch and smash in all of the glass at the front. As the water swept around the house and into the cane field, we saw our refrigerator carried past us and deposited right side up, eggs unbroken.

Water swept down the escape road to our right, leaving us no chance to get out by car. The neighbors' house, which was vacant at the time, had been completely torn apart, but the back portion of our house still stood, thanks probably to the casuarina (ironwood) trees growing along the edge of the berm in front.

As soon as the second wave had started to retreat, we ran along the beach ridge to our left, and then through the cane field by path to the main road, arriving there just ahead of the third wave.

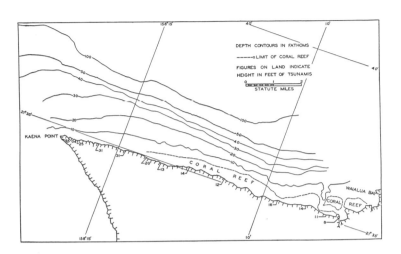

15.34 Relation of coral reefs along the northwest coast of Oahu to heights of 1946 tsunami. From Shepard, Macdonald, and Cox (1950).

15.35 The second great wave of the 1946 tsunami roaring into shore near Kawela Bay, west of north tip of Oahu. Photo by Shepard, April 1, 1946.

We found quite a group on the road. The house of one family living at the edge of Kawela Bay had been carried bodily into the cane field and dropped without the wave having done much damage (Fig. 15.36, arrow). In fact, their breakfast was still cooking when they were set down. Other unoccupied houses did not fare so well. Some of them were swept into a small pond (A), and others out into the bay by the retreat of the second wave.

15.36 Results of 1946 tsunami at Kawela Bay. Note wrecked houses in fish pond (A) and house carried intact into sugar cane field (arrow). U.S. Navy, 1946.

We watched three or four more waves come into Kawela Bay at intervals (shown later by tide gauge records) of fifteen minutes. They had steep fronts, looking very much like the tidal bore that comes up the Bay of Fundy. Just before the eighth wave, I decided that the excitement was abating and ran back to the house to try to rescue some effects, particularly necessary as we were in pajamas and raincoats. Just as I arrived, a wave that must have been the largest of the set came roaring in, and I had to run for a tree and climb it as the water surged beneath me. I hung on swaying back and forth as the water roared by into the cane field.

That was the end of the adventure, and we gradually got what we could rescue of our possessions, but had to leave behind quantities of notes and the beginning of a new book, *Submarine Geology*, which had been scattered in the cane field. We were given wonderfully hospitable treatment by new and old friends whom we shall never forget. After a few days, I got in touch with Gordon Macdonald, of the U.S. Geological Survey, and Doak Cox, the geologist of Hawaiian Planters Association, and together we started a program of investigating the tsunami effects around the different islands.

In 1946, at Kahuku Point, the waves rose to 24 feet and drove inland across a dune belt to the Kahuku Air Force Station, where they caused extensive flooding of barracks and runways (Fig. 15.37) but caused no casualties. Along this north and northwest coast, the 1957 waves were almost as high as those in 1946. However, it should be noted that the Harold

15.37 The Air Force Station at Kahuku Point, showing damage to barracks and runways by 1946 tsunami. U.S. Navy, 1946.

Palmer house, in which the Shepards were living in 1946, had been rebuilt and received no damage in 1957. This variability seems to be characteristic of tsunamis. They shift their emphasis on each occasion, even when they come from the same source and with similar intensity.

Raised coral reefs along the northwest coast of Oahu are more common than anywhere else on the islands. As mentioned previously, they were investigated to determine their age. Shells collected by Macdonald and Shepard from the coral reef that is 5 feet above sea level at Haleiwa showed ages of approximately 22,000 and 24,000 B.C. Other shells from the 12-foot algal reef, just northwest of Waimea Bay, gave ages around 32,000 years. Later studies, partly by H. H. Veeh, have shown that slightly elevated reefs at Kahuku Point are much older, perhaps

100,000 years. It is now evident that the sea stood above its present level along the north coast of Oahu, partly at times when the worldwide sea level was greatly lowered, due to the extraction of water to form the great continental glaciers. Therefore it can now be concluded that Oahu has been unstable, and that the raised reefs are due more to earth movements than to sea level fluctuations of the glacial period.

THE PALI COAST OF NORTHEAST OAHU AND KANEOHE BAY [Figs. 15.38, 15.39 and 15.40]   Before the drilling of the tunnels through the Koolau Range in 1960, the trip from Honolulu to Kaneohe Bay, on the windward side, wound up the mountains until through a gap one suddenly got a breathtaking view down the other side, showing the great cliff, called the Pali, where in 1798 King Ka-

15.38 Rock promontories of eolianite near Laie Bay, northern Oahu. U.S. Navy, 1946.

mahameha I destroyed his enemies by driving them over the escarpment. This cliff, largely the result of erosion, extends almost all along the 40-mile northeast side of the island. It has nearly vertical drops of more than 1,000 feet and is similar to the cliffs on the north side of Molokai, but in Oahu there is a lowland a mile or two wide along the base of the cliffs in most places. Some large and many small coastal communities have been built on this lowland, including Kaneohe, Kailua, and Waimanalo. On northeastern Oahu, the coast is not as straight as on the other sides. A number of promontories, notably the rock spurs, project vertically from the shore near Laie (Fig. 15.38) and Mokapu Peninsula, which juts out 5 miles, forming the south bastion of Kaneohe Bay. (Fig. 15.40).

The seas break with great force on the points near Laie. These points are made of eolianite, a consolidated dune sand, which is undergoing active erosion. A picture taken in 1946 just before the great tsunami waves, showed only a slight indication of a cave cutting through the island, which was clearly visible in 1961 (A in Fig. 15.39).

The most flourishing coral reefs in the Hawaiian Islands are found along this coast. Many of the Hawaiian reefs are mostly dead; but the reef in Kaneohe Bay (Fig. 15.40) is flourishing, making Mokuoloe

15.39 An arch (A) through an offshore island near Laie, Oahu. Photo by Shepard, 1961.

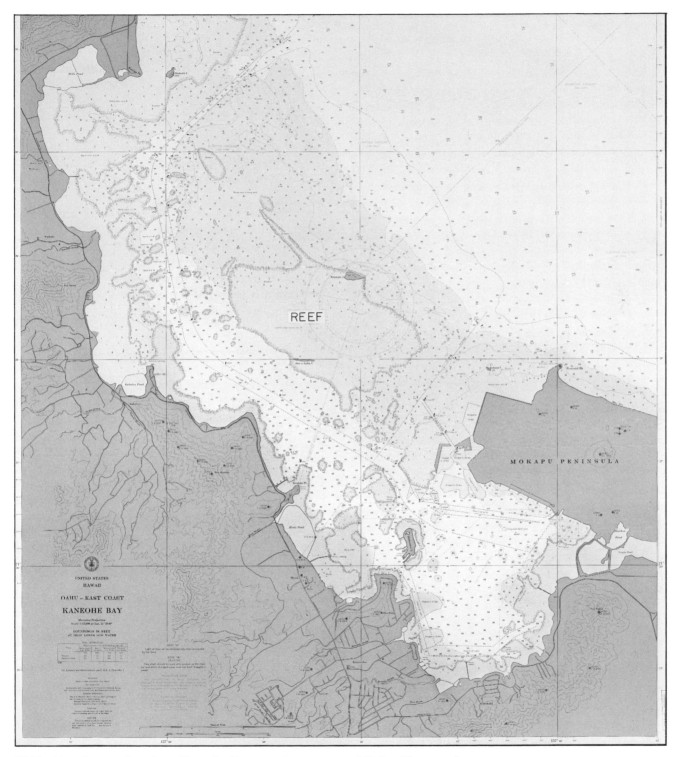

15.40 Growing coral reefs at Kaneohe Bay, northeast coast of Oahu. These reefs greatly reduced the runup of the various recent tsunamis that have hit Oahu. Channel into bay shown by dashed lines. U.S. Coast and Geodetic Survey Chart 4134, 1960.

VOLCANIC COASTS: HAWAII

15.41 Scarps cut by the 1946 tsunami in coastal dunes at Makapuu Bay at height of 37 feet above sea level, southeast Oahu. Photo by Shepard, 1946.

Island in the bay a highly appropriate place for the University of Hawaii's Marine Laboratory. This reef extends seaward for more than 2 miles but has a narrow channel parallel to the coast inside the widest part. The inner channel has to be traversed by boats with care as there are many small patch reefs. The channel swings seaward near the north end of the bay, forming an outlet to the ocean. The channel has been deepened and straightened artificially. While one might expect the channel to be well protected by reefs, small-boat operators must bear in mind that tremendous gusts of wind come down from Pali on many occasions, making the water in the channel extremely rough with short steep waves. The currents measured by Shepard during such gusts proved sufficiently powerful to transport quantities of sediment out through the passageway to the open sea.

The beaches along the northeast coast are predominantly calcareous, with the exception of sand high in volcanics at the head of Kahana Bay, a partly filled estuary north of Kaneohe. A number of narrow beaches lie inside the coral reef south of Kahuku. The beach at Kailua is used extensively for swimming. Just to the south, Lanikai Beach, according to Campbell and Moberly, was being eroded in 1964 at the northwest end and was growing at the southeast end, just the reverse of an earlier trend. Near the south of this coast, Waimanalo has the longest continuous beach in Oahu, 3.5 miles. This calcareous beach shows little seasonal change. It is bordered inland by a long line of dunes.

The 1946 tsunami showed great variation in wave lengths along the northeast coast. Inside the coral reef at Kaneohe Bay, the water rose only a foot above normal high tide. Here, as at Pearl Harbor, residents knew of the waves only if they were listening to their radios. At the same time, a few miles away on the Mokapu Peninsula, water rushed up, producing swaths in the vegetation to heights of 22 feet. Inside the coral reef at Kaneohe Bay, similar low heights were characteristic of succeeding large tsunamis. The greatest heights on the northeast coast in 1946 were in Makapuu Cove, at the south end. Here, notches were cut into the dunes to a height of 37 feet (Fig. 15.41).

SOUTHEAST COAST, OAHU   The 5-mile stretch from Makapuu Head to Koko Head, all within easy reach of Honolulu, contains many of the island's tourist attractions. At the Blow Hole (A in Fig. 15.42[1]), just north of Hanauma Bay, water shoots up, probably through a joint crack, and is activated by the large surf of the trade winds. Nearby Koko Crater (B) is the easternmost of the Pleistocene cones on Oahu. Hanauma Bay (C) is in the remnant of another Pleistocene crater, Koko Head, one side having collapsed. A coral reef has grown across the head of the bay. A 5-foot terrace extends around the northeast side of Hanauma Bay. This was cut by the waves into the volcanic tuff when the sea stood at a slightly higher level. The age of this terrace remains uncertain, as it does not contain the shells that allowed dating of the coral reef terraces on the north side of the island.

To the west of Koko Head, the indented coast is protected by a barrier beach that extends across Kuapa Pond (D in Fig. 15.42) and then farther west by a shallow coral reef that continues all the way to Diamond Head. Kuapa Pond is a drowned river valley, like Pearl Harbor, but does not have the dendritic branches.

[1] Figure 15.42 is a stereo pair, and can be seen in three dimensions with a lens stereoscope.

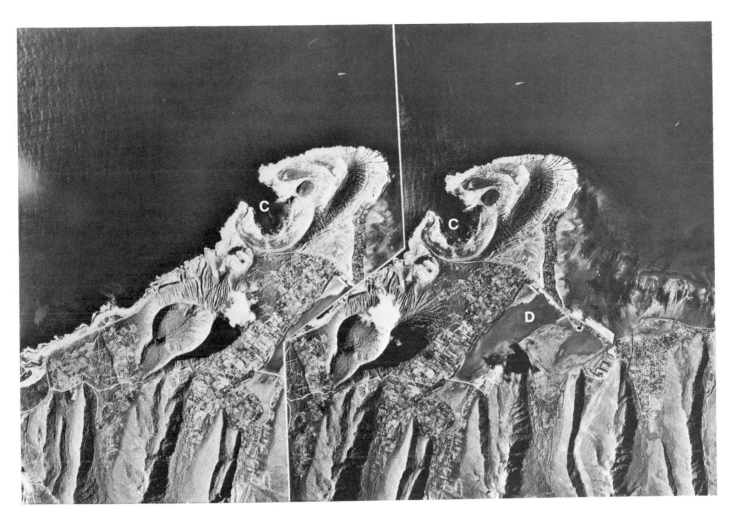

15.42 Koko Head, a chain of coastal volcanic cones showing the Blow Hole (A) and Hanauma Bay (C), the crater of an eroded volcano breached collapse of one side. A stereogram prepared from U.S. Coast and Geodetic Survey 1960 photos by the University of Illinois Committee on Aerial Photography. May be seen in three dimensions with a lens stereoscope.

The 1946 tsunami came around Makapuu Head and rose as much as 31 feet near the Blow Hole. At Kaloko, 2 miles to the east, the water reached only 15 feet, but a number of houses had been built on the low ground landward of the beach in this area. The waves swept them all away, and no further real estate development has followed. The water came in here so gently that one of the residents was able to wade through it carrying above his head a valuable picture from his home. At Hanauma Bay, the water, impeded by the coral reef, rose 14 feet. West of Koko

Head, the reef partially protected the houses on the low ground inside, but these homes were somewhat damaged by the low waves that crossed the narrow reefs that front the shore.

ISLAND OF KAUAI

Kauai (Fig. 15.43), the northwesternmost of the large islands, was the first visited by a white man. Captain Cook landed in Waimea in 1778; and 10

VOLCANIC COASTS: HAWAII

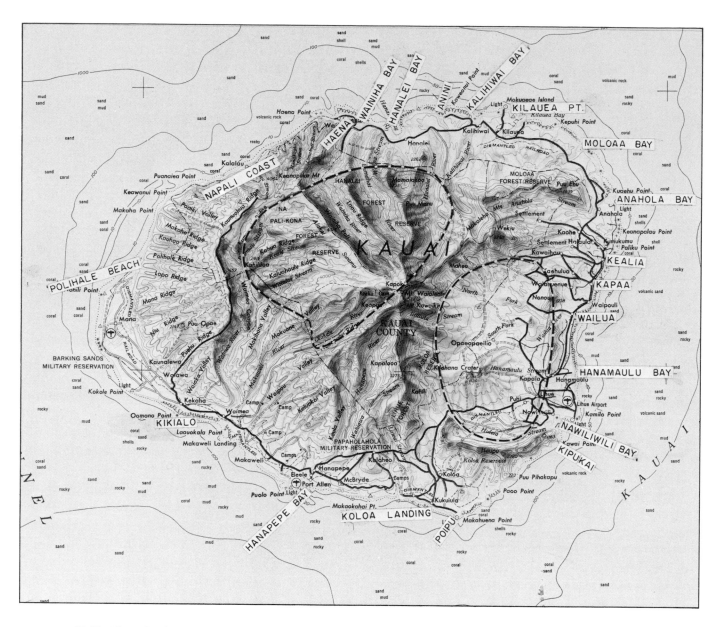

15.43 The island of Kauai showing localities described. Dashed lines show large collapse calderas. The volcanoes on Kauai are older and more dissected than those on the other islands. U.S. Geological Survey, Hawaiian Map NF 4–6, 1946.

years later his former lieutenant, Captain Vancouver, revisited the island. A kingdom of Kauai existed at this time and continued until 1810, when the island voluntarily became a vassalage of the powerful Kamahameha I.

The geology of Kauai has been best described by Macdonald, Davis, and Cox. Kauai differs from all the other large Hawaiian Islands in that it was built by the eruptions of only one volcano. As a result, Kauai is essentially a round island with an average diameter of 23 miles. The volcano has long been dormant, and erosion has cut deeply into the volcanic core. Many changes have occurred along the coast due to erosion on the north and east sides and deposition on the west. Toward the end of the volcanic eruptions that built the island, the summit of the mountain collapsed, leaving the largest caldera in the Hawaiian Islands (dashed line in Fig. 15.43). Later, another collapse on the eastern flank of the mountain further complicated the topography. After a long period of canyon erosion and cliff cutting, especially pronounced on the north side, there was a renewal of vulcanism coming from several vents scattered over the island, except on the west side. These produced cinder cones, now greatly eroded; and a few valleys were filled with lava flows. Also the old volcano was partly rebuilt. Like Oahu, Kauai has had a complicated history of coastal warping, and has evidence both of higher stands of the sea and of considerable submergence.

Kauai is rightly called "the garden island" because of the luxuriant vegetation, especially flowers, which covers all except the semiarid coast on the west side. The rainfall is the highest of any of the islands, ranging from 466 inches per year on Mt. Waialeale to 19 inches at Waimea, in the middle of the southwest coast. On one occasion, a 600-inch rain gauge on the summit of Waialeale overflowed, making a record that is exceeded only by one year at a station on the south side of the Himalayas. The mean rainfall at Waialeale is the greatest in the world. All along the north coast, the rainfall ranges from about 50 to 70 inches per year; and, along the east and southeast coasts it averages about 40 inches. The high rainfall on Waialeale accounts for the large Alakai Swamp in the flat caldera floor just west of the summit. This swamp provides the drainage for the principal source of the two largest rivers on the south side of the island, Waimea and Hanapepe, both of which have cut huge canyons into the south slope. It is only these two rivers that supply sufficient volcanic sand to produce black sand beaches at and near their mouths. Elsewhere, the beach sands, as described by Inman, Gayman, and Cox, and by Moberly, are predominantly calcareous, with short stretches that are high in volcanic sand near the mouths of a few streams. The beaches of Kauai include the widest and most extensive in all the islands.

The best development of coral reefs in Kauai is off the middle of the north coast. Additional reefs extend along part of the east coast and are developed locally on the southeast. It is notable that the westward termination of the reefs along the north coast

15.44 Nawiliwili Bay, southeast Kauai, a drowned valley, the best harbor on Kauai. Lihue (A) is the principal Kauai city. Extensive sugar plantations cover the low coastal terrace between Lihue and the airport. The cliffs of Haupu Mountain (D) are remnants of an old eroded volcano. U.S. Department of Agriculture, 1965.

occurs at the point where the mountains come to the sea, and the cliffed Napali Coast has defied road construction.

The waves of 1957 caused more destruction along parts of the north coast than those in 1946. Because of the circular coast of Kauai, the waves in each of the recent tsunamis bent around the island and met, reinforcing each other on the protected side.

NAWILIWILI BAY AND THE LIHUE AREA, KAUAI [Fig. 15.44]   Kauai has no large cities, but the largest community, Lihue (A), is located on the southeast side. The nearby port at Nawiliwili is the best harbor in the island. Until about 1950, daily passenger steamers from Oahu docked in the inner

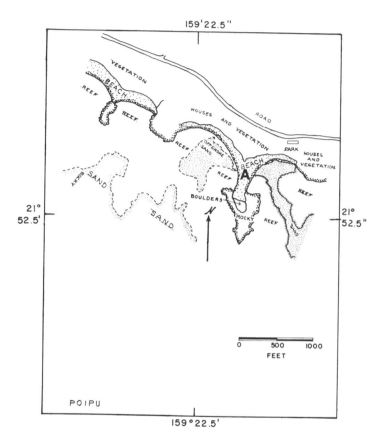

15.45 Poipu Beach (A), southern Kauai, on a tombolo between two coves, adjoins submerged reefs. Bottom character indicated. From J. F. Campbell, in Moberly *et al.* (1963).

MAKAHUENA POINT TO KUKUIULA BAY, SOUTH KAUAI Between Nawiliwili Bay and Makahuena Point, the rugged coast has much of beauty and includes three fine pocket beaches at Kipukai. Makahuena is the south point of the island; and, according to Macdonald, Davis, and Cox, it protrudes as the result of the building of a series of spatter cones by the late phase of vulcanism. Just east of the point, a series of sand dunes has been consolidated and extends below sea level, having been formed when the sea was lower than at present.

At Poipu, a few miles west of the point, two coves are separated by a tombolo (Fig. 15.45). The eastern cove that adjoins a public park has a shallow bay fronted by a slightly submerged reef. Waves coming in across this reef provide good surfing, and under small wave conditions the shallow water on the inside is a safe place for beginners to look at fish through face plates. After a severe westerly storm in January 1963, the beach was built up on the east side by sand carried in across the tombolo. The other cove, on the west side of the tombolo, has deeper water and is protected outside by a deeper reef. A great variety of colorful fish can be seen here.

Extending east from Kukuiula Bay, there is a rock bench a few feet above high tide with wave-cut stacks rising above it. It is about the same height as the bench at Hanauma Bay in Oahu and thus may represent a higher sea level; but in view of the accumulating evidence of the instability of these volcanic islands, it seems more likely that the height is a coincidence. The bench has one of the tourist attractions of the island, another Spouting Horn, formed by a lava tube through which water erupts like a geyser during large wave conditions.

PORT ALLEN TO WAIMEA, SOUTHWEST KAUAI The 6-mile coastal belt between Port Allen and Waimea includes one of the population centers in the island, Hanapepe Bay at the site of Port Allen, which is a well-protected harbor, like Nawiliwili. This coastal indentation was originally a long-armed estuary that extended well up the Hanapepe Valley, but alluvium from the river has filled all but the present rounded bay. A half-mile-long beach forms a barrier across most of the mouth of the Hanapepe River. A medium-grain-sized volcanic sand of the beach comes from the river. The beach was about 70 feet wide when visited by Shepard in 1962; but, a year later,

harbor inside the breakwater. Now only occasional tour liners, freight steamers, and fishing boats use this dock. Nawiliwili Bay is a drowned river valley cut when the sea stood lower than at present. Directly after drowning, the bay had several arms; but, unlike Pearl Harbor, all except one of these have been largely filled with alluvium. The one remaining head extends west into the drowned mouth of Huleia Stream. According to J. F. Campbell, the calcareous beach (B) in the cove at the Kauai Surf Hotel varies about 50 feet in width during the year, being cut back in winter. The 1946 tsunami rose to a height of 14 feet in the cove (C) and destroyed several small houses but did not damage the port inside the jetty, although one boat was washed ashore farther up the harbor.

Campbell found that it had been largely eroded back to the boulder rampart, except at the mouth of the river where a pocket of sand remained.

Volcanic sand is also found at the mouth of the Waimea River, 7 miles west of Hanapepe River. Captain Cook landed here in 1778, and later the Russians built a small fort, still in existence. This river is one of the largest in the Hawaiian Islands and drains the most majestic canyon, one that is often compared with the Grand Canyon. The river has filled an old estuary, so now there is no bay at its mouth comparable to those at Nawiliwili and Hanapepe. The black volcanic sand from the Waimea River dominates the beaches for 3 miles to the west, as far as Kekaha. However, the building of jetties for a small-boat harbor at Kikialo, in the middle of the stretch, has so restricted the western sand drift that the beaches beyond this point will probably lose their black color and may also retreat.

15.46 A low plain of marine deposition, near Kekaha, southwestern Kauai. Along the coast are prograding beach (dune) ridges (B). Inland, most of the plain is used for sugar plantations. One to two miles inland from the coast is a line of abandoned sea cliffs (A, A′). The streaks in the ocean are due to runoff waste from sugar mills. U.S. Department of Agriculture, 1965.

VOLCANIC COASTS: HAWAII

15.47 Polihale Beach, the widest in the Hawaiian Islands, near Nohili Point, western Kauai, showing west end of the Napali Coast in the background. Photo by Shepard, 1962.

KEKAHA TO BARKING SANDS, WEST KAUAI [Figs. 15.46 and 15.47]

The western coast of Kauai is unique in the Hawaiian Islands in consisting of a broad plain, largely due to marine deposition. One to two miles in from the present coast there is a row of definite cliffs that were cut at least 100 feet below present sea level. After the cutting, as the sea was rising there must have been a diminution of westerly storms that allowed the waves to build out the plain as a combined effect of the currents flowing northwest from the south coast and southwest from the Napali Coast. Dune and beach ridges were formed at this time. The beaches along this coastal plain are very largely calcareous, showing that the sources of volcanic sand from the Waimea River and from the many canyons of the Napali Coast are not important. The abundant organisms living in the shallow water off the coast and the patches of coral reef supply the bulk of the material. Along the coast, the loose sand alternates with beachrock, very much like the beaches of western Oahu.

The points near the west end of the island are small cuspate forelands (Fig. 15.46). In from the shore, beach ridges and troughs (B) are somewhat comparable to those inside the cuspate forelands along the Florida coast. Dunes (C) behind the beach are well developed between Nohili Point and the cliffs of the Napali Coast. These dunes rise to heights of about 100 feet, and are characterized by the creaking noise made when one walks over them, giving them the name of Barking Sands. The 3-mile Polihale Beach (Fig. 15.47), north of Nohili Point, is hundreds of feet wide, the widest in the islands. The intense midday heat along this leeward coast makes crossing the beach an unpleasant ordeal. Campbell found that the beach varies in width almost 200 feet, being widest during the summer.[2] Here, during the 1946 tsunami, the water rose 38 feet but caused little damage because of the lack of habitation.

NAPALI COAST, NORTHWEST KAUAI [Figs. 15.48, 15.49, and 15.50]

The 14 miles of virtually impassable cliffs between the end of the road at Polihale Beach and Haena are a memorable and thrilling sight, whether viewed from the sea, which is generally rough; from the air, in a nerve-wracking flight by helicopter; or from the high narrow trail cut into the precipitous cliffs for 6 miles west of Haena. The trail is dangerous during high winds, because gusts could easily blow a hiker over the edge. The cliffs come right down to the water along most of the coast (Fig. 15.48), but there are narrow volcanic beaches at the mouths of several of the canyons. Wave erosion has cut hanging valleys at the mouths of many of the canyons, but the largest stream, Kalalau, has built a fan out into the ocean at the mouth of its canyon. This fan is now partly dissected by wave erosion (Fig. 15.49).

The Napali Coast is clearly a product of wave erosion, like the cliffed north coast of Molokai and the north coast of Kohala Volcano in Hawaii. The cliffs are a continuation of those along the west coast of the island, which have been separated from the ocean by the recent formation of a coastal plain. The sea floor outside the cliffs is of a different character at Keawanui Point, where the cliffs change direction from north-northeast to northeast (Fig. 15.43). Off the former is a 6-mile-wide continental shelf that has a submerged bar 60 feet deep, 3 miles out from the coast. This bar appears to have been formed as a barrier island when it is thought that the sea stood for some time at the 60-foot level as a pause during

[2] In early December 1969, the largest storm waves on record hit the northern and western shores of the Hawaiian Islands. At this time, the wide Polihale Beach was almost entirely cut away, exposing bedrock along the shore.

15.49 Kalalau Canyon, Napali Coast, showing an alluvial fan at mouth of canyon that has been eroded by waves. Narrow beach of volcanic sand along part of the shore. Photo by Shepard, 1962.

15.48 East end of the rugged Napali Coast of northern Kauai, accessible only by foot trail. Cliffs are largely the result of wave erosion of the north flank of Waialeale Volcano. Photo by Shepard, 1950.

the postglacial rise. Along the northeast-trending coast, the shelf is narrowed to 2 miles; and submarine canyons extend in toward several of the large land canyons. The deep indentations of the continental slope, partly due to these canyons, apparently had an important effect on the height to which the 1946 tsunami rose along this coast. Where measured by the U.S. Geological Survey at three points, the water did not rise above 10 feet. This is another illustration of the way in which submarine canyons deflect wave energy to either side, as was observed in the discussion of the California coast (p. 264). Another interesting wave phenomenon along the Napali Coast is the huge water spouts that develop where a wave reflected from the precipitous coast encounters the next incoming breaker. While flying at a 100-foot level in a helicopter along the Napali Coast, Shepard saw one of these waves rise higher than the aircraft (Fig. 15.50).

15.50 Wave fountain due to reflected wave encountering the next oncoming wave. Taken from helicopter flying at 100 feet along Napali Coast. Note that fountain rose above the helicopter. Photo by Shepard, 1968.

15.51 Broadly curving Hanalei Bay on the north coast of Kauai. Outlying ridges of Waialeale Volcano in background. Tsunami of 1946 washed over pier (left) but did not greatly damage Hanalei, whereas the 1958 tsunami was very destructive. Photo by Shepard, 1947.

15.52 Pinnacles in eroded lavas near Haena, north Kauai. Dead coral reef in middle ground exposed by low tide. The 1946 tsunami rose to more than 40 feet along this part of the coast. Photo by Shepard, 1950.

HANALEI AND THE NORTH COAST OF KAUAI [Figs. 15.51 through 15.55]   Much of the most impressive coastal scenery in the Hawaiian Islands is just east of the Napali cliffs. This area has been used as the South Sea Islands setting for numerous movies. In *South Pacific*, the plantation (now a modern hotel) was on a bluff from which one can look across the broadly curving Hanalei Bay (Fig. 15.51) to a precipitous mountain range that is an offshoot of Waialeale. After a rain, scores of waterfalls cascade down the sides of these mountains. From this bluff looking to the right, one sees the remarkable pinnacles at the end of the road (Fig. 15.52). Aside from the excessive rain and low clouds, the area has everything the nature lover could desire; and, as of this writing, it is still not overrun with tourists. Swimming at Hanalei and Haena is popular except during large waves of winter storms, but one does not mind these interruptions because of the beauty of the huge breaking seas that come in across the reefs. Under ordinary conditions, swimmers can choose between surf riding where reefs are lacking and swimming over coral reefs where there is a magnificent assortment of tropical fish.

The narrow lowlands, which are suitable for habitation at the base of the mountains in the Haena to Hanalei region, represent a filled lagoon. The bays are the unfilled portions. The circular shape of Hanalei Bay is apparently due to the large waves that come in between the reefs on each side of the bay and preserve a crescent shape in the deltaic deposits of the combined Hanalei, Waioli, and Waipa Rivers. The eastern part of this crescent is a barrier formed along one side of the mouth of the Hanalei River. Just west of the town of Hanalei where the Waipa River comes to the shore, a spit often grows to the east in a few weeks' time, carrying the river water along the shore until it reaches the mouth of the Waioli River. After each flood or large storm, the Waipa breaks straight through to the bay, leaving the longshore channel deserted. Two miles to the west of Hanalei, a similar barrier has formed at the mouth of the Wainiha River. The mouth of this river alternates between the east and the west sides of the bay.

In addition to the wide crescentic beach in Hanalei Bay, two other beaches are found along the north-central coast of Kauai. One (Fig. 15.52) extends for 3 miles, starting at the end of the road and passing

15.53 Lumahai Beach, west of Hanalei Bay, north Kauai. This coarse sand beach, with its succession of berms and steep foreshore, is very unstable and reacts markedly to changing direction of wave approach. Photo by Shepard, 1947.

the small settlement called Haena, terminating at Wainiha Bay. Except for two small zones of open water, this beach is bounded by a wide coral reef with discontinuous channels on the inside. The sand is predominantly calcareous, coming from the reef outside. After large storms and tsunamis, great quantities of shells are washed onto this beach, making it one of the best collecting grounds in the Hawaiian Islands. The beach is unusual in that it extends continuously around several headlands. The other beach, Lumahai, runs straight east from the mouth of the Lumahai River (Fig. 15.53). It has almost no reef growth outside, so that the beach is pounded by the large waves of the open sea. More than half of the sand is volcanic with a large quantity of small olivene crystals that are locally concentrated, giving the sand a green color. The waves have produced a very steep foreshore slope and a series of wide berms, often as

many as five—one inside the other. The beach at Lumahai changes tremendously in width. According to Campbell, in August 1962, the west end was 350 feed wide; in July 1963, it was all gone and the waves were cutting away at the dunes on the inside. During the same period, the width of the east end built out from 135 feet to 435 feet. This shift of sand from one side of the beach to the other was due to changing wave approach, as was described for Boomer Beach in La Jolla, California (Fig. 10.14).

The tsunamis of 1946 and 1957 both caused damage to the north coast of Kauai but were not consistent in the localities damaged. This was brought home to Shepard because prior to 1957 he had spent several vacations in the summer beach residence of Joel B. Cox at Hanalei. In 1946, the waves stopped at the edge of the house; but, in 1957, the water rose far higher in the entire area and completely de-

15.54 Beach scarp near Haena, northern Kauai, cut into a dune ridge by the 1946 tsunami. Note figure of a man for scale. Coral fragments in foreground are remnants of the 1946 waves. Photo by Shepard, 1946.

molished the Cox house. In the small community of Anini, 2 miles east of Hanalei, the water also did little damage in 1946; but, in 1957, the waves destroyed several houses. In 1946, the highest waves were at Haena, where the water reached 45 feet above sea level at the park pavilion inside the break in the reef (Fig. 15.52). A 12-foot-high cliff was cut into the sand dunes inside the beach just east of the park (Fig. 15.54), and huge coral boulders were left on the beach, including the largest one transported by the 1946 waves (Fig. 15.55). During the same time, at Kilauea Lighthouse, 5 miles east of Hanalei, the water also rose to 45 feet, and reached a 38-foot level at Moloaa, at the turn in the coast. All three of these areas of considerable wave heights were inside long submarine ridges that extend out from the coast of Kauai. The waves apparently converged on these ridges, whereas they diverged over the submarine val-

ley off Hanalei. However, in 1957, the effects of this submarine topography were not as evident, indicating that it is rather dangerous to count on factors of this kind in predicting effects of future waves.

EAST COAST, KAUAI—MOLOAA TO HANA-MAULU   The east coast of Kauai north of the Lihue area has a relatively low relief, somewhat comparable to the south coast. As a result, this is an important agricultural region with large pineapple and sugar cane plantations. The ancient kings of Kauai lived at Wailua, halfway down this coast. Here, the narrow estuary of the Wailua River extends for about 2 miles in from the coast. The fern grotto on its south side, reached by boat, is a cave formed by erosion of a weathered talus beneath a dense posterosional lava flow. At the mouth of the estuary, a barrier beach has been built part way across the lagoon; and one of the

15.55 Coral block, 12 feet in diameter, the largest carried in from the reefs by the 1946 tsunami. See camera case for scale. Photo at Haena, north Kauai, by Shepard, 1946.

large hotels was constructed on this barrier, with the lagoon remnant on the landward side serving as a pond for small boats.

Farther north, small square-headed bays are located at Moloaa and Anahola, off the main road. In both of these places, stream deposition has largely filled an old estuary. At Hanamaulu, just north of Lihue (Fig. 15.44), there is another square-headed estuary at the mouth of which a small jetty and pier formerly allowed the docking of ships.

A series of relatively narrow beaches are found along the east coast of Kauai, with the longest and widest at Anahola, Kaelia, Kapaa, and Wailua. These are calcareous sand beaches. The streams that come to the shore at all these places introduce far less volcanic sand than the calcareous sand brought in by waves from the marginal reefs. Even the beach at the head of Hanamaulu Bay (E in Fig. 15.44) is mostly

calcareous despite a considerable stream coming in here and the rather remote source of reef debris.

Along the east coast, the 1946 tsunami showed quite a variation in wave heights. The coral reefs protected several of the communities, notably Kapaa. The most devastating waves were at Moloaa, to the north where the coral reef protects only the south side of the bay. Waves coming in past this reef rose to 32 feet near the coast and completely destroyed a group of native houses, throwing one of them up into a tree. The water swept on up the valley, reaching a 38-foot elevation. The beach was cut back, leaving cliffs in the alluvium at the valley mouth. At Hanamaulu, the water rose only 16 feet but cut back the beach 30 to 40 feet and swept inland for 500 feet. At a funnel-shaped bay just south of Hanamaulu, the water rose 25 feet on each side but 40 feet at the inner end of the funnel, demonstrating why tides rise to such extreme heights at the head of the Bay of Fundy.

Thus we end the tour of the Hawaiian Islands with apologies for having stressed the disasters, which occur from time to time along the shores of these beautiful islands. Because these big waves play the most important part in modification of the island coasts, they could hardly be overlooked in our attempt to consider coastal development. At least, one can venture the opinion that the tsunamis are not as great a hazard here, especially since the installation of the warning system setup in all coastal villages, as are the earthquakes that plague the southern Alaskan coast, where waves also add to the havoc produced by the shaking and the landsliding.

REFERENCES

Cox, D. C., and J. F. Mink, 1963. The tsunami of 23 May, 1960 in the Hawaiian Islands. *Bull. Seismological Soc. Amer.*, vol. 53, pp. 1191–1209.

Daws, Gavan, 1968. *Shoal of Time, A History of the Hawaiian Islands.* The Macmillan Company, New York.

Fraser, G. D., J. P. Eaton, and C. K. Wentworth, 1959. The tsunami of March 9, 1957, on the island of Hawaii. *Bull. Seismological Soc. Amer.*, vol. 49, no. 1, pp. 79–90.

Inman, D. L., W. R. Gayman, and D. C. Cox, 1963. Littoral sedimentary processes on Kauai, a subtropical high island. *Pacific Sci.*, vol. 17, pp. 106–130.

Jaggar, T. A., Jr., 1936. The bombing of Mauna Loa, 1935. *Military Engineer*, vol. 28, pp. 241–245.

———, 1937. The protection of Hilo from coming lava flows. *Volcano Letter*, no. 443.

Kuykendall, R. S., 1957. *The Hawaiian Kingdom*, 3 vols. University of Hawaii Press, Honolulu.

Macdonald, G. A., D. A. Davis, and D. C. Cox, 1960. Geology and groundwater resources of the Island of Kauai, Hawaii. *Hawaii Div. Hydrog. Bull.* 13.

———, and C. K. Wentworth, 1954. The tsunami of November 4, 1952, on the Island of Hawaii. *Bull. Seismological Soc. Amer.*, vol. 44, no. 3, pp. 463–470.

Michener, J. A., 1959. *Hawaii.* Random House, New York.

Moberly, Ralph, Jr., 1968. Loss of Hawaiian littoral sand. *Jour. Sedimentary Petrology*, vol. 38, no. 1, pp. 17–34.

———, and T. K. Chamberlain, 1964. *Hawaiian Beach Systems.* Hawaii Institute of Geophysics, University of Hawaii.

———, with D. C. Cox, T. K. Chamberlain, F. W. McCoy, Jr., and J. F. Campbell, 1963. *Coastal Geology of Hawaii.* Hawaii Institute of Geophysics, University of Hawaii.

Oostdam, B. L., 1965. Age of lava flows on Haleakala, Maui, Hawaii. *Geol. Soc. Amer. Bull.*, vol. 76, no. 3, pp. 393–394.

Shepard, F. P., 1963. *Submarine Geology*, 2d ed. Harper & Row, New York.

————, and R. F. Dill, 1966. *Submarine Canyons and Other Sea Valleys.* Rand McNally & Company, Chicago.

————, G. A. Macdonald, and D. C. Cox, 1950. The tsunami of April 1, 1946. *Bull. Scripps Inst. Oceanography*, Univ. Calif. Press, vol. 5, no. 6, pp. 391–528.

Stearns, H. T., 1966. *Geology of the State of Hawaii.* Pacific Books, Palo Alto, Calif.

————, and G. A. Macdonald, 1942. Geology and ground-water resources of the Island of Maui, Hawaii. *Terr. Hawaii, Div. Hydrog. Bull.* 7.

————, and G. A. Macdonald, 1946. Geology and ground-water resources of the Island of Hawaii. *Terr. Hawaii, Div. Hydrog. Bull.* 9.

————, and G. A. Macdonald, 1947. Geology and ground-water resources of the Island of Molokai, Hawaii. *Terr. Hawaii, Div. Hydrog. Bull.* 11.

————, and K. N. Vaksvik, 1935. Geology and ground-water resources of the Island of Oahu. *Terr. Hawaii, Div. Hydrog. Bull.* 4.

Veeh, H. Herbert, 1966. Th^{230}/U^{238} and U^{234}/U^{238} ages of Pleistocene high sea level stand. *Jour. Geophysical Res.*, vol. 71, no. 14, pp. 3379–3386.

Summary and Conclusions

16   In the preceding chapters we have followed the coasts of the United States in a clockwise direction from Maine to the state of Washington, then in the same direction around Alaska, and around each of the five large islands of Hawaii. As we proceeded we have discussed the general character of the coasts in the various areas with brief mention of the geological history that led to their development into their present form. We have also emphasized the changes that have taken place along these coasts since the making of the earliest maps and charts and have made use of numerous aerial photographs to look for changes. As many as ten dates of rephotographing the same coast from the air during the past 30 years have made this information particularly helpful. This method is most effective on low coasts where sand islands and broad sand beaches are changed radically in character by the waves of great storms. The changes of cliffed coasts are less easy to determine, although information is available from some accurate surveys. Also, comparing old photographs with those of today has given some idea of the rate at which coasts are retreating under wave attack.

The mass of material that is available is so great that we would have had to spend decades before getting it all digested and completely synthesized. Because such time has not been available for either of us to devote to this work, we have attempted in this volume to present the facts as well as possible and to draw tentative conclusions, with the realization that some or even many of them may prove erroneous. We hope that we have provided enough information from our coverage of this vast tract of coastline to make possible comparisons between the various areas, which should be valuable to those who will later cover individual coastal regions with much more detailed studies. Investigators who confine themselves to small areas sometimes suffer from failure to realize the broader picture. A land geologist who works in detail in one locale has a backlog of information from geological texts covering much of the world; but, in coastal studies, there has been very little available to give a similar broad picture. Thus we hope to stimulate detailed studies by our broad coverage. The importance of conducting future detailed studies can be appreciated when it is realized that not only are cliffs retreating sufficiently to cause huge losses of property, but many beaches are threatened with extinction. If we wish to preserve these for future generations, we will have to take strenuous measures.

SEA LEVEL CHANGES AND OTHER CAUSES OF EMBAYED COASTS   In the second chapter we attempted a classification of coasts based largely on the processes that have been of major importance in developing the various types, such as wave erosion, wave deposition, glaciation, river erosion, river deposition, volcanic activity, and movements of the earth's crust. However, almost all coasts have been influenced in their development by the worldwide rise in sea level that accompanied the melting of the great continental glaciers that once covered so much of North America and Europe. This rise was quite rapid until a few thousand years ago, and has continued very slowly and somewhat intermittently up to the present. The deglaciation tended to drown the lower stretches of river valleys, but it has also led to large-scale crustal warping because of the rebound from the depressed condition that existed due to the weighting effect of the thick ice caps.

The result of the postglacial rise in sea level, locally accentuated by crustal subsidence, is evident along most coasts of the United States as elsewhere in the world. Embayed river valleys can be seen on almost all of the aerial photographs and maps that are included as illustrations in this book. It is relatively easy to understand the existence of these drowned river valleys, but the absence of such embayments along rather large tracts of coast may require some explanation.

The following reasons appear to explain many of these exceptions: (1) Coastal areas that border mountain ranges have streams with sufficient gradient to transport enough sediment so that they have filled many of the estuaries that were present when the sea-level rise became negligible a few thousand

years ago. Examples are found along much of the California coast. (2) Large rivers, like the Mississippi, the Brazos, and Rio Grande (Figs. 9.7 and 9.25) of the Gulf Coast, and the Yukon of Alaska, have filled their former estuaries and have even built deltas into the adjacent seas. (3) Where upwarping of the earth's crust has been as great as the rise of sea level, there has been no reason for drowning of valleys. This probably applies to parts of the California coast and to the Southern California islands. (4) Faulting has produced some straight coasts, notably in California (Fig. 2.8). (5) Excessive wave erosion often straightens coasts, eliminating the former estuaries (Fig. 2.14).

Another problem in relation to coastal drowning applies to glaciated coasts. Most of them are deeply embayed, despite the fact that they have been considerably elevated due to rebound since the glaciers retreated. The explanation of the embayments of these coasts is that drowning has been the result of the erosion to great depths below sea level by the glaciers that existed in the valleys. With the melting of the ice, seawater entered the valleys and the subsequent rebound has only somewhat offset the deepning by the glaciers. Examples of glacially indented coasts are seen in Figures 3.4, 12.47, and 13.6.

One of the strange features of coastal estuaries is that they are much better developed in some areas than elsewhere, and none of the preceding explanations seem to apply. The most notable cases in the United States are the Chesapeake Bay area, which is much more deeply embayed than the coast to the south, and the Columbia River estuary, which also forms such a contrast to the relatively straight coast farther south. In both of these cases, there are large entering rivers that should have filled the embayments. As a possible explanation for this enigma, it is suggested that both of the deeply embayed areas lie close to formerly glaciated territories, and that in these marginal zones subsidence has been occurring as a result of the settling of areas which had formerly bulged around the rims of the depressed ice-covered lands. A similar explanation might apply to the large estuaries of southern England and of the adjacent French west coast, both being marginal to the European ice sheets. A similar bulge now exists in the sea floor a few hundred miles northeast of the Hawaiian Islands, where weighting has been due to piling up of lava on the sea floor.

WAVE EROSION COASTS AND RATES OF
RETREAT   Extensive cliffed areas along the west
coasts of the United States and on the windward
coasts of the Hawaiian Islands are the result of wave
erosion, much of it having occurred since the slow-
down of the postglacial rise in sea level. On the other
hand, wave erosion coasts are of very limited extent
along the East and Gulf Coasts.

Wave erosion may either straighten coasts or make
them more irregular. Where the waves are attacking
land with unconsolidated sediments or soft rock of
uniform composition, the coasts are usually straightened, as for example, the cliffs of outer Cape Cod.
However, where the waves have cut back a rocky
coast they leave jutting points (Fig. 12.16) where
the rock was more resistant and develop small steep-
walled coves (Fig. 10.11) where the rock was relatively soft.

The rates of retreat of cliffs under attack are not
well known but have been established in a few places,
mostly in unconsolidated materials. For example, the
outer cliffs of Cape Cod have been retreating at an
average of 2.5 feet per year in historical times. The
fan sediments north of La Jolla, California, were retreating at a foot per year until winter storms stopped
cutting away the beach that annually exposed the
cliffs to wave attack. Rates of one to several feet a
year are found in many other places, including the
arctic coasts of northwestern Alaska where they are
not protected by barrier islands. Erosion southwest
of Point Barrow is locally 10 feet a year. The retreat
of cliffs in the arctic is accelerated by solifluction during summer melting of the frozen soil. Ice wedges develop during the winter and force apart the ground,
allowing slumping when melting takes place in summer. Also, the thaw depressions on the arctic slopes
add to the rate of erosion. Most of the cliffs of glacial
drift along the coasts of Lake Michigan and Lake
Erie are retreating under wave attack at a foot or
more per year, except where artificial protection has
been provided. Rapid retreat of volcanic coasts occurs
where explosive eruptions have built out the land
with fragmental material, such as volcanic ash and
cinders. As an example, Bogoslof (Fig. 13.48), the
volcano along the north side of the Aleutians, has
new cones built rapidly above sea level during eruptions, but the waves often have cut away the new
islands in a few years, leaving only shoals or small
volcanic necks.

The retreat of rock cliffs is less well known. Old
photographs show that changes are rarely pronounced
within a few decades, although natural bridges and
narrow stacks may show striking differences (Figs.
10.10, 11.15). Along the glaciated hard rock coast
of Maine, it is often possible to find glacial striations
extending right down to sea level, showing that there
has been no retreat since the sea level stabilized after
the glacial period. However, rock cliffs often retreat
rapidly as a result of landslides. In such cases, it is
usual to find no retreat on either side of the landslide
over long periods. The cutting back of cliffs can be
considerably decreased by providing good drainage
of surface water. Also, the filling of cracks will help
stabilize doubtful sections of a cliff. The cracks,
when left alone, usually widen slowly; but after a
number of years a mass breaks away and falls to the
base of the cliff.

BARRIER COASTS   Approximately 47 percent
of the coasts of the United States are bordered seaward by sand barriers that are separated from the
mainland by shallow lagoons. Most of the barriers
conform in direction with the general trend of the
coast. South of New England, almost the entire East
Coast is flanked with barriers, although in some areas,
notably Florida, the lagoons have been filled with
sediment or marsh grass. The barriers continue
around most of the Gulf Coast, and individual barrier
islands of Texas have lengths up to 130 miles. On
the West Coast, barriers are much less common, except in a belt along northern Oregon and southern
Washington. Barriers are rare along the southern
Alaska coast but become important again in northern
Alaska, especially in the arctic where one barrier is
150 miles long.

Barriers appear to be the normal result of the sea
rising over a lowland, as has happened to all of our
coastal plains. During the low stages of sea level,
sand had been deposited widely over the exposed
continental shelves. During the rise, whenever there
was a pause, the waves tended to build barriers along
the coast; and many of these now exist as low sand
ridges outside the present coast. When the sea-level
rise slowed a few thousand years ago, the waves began to build sand ridges along the coast; and many
of them persisted as islands during the last slow rise.
Longshore currents built spits out from the sides of
the newly formed bays and in many places united to

form continuous sand beaches across the bay mouths, cutting them off from the ocean (Fig. 2.17).

Because of the slow rise in the past few thousand years, the lagoons on the inside of the growing barriers were temporarily deepened and widened. More recently, on the other hand, the lagoons have been filling. This is seen by comparison of present depths with those of old surveys. The Texas lagoons, for example, have shoaled at a rate of about 1.25 feet per century. Marshes have taken over large parts of lagoons, especially along the New Jersey coast. Many lagoons along the west coast of Florida have been filled with mangroves and with the sediment that accumulates around their roots. Another type of lagoon filling is the result of the building of tidal deltas on the inside of inlets (Fig. 4.8). This occurs frequently during great storms when enormous amounts of sediment are carried through the inlets and deposited near the entrance. These tidal deltas are often built up to sea level. If they develop in densely populated areas, as on the south coast of Long Island, they are often built up artificially to add to the available real estate. In some areas, tidal deltas develop on the seaward side of inlets (Fig. 6.5) due to strong outflow from the lagoons and relatively quiet water outside. Notable examples are off South Carolina and Georgia. In a few places, tidal deltas extend both seaward and landward of the inlets.

During these lagoonal changes, most barrier islands have been growing seaward. This growth may take place by development of new sand ridges on the outside (Fig. 7.7). Elsewhere the beach widens seaward, often allowing a dune ridge to grow on the inside.

Barriers may extend for many miles along a lowland coast without any breaks, as in southern Texas and parts of arctic Alaska, or there may be numerous inlets; most of them are due to storm waves, particularly hurricanes that cut gashes through the sand islands. In some places, the tides maintain passageways of unknown origin, often aided by the outflow of river water that enters the lagoon from the mainland.

Some of the barriers have seaward-pointing projections, called cuspate forelands, of which Cape Hatteras is the type example (Fig. 5.3). Cuspate forelands are best developed in two localities along the United States coasts—in the Carolinas where four of them are separated by about 100 miles (Fig. 5.1), and in northern Alaska where three of them are about 80 miles apart (Fig. 14.24). The most pointed of the cuspate forelands is also found in arctic Alaska, Point Hope (Fig. 14.20). Other well-known cuspate forelands include Cape Kennedy and Cape San Blas, on opposite sides of Florida. Most cuspate forelands are bordered seaward by a long band of shoals extending directly out from their points. The cuspate forelands of the Carolinas can be explained at least in part as due to gyral countercurrents that develop inside the powerful north-flowing Gulf Stream. Possibly the same explanation applies to the arctic examples, but here the evidence is not clear because of the ice pack.

Some low coasts lack barriers, notably west Florida north of Tarpon Springs. Barriers could not develop here because of the lack of sand-sized material, which in turn is due to the limestone formations through which the coastal rivers drain. Also, the weak waves along parts of this coast prevent any sand from being derived from farther south.

DELTAIC COASTS   Most of the large deltas of the world are found along the coasts of inland seas where waves are generally small and longshore currents likely to be less powerful than on coasts exposed to the open oceans. Thus we have the Nile, the Rhone, and the Ebro Deltas of the Mediterranean; the Volga of the Black Sea; the Hwang Ho and Yangtze Kiang of the Yellow Sea; the Euphrates of the Persian Gulf; and the Magdalena of the Caribbean. The same applies to the United States with our greatest delta, the Mississippi in the Gulf of Mexico, the Yukon in a protected part of the Bering Sea, and a tremendous row of deltas along the north slope of Alaska, east of Point Barrow. The development of the northern Alaska deltas is favored by the off-lying pack ice, which inhibits wave activity during the summer and absolutely stops it during the long winter.

Deltas build out coasts very rapidly, accounting for many miles of growth in historical times (Figs. 8.3, 9.9). On the other hand, where a distributary of a delta has abandoned its channel, the coast is likely to retreat at a rapid rate. Considering the entire deltaic development of the Mississippi we find that there has been more loss of land to Louisiana in the past few thousand years than there has been growth. Part of the loss is due to subsidence, which is common in deltas, partly due to compaction of the water-saturated muds and partly to the extra weight on the crust that is added because of the delta growth.

The fronts of most deltas are unstable, particularly where they have been built into deep bodies of water, such as fiords. One of the worst effects of the great Alaska earthquake of 1964 was due to the sliding into the fiords of the fronts of deltas that had been built mostly from the outwash of the glacial streams coming from the adjacent mountains.

Where delta lobes have been abandoned and the coast is sinking, we have an ideal place for the growth of new barriers. This accounts for the Chandeleur Islands along the east side of the Mississippi Delta and on the west for such bays as Barataria, where Grand Isle has become the land base for the huge offshore drilling program of the oil industry.

The fact that deltas are missing along most open coasts, although due largely to wave attack and the strong longshore currents, is also partly the result of the postglacial rise in sea level that has prevented the smaller rivers from filling their embayments.

COASTS RELATED TO ANIMAL AND PLANT GROWTH   Both animals and plants play an important role in coastal development in tropical and subtropical areas. Animals are largely responsible for the growth of coral reefs, although the calcareous algae often constitute a larger percentage of the volume of the reef than the corals. These reefs grow up only to the low tide level; but, with the help of storm waves, the dead coral masses are piled up above normal water level and actually form the base for most of the low coral islands in the Western Pacific. The coasts of the United States have few localities that can be considered the result of coral reefs. Slightly elevated reefs form much of the land area of the Florida keys (Fig. 6.22). These reefs grew mostly below sea level during interglacial stages when the sea stood higher than it does at present. Also, small sections of the coasts of the Hawaiian Islands represent slightly elevated reefs (Fig. 15.52), due here mostly to upwarping of the land.

Mangroves are more important in the United States in producing coastal outgrowth than coral reefs. The shallow bays along the south coasts of Florida (Fig. 2.26) are being rapidly filled by mangroves. These trees take root in shallow marine water which may become land after muddy sediment has been washed in among the roots. Both the mainland

and the numerous islands in the bays expand outward in this fashion. Some of the embayments in the Hawaiian Islands also are being filled with mangroves.

In addition to mangrove trees, marsh grass is locally a means of filling embayments. This can be seen in the Panhandle of Florida but it is also important in higher latitudes.

VOLCANIC COASTS   In the United States, the only coasts which are primarily due to vulcanism are found in Alaska and Hawaii, although elsewhere the rocks along the coast may consist of ancient lavas that have been attacked by erosion over long periods of time. Diamond Head, on the Island of Oahu, familiar to many Americans, has the typical convexity of a volcano. Here, the coast was primarily made by volcanic activity that built a cinder cone out into the ocean, but the cone has been protected from erosion by a fringing coral reef that has grown around its margin since the vulcanism ceased. The circular islands of the Aleutians (Fig. 13.49) are volcanic, some of them extinct volcanoes and others still active. Points of land in the Hawaiian Islands are usually due to lava flowing down a valley and building a lava delta into the sea (Fig. 15.15). Elsewhere, circular bays indent these volcanic coasts (Fig. 15.42) as the result of subsidence of one side of a volcano, allowing the sea to enter the crater.

COASTS DUE TO CRUSTAL MOVEMENTS   Movements of the earth's crust, such as faulting and folding, account for the configuration of a few of the coasts of the United States. The straight northeast side of San Clemente Island (Fig. 2.8), off California, is one of the clearest examples. Here, the sea floor slopes off directly outside the land cliff with no intervening shelf. This shows that a fault has carried down the adjacent sea floor, and there has not been sufficient time since this occurred for the cutting of a shelf into the side of the island. Similarly, part of the steep coast of the Santa Lucia Mountains in Central California has no bordering shelf, and is probably the result of faulting, although some coastal erosion has followed.

Faulting during recent earthquakes in southern Alaska has produced some of the cliffed coasts. In others, elevated wave-cut benches (Fig. 13.22) are the result of coastal uplift during recent Alaskan earthquakes. The lowering of the land at the head of Turnagain Inlet, in Alaska, submerged a wide tract, including the town of Portage, during the 1964 earthquake. Such submergence carries trees below the high-tide level, killing wide tracts of forest.

The importance of faulting in producing some of the cliffed coasts of western Hawaii is not clearly established, but the absence of a bordering shelf in some cliffed areas may indicate fault origin. Elsewhere, as in northern Molokai, earlier faulting may have established a line of cliffs that have subsequently retreated for several miles, due to wave erosion (Fig. 15.27).

OTHER TYPES OF COASTS   Several other types of coasts are found locally. Irregular points that protrude beyond some cliffed coasts are the result of large landslides (Fig. 12.15). These are usually of short lateral extent. The Alaska earthquakes have produced many rockfalls, which have left masses protruding for short distances beyond the coast, in contrast to the slides at the end of deltas that cause coastal indentations. Mudflows also build out the coasts locally, as at Turnagain by the Sea, near Anchorage, Alaska (Fig. 13.33).

The irregularity of some of the west Florida coast north of Tarpon Springs is due largely to limestone solution that produced caves and sinkholes when the sea level was lower than at present. The rising sea flooded these irregularities, accounting, as an example, for the unusual shape of the coast at Homosassa Bay, west Florida (Fig. 7.17).

In a very few localities, dunes have advanced into the sea, forming a dune coast (Fig. 10.54). These areas are cut back rapidly by the sea, and are dune coasts for only a short period of time after the sand has built forward into the ocean.

EFFECTS OF CATASTROPHIC WAVES Huge surging waves that are comparable to a rapid and extreme rising tide are the cause of extensive changes of coastlines and are also responsible for great loss of life and property along the shore. These catastrophic waves are known collectively as tidal waves, but this is a misnomer as they are not due to tides. They include (1) tsunami waves, due to sudden movements of the sea floor or to submarine landslides or volcanic explosions; (2) storm surges that accompany the high winds of hurricanes and other

atmospheric disturbances; and (3) waves due to rockfalls from mountain sides into bodies of water, notably fiords.

Storm surges have produced the most disastrous wave effects on the coasts of the United States. The late summer and autumn hurricanes that breed in the tropical Atlantic have devastated extensive areas along the Gulf and East Coasts. The greatest damage from these storms comes not from the wind but from wave surges that bring the sea level far above normal when the eye of the hurricane passes.

Hurricanes have been most destructive on the Gulf Coast. Hurricane Camille, which hit the Mississippi coast in August of 1969, had a high-water mark of 30 feet with accompanying winds of up to 200 miles an hour. Despite a twelve-hour warning, hundreds of lives were lost, and almost nothing was left standing along the low coastal plain. Loss was estimated at $1.4 billion in damages. Hurricane Audrey in 1957 hit a still flatter coast in western Louisiana, putting hundreds of square miles under water and drowning even more people than Camille but not causing as much property damage. In 1900, the United States' worst loss of life from a hurricane occurred when Galveston was hit by a 20-foot surge that swept over the low seawalls and virtually wiped out the entire population, killing 7,000 people. Since then, a 30-foot wall has been built around the city; and it has been almost entirely spared further damage, in spite of several storms that hit the coast in the vicinity.

The East Coast north of the Carolinas had been relatively free of hurricanes for almost a century when the 1938 storm hit the New England coast. Since then, there have been a number of hurricanes that have struck almost all parts of the East Coast. Although the Gulf hurricanes usually hit a rather small area, some of the East Coast storms have affected hundreds of miles of the coast.

The effects of hurricanes on the beaches and barriers have been emphasized in this book because they account for the most striking changes that we could find in our comparison of successive aerial photographs. The most evident effect is the cutting of scores of new inlets across the barriers (Figs. 2.13; 9.11c, 9.12d). Many of these new inlets are quickly healed by longshore currents that deposit sand across their mouths. Other inlets are maintained by tidal flow. Another striking effect on the barriers is the wave erosion on the dune ridges inside the beaches. Escarpments cut by the hurricanes are striking (Fig. 5.6). The coasts of some islands have been known to be cut back as much as a mile during one hurricane; but, after the storm, the barrier widens rapidly, generally leaving little if any net effect.

Deposition by hurricanes is also pronounced. The water that sweeps over islands or through new inlets deposits its load of sand on the inside, forming broad overwash deltas and fans in the lagoons (Fig. 2.21). These growths account for many of the wide barrier flats that are found on the lagoon side of islands. In some cases, hurricanes dig up the shallow sea floor, producing new barriers outside the low coast. This has happened during various storms that have struck near the Brazos River mouth in Texas (Fig. 9.9b).

Measures have been taken to reduce the disastrous effects of hurricanes. In addition to the building of seawalls, we have seen considerable improvement in the warning system. Substantially constructed tracking planes follow the progress of the storm center, determining its course and rate of progress. This provides lengthy warning in most cases, although it was not enough for Hurricane Camille where the track changed rather abruptly so that only twelve hours' advance notice was given. Attempts are also being made to seed hurricanes with chemicals dropped from high-flying planes. Ordinary explosives have far too little power to have any effect on the tremendous mass of whirling air currents that constitute a hurricane.

Tsunamis, the product of sudden movements of the sea floor, mostly faulting at the time of earthquakes, are long-period waves with crests that advance across the deep ocean at speeds of 400 to 500 miles per hour. They can be caused also by submarine volcanic activity or large submarine landslides. The significant feature about tsunamis is that they are capable of traveling for thousands of miles with very little loss of energy. Thus we have seen that faulting accompanying earthquakes in South America or near the Alaska coast has produced waves that surge up as high as 50 feet in places on the coasts of the Hawaiian Islands. These islands have had four destructive sets of waves between 1946 and 1960, as well as many small surges from the same cause. The West Coast of the conterminous United States had received almost no serious tsunami damage until the sea floor faulting in the 1964 Alaskan earthquake

sent a train of waves south to wreak havoc on Crescent City in Northern California and to damage a few coastal towns in Oregon. The tsunami following that earthquake caused even more serious damage to many Alaskan cities. Here the causes were complicated, as there were both faulting movements on the sea floor and sliding out of the fronts of deltas.

From the study of the tsunamis that have hit the Hawaiian Islands, it has been possible to draw a few tentative conclusions. The water uprush was, as would be expected, higher on the sides facing the advancing waves, but very high water marks were also found on the far sides of some projecting points. The waves were generally higher inside submarine ridges and lower inside submarine valleys, although the relationship was not as striking in the last three tsunamis in Hawaii as it was in 1946. Coral reefs have had a decided effect on wave height. Apparently the reefs reflect the waves very effectively. The widest of the island reefs, at Kaneohe Bay, Oahu, have so far prevented all damage to shore property on the inside. In general, waves become intensified in moving up funnel-shaped embayments, as is also true of normal ocean tides.

Despite the frequency of large earthquakes off the Southern California coast, no appreciable tsunamis have developed from them. This is probably due to the fact that the surficial movement accompanying most California earthquakes is in a horizontal direction, whereas it requires a vertical movement to set up large waves. Unfortunately for Alaska and Hawaii, vertical movements are the predominant cause for the Alaskan earthquakes.

Future loss of life from tsunamis can be avoided where the source of the waves has been the result of faulting movement on the sea bottom at a considerable distance from where the waves strike. The faults that cause the waves set up earthquakes, and within about an hour the location of these earthquakes can be determined by coordinated efforts of seismograph station personnel. Knowing the rate of travel across the deep ocean, it is possible to predict accurately the time of the first arrival. Because of the damage to the Hawaiian Islands in 1946, warning sirens have been set up around the exposed coasts of the islands. These warnings and police patrols have saved many lives; but, unfortunately, in 1960, the residents of Hilo failed to make much use of the warning, thinking that it might be just another false alarm. Other methods have been adopted, such as setting aside the low areas as parks and establishing strict building codes. It has proven very effective to have upper stories of coastal homes firmly supported by columns which can withstand the waves, even when the thin partitions of the lower floor have been washed away.

Landslide surges are due to rockfalls into the ocean or lakes from precipitous slopes. The great masses of rock hitting the water below send waves forward that may rise higher than any of the waves of hurricane tides or tsunamis. The Lituya Bay rockfall at the time of the 1958 Alaskan earthquake produced the greatest wave runup on record. The water swept to 1,740 feet on the slopes across the fiord from the rockfall and cut away the forest up to that level. Lituya Bay has had other great waves, all of them worse than those known in other areas, such as the Norwegian fiords. Destruction from waves of this type has been very small up to date, but the location of towns along the fiords raises a threat of possible future destruction on a major scale. Fortunately, the waves from this cause have not been known to travel far from the source, although at the time of the 1958 rockfall in Lituya Bay the wave moved down the length of the bay beyond its point of high surge, cutting a swath in the trees up to about 100 feet. No effects were reported out beyond the entrance of the bay.

BEACHES   Most of the coasts of the United States are flanked with beaches, especially the barrier coasts already discussed. Along formerly glaciated coasts, beaches are very scarce, partly because the glaciers have carried away so much of the sand-sized sediment and have stripped the rock formations of their soil and other sediment cover. Beaches are also largely lacking off rocky points where the waves tend to converge and remove all of the sand.

The beaches of barrier islands are often not readily available to the public for recreation because of the lagoons that separate them from the mainland. In highly populated areas, like the coasts of Florida, this is no problem because of bridge building. Also, ferries provide transportation elsewhere.

Beaches are also found along many straight cliffed coasts, notably in Southern California (Fig. 2.14). Here, the beaches are likely to be narrow, particularly in winter during the storm season. These cliff-base beaches generally receive their sand from floodwaters that carry sediment down to the shore through the intermittent canyons that cut the cliffs.

Along rocky coasts, beaches are located in many of the cove indentations. Here crescentic beaches are the usual type. It is a common rule that cove beaches have coarser sand than the nearby long straight beaches. This is explained by the coarse grain of the sand cut by the waves from the cliffs inside and adjacent to the coves, whereas the sand brought down river valleys to form the long straight beaches is largely made of the fine material found in the streams when they finally reach the coast.

Submarine canyons that extend in close to the coast have an important effect on beaches. The sand that is carried along the shore is likely to be trapped by the canyon head; and, once caught, it generally flows down the canyon out into deep water. As a result, beaches downcurrent from canyon heads are likely to be missing or very narrow.

Most beaches, where not interfered with by man, are essentially in equilibrium; that is, erosion during stormy periods is roughly equal to progradation during periods of small waves. During the latter, the sand that had previously been carried along the shore is moved landward onto the beaches.

PRESERVING OUR BEACHES FROM DE-STRUCTION BY MAN   The monetary value of beaches and coastal property in the United States is hard to reckon, but by any standard it is enormous. A large percentage of the population take their vacations where they can relax on the beach or swim in the adjacent water. Most of these vacationers fail to realize that the works of man are doing far more to eliminate this valuable heritage than to preserve it. Every dam that is built across a stream that would normally supply sand to the shore is decreasing the size of the adjacent beaches. The same is true of the storage basins that have been used extensively in Southern California to catch floodwaters coming from the mountains. Much sand is deposited in these basins rather than reaching the shore.

The construction of harbor jetties is an even more important cause of beach erosion. If the longshore current is predominantly in one direction, sand will build out on the upcurrent side of the jetties, often making the beach on that side too wide, as at Santa Barbara (Fig. 10.38). On the downcurrent side, the beach is cut away by winter storms, but the ordinary replenishment that would come in summer is not possible because the sand is stored on the other side of the jetties. As a result, many downcurrent beaches have been destroyed. This is particularly true in Southern California where most harbors require jetties (Fig. 10.40 and 10.41). Examples of erosion on the East Coast due to jetty building are found at Cape May, New Jersey (Fig. 4.11), and at Ocean City, Maryland (Fig. 4.15). South Cape May has virtually disappeared during the past 50 years due to the jetties to the northeast and to the southerly current. Assateague Island has been eroded at least 1,500 feet because of the Ocean City jetties. Loss of most of a small peninsula, formerly a seaside resort, at Tillamook, Oregon (Fig. 12.28) can be laid to the long jetty built on the north side of the harbor entrance. The loss of beaches southwest of Santa Monica, California, resulted from building a breakwater parallel to the shore, producing a wave shadow in which the drifting sand was deposited (Fig. 10.31). The effect of a breakwater built just up-canyon from the head of a submarine canyon is illustrated by the changes in the shoreline at Redondo, California (Fig. 10.30). Another special effect of jetties is seen at the mouth of the Columbia River estuary (Fig. 12.38 and 12.40). Clatsop Plain in Oregon, south of the jetties, was at first built seaward as a result of the south jetty, but after the north jetty was constructed the beach was cut back.

In solving the problem of engineering construction and its effects on beaches, it is important to have a clear knowledge of the currents. We know how they flow in many places, as for example, the south flow along the California coast and along much of the southeastern coast of the United States. In many other areas there is conflicting evidence, such as along the Texas coast where the jetties indicate a north drift, but some of the studies of the beach sediment suggest a south drift. Also, the protruding side of a barrier adjacent to a pass indicates that the drift is toward the indented side (Fig. 6.2); but we find that some of these protrusions change sides from time to time, leaving it an open question as to which way the predominant current is flowing. All of these points indicate the importance of making long-continued studies of shore currents to help improve information on how to preserve beaches. Solutions of the problem cannot do away with harbor jetties, which are as important as the beaches. We have to learn better methods of bypassing sand downcurrent from the jetties and attempt to build new jetties at points where beaches are least likely to be affected.

In conclusion, we hope that this discussion will lead to more study of all of the problems of coastal changes. Most of the wild life of this country has been lost because of the former policy of allowing unrestricted hunting and, more recently, because of the cumulative effects of pollution. DDT and many other industrial wastes are destroying much of the life of streams and lakes, and even the ocean life may be dying because of this poisoning. Our atmosphere is constantly becoming more unhealthy to breathe. Many of our beaches are becoming almost useless because of sewage or oil spillage, as at Santa Barbara. Let's not lose our remaining beaches and doom many of our coastal communities to the attack of the sea because we fail to take adequate measures to preserve them.

GEOLOGICAL TIME SCALE

Era	Period	Epoch	Approximate age in years
CENOZOIC	QUATERNARY	Recent	10,000
		Pleistocene	
			2,000,000
	TERTIARY	Pliocene	7,000,000
		Miocene	22,000,000
		Oligocene	32,000,000
		Eocene	52,000,000
		Paleocene	62,000,000
MESOZOIC	CRETACEOUS		130,000,000
	JURASSIC		165,000,000
	TRIASSIC		195,000,000
PALEOZOIC	PERMIAN		
	PENNSYLVANIAN		
	MISSISSIPPIAN		
	DEVONIAN		
	SILURIAN		
	ORDOVICIAN		
	CAMBRIAN		
			500,000,000

Glossary

ABLATION. Thinning of a glacier by melting, which occurs mostly during the summer.

ALLUVIAL FAN (OR CONE). Where a stream emerges from a narrow valley or canyon, it deposits a large part of its sediment load over the plain in a fan shape. If the slope of this deposit is quite steep, it is called an *alluvial cone.*

ATOLL. A ringlike coral island or series of islands enclosing a central lagoon.

BACKWASH. The seaward return of water from a wave after it has just reached its greatest runup on the shore, generally at right angles to the shoreline.

BAR. A slightly submerged sand or gravel ridge, often found at the mouth of a bay.

BARRIER. A sand beach, island, or spit extending roughly parallel to the coast and separated from the mainland by a lagoon. Present along large parts of the Atlantic, Gulf Coasts, and along much of the arctic coast of Alaska.

BARRIER BEACH. A straight or gently curved beach separated from the mainland by a lagoon.

BARRIER FLAT. A marshy flat on the lagoon side of a barrier spit or island, largely formed by sand or silt carried across the barrier through sluiceways during major storms (Fig. 9.15).

BARRIER SPIT. A barrier connected with the mainland at one end, extending part way across a bay or estuary.

BAY BARRIER. A sandy barrier that separates or nearly separates a bay from the ocean (Fig. 2.17).

BEACH DRIFTING. The transfer of sand or gravel along the shore by littoral currents.

BEACH RIDGE. During storms, coarse sediment, sand, gravel, or shells may pile up just landward of the beach. Very similar ridges may form behind the beach, composed of sand blown from the beach (*see* Dune ridge).

BEACHROCK. In tropical beaches where there is much shell or coral detritus, the loose beach sediment may be cemented into a firm rock, often within a few years of deposition. In the United States, beachrock is found in the Florida Keys and along many Hawaiian beaches.

BERM. A nearly horizontal upper part of the beach or one sloping away from the ocean.

BLOWOUT DUNE. A break in the plant cover of coastal dunes allows landward transfer of the dune sand developing a depressed passage (blowout) across the dune ridge and generally building a higher U-shaped dune inland from the coastal dune ridge.

BOMB. A mass of semifluid lava forcibly ejected from a vent and shaped to a spindlelike form while hardening during air transport.

CARBON-14. A carbon isotope, atomic weight 14, with a half-life of 5,700 years. The percentage of carbon-14 present in ancient wood or shell permits dating events back to about 30,000 years before the present.

CAROLINA BAYS. Elliptical tracts of marshland on the southeast coastal plain (Fig. 5.15) and northern Alaska (Fig. 14.25). They have been explained as developing in present or former permafrost areas as result of vegetation mats and prevailing wind directions, or due to meteorite impact, wave action, upwelling springs, or to eddy currents.

CAY. Low island of coral, algal limestone, or calcareous sand, generally called *key* in North America, as "the Florida Keys."

CHENIER. A beach ridge generally including much shell detritus piled up on a flat coastal plain during a hurricane or major storm. The name comes from Louisiana where oak trees (*chêne,* in French) grow along the ridges.

CINDER CONE. A steep-sided subcircular hill, usually with a small crater in the center, piled up during an explosive volcanic eruption. The angle of slope is the angle of rest of the loose material composing the cone.

CIRQUE. An amphitheaterlike valley head excavated by an alpine glacier. Where the glacier has now vanished, a small cirque lake commonly occupies the deeper part of the steep-walled amphitheater.

CLAY DUNE. In the Laguna Madre of southern Texas, salts such as gypsum (hydrated calcium sulphate) are precipitated during the summer dry season. This salt then binds together masses of clay, forming grains of sand size; and these may be piled up into dunes by the wind.

COL. A low pass in a formerly glaciated mountain range where a drainage divide has been lowered by glacial erosion.

CONTINENTAL SHELF. A shallow portion of the sea floor adjoining continents and extending from the low tide level seaward to a break in slope, generally 300 to 700 feet below sea level. Widths vary from less than a mile to several hundred miles.

COQUINA. A limestone composed of cemented shells or shell fragments formed in very shallow water or on the shore, a kind of beachrock common on the Atlantic coast of Florida.

CORAL REEF. A limestone shoal water area built in subtropical or tropical seas by corals, marine algae, and other calcium carbonate-secreting organisms.

COUNTERCURRENT. A current, commonly near shore, moving in a direction opposite to that of the predominant oceanic current. For example, the southwestward-flowing littoral currents along the southeastern United States, shoreward from northeastward-flowing Gulf Stream.

CREVASSE (GLACIAL). Systems of fractures in a moving glacier formed where one part of the glacier moves faster than that adjoining, where it moves over an uneven base, or where a valley glacier emerges from the mountains and spreads out on a broad plain, forming a piedmont glacier.

CREVASSE (RIVER CHANNEL). A break in the natural levees along a stream caused by erosion during a flood or excavation by man.

CUSPATE BAR. A series of loops in a longshore bar, as in Horn Island, Mississippi (Fig. 7.35).

CUSPATE FORELAND. A projecting point in a barrier coast, such as the Carolina capes and Cape Krusenstern and Point Barrow in northern Alaska.

CUSPATE SAND KEY. A cuspate sand deposit formed by an out-flowing tide outside a tidal inlet. If the sand key is angular it is called *cuspate*, but where it is rounded it may be called *lunate*.

CUSPATE SPIT. Cuspate projections of a beach into a lagoon.

DELTA. The deposit formed at the mouth of a river where it enters a standing body of water and builds out the coast.

DENDRITIC. Term applied to a drainage pattern suggestive of the pattern of tree branches. Most rivers traversing areas of weak or unconsolidated rock in horizontal layers have this pattern, and it is also evident in many estuaries, such as Chesapeake Bay.

DIATOMITE. A lightweight rock composed of minute spicules of silicon dioxide precipitated by diatoms (microscopic marine plants). The principal North American examples are in the Miocene Monterey Shale in central and southern California.

DISTRIBUTARY. In the lower part of its course, a river may break up into several channels which enter the sea or other bodies of water at different places. Distributary channels are found in most deltas.

DRUMLIN. Elongate oval hill formed of debris accumulated beneath a slowly advancing glacier. The long axis of the hill and steeper frontal slope mark the direction of movement of the subsequently vanished glaciers.

DUNE RIDGE. A ridge of sand blown a short distance inland from the beach. Where the shore is being extended into the sea (prograded), there may be a series of subparallel dune ridges, as at Cape Henry, Virginia (Fig. 4.27).

EBB TIDE. Falling tide between high and low tidal stages. At such times, currents flow out of bays into the ocean.

END MORAINE. Debris deposited at the terminus of a glacier and forming a ridge remaining to mark a particular glacial stage after the glacier has melted back or vanished.

EOLIANITE. Sand dunes that have been cemented to become rock, often composed of minute shells or shell fragments.

EPICENTER. The point of the earth's surface directly above the center of disturbance (*focus*) of an earthquake.

EQUILIBRIUM BEACH.   A beach where littoral currents supply an adequate quantity of sand or gravel during small wave periods to replace that removed by beach erosion during storms. Equilibrium may be disturbed by (1) human activities, such as jetty building, or (2) opening of new tidal inlets where sand is carried into lagoons forming tidal deltas or (3) a change of wave or current regime.

ESCARPMENT.   A cliffed terminus of an elevated area, such as a fault scarp, as on the northeast coast of San Clemente Island off California (Fig. 2.8), or on an erosional escarpment, such as the cliffed north shore of Molokai Island, Hawaii (Fig. 15.26). An escarpment may be entirely below sea level, as the Gorda Escarpment in the Pacific Ocean off California on the south side of the San Andreas Fault.

ESTUARY.   The drowned valley of a river including its tributaries, generally elongate at an angle to the shoreline. Some other authors include in the definitions lagoons elongate parallel to the shoreline.

EUSTATIC.   Refers to a worldwide rise or fall in sea level resulting, for example, from the return to the ocean of meltwater at the end of a glacial episode. This is independent of local elevation or depression of coastal lands.

FAULT.   A fracture along which there has been differential movement of the blocks on opposite sides. The movement may be principally vertical, so that one block is elevated, or lateral, in which case there is a different direction of movement of the blocks on either side, as in the San Andreas Fault of California. Movement may involve both vertical and lateral components.

FAULT BLOCK.   The elevated mass of rock on the upthrow side of a fault surface.

FETCH.   The distance of open water across which wind may blow. The longer the fetch the higher the resulting waves.

FIORD.   A valley cut below sea level by an alpine glacier, which becomes an arm of the sea as the glacier melts back. Examples in northeastern Maine (Fig. 3.4), the Puget Sound area (Fig. 12.48), Washington and southern Alaska (Fig. 13.4). Sometimes spelled "fjord."

FLOATING ISLANDS.   Masses of marsh vegetation choking interdistributary bays of the Mississippi or other large deltas (Fig. 8.6a). At the time of a great flood or during subsidence, these may be dislodged and float out to sea.

FLOOD TIDE.   Rising ocean surface preceding high tide stage; often produces a current that flows into a bay.

FRINGING REEF.   Reef building by marine organisms, commonly corals and algae, in shallow water along the shore, as on several Hawaiian Islands. In the Cedar Keys area of the Florida Gulf Coast, many fringing reefs are made of oyster shells.

FUMAROLE.   A vent or hole through which a column of superheated steam with associated gases rise, usually in recent lava flows or ash flows, as in the Valley of Ten Thousand Smokes, near Mt. Katmai, Alaska.

GLACIAL DRIFT.   Sediment accumulated as a result of glaciation, under a glacier, at its margins or beyond, as glaciofluvial and glacial marine deposits.

GLACIAL MARINE. Deposits formed in seawater at or near the margins of an ice sheet or glacier, as in Alaskan fiords, or the Ross Shelf ice adjoining Antarctica. Also included are sediments dropped from icebergs.

GLACIAL TILL. A "boulder clay," an unsorted and unstratified sediment deposited directly by a glacier in moraines or drumlins and not reworked by meltwater.

GLACIOFLUVIAL. A term applied to sediments introduced into an area by glaciers but transported beyond the ice front by meltwater streams. Includes outwash and valley train deposits.

GLOWING (FLAMING) AVALANCHE. An incandescent flow of super-heated ash and associated gases, which moves swiftly down the slopes of a volcano, destroying all life in its path. The French term *nué ardente* was applied to the catastrophic flow of Mt. Pelée, Martinique, destroying the city of St. Pierre. In 1912, Mt. Katmai, Alaska, had a similar flaming avalanche.

GROIN. A shore protection structure usually extended out perpendicularly from the shore (Fig. 3.19).

GYRAL. An orbital current in a bay or the open ocean, which may result in the formation of cuspate spits or cuspate forelands.

HINGE LINE. During the Pleistocene ice age, heavily glaciated areas were depressed under the weight of the ice, and marginal areas were elevated. When the glaciers melted, these movements were reversed. The hinge line is the junction between elevated and depressed areas. Also applies to line between upraised and downdropped areas due to faulting.

HOOK. A curve at the end of a spit formed by tidal currents entering a bay. Present in most tidal inlets. Sandy Hook, outside New York Harbor (Fig. 4.4) is a well-known example.

ICE FIELD (OR ICE CAP). In Alaska, as well as in Greenland and Antarctica, large upland areas are largely buried beneath glacial ice. Glacial flow generally takes place radially from the highest parts of such an ice field. The Pleistocene continental glaciers of North America and Europe were large ice fields.

ICE SHOVE. Along a shore, the cold winter ice expands as it warms toward the melting point, and pushes ice fragments or sediment masses from the shallow sea onto the shore (Fig. 14.29).

ICE-WEDGE POLYGON. During cold arctic winters, ground contracts and cracks. Snow blows into the cracks and condenses on walls, forming thin veins of ice. During summer, the upper parts of the veins thaw. By repetition of this annual cycle over a period of years, ice veins 5 to 10 feet wide may form.

INTERGLACIAL STAGE. During the Pleistocene period, four major glacial episodes are recognized in North America and Europe. In the three intervening stages, glaciers of the earth melted back even farther than they have today. During parts of interglacials, sea levels were higher than now, and marine beaches and terraces were formed at many places higher than those along the present shores.

ISOSTATIC ADJUSMENT. When an additional weight, such as a glacier or deposits of a large delta, are placed on a portion of the earth's crust, it subsides under the load. If this weight is removed, as by melting of the glacier or erosion of the delta sediments, the area will rise.

JETTY. A long wall extended seaward from the shore at a narrow entrance to a bay to increase tidal flow and keep the entrance open to shipping.

KAIMOO. An Eskimo term for an ice ridge formed along the shore of arctic areas. Its development starts from freezing of the runup of waves on sand and gravel beaches during late autumn and continues growth until it may be several feet thick and 140 feet wide. Along northern Alaskan coasts, kaimoos are used as winter trails.

KARST TOPOGRAPHY. In soluble rocks, such as limestone, dolomite, and gypsum, a complex of solution cavities (like caves and sink holes) allow surface streams to disappear, flowing into the underlying caves. In western peninsular Florida, a karst area developed during the Pleistocene time of lowered sea levels is now partly drowned by postglacial rise in sea level, leaving numerous lakes.

KETTLE HOLE. Near the margin of a receding glacier, outwash deposits of sand and gravel may bury masses of ice. As these buried blocks later melt, the sediments above collapse, forming a depression called *kettle hole*. Commonly, small lakes form in kettle holes.

KEY. A low island near the shore composed of either reef limestone deposits, as in the Florida Keys, or sand deposits, as in lunate or cuspate sand islands near the Gulf Coast of Florida.

KITCHEN MIDDEN. The waste left by prehistoric peoples, which includes bones, shells, and discarded utensils. Common along sandy shores of the world.

LAGOON. A shallow-water bay extending parallel to the coast behind a barrier. The water may vary from fresh or brackish to the normal salinity of sea water, and even to dense brine. Many lagoons have been filled with delta, tidal delta, washover, or marsh sediments.

LATERAL MORAINE. The deposit formed along the sides of a valley glacier, composed of debris carried to the glacier by avalanches from bordering cliffs. This type of moraine may survive after the glacier has melted, leaving a terrace on the side of a valley.

LAVA CONE. A cone-shaped mountain built by successive lava flows. It has gentler slopes than a cinder cone. Good examples are in the Hawaiian Islands and the Aleutians.

LAVA FAN. Arcuate coastal bulges due to lavas entering the sea, for example, in Maui, Hawaii (Fig. 15.15).

LITTORAL CURRENT. A current moving parallel to the shore, usually developed by wave fronts that have an angular approach to the shore. The current causes shifting of beach sand along the shore.

LONGITUDINAL DUNE. A dune ridge elongate in the same direction as the prevailing wind (Fig. 11.6).

LONGSHORE BAR.   A slightly submerged sand ridge generally parallel to the shore a short distance from the beach. At some places there are series of parallel longshore bars at increasing distances from the beach.

LONGSHORE CURRENT, LONGSHORE DRIFT.   *See* Littoral current *and* Beach drifting.

LUNATE BAR.   A crescent-shaped, submerged sand bar commonly developed directly outside the entrance to a harbor or estuary.

MANGROVE.   A family of trees that grow in shallow tropical waters and build out the coasts in many places. There are two important varieties. Red mangrove, *Rhizoma mengle,* can establish itself and grow in normal seawater; it forms the seaward margin of mangrove coasts. Black mangrove, *Avicenna nitida,* cannot colonize in open marine water but inhabits areas behind the red mangrove stand; it is covered only at very high tides.

MARINE TERRACE.   A wave-cut surface that may have developed when local sea level was higher than at present. There are also marine terraces well below the present sea level, formed during a glacial stage of lowered sea level.

MARL.   A loosely compacted uncemented organic limestone deposit formed either in freshwater lakes or shallow marine waters.

MEDIAL MORAINE.   Where the lateral moraines of two glaciers have joined and extended below the junction as a dark band of debris in the combined glacier (Fig. 13.20*a*).

MORAINE.   A deposit left by a glacier at its terminus (*end moraine*), along the side of a valley glacier (*lateral moraine*), down the glacier from the junction of tributaries (*medial moraine*), and as a thin glacial deposit over most of the glaciated area (*ground moraine*). Moraines are generally ridges, but a ground moraine may form a level plain.

MUDFLOW.   A deposit formed by the rapid flow of water-saturated clay or shale. A mudflow that entered the sea is shown in Figure 10.34.

NATURAL LEVEE.   When a flooded river overflows its banks, it deposits a portion of its load in low ridges adjoining the channel on each side. Successive floods build them higher.

NUNATAK.   An isolated hill or peak that projects above the surface of a glacier.

OÖLITE.   A spherical mass of calcium carbonate about the size of a sand grain formed by deposition of concentric rings in shallow agitated water.

OÖLITIC LIMESTONE.   A limestone formed largely of cemented round calcareous grains.

OUTWASH PLAIN.   A plain built by meltwater from the front of a glacier, often composed of gravel near the ice front and sand at a greater distance. Modern outwash plains flank the piedmont glaciers of southern Alaska. A Pleistocene example is the southern part of Long Island, New York.

OVERWASH PLAIN.   A plain built into the side of a coastal lagoon adjoining a barrier by overwashes (washovers) through sluiceways during hurricanes and other violent storms.

OYSTER REEF. An organic reef composed of oyster and other molluscan shells (Fig. 7.20).

PARABOLIC DUNE. A U-shaped dune in which the concave side points into the wind. It may form at the downwind end of a blowout or by the merging of two longitudinal dunes.

PARASITIC CONE. A small volcanic cone on the slope of a larger volcano. Frequently the product of a single eruption.

PERMAFROST. Permanently frozen ground of arctic areas, such as northern Alaska, where it may be more than a thousand feet thick. The ground above the permafrost thaws in summer, but the ice beneath may persist indefinitely.

PIEDMONT FAN. A fanlike deposit built by ephemeral streams on a plain adjoining a mountain area.

PIEDMONT GLACIER. Alpine valley glaciers may extend beyond a mountain front where they spread out, forming a bulbous projection. Malaspina Glacier (Fig. 13.19) in southern Alaska is the largest North American piedmont glacier.

PINGO. A relatively large mound raised by frost action above the permafrost, as in northern Alaska. Generally persists for more than one season.

PLACER. An alluvial or beach deposit of sand or gravel containing eroded particles of valuable minerals. An example is the gold deposits at Nome, Alaska.

PLUNGING BREAKER. A wave near shore that builds up, curls over developing a hollow front, and breaks with a crash (Fig. 2.10*a*).

PRIMARY COAST. A coast largely unmodified by shore processes. May be the product of rise or fall in sea level, delta growth, glacial action, volcanic eruptions, or earth movements.

PROGRADE, PROGRADATION. Where a coast is being extended seaward, as if by deposition of a succession of beach or dune ridges, it is said to be prograding (Fig. 7.9).

REBOUND. Elevation of a land area after a large glacier, the weight of which had caused it to subside, has melted away. This is a form of isostatic adjustment.

RESACA. A Spanish word used for an abandoned distributary channel of a delta, such as the Rio Grande.

RECESSION. The back melting of the frontal area of a glacier where melting is more rapid than the advance of the new glacial ice. It *does not* involve a reversal in the direction of glacial flow.

RETICULATE BARS. A crisscross pattern of slightly submerged sand ridges. Formed by littoral currents that change direction from time to time (Fig. 7.33).

RIFT. A valley depression along a large fault. Particularly applied to the San Andreas Fault of California.

RIGHT LATERAL FAULT. A fault in which the continuation of a stratum that terminates at the fault will be found to the right of the observer. The San Andreas is a right lateral fault.

RIP CURRENT. A current in which a narrow band of water moves away from shore, returning excess water carried shoreward by the ordinary wave motion. It may be recognized as a breach in a line of breaking waves. Often has velocities that are a danger to swimmers. (Fig. 11.14).

SALT DOME. Where a portion of a deeply buried salt bed has been thrust surfaceward in the form of a dome. The bending of surrounding strata toward the salt dome makes an excellent trap for oil (Fig. 9.2).

"SEA ISLAND." A name applied in Georgia to a series of barrier islands of short length but considerable breadth.

SEA VALLEY. A sea-floor valley of small depth below surroundings, like that off New York Harbor which crosses the continental shelf.

SINKHOLE. A hole due to the collapse of the roof above. A solution cavity in limestone, gypsum, salt, or dolomite. Surface streams are often carried underground along sinkholes. An area with sinkholes has karst topography.

SLOUGH. A linear depression with water channels, marshes, or narrow lakes, frequently present between parallel beach or dune ridges on a prograding coast (Fig. 12.34). Sloughs are nearly synonymous with swales.

SLUICEWAY. A narrow breach through a coastal barrier cut at times of extremely high waves and tides, as during a hurricane or other severe storm. The breach is generally closed soon after the storm (Fig. 9.11).

SOLIFLUCTION. The slow flow of surficial mud down slopes during the summer thaw in arctic areas underlain by permafrost. Its pattern is conspicuous in northern Alaska (Fig. 14.10).

SPILLING BREAKERS are waves near shore that break gradually over quite a distance (Fig. 2.10*b*).

SPIT. A small elongate point of land, mostly sand, extending into a body of water (Fig. 11.30).

STABLE AREA. An area that has not experienced recent deformation by uplift, depression, or lateral movement.

STACK. An isolated rock rising from the shallow sea floor near shore, detached from shore cliffs by erosion (Fig. 11.38).

STORM SURGE. The large inundations of the coast that often accompany great storms.

STRIATION. Parallel scratches or grooves on a surface of rock, produced by rock fragments at the base of a moving glacier. After the glacier has vanished, its former direction of advance may be determined from the striations.

SUBDELTA. A portion of a large compound delta, like that of the Mississippi River where breaches in the natural levees of old channels have provided shorter routes to the sea for new channels with the development of new deltaic lobes (Fig. 8.2).

SUBMARINE CANYON. A deep, narrow, steep-sided valley entirely below sea level but commonly located seaward of a stream valley on land.

SUBMERGED COAST. A coastal area that has recently subsided due to land movement, like parts of the Mississippi Delta (Fig. 8.6*a* and *b*). Many coasts that appear submerged have been affected only by postglacial rise in sea level, inundating stream valleys. Such coasts are not truly submerged.

SWELL. Wind-generated waves that have advanced beyond a storm area into regions of weaker winds or calms.

THAW LAKE. In arctic areas underlain by permafrost, the summer sun thaws the ground ice unevenly and areas of local thaw become small ponds.

TIDAL DELTA. When flood tides enter a tidal inlet across a barrier, they deposit part of their load in the lagoon just inside the inlet, forming a delta supplied with sediment from the ocean rather than from a river (Fig. 4.8).

TIDAL FLAT. A marshy or muddy land covered and uncovered by rise and fall of the tides. Tidal flats are largest where land slopes are low and tidal range is high, as in northern Maine (Fig. 3.3).

TIDAL INLET. A breach in a coastal barrier generally opened by a major storm and maintained by tidal flow (Fig. 3.27*a*).

TIDAL MARSH. Marshy tidal flat. Marsh may eventually occupy most of a lagoon that has been filled by tidal delta sediments (Figs. 2.19 and 2.20).

TIDAL RANGE. The difference in elevation of coastal waters at high and low tides. A maximum in North America is about 60 feet near the head of the Bay of Fundy in New Brunswick.

TIDAL SCOUR. Erosion by tidal currents may form deep channels in bay entrances or in shallow marshy lagoons, as in the channels (Fig. 4.20).

TIDAL STREAM. A flow of water through a channel in a marsh where the current is due to the rising or falling tide.

TOMBOLO. A barrier that ties an island to the mainland, such as Marblehead Neck, Massachusetts (Fig. 3.7). Some islands are attached to the mainland by two barriers (*double tombolo*).

TRANSVERSE DUNE. A sand dune ridge with a trend at right angles to the prevailing wind direction. The windward side of the ridge is less steep than the leeward (Fig. 12.21).

TREE ISLANDS. A concentration of forest trees in the saw grass swamps of the Florida Everglades. The first trees generally start in the shallow water of drowned sinkholes and provide shade and wind protection for further tree growth (Fig. 6.19).

TRIMLINE. All trees may be killed below a certain line when an alpine glacier advances into a forest or a great wave cuts a swath alongside of a bay.

TSUNAMI. A sea wave produced by a submarine fault movement, a submarine slide, or volcanic eruption (Fig. 15.35).

U-SHAPED VALLEY. A valley with steep walls and rounded floor carved by a former valley glacier.

UNDERTOW. The misconception that backwash from a wave forms a powerful seaward current beneath the next advancing wave. Such currents are largely fictitious and based on a misinterpretation of rip currents, which move seaward mostly near the surface.

UPRUSH (SWASH). The rush of water up onto a beach following the breaking of a wave.

VALLEY TRAIN. Outwash of a melting glacier carried downstream along a valley below the glacial front. For example, the valley train on which Valdez, Alaska, was located (Fig. 13.26).

VERMITOID GASTROPOD. An irregularly shaped gastropod (snail) that has the capacity to form small reeflike growths, as in the Ten Thousand Island area of southwestern Florida.

VOLCANIC CALDERA. A large circular depression in the center of a large volcanic cone generally formed by collapse of the top of a mountain but occasionally by removal of the mountain by explosive eruption. For example, Aleutian Islands, Alaska (Fig. 13.47*b*).

VOLCANIC SAND. Fine detritus erupted during volcanic explosions, with fragments the size of a pea or smaller. The particles are also called *lapilli.*

VOLCANIC TUFF. The particles smaller than sand size resulting from volcanic explosions, also called *volcanic ash.* A volume of tuff equal to 7 cubic miles was produced by the Mt. Katmai eruption of 1912.

WASHAROUND. Oval remnants of dune ridges isolated by sluiceways through which sand has been carried across a barrier. Washarounds are known on the Maryland coast (Fig. 4.16*a*) and on the south Texas coast near the Rio Grande Delta (Fig. 9.27).

WASHOVER (OR OVERWASH). The transfer of beach sand across to the lagoon side of the barrier through sluiceways during a hurricane.

WASHOVER DELTA (OR FAN). A triangular deposit on the lagoon side of a barrier transported from the beach through a gap in a barrier during a hurricane or other violent storm (Fig. 2.21).

WAVE CONVERGENCE. Where the crest of a wave is bent so that the two arms converge on a point, which produces higher waves at the point.

WAVE-CUT PLATFORM. A relatively smooth surface just below low tide extending seaward from the shore, resulting from wave erosion (Fig. 10.12). For a wave-cut platform now above sea level, see Figure 11.5.

WAVE DIVERGENCE. The opposite of wave convergence; the divergence produces low wave heights.

WAVE HEIGHT. The vertical difference between the wave crest and trough, the equivalent to the wave amplitude (Fig. 2.9).

WAVE LENGTH. The horizontal distance between similar points on two successive waves.

WAVE PERIOD. The time required for a wave crest to traverse a distance equal to one wave length.

Index

Boldface type indicates an illustration.

Overwash fans, 23, 53, 55, 89, **23**
Oxnard Plain, California, 284, 286
Oyster Bay, Long Island, New York, 65, 68, **68**
Oyster reefs, 27, 168, 178–180, 215, 241–243, **178–180, 241**
    hurricane destruction of, 179
Ozette, Lake, Washington, 379

Pacific Palisades, California, earthslide at, 281, **281**
Pack ice, 479
Padre Island, Texas, 245–248, **246–248**
Palm Beach, Florida, 25, 150, 151
    beach changes due to jetties, 25, **25**
Palmer, Harold S., 522–523
Palms, Isle of, South Carolina, 134, **134**
Palos Verdes Hills, California, 274–277, **274**
    geological history of, 275–277
    landslides of, 226–277, **276–277**
Pamlico Sound, North Carolina, 105, 113
Panama City, Florida, 185, 186, **185**
Partington Submarine Canyon, California, 313
Pass a Loutre, Mississippi Delta, Louisiana, 202, 203, 205
Patrick, D. A., 305
Patricks Point, California, 350
Paulsen, C. G., 393
Pavlof Volcano, Alaska, 441
Payne, T. G., 450, 492
Pearl Harbor, Oahu, Hawaiian Islands, 517–519
Pensacola Bay, Florida, 186–187, **187**
Perdido Bay, Florida, 187, 189–191, **187–189**
    history of development, 187, 189–191
    reticulate sand bars of, 189, **189**
Permafrost, 455, 458, 461–464, 467, 469, 473, 475, 487, 489, **462, 463, 475, 487**
    (ice) polygons, 479, 480, 485–488, **478, 486, 488**
    origin of, 480
Péwé, T. L., 487, 493
Photography, aerial (*see* Aerial photography)
Pickering Passage, Washington, 383, 384, **384**
Pinellas Peninsula, Florida, 175, **175**
Pingos, 488, **488**
Plafker, George, 417, 418, 419, 436, 451, 452
Plain of marine deposition, 531, **531**
Pleistocene shoreline, 139, **139**
Plusquellec, Paul, 75, 78, 103
Plymouth Harbor area, Massachusetts:
    charts of 1765, 40, **40**
    charts of 1960, 41, **41**
Pt. Año Nuevo, California, 320, **320**
Pt. Arena, California, 332, 333, **333**

Pt. Arguello, California, 308–309, **308**
    great loss of naval vessels at, 309
Pt. Barrow, Alaska (*see* Barrow, Pt., Alaska)
Pt. Conception, California, 291–292, 308–309, **308**
Pt. Delgado, California, 336–339, **336**
Pt. Dume, California, 281–283, **282**
Pt. Hope, Alaska, 477, 479–480, **478–479**
Pt. Hueneme, California, 286
Pt. Mugu, California, 283, 284, **283**
Pt. Pinos, California, 316
Pt. Reyes Peninsula, California, 329–331, **330**
Pt. Sur, California, 19, 314–315, **19, 315**
Poipu Beach, Kauai, Hawaiian Islands, 530, **530**
Polihale Beach, Kauai, widest beach in Hawaiian Islands, 532, **532**
Ponce de Leon Bay, Florida, 165–166, **165**
Poplar Island, Chesapeake Bay, Maryland, 100–101, **101**
Porpoise, Cape, Maine, 35, 36, **36**
Port Angeles, Washington, 383
Port Orford, Oregon, 358
Port Royal Sound, South Carolina, 137
Port St. Joe, Florida, 185
Port San Luis, California, 310–311
Port Townsend, Washington, 383
Portland, Maine, 35
Post, Austin S., 424, 452
Postglacial rebound, 30, 383
Powers, H. A., 450
Price, W. Armstrong, 89, 91, 103, 217, 225, 228, 234, 255
Price Inlet, South Carolina:
    changes at, 135, **135**
    history of, 134, **134**
Primary coasts, 7
Prince of Wales Island, Alaska, 397
Prince William Sound, Alaska, 417, 419, 421, 424–428, **420**
Pritchard Island, South Carolina, 139, 140, **139**
Prouty, William, 123, 131
Provincetown, Massachusetts, 40–43, **42**
Provincetown Harbor, Massachusetts, 42, **42**
Prudhoe Bay, Alaska, oil development at, 489
Puffin Bay, Alaska, 398, **398**
Puget Sound, Washington, 344, 383–386
    glaciers of, 383
    lowland of, 383–386, **382–385**
Punta Gorda, California, 338–340
Putnam, William C., 286, 287, 304
Puyallup River, Washington, 384

Rantz, S. F., 393

Waves (*cont'd*):
   water motion in, 13, **13**
Weaver, C. E., 341
Weeks, A. W., 236, 255
Welder, Frank A., 225
Wellfleet Harbor, Cape Cod, Massachusetts, 44, **44**
Wentworth, C. K., 517, 538
Whistler, James A. McN. (artist), 297, 298
White, William A., 106, 107, 131
Whittington Point, Maryland, 89
Wiegel, R. L., 27, 305
Wigglesworth, Edward, 56, 69
Willapa Bay, Washington, 375–377, **377**
Williams, Howel, 443, **450**
Willis, B., 393
Wilmington, California, 272, 274, 275, **272**
Wilmington, North Carolina, 118, 119, **118**
Wilson, B. W., 423, 425, 453
Winchester Bay, Oregon, 362
Winyah Bay, South Carolina, 124
   changes near, 125, 126, **125, 126**
   effects of jetties, 124
Woodring, W. P., 305, 310, 341

Woodworth, J. B., 56, 69
Worth, Lake, Florida, 150, 151, **150**
Wright, Martin, 216, 217, 220, 223, 225

Yachats, Oregon:
   cliff erosion, rate of, 364
   wave erosion at, 364
Yakutat Bay, Alaska, 411–414, **411**
   earthquake of 1899, 411–413
      effects on glaciers, 404
      47-foot uplift of, 411–413, **412, 413**
Yaquina Bay, Oregon, 364–366, **365**
Yaquina Head, Oregon, 365, 366, **365**
Yaquina River, Oregon, 364
Yukon River Delta, Alaska, 12, 455, 458–459,
      461–465, **460, 462–464**
   outline map of Yukon-Kuskokwim deltaic
      plain, **460**
   recent slow growth of, 464

Zeigler, John M., 43, 45, 69, 143, 161
Zenkovich (or Zenkovitch), V. P., 192, 193, 197,
      296, 305